RELIGION IN AMERICA

SECOND EDITION

George C. Bedell
Leo Sandon, Jr.
Charles T. Wellborn
THE FLORIDA STATE UNIVERSITY

Macmillan Publishing Co., Inc.
New York

Macmillan Publishing Co., Inc.
866 Third Avenue, New York, New York 10022

Collier Macmillan Canada, Inc.

Library of Congress Cataloging in Publication Data

Bedell, George C.
  Religion in America

  Includes bibliographical references and index.
  1. Christianity—United States.   2. United States—
Religion.   I. Sandon, Leo.   II. Wellborn, Charles.
III. Title
BR515.B48   1982   291'.0973   81-8239
ISBN 0-02-307810-3   AACR2

Printing: 1 2 3 4 5 6 7 8   Year: 2 3 4 5 6 7 8 9

Preface to the Second Edition

We are grateful for the response to the first edition of *Religion in America*. The success of the book confirms our original conviction that a text with documents is a useful teaching resource. Changes in this edition were made to incorporate suggestions for improvement and to keep the book current. The fourth chapter is expanded considerably to amplify our discussion of indigenous American religious movements. The ninth chapter is composed of almost entirely new material. The other chapters, while remaining close to the first edition, contain significant revisions.

We are also grateful for the criticism we have received from both students and teachers; we believe that your comments have contributed to an improved book. Robert L. Hall of the Florida State Department of History was helpful with both the first and second editions as a consultant on the topic of Afro-American religion. We also wish to express our gratitude to Linda Carr Schmidt for her excellent typing and editorial work, which was largely a labor of love. The competence of Barbara Nonas, production editor for the second edition, contributed much to the quality of the manuscript. Our appreciation is expressed a second time to our editor, Kenneth Scott, for his patience and wise guidance.

G.C.B.
L.S.
C.T.W.

Preface to the First Edition

Although there are a number of excellent volumes in the field of religion in America, no one of them taken alone is suitable for an introductory course for undergraduates. At least that has been our experience as teachers. For example, we have attempted to use some of the available histories of American religion, but they have failed in two important ways: they were much too detailed for beginning religion students, and their methodology was, of course, exclusively historical. On the other hand, we found books on the sociology of religion in America to be much too circumscribed in methodology, and, in one notable case, the data and interpretations of the data seemed particularly dated. We tried several anthologies but they also fell short: one well-known anthology uses exclusively Protestant sources; another is much too long and neglects the Jewish tradition; still another contains only theological writings; a fourth, though well balanced in most every way, must be supplemented with interpretive comment; and a fifth anthology, although it deals effectively with current issues in American religion, contains little historical depth. Over the years, we have tried various combinations of these books, and although we, as teachers, have been enriched by having to master the assigned texts, our students have not always been so fortunate.

We have therefore attempted to do what none of those books does by itself. Or to put it another way, we have tried in some sense to do in one book what all of them do. That is to say, we have used several methodologies instead of one—the methodologies of history, sociology, phenomenology, theology, psychology, and anthropology. Next, we have attempted to deal equitably with all three major American Traditions—Protestantism, Catholicism, and Judaism—not just one or two. We also take note of some of the more important minor religious groups and communities that have appeared on the American scene. Third, we hoped to design a book that would be useful in several academic settings, the public or non-sectarian institution as well as the seminary or denominational college. Although this book is designed primarily for the student of religion, we hope it will be adopted in classes in American studies and perhaps even in American history. Accordingly, we have sought to be as objective as possible about partisan religious matters. That does not mean that we have avoided controversy. As anyone knows, controversy has frequently occupied the center stage of religion in America. Our only aim has been to portray the events and forces of American religion faithfully and impartially.

Because of our approach, we have done little that is novel or original. Indeed, we are, in large part, dependent upon the excellent work of those whose books we have attempted to use in the past. We simply hope that we have combined the best features from all of their books into a single, useful textbook. In a word, our volume is born of desire. We want a book that can be used in our own introductory course in American religion, and we suspect others are looking for the same thing.

A note about the book's structure. Drawing from our own experience in teaching undergraduate classes in American religion, we long ago arrived at a set of significant factors or motifs that can be used as keys to understanding the forces that have shaped American religion: the public or civil religion of Americans, disestablishment and religious liberty, revivalism, indigenous religious groups, theology or religious thought, missions and humanitarian endeavors, black religion, interfaith and ecumenical relations, and contemporary trends in American religion. These motifs, in fact, became chapter headings. Then each chapter was developed in the following way: first, there is a thorough but summary exposition of the motif under consideration, which is then followed by a short historical sketch of the motif.

Original source materials or documents are distributed throughout each chapter. They serve to illumine the text rather than the other way around. Or, to put it still another way, this volume is more than a collection of readings. We do not want to add to the growing list of anthologies. Moreover, we have attempted to select source materials not generally found in other volumes. In some cases, however, some oft-anthologized documents seemed so germane to the topic under discussion that it would have been foolish to select other less appropriate materials.

Because this book is only an introduction, there is obviously much more that could have been said on any given subject. But our purpose will have been well served if those who use this work will want to continue their study of the altogether fascinating phenomenon of American religion.

Finally, we want to extend our thanks to a number of people who have assisted us in various ways. To our friends and colleagues who read the manuscript at various stages and made helpful comments—Professors Edwin Scott Gaustad, Michael Gannon, and Franklin Littell. To Professors Lawrence Cunningham and Richard Rubenstein for their consultation on source materials. To Louise Clay of the Strozier Library at Florida State University, who helped ferret out some seemingly inaccessible materials. To Bettie Bedell and Kathy Bird for their cheerful and vigorous production of typed script. To our editors, Ken Scott and, before him, Charlie Smith, who have been a great deal of help in seeing this project through. To our students who did some preliminary digging—Melanie Young, Tom Goldenson, Donna Gaither, Mark Freshwater, and Don James. To Marc Ellis we are indebted for sustained editorial assistance and manuscript proofreading. Then, of course, there were the hundreds of undergraduates who labored with us in the formative stages of "Religion 310." Little did they know their anguish and hours would result in this project. We trust it was all worth it.

G. C. B.
L. S.
C. T. W.

Contents

Documents

Introduction

The United States has been regarded by some observers as one of the most religious nations in history. The Frenchman Alexis de Tocqueville, who visited America in the 1830s, wrote a remarkable account of American life and manners. He found "the religious atmosphere" to be the first thing that strikes a visitor from abroad and concluded that "there is no country in the world where the Christian religion retains a greater influence over the souls of men than in America."[1] In the 1950s the same sorts of data confronted the contemporary observer. Church spires and towers were visible in every hamlet and neighborhood in the land. Public officials expressed themselves in language liberally garnished with religious terms and images. Membership in a religious denomination enabled the mobile American family to move with ease and confidence into the life of a new community. It is not surprising, then, that a Supreme Court Justice could write in the 1950s that "we are a religious people" and that our institutions "presuppose a Supreme Being."[2]

In the 1960s, however, a gradual but noticeable erosion had begun to take place in church attendance. In 1971 the Gallup Poll released the results of a survey of churchgoing America. Though the figures for the United States were much higher than those of other nations, there had still been a decided decline in attendance from the boom of the 1950s, when as much as 49 per cent of the adult population could be found in church on any given Sabbath. By 1970 only a little over 50 million adults, or 42 per cent of the population, would be in church once each week.[3] A year later attendance had dropped two more percentage points, to 40 per cent. Several years later the Gallup Poll reported that the drop in attendance could "almost entirely" be attributed to the decline in attendance among Roman Catholics:

> In 1973, . . . the percentage of Catholics who attended church in a typical week was 55 per cent, compared with 71 per cent in 1964.
>
> Protestant church attendance, according to the poll, reflected virtually no change over the same period. In 1973, 37 per cent of the nation's Protestants attended service in an average week, compared with 38 per cent in 1964.

---

[1] Alexis de Tocqueville, *Democracy in America*, edited by J. P. Mayer and Max Lerner (New York: Harper & Row, 1966), pp. 268 and 271.

[2] Justice William O. Douglas, *Zorach v. Clauson*, 343 U.S. 306, 313 (1952). In subsequent opinions Mr. Justice Douglas, in effect, qualified his attitude about the place of religion in public life but consistently manifested a keen interest in the subject. See his *The Bible and the Schools* (Boston: Little, Brown, and Company, 1966).

[3] "Religion in America," *The Gallup Opinion Index*, April 1971, p. 43.

Synagogue attendance also showed little change over the last ten years, with 19 per cent attending service in a typical week in 1973 compared with 17 per cent a decade earlier.[4]

In 1976 Gallup reported that attendance had crept back up to 42 per cent.[5]

But whatever the record of attendance, financial support, or membership might have been during the 1960s and the 1970s, the churches were still highly conspicuous on the national landscape and Americans continued to talk incessantly of religion. A 1968 survey indicated that 98 per cent of the people still believed in God; 73 per cent believed in some sort of afterlife; 65 per cent believed in a system of rewards and punishment; and 60 per cent believed in the devil.[6] Ten years later, another survey revealed that affiliation with organized religion declined during that decade: over 41 per cent of all Americans were "unchurched." Even so, reported *The New York Times*, they shared convictions with churchgoers to a remarkable degree:

For example, 93 per cent of the churchgoers said they believed in God and 68 per cent of the unchurched agreed. Eighty-nine per cent of the churchgoers polled said they believed Jesus was the Son of God, and 83 per cent said they believed in life after death. Corresponding figures for the unchurched were 64 per cent and 57 per cent.[7]

One may therefore safely conclude that, although there was a decrease in interest in the institutional forms of religion—and that largely occurred among younger people—religion as a matter of general interest continued to thrive. One notable development was the marked increase in registration for updated and academically respectable religion courses being taught in colleges and universities, both public and private, by highly trained scholars. Astrology, mysticism, and the occult enjoyed renewed interest among all groups. Even (or especially?) members of the then-popular counterculture looked for new ways of expressing the religious impulse. One journalist observed,

There appears to be little support for those who, a decade ago, were predicting the demise of American spirituality under the weight of secularism. Since the "God is Dead" movement and the radical turning away from religion by the students of the 1960s, the nation has experienced a wave of evangelical activity which has included succeeding generations of youth.[8]

[4] *The New York Times*, January 13, 1974, p. 64.
[5] *The New York Times*, December 31, 1976, p. 10.
[6] *The New York Times*, December 28, 1968, Sec. 4, p. 9.
[7] "An 'unchurched' person, for purposes of the poll, was defined as one who has not attended a church service, other than for a special occasion such as a funeral, wedding or Christmas program, in the last six months." See *The New York Times*, June 20, 1978, p. 14.
[8] Kenneth A. Briggs in *The New York Times*, September 12, 1976, p. 41.

The reason for this high degree of religiosity is hotly debated among students of American culture, but thus far no consensus has emerged from the many theologians, sociologists, historians, and religion scholars who have attempted to solve the problem. The only kind of agreement that can be reached is that religion is and always has been a basic ingredient in our national life. One reason that consensus had been so elusive, however, had to do with definition. Nearly everyone agrees that religion is present, but few can agree on what it is.

The Problem of Definition

Part of the difficulty of talking about religion in America may be attributed to the ambiguity and complexity of the term *religion* itself. After all, what is the nature and function of religion? Wilfred Cantwell Smith writes that "the term is notoriously difficult to define. At least, there has been in recent decades a bewildering variety of definitions; and no one of them has commanded wide acceptance."[9]

The problem becomes incredibly more complex when we attempt to define the relationships that occur between religion and the culture in which it exists. At one end of the scale will be those who see little, if any, difference between "religion," on the one hand, and "culture" on the other. For them religion and culture meld into one another. At the opposite pole are those who see religion and culture in conflict, and even this group is divided—some believing cultural phenomena to be the enemy of true religion, others believing religion to be the enemy of free cultural expression. It is therefore easy to see why innumerable variations might be developed on the theme of the relationship between religion and culture. But we must realize that whatever the nature of the relationship between religion and culture might be, it is not one-sided. Religion is not purely the product of its cultural setting; by the same token, culture is not totally molded by religion. The relationship is more complex—a constant interaction in which religious phenomena are never free from cultural influences nor cultural patterns ever divorced from religious concepts. It may not be analytically neat or satisfying, but it is almost certainly accurate to say that religion and culture are constantly in the process of shaping each other.[10]

For purposes of clarification, however, every student of religion in America must attempt to develop a personal working definition of

[9] Wilfred Cantwell Smith, *The Meaning and End of Religion* (New York: New American Library, 1964), p. 21.

[10] The classic discussion of the subject is found in H. Richard Niebuhr's *Christ and Culture* (New York: Harper & Row, 1951). Although Niebuhr confines himself to a discussion of Western traditions, the theoretical model he develops is helpful in discussions of the problem in other contexts as well.

religion. Simply to acknowledge the difficulty without attempting to solve the problem is, of course, intellectual laziness.

Personal Religion

One of the most prevalent and popular connotations of the term *religion* had to do with the inviolability of thought and conviction. From this perspective, religion is uniquely personal and private. In American religion today so much emphasis is sometimes placed on the authority of the individual conscience in religious and moral matters that rational dialogue among persons about such issues is effectively shut off. When this happens, we fall victim to privatism. Privatism expresses itself in such attitudes as "any man's religion is purely his own business" or "what a man believes about religion is his own cup of tea." William F. Buckley, Jr., the newspaper columnist, once summed up the privatist attitude by quoting Hugh Hefner, the popular *Playboy* philosopher: "A man's morality, like his religion, is a purely personal affair, best left to his own conscience."[11]

Kinship with such privatism could be discerned in such phenomena as the "death of God" movement and in some forms of the so-called New Morality of the 1960s. This is not meant as a value judgment on these approaches. What is apparent is that they frequently emphasized purely private dimensions of religion as normative. Some death of God theologians took a private experience and projected it as public reality.[12] Some forms of the New Morality narrowed drastically the scope of ethical responsibility to the realm of private and personal relationships. Both movements reflected the concept of religion as primarily personal and individual.

Obviously, there is a deeply personal dimension to religion, and clearly the individual conscience plays a definitive role in marking off any individual's religion. This understanding of religion had deep roots in the American historical experience. Though it is probably stretching it a bit to try to draw a direct relationship between Hefner's privatism and the intensely personal religion of mainstream American Protestantism, they are roughly at the same end of the religion spectrum. Most Americans, even those who are members of religious groups that stress the corporate nature of religion, are as protective of the priority of the individual in religious matters as they are of the individual's rights in political matters. The proponents of privatism take this position to its extreme when they say that what a person believes and does about religion should be no one else's concern.

Personal religion, as opposed to privatism, was deeply ingrained into

[11]William F. Buckley, Jr., *The Tampa Tribune*, October 3, 1966, p. 11A.
[12]William Hamilton, "An experience of the absence of God," in his essay "The Death of God Theology," *The Christian Scholar*, Vol. 48 (Spring 1965), p. 30.

American religious experience by at least two early groups: (1) left-wing colonial Protestants[13] and (2) the Revolutionary political leaders whose thoughts about government were greatly influenced by the Enlightenment[14] political theory.

The first major American spokesman for a profoundly personal religion was Roger Williams (1604-1684), who began as a Puritan,[15] later became a Baptist,[16] and eventually rejected organized religious groups altogether. He argued for *absolute* freedom of conscience as the only meaningful alternative to governmental interference with religious practice and belief. For him there could be no compromise. His basic assumption was that since religion is so intensely personal no one should tamper with anyone else's religion, though he never believed that men ought not to discuss and, indeed, argue about religion. His antagonists had suggested that the individual sometimes must be saved *by force* from making the kinds of errors in belief that would inevitably damn him or her—that it is better to coerce right belief than to allow one to fall into perdition. But Williams countered with the contention that coercion has not only proved to be ineffective, but wrong, as is illustrated by the many martyrs killed by well-meaning but wrongheaded magistrates in the past. In addition, he said, the free conscience of the individual is most likely to worship God in sincerity and truth because only the inner man may really come to know God.

Williams was careful to note that "enforced uniformity of Religion throughout a Nation or civil state confounds the Civil and Religious" spheres, which should remain completely seperate. Culture—in this case government—must refrain from interfering with religion, because the purposes and functions of government are not the salvation and redemption of souls but rather keeping peace in the civil order. What, then, of the church as a social institution? Williams became so insistent about the sanctity of conscience that he effectively cut the ground out from under churches altogether; he ended up denying religious groups as necessary social institutions.[17]

But Williams was not the only one to speak for the religion of con-

[13] Religious groups, originally from England, who broke away and formed independent and autonomous groups, separate even from the dominant congregational churches in New England, which themselves had separated from the Church of England.

[14] The eighteenth-century movement in Europe and America that stressed the ability of human reason to explain all the mysteries of the universe, including religious phenomena. A principal tenet of the Enlightenment was toleration for religious as well as political diversity.

[15] A type of English churchman who wished to "purify" the Church of England of its imperfections during the seventeenth century.

[16] Left-wing separatists who taught that the individual believer must consciously profess faith and who thus rejected infant baptism as practiced by the Church of England. Baptist got their start in America with Williams and his associates, but the movement did not grow rapidly until the period following the American Revolution. Today they are the largest "family" of Protestants in America.

[17] See Edmund S. Morgan, *Roger Williams: The Church and the State* (New York: Harcourt Brace Jovanovich, 1967), p. 137 and elsewhere. Also see H. W. Schneider, *The Puritan Mind* (Ann Arbor: University of Michigan Press, 1966), p. 57.

science. Others developed the same theme, most notably the Quakers. William Penn's (1644–1718) "case of liberty of conscience" was based on many of the same premises that Williams invoked. Penn objected to coercion in religious matters because men thereby invade the area reserved to God: the inner man. In the first place, argued Penn, God creates the conscience in that He places in every man "a Principle . . . to inform him of his duty, and to enable him to do it." One must therefore be careful not to meddle with this God-given principle. Such meddling could only result in damage to the victim, for without a free conscience "there is no Conviction, so no Conversion, or Regeneration." The clincher of Penn's argument was that the conscience is, in the last analysis, divine—that anyone interfering with the operation of conscience within a man is, in short, interfering with god Himself! In contrast to Williams, who saw the conscience to be the locus of God's activity, Penn considered the conscience to be a particle of God, or, as he called it, "a divine spark."[18]

A century after Williams and Penn, the New England transcendentalists[19] carried personal religion to its logical end. Ralph Waldo Emerson (1803–1882), one of their spokesmen, described religion as "self-reliance":

> To believe your own thought, to believe that what is true for you in your private heart is true for all men—that is genius. Speak your latent conviction, and it shall be the universal sense; for the inmost in due time becomes the outmost, and our first thought is rendered back to us by the trumpets of the Last Judgment. . . . A man should learn to detect and watch that gleam of light which flashes across his mind from within, more than the lustre of the firmament of bards and sages.[20]

For Emerson no man really needs the help of others or even past generations to discover the truth; his most trusted guide is his own heart of hearts.

The notion that religion is essentially personal was also supported by men whose ideas about such matters were shaped not so much by theological or ecclesiastical[21] traditions as by Enlightenment political theory. James Madison (1751–1836) in his historic "Memorial and Remonstrance" stated as incontestable and self-evident that religion must be left up to the individual because no one else can respond to God's graciousness on his behalf. Nor can belief be taken away from him by any

---

[18] William Penn, "Primitive Christianity Revived," in Shelton Smith, Robert T. Handy, and Lefferts A. Loetscher (eds.), *American Christianity* (New York: Charles Scribner's Sons, 1960), Vol I, p. 241. There were, of course, other religious leaders in the colonial period who took up similar positions with regard to the nature of religion.

[19] A religious and literary movement in reaction to eighteenth-century rationalism; a general cast of thought rather than a systematically formulated philosophy or theology which derived much of its impetus from a variety of sources—English and German romanticism, Eastern and Western mystics, Neo-Platonism, and so on.—Transcendentalists believed they possessed a direct and intuitive grasp of divinity, which permeated the universe.

[20] Ralph Walso Emerson, *The Essays of Ralph Waldo Emerson* (New York: Random House, 1944), p. 27.

[21] *Ecclesiastical* is a technical word that refers to church organization or government.

external authority. It is, as Madison said, "inalienable" along with other rights such as freedom of speech and assembly. Ultimately, the worship of God not only takes precedence over any duties owed the civil government, but it is necessary for a healthy body politic. Said Madison, "Before any man can be considered as a member of Civil Society, he must be considered as a subject of the Governor of the Universe."[22]

That men like Madison and Thomas Jefferson (1743–1826) should hold positive attitudes toward religion comes as a surprise to some. It is true that both disrupted the institutional church and that Jefferson won for himself the epithet "infidel" because of his sympathy with the anticlerical French Revolution. But both Madison and Jefferson saw the value and necessity of religion. The latter even chaired a committee to raise money for the minister at St. Paul's Church in Charlottesville.[23]

The kind of religion Jefferson wished to promote and support in the new republic was primarily a personal faith. He held that no ruler, whether temporal or ecclesiastical, has any authority whatever over the consciences of men: "The rights of conscience we never submitted, we could not submit. We are answerable for them to our God." For Jefferson it was a practical matter: other people's beliefs and thoughts could not possibly injure him. He wrote: "It does me no injury for my neighbor to say there are twenty gods, or no God. It neither picks my pocket nor breaks my leg." The only effect of constraint in religion is to make one a hypocrite. Contrarily, true religion is gained when "reason and free inquiry" are free to ferret out error and falsehood.[24]

The religious ideas of Madison and Jefferson were consistent with their political views. Just as each man is intrinsically entitled to the right of free conscience in religious matters, so each citizen is possessed of inalienable political freedoms. The intermeshing of these religious and political views in early America helped to produce the distinctively American idea of the free, rational, independent individual.

With the passage of time, the left-wing traditions of Williams, Penn, and Emerson were mixed with the Enlightenment theories propounded by men like Madison and Jefferson, and then a third ingredient was thrown in for good measure: pietism. During the eighteenth century, through the efforts of the Wesleys, Jonathan Edwards, George Whitefield, the Tennants, and others, the individual and his personal religious health became the focal point of feverish religious activity in a way that has been unparalleled in history. As we shall show in Chapter 3, revivalism and its concern for the individual has pulsated unalteringly in American history for over two hundred years.

[22] James Madison, "A Memorial and Remonstrance," *The Complete Madison: His Basic Writings*, edited by Saul K. Padover (New York: Harper & Row, 1953), p. 299.
[23] Jefferson drafted subscriptions for the support of clergy in Virginia and supported them generously, especially for the Rev. Charles Clay, Anglican priest in charge of St. Paul's. See *The Papers of Thomas Jefferson* (Princeton: Princeton University Press, 1950), Vol. II, pp. 6–8.
[24] Saul K. Padover (ed.), *The Complete Jefferson* (New York: Books for Libraries, 1943), p. 675.

Finally, the combination of these strands must be seen within their natural and geographic setting: the American frontier, with its strong emphasis on individualism and personal independence. The result is what we today recognize as the *personal* religion of many, if not most, Americans. There are other connotations we give to the word *religion*, but Americans cannot help but believe religion to be personal and private. Walt Whitman (1819–1892) successfully caught the nuances of meaning that we have been speaking of:

> Only in the perfect uncontamination and solitariness of individuality may the spirituality of religion positively come forth at all. Only here, and on such terms, the meditation, the devout ecstasy, the soaring flight. Only here, communion with the mysteries, the eternal problems. Whence? Whither? Alone, and identity, and the mood—and the soul emerges, and all statements, churches, sermons, melt away like vapors. . . . Bibles may convey and priests expound, but it is exclusively for the noiseless operation of one's isolated Self, to enter the pure ether of veneration, reach the divine level, and commune with the unutterable.[25]

William James (1842–1910), the great American philosopher, noted the futility of trying to arrive at a universally acceptable definition of religion, but he also concluded that "personal religion will prove itself more fundamental" than other definitions. Churches, "when once established, live at second-hand upon tradition, but the *founders* of every church owed their power originally to the fact of their direct personal communion with the divine." Though James acknowledged that his subject, the *psychology* of religion, necessarily predisposed him to take a personalist definition of religion, he nevertheless argued that the personal *is* the most fundamental element in religiousness. For him religion consists of *"the feelings, acts, and experiences of individual men in their solitude, so far as they apprehend themselves to stand in relation to whatever they may consider the divine."*[26]

What all of this implies is that anyone attempting to understand religion in America today must recognize strong and pervasive brushstrokes of individualism, personal conscience, and private judgment in religious matters which help to make up the overall picture.

Ecclesial Religion

Another strong current in the American religious stream has been organized religion. Americans, notorious joiners anyway, have in recent decades shown a penchant for churchgoing, though their sense of what the church is has seldom coincided with what their European forebears meant when they spoke of the Church: an entity stretching continuously

[25] Walt Whitman, "Democratic Vistas," *Walt Whitman: Complete Poetry and Selected Prose and Letters*, edited by Emory Holloway (London: Nonesuch, 1967), p. 693.

[26] William James, *The Varieties of Religious Experience* (New York: New American Library, 1961), p. 42.

and unbrokenly back through the ages to Jerusalem. Rather, for Americans, the image of the social contract has dominated the discussion: the church or synagogue has been a group of like-minded people, gathered together around mutual concerns. Indeed, the necessity for phrases like *organized religion* or *institutional religion* bespeaks the tendency to treat the church as a society rather than as an organic body. An additional significant factor is that Americans have almost always felt free to switch from one religious group to another with relative ease and impunity.[27] Although attaining or changing church membership has never presented serious barriers for prospective new members, belonging to religious groups has not always been as popular as it is today. Just after the Civil War only about 26 per cent of the population acknowledged affiliation with an organized body. By the 1920s 47 per cent were churched, but in the 1930s membership went into a slight decline. Today about 64 per cent of the population, or about 125 million persons, acknowledge membership in some form of institutionalized religion.[28]

Will Herberg asserts that the recent popularity of organized religion may be attributed to the sociological need for "self-identification" in the increasingly impersonal modern society—that belonging to a religious group gives one a sense of stability:

> although this process of self-identification and social location is not in itself intrinsically religious, the mere fact that in order to be "something" one must be either a Protestant, a Catholic, or a Jew means that one begins to think of oneself as religiously identified and affiliated. *Naming* oneself a Protestant, a Catholic, or a Jew carries with it a distinctive attitude to "one's" church, an attitude that is definitely favorable. Since one "is" a Protestant, a Catholic, or a Jew, and recognizes oneself as such, one tends to think of oneself as somehow part of a church and involved in its activities and concerns.[29]

Thus church membership functions for many Americans as a "badge of belonging," a token of identity.

The most startling fact Herberg adduces is that a significantly larger number of people claim church membership in opinion polls and popular surveys that can be found on denominational rosters. Although, as we have seen, 64 per cent of the population was recently claimed by denominational rolls, about 70 to 75 per cent of the population *regard themselves* as church members and another 20 or 25 per cent *locate themselves* in one of the broad religious traditions of America—Protestant, Catholic, or Jew. Though "locating themselves" may not be con-

[27] For an excellent discussion of the "switching syndrome," see Rodney Stark and Charles Y. Glock, *American Piety: The Nature of Religious Commitment* (Berkeley: University of California Press, 1968), pp. 183–203.

[28] Edwin Scott Gaustad, "America's Institutions of Faith," *The Religious Situation: 1968*, edited by Donald R. Cutler (Boston: Beacon Press, 1968), p. 848. Gaustad's article is a thorough and responsible treatment of the *facts* concerning the institutionalized forms of religion in America.

[29] From *Protestant-Catholic-Jew* by Will Herberg. Copyright © 1955, 1960 by Will Herberg. Reprinted by permission of Doubleday & Company, Inc.

strued precisely as church *membership*, it is instructive that belonging to one tradition instead of another or just the fact of belonging in itself is important enough for people to report to pollsters.[30]

Though the variety of American religious groups is dazzling, the variations should not blind us to the relative stability of the situation. Edwin Scott Gaustad notes that the

> institutions of religion are not scattered in hundreds of meaningless fragments. While the ecclesiastical patterns may bear some resemblance to a crazy quilt, the design is not totally devoid of meaning. . . . Ten denominational families or traditions of Christendom account for 90% of all religious group membership in America. If the Jewish population is added, we account for 94% of the total number with religious affiliation. . . .
>   The ten major traditions are these: Roman Catholic, 46¼ millions; Baptist, 23½ millions; Methodist, 14¼ millions; Lutheran, 8¾ millions; Presbyterian, 4½ millions; Christian, 4¼ millions; Episcopal, 3½ millions; Eastern Orthodoxy, 3¼ millions; Latter Day Saints, 2 millions; and the United Church of Christ, 2 millions. The Jews belong in this list too, but since membership figures present special problems, it is necessary to speak of Jewish population rather than Jewish religious affiliation. These 11 groups, then, encompass all but about 6% of institutional religious membership in America.[31]

Membership figures in religious groups must, of course, be employed only as general guides to denominational strength, because methods and accuracy of record keeping vary so widely. Many groups, such as Catholics, Episcopalians, and Lutherans, count all family members, including baptized infants, in their membership totals. Other groups, such as Baptists and Disciples of Christ, include only those above "age of accountability" who have made professions of faith and "joined" the churches. In addition, a majority of churches carry on their rolls the names of many people who have been inactive, some for years.

Of course, the churches, as institutions ready to accept and include people as members, have been on American shores since the beginning. Indeed, it was against a churchly or right-wing tradition that Roger Williams rebelled. While he was propounding his radical views about the freedom of religion, the great Puritan divines of New England were writing about religion as essentially a covenant relationship between God and his *people*. Though they sought the "middle way" between separatism and loyalty to the Church of England, the Puritan fathers would never have thought of practicing religion outside boundaries of the "visible" church. In 1648, when "The Cambridge Platform" was designed by the New Englanders, the aim was to draw up a set of statements about religion that all could agree upon. In the logic of the Platform, religious people—or "saints" as they were called—were defined as those who had not only personally "owned" the covenant but who had also

[30] Ibid., pp. 48–49.
[31] Gaustad, op. cit., pp. 836–937.

bound themselves to the New Israel planted in this hemisphere, that is, made themselves active members of the institutionalized form of religion in the new world.

In addition to the Puritans of New England, Anglicans in the South and in the Middle Atlantic colonies, Dutch Reformed people in New York, and a smattering of Jews and Catholics here and there all contributed to the early growth in this country of religion in the form of *ecclesial* institutions.[32] However, not all Jews in America have considered themselves to be religious Jews. Though many Jews claim something called Jewishness, it is not the synagogue or the temple or the religion of Judaism they are talking about. Instead, they are claiming something else, an ethnic tradition perhaps.[33] The point becomes clearer when one substitutes, say, *Baptist* for *Jew*. To say that one is a Baptist but no longer a religious Baptist is a virtually meaningless utterance. You *may* be making a highly figurative allusion: that your friend is no longer evangelical, morally rigorous, or some such thing. But there is no way to give up membership in the Baptist church and still be thought of as a Baptist. Jews, on the other hand, can continue to think of and call themselves Jews although they have no affiliation or intention of affiliating with a Jewish ecclesial group. Or to put it still another way: a Baptist (or any other Christian in America) has to work at being a Baptist, because being a Baptist is pretty much a voluntary matter. But an atheistic or skeptical Jew is still recognized as a Jew by others, as the death camps proved, even if he or she should disavow Judaism as a religion. In short, what Jewishness consists of has never been satisfactorily resolved by anyone. We simply have to acknowledge that, when talking about Jews, we are dealing with a unique religio-cultural phenomenon in America.

In addition to the special problem of what constitutes Jewishness, there is another curious ambiguity about American ecclesial institutions. The ambiguity arises out of the relationship between that peculiarly American creation the denomination and its local manifestation, the congregation. For example, the question "What church do you belong to?" may be answered in at least one of two ways. You may answer that you are a Methodist, by which you are, by inference, giving your denominational preference. Or you may reply that you belong to a *specific* local manifestation of the denomination—the *First* Methodist Church, *Trinity* Methodist Church, the *Southside* Methodist Church, and so on. By contrast, in Europe, where the Christian establishment prevailed for hundreds of years, if you lived in a particular geographical locale, you were a member of *that* parish. You had no options because

[32] The word *ecclesial* is handy because it does not have the specifically Christian and clerical connotations that the word *ecclesiastical* carries. Taken from the Greek, *ecclesial* refers to religion as found in gathered social entities such as churches, synagogues, temples, meetings, and other institutionalized forms of faith.

[33] Nor, might we add, is it a racial term. There is no such thing as the Jewish race. Jews are found among many different people of varying characteristics the world over.

there *were* no options. After the Reformation the parochial system continued throughout Europe, even within areas predominantly Lutheran, Calvinist, or Anglican. But in America, where religion has been disestablished, denominations (and congregations within a single denomination) are in *competition* with one another. The location of one's residence has not been the determining factor of church membership. Frequently members of one congregation will drive by other church buildings, of their own denomination as well as others, to get to the house of worship they prefer. Only the Catholics have attempted to maintain the concept of the parish and even they do not scrupulously enforce parish boundaries.

Typical Americans, then, if they attach themselves to the church, usually think of their attachment in terms of the local group of their own choice. William A. Clebsch, an astute observer of the American scene, has written a perceptive account of the "stubborn congregationalism of American religion." Although denominations have "thrown up centralized bureaucracies in national headquarters populated by executives" who attempt to exercise suzerainty over far-flung ecclesiastical domains, the "church" for the lay constituency has more often been identified with the local congregation than with a national or international denomination. Clebsch attributes the intense local loyalty to the relative stability of the lay constituency and the marked mobility of the clergy: "By and large professional religionists in America, most notably among Methodists, (have) lived like butterflies," settling first on one congregation and then another.[34]

So if we think much about *ecclesial* religion in America, as opposed to personal and private religion, we are more likely to think of it in terms of the local congregation. Clebsch was writing principally of Protestants, but Herberg has also shown how no one supracongregational authority has ever been able to gain power over Jewish synagogues and temples: "Jewish religious polity is ultracongregational, and this is equally true of all three 'denominations.' . . . The various rabbinical and synagogal associations have no formal power over their constituents and can make no decisions binding on the individual congregations."[35]

Only Catholics, Christian Scientists, and Mormons have been able to regulate local affairs from centralized offices with any degree of efficiency, and sometimes even they falter.

There are a number of inferences we may draw from this highly ambiguous situation with regard to American ecclesial religion, but the most obvious conclusion is that Americans are not terribly "churchy." As John W. Turnbull has noted, "the American does not think much in terms of 'the Church' because even when 'the churches' present themselves to him, they do not do so as clear entities. . . . Each denomination

[34] William A. Clebsch, *From Sacred to Profane America* (New York: Harper & Row, 1968), pp. 74f.
[35] Herberg, op. cit., p. 209.

(at least within Protestantism) is . . . imperfectly distinguished from the others." In addition, there simply is no clear-cut attachment to "the Church" as one vast presence because, in America, "we have never had a body which, however pretentious its claim and however imperfect its performance, even attempted to represent such a reality."[36]

A subset of ecclesial religion which will be used in this book is represented by the term *main line*. The term is derived from railroad usage where the main line is the principal route as opposed to a branch line or a side track. *Main line* has an unfortunate elitist connotation in American social history in that it originally connoted the aristocratic district just outside Philadelphia served by the Pennsylvania Railroad. We are using main-line to designate those Protestant, Catholic, and Jewish groups, that by the early 1980s, were being viewed as "traditional," inherited, and normative and that constitute a category commonly referred to as main-line by journalists, historians, and sociologists. Main-line bodies tend not to be exclusivist in their religious claims and are not anti-ecumenical. Following an "Exclusivist-Ecumenical Gradient," established members of the main-line denominations are, in order:

Reform Jews; United Church of Christ; United Methodist Church; United Presbyterian Church; American Baptist Convention; Episcopal Church; Reformed Church in America.

More ambiguous in their main-line status would be

Greek Orthodox; Russian Orthodox; Conservative Jews; Roman Catholic Church; American Lutheran Church; Lutheran Church-Missouri Synod; Southern Baptist Convention; Black Muslims.

Those who clearly are not main-line would be

Church of Christ, Scientist; Church of God; Seventh-Day Adventists; Latter-Day Saints (Mormons); Churches of Christ; Orthodox Jews; Evangelicals and Pentecostals; Jehovah's Witnesses.[37]

In sum, for most Americans, the word *religion* calls up connotations dealing with the personal, individualized element but also with a rather elastic ecclesial dimension. This does not preclude the recognition of other factors that enter into the comprehensive self-understanding of American religion. Obviously, some Americans perceive religion primarily in terms of creedal affirmations or theological beliefs, whereas for others religion may center on ritual observances or traditional cul-

---

[36]John W. Turnbull, "Some Notes on Religious America," *Student World*, Vol. 55 (1962), pp. 416–417.

[37]The Exclusivist-Ecumenical Gradient was taken from Dean M. Kelley, *Why Conservative Churches Are Growing* (New York: Harper & Row, 1977), p 89. For a more extensive discussion of the term *main line*, see Martin E. Marty, *A Nation of Behavers* (Chicago: University of Chicago Press, 1976), pp. 52–79.

tural patterns. What is evident is that religion is a complex phenomenon, a "many-splendored thing," which must be studied with full awareness of its multiple facets.

Failure to keep this complexity in mind exposes us to the danger of reductionism in the study of religion. Reductionism implies that we may understand a phenomenon like religion by approaching it from only one disciplinary perspective. For instance, a scholar may insist that the full scope of religion in America may be understood through a system of rigorous sociological analysis or, perhaps, by applying the methods and models of psychological study. Many religiously oriented scholars have made the similar mistake of insisting that religion must only be studied theologically. Realistically, if religion is the complex thing we have just been describing, it must be studied from many angles. Sociology, anthropology, theology, history, psychology—all will make their contributions to understanding; but no one of these can hope to comprehend the phenomenon alone. The disciplines must supplement each other.

One form of religiousness that is particularly open to this multidisciplinary approach is the so-called civil religion. Scholars have in recent years increasingly turned their attention to the role religion plays in our self-consciousness as a nation. The term *civil religion* is derived from *The Social Contract* by the great French philosopher Jean–Jacques Rousseau. Although we will, in this study, address ourselves to many other problems, motifs, and structures in American religion, civil religion is a basic and fundamental phenomenon requiring searching and extended scrutiny.

Civil Religion

1

Some of the most penetrating analyses of American life have been made by visitors from other shores. G. K. Chesterton (1874–1936), English Catholic and belletrist, after a visit to this country declared that

> America is the only nation in the world that is founded on a creed. That creed is set forth with dogmatic and even theological lucidity in the Declaration of Independence; perhaps the only piece of practical politics that is also theoretical politics and good literature. It enunciates that all men are equal in their claim to justice, that governments exist to give them that justice, and that their authority is for that reason just. It certainly does condemn anarchism, and it does also by inference condemn atheism, since it clearly names the Creator as the ultimate authority from whom these equal rights are derived. Nobody expects a modern political system to proceed logically in the application of such dogmas, and in the matter of God and Government it is naturally God whose claim is taken more lightly. The point is that there is a creed, if not about divine, at least about human things.[1]

Chesterton's comment comes as a brilliant flash of insight into our national life when one reflects on the sacred character Americans have attributed to the Declaration of Independence and national institutions. But as one surveys the literature, one discovers that Chesterton's point was hardly new. Americans had for generations assigned a very special, if not religious, meaning to the course of the nation's history and destiny under God. So convinced were they of this fact that in 1954 Congress added the phrase _under God_ to the Pledge of Allegiance. This action was taken during the administration of Dwight D. Eisenhower (1890–1969), who himself was a fascinating embodiment of our civil religion. During his campaign for the presidency he was fond of telling people that he was engaged in a "crusade."[2] His speeches were filled with religious terms and imagery. It therefore came as no real surprise that God was the first word he spoke in his inaugural address. One historian writes that on the night before the inauguration, the president-elect told the group of men that were to make up his cabinet that "one flame seems to be missing. Perhaps it is a feeling of prayer."[3] The next day he turned away from the _two_ Bibles on which he had taken the oath of office, faced the assembled crowd before the Capital steps and the millions

---

[1] G. K. Chesterton, "What I Saw in America," _The Man Who Was Chesterton_, edited by Raymond T. Bond (New York: Dodd, Mead, 1954), p. 188.

[2] Paul Hutchinson, "The President's Religious Faith," _The Christian Century_, Vol. 71, No. 12 (March 24, 1954), p. 367.

[3] Davis Newton Lott, _The Presidents Speak: The Inaugural Addresses of the American Presidents from Washington to Nixon_ (New York: Holt, Rinehart and Winston, 1969), p. 257.

who were viewing him on their television sets around the country, and asked permission to give "a little private prayer of my own."[4] Paul Hutchinson has noted that:

> Uttered by some men, a prayer inserted at that moment would have sounded like a calculated play to the church-going galleries. This prayer did not. It was too direct, too faulty in diction—ritualists could grimace at "Thou will"—to be anything but what it was, the intuitive expression of a humble man who, in assuming tasks new to his experience, acknowledged his need for divine aid.[5]

Eisenhower then launched into his address, during which he called on all Americans to renew their faith:

> This faith is the abiding creed of our fathers. It is our faith in the deathless dignity of man, governed by eternal moral and natural laws.
> This faith defines our full view of life. It establishes, beyond debate, those gifts of the Creator that are man's inalienable rights, and that make all men equal in His sight. . . .
> This faith rules our whole way of life. It decrees that we, the people, elect leaders not to rule but to serve.[6]

Toward the end of his speech he said that all good citizens need to renew their "conscious faith in our country and in the watchfulness of a Divine Providence."[7] Some theologically scrupulous observers wryly commented that the president might have difficulty in placing faith in the country *as well as God.*

The "religious" gesture Eisenhower was making, however, was by no means new and strange to the American public. Ever since Washington was sworn into office, every American president has made some overt recognition of the supposed special relationship between nation and God. Even the theologically independent Thomas Jefferson admitted the necessity for God's help:

> I shall need, too, the favour of that Being in whose hands we are, who led our fathers, as Israel of old, from their native land and planted them in a country flowing with all the necessaries and comforts of life; who has covered our infancy with His providence and our riper years with His wisdom and power, and to whose goodness I ask you to join in supplication with me that He will so enlighten the minds of your servants, guide their councils, and prosper their measures that whatsoever they do shall result in your good, and shall secure to you the peace, friendship, and approbation of all nations.[8]

As Hutchinson has said, the cynic might be inclined to dismiss these invocations of divine aid as sheer hypocrisy. Indeed, the motivations behind these utterances are unquestionably mixed, as are all human mo-

---

[4] Ibid.
[5] Hutchinson, op. cit., p. 362.
[6] Lott, op. cit., p. 258.
[7] Ibid., p. 259.
[8] From Jefferson's Second Inaugural, delivered March 4, 1805. Lott, op. cit., p. 22.

tives. But the serious student of religion cannot take these actions lightly. We know them to be evidence of something much more profound than mere grandstanding. We have said that they are evidences of civil religion, but just what is that? How did it begin? What is its structure today?

Religion and the Political Order

Toqueville correctly observed that "every religion has some political opinion linked to it by affinity." (Note: not just *any* "political opinion" but a congenial political opinion.) He believed that "the spirit of man, left to follow its bent, will regulate political society and the City of God in uniform fashion; it will . . . seek to *harmonize* earth with heaven."[9] Toqueville's observation is sound enough, except that for America he might have turned it around: in this country it appears that the government has a congenial religious opinion linked to it, a civil religiousness. At least, to the latter-day observer, "the religion of the republic" seems to have come into being with the formation of the republic in the late eighteenth century. But Toqueville was on dead center when he described the religion of the New World as a religiousness "which I can only describe as democratic and republican."[10]

A brief look at the historical data is instructive. In the beginnings of the American experience most colonies attempted, some more successfully than others, to establish various forms of ecclesial religion. In New England the Puritans linked civil government intimately with what was later to become the Congregational church. In Virginia, the Carolinas, and Maryland (and, to a lesser degree, in Georgia and New York) the Anglican church (later to become the Episcopal church) was given the preferred status. In 1791, however, disestablishment (the severing of legal ties between church and state) became the national rule with the adoption of the First Amendment to the Constitution, which holds that "Congress shall make no law respecting an establishment of religion, or prohibiting the free exercise thereof." As we shall see later, the full implication of these words is still being worked out in contemporary law and judicial opinions, but they obviously meant that no form of ecclesial religion—or to be more historically precise, no form of the *Christian* religion—would be allowed to occupy the most favored position in the newly founded republic. Michaelson writes, "The fathers understood themselves to be launching a new secular society in which the state would play a limited role in human affairs, religion would not be used by the state to sanctify itself, and 'the free exercise' of religion would be encouraged."[11] Similar disestablishment at the state level had already

[9] Alexis de Toqueville, *Democracy in America*, edited by J. P. Mayer and Max Lerner (New York: Harper & Row, 1966), p. 265.
[10] Ibid.
[11] Robert Michaelson, *Piety in the Public School* (New York: Macmillan, 1970), p. 38.

occurred in several of the colonies and, although it took several decades (the Congregational church in Massachusetts was not fully separated from the state until 1831), the pattern eventually prevailed in the entire American political structure.[12]

Having come to take such an arrangement for granted, so much so that "separation of church and state" is a kind of modern American political shibboleth, it is difficult for many people to comprehend the reasoning and attitudes that led the early Puritans, for instance, to wish to establish their religion as the official religion in the colonies. We are accustomed to think of the Puritans as simply perversely intolerant, but such an image tends to obscure most of the real issues involved in the matter.

The Puritans

Colonial New England was dominated by transplanted English Puritans. These Puritans were Calvinist in their religious doctrines; that is, they accepted the teachings of the French Protestant reformer John Calvin, who laid primary emphasis on the sovereignty of God and the helplessness of sinful persons apart from providential grace. God chooses or "elects" certain persons to be saved, not on the basis of their merit but purely as an act of mercy and love. Persons cannot know certainly that they are counted among the elect, but if they respond to God in faith and obedience, striving to live righteous lives, they may hope that these things are indications of their election. God's way of accomplishing his work on earth is through the elect, who are appointed to carry out his plan. They do this by applying the doctrines and commandments of the Bible to every detail of life.

The particular kind of Calvinism brought to this country by the colonial Puritans was the so-called covenant or federal theology, of which the leading English exponent was William Ames (1576–1633) and whose most distinguished representative in New England was John Cotton of Massachusetts (1584–1652). Ames and Cotton taught that God has entered into a covenant or agreement with his people. He undertakes to save His people from their sins and, in response to this gracious divine act, men are to obey Him and to seek to transform society according to His will. Puritans found in the Bible the model for a total community—a "holy commonwealth"—which involved all aspects of life both personal and social. Thus Richard Baxter (1615–1691), one of the greatest of the English Puritan preachers, wrote in 1659, "It is this theocratical policy or Divine Commonwealth, which is the unquestionable reign of Christ on earth, which all Christians are agreed may be

---

[12]Sidney Mead points out that, ironically, "under the system of official separation of church and state, the denominations eventually found themselves as completely identified with nationalism and their country's political systems as had ever been known in Christendom." See Sidney E. Mead, *The Lively Experiment* (New York: Harper & Row, 1963), p. 157.

justly sought; and that temporal dignity of Saints, which undoubtedly must bless the world."[13]

Under the leadership of Henry VIII, and for a variety of reasons more political than religious, the established Church of England had broken away from the Roman Church in 1534. In the latter half of that century the Puritan movement began as an agitation within the Church of England, seeking to "purify" the church by eliminating remaining Catholic doctrines and practices. The English Puritans wished also to see the transformation of England's total society in accordance with their understanding of God's will.

Such a task proved impossible in England, where the Puritans were surrounded by a society hostile to their ideas and under a government legally bound to an "impure" church. Many of the more radical and activist Puritans underwent a considerable amount of persecution. Then the New World came into view as a possible solution. Though many stayed on in England and became involved in the bloody events of the Cromwellian revolution, some remaining loyal to the Church of England while others opted for complete separation, there were many who saw in the New World a unique opportunity to accomplish what they had not been able to do in England. Free from the pressure of a "godless" culture and far removed from the inhibiting hand of the English crown, God's people might build the kind of society God had decreed—a Holy Commonwealth.[14]

---

[13] Richard Baxter, *The Holy Commonwealth* (1659), p. 221.

[14] It should be noted in passing that there were initially three principal types of English churchmen who came to the New World, all of whom were "puritan" in one way or another. (1) In Virginia they were loyal to the Church of England and believed that the episcopacy (bishops) was necessary for the continuity and health of the church, though they were greatly influenced by the writings of John Calvin. They were what has commonly been called "low churchmen" as compared to the "high churchmen" back home, who wanted to keep the church more closely tied to the crown and to Catholic tradition and practice. (2) Those who came to Massachusetts Bay considered themselves loyal British subjects and loyal churchmen. But they saw no necessity whatever for bishops. The congregation, they believed, should become the locus of ecclesiastical authority. They nevertheless did not immediately or openly break their relationship with the mother church. (3) Those who came to Plymouth in 1620 were separatists. That is, they could see no virtue in maintaining any kind of relationship with the Church of England. To purify it meant to separate from it. [For a discussion of the problem, see H. Shelton Smith, Robert T. Handy, Lefferts A. Loetscher, *American Christianity* (New York: Scribner, 1960), Vol. I, p. 87.] Within a short time, however, the position of those at Plymouth and Massachusetts Bay coalesced, and *all* the Puritans of New England became Congregationalists who had, for all intents and purposes, separated themselves from the jurisdiction of the Church of England, whereas Anglicans in the South and Mid-Atlantic colonies remained loyal to the Church of England, with its episcopal form of government. There were, however, no American bishops until after the Revolution, and during the colonial period Anglican churches in this country were governed by local boards of laymen called vestries, which has given the Anglican church in America (the Protestant Episcopal Church) a decidedly congregational flavor. There were no bishops in the colonies primarily because of the efforts of Nonconformists in England and America. Various officals made repeated suggestions that the Crown send out bishops to America, but the Nonconformists were able to persuade the Crown of the impropriety of such an act. As the Revolution approached, the more militant non-Anglicans in America adamantly resisted the idea of the episcopacy on the ground that bishops were but stalking horses for establishing the monarchy in America. [For the classic description of the problem of the episcopacy in the colonies, see Carl Bridenbaugh, *Mitre and Sceptre* (New York: Oxford University Press, 1967).]

The early Puritans carried this vision to the shores of New England. They were determined to avoid the pitfalls and problems that had dogged their dream in the mother country. Because society's chief purpose was to do the will of God, there could be no legitimate separation between church and state, for both institutions must interpret and implement divinely given laws. Because natural man is sinful, however, it followed that God's will could be truly done in the community only if the government of both church and state rested securely in the hands of the elect. Only holy and regenerate men could interpret and enforce God's laws. And there could be no real distinction between civil and sacred law. A person who violated or disobeyed *any* law of the community, whether it be that against theft or that which required all men to attend "divine service," threatened to undermine the foundations of the Commonwealth. For those who were not Puritans but still resided in the community, the alternatives were clear: either obey the laws, or leave! Because the leadership did not require all residents to join the church, the Puritans did not see this as intolerance. After all, there was plenty of virgin space to which the dissenter might go. Moreover, the Puritans were sure in their own minds that they represented God's Chosen, carving out a new and revolutionary kind of society in a world opened up to them by divine providence, just as Canaan had once been opened up to Israel. To allow perverse individuals, in the name of abstract concepts like liberty or freedom, to inhibit the progress of God's plan by denying, twisting, or misinterpreting biblical teachings simply did not make sense. When the perverse member of society continued in his perversity, it was the duty of the magistrate to punish the wrongdoer. The Quakers especially suffered.

At this point it is to be noted that we certainly cannot fully understand the Puritans unless we recognize that they took religious heresy with great seriousness. They believed that the perversion of Christian teaching might well result in the eternal damnation of human's souls. It is relatively easy, for example, to be tolerant of witches if one does not believe in their existence. But if one is convinced, as many of the Puritans were, that witches are actually people who have entered into league with the Devil, the situation changes. If a person believes in witches, how tolerant is he going to be toward one who is a next-door neighbor, threatening to corrupt or damn his wife and child?

The contemporary American situation is not totally divorced from this historical background. Although few moderns believe seriously in witches or become overly concerned about religious heresy, many Americans view *political* heresy in much the same way as the Puritans looked at spiritual unbelief. For many citizens, political heretics— anarchists, Communists, the Klan, for example—represent flagrant challenges to officially sanctioned democratic values. Political heretics, like the religious heretics of old, must, these people think, be stopped before they rip apart the fabric of the national community. Such a view has some connection with the Puritan legacy.

The Puritan view was more clearly articulated and effectively implemented in this country than the views of other groups. It is still true, however, that the kind of total religious disestablishment that took place in the Revolutionary and early national period of the United States was a startling development for a Western nation. From the time of Constantine, the Christian church enjoyed in one form or another a privileged position with every government in Europe. An intensive alliance was contracted during the fourth century of the Christian era. A highly sophisticated network of laws, both civil and canon, provided rulers in both orders with what were believed to be divine sanctions. Pagan cultures became saturated with Christian belief and symbol, and "Christendom" came into being—an entity that existed, without challenge, until the eighteenth century. Then the American and French revolutions sundered the identification of sacred and temporal power in the West. (In the East, the Russian Revolution had the same effect during the present century.) In a sense, with these political revolutions, a religious vacuum was created, but only temporarily. A new kind of national religiousness surged in to fill the gap created by disestablishment. It has been given a variety of names in America, but all of them describe roughly the same phenomenon, though each term carries a slightly different connotation. Will Herberg calls it the "American Way of Life" and sees it as inimical to authentic religion, which is most likely to be found, he says, in the ecclesial bodies.[15] Sidney Mead names it the "religion of the republic," by which he conjures up an antiparticularist creed espoused by men like Franklin and Jefferson who helped to shape the Constitution and who viewed suspiciously the exclusivistic tendencies of the traditional ecclesial bodies.[16] Robert N. Bellah prefers the term *civil religion*, which he borrows from Rousseau. Bellah is attempting to describe the sociological fact as he finds it, without making any sort of judgment for or against it. These three authors—Herberg, Mead, and Bellah—provide significant contrasts in their perception of the phenomenon we are now dealing with.

Recent Discussions

In 1955 Herberg published *Protestant-Catholic-Jew: An Essay in Religious Sociology*. In the preface he acknowledged that he was not attempting "a comprehensive treatise on the sociology of religion in

---

[15] See Will Herberg, *Protestant-Catholic-Jew: An Essay in American Religious Sociology* (Garden City, N.Y.: Doubleday, 1960).

[16] See Sidney E. Mead, "The Post-Protestant Concept and America's Two Religions," *Religion in Life*, Vol. 33 (Spring 1964).

the United States, but a study of one aspect of the religious situation in this country"—namely, the thesis that ecclesial religion in America, though made up of many groups and sects, has tended to fall into three capacious melting pots rather than one; hence the name of the book. In the course of his analysis[17] he also closely scrutinized and roundly attacked public religiousness, or, as he preferred to call it, the "American Way of Life," because, in his judgment, it is a combination of free-wheeling free enterprise, democracy, and pop psychology with a fatuous, self-confident version of the Judaeo-Christian tradition. Herberg's attack is appealing because he lashes out at the hypocrisy in the kind of religiousness he describes, but by taking a polemical stand, he necessarily qualifies his effectiveness as a sociologist. His zeal to polemicize allows him to caricature civil religion and to set up straw men that are easy enough to demolish. A partial answer to his criticism, as Bellah suggests, is that all religious traditions have their deformations and distortions, America's civil religion being no exception.

In 1964 Sidney Mead published an article entitled "The Post-Protestant Concept and America's Two Religions," in which he attempted to unravel the tangled question of the relation between the churches and the common faith of Americans. For a number of years he had written about religion in America and had concluded that the tradition in this country, which informs the life of the ecclesial groups and provides the basic religious attitude for the public at large, is a cluster of Enlightenment political ideas embodied in the Constitution.

The occasion for Mead's article was the rather popularly held sentiment among some scholars and theologians that America had entered a "Post-Protestant" era. Mead disagreed. He claimed that the contemporary situation could not be accurately described as "Post-Protestant" for the simple reason that the nation had never been Protestant in the way that Herberg and others had supposed. That America had been affected by the Protestant sects and churches more than by the Catholic and Jewish traditions, Mead agreed. In that rather obvious sense, America has been largely Protestant. But if one means that Protestantism has provided the ideological premises upon which the nation's public and political life was built, then it could never be said to have been Protestant. The very idea of religious freedom incorporated in the Bill of Rights expressly prohibits the kind of exclusivistic ideology that is at the heart of Protestantism. Accordingly, the nation, as a political and social entity, has turned its back on the particularism of sects, no matter what the sectarian hue might be. We must understand, says Mead, that the theology of the denominations has not been the ideology of the republic. The republic generated its own brand of "theology" consistent with eighteenth-century rationalism. Thus, we could not be in a "Post-Protestant" phase of our history today because we have never been Protestant in the first place.

[17]Herberg, op. cit., p. vii.

Toward the end of his article Mead suggests that the ecclesial groups, by muting their particularist claims and by adopting what Mead calls the "theology of the republic," could effectively overcome the tendency toward denominational competition. The religion of the republic in effect could become an instrumentality for ecumenical rapprochement. Unity for churches in America will be found when all the conflicting groups learn to adjust to the broad and general claims of American civil religion.

Mead's attitude toward civil religion represents a position that is almost the precise opposite of Herberg's. His desire to subsume the religion of the churches under the umbrella of civil religion is exactly the insidious form of idolatry that Herberg found so disturbing. But in contrast to both Mead and Herberg, we might well want to ask why it is necessary for either civil or ecclesial religion to assume a predominant role. Could not the relationship be treated in a more dialectical way—in which the churches continue to exist as independent bodies with their own particular claims, and civil religion is recognized as a viable religious force for the public at large? Surely the framers of the American state maintained both a sense of civil religion and of the value of Christianity. But at the same time, they sought to preserve and purify both by separating them through disestablishment, forbidding religious tests for public office, the guarantee of religious freedom, and the like. And although civil religion and Christianity continue to be imperfectly distinguished from one another in our culture, it should not blind us to the fact that there is room for both, and a *necessity* for both, in our system.

It remained for Robert N. Bellah to sort out some of the imponderables and give what is perhaps a more balanced account of the problem. In his work we shall see that civil religion in America is a fairly well-formulated set of beliefs, values, symbols, and institutions in which our society expresses its sense of meaning and destiny and to which it demands assent and loyalty as a condition of citizenship. It articulates the transcendent foundations upon which our society rests and finds its unity. It is the source of whatever public virtue we may possess and is the basis for public ceremony and civil order.

In 1967 Bellah published an article that immediately captured the attention of religion scholars in this country. Although the ideas he addressed himself to had been dealt with in prior efforts by others, no one had put them together in so lucid and impartial a fashion. For Bellah, American civil religion is to be neither praised nor blamed but described. Sociological impartiality was temporarily abandoned only at the end of the essay, when he set forth the conditions upon which civil religion can remain a viable force in the national life. He called the late 1960s a "time of trial" when, as we all recall, the vitality of the nation's faith was sorely tested by revolutionary forces at home and abroad.

From "Civil Religion in America" by Robert N. Bellah

While some have argued that Christianity is the national faith, and others that church and synagogue celebrate only the generalized religion of "the American Way of Life," few have realized that there actually exists alongside of and rather clearly differentiated from the churches an elaborate and well-institutionalized civil religion in America. This article argues not only that there is such a thing, but also that this religion—or perhaps better, this religious dimension—has its own seriousness and integrity and requires the same care in understanding that any other religion does.

The Kennedy Inaugural

Kennedy's inaugural address of 20 January 1961 serves as an example and a clue with which to introduce this complex subject. That address began:

> We observe today not a victory of party but a celebration of freedom—symbolizing an end as well as a beginning—signifying renewal as well as change. For I have sworn before you and Almighty God the same solemn oath our forebears prescribed nearly a century and three quarters ago.
>
> The world is very different now. For man holds in his mortal hands the power to abolish all forms of human poverty and to abolish all forms of human life. And yet the same revolutionary beliefs for which our forebears fought are still at issue around the globe—the belief that the rights of man come not from the generosity of the state but from the hand of God.

And it concluded:

> Finally, whether you are citizens of America or of the world, ask of us the same high standards of strength and sacrifice that we shall ask of you. With a good conscience our only sure reward, with history the final judge of our deeds, let us go forth to lead the land we love, asking His blessing and His help, but knowing that here on earth God's work must truly be our own.

These are the three places in his brief address in which Kennedy mentioned the name of God. If we could understand why he mentioned God, the way in which he did it, and what he meant to say in those three references, we would understand much about American civil religion. But this is not a simple or obvious task, and American students of religion would probably differ widely in their interpretation of these passages.

Let us consider first the placing of the three references. They occur in the two opening paragraphs and in the closing paragraph, thus providing a sort of frame for the more concrete remarks that form the middle part of the speech. Looking be-

SOURCE: Robert N. Bellah, "Civil Religion in America, " *Daedalus*, Vol. 96, No. 1 (Winter 1967). Reprinted by permission of *Daedalus*, Journal of the American Academy of Arts and Sciences, Cambridge, Massachusetts.

yond this particular speech, we would find that similar references to God are almost invariably to be found in the pronouncements of American presidents on solemn occasions, though usually not in the working messages that the president sends to Congress on various concrete issues. How, then, are we to interpret this placing of references to God?

It might be argued that the passages quoted reveal the essentially irrelevant role of religion in the very secular society that is America. The placing of the references in this speech as well as in public life generally indicates that religion has "only a ceremonial significance;" it gets only a sentimental nod which serves largely to placate the more unenlightened members of the community, before a discussion of the really serious business with which religion has nothing whatever to do. A cynical observer might even say that an American president has to mention God or risk losing votes. A semblance of piety is merely one of the unwritten qualifications for the office, a bit more traditional than but not essentially different from the present-day requirement of a pleasing television personality.

But we know enough about the function of ceremonial and ritual in various societies to make us suspicious of dismissing something as unimportant because it is "only a ritual." What people say on solemn occasions need not be taken at face value, but it is often indicative of deep-seated values and commitments that are not made explicit in the course of everyday life. Following this line of argument, it is worth considering whether the very special placing of the references to God in Kennedy's address may not reveal something rather important and serious about religion in American life.

It might be countered that the very way in which Kennedy made his references reveals the essentially vestigial place of religion today. He did not refer to any religion in particular. He did not refer to Jesus Christ, or to Moses, or to the Christian church; certainly he did not refer to the Catholic Church. In fact, his only reference was to the concept of God, a word which almost all Americans can accept but which means so many different things to so many different people that it is almost an empty sign. Is this not just another indication that in America religion is considered vaguely to be a good thing, but that people care so little about it that it has lost any content whatever? Isn't Eisenhower reported to have said, "Our government makes no sense unless it is founded in a deeply felt religious faith—and I don't care what it is," and isn't that a complete negation of any real religion?

These questions are worth pursuing because they raise the issue of how civil religion relates to the political society, on the one hand, and to private religious organizations, on the other. President Kennedy was a Christian, more specifically a Catholic Christian. Thus, his general references to God do not mean that he lacked a specific religious commitment. But why, then, did he not include some remark to the effect that Christ is the Lord of the world or some indication of respect for the Catholic Church? He did not because these are matters of his own private religious belief and of his relation to his own particular church; they are not matters relevant in any direct way to the conduct of his public office. Others with different religious views and commitments to different churches or denominations are equally qualified participants in the political process. The principle of separation of church

and state guarantees the freedom of religious belief and association, but at the same
time clearly segregates the religious sphere, which is considered to be essentially
private, from the political one.

Considering the separation of church and state, how is a president justified in
using the word *God* at all? The answer is that the separation of church and state has
not denied the political realm a religious dimension. Although matters of personal
religious belief, worship, and association are considered to be strictly private affairs,
there are, at the same time, certain common elements of religious orientation that
the great majority of Americans share. These have played a crucial role in the development of American institutions and still provide a religious dimension for the
whole fabric of American life, including the political sphere. This public religious
dimension is expressed in a set of beliefs, symbols, and rituals that I am calling the
American civil religion. The inauguration of a president is an important ceremonial
event in this religion. It reaffirms, among other things, the religious legitimation of
the highest political authority.

Let us look more closely at what Kennedy actually said. First he said, "I have
sworn before you and Almighty God the same solemn oath our forebears prescribed
nearly a century and three quarters ago." The oath is the oath of office, including
the acceptance of the obligation to uphold the Constitution. He swears it before the
people (you) and God. Beyond the Constitution, then, the president's obligation
extends not only to the people but to God. In American political theory, sovereignty
rests, of course, with the people, but implicitly, and often explicitly, the ultimate
sovereignty has been attributed to God. This is the meaning of the motto, "In God
we trust," as well as the inclusion of the phrase "under God" in the pledge to the
flag. What difference does it make that sovereignty belongs to God? Though the will
of the people as expressed in majority vote is carefully institutionalized as the
operative source of political authority, it is deprived of an ultimate significance. The
will of the people is not itself the criterion of right and wrong. There is a higher
criterion in terms of which this will can be judged; it is possible that the people may
be wrong. The president's obligation extends to the higher criterion.

But the religious dimension in political life as recognized by Kennedy not only
provides a grounding for the rights of man which makes any form of political ab-
solutism illegitmate, it also provides a transcendent goal for the political process.
This is implied in his final words that "here on earth God's work must truly be our
own." What he means here is, I think, more clearly spelled out in a previous paragraph, the wording of which, incidentally, has a distinctly Biblical ring:

> Now the trumpet summons us again—not as a call to bear arms, though arms we
> need—not as a call to battle, though embattled we are—but a call to bear the
> burden of a long twilight struggle, year in and year out, "rejoicing in hope,
> patient in tribulation"—a struggle against the common enemies of man: tyranny,
> poverty, disease and war itself.

The whole address can be understood as only the most recent statement of a theme
that lies very deep in the American tradition, namely the obligation, both collective
and individual, to carry out God's will on earth. This was the motivating spirit of
those who founded America, and it has been present in every generation since. Just

below the surface throughout Kennedy's inaugural address, it becomes explicit in the closing statement that God's work must be our own. That this very activist and non-contemplative conception of the fundamental religious obligation, which has been historically associated with the Protestant position, should be enunciated so clearly in the first major statement of the first Catholic president seems to underline how deeply established it is in the American outlook. Let us now consider the form and history of the civil religious tradition in which Kennedy was speaking.

The Idea of a Civil Religion

The phrase *civil religion* is, of course, Rousseau's. In Chapter 8, Book 4, of *The Social Contract*, he outlines the simple dogmas of the civil religion: the existence of God, the life to come, the reward of virtue and the punishment of vice, and the exclusion of religious intolerance. All other religious opinions are outside the cognizance of the state and may be freely held by citizens. While the phrase *civil religion* was not used, to the best of my knowledge, by the founding fathers, and I am certainly not arguing for the particular influence of Rousseau, it is clear that similar ideas, as part of the cultural climate of the late-eighteenth century, were to be found among the Americans.

The words and acts of the founding fathers, especially the first few presidents, shaped the form and tone of the civil religion as it has been maintained ever since. Though much is selectively derived from Christianity, this religion is clearly not itself Christianity. For one thing, neither Washington nor Adams nor Jefferson mentions Christ in his inaugural address; nor do any of the subsequent presidents, although not one of them fails to mention God. The God of the civil religion is not only rather "unitarian," he is also on the austere side, much more related to order, law, and right than to salvation and love. Even though he is somewhat deist in cast, he is by no means simply a watchmaker God. He is actively interested and involved in history, with a special concern for America. Here the analogy has much less to do with natural law than with ancient Israel; the equation of America with Israel in the idea of the "American Israel" is not infrequent.

What we have, then, from the earliest years of the republic is a collection of beliefs, symbols, and rituals with respect to sacred things and institutionalized in a collectivity. This religion—there seems no other word for it—while not antithetical to and indeed sharing much in common with Christianity, was neither sectarian nor in any specific sense Christian. At a time when the society was overwhelmingly Christian, it seems unlikely that this lack of Christian reference was meant to spare the feelings of the tiny non-Christian minority. Rather, the civil religion expressed what those who set the precedents felt was appropriate under the circumstances. It reflected their private as well as public views. Nor was the civil religion simply "religion in general." . . .

But the civil religion was not, in the minds of Franklin, Washington, Jefferson, or other leaders, with the exception of a few radicals like Tom Paine, ever felt to be a substitute for Christianity. There was an implicit but quite clear division of function between the civil religion and Christianity. Under the doctrine of religious liberty, an exceptionally wide sphere of personal piety and voluntary social action was left to the churches. But the churches were neither to control the state nor to be controlled by it. The national magistrate, whatever his private religious views, operates under the rubrics of the civil religion as long as he is in his official capacity, as we have already seen in the case of Kennedy. This accommodation was undoubtedly the product of a particular historical moment and of a cultural background dominated by Protestantism of several varieties and by the Enlightenment, but it has survived despite subsequent changes in the cultural and religious climate.

Civil War and Civil Religion

Until the Civil War, the American civil religion focused above all on the event of the Revolution, which was seen as the final act of the Exodus from the old lands across the waters. The Declaration of Independence and the Constitution were the sacred scriptures and Washington the divinely appointed Moses who led his people out of the hands of tyranny.

With the Civil War, a new theme of death, sacrifice, and rebirth enters the civil religion. It is symbolized in the life and death of Lincoln. Nowhere is it stated more vividly than in the Gettysburg Address, itself part of the Lincolnian "New Testament" among the civil scriptures. Robert Lowell has recently pointed out the "insistent use of birth images" in this speech explicitly devoted to "these honored dead": "brought forth," "conceived," "created," "a new birth of freedom." He goes on to say:

> The Gettysburg Address is a symbolic and sacramental act. Its verbal quality is resonance combined with a logical, matter of fact, prosaic brevity. . . . In his words, Lincoln symbolically died, just as the Union soldiers really died—and as he himself was soon really to die. By his words, he gave the field of battle a symbolic significance that it had lacked. For us and our country, he left Jefferson's ideals of freedom and equality joined to the Christian sacrificial act of death and rebirth. I believe this is a meaning that goes beyond sect or religion and beyond peace and war, and is now part of our lives as a challenge, obstacle and hope.

Lowell is certainly right in pointing out the Christian quality of the symbolism here, but he is also right in quickly disavowing any sectarian implication. The earlier symbolism of the civil religion had been Hebraic without being in any specific sense Jewish. The Gettysburg symbolism (". . . those who here gave their lives, that that nation might live") is Christian without having anything to do with the Christian church.

The symbolic equation of Lincoln with Jesus was made relatively early. Herndon, who had been Lincoln's law partner, wrote:

> For fifty years God rolled Abraham Lincoln through his fiery furnace. He did it to try Abraham and to purify him for his purposes. This made Mr. Lincoln humble, tender, forbearing, sympathetic to suffering, kind, sensitive, tolerant; broadening, deepening and widening his whole nature; making him the noblest and loveliest character since Jesus Christ. . . . I believe that Lincoln was God's chosen one.

With the Christian archetype in the background, Lincoln, "our martyred president," was linked to the war dead, those who "gave the last full measure of devotion." The theme of sacrifice was indelibly written into the civil religion.

The new symbolism soon found both physical and ritualistic expression. The great number of the war dead required the establishment of a number of national cemeteries. Of these, the Gettysburg National Cemetery, which Lincoln's famous address served to dedicate, has been overshadowed only by the Arlington National Cemetery. Begun somewhat vindictively on the Lee estate across the river from Washington, partly with the end that the Lee family could never reclaim it, it has subsequently become the most hallowed monument of the civil religion. Not only was a section set aside for the Confederate dead, but it has received the dead of each succeeding American war. It is the site of the one important new symbol to come out of World War I, the Tomb of the Unknown Soldier; more recently it has become the site of the tomb of another martyred president and its symbolic eternal flame.

Memorial Day, which grew out of the Civil War, gave ritual expression to the themes we have been discussing. As Lloyd Warner has so brilliantly analyzed it, the Memorial Day observance, especially in the towns and smaller cities of America, is a major event for the whole community involving a rededication to the martyred dead, to the spirit of sacrifice, and to the American vision. Just as Thanksgiving Day, which incidentally was securely institutionalized as an annual national holiday only under the presidency of Lincoln, serves to integrate the family into the civil religion, so Memorial Day has acted to integrate the local community into the national cult. Together with the less overtly religious Fourth of July and the more minor celebrations of Veterans Day and the birthdays of Washington and Lincoln, these two holidays provide an annual ritual calendar for the civil religion. The public-school system serves as a particularly important context for the cultic celebration of the civil rituals.

The Civil Religion Today

In reifying and giving a name to something that, though pervasive enough when you look at it, has gone on only semiconsciously, there is risk of severely distorting the data. But the reification and the naming have already begun. The religious critics of "religion in general," or of the "religion of the 'American Way of Life,'" or of "American Shinto" have really been talking about the civil religion. As usual in religious polemic, they take as criteria the best in their own religious tradition and as typical the worst in the tradition of the civil religion. Against these critics, I would argue that the civil religion at its best is a genuine apprehension of universal and transcendent religious reality as seen in or, one could almost say, as revealed through the experience of the American people. Like all religions, it has suffered various deformations and demonic distortions. At its best, it has neither been so general that it has lacked incisive relevance to the American scene nor so particular that it has placed American society above universal human values. I am not at all convinced that the leaders of the churches have consistently represented a higher level of religious insight than the spokesmen of the civil religion.

The civil religion has not always been invoked in favor of worthy causes. On the domestic scene, an American-legion type of ideology that fuses God, country, and flag has been used to attack nonconformist and liberal ideas and groups of all kinds. Still, it has been difficult to use the words of Jefferson and Lincoln to support special interests and undermine personal freedom. The defenders of slavery before the Civil War came to reject the thinking of the Declaration of Independence. Some of the most consistent of them turned against not only Jeffersonian democracy but Reformation religion; they dreamed of a South dominated by medieval chivalry and divine-right monarchy. For all the overt religiosity of the radical right today, their relation to the civil religious consensus is tenuous, as when the John Birch Society attacks the central American symbol of Democracy itself.

With the respect to America's role in the world, the dangers of distortion are greater and the built-in safeguards of the tradition weaker. The theme of the American Israel was used, almost from the beginning, as a justification for the shameful treatment of the Indians so characteristic of our history. It can be overtly or implicitly linked to the idea of manifest destiny which has been used to legitimate several adventures in imperialism since the early nineteenth century. Never has the danger been greater than today. The issue is not so much one of imperial expansion, of which we are accused, as of the tendency to assimilate all governments or parties in the world which support our immediate policies or call upon our help by invoking the notion of free institutions and democratic values. Those nations that are for the moment "on our side" become "the free world." A repressive and unstable military dictatorship in South Viet-Nam becomes "the free people of South Viet-Nam and their government." It is then part of the role of America as the New Jerusalem and "the last best hope of earth" to defend such governments with treasure and eventually with blood. When our soldiers are actually dying, it becomes possible to consecrate the struggle further by invoking the great theme of sacrifice. . . . The civil religion has exercised long-term pressure for the humane solution of our greatest domestic problem, the treatment of the Negro American. It remains to be seen how relevant it can become for our role in the world at large, and whether we can effectually stand for "the revolutionary beliefs for which our forebears fought," in John F. Kennedy's words.

The Third Time of Trial

In conclusion it may be worthwhile to relate the civil religion to the most serious situation that we as Americans now face, what I call the third time of trial. The first time of trial had to do with the question of independence, whether we should or could run our own affairs in our own way. The second time of trial was over the issue of slavery, which in turn was only the most salient aspect of the more general problem of the full institutionalization of democracy within our country. This second problem we are still far from solving though we have some notable successes to our credit. But we have been overtaken by a third great problem which has led to a third great crisis, in the midst of which we stand. This is the problem of responsible action in a revolutionary world, a world seeking to attain many of the things, material and spiritual, that we have already attained. Americans have, from the beginning, been aware of the responsibility and the significance our republican experiment has for the whole world. The first internal political polarization in the new nation had to do with our attitude toward the French Revolution. But we were small and weak then, and "foreign entanglements" seemed to threaten our very survival. During the last century, our relevance for the world was not forgotten, but our role was seen as purely exemplary. Our democratic republic rebuked tyranny by merely existing. Just after World War I we were on the brink of taking a different role in the world, but once again we turned our back.

Since World War II the old pattern has become impossible. Every president since Roosevelt has been groping toward a new pattern of action in the world, one that would be consonant with our power and our responsibilities. For Truman and for the period dominated by John Foster Dulles that pattern was seen to be the great Manichaean confrontation of East and West, the confrontation of democracy and "the false philosophy of Communism" that provided the structure of Truman's inaugural address. But with the last years of Eisenhower and with the successive two presidents, the pattern began to shift. The great problems came to be seen as caused not solely by the evil intent of any one group of men, but as stemming from much more complex and multiple sources. For Kennedy, it was not so much a struggle against particular men as against "the common enemies of man: tyranny, poverty, disease and war itself."

But in the midst of this trend toward a less primitive conception of ourselves and our world, we have somehow, without anyone really intending it, stumbled into a military confrontation in [Southeast Asia] where we have come to feel that our honor is at stake. We have in a moment of uncertainty been tempted to rely on our overwhelming physical power rather than on our intelligence, and we have, in part, succumbed to this temptation. Bewildered and unnerved when our terrible power fails to bring immediate success, we are at the edge of a chasm the depth of which no man knows.

Without an awareness that our nation stands under higher judgment, the tradition of the civil religion would be dangerous indeed. Fortunately, the prophetic voices have never been lacking. Our present situation brings to mind the Mexican-American war that Lincoln, among so many others, opposed. The spirit of civil disobedience that is alive today in the civil rights movement and the opposition to . . . war was already clearly outlined by Henry David Thoreau when he wrote, "If the law is of such a nature that it requires you to be an agent of injustice to another, then I say, break the law." Thoreau's words, "I would remind my countrymen that they are men first, and Americans at a late and convenient hour," provide an essential standard for any adequate thought and action in our third time of trial. As Americans, we have been well favored in the world, but it is as men that we will be judged.

Behind the civil religion at every point lie Biblical archetypes: Exodus, Chosen People, Promised Land, New Jerusalem, Sacrificial Death and Rebirth. But it is also genuinely American and genuinely new. It has its own prophets and its own martyrs, its own sacred events and sacred places, its own solemn rituals and symbols. It is concerned that America be a society as perfectly in accord with the will of God as men can make it, and a light to all the nations.

It has often been used and is being used today as a cloak for petty interests and ugly passions. It is in need—as is any living faith—of continual reformation, of being measured by universal standards. But it is not evident that it is incapable of growth and new insight.

It does not make any decision for us. It does not remove us from moral ambiguity, from being, in Lincoln's fine phrase, an "almost chosen people." But it is a heritage of moral and religious experience from which we still have much to learn as we formulate the decisions that lie ahead.

The publication of Bellah's article in 1967 started a debate that is still going on. Some observers of American culture hailed his essay as having successfully delineated and illumined a phenomenon that many had been alluding to but had not yet fully described. Others had written about it from slightly different vantage points and had missed the mark. The publication of the Bellah piece struck a responsive chord, especially in academic circles.

Not everyone was quite so positive, however. Bellah later noted that his formulation of civil religion "frequently generated negative reaction ranging from a vague uneasiness to outright hostility. Some have wished to deny categorically that there is anything there worth discussing at all."[18] But whatever the reaction, it nonetheless became a topic of symposia and was widely discussed in essays, in the popular press, in pulpits, and, now, in textbooks; no amount of criticism could make it go away. In a sense, the question of whether civil religion is a positive or negative force is beside the point. As Bellah says,

> if there is any utility in the notion of civil religion it is as an analytical tool for the understanding of something that exists which, like all things human, is some-times good and sometimes bad, but which in any case is apt to be with us for a very long time. I do not expect universal agreement even with that statement, but I do hope it is clear that it is not my purpose to praise civil religion in general or American civil religion in particular.[19]

What seems to have disturbed most detractors was the possibility for distortion and idolatry. Although Bellah warned toward the end of the original essay that civil religion can be used to cloak "petty interests and ugly passions" and that all of the nation's activities must be brought under "prophetic" scrutiny, some have felt that civil religion, as Bellah articulated it, could eventually lead to a deification of the tradition. "Their main interest," he noted, "was to deplore what they took to be a misplaced sacredness."[20] They apparently thought that he was making the uncritical judgment that civil religion is a "good thing."

One such critic was Senator Mark O. Hatfield, Republican from Oregon. At a National Prayer Breakfast in 1973 he lashed out at the way in which the nation had apparently succumbed to a type of "folk religion, devoid of moral content." Rather than seeing civil religion as

[18] Robert Bellah, "American Civil Religion in the 1970s," in *American Civil Religion*, edited by Russell E. Richey and Donald G. Jones (New York: Harper & Row, 1974), pp. 255–256.
[19] Ibid., p. 257.
[20] Ibid.

a sociological phenomenon that exists alongside of and in addition to the historic ecclesial groups of the Judaeo-Christian tradition, he saw it as a competitor for people's faith. The National Prayer Breakfast, begun in 1953, had been an occasion for celebration of the nation's heritage, its goodness. The noncontroversial affair usually attracted political and religious leaders from all over the country. When he was invited to speak, Senator Hatfield explained that, if he accepted the invitation, he would be compelled to "speak his mind." Assured that he should do so, he agreed to appear on the program, which included the usual prayers, scripture reading, and speeches. In the audience were President and Mrs. Nixon, Billy Graham, members of Congress, justices of the Supreme Court, cabinet members, and other important persons.

_____ *Document 2*

"The Sin That Scarred Our National Soul" by Mark O. Hatfield

My brothers and sisters, as we gather at this prayer breakfast, let us beware of the real danger of misplaced allegiance, if not outright idolatry, to the extent that we fail to distinguish between the god of an American civil religion and the God who reveals himself in the holy Scriptures and in Jesus Christ.

If we as leaders appeal to the god of civil religion, our faith is in a small and exclusive deity, a loyal spiritual adviser to power and prestige, a defender of only the American nation, the object of a national folk religion devoid of moral content. But if we pray to the biblical God of justice and righteousness, we fall under God's judgment for calling upon his name but failing to obey his commands.

Our Lord Jesus Christ confronts false petitioners who disobey the Word of God: "Why do you call me 'Lord, Lord' and do not the things I say?" (Luke 6:46). God tells us that acceptable worship and obedience are expressed by specific acts of love and justice:

> Is not this what I require of you . . . to loose the fetters of injustice . . . to snap every yoke and set free those who have been crushed? Is it not sharing your food with the hungry, taking the homeless poor into your house, clothing the naked when you meet them, and never evading a duty to your kinsfolk? [Isa. 58:6-7].

We sit here today as the wealthy and the powerful. But let us not forget that those who follow Christ will more often find themselves not with comfortable majorities, but with miserable minorities. Today our prayers must begin with repentance. Individually, we must seek forgiveness for the exile of love from our hearts. And corporately, as a people, we must turn in repentance from the sin that has scarred our national soul. "If my people . . . shall humble themselves, and pray, and seek my face, and turn from their wicked ways . . . then I will forgive their sins, and will heal their land" (II Chron. 7:14).

SOURCE: Mark O. Hatfield, "The Sin That Scarred Our National Soul," *The Christian Century*, Vol. XC, No. 8 (February 1, 1973), p. 221.

We need a "confessing church"—a body of people who confess Jesus as Lord and are prepared to live by their confession. Lives lived under the lordship of Jesus Christ at this point in our history may well put us at odds with values of our society, abuses of political power, and cultural conformity of our church. We need those who seek to honor the claims of their discipleship—those who live in active obedience to the call: "Do not be conformed to this world, but be transformed by the renewing of your minds" (Rom. 12:2). We must continually be transformed by Jesus Christ and take his commands seriously. Let us be Christ's messengers of reconciliation and peace, giving our lives over to the power of his love. Then we can soothe the wounds of war, and renew the face of the earth and all mankind.

Acknowledging that the "crisis" confronting American civil religion in 1967 had been deepened by the disclosures of Watergate, Bellah nevertheless insisted in a 1974 article that his original analysis was still valid and useful. One might not like the phenomenon, but that does not make it any less real. He did, however, suggest a program to prevent the very idolatry that Senator Hatfield and others attacked. The civil religion tradition, he said, must be subjected to "searing criticism" by using even the radically different traditions available to us today in order to prevent civil religion from becoming the type of "folk religion" that would mask and sanctify political exploitation.[21]

Rosemary Radford Ruether, writing in 1977 just before the Carter inaugural, explained how the prophetic element within the civil religion tradition itself can be used to correct distortions. Her remarks were in the form of a challenge to the new president: would he, as the primary spokesman for that tradition, use it as a means of obscuring justice or of liberating those in bondage?

Document 3

"Mystification or Liberation?" by Rosemary Radford Ruether

The problem of civil religion in the rhetoric of American politicians is not that of too much or too little God-talk, but of what kind. God-talk tends to be used by politicians to mystify social reality. We talk of God "crowning our good with brotherhood from sea to shining sea." This kind of language carries several assumptions (aside from the assumption that all Americans are "brothers"). It assumes that an idyllic social and physical community has already been established as our reality and heritage. It assumes that God is the author of American success; therefore, American success is basically natural, innocent and good.

All this is social ideology with divine sanctions. It obscures a lot of our real history. We would never be allowed to mention that much of our prosperity has come from vicious exploitation—of slaves, of workers, of the human labor and raw materials of

SOURCE: Rosemary Radford Ruether, "Mystification or Liberation?" *The Christian Century*, Vol. XCIV, No. 1 (January 5–12, 1977), p. 4.

[21] Ibid., p. 266.

many other parts of the globe. That brotherhood (let alone sister-brotherhood) does not reign from city to polluted city also is unmentionable. A rosy glow of utopia is imposed on our reality as the true American identity, blocking out critical thinking or making it "unpatriotic."

There is an alternative way to use the God-language of our civil religion, with its blend of Christian and Enlightenment roots. That is to use the divine sanction and the vision of reconciled nature and humanity not as ideology but as prophetic criticism. One does not speak of these hopes of justice and peace as though they were an achieved reality, but as a divine mandate. This is what God demands of us. But precisely as we become aware of these hopes as divine commands we are also aware of our failures to achieve them. Prophetic criticism is reality-discerning rather than reality-obscuring. It points a glaring light upon our realities at the same time that it calls us to an alternative. This is the language of Martin Luther King, Jr., the most skilled exponent in recent American history (perhaps all of American history) of American civil religion as prophetic criticism and liberation:

> I have a dream that one day this nation will rise up and live out the true meaning of its creed, "We hold these truths to be self-evident that all men are created equal." I have a dream that one day on the red hills of Georgia, sons of former slaves and sons of former slave owners will be able to sit down together at the table of brotherhood.
>
> I have a dream that one day even the state of Mississippi, a state sweltering with the heat of injustice, sweltering with the heat of oppression, will be transformed into an oasis of freedom and justice. I have a dream that my four little children will one day live in a nation where they will not be judged by the color of their skins, but by the content of their character. . . .
>
> I have a dream that one day "every valley will be exalted and every hill and mountain shall be made low. The rough places will be made plain and the crooked places will be made straight, and the glory of the Lord shall be revealed and all flesh shall see it together."

Can Mr. Carter speak of that dream as judgment and liberation? Or only as mystification and false piety?

The Historical Data

Whatever one's attitude toward the phenomenon of civil religion might be, it should be clear by now that America's civil religion did not spontaneously burst upon the scene a few years ago with the publication of the Bellah article nor did it even start abruptly at the time of the Revolution. The seeds of our civil religion were there from the beginning. Nearly all the colonial religious leaders thought of themselves as participating in the birth of a *New* Isreal and couched their rhetoric in the language of the Old Testament. They constantly used the exodus metaphor around which to organize their thoughts about their life in America.

They thought of themselves as having been freed from the bondage and decadence of the Old World in order to enter into the New World—a land flowing with natural riches and spiritual freedom[22] It is important to realize that this attitude was typical not only of the New England Puritans but of virtually all colonial religious groups. In a real sense, the overwhelming majority of the new settlers, whatever their religious connection, shared in the Puritan dream of a decisively new, and better, world. This was true, for instance, of southern colonists, most of them loyal but low church members of the Church of England, whose sense of mission was nearly as strong as that of the New Englanders. In requesting a clergyman for South Carolina, the first governor wrote back home: "The Israelites' prosperity decayed when their prophets were wanting, for where the ark of God is, there is peace and tranquility."[23]

As Sidney Mead points out, however, a sense of destiny or divine favor is not peculiar to America. All nations, tribes, and peoples have thought of themselves as occupying a special place in the scheme of things.[24] But the fact that Americans chose to assimilate their history to the exodus, the archetypal story of our civilization, lifted the events of a bobtailed rebellion to the level of cosmic mythology.

The contours of the American belief in destiny are not difficult to trace, according to Mead. First, America has placed its faith in a God of "will and purpose," which means, among other things, that there is "order and ultimate meaning in the universe," which may be discerned by the faithful. Next, there is belief in "the people" as the elect of God. Because they are actors on the stage of history, "the people" become the *instruments* for His will and purpose on the historical level. We may even say that the voice of the people is the voice of God, if we can agree with Lincoln,

> that while some of the people can be fooled and hence be wrong all of the time, and all of the people can be fooled and hence be wrong part of the time, nevertheless in the long run it appears that all of the people cannot be fooled and hence be wrong all of the time. This means that the whimsies of the multitude at any point in history need not bespeak the will of the Almighty, but rather that for men there is no higher court of appeal in the long run than the "will of the people"— the stuff of history itself. Ultimately, then, "the people shall be judge."[25]

The last element of the American belief in destiny rests on the concept of liberty. As long as a condition of freedom prevails, the people are able to be the agents of God in history. According to Mead, the Christian substructure for this belief rests in the idea that the Spirit

[22] As Robert Michaelson points out, because the American memory has been so "liberally inhabited by images and myths" derived from the Bible some have argued that it must be taught in public schools if we are to survive as a unified culture. See Michaelson, op. cit, p. 32.

[23] Edward McCrady, *An Historic Church: The Westminster Abbey of South Carolina—A Sketch of St. Philip's Church, Charleston, S.C.* (Charleston, S.C.: Lucas and Richardson Co., 1901), p. 6.

[24] Mead, *The Lively Experiment*, p. 75.

[25] Ibid., p. 81.

of God cannot be "fenced in." In like manner, "the people" must not be "fenced in." Just at the moment when they lose their ability to speak or move about freely, the nation is in gravest danger of departing from God. Jefferson cogently expressed this belief in his "Act for Establishing Religious Freedom in Virginia." He was convinced that

> truth is great and will prevail if left to herself; that she is the proper and sufficient antagonist to error, and has nothing to fear from the conflict unless by human interposition disarmed of her natural weapon, free argument and debate; errors ceasing to be dangerous when it is permitted freely to contradict them.[26]

As Mead says, this conception of freedom is not a concession to the relativist notion that all religions are equally right. Quite the opposite is being argued: only through the free competition of contrasting ideas and practices will truth emerge.

The concept of destiny, then, is a common motif in the nation's history and was most certainly present among the earliest colonists. We know, for example, from William Bradford's (1590–1657) *History of the Plymouth Plantation* that he believed God to be the guiding force behind his expedition. Indeed, the Mayflower Compact, which he recorded, is one of the first major documents of American civil religion.

_____ *Document 4*

The Mayflower Compact.

In the Name of God, Amen. We whose names are underwritten, the loyal subjects of our dread sovereign lord, King James, by the grace of God of Great Britain, France, and Ireland, king, defender of the faith, etc., having undertaken, for the glory of God and advancement of the Christian faith and honor of our king and country, a voyage to plant the first colony in the northern parts of Virginia, do by these presents solemnly and mutually in the presence of God and one of another, covenant and combine ourselves together into a civil body politic, for our better ordering and preservation and furtherance of the ends aforesaid; and by virtue hereof to enact, constitute and frame such just and equal laws, ordinances, acts, constitutions and offices, from time to time, as shall be thought most meet and convenient for the general good of the colony, unto which we promise all due submission and obedience. In witness whereof we have hereunder subscribed our names at Cape Cod, the 11th of November, in the year of the reign of our sovereign lord, King James, of England, France and Ireland the eighteenth, and of Scotland the fifty-fourth.

_____

Clearly, the compact is nothing more than an adaptation of the Puritan church covenant to the civil order. In the voyage from Holland to America, some of the group began to split into factions. Those who

[26] Quoted by Mead, ibid., p. 82.

emerged as leaders decided that some sort of legal framework would have to be provided in order to avert civil disorder, and it was natural for them to turn to church government for a plan. The covenant offered them an ideal pattern because it not only bound them to one another but to God as well. The logic of the Puritan idea of the covenant—which they, in turn, had derived from the Old Testament—was as follows: when God covenants with a people to be their God, the people themselves are thereby bound to one another, through God, in a sacred relationship that can be frustrated only at the price of shattering the original covenant with God. A covenant, then, has more than one dimension; it is both horizontal and vertical. It was this idea that lay behind the Mayflower Compact and a few years later behind "A model of Christian Charity" set forth by John Winthrop (1587–1649), the first governor of the Massachusetts Bay Colony. In 1630 Winthrop led a small band of Puritans to the New World, and while still off the coast, he delivered a sermon in which he delineates the design for a form of government based upon the concept of the covenant.

Document 5 ———————————————————————————————

From "A Model of Christian Charity" by John Winthrop

. . . Thus stands the cause between God and us. We are entered into Covenant with him for this work, we have taken out a Commission, the Lord hath given us leave to draw our own Articles. We have professed to enterprise these Actions upon these . . . ends, we have hereupon besought him of favor and blessing. Now if the Lord shall please to hear us, and bring us in peace to the place we desire, then hath he ratified this Covenant and sealed our Commission, [and] will exact a strict performance of the articles contained in it; but if we shall neglect the observation of these Articles which are the ends we have propounded, and dissembling with our God, shall fall to embrace this present world and prosecute our carnal intentions, seeking great things for ourselves and our posterity, the Lord will surely break out in wrath against us, be revenged of such a perjured people, and make us know the price of the breach of such a Covenant.

Now the only way to avoid this shipwreck and to provide for our posterity is to follow the Counsel of Micah, to do Justly, to love mercy, to walk humbly with our God. For this end, we must be knit together in this work as one man; we must entertain each other in brotherly Affection; we must be willing to abridge ourselves of our superfluities, for the supply of others' necessities; we must uphold a familiar Commerce together in all meekness, gentleness, patience and liberality; we must delight in each other, make others' Conditions our own, rejoice together, mourn together, labor and suffer together, always having before our eyes our Commission and Community in the work, our Community as members of the same body. So

SOURCE: John Winthrop, "A Model of Christian Charity," *Winthrop Papers*, Vol. II (Boston: Massachusetts Historical Society, 1931).

shall we keep the unity of the spirit in the bond of peace. The Lord will be our God and delight to dwell among us, as his own people and will command a blessing upon us in all our ways, so that we shall see much more of his wisdom, power, goodness, and truth than formerly we have been acquainted with. We shall find that the God of Israel is among us, when ten of us shall be able to resist a thousand of our enemies, when he shall make us a praise and glory, that men shall say of succeeding plantations: the Lord make it like that of New England. For we must Consider that we shall be as a City upon a Hill, the eyes of all people are upon us. So that if we shall deal falsely with our God in this work we have undertaken and so cause him to withdraw his present help from us, we shall be made a story and a by-word through the world; we shall open the mouths of enemies to speak evil of the ways of God and all professors for God's sake; we shall shame the faces of many of God's worthy servants, and cause their prayers to be turned into Curses upon us till we be consumed out of the good land whither we are going. And to shut up this discourse with that exhortation of Moses, that faithful servant of the Lord, in his last farewell to Israel, . . . Beloved, there is now set before us life and good, death and evil in that we are Commanded this day to love the Lord our God, and to love one another, to walk in his ways and to keep his Commandments and his Ordinance and his laws and the Articles of our Covenant with him, that we live and be multiplied, and that the Lord our God may bless the land whither we go to possess it. But if our hearts shall turn away so that we will not obey, but shall be seduced and worship . . . other gods, our pleasures, and profits, and serve them, it is propounded unto us this day, we shall surely perish out of the good Land whither we pass over this vast Sea to posess it.

Therefore, let us choose life, that we, and our Seed, may live; obeying his voice, and leaving to him, for he is our life, and our prosperity.

A century following the establishment of the Massachusetts Bay Colony, Jonathan Edwards (1703–1758) saw the Great Awakening, the remarkable spiritual renewal in the eighteenth century, as clear proof that America was indeed the Promised Land. In *The History of the Work of Redemption* (1739), a wide-ranging but never completed account of God's treatment of mankind from Adam to the Awakening, Edwards held that there were three reasons to believe that people in America were standing on the threshold of the last days: (1) the "reformation in doctrine and worship in countries called Christian" (it was no mere coincidence, said he, that the discovery of America and the Reformation took place roughly the same time!); (2) the propagation of the gospel among heathen (it was now transparent that, before the earth could be redeemed, God would require all men in the Western Hemisphere to be evangelized); and (3) the American revival.[27]

[27]Jonathan Edwards, *The Works of President Edwards* (London: Hughes & Baynes, 1817), Vol. V, p. 221.

Edwards acknowledged that his own era fell far short of perfection but nevertheless held that all signs were hopeful. There would simply be a period of great stress and tribulation before the final revolution and establishment of Christ's Kingdom on earth in America:

> However small the propagation of the gospel among the Heathen here in America has been hitherto; yet I think we may well look upon the discovery of so great a part of the world, and bringing the gospel into it, as one thing by which divine providence is preparing the way for the future glorious times of the church, when Satan's kingdom shall be overthrown throughout the whole habitable globe, on every side, and on all its continents. When those times come, then doubtless the gospel shall have glorious success, and all the inhabitants of this new-discovered world shall become subjects of the kingdom of Christ, as well as all the other ends of the earth. In all probability, providence has so ordered it, that the mariner's compass (which is an invention of later times, whereby men are enabled to sail over the widest ocean, when before they durst not venture far from land), should prove a preparation for what God intends to bring to pass in the glorious times of the church, *viz.*, the sending forth the gospel wherever any of the children of men dwell, how far soever off, and however separated by wide oceans from those parts of the world which are already Christianized.[28]

Edwards, generally regarded to be the greatest theologian produced in America, published *Thoughts on the Revival* in 1742. With typical Edwardsean reasoning, he held that the effectiveness of the Great Awakening could be determined by observing its results. It is axiomatic, said he, that "the visible fruit that is to be expected of a pouring out of the Spirit of God on a country, is a visible reformation in that country."[29] Such a work had begun in New England. He called it a "strange revolution, an unexpected, surprising overturning of things, suddenly brought to pass; such as never has been seen in *New England*, and scarce even has been heard of in any land." This mighty work, a new creation, was "infinitely more glorious than the old. I am bold to say, that the work of God in the conversion of one soul . . . , is a more glorious work of God than the creation of the whole material universe."[30] But the merit of the present revival, he maintained, was that there was not just one soul saved, but thousands. He asked, "Now, when there are many thousands of souls thus converted and saved, shall it be esteemed worth but little notice, and be mentioned with coldness and indifference here on earth, by those among whom such work is wrought?"[31] Of course not. America was blessed, because *America was to be the vessel of redemption.*

[28] Ibid., p. 222.
[29] Ibid., Vol. VI, p. 46.
[30] Ibid., p. 47.
[31] Ibid., p. 48.

Document 6

From *Thoughts on the Revival* by Jonathan Edwards

The Latter-Day Glory, is probably to begin in America

It is not unlikely that this work of God's Spirit, so extraordinary and wonderful, is the dawning, or at least, a prelude of that glorious work of God, so often foretold in scripture, which, in the progress and issue of it, shall renew the world and mankind. If we consider . . . what the state of things now is, and has for a considerable time been, in the church of God, and the world of mankind; we cannot reasonably think otherwise, than that the beginning of this great work of God must be near. And there are many things that make it probable that his work will begin in *America* . . . .

God has made as it were two worlds here below, two great habitable continents, far separated one from the other: The latter is as it were now but newly created; it has been till of late, wholly the possession of *Satan*, the church of God having never been in it, as it has been in the other continent, from the beginning of the world. This new world is probably now discovered, that the new and most glorious state of God's church on earth might commence there; that God might in it begin a new world in a spiritual respect, when he creates the *new heavens* and *new earth*.

God has already put that honour upon the other continent, that Christ was born there literally, and there made the *purchase of redemption*. So, as Providence observes a kind of equal distribution of things, it is not unlikely that the great spiritual birth of Christ, and the most glorious application of redemption, is to begin in this [continent] . . . .

The old continent has been the source and original of mankind, in several respects. The first parents of mankind dwelt there; and there dwelt *Noah* and his sons; there the second *Adam* was born, and crucified and raised again: And it is probable that, in some measure to balance these things, the most glorious renovation of the world shall originate from the new continent, and the church of God in that respect be from hence. And so it is probable that will come to pass in spirituals, which has taken place in temporals, with respect to *America*; that whereas, til of late, the world was supplied with its silver, and gold, and earthly treasures from the old continent, now it is supplied chiefly from the new; so the course of things in spiritual respect will be in like manner turned.—And it is worthy to be noted, that *America* was discovered about the time of the reformation, or but little before: Which reformation was the first thing that God did towards the glorious renovation of the world, after it had sunk into the depths of darkness and ruin, under the great anti-christian apostasy. So that, as soon as this new world stands forth in view, God presently goes about doing some great thing in order to make way for the introduction of the church's latter-day glory—which is to have its first seat in, and is to take its rise from that new world.

It is agreeable to God's manner, when he accomplishes any glorious work in the

SOURCE: Jonathan Edwards, *The Works of President Edwards* (London: Hughes & Baynes, 1817), Vol. 6, pp. 54–59.

world, in order to introduce a new and more excellent state of his church, to begin
where no foundation had been already laid, that the power of God might be the
more conspicuous; that the work might appear to be entirely God's and be more
manifestly a creation out of nothing; . . . When God is about to turn the earth into
a paradise, he does not begin his work where there is some good growth already,
but in the wilderness, where nothing grows, and nothing is to be seen but dry sand
and barren rocks; that the light may shine out of darkness, the world be replenished
from emptiness, and the earth watered by springs from a droughty desert; agreeable
to many prophecies of scripture, as Isa. . . . xliii. 20. I will give waters in the wilderness, and rivers in the desert, to give drink to my people, my chosen. And many
other parallel scriptures might be mentioned. Now as when God is about to do
some great work for his church, his manner is to begin at the lower end; so, when he
is about to renew the whole habitable earth, it is probable and that he will begin
in this utmost, meanest, youngest and weakest part of it, where the church of God
has been planted last of all; and so the first shall be last, and the last first. . . .

There are several things that seem to me to argue, that the sun of righteousness,
the sun of the new heavens and new earth, when he rises—and *comes forth as the
bridegroom of his church* . . . —shall rise in *the* west, contrary to the course of
things in the old heavens and earth. The movements of Providence shall in that day
be so wonderfully altered in many respects, that God will as it were change the
course of nature, in answer to the prayers of his church; as he caused the sun to go
from the west to the east when he promised to do such great things for his church.
. . . The sun of righteousness has long been going down from the east to west;
and probably when the time comes of the church's deliverance from her enemies . . . ,
the light will rise in the west, till it shines through the world like the sun in its
meridian brightness.

. . . And if we may suppose that this glorious work of God shall begin in any part
of *America,* I think, if we consider the circumstances of the settlement of *New
England*, it must needs appear the most likely, of all *American colonies*, to be the
place whence this work shall principally take its rise. And, if these things be so, it
gives us more abundant reason to hope that what is now seen in *America*, and
especially in *New England*, may prove the dawn of that glorious day; and the very
uncommon and wonderful circumstances and events of this work, seem to me
strongly to argue that God intends it as the beginning or forerunner of something
vastly great.

Samuel Adams (1723-1797) was one of the first prominent *political*
figures to articulate America's civil religion. By putting the conflict
with England in a biblical framework, he was using language that had
already been set up by religious leaders for generations. From the time
of the Revolution forward, it would be difficult to determine where the
Christian tradition left off and the religion of the republic began. But
it is clear that the nation had found its feet theologically.

Adams, a forceful and persuasive speaker, helped stir up the fervor
among the people. Because of his platform reputation, he was asked to
deliver a speech on American independence at the State House in Phila-

delphia on August 1, 1776. He likened America to ancient Israel, as so many had done before him, and declared that there was yet much to do in the way of political reformation. As his forebears had thrown off the "yoke of Popery,"[32] so his generation was offered the opportunity to cast off the bondage of political servitude.

_____ *Document 7*

From "American Independence" by Samuel Adams

Countrymen and brethren: I would gladly have declined an honor to which I find myself unequal. I have not the calmness and impartiality which the infinite importance of the occasion demands. I will not deny the charge of my enemies, that resentment for the accumulated injuries of our country and an ardor for her glory . . . may deprive me of that accuracy of judgment and expression which men of cooler passions may possess. Let me beseech you then, to hear me with caution, to examine without prejudice, and to correct the mistakes into which I may be hurried by my zeal . . . .

Our forefathers threw off the yoke of Popery in religion; for you is reserved the honor of leveling the popery of politics . . . . This day, I trust, the reign of political protestantism will commence. We have explored the temple of royalty, and found that the idol we have bowed down to, has eyes which see not, ears that hear not our prayers, and a heart like the nether millstone. We have this day restored the Sovereign, to whom alone men ought to be obedient. He reigns in Heaven, and with a propitious eye beholds his subjects assuming that freedom of thought, and dignity of self-direction which he bestowed on them. . . .

We are now on this continent to the astonishment of the world three millions of souls united in one common cause. We have large armies, well disciplined and appointed, with commanders inferior to none in military skill, and superior in activity and zeal. We are furnished with arsenals and stores beyond our most sanguine expectations, and foreign nations are waiting to crown our success by their alliances. There are instances of, I would say, an almost astonishing Providence in our favor; our success has staggered our enemies, and almost given faith to infidels; so that we may truly say it is not our own arm which has saved us.

The hand of heaven appears to have led us on to be, perhaps, humble instruments and means in the great Providential dispensation which is completing. We have fled from the political Sodom; let us not look back, lest we perish and become a monument of infamy and derision to the world! . . .

And, brethren and fellow-countrymen, if it was ever granted to mortals to trace the designs of Providence, and interpret its manifestations in favor of their cause, we may, with humility of soul, cry out, Not unto us, not unto us, but to thy Name

SOURCE: *American Eloquence*, edited by Frank Moore (New York: D. Appleton and Company, 1876), pp. 324–330.

[32]*Popery* was a term of opprobrium for the Catholic Church used by militant Protestants and other anti-Catholics.

be the praise. The confusion of the devices among our enemies, and the rage of the elements against them, have done almost as much towards our success as either our councils or our arms.

The time at which this attempt on our liberties was made, when we were ripened into maturity, had acquired a knowledge of war, and were free from the incursions of enemies in this country, the gradual advances of our oppressors enabling us to prepare for our defence, the unusual fertility of our lands and clemency of the seasons, the success which at first attended our feeble arms, producing unanimity among our friends and reducing our internal foes to acquiescense—these are all strong and palpable marks and assurances, that Providence is yet gracious unto Zion, that it will turn away the captivity of Jacob.

Our glorious reformers, when they broke through the fetters of superstition, effected more than could be expected from an age so darkened. But they left much to be done by their posterity. They lopped off, indeed, some of the branches of popery, but they left the root and stock when they left us under the domination of human systems and decisions, usurping the infallibility which can be attributed to Revelation alone. They dethroned one usurper only to raise up another; they refused allegiance to the Pope, only to place the civil magistrate in the throne of Christ, vested with authority to enact laws, and inflict penalties in his kingdom. And if we now cast our eyes over the nations of the earth we shall find, that instead of possessing the pure religion of the gospel, they may be divided either into infidels who deny the truth, or politicians who make religion a stalking horse for their ambition, or professors, who walk in the trammels of orthodoxy, and are more attentive to traditions and ordinances of men than to the oracles of truth.

Thus by the beneficence of Providence, we shall behold our empire arising, founded on justice and the voluntary consent of the people, and giving full scope to the exercise of those faculties and rights which most ennoble our species. Besides the advantages of liberty and the most equal constitution, heaven has given us a country with every variety of climate and soil, pouring forth in abundance whatever is necessary for the support, comfort, and strength of a nation. Within our own borders we possess all the means of sustenance, defence, and commerce; at the same time, these advantages are so distributed among the different States of this continent, as if nature had in view to proclaim to us—be united among yourselves, and you will want nothing from the rest of the world. . . .

Protestant patriots and preachers were not the only ones to celebrate America's vocation as the chosen of God. Among Revolutionary leaders were members of distinguished Catholic families—such as the Carrolls of Maryland and others—who found themselves united with Protestants and freethinkers in the struggle against the British crown. Indeed, John Carroll (1735–1815) of Maryland, later to be consecrated the first Catholic bishop in America (1790), threw himself unreservedly into the Revolutionary cause, thereby helping to create considerable friendliness between Protestants and Catholics in the early days of the republic. In 1778 the Alliance with France was signed, and French Catholics, lately come to America, were also able to ride the wave of good feeling into the mainstream of American life. Having been tolerated and harassed in the past because of their historic faith, colonial Catholics welcomed the relief and recognition as bona fide citizens in the New World. Accordingly, on July 4, 1779, Conrad Alexander Gerard, minister plenipotentiary of France, invited members of the Continental Congress to a solemn *Te Deum* to be sung at St. Mary's Chapel in Philadelphia. The Rev. Seraphin Bandot, chaplain to the French legation, preached a sermon that received wide attention because of its unabashed patriotic theme and fervor. It was "probably the first Catholic discourse communicated by the press to the people of the Thirteen United States."[33]

_____ *Document 8*

Sermon Delivered by Reverend Seraphin Bandot

Gentlemen: We are assembled to celebrate the anniversary of that day which Providence had marked in his Eternal Decrees, to become the epoch of liberty and independence to thirteen United States of America. That Being, whose Almighty hand holds all existence beneath its dominion, undoubtedly produces in the depths of His wisdom, those great events which astonish the universe, and of which the most presumptuous, though instrumental in accomplishing them, dare not attribute to themselves the merit. But the finger of God is still more peculiarly evident in that happy, that glorious revolution, which calls forth this day's festivity. He hath struck the oppressors of a people free and peaceable, with the spirit of delusion which renders the wicked artificers of their own proper misfortunes. Permit me, my dear brethren, citizens of the United States, to address you on this occasion. It is that God, that all-powerful God who hath directed your steps, when you knew not where to apply for counsel: who, when you were without arms, fought for you with the sword of Justice; who, when you were in adversity, poured into your hearts the spirit of courage, of wisdom and of fortitude, and who hath at length raised up for your support a youthful sovereign, whose virtues bless and adorn a sensible, a faithful, and a generous nation. This nation has blended her interests with your interests, and her sentiments with yours. She participates in all your joys, and this day unites her voice to yours, at the foot of the altars of the Eternal God, to celebrate that glorious revolution, which has placed the sons of America among the free and independent nations of the earth.

We have nothing now to apprehend but the anger of Heaven, or that the measure of our guilt should exceed His mercy. Let us then prostrate ourselves at the feet of the immortal God who holds the fate of empires in His hands and raises them up at His pleasure, or breaks them down to dust. Let us conjure him to enlighten our enemies, and to dispose their hearts to enjoy that tranquillity and happiness which

SOURCE: John Gilmary Shea, *History of the Catholic Church in the United States: 1763–1815* (Akron: D. H. McBride & Co., 1888), Vol. 2, pp. 175–176.

[33] John Gilmary Shea, *History of the Catholic Church in the United States: 1763–1815* (Akron: D. H. McBride & Co., 1888), Vol. 2, p. 175.

the revolution we now celebrate has established for a great part of the human race. Let us implore him to conduct us by that way which His providence has marked out for a union at so desirable an end. Let us offer unto him hearts imbued with sentiments of respect, consecrated by religion, by humanity, and by patriotism. Never is the august ministry of His altars more acceptable to His Divine Majesty than when it lays at His feet homages, offerings and vows, so pure, so worthy the common parent of mankind. God will not reject our joy, for He is the author of it: nor will He reject our prayers, for they ask but the full accomplishment of the decrees He hath manifested. Filled with this spirit let us, in concert with each other, raise our hearts to the Eternal. Let us implore His infinite mercy to be pleased to inspire the rulers of both nations with the wisdom and force necessary to perfect what it hath begun. Let us, in a word, unite our voices to beseech Him to dispense His blessings upon the councils and the arms of the allies, and that we may soon enjoy the sweets of a peace which will cement the union, and establish the prosperity of the two empires. It is with this view that we shall cause that canticle to be performed which the custom of the Catholic Church hath consecrated to be at once a testimonial of public joy, a thanksgiving for benefits received from Heaven, and a prayer for the continuance of its mercies.

It is a well-worn observation that the Revolutionary period is the defining point in our nation's history. It possesses a quality that no other time does, including the first colonizations and the Civil War. In religious parlance, the Revolution was a "sacred" time, a *time of origins*, when our "world" was created. The Revolutionary leaders performed the "formative acts" against which all subsequent events in the nation's history must be tested.[34] Accordingly, the most damaging criticism that can be made of any political act taken by an American citizen is that it is inconsistent with the time of origins, the Revolutionary period, and the "creative acts" performed by the Founding Fathers. Such an act would be considered "profane" at the very least and heretical at the worst. The touchstone for making such a determination is, of course, the Holy Writ, or the Constitution and Bill of Rights.

First among the Founding Fathers was George Washington (1732–1799), whose policies and actions set precedents and established patterns that have subsequently been re-enacted on innumerable occasions. Not only is his birthday a national holiday (holy day), but his name and spirit are invoked at Independence Day celebrations and other special days in our national "liturgical calendar."

Washington, though favorably inclined toward the more rational brand of Christianity popular among many intellectuals in his day, was definitely a religious man. He was not totally captivated, as some have suggested, by deism, though he did believe that reason and revelation

[34] Sidney Mead calls the Revolution "the hinge upon which the history of Christianity in America really turns." See *The Lively Experiment*, op. cit., p. 52. By contrast, we contend that the Revolutionary epoch is the pivotal event for the *whole* national community, Christianity included.

were not incompatible. Moreover, he was baptized and married in the Anglican church and was actively involved in its support all his life as vestryman and lay leader. On the day of his inauguration, he attended "divine service performed by the Chaplain of the Congress" at St. Paul's Church and was joined in this act by the vice-president and members of Congress. As president, he issued proclamations calling for national days of fasting and thanksgiving as the young nation found its way through crises and to prosperity. It is no mere coincidence, then, that Washington, the father of the nation, becomes a model for all three strands of religiousness in America: (1) he thought of religion as an intensely personal matter; (2) he participated in the affairs of the institutional church; but, most important for the present discussion, (3) he believed religion to perform a vital function in the public or civil domain. In his First Inaugural Address, delivered April 30, 1789, at Federal Hall in New York, he acknowledged the guiding hand of Providence in the nation's founding and prayed for continued divine direction. No president since then has failed to do the same. Indeed, it was another president, Benjamin Harrison, who saw most clearly the ritualistic and religious significance of the inaugural event. He noted in his own Inaugural Address a century after Washington's that, although "there is no institutional or legal requirement" that a president take his oath of office "in the presence of the people," still "there is so manifest an appropriateness for it to be done in public that, beginning with Washington, it has always been done." It was, he said, "a solemn ceremonial . . . taken in the presence of the people [effecting] a mutual covenant" between the chief executive and the people:

> My promise is spoken; yours unspoken, but not less real and solemn. The people of every State have their representatives. Surely I do not misinterpret the spirit of the occasion when I assume that the whole body *covenant* with me and with each other to-day to support and defend the Constitution and the Union of the States. . . . Entering thus solemnly into *covenant* with each other, we may reverently invoke and confidently expect the favor and help of Almighty God— that He will give to me wisdom, strength, and fidelity, and to our people a spirit of fraternity and a love of righteousness and peace.[35]

Washington's words and actions, then, established the pattern to come. Every president since then has sensed the profoundly religious nature of the inaugural event, which has been inextricably linked to the notions of covenant, election, and Providence. As Michaelson has appositely written, "There is a thin line which divides nationalism from religion, a patriotic rite from a religious one."[36]

As soon as Washington was sworn into office, messages poured into the executive offices congratulating the lately triumphant military leader on his accession to political leadership. Especially noteworthy were the

[35] Lott, op. cit., p. 155, Emphasis added.
[36] Michaelson, op. cit., p. 213.

communications received from ecclesial religious groups. They are remarkably alike in their form and content, no matter which of the
religious groups was writing. The next brief reading is a message from
Jewish groups in several states.

Document 9

The Address of the Hebrew Congregations in the Cities of Philadelphia, New York, Richmond, and Charleston to the President of the United States

Sir: It is reserved for you to unite in affection for your character and person
every political and religious denomination of men; and in this will the Hebrew congregations aforesaid yield to no class of their fellow citizens.

We have been hitherto prevented by various circumstances peculiar to our situation from adding our congratulations to those which the rest of America have
offered on your elevation to the chair of the Federal Government. Deign, then,
illustrious Sir, to accept this our homage.

The wonders which the Lord of Hosts hath worked in the days of our forefathers
have taught us to observe the greatness of His wisdom and His might throughout the
events of the late glorious revolution; and while we humble ourselves at His footstool in thanksgiving and praise for the blessing of His deliverance, we acknowledge
you, the leader of American armies, as His chosen and beloved servant. But not to
your sword alone is present happiness to be ascribed; that, indeed, opened the way
to the reign of freedom; but never was it perfectly secure till your hand gave birth
to the Federal Constitution and you renounced the joys of retirement to seal by
your administration in peace what you had achieved in war.

To the eternal God, who is thy refuge, we commit in our prayers the care of thy
precious life; and when, full of years, thou shalt be gathered unto thy people, thy
righteousness shall go before thee, and we shall remember, amidst our regret, "that
the Lord hath set apart the Godly for himself," whilst thy name and thy virtues will
remain an indelible memorial of our minds.

MANUEL JOSEPHSON,
For and in behalf and under the authority of the
several congregations aforesaid.

SOURCE: Lee M. Friedman, *Jewish Pioneers and Patriots* (Philadelphia: The Jewish Publication
Society, 1943), p. 29.

Following the ratification of the Constitution and the adoption of
the Bill of Rights, America settled down to the task of becoming the
nation people had dreamed about for several generations. The most
intriguing desideratum for consideration by the young nation was the
vast expanse of land to the West. Unexplored regions, teeming with
natural resources and affording their inhabitants room to stretch and
work out their own styles of life, beckoned to a new generation of

pioneers. The idea was celebrated in verse, hailed by newspaper editors, and extolled by politicians. The poet-diplomat Joel Barlow (1754–1812), in an Independence Day address in 1809, sounded the theme before the president and his cabinet:

> The form of government we have chosen, the geographical position we occupy, as relative to the most turbulent powers of Europe, whose political maxims are widely different from ours; the vast extent of continent that is or must be comprised within our limits, containing not less than sixteen hundred millions of acres, and susceptible of a population of two hundred millions of human beings; our habits of industry and peace, instead of violence and war . . . all these are circumstances that render our situation as novel as it is important.[37]

Though the phrase *Manifest Destiny* had not yet been coined, the substance of the idea was there. The old idea of divine Providence was at work, but it had been extensively modified by a young nation beginning to feel its own power. Whereas Edwards and Washington might have spoken with humility about God's gracious and special dealing with the men who settled the New World and formed the new state, early-nineteenth-century Americans began to speak about the nation's special vocation as continental savior, ordained by God to spread the goodness of democracy (with guns, if necessary) to the Pacific Ocean. During the 1840s, the Texas revolution, improved industrial capabilities, and other factors combined with the general confidence in providential guidance to create the messianic vision called "Manifest Destiny." Many sensed what was going on, but it was the magazine editor J. Sullivan Cox who in 1846 articulated what others only felt. What all nations need, he said, is a "celestial beacon" to direct their course: "There is a moral sense—a soul in the state, which longs for something more than tariffs, the bank, and the bankrupt bills of a temporizing present; which looks for some celestial beacon to direct the course of popular movement through the eternal future!"[38] Did America have a "beacon" to guide it? By all means:

> Something of the same spirit now glows in the bosom of every member of this western commonwealth in America. Call it what you will, *destiny*, or what not; it is leading us as a cloud by day and a pillar of fire by night. It beckons to us from the dim and shadowy distance, and bids us, All Hail! It illumines our faces with hope, lights our eye with enterprise. Who can define it? As well define infinity, space, eternity; yet who so heartless as not to feel it. It has been called manifest. Its effects *are* manifest. They are seen in the throbbing pulse of America. It whelms and controls us, yet who would stem its rushing stream.[39]

[37] As quoted by Ernest Lee Tuveson, *Redeemer Nation: The Idea of America's Millennial Role* (Chicago: University of Chicago Press, 1968), p. 124. Tuveson's excellent work informs the next few paragraphs of the present work.

[38] J. Sullivan Cox, "Imaginary Commonwealth," *The United States Magazine and Democratic Review*, Vol. 19 (New York, 1846), p. 184.

[39] Ibid.

Although the motives for speaking in such lofty ways might well be mixed, the surface meaning is clearly religious. In America, Cox concluded, "a mighty work is to be fulfilled," because there are no more worlds to conquer, "no more continents to be revealed."[40]

In 1858 an unsigned article appeared in *Harper's* entitled "Providence in American History," the central thesis of which was "the intense conviction" that America, as a nation, was performing a work for the rest of the world.[41] By then, continental messianism had given way to global messianism, and it was not just a case of suprahistorical power so blessing the nation.[42] Americans themselves had helped bring it about by their "intelligence, sagacity, energy, restlessness, and indomitable will"—traits that fortune had liberally bestowed upon Anglo-Saxon peoples! Here we have something more than belief in Providence; the inherently superior capacities of a "race" are combined with the benevolence of a gracious deity. The author says that Anglo-Saxons had proved themselves by mastering physical nature "without being mastered by it," as though no other peoples had ever done that before:

> a race that fears nothing, claims everything within reach, enjoys the future more than the present, and believes in a destiny of incomparable and immeasurable grandeur. Without the least extravagance it may be said that there never was such a character—such elements of activity, foresight, sovereignty—acting on a theater so broad, so ample, so wonderful. It is the only country that holds out any general prospect to humanity—that offers ideas, sentiments, hopes for general diffusion—that has an educative power for the world in its principles and institutions.[43]

In addition to the fact that the credibility of "the American dream" is, in our own day, undergoing severe stress, it is doubly difficult for us to fathom the apparent racism inherent in this kind of writing. Yet this essay is not atypical of the period. Even the storm clouds of the approaching Civil War could not dampen the author's ardor. He goes on to plead that no thoughtful reader could fail to see "the insignia of Providence" in the history of the young nation: "True now as true of old in Horeb: *'Put off thy shoes from off thy feet; for the place whereon thou standest is holy ground.'* "[44]

The doctrine of Manifest Destiny was not the exclusive possession of politicians, poets, and newspaper pundits. Religious leaders also employed their pens in praise of America, much as they had always done. Among the most ardent of these was an immigrant professor of ecclesiastical history, Philip Schaff (1819–1893). This brilliant Reformed scholar moved to the United States in 1844. With John W. Nevin

[40] Ibid., p. 185.
[41] *Harper's New Monthly Magazine*, Vol. 17 (October 1858), p. 695.
[42] *Messianism* is the belief that one is a savior. In this case, some people thought America had become the savior of the entire world.
[43] *Harper's New Monthly Magazine*, p. 699.
[44] Ibid., p. 700.

(1803–1886) he helped to shape what has come to be known as "the Mercersburg theology," standing staunchly for the churchly tradition of Lutheranism against the multitudes of evangelical sects found in America. In addition, Schaff prophetically spoke of a future blending of Protestantism and Catholicism, a notion that has not been seriously entertained by many others until our own day.

As in the case of many first-generation Americans, Schaff often spoke affectionately of his adopted country. In 1854 he published a book entitled *America: A Sketch of Its Political, Social, and Religious Character*. The book grew out of a series of lectures he had given during a return visit to his native Germany. In the preface he remarked that whatever might happen to Europe, American would be "without question, emphatically a land of the future." But Schaff was not as uncritical in his praise as others had been and would be. He brought to bear his incisive intelligence on the matter. He said, for example, that it was because of no particular merit that Americans were chosen for this special purpose; "they are in themselves not a whit better than the Europeans." Rather, it was "the favor of Providence; and it should not make them vain, but earnest and humble, that they may faithfully and conscientiously fulfill their mission."[45] A far cry from some of the rank chauvinism produced in other quarters.

_____ *Document 10*

From *America* by Philip Schaff

The United States of North America—whose citizens are called *Americans* in an emphatic sense—because the bearers of the historical life and progress of the whole Western Hemisphere—are a wonder in the annals of the human race. Their development, in its rapidity and gigantic proportions, far outstrip all former experience, and their significance for the future mocks the boldest calculation. Though not an hundred years old, they have become already, by natural force of expansion, one of the mightiest empires of the civilized world, with the control of one entire continent and two oceans, and spread, in the most peaceful manner, the meshes of their influence over Europe, Asia and Africa. And yet their history up to this time is only a faint prelude of what is to come, and the Americans of the twentieth century will look upon the present age of their country, with feelings akin to those with which modern Europeans regard the exodus of the threshold of the Middle Ages. The "Young Giant," has not yet, so to speak, sown all his wild oats, and along with many heroic deeds, commits also some wanton and extravagant pranks, which prove,

SOURCE: Philip Schaff, *America: A Sketch of Its Political, Social, and Religious Character*, edited by Perry Miller (Cambridge, Mass.: Harvard University Press, 1961), pp. 209–213.

[45] Philip Schaff, *America: A Sketch of Its Political, Social, and Religious Character*, edited by Perry Miller (Cambridge, Mass.: Harvard University Press, 1961), p. 16.

however, the exuberant vigor of his youthful powers. Providence, who creates nothing in vain, has there made physical preparations on the grandest scale, and formed an immeasurable territory, containing the most fruitful soil, the most valuable mineral treasures and the most favorable means of commercial intercourse, as a tempting asylum for all European nations, churches and sects, who, there freed from the fetters of antiquated institutions, amid circumstances and conditions altogether new, and with renovated energies, swarm, and jostle each other, and yet, in an incredibly short space of time, are moulded by the process into one powerful nationality. Whilst Europe had first to work her way up out of heathen-barbarism, America, without earning it, has appropriated the civilization and church history of two thousand years, as an inheritance, and already put out at the highest rate of interest for the benefit of after generations.

For, these Americans have not the least desire to rest on the laurels of the past and comfortably enjoy the present; they are full of ambition and national pride, and firmly resolved to soar above the Old World. They are a people of the boldest enterprise and untiring progress—Restlessness and Agitation personified. Even when seated, they push themselves to and fro on their rockingchairs; they live in a state of perpetual excitement in their business, their politics and their religion, and remind one of the storm-lashed sea. . . . They are excellently characterized by the expressions, "Help yourself" and "Go ahead," which are never out of their mouths. It is also a very significant fact, that they have invented the magnetic telegraph, or at least perfected it, and are far advanced in the useful arts. For there the car of the world's history moves swifter on the pinions of steam and electricity, and "the days become shortened."

The grandest destiny is evidently reserved for such a people. We can and must, it is true, find fault with many things in them and their institutions—slavery, the lust of conquest, the worship of Mammon, the rage for speculation, political and religious fanaticism and party-spirit, boundless temerity, boasting, quackery, and—to use the American word for it—humbug, as well as other weaknesses and dangers, that are moreover wanting to no country in Europe. But we must not overlook the healthy, vital energies, that continually re-act against these diseases: the moral, yea Puritanical earnestness of the American character, its patriotism and noble love of liberty in connection with deep-rooted reverence for the law of God and authority, its clear, practical understanding, its talent for organization, its inclination for improvement in every sphere, its fresh enthusiasm for great plans and schemes of moral reform, and its willingness to make sacrifices for the promotion of God's kingdom and every good work. The acquisition of riches is to them only a help toward higher spiritual and moral ends; the grain derived from the inexhaustible physical resources of their glorious country only the material ground-work toward the furtherance of civilization. They wrestle with the most colossal projects. The deepest meaning and aim of their political institutions are to actualize the idea of *universal* sovereignty, the education of every individual for intellectual and moral self-government and thus for true freedom. They wish to make culture, which in Europe is everywhere aristocratic and confined to a comparatively small portion of society, the common property of the people, and train up if possible every youth as a gentleman and every girl as a lady; and in the six States of New England at least, they have attained this object in a higher degree than any country in the Old World, England and Scotland not even excepted.

In short, if anywhere in the wide world a new page of universal history has been unfolded and a new fountain opened, fraught with incalculable curses or blessings for future generations, it is in the Republic of the United States with her starspangled banner. Either humanity has no earthly future and everything is tending to destruction, or this future lies—I say not exclusively, but mainly—in America, according to the victorious march of history, with the sun from east to west.

If the Revolution was the defining point in our history, a time when in a sense the shape of the political and social narrative was set, the Civil War may be regarded as the first major crisis in the national drama.[46] Or to change the metaphor and use the language of religious study, armed rebellion came close to desacralizing the American myth, as we know it. But men like Abraham Lincoln (1809–1865) were too intent on preserving the integrity of the myth to let it happen, and his death was a sacrifice on behalf of that belief. In his Annual Message to Congress on December 1, 1862, Lincoln said:

> Fellow-citizens, *we* cannot escape history. We of this Congress and this administration, will be remembered in spite of ourselves. . . . The fiery trial through which we pass, will light us down, in honor or dishonor, to the latest generation . . . . We shall nobly save, or meanly lose, the last best hope of earth. . . . The way is plain, peaceful, generous, just—a way which if followed, the world will forever applaud, and God must forever bless.[47]

They could not "escape history" but they could at least try to do God's will on earth. It is important to note, in this connection, that little time elapsed after Lincoln's tragic death until Memorial Day was fixed in our national liturgical calendar and the assassinated president was regarded as a martyred savior god. The myth had been not only preserved but deepened by his sacrificial death; the most obvious mythological parallel was Calvary, just as the seventeenth-century emigrations from Europe were looked upon as an Exodus event.

Though his parents were religious people and joined the Baptist church, Lincoln himself consistently shunned institutionalized religion, largely because of the bitter recriminations he had observed between denominations.[48] Moreover, as he said, he doubted "the possibility, or

---

[46] Sidney Mead calls the Civil War the "center of American history." It occupies the center because, as Lincoln put it, the nation could not afford to have "the mystic chords of memory that bind the Union together [be] cut by the simple expedient of dividing the country along a geographical line." See Mead, *The Lively Experiment*, op. cit., p. 12.

[47] Abraham Lincoln, *The Living Lincoln*, edited by Paul M. Angle and Earl Schenck Miers (New Brunswick, N.J.: Rutgers University Press, 1955), p. 522.

[48] On July 31, 1846, Lincoln addressed himself to the voters in the Seventh Congressional District. Someone had called him "an open scoffer at Christianity," to which he replied, "That I am not a member of any Christian church is true; but I have never denied the truth of Scriptures; and I have never spoken with intentional disrespect of religion in general, or of any denomination in particular." See Angle and Miers, op. cit., p. 89

propriety, of settling the religion of Jesus Christ in the models of man-made creeds and dogmas"; he saw no way of his assenting "to long and complicated creeds and catechisms" without severe mental reservations.[49] Nevertheless, he was an intensely religious person and was deeply immersed in the Bible, which was a source for enlightenment and meditation all his life. In the year before he died he wrote to a friend, "I am profitably engaged in reading the Bible. Take all of this book upon reason that you can and the balance upon faith and you will live and die a better man."[50] In addition to being an active proponent of the civil religion, he is also a choice example of personal religion.

The maturation of Lincoln's religious life occurred when he assumed the presidency. The crisis under which the nation struggled cried out for interpretation and understanding, and the only way he knew to give meaning to the events of the day was to place them in a biblical perspective.[51] Like the prophets of old, he attempted to plumb the mystery of the Divine Will, and, like them, discovered how mystifying the experience could be. He never questioned God's ultimate justice and sovereignty, but he did have difficulty in tracing the outline of God's hand in daily affairs. He frequently told his associates that the question was not one of asking God to be on his side but of making sure that he and the nation were on God's side:

> I am approached with the most opposite opinions and advice, and that by religious men who are equally certain that they represent the divine will. I am sure that either the one or the other class is mistaken in that belief and perhaps in some respects both. I hope it will not be irreverent for me to say that if it is probable that God would reveal his will to others on a point so connected with my duty, it might be supposed he would reveal it directly to me; for, unless I am more deceived in myself than I often am, it is my earnest desire to know the will of Providence in this matter. And if I can learn what it is, I will do it.[52]

As the war wore on, though he was anguished by the horrors he saw, he never departed from his way of reading the meaning behind events.

[49] Henry Rankin, a contemporary of Lincoln's, as quoted by William J. Wolf, *The Almost Chosen People* (Garden City, N.Y.: Doubleday & Company, 1959), p. 51. Wolf's excellent essay on Lincoln's religion derives its title from a typical remark he made to the State Senate of New Jersey on February 21, 1861: "I shall be most happy indeed if I shall be an humble instrument in the hands of the Almighty, and of this, his almost chosen people." See Angle and Miers, op. cit., p. 378.

[50] Lord Charnwood (Godfrey Rathbone Benson), *Abraham Lincoln* (New York: Holt, Rinehart & Winston, 1960), p. 477.

[51] Toward the end of World War I, the Presbyterian Woodrow Wilson was to tell a group of British churchmen: "You are quite right . . . , in saying that I do recognize the sanctions of religion in these times of perplexity with matters so large to settle that no man can feel that his mind can compass them. I think one would go crazy if he did not believe in Providence. It would be a maze without a clue. Unless there were some supreme guidance we would despair of the results of human counsel." Ray Stannard Baker and William E. Dodd (eds.), *The Public Papers of Woodrow Wilson* (New York: Harper & Row, 1925), Vol. III, p. 339.

[52] Philip Van Doren Stern, *The Life and Writings of Abraham Lincoln* (New York: Random House, 1940), p. 720.

After the disastrous second battle of Bull Run, he meditated upon the nature of the Divine Will:

> The will of God prevails. In great contests each party claims to act in accordance with the will of God. Both may be, and one must be, wrong. God cannot be for and against the same thing at the same time. In the present civil war, it is quite possible that God's purpose is something different from the purpose of either party; and yet the human instrumentalities, working just as they do, are of the best adaptation to effect his purpose. I am almost ready to say that this is probably true; that God wills this contest, and wills that it shall not end yet. By his mere great power on the minds of the now contestants, he could have either saved or destroyed the Union without a human contest. Yet the contest began. And, having begun, he could give the final victory to either side any day. Yet the contest proceeds.[53]

At about the time he was writing these thoughts he made "a solemn vow with God" to free the slaves as soon as a Union victory would "give stature" to such a decision.[54] Though his action had obvious dangers in it (everything could backfire), there was no superstition involved. Lincoln was simply acting in the best Puritan tradition, in the conviction that Providence had chosen America for a special destiny and that freedom for all men, including black men, was decreed. Behind him stood the dim lineaments of men like Winthrop and Edwards. Edmund Wilson aptly remarks that

> Lincoln's conception of the progress and meaning of the Civil War was indeed an interpretation that he partly took over from others but that he partly made others accept. . . . Like most of the important products of the American mind at that time, it grew out of the religious tradition of the New England theology of Puritanism.[55]

The framework of New England covenant theology can also be seen in the Second Inaugural, which, after the Gettysburg Address, contains Lincoln's most memorable words. Even he knew that, for he said of the speech,

> I expect it to wear as well as, perhaps better than, any thing I have produced; but I believe it is not immediately popular. Men are not flattered by being shown that there has been a difference of purpose between the Almighty and them. To deny it, however, in this case, is to deny that there is a God governing the world. It is a truth which I thought needed to be told, and, as whatever of humiliation there is in it falls most directly on myself, I thought others might afford for me to tell it.[56]

Brief though it is, the speech contains the tempered wisdom of a man

[53] Ibid., pp. 728–729.
[54] Wolf, op. cit., p. 148.
[55] Edmund Wilson, *Eight Essays* (Garden City, N.Y.: Doubleday, 1954), p. 189.
[56] Angle and Miers, op. cit., p. 640.

who had suffered in the extreme as he wrestled with the problem of placing the tragic affairs of the nation within the context of Divine Wisdom.

Document 11

Abraham Lincoln's Second Inaugural Address

Fellow-Countrymen:

At this second appearing to take the oath of the Presidential office there is less occasion for an extended address than there was at the first. Then a statement in detail of a course to be pursued seemed fitting and proper. Now, at the expiration of four years, during which public declarations have been constantly called forth on every point and phase of the great contest which still absorbs the attention and engrosses the energies of the nation little that is new could be presented. The progress of our arms, upon which all else chiefly depends, is as well-known to the public as to myself, and it is, I trust, reasonably satisfactory and encouraging to all. With high hope for the future, no prediction in regard to it is ventured.

On the occasion corresponding to this four years ago all thoughts were anxiously directed to an impending civil war. All dreaded it, all sought to avert it. While the inaugural address was being delivered from this place, devoted altogether to *saving* the Union without war, insurgent agents were in the city seeking to *destroy* it without war—seeking to dissolve the Union and divide effects by negotiation. Both parties deprecated war, but one of them would *make* war rather than let the nation survive, and the other would *accept* war rather than let it perish, and the war came.

One-eighth of the whole population were colored slaves, not distributed generally over the Union, but localized in the southern part of it. These slaves constituted a peculiar and powerful interest. All knew that this interest was somehow the cause of war. To strengthen, perpetuate, and extend this interest was the object for which the insurgents would rend the Union even by war, while the Government claimed no right to do more than to restrict the territorial enlargement of it. Neither party expected for the war the magnitude or the duration which it has already attained. Neither anticipated that the *cause* of the conflict might cease with or even before the conflict itself should cease. Each looked for an easier triumph, and a result less fundamental and astounding. Both read the same Bible and pray to the same God, and each invokes His aid against the other. It may seem strange that any men should dare to ask a just God's assistance in wringing their bread from the sweat of other men's faces, but let us judge not, that we be not judged. The prayers of both could not be answered. That of neither has been answered fully. The Almighty has His own purposes. "Woe unto the world because of offenses; for it must needs be that offenses come, but woe to that man by whom the offense cometh." If we shall suppose that American slavery is one of those offenses which, in the providence of God, must needs come, but which, having continued through His appointed time,

SOURCE: From *The Living Lincoln: The Man, His Mind, His Times, and the War He Fought, Reconstructed from His Own Writings,* by Paul Angle and Earl Schenck Miers (New Brunswick, N.J.: Rutgers University Press, 1955), pp. 628–630.

He now wills to remove, and that He gives to both North and South this terrible war as the woe due to those by whom the offense came, shall we discern therein any departure from those divine attributes which the believers in a living God always ascribe to Him? Fondly do we hope, fervently do we pray, that this mighty scourge of war may speedily pass away. Yet, if God wills that it continue until all the wealth piled by the bondsman's two hundred and fifty years of unrequited toil shall be sunk, and until every drop of blood drawn with the lash shall be paid by another drawn with the sword, as was said three thousand years ago, so still it must be said "the judgments of the Lord are true and righteous altogether."

With malice toward none, with charity for all, with firmness in the right as God gives us to see the right, let us strive on to finish the work we are in, to bind up the nation's wounds, to care for him who shall have borne the battle and for his widow and his orphan, to do all which may achieve and cherish a just and lasting peace among ourselves and with all nations.

When Lincoln referred to America as God's "almost chosen people," he was expressing his judgment that American practices had fallen far short of the principles set forth in the Constitution and the Bill of Rights. It is instructive to compare his insights with those of men who followed him. For example, President Eisenhower, who was cited by both Herberg and Mead as an important civil religion figure, has often been compared to Lincoln. Former Chief Justice Earl Warren once claimed at a prayer breakfast that President Eisenhower possessed "Abraham Lincoln's simple faith." But, as one observer has noted, the comparison failed because Lincoln's faith was not simple; "it was a faith arrived at through long days and nights of wrestling with the intractable facts which posed the all but insoluble problems of administration."[57]

One might counter that Eisenhower's faith was arrived at through similar circumstances, which may very well have been so. But Eisenhower himself shunned the complex and sophisticated form of faith displayed in Lincoln's Second Inaugural. Instead, he described his ideal in the speech at Abilene, his boyhood home:

> If each of us in his own mind would dwell more upon these simple virtues—integrity, courage, self-confidence and unshakable belief in the Bible—would not some of these problems [confronting the nation] tend to simplify themselves? Would not we, after having done our very best with them, be content to leave the rest with the Almighty, and not to charge all our fellow-men with the fault of bringing us where we are?[58]

The great contribution Lincoln made to any discussion of civil religion lies in his calling attention to the idolatry implicit in too closely identifying the will of God with national aims. He would have agreed in principle with the anonymous author who wrote in *Harper's* in 1858:

[57]Hutchinson, op. cit., p. 369.
[58]Ibid.

Let us not, then, be understood as arguing that the thoughtful mind of our country has identified the sense of Providence with specific measures of national debate. . . . Such a view would imply that men could penetrate beforehand the counsels of the Infinite. . . . We simply mean that [the] American mind has been deeply impregnated with the sentiment of Providence in the whole history of our colonization and civilization. It has not explained the past on the theory of lucky accidents and fortunate circumstances. Nor has it attempted to solve the problems of our existence and progress by a glorification of human sagacity and skill in statesmanship.[59]

The nation's perennial temptation, he continued, is to rely completely on its own capacities and political institutions. If the nation calls on God only in "the hours of darkness and danger, then it would idolize itself and its machinery, forget its homage to Providence, and war against the order of the universe."[60]

The issue was complex and clouded. Could one believe in the doctrine of national election and still avoid chauvinism? Some of the most egregious offenders in this regard were men who were theologically adept and should have known better. One might be willing to dismiss the jingoism of a politician seeking votes at the hustings but not that of a clergyman whose professional competence should make him careful not to confound God with nation. In 1863 Henry Ward Beecher (1813–1887), pastor of Plymouth Congregational Church in Brooklyn and one of the most prominent preachers of his day, pointed out that God "in his good providence" had, in effect, joined forces with the Union in its cause: "while the South is draining itself dry of its resources . . . the Northern states are growing rich by war." Why? Because "God is storing us with wealth by which we are to be prepared to meet the exigencies which war shall bring upon us." And what are the exigencies? Beecher was most explicit:

We are to have the charge of this continent. The South has been proved, and has been found wanting. She is not worthy to bear rule. She has lost the scepter in our national government; she is to lose the scepter in the States themselves; and this continent is to be from this time forth governed by Northern men, with Northern ideals, and with a Northern gospel.

Beecher then went on to claim that "this continent is to be cared for by the North simply because the North has been true to the cause of Christ . . . in a sufficient measure."[61] Apparently the South had been unfaithful. Lincoln would have cringed at such a thought! Rebellion, for him, was inexcusable. Freedom for the slaves was absolutely mandatory, but *no one* could be so confident of God's partiality as to claim that the South had not trusted in the very same God to whom Northerners had made *their* petitions.

[59] *Harper's New Monthly Magazine*, op. cit., p. 695.
[60] Ibid., p. 694.
[61] As quoted by Mead, *The Lively Experiment*, op. cit., pp. 143–144.

It might be argued that Beecher was merely a "popularizer," given to brushing over subtleties of thought, but this explains nothing. One of the more sophisticated theological minds of his day took a similar reading of history. Horace Bushnell (1802–1876), whose theology is still highly regarded in many circles, spoke of the United States in similar terms:

> There was never a finer way of government for a people than God has given us, ... the whole shaping of the fabric is Providential. God, God is in it, everywhere. He is Founder before the founders, training both them and us, and building in the Constitution, before it is produced without. Our whole civil order is the ordinance of God—saturated all through with flavors of historical religion, sanctioned every way by the sanction, and sanctified by the indwelling concourse of God.[62]

Bushnell was not able to combine his belief in divine guidance with anything approaching Lincoln's realistic assessment of the Union's performance. Lincoln agonized over the blunders he and others had made. So far as Bushnell was concerned the Union could do no wrong:

> We associate God and religion with all that we are fighting for. ... Our cause, we love to think, is especially God's and so we are connecting all most sacred impressions with our government itself, weaving in a woof of holy feeling among all the fibres of our constitutional polity and government. ... Oh! it is religion, it is God—every drum-beat is a hymn, the cannon thunder God, the electric silence, darting victory along the wires, is the inaudible greeting of God's favoring word and purpose.[63]

Men, like Barlow, Cox, and Bushnell, among many others, touted the nation's "right" to continental leadership. All were so caught up in developing the land's potential that they took little time to look outward. But as the confidence in America's divine mission in the New World was enlarged to include the whole world, "Manifest Destiny" was expanded to the international realm.

Since James Monroe had promulgated his famous "doctrine," the country had scrupulously avoided any unnecessary foreign alliances, but with the Spanish-American War, the latent internationalism of Manifest Destiny became overt and active. As in our own day, however, the nation was sharply divided about the war. Indiana Senator Albert J. Beveridge defended our "annexation" of the Philippines as a divinely ordained act:

> We will not renounce our part in the mission of the race, trustee, under God, of the civilization of the world. ... He has made us ... the master organizers of the world to establish system where chaos reigns. ... He has made us adept in government that we may administer among savage and servile peoples. ... And of all our race, He has marked the American people as His chosen Nation to fi-

[62] Horace Bushnell, *Popular Government by Divine Right* (Hartford: L. E. Hunt, n.d.), p. 12.
[63] Ibid., p. 15.

nally lead in the regeneration of the world. This is the divine mission of America, and it holds for us all the profit, all the glory, all the happiness possible to man. We are trustees of the world's progress, guardians of its righteous peace. The judgment of the Master is upon us: "Ye have been faithful over a few things; I will make you ruler over many things."[64]

Others were not so sanguine about our impartiality toward the Philippines nor so sure about God's partiality toward us. Mark Twain (1835–1910) was deeply offended by such action. To him "pacification" of the islands seemed nothing more than a further extension of something America had hoped to be rid of—European colonialism. Twain complained: "I pray you to pause and consider. Against our traditions we are now entering upon an unjust and trivial war, a war against a helpless people, and for a base object—robbery."[65]

The argument sounds strangely familiar today. In the light of America's recent involvement in Southeast Asia, many critics of the nation's foreign policy would be sympathetic to Twain's outlook, maintaining that the contemporary forms of American messianism have become mercenary and meddlesome rather than salvific. Opponents of this view point out, however, that it would be irresponsible to retire from world politics into a new form of isolationism, that the alternatives to the governments we presently support would be worse than those now in power.

As we have already seen, Bellah, in his essay, maintains that American civil religion is currently in a period of testing, what he calls "the third time of trial." The first time of trial was during the American Revolution, when we had to discover whether or not we could run our own affairs. The second time of trial was the Civil War, when we had to decide whether or not personal liberty was to be enjoyed universally in America. We are still attempting to solve that crisis. The third time of trial is contemporary. As a nation we must decide whether or not we shall use our vast powers and capabilities to live responsibly in a "revolutionary world, a world seeking to attain many of the things, material and spiritual, that we have already attained."[66]

A good many people believe it is already too late, that we have lost contact with our own revolutionary heritage by casting our lot with the powers of oppression. Or, to put it in the language of religion, a good many believe that we have lost our faith in the nation. When people lose faith, there are hints of defection from the "Church" (or, in this case, the Nation)—an act that has traditionally been called apostasy. Indeed, some young men fled to Canada and other places rather than fight a war they considered to be morally corrupt and politically indefensible. Mead

[64] Mead, *The Lively Experiment*, op. cit., pp. 153–154.
[65] Mark Twain, "Two Fragments from a Suppressed Book Called 'Glances at History,' or 'Outlines of History,' " in *Letters from the Earth*, edited by Bernard De Voto (New York: Harper & Row, 1962).
[66] Bellah, op. cit., p. 15.

writes, "So long as there is widespread confidence among the people that the direction and way are basically right, the system is sound and can function even in adversity."[67] But when the confidence is shaken, the threat of heresy and apostasy becomes greater. It is, as Mead says, "essentially a matter of faith." But when one can no longer hold onto that faith, the resulting despair can often lead to simplistic solutions.

The most consistent critic of American foreign policy in recent years was J. William Fulbright, Democrat of Arkansas. Elected to the Senate in 1945, he was given a seat on the Foreign Relations Committee four years later. When he became its chairman in 1959, Walter Lippmann prophetically observed, "The windows of the Senate will be open to the fresh air of a new time." Some have found the air exhilarating, others abrasive, but in any case he has provided his colleagues, four presidents, and the American public with alternative viewpoints to prevailing policies.

Fulbright became increasingly alarmed at the nation's drift toward what he called "the arrogance of power." He became aware of the difficulties in defining precisely the relationship between the executive and legislative branches in the area of foreign policy, that there is no clearcut constitutional directive or tradition by which to settle the distribution of power, and so he used the power of the mass media to try to persuade the various administrations to change their views by stirring up public opinion. The Foreign Relations Committee thus became a kind of educational agency in that it provided him a forum for public debate, and Fulbright personally kept up steady pressure by public speeches and popular essays through which he presented his own views.

Though he may know little, if anything, about civil religion by that name, Fulbright is certainly familiar with the phenomenon as such. The following essay demonstrates that. Indeed, he might even be called a "prophet" of the tradition in that he brings judgment to bear on the incipient idolatry expressed by some of the leading practitioners of American civil religion.

Document 12

From *The Arrogance of Power* by J. William Fulbright

America is the most fortunate of nations—fortunate in her rich territory, fortunate in having had a century of relative peace in which to develop that territory, fortunate in her diverse and talented population, fortunate in the institutions devised by the founding fathers and in the wisdom of those who have adapted those institutions to a changing world.

SOURCE: From *The Arrogance of Power*, by J. William Fulbright. Copyright ©1966 by J. William Fulbright. Reprinted by permission of Random House, Inc.

[67]Mead, *The Lively Experiment*, op. cit., p. 85.

For the most part America has made good use of her blessings, especially in her internal life but also in her foreign relations. Having done so much and succeeded so well, America is now at that historical point at which a great nation is in danger of losing its perspective on what exactly is within the realm of its power and what is beyond it. Other great nations, reaching this critical juncture, have aspired to too much, and by over-extension of effort have declined and then fallen.

The causes of the malady are not entirely clear but its recurrence is one of the uniformities of history: power tends to confuse itself with virtue and a great nation is peculiarly susceptible to the idea that its power is a sign of God's favor, conferring upon it a special responsibility for other nations—to make them richer and happier and wiser, to remake them, that is, in its own shining image. Power confuses itself with virtue and tends also to take itself for omnipotence. Once imbued with the idea of a mission, a great nation easily assumes that it has the means as well as the duty to do God's work. The Lord, after all, surely would not choose you as His agent and then deny you the sword with which to work His will. German soldiers in the First World War wore belt buckles imprinted with the words, "*Gott mit uns.*" It was approximately under this kind of infatuation—an exaggerated sense of power and an imaginary sense of mission—that the Athenians attacked Syracuse and Napoleon and then Hitler invaded Russia. In plain words, they overextended their commitments and they came to grief.

I do not think for a moment that America, with her deeply rooted democratic traditions, is likely to embark upon a campaign to dominate the world in the manner of a Hitler or Napoleon. What I do fear is that she may be drifting into commitments which, though generous and benevolent in intent, are so far-reaching as to exceed even America's great capacities. At the same time, it is my hope—and I emphasize it because it underlies all of the criticisms and proposals to be made in these pages—that America will escape those fatal temptations of power which have ruined other great nations and will instead confine herself to doing only that good in the world which she *can* do, both by direct effort and by the force of her own example.

The stakes are high indeed: they include not only America's continued greatness but nothing less than the survival of the human race in an era when, for the first time in human history, a living generation has the power of veto over the survival of the next.

The Power Drive of Nations

Many of the wars fought by man—I am tempted to say most—have been fought over . . . abstractions. The more I puzzle over the great wars of history, the more I am inclined to the view that the causes attributed to them—territory, markets, resources, the defense or perpetuation of great principles—were not the root causes at all but rather explanations or excuses for certain unfathomable drives of human nature. For lack of a clear and precise understanding of exactly what these motives are, I refer to them as the "arrogance of power"—as a psychological need that nations seem to have in order to prove that they are bigger, better, or stronger than other nations. Implicit in this drive is the assumption, even on the part of normally peaceful nations, that force is the ultimate proof of superiority—that when a nation shows that it has the stronger army, it is also proving that it has better people, better institutions, better principles, and, in general, a better civilization.

Evidence for my proposition is found in the remarkable discrepancy between the apparent and hidden causes of some modern wars and the discrepancy between their causes and ultimate consequences.

The United States went to war in 1898 for the stated purpose of liberating Cuba from Spanish tyranny, but after winning the war—a war which Spain had been willing to pay a high price to avoid—the United States brought the liberated Cubans under an American protectorate and incidentally annexed the Philippines, because, according to President McKinley, the Lord told him it was America's duty "to educate the Filipinos, and uplift and civilize and Christianize them, and by God's grace do the very best we could by them, as our fellowmen for whom Christ also died."

Isn't it interesting that the voice was the voice of the Lord but the words were those of Theodore Roosevelt, Henry Cabot Lodge, and Admiral Mahan, those "imperialists of 1898" who wanted America to have an empire just because a big, powerful country like the United States *ought* to have an empire? The spirit of the times was expressed by Albert Beveridge, soon thereafter to be elected to the United States Senate, who proclaimed Americans to be a "conquering race": "We must obey our blood and occupy new markets and if necessary new lands," he said, because "In the Almighty's infinite plan. . . debased civilizations and decaying races" must disappear "before the higher civilization of the nobler and more virile types of man."

The attitude above all others which I feel sure is no longer valid is the arrogance of power, the tendency of great nations to equate power with virtue and major responsibilities with a universal mission. The dilemmas involved are pre-eminently American dilemmas, not because America has weaknesses that others do not have but because America is powerful as no nation has ever been before, and the discrepancy between her power and the power of others appears to be increasing. One may hope that America, with her vast resources and democratic traditions, with her diverse and creative population, will find the wisdom to match her power; but one can hardly be confident because the wisdom required is greater wisdom than any great nation has ever shown before.

During the late sixties and early seventies, the nation drifted aimlessly. Although the 1964 Civil Rights Act had promised an end to racial injustice at home, a sizable portion of the black population still suffered intolerance. Poverty still afflicted millions of people here, in the middle of the world's most affluent society. Abroad, the Vietnam war became the most embarrassing and tragic conflict in the history of the Republic. Young Americans on college campuses rebelled against its pointlessness and took to the streets. The last straw for almost everyone was the way in which the Nixon administration tried to deny responsibility for the robbery of the Democratic National Headquarters. The incident even added a new term to the American vocabulary, as *Watergate* came to denote not just ordinary political skullduggery but pervasive and profound political corruption.

In 1976, the Democrats—looking for a way to rejuvenate the conscience and confidence of the nation—nominated an obscure Southern governor to carry its banner in the national elections. There had never been another candidate so overtly religious as Jimmy Carter. If inaugural addresses have been among the most obvious expressions of civil religion, one would logically have expected Carter's speech to be filled with the type of Southern Baptist religious rhetoric the nation had become familiar with during the campaign. And yet, in some very notable ways, there were not, in Carter's address, the usual references to America's chosen place in history or the obligatory invocation of God's blessing on the land. Perhaps it was not necessary for him to include these because everyone knew that the new president's personal faith would be expected to anchor his decisions. In a curious way, however, his relatively short speech was homiletic in nature and falls into its place as one of the important documents of the civil religion tradition. He called upon his fellow countrymen to create "a new national spirit of unity and trust." He talked about having "faith in our country—and in one other." And although he did quote the prophet Micah as John Winthrop had done some 350 years earlier, there was no direct mention of God or Providence, of America as the New Israel or Promised Land. It was almost as if he did not have to because of the character of his own personal religiousness.

Document 13

Jimmy Carter's Inaugural Address

For myself and for our nation, I want to thank my predecessor for all he has done to heal our land. In this outward and physical ceremony we attest once again to the inner and spiritual strength of our nation.

As my high school teacher, Miss Julia Coleman, used to say, "We must adjust to changing times and still hold to unchanging principles."

Here before me is the Bible used in the inauguration of our first President in 1789, and I have just taken the oath of office on the Bible my mother gave me just a few years ago, opened to a timeless admonition from the ancient prophet, Micah:

"He hath showed thee, O man, what is good; and what doth the Lord require of thee, but to do justly, and to love mercy, and to walk humbly with thy God." (Micah 6:8)

This inauguration ceremony marks a new beginning, a new dedication within our Government, and a new spirit among us all. A President may sense and proclaim that new spirit, but only a people can provide it.

Two centuries ago our nation's birth was a milestone in the long quest for free-

SOURCE: *The New York Times*, January 21, 1977.

dom, but the bold and brilliant dream which excited the founders of our nation still awaits its consummation. I have no new dream to set forth today, but rather urge a fresh faith in the old dream.

Ours was the first society openly to define itself in terms of both spirituality and human liberty. It is that unique self-definition which has given us an exceptional appeal—but it also imposes on us a special obligation, to take on those moral duties which, when assumed, seem invariably to be in our own best interests.

You have given me a great responsibility—to stay close to you, to be worthy of you and to exemplify what you are. Let us create together a new national spirit of unity and trust. Your strength can compensate for my weakness, and your wisdom can help to minimize my mistakes.

Let us learn together and laugh together and work together and pray together, confident that in the end we will triumph together in the right.

The American dream endures. We must once again have faith in our country—and in one another. I believe America can be better. We can be even stronger than before.

Let our recent mistakes bring a resurgent commitment to the basic principles of our nation, for we know that if we despise our own Government we have no future. We recall in special times when we have stood briefly, but magnificently, united; in those times no prize was beyond our grasp.

But we cannot dwell upon remembered glory. We cannot afford to drift. We reject the prospect of failure or mediocrity or an inferior quality of life for any person.

Our Government must at the same time be both competent and compassionate.

We have already found a high degree of personal liberty, and we are now struggling to enhance equality of opportunity. Our commitment to human rights must be absolute, our laws fair, our natural beauty preserved; the powerful must not persecute the weak, and human dignity must be enhanced.

We have learned that "more" is not necessarily "better," that even our great nation has its recognized limits and that we can neither answer all questions nor solve all problems. We cannot afford to do everything, nor can we afford to lack boldness as we meet the future. So together, in a spirit of individual sacrifice for the common good, we must simply do our best.

Our nation can be strong abroad only if it is strong at home, and we know that the best way to enhance freedom in other lands is to demonstrate here that our democratic system is worthy of emulation.

To be true to ourselves, we must be true to others. We will not behave in foreign places so as to violate our rules and standards here at home, for we know that this trust which our nation earns is essential to our strength.

The world itself is now dominated by a new spirit. Peoples more numerous and more politically aware are craving and now demanding their place in the sun—not just for the benefit of their own physical condition, but for basic human rights.

The passion for freedom is on the rise. Tapping this new spirit, there can be no nobler nor more ambitious task for America to undertake on this day of a new beginning than to help shape a just and peaceful world that is truly humane.

We are a strong nation and we will maintain strength so sufficient that it need not be proven in combat—a quiet strength based not merely on the size of an arsenal, but on the nobility of ideas.

We will be ever vigilant and never vulnerable, and we will fight our wars against poverty, ignorance and injustice, for those are the enemies against which our forces can be honorably marshaled.

We are a proudly idealistic nation, but let no one confuse our idealism with weakness.

Because we are free we can never be indifferent to the fate of freedom elsewhere. Our moral sense dictates a clearcut preference for those societies which share with us an abiding respect for individual human rights. We do not seek to intimidate, but it is clear that a world which others can dominate with impunity would be inhospitable to decency and a threat to the well-being of all people.

The world is still engaged in a massive armaments race designed to insure continuing equivalent strength among potential adversaries. We pledge perseverence and wisdom in our efforts to limit the world's armaments to those necessary for each nation's own domestic safety. We will move this year a step toward our ultimate goal—the elimination of all nuclear weapons from this earth.

We urge all other people to join us, for success can mean life instead of death.

Within us, the people of the United States, there is evident a serious and purposeful rekindling of confidence, and I join in the hope that when my time as your President has ended, people might say this about our nation:

That we had remembered the words of Micah and renewed our search for humility, mercy and justice;

That we had torn down the barriers that separated those of different race and region and religion, and where there had been mistrust, built unity, with a respect for diversity;

That we had found productive work for those able to perform it;

That we had strengthened the American family, which is the basis of our society;

That we had insured respect for the law, and equal treatment under the law, for the weak and the powerful, for the rich and the poor;

And that we had enabled our people to be proud of their own Government once again.

I would hope that the nations of the world might say that we had built a lasting peace, based not on weapons of war but on international policies which reflect our own most precious values.

These are not just my goals. And they will not be my accomplishments, but the affirmation of our nation's continuing moral strength and our belief in an undiminished, ever expanding American dream.

Summary

This chapter has consisted of two major parts: (1) a theoretical discussion of the morphology of civil religion in which its structure and shape were abstracted from the flux of historical data and (2) a historical survey of the various persons, events, and writings that have expressed American civil religion since its inception.

In the theorectical section, we first attempted to account for the origin of our particular brand of civil religion, concluding that it arose out of the interplay between the very special circumstances in America, both political and religious. On the one hand, the Enlightenment theories of government insisted on a separation of civil and ecclesiastical powers so that no one church was allowed to gain the upper hand in any social way, which simply meant that an unofficial and undetected form of religiousness swept into the vacuum created by disestablishment and took hold of the American people. This religiousness is what we call civil religion. On the other hand, the Judaeo-Christian tradition supplied some of the fundamental motifs and metaphors for American civil religion: the "exodus" from the Old World to the Promised Land, the death and resurrection theme implicit in the Civil War, the faith in the divine Providence watching over our destiny, and others.

Reference to the work of three scholars offered three different ways of assessing the function and value of civil religion. First cited was Will Herberg, who cautions that "the American Way of Life" (his term for civil religion) often comes close to idolatry. The problem, he says, is that contemporary Americans have domesticated God and made of Him a tribal deity. This deity's most useful functions have been to reinforce the self-serving aspects of the "democratic free enterprise" system and to serve as a psychological crutch for the insecure. Moreover, says Herberg, church membership has become a means of self-identification in modern mass society, and the voluntarism[68] of American religion—at one time a healthy ingredient in our national life—has lapsed into a belief in the value of belief. Herberg holds no special brief *against* modern secular society as such. He only says that the wellsprings of modern life will soon dry up if contemporary Americans do not rediscover the vital faith that stands at the heart of Judaism and Christianity, if they allow secular institutions to provide pseudoreligious answers to modern spiritual problems.

Sidney Mead, on the other hand, sees "the religion of the Republic" as a possible solution for the inevitable conflicts that exist among the denominations. By definition, he says, the ecclesial religious groups are particularistic and exclusivistic. Although the ecumenical movement[69] may be an encouraging movement toward overcoming conflict, it by no means accomplishes what the First Amendment can. The religion clauses of the First Amendment encourage both pluralism and inclusiveness. All religious groups are equally protected before the law and may pursue their own policies with the guarantee of complete freedom. Even

---

[68]The principle that religion is a voluntary matter, freely engaged in or not by the individual.

[69]The movement toward reunion among the various denominations and churches, which in the beginning, it is presumed, were one. See Chapter 8.

if the ecumenical movement should eventually encompass all Christian denominations, a highly unlikely event, there are still Jews, Ethical Culturalists, Buddhists, nonbelievers, and various others who would inevitably be excluded from the superchurch. That is because all groups within the Judeo-Christian tradition are by nature exclusivistic: they must by necessity hold that they own the truth. Even the superchurch would have to draw the line somewhere. Mead therefore opts for the broad, inclusive policy embodied in the First Amendment. Out of the philosopy behind the First Amendment, he contends, there has arisen a faith among the American people that, on the one hand, holds fast to the policy of pluralism while at the same time holding, in a rather imprecise consensus, the conviction that the God of our Fathers has been watching over the nation and that He will one day judge our actions. This belief is not contained in any creed or confession to which the people adhere; it simply is the conviction of most American people. Thus all believers, whatever their stripe (including nonbelievers!), could come together under the spacious umbrella of what he calls "the religion of the Republic." Denominational lines, which are largely meaningless to the majority of the people, would melt away.

Robert Bellah holds a mediating position between Herberg and Mead. He sees that the denominations and the civil religion can coexist, and indeed, must coexist according to the system we have devised. Civil religion and ecclesial religion are not necessarily competitive. If anything, ecclesial religion may provide some of the substance for civil religion and may act as a critic of any attempt to divinize political power. On the other hand, the government will keep itself free from any encroachment upon the integrity of the denominations. For Bellah the main problem today is whether or not the nation, in this "third time of trial," will be able to make the ideals and goals of America a reality in the lives of those who desperately seek freedom from oppression both at home and abroad. The great danger is that people will be satisfied to make compromises with those principles that brought our civil religion into being in the first place.

The theoretical section closed with two warnings—one from a contemporary theologian, Rosemary Radford Ruether, who wants to preserve the prophetic element in civil religion, and the other from Senator Mark Hatfield, who sounds like a prophet himself, warning against the idolatry he believes to be inherent in civil religion.

Next, in the historical section of this first chapter, we attempted to sketch the development of civil religion from the earliest colonial days up to the present. Along the way we recorded many of the documents that have given expression to American civil religion. From the idea of the covenant found in the Mayflower Compact we discerned the earliest intimations of what would later turn into the doctrine of Manifest Destiny—the fundamental point being that God covenants with a people to be their God, if they will be His people. In the Edwards piece we saw how even his powerful intellect was so persuaded of the election of the American nation that he believed the Kingdom in all its fullness would actually come to this section of God's earth soon, because of the highly successful revivals in mid-eighteenth-century New England. The theme of Providence was then picked up and enunciated by politicians as well as preachers and theologians. Washington, in the First Inaugural, began his administration with an invocation of God's blessing upon his endeavors and so established a custom that has existed unbroken down through the years. First one president, then another has spoken of America's special place in the order of things, even up to our own day. But in order to show how the tradition can create its own critics, we excerpted sections from a book by a United States senator whose degree of patriotism has been most eloquently displayed in his quarrel with American foreign policy. Senator Fulbright has cautioned us against the arrogance that so easily accompanies political power. In the language of religion, he is suggesting that the nation has engaged in a most serious kind of apostasy from its stated ideals. It has not humbled itself before the hard facts of history but has become arrogant in its misuse of unparalleled power. That debate is long from over.

A thorough examination of the religious elements in the Constitution and Bill of Rights is necessary if one is really to appreciate the unique quality of American civil religion. That is our next concern.

2

Religious Liberty and the Free Church

In recent years the United States Supreme Court has held

- That school boards may not prescribe any sort of opening religious exercises for public schools.
- That an illegal drug like peyote can be ingested by members of a religious group so long as it is part of their cultic practice.
- That a famous boxer who is also a member of an Islamic sect in which holy wars are the only justifiable wars was a legitimate conscientious objector to the Vietnam war.
- That the government can pay for lunches, bus transportation, and even some kinds of textbooks for parochial school children.
- That the government can help pay for buildings on church-related college campuses so long as the buildings are used for secular purposes.
- But that the government cannot pay for the salaries of parochial school teachers, or even guidance counsellors who work at church-related schools.
- That "released-time" programs on public school property are illegal.
- But that "released-time" programs for religious training off of public school property are acceptable.
- That people whose religion forbids their working on Saturday may receive unemployment compensation if their employers require them to work on Saturday.
- That an agnostic can be a conscientious objector if he objects to war with a sincerity and fervor resembling religious faith.
- That church property is tax exempt but that church-owned property used for a commercial purpose such as a church-owned parking lot is not.

The subtleties of the decisions are, of course, overlooked in a quick survey of this kind. The closeness of some of the decisions is ignored. (Some of the decisions could even be significantly modified before this book gets off the press.) But the overwhelming effect of reading the opinions of the courts in recent years is to make one conscious of just how central religious liberty is to the American political and social system. We do live in "a new order for the ages."

Novus Ordo Seclorum

Novus ordo seclorum, "a new order for the ages," is the motto found on the reverse side of the Great Seal of the United States. No doubt each American who pauses long enough to think about its meaning will consider all the various freedoms acheived during the American revolution, but certainly everyone can now agree that none was more significant than religious freedom, a radically new idea when the nation was founded. Not everyone in the eighteenth century was favorably inclined towards religious liberty. Many thought that religious toleration, where some form of Protestantism would remain the "established" religion, was preferable to outright *dis*establishment and religious freedom.[1] But the arguments of the libertarians prevailed. They were convinced that the alliance between civil and ecclesiastical governments had to be permanently broken because that alliance had been too powerful and too prone to misuse its authority. Accordingly, disestablishment was urgently pursued by men like Jefferson and Madison. Although they were incapable of grasping the full significance of their words and actions, they were correct to think of themselves as creating "a new order for the ages."

Our problem today is just the opposite. We are so accustomed to living with disestablishment that we fail to see how unique a phenomenon it is in world history. We would do well to listen to visitors like Lord Bryce, who noted that "of all the differences between the Old World and the New, this is the most significant."[2] The effect of the Establishment and Free Exercise clauses of the First Amendment was to turn upside down the old medieval system of privilege: former masters had to become public servants, whose tenure and power were to be held at the discretion of the people or in the case of the churches, at the discretion of the membership. In other words, leaders, whether political or religious, were in most cases subject to the democratic process.[3] Moreover,

[1] Indeed, some nineteenth-century constitutional historians held that the establishment clause of the First Amendment was only intended to prohibit the federal government from acting upon the subject and that the whole power over the subject of establishment is left exclusively to state governments. For example, Joseph Story, an associate justice of the Supreme Court, wrote: "Probably [at] the adoption of the constitution and of the [First Amendment], the general, if not the universal, sentiment in America was, that Christianity ought to receive encouragement from the state, so far as was not incompatible with the private rights of conscience, and the freedom of religious worship. An attempt to level all religions, and to make it a matter of state policy to hold all in utter indifference, would have created universal disapprobation, if not universal indignation." See Joseph Story, *Commentaries on the Constitution of the United States* (Boston: 1833), paragraph 1868.

[2] James Bryce, *The American Commonwealth* (New York: Macmillan, 1901), p. 695.

[3] Only the Roman Catholics continued the old medieval hierarchical system. But even they felt the bracing winds of religious freedom during the Revolutionary period, when lay trustees, who held title to most Catholic property in the United States, began to exercise a modest amount of influence in church affairs. It was not until the Irish immigrations during the first half of the nineteenth century that the controversy over trusteeship was successfully squelched

all magistrates, whether civil or ecclesiastical, would henceforth be subject to criticism from the ordinary person. For generations the established rulers had operated beyond the reach and influence of the laity. All power, if not actually concentrated in the person of a single ruler, had been comfortably shared by magistrates in the two orders, religious and civil. Even during those periods when church and state were vying for supremacy, during the worst moments of the medieval investiture controversies,[4] no one ever really supposed that spiritual and temporal powers were not ultimately and intimately connected. All rulers were divinely appointed to rule. Had not Paul warned the church at Rome: "Let every person be subject to the governing authorities. For there is no authority except from God, and those that exist have been instituted by God. Therefore he who resists the authorities resists what God has appointed, and those who resist will incur judgment"?[5]

As Christianity grew and spread, the great teachers of the church followed Paul fairly closely in this matter. In *The City of God,* Augustine said that all Christians live in two cities: one of God, the other of man. In the city of man (the political order) men must keep the law because God ordains it for the twin purposes of keeping in check their unruly passions and of promoting justice in human society. Or, to put it another way, God gives secular law because men are sinners. Augustine held that

> the Christian obeys the state no less than the pagan, but his outlook is different. . . . The Christian lives in the state and enjoys its goods and contributes to those goods and obeys it; in mind and spirit he lives also in the city of God. He lives one life inside the other, and because he lives as citizen of the city of God his citizenship of the state is informed with a new spirit. He owes double allegiance, one allegiance inside the other, to the state and to the city of God.[6]

Augustine thus provided the rationale for what soon became the medieval accommodation between church and state.

---

by the Irish bishops, who had gained control. Their fierce loyalty to the nation did not keep them from being as intensely loyal to Rome. This interesting combination helped to shape the future course for American Catholicism. See Will Herberg, *Protestant-Catholic-Jew: An Essay in American Religious Sociology* (Garden City, N.Y.: Doubleday, 1960), pp. 138f.

[4] Disputes during the eleventh and twelfth centuries over who should "invest" bishops and abbots in their offices, secular or religious princes. The pope sought to wrest the power from secular lords.

[5] Romans 12:1–2, *Revised Standard Version* (New York: Thomas Nelson & Sons, 1952).

[6] As summarized by R.H. Barrow, *Introduction to St. Augustine* (London: Faber and Faber, 1950), p. 236. Augustine has sometimes been cited for advocating separation of church and state. As Barrow notes, Augustine clearly defines the sphere of the state and the sphere of the church, but to say that he is a protoseparationist is a bit anachronistic. To do so is to forget that Augustine wrote in a half-pagan world. Indeed, he brought the Christian and the state much closer than they had ever been before, for "he shows the Christian that he owes full allegiance to the state (subject to one proviso) and that he can live a Christian life within its limited objective." Ibid., p. 239.

Later on, Martin Luther and John Calvin took positions similar to Augustine's. "If the Emperor calls me," said Luther, "God calls me."[7] Although it is a matter of lively debate precisely how he and Calvin thought of the relationship between church and state, there is no debate at all about their thoughts on establishment. They, like everyone else in that day, *assumed* Christianity to be the official religion of the state. The only question was one of preference: which brand of Christianity was to prevail, Roman or Reformed? Once that was determined, they believed that the good churchman was always to obey the civil as well as the ecclesiastical prince, because all rulers ultimately derive their power from God. More than that, Luther and Calvin taught that both kinds of rulers were to collaborate with and mutually aid one another in carrying out their respective God-given duties. Therefore, to equate, as is so often done, historic European Protestantism with the rather democratic Protestant denominational life as we know it in the United States is misleading. Admittedly, American Protestantism is a legitimate and natural heir to the movements begun by the great European Reformers, but when exported to these shores, Protestantism underwent significant alterations.

Of all the types of Protestantism that emerged in Europe in the sixteenth century, the type that turned out to be the most congenial on American soil was the radical, left wing of the Reformation. These Protestants were, by conviction, totally opposed to any alliance between church and state. Their experiences had taught them that magistrates were good for only one thing, persecution and harassment. Even so fervent a reformer as Martin Luther had vigorously objected to the left wing for its lawlessness and enjoined civil authorities to use violence to rid the world of this new infidelity.

The Anabaptists, as these radicals were first known, comprised "the continental fountainhead" for a "deep river of religion" that eventually washed over the American continent. They eschewed any intermediaries between man and God. As Edwin Scott Gaustad points out, "the less mediation the better, whether that mediation be by state, by society, by school, or even by church." For them, the only legitimate religious authority was to be derived from one's own direct encounter with God and not through some magistrate, either civil or religious. Quakers and Baptists were the most conspicuous representatives in colonial America, though there were others: Mennonites, Independents, Separate Congregationalists, and, later on, Methodists.[8] Although the Quak-

---

[7] As quoted by Roland Bainton, *Here I Stand* (New York: Abingdon-Cokesbury, 1940), p. 238. For an account of Calvin's stance, see Francois Wendel's *Calvin* (New York: Harper & Row, 1963), p. 79.

[8] Edwin Scott Gaustad, "A Disestablished Society: Origins of the First Amendment," *A Journal of Church and State,* Vol. 11 (Autumn 1969), pp. 409–410. See also Franklin H. Littell, *The Origins of Sectarian Protestantism: The Anabaptist View of the Church* (New York: Macmillan Publishing Co., 1960).

ers and Mennonites are barely noticeable in any numerical profile of American Protestantism today, Baptists and Methodists are by far the largest Protestant families. Left-wing Protestantism did indeed take hold in America, and, after disestablishment, grew like wildfire.

In the last analysis, however, it was the First Amendment that created the milieu in which our kind of denominational life could come into being and flourish. The Reformation was most certainly a first step toward modification of excessive ecclesiastical power and hence a move toward disestablishment. But the Bill of Rights, adopted on November 3, 1971, was the real breakthrough.[9] By means of that document Americans were assured that they could follow the dictates of their consciences in matters of religion. From that time forward it was difficult, if not impossible, for any one religious group to prescribe religious beliefs or practices for any other group or individual.

Although a good many believed that the First Amendment was the first step toward the ultimate demise of religion, the framers were convinced that institutional religion would not be hurt but stimulated. Jefferson stated in 1781 that "difference of opinion is advantageous to religion."[10] Though one might want to argue that point, he held that in a society where no one religious group is allowed to gain official sanction from the government, all groups are compelled to compete, as it were, in the open marketplace and thus gain vitality through competition. By relying on governmental backing, the churches of Europe, on the other hand, would eventually lose what vigor they possessed.

An additional advantage to disestablishment, Jefferson held, was that "the several sects perform the office of *censor morum*" or automatic check on each other. The pressures of open and free disagreement between the various groups would keep them "honest," and the government would have to watch the contest from a safe distance away. In short, uniformity in religion was not only undesirable but unattainable so far as Jefferson was concerned: "Millions of innocent men, women, and children, since the introduction of Christianity, have been burnt, tortured, fined, imprisoned; yet we have not advanced one inch towards uniformity."[11]

The American "free church" tradition must therefore be distinguished from the "free church" or "nonconforming" sects of Europe. There these groups have persisted as "outsiders" in that they have been "permitted" to operate with varying degrees of freedom but always with a handicap in relation to the established church. Here in America, on the other hand, *all* groups are in some sense "free churches," and as Sidney Mead points out, the word *free* has a different value for us. We

[9] There were other agents as well: geographic, economic, demographic, and so on. See H. Richard Niebuhr's classic study, *The Social Sources of Denominationalism* (New York: World Publishing Company, 1957).

[10] Saul K. Padover (ed.), *The Complete Jefferson* (New York: Books for Libraries, 1943), p. 675.

[11] Ibid.

are talking about a situation where *all* groups are completely "indepen-dent of the state and autonomous in relation to it."[12]

The Supreme Court

The institution charged with protecting the concept of religious liberty in America has, of course, been the Supreme Court. Because disestab-lishment was such a novelty at the time, no one at the Constitutional conventions could have predicted all the ways in which the issue of re-ligious liberty would subsequently be joined. No one was wise enough to draw up statutes and constitutional provisions that would have been either broad enough or precise enough to anticipate the myriad prob-lems that would inevitably arise. The best one could do was to draw up several general principles and hope that the Supreme Court would have the wisdom to apply them with equity to specific cases.

Moreover, no one yet knows the final or ultimate shape of religious liberty in America. Today the Court is still attempting to define the nature of religious freedom. The judges not only seek to discover what the intentions of the Founding Fathers might have been, but they also attempt to square present policy against the *ideal* of religious freedom. Though the natural law tradition, which teaches that values like justice are rationally clear, has fallen into disrepute among a good many mod-ern thinkers, the Court nevertheless operates on the assumption that perfect justice is an appropriate goal toward which to strive. Thus, the Court has not been satisfied merely to read precedent into new and changing situations; it has also attempted to spell out the particulars of a justice that is always coming into being. It is as though the Court must look both ways at once: backward to the wisdom of previous gen-erations and forward to that ideal form of justice that hovers just over the horizon, waiting to be brought into being at every moment.

What Chief Justice Earl Warren wrote several years ago about the Eighth Amendment could be applied with validity to the First: "The words of the Amendment are not precise . . . their scope is not static. The Amendment must draw its meaning from the evolving standards of decency that mark the progress of a maturing society."[13] Indeed, the entire Bill of Rights has proved to be a remarkably strong but elastic document through the nearly two hundred years of its existence. Be-cause it has been relevant to almost every conceivable circumstance, it has managed to remain the vital instrument it was when first adopted. Although its flexibility has been severely tested in recent years, it has not been found wanting. Thus, the Court's most vigorous critics have been those who have felt that it has been too accommodating to the

---

[12] Sidney E. Mead, *The Lively Experiment* (New York: Harper & Row, 1963), p. 103.

[13] As quoted by Leo Pfeffer, "The Case for Separation," *Religion in America,* edited by John Cogley (New York: World Publishing Company, 1962), p. 55.

changing times, instead of being too inflexible. But the Court has none-theless continued to attempt to deal effectively with each new challenge to religious liberty.

Metaphors and Doctrine

Throughout the history of the Court, various controlling metaphors or phrases have emerged from time to time. These metaphors have tended to dominate its thinking. This has been especially so in the opinions regarding the religion clauses of the First Amendment. These phrases have not always been precisely defined, but they have carried a kind of tacit logic, appealing to a wide spectrum of people. In time, the phrases have gained the power of doctrine, so that subsequent opinions have had to agree with or at least take into consideration the general intention of the phrases as first used.

THE WALL OF SEPARATION *can never be broken*

Until recently, one of the most important of these phrases has been the *wall of separation*, an expression that was first coined by Roger Williams but that was adopted by Jefferson when he wrote to a group of Danbury, Connecticut, Baptists in 1802:

> Believing with you that religion is a matter which lies solely between man and his God, that he owes account to none other for his faith or his worship, that the legislative powers of government reach actions only, not opinions, I contemplate with sovereign reverence that act of the whole American people which declared that their legislature should "make no law respecting the establishment of religion, or prohibiting the free exercise thereof," thus building a *wall of separation between church and state*.[14]

The Court incorporated this letter into the body of the 1878 *Reynolds* opinion, which meant not only that it adopted the wall metaphor as a useful constitutional gloss, but that it also reaffirmed what it had long held, the distinction between belief and action. That is to say, Jefferson inferred you can "believe" anything you want to or entertain any idea intellectually, but so long as it remains in that preactive state, you are not subject to governmental interference. Once the belief is translated into action, you are subject to the police powers of the government.

Reynolds, a Mormon, had raised the question whether a federal statute against polygamy could be constitutionally applied to him because of his faith. The trial court chose not to deal with that question but rather to hold that polygamy was detrimental to the general welfare. The Supreme Court agreed. Its reasoning was straightforward, if questionable: history showed that "Congress was deprived of all legislative power over mere opinion [or religious belief], but was left free to reach actions which were in violation of social duties or subversive of good

---

[14] Padover, op. cit., pp. 518–519. Emphasis added.

order." Because Reynolds did not deny that he had more than one wife and because American society at large had long before decided that polygamy was unacceptable, he was adjudged guilty. The author of the majority opinion in the case concluded his argument by holding that, because the distinction between belief and action came from "an acknowleged leader of the advocates" for separation (Jefferson), the distinction "may be accepted almost as an authoritative declaration of the scope and effect of the First Amendment."[15] Built into the verbiage of the Court from that time to this has been the wall metaphor.

It was not until another sixty years had passed, however, that the Court was required to be more precise about what the "wall" of separation might really consist of. Although it had decided several cases involving the Establishment Clause of the First Amendment, the crucial test came in *Everson v. Board of Education* (1947), one of the most significant cases of recent times.

Everson brought suit to have declared unconstitutional a New Jersey statute authorizing local school boards to reimburse parents whose children were bused to schools owned and operated by the Roman Catholic Church. He contended that the state had no business reimbursing the parents because it indirectly constituted an "establishment" of religion. But the Court decided, by a vote of 5 to 4, against Everson: public subsidies for busing students to Catholic parochial schools is not unconstitutional. In the course of the majority opinion Mr. Justice Black wrote:

> This Court has said that the parents may, in the discharge of their duty under state compulsory education laws, send their children to a religious rather than a public school if the school meets the secular education requirements which the state has power to impose. It appears that these parochial schools meet New Jersey's requirements. The state contributes no money to the schools. It does not support them. Its legislation, as applied, does no more than provide a general program to help parents get their children, regardless of their religion, safely and expeditiously to and from accredited schools.
> The First Amendment has erected *a wall between church and state*. That wall must be kept high and impregnable. We could not approve the slightest breach. New Jersey has not breached it here.[16]

The logic was simple: money is given to parents of students who are sent to constitutionally acceptable schools; no money is granted to the schools themselves.

In the next year, 1948, another major case involving the question of church–state relations was decided, *McCollum v. Board of Education.* Here the Court, in an 8 to 1 decision, accepted the theory of separation developed in the *Everson* case and used that theory to nullify a "released time" program in Illinois. The Illinois plan made it possible for students to receive sectarian instruction on school time and on school

[15] *Reynolds v. United States*, 98 U.S. 145 (1878).
[16] *Everson v. Board of Education*, 330 U.S. 1, 18 (1947). Emphasis added.

property. In a concurring opinion Mr. Justice Frankfurter (1882–1965) wrote that the wall metaphor could be "illuminatingly" applied in the *McCollum* case:

> Separation means separation, not something less. Jefferson's metaphor in describing the relation between Church and State speaks of a "wall of separation," not a fine line easily overstepped. The public school is at once the symbol of our democracy and the most pervasive means for promoting our common destiny. In no activity of the State is it more vital to keep out divisive forces than its schools, to avoid confusing, not to say fusing, what the Constitution sought to keep strictly apart.[17]

The Illinois plan, said he, was clearly unconstitutional.

But in a second concurring opinion, Mr. Justice Jackson (1892–1954) suggested that the wall metaphor was not too helpful in deciding this type of case. He stoutly resisted Mrs. McCollum's desire "to lay down a sweeping constitutional doctrine" that would prohibit any sort of released time program. He said that such a decree would ignore the fact that individual programs and circumstances will vary widely and would eventually turn the Court into a kind of "super board of education" for every school district in the nation. Yet, said Jackson, the justices must find some principle that would work, some principle sounder than their own "prepossessions" about what the law ought to be, some firm base on which to found the law. Otherwise they were "likely to make the legal 'wall of separation between church and state' as winding as the famous serpentine wall designed by Mr. Jefferson for the University he founded"![18]

Four years later in another major suit, *Zorach v. Clauson* (1952), the Court again used the wall metaphor, but by this time cracks had begun to appear in it. As a figure of speech, it had begun to lose its usefulness because the problem called for a subtler and more elastic doctrine than "the wall of separation" could provide. Some other phrase would have to be found.

Like the *McCollum* case, *Zorach* involved a "released-time" program, but with a significant difference: New York authorities would permit religious instruction to take place during school time, but *off* school property. In the *McCollum* case, it will be remembered, religious instruction was to be given by sectarian teachers at the schools on regular time. The New York authorities, however, insisted in *Zorach* that no public funds or facilities were being used for their program.

In the majority opinion the Court reiterated its belief that church and state should be unequivocally separated from one another, but then it made an important qualification. Mr. Justice Douglas wrote, "The First Amendment . . . , does not say that in every and all respects there shall be a separation of Church and State. Rather, it studiously defines

---

[17] *McCollum v. Board of Education*, 333 U.S. 203, 231 (1948).
[18] Ibid. at 238.

the manner, the specific ways, in which there shall be no concert or union or dependency one on the other."[19] In other words, when the principle of separation is invoked, the implication is that separation should be unqualified and complete. But, he suggested, there are situations where enforced separation is arbitrary and capricious. Religion and government are not necessarily "aliens to each other—hostile, suspicious, and even unfriendly." Rather, there are occasions when government and religion are legally supportive of one another. If the "wall of separation" were dogmatically and rigidly held in every situation, "Churches would not be required to pay even property taxes. Municipalities would not be permitted to render police or fire protection to religious groups. Policemen who helped parishioners into their places of worship would violate the Constitution."[20] Moreover, he argued, religion is necessary to the health of the republic:

> We are a religious people whose institutions presuppose a Supreme Being. . . . When the state encourages religious instruction or cooperates with religious authorities by adjusting the schedule of public events to sectarian needs, it follows the best of our traditions. . . . To hold that it may not would be to find in the Constitution a requirement that the government show a callous indifference to religious groups. That would be preferring those who believe in no religion over those who do believe.[21]

During the 1960s none of the cases in the domain of church—state relations employed the "wall" metaphor as a guide or rule.[22] Though it had served adequately for an important period in the Court's history, the metaphor had lost its usefulness. The justices were then compelled

[19] *Zorach* v. *Clauson*, op. cit., 343 U.S. at 312.

[20] Ibid. By 1970 Douglas had changed from an "accommodationist" to a "strict separationist." As the lone dissenter in *Walz* v. *City of New York,* Douglas argued that tax exemption constituted indirect support of religious establishment. In *Zorach* he said churches could be taxed because the line between government and religion cannot always be tightly drawn. But in the *Walz* dissent he said churches should be taxed in order to *insure* their mutual independence. He rejected the majority theory offered by Chief Justice Burger that, because the two spheres are necessarily and incorrigibly entangled, exemption would decrease the risk of governmental interference in the internal affairs of the churches. The weightier argument, he said, is that, by granting exemption to churches, the government forces the nonbeliever to support religious institutions against his wishes. Or, exemption constitutes indirect establishment. Mr. Justice Douglas's pilgrimage to the "strict separationist" position was by way of *Engel* v. *Vitale* (1962), more popularly known as "the New York Regents' Prayer Case." In the *Engel* case he wrote a concurring opinion in which he repudiated his earlier vote with the majority in *Everson*. He claimed that governmental financing of any kind of religious exercise was "an unconstitutional undertaking" and listed a number of ways in which this might occur: the use of *God* in the pledge of allegiance, "Bible reading in the schools of the District of Columbia," and even the availability "to students in private as well as public schools" of federally assisted lunch programs. As one observer suggested, it seemed that Douglas wanted to "root out . . . every vestige, direct or indirect, of religion in public affairs." See David W. Louisell, "The Man and the Mountain: Douglas on Religious Freedom," *Yale Law Journal,* Vol. 73 (1964), p. 991.

[21] *Zorach* v. *Clauson*, op. cit., 343 U.S. at 313–314.

[22] In 1971 Chief Justice Burger remarked that "the line of separation, far from being a 'wall,' is a blurred, indistinct and variable barrier depending on all the circumstances of a particular relationship." See *Lemon* v. *Kurtzman*, 403 U.S. 602, 614 (1971).

to develop another, more responsive doctrine for dealing with the more complex questions that arose during the 1960s.

First of all, the metaphor had lost its usefulness, says Robert Michaelson, because it does not appear anywhere in the Constitution or Bill of Rights.[23] Instead, as we have already seen, it appears in an unofficial letter from Jefferson to a group of Connecticut churchmen in 1802, after the Constitution was adopted. It therefore does not possess the intrinsic power of the original constitutional prose. For that matter, the words *church* and *state* do not appear anywhere in the original charter. These two words, though frequently used by writers on the subject in America, are much more aptly applied to the European situation than ours. The United States is not a "state" in their sense, nor is there any one entity we can point to as "the church." Our denominational groups, which we sometimes call churches, are by and large voluntary societies whose membership is fluid and arbitrary. We freely decide whether or not we shall "join" a "church," whereas in Europe "the church" is an organic body, which "grows" out of the very cultural "soil" in which it is "rooted." In most European countries, every citizen stands in some official relation to "the church." Here the more neutral term *religion* is a much more apposite term for describing the phenomenon as it occurs. Moreover, we are simply not concerned about the two items that really made a church "the church": ideology and the sacred ministry. First, Americans are patently suspicious of anyone who assigns much importance to dogma and doctrine. If we "believe" in anything, it is likely to be a belief in pluralism, which automatically assumes that any one person's belief, as vague as it may be, is as sound as anyone else's. Second, we are not so ready to concede that the ordained clergy possess some "higher" or more privileged position in the congregation or denomination than laymen do. All members, whether clerical or lay, are considered to be on more or less an equal footing. Denominational executives are respectfully tolerated or, in cases where they have adopted stands unpopular with the local constituency, ignored. So the church-state terminology simply fails to reflect the American situation, because we do not have "the church."

Next, the phrase *wall of separation* conveys a sense of alienation, which is not truly descriptive of what actually occurs in America. There is a great deal of unofficial commerce between the temporal and religious spheres that ignores any sort of artificial barrier such as a wall. Thus the phrase is simply not flexible enough to encompass the kaleidoscopic quality of American religion. We require something much more pragmatic and pliable than that. Michaelson suggests that Madison's phrase *the line of separation* might have been a happier expression with which to operate. At any rate, the Court needed to come up

---

[23] Robert Michaelson, *Piety in the Public School* (New York: Macmillan, 1970), pp. 199, 216, and elsewhere. See also Paul G. Kauper, *Religion and the Constitution* (Baton Rouge: Louisiana State University Press, 1964), p. 76.

with another metaphor or doctrine, and it found a concept that has been most helpful, at least until the present. This was the concept of neutrality.[24]

NEUTRALITY

The seeds of the doctrine of neutrality were sown in the historic Cincinnati school case of 1872 in which Judge Alphonso Taft held that the American ideal was one of "absolute equality before the law, of religious opinions and sects. . . . The government is neutral, and, while protecting all, it prefers none, and it disparages none."[25]

The term was not given its authority as judicial doctrine until the 1947 *Everson* case. The concept had been used from time to time in previous opinions, but in *Everson* it became the controlling principle. Typically, the term was invoked on both sides of the issue. Mr. Justice Black (1886–1971) wrote for the majority that the First Amendment "requires the state to be *neutral* in its relations with groups of religious believers and non-believers; it does not require the state to be their adversary. State power is no more to be used so as to handicap religions than it is to favor them."[26] Then, in dissent, Mr. Justice Jackson held that public schools are organized

> on the premise that secular education can be isolated from all religious teaching so that the school can inculcate all needed temporal knowledge and also maintain a strict and *lofty neutrality* as to religion. The assumption is that after the individual has been instructed in worldly wisdom he will be better fitted to choose his religion.[27]

The nub of the matter then lay in the facts as developed in the case and the justices' determination of the most neutral course for the government to take.

The doctrine reached fruition in the Bible reading and Lord's Prayer cases of 1962 and 1963. In *Engel v. Vitale,* sometimes known as "the New York Regents' Prayer Case," the Court ruled that a prayer composed by the Regents could not be used at the opening exercises in the public schools of New York. The prayer itself was innocuous enough: "Almighty God, we acknowledge our dependence upon Thee, and we beg Thy blessings upon us, our parents, our teachers and our Country."[28] But the Court held that, innocuous or not, the practice was "wholly inconsistent with the Establishment Clause" and that

> the constitutional prohibition against laws respecting an establishment of religion must at least mean that in this country it is no part of the business of gov-

[24] Michaelson, op. cit., pp. 216–217.
[25] As quoted by Mr. Justice Clark in *Abington* v. *Schempp*, 374 U.S. 203, 215 (1963).
[26] *Everson* v. *Board of Education*, op. cit., 330 U.S. at 18. Emphasis added.
[27] 330 U.S. at 23–24. Emphasis added.
[28] *Engel* v. *Vitale*, 370 U.S. 421, 422 (1962).

ernment to compose official prayers for any group of the American people to recite as a part of a religious program carried on by the government.[29]

Thus the state of New York had not remained neutral: "When the power, prestige and financial support of government is placed behind a particular religious belief, the indirect coercive pressure upon religious minorities to conform to the prevailing officially approved religion is plain."[30]

The *Engel* case provoked a stormy response from the public. Members of Congress quickly promised to pass a constitutional amendment to make prayer in the public schools permissible. When the *Schempp* and *Murray* decisions were delivered the next year, the justices couched their opinions in such a way as to avoid the kind of violent criticism they received in the Regents' Prayer Case. Mr. Justice Goldberg, in a concurring opinion, noted:

> Neither government nor this Court can or should ignore the significance of the fact that a vast portion of our people believe in and worship God and that many of our legal, political and personal values derive historically from religious teachings. Government must inevitably take cognizance of the existence of religion and, indeed, under certain circumstances the First Amendment may require that it do so.[31]

Mr. Justice Clark spoke of the "wholesome" neutrality pursued by the Court. He warned that history has shown the ways in which powerful religious groups have often sought to fuse their power with the power of government. The First Amendment clearly prohibits that. Instead, he argued, religion has been able to maintain its "exalted" place in American life precisely because the transactions of religion have been performed in

> the home, the church and the inviolable citadel of the individual heart and mind. We have come to recognize through bitter experience that it is not within the power of government to invade that citadel, whether its purpose or effect be to aid or oppose, to advance or retard. In the relationship between man and religion, the State is firmly committed to a position of neutrality.[32]

To the argument that the Court, because it proscribed prayer and Bible reading, was, in effect, establishing a "religion of secularism," Clark replied:

> We agree of course that the State may not establish a "religion of secularism" in the sense of affirmatively opposing or showing hostility to religion, thus "preferring those who believe in no religion over those who do believe" . . . We do not agree, however, that this decision in any sense has that effect. In addition, it

[29] 370 U.S. at 425.
[30] Ibid. at 431.
[31] *Abington* v. *Schempp*, op. cit., 374 U.S. at 306.
[32] Ibid. at 226.

might well be said that one's education is not complete without a study of comparative religion or the history of religion and its relationship to the advancement of civilization. It certainly may be said that the Bible is worthy of study for its literary and historic qualities. Nothing we have said here indicates that such study of the Bible or of religion, when presented objectively as part of a secular program of education, may not be effected consistently with the First Amendment. But the exercises here do not fall into those categories. They are religious exercises, required by the States in violation of the command of the First Amendment that the Government maintain strict neutrality, neither aiding nor opposing religion.[33]

It was after these particular decisions that public schools, colleges, and universities began to review their curricula to determine where studies in religion might be introduced, for as Mr. Justice Goldberg put it, "teaching *about* religion, as distinguished from teaching *of* religion" was lawful.[34]

The discussion of neutrality was further extended in the 1963 *Sherbert* decision involving a conflict between a Seventh Day Adventist and the unemployment compensation laws of South Carolina. The statutes provided compensation only for persons willing to accept regular employment under normal circumstances, and for most firms this meant some Saturday work. The Court held that South Carolina, in the interest of religious liberty, had to accommodate its unemployment laws to the religious beliefs and practices of Seventh Day Adventists and provide Mrs. Sherbert with compensation on the Saturdays she could not work because of her religious convictions. Although this opened the Court to the charge that it might be, in some sense, "establishing" the Adventist group, the Court believed itself to be acting in the interest of neutrality:

> the extension of unemployment benefits to Sabbatarians in common with Sunday worshippers reflects nothing more than the governmental obligation of neutrality in the face of religious differences, and does not represent that involvement of religious with secular institutions which it is the object of the Establishment Clause to forestall.[35]

This case illustrates, about as well as any, the suggestion made by Paul G. Kauper that the ideas contained in Supreme Court decisions should not be pressed to their absolute limit.[36] They will not stand up under that kind of rigorously logical extension. Rather, we must see the Court's work in a less fundamentalistic way. Court decisions are rendered only after the facts of a specific case have been developed and presented. Arguments are made pro and con. The Court *then* strives, in its collective wisdom, to develop a workable solution that does the least violence to the ideas and ideals contained in the Constitution. Its ap-

[33] Ibid. at 225.
[34] Ibid. at 306.
[35] *Sherbert* v. *Verner*, 374 U.S. 398, 409 (1963).
[36] Kauper, op. cit., p. 75.

proach is, of necessity, pragmatic more than conceptual; it has little interest in building a body of legal theory, but merely wishes to discover the best way for justice to be nurtured. Therefore, the wall metaphor was dropped when it was no longer useful as legal doctrine and the concept of neutrality emerged as a much more flexible and resilient device. The Court is constantly searching for new and better ways of dealing with the problems brought before it.

Recently, still another term has been used to elucidate the very complex and sticky problem of church-state relations.

ENTANGLEMENT

In 1970 Chief Justice Warren Burger delivered his first major opinion regarding church-state relations in *Walz v. Tax Commission* and stated, "No perfect or absolute separation is really possible; the very existence of the Religion Clauses is an involvement of sorts—one that seeks to make boundaries to avoid *excessive entanglement.*"[37] How useful this concept will be remains to be seen, but it became the central principle around which this important case was decided.

Frederick Walz had attacked tax exemptions for all church-owned buildings in New York City on the ground that exemptions, in effect, constituted an indirect establishment of religion. But the Chief Justice held:

> The grant of a tax exemption is not sponsorship since the government does not transfer part of its revenue to churches but simply abstains from demanding that the church support the state. No one has ever suggested that tax exemption has converted libraries, art galleries, or hospitals into arms of the state or put employees "on the public payroll." There is no genuine nexus between tax exemption and establishment of religion.[38]

But then Burger stated:

> Determining that the legislative purpose of tax exemption is not aimed at establishing, sponsoring, or supporting religion does not end the inquiry, however. We must also be sure that the end result—the effect—is not an excessive government entanglement with religion. The test is inescapably one of degree. Either course, taxation of churches or exemption, occasions some degree of involvement with religion. Elimination of exemption would tend to expand the involvement of government by giving rise to tax valuation of church property, tax liens, tax foreclosures, and the direct confrontations and conflicts that follow in the train of these legal processes.[39]

Involvement or entanglement of that sort is the very thing Burger wanted the government to avoid, if at all possible. Although "separa-

---

[37] *Walz* v. *Tax Commission*, 397 U.S. 664, 670 (1970).
[38] 397 U.S. at 675.
[39] Ibid.

tion . . . cannot mean absence of all contact," the government must seek minimal contact with religion. Mere neutrality is not enough.

Mr. Justice Douglas, in his lone dissent to the decision, maintained that tax exemption was nothing more or less than subsidization of the churches and quoted a Brookings Institution report in his favor: "Tax exemption, no matter what its form, is essentially a government grant or subsidy. Such grants would seem to be justified only if the purpose for which they are made is one for which the legislative body *would be equally willing to make* a direct appropriation from public funds equal to the amount of the exemption."[40]

It is quite to the contrary, replied Mr. Justice Brennan; tax exemptions and subsidies are "qualitatively different" because exemptions keep at a minimum the contact between the two spheres, whereas subsidies mean constant confrontation between them. Mr. Justice Harlan agreed and elaborated:

> Subsidies, unlike exemptions, must be passed on periodically and thus invite more political controversy than exemptions. Moreover, subsidies or direct aid, as a general rule, are granted on the basis of enumerated and more complicated qualifications and frequently involve the state in administration to a higher degree, though to be sure, this is not necessarily the case.[41]

Most of the justices therefore disagreed with Douglas. Tax exemption, though it bears similarities to subsidization, is "qualitatively different" because it keeps *entanglement* down to a minimum.

The argument about subsidies as compared to exemptions is particularly interesting, because during the very next term (1971), the Court had to deal with federal grants to church-related colleges and universities, and once again the doctrine of entanglement was brought to bear. The case in question was *Tilton v. Richardson*. It tested the Higher Education Act of 1963, which provided construction grants for colleges and universities, excluding "any facility used or to be used for sectarian instruction or as a place for religious worship, or . . . primarily in connection with any part of a program of a school or department of divinity."[42] Burger again wrote the majority opinion for a badly divided (5-4) Court. He first pointed out: "The simplistic argument that every form of financial aid to church sponsored activity violates the Religion Clauses was rejected long ago" in a case involving federal construction grants to hospitals, including those owned and operated by religious groups.[43] The Court held that the grants were intended to advance a goal that was primarily secular: the provision of additional hospital beds for the general populace. See *Bradfield* v. *Roberts*, 175 U.S. 291

---

[40] Ibid. at 709.
[41] Ibid. at 699.
[42] *Tilton* v. *Richardson*, 403 U.S. 672 (1971).
[43] 403 U.S. at 679.

(1899). Accordingly, the crucial question was not "whether some benefit accrues to a religious institution" as a consequence of the government
grant, but "whether its principal or primary effect advances religion."[44]
He then argued that the federal act is not unconstitutional because the
entanglement is not excessive. To be sure there is entanglement, but it
is not yet in dangerous proportions. But, asked the dissenters, does this
not contradict the previous year's *Walz* decision, which granted tax
exemption to churches precisely because exemption is "qualitatively
different" from a grant? On the one hand, in *Walz,* the Court seemed to
be eschewing grants because they increased the entanglement between
church and state. On the other hand, with the *Tilton* decision, grants became permissible.

Burger replied that a distinction would have to be made between secondary and higher education, that "college students are less impression-
able and less susceptible to religious indoctrination" than elementary
school children and are better equipped to respond critically to the
ideas they have to face in the classroom. Moreover, he said, the nature
of the subject matter or disciplines taught in colleges and universities
tends "to limit the opportunities for sectarian influence." The government can thereby afford to risk a greater degree of "entanglement"
with colleges and universities than with secondary schools.[45]

Burger then offered a final reason for permitting the grants: the
type of financial support offered under the federal program—"one-
shot" building grants as contrasted with a continuing subsidy for an on-
going program of some kind—means that there are no permanent "financial relationships or dependencies, no annual audits, and no government analysis of an institution's expenditures on secular as distinguished from religious activities. Inspection as to use is a minimal
contact."[46]

Mr. Justice Douglas was not convinced: "Money saved from one
item in a budget is free to be used elsewhere. By conducting religious
services in another building the school has—rent free—a building for
nonsectarian use." And because the government must be sure that a
building is not being used for sectarian puposes, "how can the Government know what is taught in the federally financed building without a
continuous auditing of classroom instruction?" The problem of surveillance would create "an entanglement of government and religion which
the First Amendment was designed to avoid."[47]

On the same day that the *Tilton* decision was handed down, the
Court rendered a second church-state decision—*Lemon* v. *Kurtzman.*
This time it was unanimous in striking down Rhode Island and Pennsylvania statutes that appropriated state funds for paying secondary parochial school teachers. Those laws created exactly the kind of continuing

[44] Ibid.
[45] Ibid. at 686.
[46] Ibid. at 688.
[47] Ibid. at 694–695.

involvement between religion and government that the Court considered intolerable. Once again, the chief justice spoke for the others as they tried to find a way of mediating the conflict between church and state:

> The objective is to prevent, as far as possible, the intrusion of either into the precincts of the other.
> Our prior holdings do not call for a total separation between church and state; total separation is not possible in an absolute sense. Some relationship between government and religious organizations is inevitable. . . . Fire inspections, building and zoning regulations, and state requirements under compulsory school-attendance laws are examples of necessary and permissible contacts.[48]

But he then contended that "the substantial religious character of the church-related schools gives rise to entangling church-state relationships of the kind the Religion Clauses sought to avoid." First of all, they were located near or next to parish churches. Religious symbols and religious activities abounded at the schools. Two-thirds of the teachers were nuns. Because the trial court had shown "that the parochial schools constituted 'an integral part of the religious mission of the Catholic Church'," the inescapable judgment was that excessive entanglement could only result from faculty salary subsidies.[49]

Of course, the Court had said in the *Allen* decision of 1968 that a state could provide textbooks on secular subjects for parochial schools, but Burger argued that teachers, as such, "have a substantially different ideological character than books. In terms of potential for involving some aspect of faith or morals in secular subjects, a textbook's content is ascertainable, but a teacher's handling of a subject is not."[50] Even if the parochial school teacher would, in good faith, intend to remain indifferent in controversial areas, "we simply recognize that a dedicated religious person . . . , will inevitably experience great difficulty in remaining religiously neutral." Under the Rhode Island and Pennsylvania plans, such teachers would have to be constantly scrutinized by the government in order to make sure that the constitutional limits had not been violated. Such scrutiny would create an intolerable degree of church-state involvement.[51]

Finally, salary subsidies are fundamentally different from building grants, because they possess "self-perpetuating and self-expanding propensities." Of necessity, they would have to be reviewed continually and "[t]he history of government grants of a continuing cash subsidy indicates that such programs have almost always been accompanied by varying measures of control and surveillance," thus creating an excessive entanglement between religion and government.[52]

[48] *Lemon* v. *Kurtzman*, op cit., 403 U.S. at 614.
[49] Ibid. at 615–620.
[50] Ibid. at 617.
[51] Ibid. at 618.
[52] Ibid. at 621.

The reader by now must have some feeling for the complex nature of the Court's task in the area of church-state relations. The need for guidelines and principles is clear. Up to this point, "the wall of separation," "neutrality," and "entanglement" have all served their time and have served well. But it is also manifest that litigation in this highly sensitive area will continue and that other methods will have to be developed in order to sort out the controversies as they reach the Supreme Court.

THE THREE-PART TEST

Sensing a need for further tools with which to attack the religious freedom question, the Court constructed a three-part test that it now applies to the facts in cases brought before it on the Religion Clauses.

> First, the statute must have a secular legislative purpose; second, its principal or primary effect must be one that neither advances nor inhibits religion, . . . finally, the statute must not foster "an excessive government entanglement with religion."[53]

Although this test may not fit every factual situation that will make its way to the Supreme Court, some members of the Court have found it a useful device in dealing with major cases involving the Religion Clauses. Mr. Justice Blackmun found it so in writing his opinion in *Roemer* v. *Board of Public Works of Maryland*[54] In that case, the Court upheld a Maryland statute that provides state aid to any private accredited institution of higher education which does not award "only seminarian or theological degrees." The aid is to be in the form of an annual subsidy to the colleges based upon the number of students and excluding those who are pursuing a theological degree or who are preparing themselves for religious vocation. The grants are "noncategorical" but cannot be used by the institution for sectarian purposes. At the end of each fiscal year, the colleges are required to report their use of the funds and to identify the nonsectarian activities directly aided by the state funds.

A group of private citizens in Maryland brought suit against the state on the grounds that the state program violated the Establishment Clause of the First Amendment because four of the colleges—those owned and operated by the Roman Catholic Church—were constitutionally ineligible to receive the kind of state support given to them. The trial court applied *the three-part test* and found that the statute did, however, pass constitutional muster. But the decision was badly split, 5–4, and amply

---

[53]*Lemon* v. *Kurtzman*, 403 U.S. 602, 612-613.
[54]*Roemer* v. *Board of Public Works of Maryland*, 426 U.S. 736 (1976).

demonstrates the difficulty the Court frequently faces in reaching a decision on the Religion Clauses.[55]

In applying the three-pronged test to the facts in the *Roemer* case, the Court found that the first prong was not really at issue. Everyone could agree from the outset that "the purpose of Maryland's aid program is the secular one of supporting private higher education generally, as an economic alternative to a wholly public system."[56] The focus of the debate in the case was therefore shifted to the other two prongs: did the statute have the *effect* of advancing religion and did it cause an "excessive entanglement" between church and state?

In an earlier case, the Court held that *no* state aid may go to institutions that are so "pervasively sectarian" that secular activities on the campus cannot be separated from sectarian ones. Furthermore, if secular activities *can*, indeed, be separated out, they alone can be funded.[57] Using the same logic in the *Roemer* case, the Court found that the four colleges in question were *not* pervasively sectarian. It is instructive to see how the Court examined each facet of the case:

- Despite the fact that the colleges formally are affiliated with the Roman Catholic Church, they could be "characterized by a high degree of institutional autonomy."
- Although they have Catholic chaplains, chapel attendance is not required.
- Religion courses are taught on campus, but primarily as an integral part of a comprehensive liberal arts curriculum that includes courses in non-Western religions.
- "Nontheology" courses are taught in an atmosphere of academic freedom and without sectarian influence.
- Although some instructors begin classes with prayer, there is no policy requiring it.

The Supreme Court agreed with the trial court that these colleges were not " pervasively sectarian."[58]

The Court then addressed the second prong of the three-pronged test: whether the aid extended the colleges had the primary effect of advancing or inhibiting religion. The facts in *Roemer*, according to the Court, showed that the Maryland statute expressly prohibits the use of funds for "sectarian purposes," and it must therefore be assumed that the colleges and the Maryland Council for Higher Education (the governmental agency charged with administering the act) "will exercise their delegated

---

[55] Mr. Justice Blackmun wrote a "plurality" decision for the Court which means that, although five justices found the Maryland statute to be constitutional, only two justices signed the Blackmun opinion while two others joined in a concurring opinion—a majority of five.

[56] 426 U.S. at 754.

[57] *Hunt* v. *McNair*, 413 U.S. 734, 743 (1973).

[58] 426 U.S. at 758–759.

control over the use of funds in compliance with the statutory, and therefore the constitutional, mandate. It is to be expected that they will give a wide berth to 'specifically religious activity,' and thus minimize constitutional questions."[59]

Finally, the third prong of the test was also satisfied: that no "excessive entanglement" of church and state is caused by the Maryland program. The colleges, as the Court found, perform "essentially secular educational functions." Even the fact that the subsidy is an annual one does not necessarily indicate that there is "excessive entanglement," because the contacts between the colleges and the Council for Higher Education "are not likely to be any more entangling than the inspections and audits incident to the normal process of the colleges' accreditations by the State."[60] Furthermore, the state can identify and subsidize separate secular functions at the colleges without having to have on-site inspections "to prevent diversion of the funds to sectarian purposes."[61]

Furthermore, the Court held that the statute did not contribute to political divisiveness, a sure sign of "excessive entanglement." That is because the aided institutions are colleges and not elementary or secondary schools. Moreover, the aid program was designed to help private colleges and universities generally, more than two-thirds of which have no religious affiliation whatsoever. The Court then concluded that "the substantial autonomy" of the Catholic colleges would help to mitigate political divisiveness, because "controversies surrounding the aid program are not likely to involve the Catholic Church itself, or even the religious character of the schools, but only their 'fiscal responsibility and educational requirements.' "[62]

Predictably the dissenters in *Roemer* said that the facts in the cases persuaded them that the Maryland program sounded too much like establishment for them. They found it impermissible to make "general subsidies" to the four colleges because they tend to promote a type of interdependence between church and state that the First Amendment sought to avoid.

In his dissent, Mr. Justice Brennan told his colleagues that he had not changed his mind from a dissent in an earlier case:

> I believe that the Establishment Clause forbids . . . Government to provide funds to sectarian universities in which the propagation and advancement of a particular religion are a function or purpose of the institution. . . .
> I reach this conclusion for [these] reasons. . . : the necessarily deep involvement of government in the religious activities of such an institution through the policing of restrictions, and the fact that subsidies of tax monies directly to a sectarian institution necessarily aids the proselytizing function of the institution.

[59] Ibid. at 760.
[60] Ibid. at 764.
[61] Ibid. at 765.
[62] Ibid. at 765–766.

... I do not believe that [direct] grants to such a sectarian institution are permissible. The reason is not that religion "permeates" the secular education that is provided. Rather, it is that the secular education is provided within the environment of religion; the institution is dedicated to two goals, secular education *and* religious instruction. When aid flows directly to the institution, both functions benefit.[63]

The *Roemer* decision therefore demonstrates how the Court used the three-pronged test to determine the constitutionality of a statute affecting the Religion Clauses. Although this test may eventually be discarded in favor of some other device, it is a fairly straightforward way of looking at the facts in a given case:

- The statute must have a secular purpose.
- Its primary effect must be neither to advance nor to inhibit religion.
- It must not foster excessive entanglement between church and state.

The Religion Clauses and the Religious Test

In order for a case on a religious liberty question to be heard by the United States Supreme Court, complainants must base their claims either on the so-called Religion Clauses of the First Amendment or on Article VI of the Constitution. The First Amendment reads in part: "Congress shall make no law respecting an *establishment* of religion or prohibiting the *free exercise* thereof."[64] In the body of the Constitution, Article VI says, among other things, that "no religious Test shall ever be required as a Qualification to any Office of Public Trust under the United States."[65] At one of these points, the issue of religious liberty is always joined.

It is now our purpose to look briefly at excerpts from several representative opinions that show how the judiciary has dealt with the problems of religious liberty, what they have said that "establishment" and "free exercise" mean and how "religious tests" are proscribed.

ESTABLISHMENT

As we have already noted, the single most significant factor in the history of American ecclesial institutions has been the constitutional prohibition of an established church. But this was by no means the original intention in most colonies. In Massachusetts, Virginia, New York, and Delaware, the colonists came to this country with the idea of establishing some form of religion in their respective places. But by the time the

---

[63] Ibid. at 771–772. Emphasis in original. See also *Lemon* v. *Kurtzman*, 403 U.S. 602, 642.
[64] Emphasis added.
[65] Emphasis added.

nation came into being in 1789, most Americans saw the desirability of forbidding any sort of establishment. It was, in fact, so desirable that they wrote the prohibition into their governmental structure with the first clause of the First Amendment of the Constitution.

A number of establishment cases were decided prior to 1947, but the *Everson* case of that year has endured as one of the most influential cases on establishment in the Court's history. *Everson* was the school bus case in which the Court held that the New Jersey statute providing state support for bus transportation to parochial schools was constitutional. Justice Hugo Black delivered the majority opinion.

Document 14 ─────────────────────────────────

From *Everson* v. *Board of Education*
Mr. Justice Black for the Court

The New Jersey statute is challanged as a "law respecting an establishment of religion." . . . These words of the First amendment reflected in the minds of early Americans a vivid mental picture of conditions and practices which they fervently wished to stamp out in order to preserve liberty for themselves and for their posterity. Doubtless their goal has not been entirely reached; but so far has the Nation moved toward it that the expression "law respecting an establishment of religion," probably does not so vividly remind present-day Americans of the evils, fears, and political problems that caused that expression to be written into our Bill of Rights. Whether this New Jersey law is one respecting the "establishment of religion" requires an understanding of the meaning of that language, particularly with respect to the imposition of taxes. Once again, therefore, it is not inappropriate briefly to review the background and environment of the period in which that constitutional language was fashioned and adopted.

A large proportion of the early settlers of this country came here from Europe to escape the bondage of laws which compelled them to support and attend government favored churches. The centuries immediately before and contemporaneous with the colonization of America had been filled with turmoil, civil strife, and persecutions, generated in large part by established sects determined to maintain their absolute political and religious supremacy. With the power of government supporting them, at various times and places, Catholics had persecuted Protestants, Protestants had persecuted Catholics, Protestant sects had persecuted other Protestant sects, Catholics of one shade of belief had persecuted Catholics of another shade of belief, and all of these had from time to time persecuted Jews. In efforts to force loyalty to whatever religious group happened to be on top and in league with the government of a particular time and place, men and women had been fined, cast in jail, cruelly tortured and killed. Among the offenses for which these punishments had been inflicted were such things as speaking disrespectfully of the views of ministers of government-established churches, non-attendance at those churches, ex-

SOURCE: *Everson* v. *Board of Education*, 330 U.S. 1, 8–18 (1947).

pressions of non-belief in their doctrines, and failure to pay taxes and tithes to support them.

These practices of the old world were transplanted to and began to thrive in the soil of new America. The very charters granted by the English Crown to the individuals and companies designated to make the laws which would control the destinies of the colonials authorized these individuals and companies to erect religious establishments which all, whether believers or non-believers, would be required to support and attend. An exercise of this authority was accompanied by a repetition of many of the old world practices and persecutions. Catholics found themselves hounded and proscribed because of their faith; Quakers who followed their conscience went to jail; Baptists were peculiarly obnoxious to certain dominant Protestant sects; men and women of varied faiths who happened to be in a minority in a particular locality were persecuted because they steadfastly persisted in worshipping God only as their own consciences dictated. And all of these dissenters were compelled to pay tithes and taxes to support government-sponsored churches whose ministers preached inflammatory sermons designed to strengthen and consolidate the established faith by generating a burning hatred against dissenters.

These practices became so commonplace as to shock the freedom-loving colonials into a feeling of abhorrence. . . . It was these feelings which found expression in the First Amendment. No one locality and no one group throughout the Colonies can rightly be given credit for having aroused the sentiment that culminated in adoption of the Bill of Rights' provisions embracing religious liberty. But Virginia, where the established church had achieved a dominant influence in political affairs and where many excesses attracted wide public attention, provided a great stimulus and able leadership for the movement. The people there, as elsewhere, reached the conviction that individual religious liberty could be achieved best under a government which was stripped of all power to tax, to support, or otherwise to assist any or all religions, or to interfere with the beliefs of any religious individual or group.

The movement toward this end reached its dramatic climax in Virginia in 1785–86 when the Virginia legislative body was about to renew Virginia's tax levy for the support of the established church. Thomas Jefferson and James Madison led the fight against this tax. Madison wrote his great Memorial and Remonstrance against the law. In it, he eloquently argued that a true religion did not need the support of law; that no person, either believer or non-believer, should be taxed to support a religious institution of any kind; that the best interest of a society required that the minds of men always be wholly free; and that cruel persecutions were the inevitable result of government-established religions. Madison's Remonstrance received strong support throughout Virginia, and the Assembly postponed consideration of the proposed tax measure until its next session. When the proposal came up for consideration at that session, it not only died in committee, but the Assembly enacted the famous "Virginia Bill for Religious Liberty" originally written by Thomas Jefferson.

This Court has previously recognized that the provisions of the First Amendment, in the drafting and adoption of which Madison and Jefferson played such leading roles, had the same objective and were intended to provide the same protection against governmental intrusion on religious liberty as the Virginia statute.

The "establishment of religion" clause of the First Amendment means at least this: Neither a state nor the Federal Government can set up a church. Neither can pass laws which aid one religion, aid all religions, or prefer one religion over another. Neither can force nor influence a person to go to or to remain away from church against his will or force him to profess a belief or disbelief in any religion. No person can be punished for entertaining or professing religious beliefs or disbeliefs, for church attendance or non-attendance. No tax in any amount, large or small, can be levied to support any religious activities or institutions, whatever they may be called, or whatever form they may adopt to teach or practice religion. Neither a state nor the Federal Government can, openly or secretly, participate in the affairs of any religious organizations or groups and vice versa. In the words of Jefferson, the clause against establishment of religion by law was intended to erect "a wall of separation between Church and State." . . .

We must consider the New Jersey statute in accordance with the foregoing limitations imposed by the First Amendment. But we must not strike that state statute down if it is within the state's constitutional power even though it approaches the verge of that power. . . . New Jersey cannot consistently with the "establishment of religion" clause of the First Amendment contribute tax-raised funds to the support of an institution which teaches the tenets and faith of any church. On the other hand, other language of the amendment commands that New Jersey cannot hamper its citizens in the free exercise of their own religion. Consequently, it cannot exclude individual Catholics, Lutherans, Mohammedans, Baptists, Jews, Methodists, Non-believers, Presbyterians, or the members of any other faith, *because of their faith, or lack of it*, from receiving the benefits of public welfare legislation. While we do not mean to intimate that a state could not provide transportation only to children attending public schools, we must be careful, in protecting the citizens of New Jersey against established churches, to be sure that we do not inadvertently prohibit New Jersey from extending its general State law benefits to all its citizens without regard to their religious belief.

Measured by these standards, we cannot say that the First Amendment prohibits New Jersey from spending tax-raised funds to pay the bus fares of parochial school pupils as a part of a general program under which it pays the fares of pupils attending public and other schools. It is undoubtedly true that children are helped to get to church schools. There is even a possibility that some of the children might not be sent to the church schools if the parents were compelled to pay their children's bus fares out of their own pockets when transportation to a public school would have been paid for by the State. The same possibility exists where the state requires a local transit company to provide reduced fares to school children including those attending parochial schools, or where a municipally owned transportation system undertakes to carry all school children free of charge. . . . Similarly, parents might be reluctant to permit their children to attend schools which the state had cut off from such general government services as ordinary police and fire protection, connections for sewage disposal, public highways and sidewalks. Of course, cutting off church schools from these services, so separate and so indisputably marked from the religious function, would make it far more difficult for the schools to operate. But such is obviously not the purpose of the First Amendment. That Amendment requires the state to be a neutral in its relations with groups of religious believers and non-believers; it does not require the state to be their adversary. State power is no more to be used so as to handicap religions, than it is to favor them.

FREE EXERCISE

No right is more clearly etched in the American political conscience than the free exercise of religion. There have, of course, been moments in the course of our history when this freedom has been subjected to severe strain. In the *Reynolds* case, as we have already seen, the federal government moved against the Mormons because of their practice of polygamy.[66] In that instance, the Court made a rigid distinction between belief and practice and decided that Reynold's beliefs were protected but that the practice growing out of those beliefs—polygamy—was "subversive of good order."[67]

Although the Court has continued to rely on the distinction between belief and action in "free exercise" cases, it has found that the line between the two cannot always be so clearly or rigidly drawn as in the *Reynolds* case. Usually, when a free exercise issue makes its way into court, an individual or group is complaining that some law, rule, or ordinance is creating a hardship on them and violates their religious scruples. Thus, the Court has been required to balance the secular demand of the law against the religious liberty asserted by the individual.

The case of *Wisconsin* v. *Yoder* is a classic illustration of how the Court deals with such an issue. The state of Wisconsin requires all children to attend school until they reach age sixteen, but members of the Amish Church—of which Yoder was a member—consider such a requirement to be inconsistent with their beliefs. When he and others refused to send their children on to high school, they were fined $5 each, and the issue was joined. Was the state's interest in requiring students to attend high school strong enough to override the assertion by Yoder and the others that such a requirement violated their free exercise of religion? Interestingly enough, the Amish had no quarrel with requiring school attendance through age 14; they only contested the requirement that their children attend the ninth and tenth grades. Once children have entered adolescence, the Amish wish to keep them secluded from the distractions of secular society so that their habits and customs can be formed in the bosom of the Amish community. As the Court noted, the Amish "believed that by sending their children to high school, they would not only expose themselves to the danger of the censure of the church community, but [would] also endanger their own salvation and that of their children."[68]

---

[66]*Reynolds* v. *United States*, 98 U.S. 145 (1878).
[67]Ibid.
[68]*Wisconsin* v. *Yoder*, 406 U.S. 205, 209 (1972).

A number of free exercise cases have reached the Supreme Court, but none more compelling than the *Yoder* case. It attracted nationwide attention at the time and was hailed as a landmark decision in favor of religious liberty.

Document 15

From *Wisconsin* v. *Yoder*
Chief Justice Burger for the Court

... In support of their position, respondents [Yoder, Miller, and Yutzy] presented as expert witnesses scholars on religion and education whose testimony is uncontradicted. They expressed their opinions on the relationship of the Amish belief concerning school attendance to the more general tenets of their religion, and described the impact that compulsory high school attendance could have on the continued survival of Amish communities as they exist in the United States today. The history of the Amish sect was given in some detail, beginning with the Swiss Anabaptists of the 16th century who rejected institutionalized churches and sought to return to the early, simple, Christian life de-emphasizing material success, rejecting the competitive spirit, and seeking to insulate themselves from the modern world. As a result of their common heritage, Old Order Amish communities today are characterized by a fundamental belief that salvation requires life in a church community separate and apart from the world and worldly influence. This concept of life aloof from the world and its values is central to their faith.

A related feature of Old Order Amish communities is their devotion to a life in harmony with nature and the soil, as exemplified by the simple life of the early Christian era that continued in America during much of our early national life. Amish beliefs require members of the community to make their living by farming or closely related activities. Broadly speaking, the Old Order Amish religion pervades and determines the entire mode of life of its adherents. Their conduct is regulated in great detail by the *Ordnung*, or rules, of the church community. Adult baptism, which occurs in late adolescence, is the time at which Amish young people voluntarily undertake heavy obligations, not unlike the Bar Mitzvah of the Jews, to abide by the rules of the church community.

Amish objection to formal education beyond the eighth grade is firmly grounded in these central religious concepts. They object to the high school, and higher education generally, because the values they teach are in marked variance with Amish values and the Amish way of life; they view secondary school education as an impermissible exposure of their children to a "worldly" influence in conflict with their beliefs. The high school tends to emphasize intellectual and scientific accomplishments, self-distinction, competitiveness, worldly success, and social life with other students. Amish society emphasizes informal learning-through-doing; a life of "goodness," rather than a life of intellect; wisdom, rather than technical knowledge, community welfare, rather than competition; and separation from, rather than integration with, contemporary worldly society.

SOURCE: *Wisconsin* v. *Yoder*, 406 U.S. 205, 209–230; 235–236 (1972).

Formal high school education beyond the eighth grade is contrary to Amish beliefs, not only because it places Amish children in an environment hostile to Amish beliefs with increasing emphasis on competition in class work and sports and with pressure to conform to the styles, manners, and ways of the peer group, but also because it takes them away from their community, physically and emotionally, during the crucial and formative adolescent period of life. During this period, the children must acquire Amish attitudes favoring manual work and self-reliance and the specific skills needed to perform the adult role of an Amish farmer or housewife. They must learn to enjoy physical labor. Once a child has learned basic reading, writing, and elementary mathematics, these traits, skills, and attitudes admittedly fall within the category of those best learned through example and "doing" rather than in a classroom. And, at this time in life, the Amish child must also grow in his faith and his relationship to the Amish community if he is to be prepared to accept the heavy obligations imposed by adult baptism. In short, high school attendance with teachers who are not of the Amish faith—and may even be hostile to it—interposes a serious barrier to the integration of the Amish child into the Amish religious community. Dr. John Hostetler, one of the experts on Amish society, testified that the modern high school is not equipped, in curriculum or social environment, to impart the values promoted by Amish society.

The Amish do not object to elementary education through the first eight grades as a general proposition because they agree that their children must have basic skills in the "three R's" in order to read the Bible, to be good farmers and citizens, and to be able to deal with non-Amish people when necessary in the course of daily affairs. They view such a basic education as acceptable because it does not significantly expose their children to worldly values or interfere with their development in the Amish community during the crucial adolescent period. While Amish accept compulsory elementary education generally, wherever possible they have established their own elementary schools in many respects like the small local schools of the past. In the Amish belief higher learning tends to develop values they reject as influences that alienate man from God.

On the basis of such considerations, Dr. Hostetler testified that compulsory high school attendance could not only result in great psychological harm to Amish children, because of the conflicts it would produce, but would also, in his opinion, ultimately result in the destruction of the Old Order Amish church community as it exists in the United States today. The testimony of Dr. Donald A. Erickson, an expert witness on education, also showed that the Amish succeed in preparing their high school age children to be productive members of the Amish community. He described their system of learning through doing the skills directly relevant to their adult roles in the Amish community as "ideal" and perhaps superior to ordinary high school education. The evidence also showed that the Amish have an excellent record as law-abiding and generally self-sufficient members of society. . . .

I

. . . There is no doubt as to the power of a State, having a high responsibility for education of its citizens, to impose reasonable regulations for the control and duration of basic education. Providing public schools ranks at the very apex of the func-

tion of a State. Yet even this paramount responsibility was, in *Pierce* [v. *Society of Sisters*, 268 U.S. 510 (1925)] , made to yield to the right of parents to provide an an equivalent education in a privately operated system. There the Court held that Oregon's statute compelling attendance in a public school from age eight to age 16 unreasonably interfered with the interest of parents in directing the rearing of their offspring, including their education in church-operated schools. As that case suggests, the values of parental direction of the religious upbringing and education of their children in their early and formative years have a high place in our society.
. . . Thus a State's interest in universal education, however highly we rank it, is not totally free from a balancing process when it impinges on fundamental rights and interests, such as those specifically protected by the Free Exercise Clause of the First Amendment, and the traditional interest of parents with respect to the religious upbringing of their children so long as they, in the words of *Pierce*, "prepare [them] for additional obligations.". . .

It follows that in order for Wisconsin to compel school attendance beyond the eighth grade against a claim that such attendance interferes with the practice of a legitimate religious belief, it must appear either that the State does not deny the free exercise of religious belief by its requirement, or that there is a state interest of sufficient magnitude to override the interest claiming protection under the Free Exercise Clause. Long before there was general acknowledgment of the need for universal formal education, the Religion Clauses had specifically and firmly fixed the right to free exercise of religious beliefs, and buttressing this fundamental right was an equally firm, even if less explicit, prohibition against the establishment of any religion by government. The values underlying these two provisions relating to religion have been zealously protected, sometimes even at the expense of other interests of admittedly high social importance. . . .

The essence of all that has been said and written on the subject is that only those interests of the highest order and those not otherwise served can overbalance legitimate claims to the free exercise of religion. We can accept it as settled, therefore, that, however strong the State's interest in universal compulsory education, it is by no means absolute to the exclusion or subordination of all other interests. . . .

II

We come then to the quality of the claims of the respondents concerning the alleged encroachment of Wisconsin's compulsory school-attendance statute on their rights and the rights of their children to the free exercise of the religious beliefs they and their forbears have adhered to for almost three centuries. In evaluating those claims we must be careful to determine whether the Amish religious faith and their mode of life are, as they claim, inseparable and interdependent. A way of life, however virtuous and admirable, may not be interposed as a barrier to reasonable state regulation of education if it is based on purely secular considerations; to have the protection of the Religion Clauses, the claims must be rooted in religious belief. Although a determination of what is a "religious" belief or practice entitled to constitutional protection may present a most delicate question, the very concept of ordered liberty precludes allowing every person to make his own standards on matters of conduct in which society as a whole has important interests. Thus, if the Amish asserted their claims because of their subjective evaluation and rejection of the contemporary secular values accepted by the majority, much as Thoreau rejected the social values of his time and isolated himself at Walden Pond, their claims would not rest on a religious basis. Thoreau's choice was philosophical and personal rather than religious, and such belief does not rise to the demands of the Religion Clauses.

Giving no weight to such secular considerations, however, we see that the record in this case abundantly supports the claim that the traditional way of life of the Amish is not merely a matter of personal preference, but one of deep religious conviction, shared by an organized group, and intimately related to daily living. That the Old Order Amish daily life and religious practice stem from their faith is shown by the fact that it is in response to their literal interpretation of the Biblical injunction from the Epistle of Paul to the Romans, "be not conformed to this world . . . ." This command is fundamental to the Amish faith. Moreover, for the Old Order Amish, religion is not simply a matter of theocratic belief. As the expert witnesses explained, the Old Order Amish religion pervades and determines virtually their entire way of life, regulating it with the detail of the Talmudic diet through the strictly enforced rules of the church community.

The record shows that the respondents' religious beliefs and attitude toward life, family, and home have remained constant—perhaps some would say static—in a period of unparalleled progress in human knowledge generally and great changes in education. The respondents freely concede, and indeed assert as an article of faith, that their religious beliefs and what we would today call "life style" have not altered in fundamentals for centuries. Their way of life in a church-oriented community, separated from the outside world and "worldly" influences, their attachment to nature and the soil, is a way inherently simple and uncomplicated, albeit difficult to preserve against the pressure to conform. Their rejection of telephones, automobiles, radios, and television, their mode of dress, of speech, their habits of manual work do indeed set them apart from much of contemporary society; these customs are both symbolic and practical.

As the society around the Amish has become more populous, urban, industrialized, and complex, particularly in this century, government regulation of human affairs has correspondingly become more detailed and pervasive. The Amish mode of life has thus come into conflict increasingly with requirements of contemporary society exerting a hydraulic insistence on conformity to majoritarian standards. So long as compulsory education laws were confined to eight grades of elementary basic education imparted in a nearby rural schoolhouse, with a large proportion of students of the Amish faith, the Old Order Amish had little basis to fear that school attendance would expose their children to the worldly influence they reject. But modern compulsory secondary education in rural areas is now largely carried on in a consolidated school often remote from the student's home and alien to his daily home life. As the record so strongly shows, the values and programs of the modern secondary school are in sharp conflict with the fundamental mode of life mandated by the Amish religion: modern laws requiring compulsory secondary education have accordingly engendered great concern and conflict. The conclusion is inescapable that secondary schooling, by exposing Amish children to worldly influences

in terms of attitudes, goals, and values contrary to beliefs, and by substantially interfering with the religious development of the Amish child and his integration into
the way of life of the Amish faith community at the crucial adolescent stage of development, contravenes the basic religious tenets and practice of the Amish faith,
both as to the parent and the child.

The impact of the compulsory-attendance law on respondents' practice of the
Amish religion is not only severe, but inescapable, for the Wisconsin law affirmatively compels them, under threat of criminal sanction, to perform acts undeniably
at odds with fundamental tenets of their religious beliefs. . . . Nor is the impact of
the compulsory attendance law confined to grave interference with important
Amish religious tenets from a subjective point of view. It carries with it precisely
the kind of objective danger to the free exercise of religion that the First Amendment was designed to prevent. As the record shows, compulsory school attendance
to age 16 for Amish children carries with it a very real threat of undermining the
Amish community and religious practice as they exist today; they must either
abandon belief and be assimilated into society at large, or be forced to migrate
to some other and more tolerant region.

In sum, the unchallenged testimony of acknowledged experts in education and
religious history, almost 300 years of consistent practice, and strong evidence of a
sustained faith pervading and regulating respondents' entire mode of life support
the claim that enforcement of the State's requirement of compulsory formal education after the eighth grade would gravely endanger if not destroy the free exercise
of respondents' religious beliefs.

III

. . . Wisconsin concedes that under the Religion Clauses religious beliefs are absolutely free from the State's control, but it argues that "actions," even though
religiously grounded, are outside the protection of the First Amendment. But our
decisions have rejected the idea that religiously grounded conduct is always outside
the protection of the Free Exercise Clause. It is true that activities of individuals,
even when religiously based, are often subject to regulation by the States in the
exercise of their undoubted power to promote the health, safety, and general welfare, or the Federal Government in the exercise of its delegated powers. . . .But to
agree that religiously grounded conduct must often be subject to the broad police
power of the State is not to deny that there are areas of conduct protected by the
Free Exercise Clause of the First Amendment and thus beyond the power of the
State to control, even under regulations of general applicability. . . . This case,
therefore, does not become easier because respondents were convicted for their
"actions" in refusing to send their children to the public high school; in this context belief and action cannot be neatly confined in logic-tight compartments. . . .

Nor can this case be disposed of on the grounds that Wisconsin's requirement for
school attendance to age 16 applies uniformly to all citizens of the State and does
not, on its face, discriminate against religions or a particular religion, or that it is
motivated by legitimate secular concerns. A regulation neutral on its face may, in
its application, nonetheless offend the constitutional requirement for governmental
neutrality if it unduly burdens the free exercise of religion. . . .

We turn, then, to the State's broader contention that its interest in its system of compulsory education is so compelling that even the established religious practices of the Amish must give way. Where fundamental claims of religious freedom are at stake, however, we cannot accept such a sweeping claim; . . .

The State advances two primary arguments in support of its system of compulsory education. It notes, as Thomas Jefferson pointed out early in our history, that some degree of education is necessary to prepare citizens to participate effectively and intelligently in our open political system if we are to preserve freedom and independence. Further, education prepares individuals to be self-reliant and self-sufficient participants in society. We accept these propositions.

However, the evidence adduced by the Amish in this case is persuasively to the effect that an additional one or two years of formal high school for Amish children in place of their long-established program of informal vocational education would do little to serve those interests. Respondents' experts testified at trial, without challenge, that the value of all education must be assessed in terms of its capacity to prepare the child for life. It is one thing to say that compulsory education for a year or two beyond the eighth grade may be necessary when its goal is for the preparation of the child for life in modern society as the majority live, but it is quite another if the goal of education be viewed as the preparation of the child for life in the separated agrarian community that is the keystone of the Amish faith. . . .

The State attacks respondents' position as one fostering "ignorance" from which the child must be protected by the State. No one can question the State's duty to protect children from ignorance but this argument does not square with the facts disclosed in the record. Whatever their idiosyncrasies as seen by the majority, the Amish community has been a highly successful social unit within our society, even if apart from the conventional "mainstream." Its members are productive and very law-abiding members of society; they reject public welfare in any of its usual modern forms. The Congress itself recognized their self-sufficiency by authorizing exemption of such groups as the Amish from the obligation to pay social security taxes.

It is neither fair nor correct to suggest that the Amish are opposed to education beyond the eighth grade level. What this record shows is that they are opposed to conventional formal education of the type provided by a certified high school because it comes at the child's crucial adolescent period of religious development. Dr. Donald Erickson, for example, testified that their system of learning-by-doing was an "ideal system" of education in terms of preparing Amish children for life as adults in the Amish community, and that "I would be inclined to say they do a better job in this than most of the rest of us do." As he put it, "These people aren't purporting to be learned people, and it seems to me the self-sufficiency of the community is the best evidence I can point to—whatever is being done seems to function well.

We must not forget that in the Middle Ages important values of the civilization of the Western World were preserved by members of religious orders who isolated themselves from all worldly influences against great obstacles. There can be no assumption that today's majority is "right" and the Amish and others like them are "wrong." A way of life that is odd or even erratic but interferes with no rights or interests of others is not to be condemned because it is different.

The State, however, supports its interest in providing an additional one or two years of compulsory high school education to Amish children because of the possibility that some such children will choose to leave the Amish community, and that if this occurs they will be ill-equipped for life. The state argues that if Amish children leave their church they should not be in the position of making their way in the world without the education available in the one or two additional years the State requires. However, on this record, that argument is highly speculative. There is no specific evidence of the loss of Amish adherents by attrition, nor is there any showing that upon leaving the Amish community Amish children, with their practical agricultural training and habits of industry and self-reliance, would become burdens on society because of educational shortcomings. Indeed, this argument of the State appears to rest primarily on the State's mistaken assumption, already noted, that the Amish do not provide any education for their children beyond the eighth grade, but allow them to grow in "ignorance." To the contrary, not only do the Amish accept the necessity for formal schooling through the eighth grade level, but they continue to provide what has been characterized by the undisputed testimony of expert educators as an "ideal" vocational education for their children in the adolescent years.

There is nothing in this record to suggest that the Amish qualities of reliability, self-reliance, and dedication to work would fail to find ready markets in today's society. Absent some contrary evidence supporting the State's position, we are unwilling to assume that persons possessing such valuable vocational skills and habits are doomed to become burdens on society should they determine to leave the Amish faith, nor is there any basis in the record to warrant a finding that an additional one or two years of formal school education beyond the eighth grade would serve to eliminate any such problem that might exist.

Insofar as the State's claim rests on the view that a brief additional period of formal education is imperative to enable the Amish to participate effectively and intelligently in our democratic process, it must fall. The Amish alternative to formal secondary school education has enabled them to function effectively in their day-to-day life under self-imposed limitations on relations with the world, and to survive and prosper in contemporary society as a separate, sharply identifiable and highly self-sufficient community for more than 200 years in this country. In itself this is strong evidence that they are capable of fulfilling the social and political responsibilities of citizenship without compelled attendance beyond the eighth grade at the price of jeopardizing their free exercise of religious belief. When Thomas Jefferson emphasized the need for education as a bulwark of a free people against tyranny, there is nothing to indicate he had in mind compulsory education through any fixed age beyond a basic education. Indeed, the Amish communities singularly parallel and reflect many of the virtues of Jefferson's ideal of the "sturdy yeoman" who would form the basis of what he considered as the ideal of a democratic society. Even their idiosyncratic separateness exemplifies the diversity we profess to admire and encourage.

The requirement for compulsory education beyond the eighth grade is a relatively recent development in our history. Less than 60 years ago, the educational requirements of almost all of the States were satisfied by completion of the elementary grades, at least where the child was regularly and lawfully employed.

The independence and successful social functioning of the Amish community for a period approaching almost three centuries and more than 200 years in this country are strong evidence that there is at best a speculative gain, in terms of meeting the duties of citizenship, from an additional one or two years of compulsory formal education. Against this background it would require a more particularized showing from the State on this point to justify the severe interference with religious freedom such additional compulsory attendance would entail.

We should also note that compulsory education and child labor laws find their historical origin in common humanitarian instincts, and that the age limits of both laws have been coordinated to achieve their related objectives. In the context of this case, such considerations, if anything, support rather than detract from respondents' position. The origins of the requirement for school attendance to age 16, an age falling after the completion of elementary school but before completion of high school, are not entirely clear. But to some extent such laws reflected the movement to prohibit most child labor under age 16 that culminated in the provisions of the Federal Fair Labor Standards Act of 1938. It is true, then, that the 16-year child labor age limit may to some degree derive from a contemporary impression that children should be in school until that age. But at the same time, it cannot be denied that, conversely, the 16-year education limit reflects, in substantial measure, the concern that children under that age not be employed under conditions hazardous to their health, or in work that should be performed by adults.

The requirement of compulsory schooling to age 16 must therefore be viewed as aimed not merely at providing educational opportunities for children, but as an alternative to the equally undesirable consequence of unhealthful child labor displacing adult workers, or, on the other hand, forced idleness. The two kinds of statutes—compulsory school attendance and child labor laws—tend to keep children of certain ages off the labor market and in school; this regimen in turn provides opportunity to prepare for a livelihood of a higher order than that which children could pursue without education and protects their health in adolescence.

In these terms, Wisconsin's interest in compelling the school attendance of Amish children to age 16 emerges as somewhat less substantial than requiring such attendance for children generally. For, while agricultural employment is not totally outside the legitimate concerns of the child labor laws, employment of children under parental guidance and on the family farm from age 14 to age 16 is an ancient tradition that lies at the periphery of the objectives of such laws. There is no intimation that the Amish employment of their children on family farms is in any way deleterious to their health or that Amish parents exploit children at tender years. Any such inference would be contrary to the record before us. Moreover, employment of Amish children on the family farm does not present the undesirable economic aspects of eliminating jobs that might otherwise be held by adults.

IV

. . . Aided by a history of three centuries as an identifiable religious sect and a long history as a successful and self-sufficient segment of American society, the Amish in this case have convincingly demonstrated the sincerity of their religious beliefs, the interrelationship of belief with their mode of life, the vital role that belief and daily conduct play in the continued survival of Old Order Amish communities and their religious organization, and the hazards presented by the State's enforcement of a statute generally valid as to others. Beyond this, they have carried the even more difficult burden of demonstrating the adequacy of their alternative mode of continuing informal vocational education in terms of precisely those over-all interests that the state advances in support of its program of compulsory high school education. In light of this convincing showing, one that probably few other religious groups or sects could make, and weighing the minimal difference between what the State would require and what the Amish already accept, it was incumbent on the State to show with more particularity how its admittedly strong interest in compulsory education would be adversely affected by granting an exemption to the Amish.

Nothing we hold is intended to undermine the general applicability of the State's compulsory school-attendance statutes or to limit the power of the State to promulgate reasonable standards that, while not impairing the free exercise of religion, provide for continuing agricultural vocational education under parental and church guidance by the Old Order Amish or others similarly situated. The States have had a long history of amicable and effective relationships with church-sponsored schools, and there is no basis for assuming that, in this related context, reasonable standards cannot be established concerning the content of the continuing vocational education of Amish children under parental guidance, provided always that state regulations are not inconsistent with what we have said in this opinion.

RELIGIOUS TESTS

It is difficult to imagine that any state today would require a "religious test" of a public office holder. Yet, until the Supreme Court ruled it unconstitutional in 1961, Maryland had such a requirement written into its constitution: "[No] religious test ought ever to be required as a qualification for any office of profit or trust in this State, *other than a declaration of belief in the existence of God*," Roy R. Torcaso brought a mandamus proceeding against Clayton K. Watkins, clerk of a circuit court in Maryland, to compel Watkins to issue him a notary commission. Torcaso had been refused a commission because of his reluctance to declare his belief in the existence of God as required by the state constitution. Mr. Justice Black held that, among other things, this violated Article VI of the federal Constitution.

Document 16 _____

From *Torcaso* v. *Watkins*
Mr. Justice Black for the Court

There is, and can be, no dispute about the purpose or effect of the Maryland Declaration of Rights requirement before us—it sets up a religious test which was

SOURCE: *Torcaso* v. *Watkins*, 367 U.S. 488, 490–491, 494–495 (1961).

designed to and, if valid, does bar every person who refuses to declare a belief in God from holding a public "office of profit or trust" in Maryland. The power and authority of the State of Maryland thus is put on the side of one particular sort of believers—those who are willing to say they believe in "the existence of God." It is true that there is much historical precedent for such laws. Indeed, it was largely to escape religious test oaths and declarations that a great many of the early colonists left Europe and came here hoping to worship in their own way. It soon developed, however, that many of those who had fled to escape religious test oaths turned out to be perfectly willing, when they had the power to do so, to force dissenters from their faith to take test oaths in conformity with that faith. This brought on a host of laws in the new Colonies imposing burdens and disabilities of various kinds upon varied beliefs depending largely upon what group happened to be politically strong enough to legislate in favor of its own beliefs. The effect of all this was the formal or practical "establishment" of particular religious faiths in most of the Colonies, with consequent burdens imposed on the free exercise of the faiths of nonfavored believers.

There were, however, wise and far-seeing men in the Colonies—too many to mention—who spoke out against test oaths and all the philosophy of intolerance behind them. One of these, it so happens, was George Calvert (the first Lord Baltimore), who took a most important part in the original establishment of the Colony of Maryland. He was a Catholic and had, for this reason, felt compelled by his conscience to refuse to take the Oath of Supremacy in England at the cost of resigning from high governmental office. He again refused to take that oath when it was demanded by the Council of the Colony of Virginia, and as a result he was denied settlement in the Colony. A recent historian of the early period of Maryland's life has said that it was Calvert's hope and purpose to establish in Maryland a colonial government free from the religious persecutions he had known—one "securely beyond the reach of oaths." . . .

When our Constitution was adopted, the desire to put the people "securely beyond the reach" of religious test oaths brought about the inclusion in Article VI of that document of a provision that "no religious Test shall ever be required as a Qualification to any Office or public Trust under the United States." . . . Not satisfied, however, with Article VI and other guarantees in the original Constitution, the First Congress proposed and the States very shortly thereafter adopted our Bill of Rights, including the First Amendment. That Amendment broke new constitutional ground in the protection it sought to afford to freedom of religion, speech, press, petition and assembly.

We repeat and again reaffirm that neither a State nor the Federal Government can constitutionally force a person "to profess a belief or disbelief in any religion." Neither can constitutionally pass laws or impose requirements which aid all religions as against non-believers, and neither can aid those religions based on a belief in the existence of God as against those religions founded on different beliefs.

In upholding the State's religious test for public office the highest court of Maryland said . . .

The petitioner is not compelled to believe or disbelieve, under threat of punishment or other compulsion. True, unless he makes the declaration of belief he cannot hold public office in Maryland, but he is not compelled to hold office.

The fact, however, that a person is not compelled to hold public office cannot possibly be an excuse for barring him from office by state-imposed criteria forbidden by the Constitution. . . .

This Maryland religious test for public office unconstitutionally invades the appellant's freedom of belief and religion and therefore cannot be enforced against him. . . .

Historical Evidence

Our purpose now is to investigate some of the more significant papers in the long history of America's search for and establishment of religious liberty. The following collection of documents is by no means exhaustive. There are others, equally important, that could have been included. But in attempting to capture the fundamental thrust of religious freedom outside the courts, we have cited persons and words that come from various periods and sectors of the American past—Christians and Jews, believers and agnostics, political radicals and ecclesiastical conservatives. Considering the disparate nature of the sources, a remarkable consensus emerges.

The first major figure in the history of religious liberty is, of course, Roger Williams. But in saying this we must be sure to see him in context. There has been a tendency among historians to see him as some kind of liberal secular democrat whose commitment to religious freedom marks him off from his contemporaries.[69] True, he was unusual and set off from his contemporaries, but he was no liberal secular democrat. His great passion was the purity and independence of the church from all outside political influences, being convinced that the union of civil and secular power could only result in destroying the church. That is why John Courtney Murray (1904–1967) points out that "he was no child of the Enlightenment, born before his time."[70] In contrast to Williams, Jefferson, a thoroughgoing humanist, wanted to protect the government from the insidious encroachments of ecclesiastical power.

The fact that Williams thought that church and state should be separated is in itself noteworthy. It was, after all, only the beginning of the seventeenth century. Most people of his theological persuasion (Calvinist) were quite willing to have the civil magistrate enforce religious uniformity. The only problem they had to solve was the *type* of uniformity. But Williams believed otherwise: To insist on uniformity

---

[69] Perry Miller sharpened the focus for us on this question in *Roger Williams* (Indianapolis: Bobbs-Merrill, 1953).

[70] John Courtney Murray, *We Hold These Truths* (Garden City, N.Y.: Doubleday, 1964), pp. 64, 72.

accomplished nothing but bloodshed and civic chaos. To his mind the only solution was to separate religion and government, for common sense shows that church and state operate on altogether different levels. To put them into some kind of liaison was therefore destructive for both, but especially for the church. Furthermore, he held, the two orders perform different functions according to the divine plan of things. They "represent" the radical disjunction between the Old Testament and the New Testament. The civil government, like the Old Testament, was transitory and would some day pass away; the religious order, like the New Testament, was ordained of God for eternal life with Christ. This problem, of course, was given its classic form by St. Augustine in the *City of God*.

Also, like Augustine, William's one great aim was peace. In his pamphlet "The Hireling Ministry None of Christ's" (1652) he said that the only way out of the turmoil of his day was for government to remain neutral with regard to religion so that people could worship and practice their beliefs as they chose. Such impartiality, he said, not only would be a boon to the individual believers, but would create the peace all so desperately longed for. That does not mean that he believed "all religions ought to be equally free because, for all anybody knows, they may all be equally true or false."[71] (That was Jefferson's way.) By contrast, Williams was willing to risk the specter of "false" religion because taking the risk secured tranquility. Besides that, men should leave judgment in such matters to God.

Thus we must agree with those who point out that Williams was no eighteenth-century rational libertarian but a rigorously committed Calvinist whose experience drove him to support the separation of church and state. Accordingly, his influence on the designers of the Constitution was, at best, indirect. Their primary source of inspiration was Enlightenment political philosophy, especially that variety espoused by John Locke. Yet William's shadow, like those of many others who suffered persecution, falls toward the First Amendment, if it does not actually reach it. Not only his life, but his rough-hewn words are eloquent testimony to the struggle for religious liberty.

Roger Williams was born in London around 1603. In 1628 he received holy orders in the Church of England and became acquainted with leaders of the Puritan movement. In 1631 he emigrated to Massachusetts Bay and by that time had become convinced of the desirability of completely separating church and state. No sooner had he arrived than he was embroiled in bitter controversy over the propriety of civil magistrates enforcing "the first table," or the first four of the Ten Commandments—those having to do with one's duty toward God and religion. It was appropriate, he thought, for them to enforce the last six commandments, or second table—those having to do with one's duty toward one's

---

[71] Murray, op. cit., p. 69.

neighbor. Because of his views and behavior he was banished by the General Court in 1635.

During the severe winter months he left Massachusetts and in 1636 established the colony of Rhode Island, where, after a brief period as a Baptist, he became a Seeker. That is, he wondered, finally, whether any sort of religious institution was possible. He never abandoned Christianity as such, but he was completely disenchanted with churches and creeds. In 1644 he wrote *The Bloody Tenet of Persecution*, an exposition of his side of the controversy with the governing powers in Massachusetts, especially John Cotton.

Document 17

From *Bloody Tenet of Persecution for the Cause of Conscience Discussed in a Conference Between Truth and Peace* by Roger Williams

The Argument

. . . that the blood of so many hundred thousand souls of Protestants and Papists, spilt in the Wars of present and former Ages, for their respective Consciences, is not required nor accepted by Jesus Christ the Prince of Peace. . . .

. . . All Civil States with their Officers of justice in their respective constitutions and administrations are proved essentially Civil, and therefore not Judges, Governors or Defenders of the Spiritual or Christian State and Worship.

. . . It is the will and command of God, that (since the coming of his Son the Lord Jesus) a permission of the most paganish, Jewish, Turkish, or Antichristian consciences and worships, be granted to all men in all Nations and Countries: and they are only to be fought against with that Sword which is only (in Soul matters) able to conquer, to wit, the Sword of God's Spirit, the Word of God.

. . . The state of the Land of Israel, the Kings and people thereof in Peace and War, is proved figurative and ceremonial, and no pattern nor precedent for any Kingdom or civil state in the world to follow.

. . . God requireth not an uniformity of Religion to be enacted and enforced in any civil state; which enforced uniformity (sooner or later) is the greatest occasion of civil War, ravishing of conscience, persecution of Christ Jesus in his servants, and of the hypocrisy and destruction of millions of souls.

. . . In holding an enforced uniformity of Religion in a civil state, we must necessarily disclaim our desires and hopes of the Jews' conversion to Christ.

. . . An enforced uniformity of Religion throughout a Nation or civil state, con-founds the Civil and Religious, denies the principles of Christianity and civility, and that Jesus Christ is come in the Flesh.

. . . The permission of other consciences and worships than a state professeth, only can (according to God) procure a firm and lasting peace, (good assurance being taken according to the wisdom of the civil state for uniformity of civil obedience from all sorts).

SOURCE: Roger Williams, *The Bloody Tenet of Persecution for the Cause of Conscience Discussed in a Conference Between Truth and Peace* (London, 1644).

. . . I acknowledge that to molest any person, Jew or Gentile, for either professing doctrine, or practising worship merely religious or spirtitual, is to persecute him, and such a person (what ever his doctrine of practice be true or false) suffereth persecution for conscience.

The church or company of worshippers (whether true or false) is like unto a Body or College of Physicians in a City; like unto a Corporation, Society, or Company of East-Indie or Turkie-Merchants, or any other Society or Company in London: which Companies may hold their Courts, keep their Records, hold disputations; and in matters concerning their Society, may dissent, divide, break into Schisms and Factions, sue and implead each other at the Law, yea, wholly break up and dissolve into pieces and nothing, and yet the peace of the City not be in the least measure impaired or disturbed; because the essence or being of the City, and so the well-being and peace thereof is essentially distinct from those particular Societies; the City Courts, City Laws, City punishments distinct from theirs. The City was before them, and stands absolute and entire, when such a Corporation or Society is taken down.

. . . as God needeth not the help of a material sword of steel to assist the sword of the Spirit in the affairs of conscience, so those men, those Magistrates, Yea, the Commonwealth which makes such Magistrates, must needs have power and authority from Christ Jesus to fit Judge and to determine in all the great controversies concerning doctrine, discipline, government, etc. . . .

Either there is no lawful Commonwealth nor civil State of men in the world, which is not qualified with this spiritual discerning. . . .

Or, . . . the Commonwealth and Magistrates, thereof must judge and punish as they are persuaded in their own belief and conscience, (be their conscience Paganish, Turkish, or Antichristian) what is this but to confound Heaven and Earth together, and not only to take away the being of Christianity out of the World, but to take away all civility, and the world out of this world, and to lay all upon heaps of confusion? . . .

Christ Jesus would not be pleased to make use of the Civil Magistrate to assist him in his Spiritual Kingdom; nor would he yet be daunted or discouraged in his Servants by all their threats and terrors: for Love is strong as death, and the coals thereof give a most vehement flame, and are not quenched by all the waters and floods of mightiest opposition.

Christ's Church is like a chaste and loving wife, in whose heart is fixed her Husband's love, who hath found the tenderness of his love towards her, and hath been made fruitful by him, and therefore seeks she not the smiles, nor fears the frowns of all the Emperors in the World to bring her Christ unto her, or keep him from her.

As it is most true that Magistracy in general is of God for the preservation of Mankind in civil order and peace, (the World otherwise would be like the Sea, wherein Men, like Fishes would hunt and devour each other, and the greater devour the less:) so also it is true, that Magistracy in special for the several kinds of it is of Man. Now what kind of Magistrate soever the people shall agree to set up, whether he receive Christianity before he be set in office, or whether he receive Christianity after, he receives no more power of Magistracy, than a Magistrate that hath received no Christianity. For neither of them both can receive more, than the Commonwealth, the Body of People and civil State, as men, communicate unto them, and betrust with them.

All lawful Magistrates in the World, both before the coming of Christ Jesus, and since . . . are but Derivatives and Agents immediately derived and employed as eyes and hands, serving for the good of the whole: Hence they have and can have no more Power, than fundamentally lies in the Bodies or Fountains themselves, which Power, Might, or Authority, is not Religious, Christian, etc. but natural, humane and civil.

And hence it is true, that a Christian Captain, Christian Merchant, Physician, Lawyer, Pilot, Father, Master, and (so consequently) Magistrate, etc. is no more a Captain, Merchant, Physician, Lawyer, Pilot, Father, Master, Magistrate, etc. than a Captain, Merchant, etc. of any other Conscience or Religion.

. . . In his season God will glorify himself in all his truths: but to gratify thy desire, thus: A pagan or Antichristian Pilot may be as skillful to carry the Ship to its desired Port, as any Christian Mariner or Pilot in the World, and may perform that work with as much safety and speed: yet have they not command over the souls and consciences of their passengers or mariners under them, although they may justly see to the labor of the one, and the civil behavior of all in the ship: A Christian Pilot he performs the same work (as likewise doth the Metaphorical Pilot in the ship of the Commonweal) from a principle of knowledge and experience: but more than this, he acts from a root of the fear of God and love to mankind, in his whole course. Secondly, his aim is more to glorify God than to gain his pay, or make his voyage. Thirdly, he walks heavenly with Men, and God, in a constant observation of God's hand in storms, calms, etc. so that the thread of Navigation being equally spun by a believing or unbelieving Pilot, yet is it drawn over with the gold of Godliness and Christianity by a Christian Pilot, while he is holy in all manner of Christianity. . . . But lastly, the Christian Pilot's power over the Souls and consciences of his Sailors and Passengers is not greater than of the Antichristian, otherwise than he can subdue the souls of any by the two-edged sword of the Spirit, the Word of God, and by his holy demeanor in his place, etc. . . .

As the Revolutionary period drew near, spokesmen on behalf of religious liberty arose from all sides and from within all ecclesial religious traditions. In New England, members of the so-called Standing Order, or Congregationalism, became more and more suspicious that the English Crown, if it retained control over America, would seek to impose bishops and hence Anglicanism upon the colonies. But in their zeal to avoid an episcopal establishment, the Congregationalists failed to understand that they, at the same time, were perpetuating their own kind of establishment in New England. Since the beginning, the Standing Order had been supported by general taxation and backed by the power of the civil government.

One of the staunchest opponents of the Congregational system was Issac Backus (1724–1806), a Massachusetts Baptist clergyman who devoted a good portion of his professional career to the cause of religious liberty. From the preaching of George Whitefield, Backus early gained a distaste for governmental interference in religious affairs. He sought to follow Whitefield's lead, became a revivalist himself, and produced a number of pamphlets on behalf of the struggle for religious liberty. As head of the Warren Association, an energetic group of prominent New England Baptists who opposed the privileged status of the Standing Order, Backus appeared several times before the Massachusetts Assembly to plead his case. His basic contention was a variation of the familiar "taxation-without-representation" argument used by colonial leaders against the policies of George III. But another patriot, John Adams, a defender of Congregationalism, pointed out that the Baptists "might as well expect a change in the solar system" as to expect the Congregationalists to give up establishment.[72]

In 1787 Backus appeared before the Constitutional Convention in Philadelphia to support the proposed constitutional prohibition of religious tests for public officeholders:

> Nothing is more evident, both in reason, and in the holy scriptures, than that religion is ever a matter between God and individuals: and therefore no men or man can impose any religious test, without invading the essential prerogatives of our Lord Jesus Christ. Ministers first assumed this power under the Christian name; and then Constantine approved of the practice, when he adopted the profession of Christianity, as an engine of state policy. And let the history of all nations be searched, from that day to this, and it will appear that the imposing of all religious tests hath been the greatest engine of tyranny in the world.[73]

The following document, produced in 1773, shows Backus at his best; it is a closely reasoned and lucid argument for the separation of powers.

_____ *Document 18*

From *An Appeal to the Public for Religious Liberty* by Issac Backus

It is needful to observe that God has appointed two kinds of government in the world which are distinct in their nature and ought never to be confounded together— one of which is called civil and the other ecclesiastical government. And though we shall not attempt a full explanation of them, some essential points of difference between them are necessary to be mentioned in order truly to open our grievances.

SOURCE: Issac Backus, *An Appeal to the Public for Religious Liberty* (Boston, 1773).

[72] As quoted by Anson Phelps Stokes and Leo Pfeffer, *Church and State in the United States* (New York: Harper & Row, 1964), p. 44.
[73] Ibid., p. 45.

Section I

Some essential points of difference between civil and ecclesiastical government.

All acts of execution of power in the civil state are to be performed in the name of the king or state they belong to, while all our religious acts are to be done in the name of the Lord Jesus, and so are to be performed heartily as to the Lord and not unto men. . . . It is often pleaded that magistrates ought to do their duty in religious as well as civil affairs. That is readily granted; but what is their duty therein? Surely it is to bow to the name of Jesus and to serve him with holy reverence; and if they do to the contrary they may expect to perish from the way. . . . But where is the officer that will dare to come in the name of the Lord to demand, and forcibly to take, a tax which was imposed by the civil state? Can any man in the light of truth maintain his character as minister of Christ, if he is not contented with all that Christ's name and influence will procure for him, but will have recourse to the kings of the earth to force money from the people to support them under the name of an ambassador of the God of heaven? . . .

In all civil governments some are appointed to judge for others and have power to compel others to submit to their judgment, but our Lord has most plainly forbidden us either to assume or submit to any such thing in religion. . . . He declares that the cause of his coming into the world was to bear "witness unto the truth," and says he, "Everyone that is of the truth heareth my voice." This is the nature of his kingdom which he says "is not of this world" and gives that as the reason why his servants should not fight or defend him with sword. . . . And it appears to us that the true difference and exact line between ecclesiastical and civil government is this: that the church is armed with light and truth to pull down the strongholds of iniquity and to gain souls to Christ and his church, to be governed by his rules therein, and again to exclude those from their communion who will not be governed; while the state is armed with the sword to guard the peace and the civil rights of all persons and societies and to punish those who violate the same. And where these two kinds of government and the weapons which belong to them are well distinguished and improved according to the true nature and end of their institution, the effects are happy, and they do not at all interfere with each other; but where they have been confounded together, no tongue nor pen can fully describe the mischiefs that have ensued. . . .

Section II

A brief view of how civil and ecclesiastical affairs are blended together among us to the depriving of many people of that liberty of conscience which he has given them. . . . We view it to be our incumbent duty "to render unto Caesar" the things that are his but that it is of as much more importance not to render unto him anything that belongs only to God, who is to be obeyed rather than man. And as it is evident to us that God always claimed it as his sole prerogative to determine by his own laws what his worship shall be, who shall minister in it, and how they shall be supported: so it is evident that their prerogative has been, and still is, encroached upon in our land. For,

1. Our legislatures claim power to compel every town and parish within their jurisdiction to set up and maintain a pedobaptist worship among them, although it is well known that infant baptism is never expressed in the Bible. . . .

2. Our ascended Lord gives "gifts unto men" in a sovereign way as seems good to him and he requires "every man, as he has received the gift, even so to minister the same"; . . . But the Massachusetts legislature, while they claim a power to compel each parish to settle a minister, have also determined that he must be one who has either an academical degree or a testimonial in his favor from a majority of the ministers in the country where the parish lies. So that let Christ give a man ever so great gifts, yet hereby these ministers derive a noble power from the state to forbid the improvement of the same if he follows not their schemes. . . .

3. Though the Lord hath "ordained that they which preach the gospel shall live by the gospel" or by the free "communications to them" which his gospel will produce . . . yet the ministers of our Lord have chosen to "live by the law"; and as a reason therefor one of their most noted writers [Cotton Mather], instead of producing any truth of God, recites the tradition of a man who said, "Ministers of the gospel would have a poor time of it, if they must rely on a free contribution of the people for their maintenance." And he says, ". . . it is enacted that there shall be a public worship of God in every plantation; that the person elected by the majority of the inhabitants shall be so, shall be looked upon as the minister of the place; that the salary for him, which they shall agree upon, shall be levied by a rate upon all inhabitants. In consequence of this, the minister thus chosen by the people is (not only Christ's but also) in reality the King's minister; and the salary raised for him is raised in the King's name."

Now who can hear Christ declare that his kindgom is "not of this world," and yet believe that this blending of the church and state together can be pleasing to him? For though their laws call them "orthodox ministers," yet the grand test of orthodoxy is the major vote of the people, be they saints or sinners, believers or unbelievers. . . .

Hence their ministers and churches must become subject to the court and the majority of the parish in order to have their salary raised in the "king's name." But how are either of them in the meantime subject to the authority of Christ in his church? . . . for though there is a show of equity in allowing every society to choose its own minister, yet let them be ever so unanimous for one who is of a different mode from the court, their choice is not allowed. . . .

Another argument which these ministers often mention is the apostolic direction to us to pray for all that are in authority that we may lead a quiet and peaceable life in all godliness and honesty. But do they pray and act according to that direction? . . . when it comes to be calmly represented that religion is a "voluntary obedience unto God" which, therefore, force cannot promote, how soon do they shift the scene and tell us that religious liberty is fully allowed to us, only the state have in their wisdom thought fit to tax all the inhabitants to support an order of men for the good of civil society. A little while ago it was for religion, and many have declared that without it we should soon have no religion left among us; but now tis to maintain civility. Though, by the way, it is well known that no men in the land have done more to promote uncivil treatment of dissenters from themselves than some of these pretended ministers of civility have done. In 1644 the court at Boston passed an act to punish men with banishment if they opposed infant baptism or departed from any of their congregations if it was going to be administered. And after they acted upon this law, one of their chief magistrates observed that such methods tended to make hypocrites. To which a noted minister replied, That if it did so, yet such were better than profane persons, because, said he, "hypocrites give God part of his due, the outward man, but the profane person giveth God neither outward nor inward man." By which it seems that in that day they were zealous to have the outward man, if no more, given to God; but now that conduct is condemned as persecution by their children, who profess to allow us full liberty of conscience because they do not hinder our giving our inward man to God, only claim a power to seize our outward man to get money for themselves. And though many of us have expended ten or twenty times as much in setting up and supporting that worship which we believe to be right as it would have cost us to have continued in the fashionable way, yet we are often accused of being covetous for dissenting from that way and refusing to pay more money out of our little incomes to uphold men from whom we receive no benefit but rather abuse. How far is this from leading "a peaceable life," either of godliness or honesty!

The debate over religious liberty that took place in all the colonial legislatures toward the end of the eighteenth century came to a head in the Virginia Assembly immediately prior to the adoption of the U.S. Constitution. Through the give and take of political debate Virginia arrived at a plan of separation that became a model for the framers of the federal Constitution. The names of those who took a leading role in developing the plan are familiar—Thomas Jefferson, James Madison, George Mason, Patrick Henry.

The Church of England, of course, had been able to assert itself as the establishment in Virginia from the time of its founding in 1607. Clergy salaries and parochial expenses were controlled and supported by the Assembly. Though toleration was granted to "dissenting" groups, their preachers were required to hold services only in those meeting houses designated in the licenses awarded by the civil government. But during the Great Awakening things began to change. Methodism took root in Virginia, Baptists and Presbyterians began to arrive in great numbers in the Shenandoah Valley, and the religious complexion of the colony lost its heavily Anglican cast. The most active denominational groups against the privileged status of Anglicanism in Virginia were the Hanover Presbytery, formed in 1755 under the leadership of the Rev. Samuel Davis (1723–1761), and the Baptist General Association under the leadership of the Rev. John Leland (1754–1841). Both groups resisted mere toleration and made repeated appeals to the Assembly for nothing short of absolute religious freedom. They were not so much concerned with the theological niceties of religious freedom as with its practical necessity. The dissenters found a sympathetic audience among the leading politicians of the colony, although many of them were of the Anglican persuasion. They were the politicians who had absorbed the theories of the great political philosophers of the Enlightenment.

Several noteworthy legislative actions were taken. In 1776, three weeks before the adoption of the Declaration of Independence, the Virginia Assembly passed its own Declaration of Rights, which advocated, among other things, "the free exercise of religion." This bill was mainly the work of George Mason.

In 1779 the Assembly took another giant step toward religious liberty when it quit paying salaries to Anglican clergy in Virginia. But six years later Patrick Henry almost convinced the Commonwealth to take a backward step. He successfully steered through two readings in the Assembly "A bill establishing a provision for teachers of the Christian Religion." Simply put, the bill would have taxed everyone for the support of the denomination designated by the individual taxpayer. Henry's impulse seemed harmless enough. His proposed legislation supported religion by statute because religion seemed to be a good thing for the body politic, but it would prevent any one ecclesial group from gaining the upper hand over its "competitors." James Madison, however, saw the flaw in the Henry bill and was able to postpone its passage until the next session of the Assembly. In the meantime, he composed the critically important *Memorial and Remonstrance Against Religious Assessments*, which protested governmental aid for any and all religious groups. It turned the tide of sentiment against the Henry bill, which was defeated when the Assembly reconvened. Madison then called for a vote on another crucial piece of legislation, Jefferson's Bill for Establishing Religious Freedom. It had languished on the calendar since 1779, when he first introduced it. Jefferson's bill passed and the decisive blow was thus struck for religious liberty in America. All subsequent struggle concerning religious freedom may well be said to have been an attempt to fathom the depths sounded in Madison's historic words. It is one of the most durable and seminal documents in American history.

_____ *Document 19*

Memorial and Remonstrance Against Religious Assessments
by James Madison

We, the subscribers, citizens of the said Commonwealth, having taken into serious consideration, a Bill printed by order of the last session of General Assembly, entitled "A Bill establishing a provision for teachers of the Christian Religion," and conceiving that the same, if finally armed with the sanctions of a law, will be a dangerous abuse of power, are bound as faithful members of a free State, to remonstrate against it, and to declare the reasons by which we are determined. We remonstrate against the said Bill,

SOURCE: *Everson v. Board of Education*, 330 U.S. 1, 63–72 (1947).

1. Because we hold it for a fundamental and undeniable truth, "that religion, or the duty which we owe to our Creator, and the manner of discharging it, can be directed only by reason and conviction, not by force or violence." The Religion then of every man must be left to the conviction and conscience of every man; and it is the right of every man to exercise it as these may dictate. This right is in its nature an unalienable right. It is unalienable; because the opinions of men, depending only on the evidence contemplated by their own minds, cannot follow the dictates of other men: It is unalienable also; because what is here a right towards men, is a duty towards the Creator. It is the duty of every man to render to the Creator such homage, and such only, as he believes to be acceptable to him. This duty is precedent both in order of time and degree of obligation, to the claims of Civil Society. Before any man can be considered as a menber of Civil Society, he must be considered as a subject of the Governor of the Universe: And if a member of Civil Society, who enters into any subordinate Association, must always do it with reservation of his duty to the general authority; much more must every man who becomes a member of any particular Civil Society, do it with a saving of his allegiance to the Universal Sovereign. We maintain therefore that in matters of Religion, no man's right is abridged by the institution of Civil Society, and that Religion is wholly exempt from its cognizance. True it is, that no other rule exists, by which any question which may divide a Society, can be ultimately determined, but the will of the majority; but it is also true, that the majority may trespass on the rights of the minority.

2. Because if religion be exempt from the authority of the Society at large, still less can it be subject to that of the Legislative Body. The latter are but the creatures and vicegerents of the former. Their jurisdiction is both derivative and limited: it is limited with regard to the co-ordinate departments, more necessarily it is limited with regard to the constituents. The preservation of a free government requires not merely, that the metes and bounds which separate each department of power may be invariably maintained; but more especially, that neither of them be suffered to overlap the great Barrier which defends the rights of the people. The Rulers who are guilty of such an encroachment, exceed the commission from which they derive their authority, and are Tyrants. The People who submit to it are governed by laws made neither by themselves, nor by an authority derived from them, and are slaves.

3. Because it is proper to take alarm at the first experiment on our liberties. We hold this prudent jealousy to be the first duty of citizens, and one of [the] noblest characteristics of the late Revolution. The freemen of America did not wait till usurped power had strengthened itself by exercise, and entangled the question in precedents. They saw all the consequences in the principle, and they avoided the consequences by denying the principle. We revere this lesson too much, soon to forget it. Who does not see that the same authority which can establish Christianity, in exclusion of all other Religions, may establish with the same ease any particular sect of Christians, in exclusion of all other Sects? That the same authority which can force a citizen to contribute three pence only of his property for the support of any one establishment, may force him to conform to any other establishment in all cases whatsoever?

4. Because, the bill violates that equality which ought to be the basis of every law, and which is more indispensable, in proportion as the validity or expediency of any law is more liable to be impeached. If "all men are by nature equally free and independent," all men are to be considered as entering into Society on equal conditions; as relinquishing no more, and therefore retaining no less, one than another, of their natural rights. Above all are they to be considered as retaining an "equal title to the free exercise of Religion according to the dictates of conscience." Whilst we assert for ourselves a freedom to embrace, to profess and to observe the Religion which we believe to be of divine origin, we cannot deny an equal freedom to those whose minds have not yet yielded to the evidence which has convinced us. If this freedom be abused, it is an offence against God, not against man: To God, therefore, not to men, must an account of it be rendered. . . .

5. Because the bill implies either that the Civil Magistrate is a competent Judge of Religious truth; or that he may employ Religion as an engine of Civil policy. The first is an arrogant pretension falsified by the contradictory opinions of Rulers in all ages, and throughout the world: The second an unhallowed perversion of the means of salvation.

6. Because the establishment proposed by the Bill is not requisite for the support of the Christian Religion. To say that it is, is a contradiction to the Christian Religion itself; for every page of it disavows a dependence on the powers of this world: it is a contradiction to fact; for it is known that this Religion both existed and flourished, not only without the support of human laws, but in spite of every opposition from them; and not only during the period of miraculous aid, but long after it had been left to its own evidence, and the ordinary care of Providence: Nay, it is a contradiction in terms; for a Religion not invented by human policy, must have pre-existed and been supported, before it was established by human policy. It is moreover to weaken in those who profess this Religion a pious confidence in its innate excellence, and the patronage of its Author; and to foster in those who still reject it, a suspicion that its friends are too conscious of its fallacies, to trust it to its own merits.

7. Because experience witnesseth that ecclesiastical establishments, instead of maintaining the purity and efficacy of Religion, have had a contrary operation. During almost fifteen centuries, has the legal establishment of Christianity been on trial. What have been its fruits? More or less in all places, pride and indolence in the Clergy; ignorance and servility in the laity; in both, superstition, bigotry and persecution. Enquire of the Teachers of Christianity for the ages in which it appeared in its greatest lustre; those of every sect, point to the ages prior to its incorporation with Civil policy. Propose a restoration of this primitive state in which its Teachers depended on the voluntary rewards of their flocks; many of them predict its downfall. On which side ought their testimony to have greatest weight, when for or when against their interest?

8. Because the establishment in question is not necessary for the support of Civil Government. It is urged as necessary for the support of Civil Government only as it is a means of supporting Religion, and it be not necessary for the latter purpose, [if] it cannot be necessary for the former. If Religion be not within [the] cognizance of Civil Government, how can its legal establishment be said to be necessary to Civil

Government? What influence in fact have ecclesiastical establishments had on Civil Society? In some instances they have been seen to erect a spiritual tyranny on the ruins of Civil authority; in many instances they have been seen upholding the thrones of political tyranny; in no instance have they been seen the guardians of the liberties of the people. Rulers who wished to subvert the public liberties, may have found an established clergy convenient auxiliaries. A just government, instituted to secure & perpetuate it, needs them not. Such a government will be best supported by protecting every citizen in the enjoyment of his Religion with the same equal hand which protects his person and his property; by neither invading the equal rights by any Sect, nor suffering any Sect to invade those of another.

9. Because the proposed establishment is a departure from that generous policy, which, offering an asylum to the persecuted and oppressed of every Nation and Religion, promised a lustre to our country, and an accession to the number of its citizens. What a melancholy mark is the Bill of sudden degeneracy? Instead of holding forth an asylum to the persecuted, it is itself a signal of persecution. It degrades from the equal rank of Citizens all those whose opinions in Religion do not bend to those of the Legislative authority. Distant as it may be, in its present form, from the Inquisition it differs from it only in degree. The one is the first step, the other the last in the career of intolerance. The magnanimous sufferer under this cruel scourge in foreign Regions, must view the Bill as a Beacon on our Coast, warning him to seek some other haven, where liberty and philanthropy in their due extent may offer a more certain repose from his troubles.

10. Because, it will have a like tendency to banish our Citizens. The allurements presented by other situations are every day thinning their number. To superadd a fresh motive to emigration, by revoking the liberty which they now enjoy, would be the same species of folly which has dishonoured and depopulated flourishing kingdoms.

11. Because, it will destroy that moderation and harmony which the forebearance of our laws to intermeddle with Religion, has produced amongst its several sects. Torrents of blood have been spilt in the old world, by vain attempts of the secular arm to extinguish Religious discord, by proscribing all differences in Religious opinions. Time has at length revealed the true remedy. Every relaxation of narrow and rigorous policy, wherever it has been tried, has been found to assuage the disease. The American Theatre has exhibited proofs, that equal and complete liberty, if it does not wholly eradicate it, sufficiently destroys its malignant influence on the health and prosperity of the State. If with the salutary effects of this system under our own eyes, we begin to contract the bonds of Religious freedom, we know no name that will too severely reproach our folly. At least let warning be taken at the first fruit of the threatened innovation. The very appearance of the Bill has transformed that "Christian forebearance, love and charity," which of late mutually prevailed, into animosities and jealousies, which may not soon be appeased. What mischiefs may not be dreaded should this enemy to the public quiet be armed with the force of a law?

12. Because the policy of the bill is adverse to the diffusion of the light of Christianity. The first wish of those who enjoy this precious gift, ought to be that it may be imparted to the whole race of mankind. Compare the number of those

who have as yet received it with the number still remaining under the dominion of false Religion; and how small is the former! Does the policy of the Bill tend to lessen the disproportion? No; it at once discourages those who are strangers to the light of [revelation] from coming into the Region of it; and countenances, by example the nations who continue in darkness, in shutting out those who might convey it to them. Instead of levelling as far as possible, every obstacle to the victorious progress of truth, the Bill with an ignoble and unchristian timidity would cirumscribe it, with a wall of defense, against the encroachments of error.

13. Because attempts to enforce by legal sanctions, acts obnoxious to so great a proportion of Citizens, tend to enervate the laws in general, and to slacken the bands of Society. If it be difficult to execute any law which is not generally deemed necessary or salutary, what must be the case where it is deemed invalid and dangerous? and what may be the effect of so striking an example of impotency in the Government, on its general authority.

14. Because a measure of such singular magnitude and delicacy ought not to be imposed, without the clearest evidence that it is called for by a majority of citizens; and no satisfactory method is yet proposed by which the voice of the majority in this case may be determined, or its influence secured. . . .

15. Because, finally, "the equal right of every citizen to the free exercise of his Religion according to the dictates of conscience" is held by the same tenure with all our other rights. If we recur to its origin, it is equally the gift of nature; if we weigh its importance it cannot be less dear to us; if we consult the Declaration of those rights which pertain to the good people of Virginia, as the "basis and foundation of Government," it is enumerated with equal solemnity, or rather studied emphasis. Either then, we must say, that the will of the Legislature is the only measure of their authority; and that in the plenitude of this authority, they may sweep away all our fundamental rights; or, that they are bound to leave this particular right untouched and sacred: Either we must say, that they may control the freedom of the press, may abolish the trial by jury, may swallow up the Executive and Judiciary Powers of the State; nay that they may despoil us of our very right of suffrage, and erect themselves into an independent and hereditary assembly: or we must say, that they have no authority to enact into law the Bill under consideration. We the subscribers say, that the General Assembly of this Commonwealth have no such authority: And that no effort may be omitted on our part against so dangerous an usurpation, we oppose to it, this remonstrance; earnestly praying, as we are in duty bound, that the Supreme Lawgiver of the Universe, by illuminating those to whom it is addressed, may on the one hand, turn their councils from every act which would affront his holy prerogative, or violate the trust committed to them: and on the other, guide them into every measure which may be worthy of [blessing, may re] dound to their own praise, and may establish more firmly the liberties, the prosperity, and the Happiness of the Commonwealth.

With the great waves of immigration that swept into the country in the nineteenth century, the "spectre" of Papist domination of the political order and the consequent loss of religious liberty arose in the imagination of many Americans. Before the Civil War over 2 million Catholics had arrived and settled in the big urban centers along the eastern seaboard. After the Civil War hundreds of thousands more would come from Eastern Europe and invade the big cities of the Midwest.

Suspicions were first aroused not just in the minds of the ignorant masses, who might not have known better, but also in the minds of well-informed and intelligent men like Samuel F. B. Morse, Lyman Beecher, (1775–1863), Horace Bushnell, and Josiah Strong. They warned that the Protestant majority might not be able to maintain control in the face of the massive Catholic incursions. The most acute response came early in the century from the "Nativists," those who appealed to bigotry and fear in order to make life uncomfortable for the Catholic "hordes." Nativism eventually emerged as a viable political power in the form of the infamous Order of United Americans, or "Know-Nothing" party of the 1840s and 1850s. The passions of the people became so inflamed by their demagogic tactics that unruly and ugly mobs burned and pillaged churches, rectories, convents, and other church buildings. Beatings occurred and riots broke out in Philadelphia, Boston, and other cities. In 1854 the persecution reached its vicious climax when almost a hundred Catholics were killed in Louisville. Only the onset of the Civil War turned men's hatred and hostility toward other enemies.

Naturally, when persecution first came, Catholics tended to withdraw into their own neighborhoods and groups. They established their own schools, orphanages, welfare agencies, and hospitals in order to "care for their own." There were even some attempts to withdraw further from the American mainstream by creating dioceses along lines of language and nationality, rather than geography. But fortunately for all, the sentiment of the American hierarchy was against that kind of a siege mentality. They felt that the newly arrived Catholic immigrant should be able to find his way into the center of American political, social, and economic life without losing his identity as a Catholic. They had confidence that justice would ultimately prevail and that the principles behind the First Amendment would overcome the bigotry.

According to Will Herberg, Catholicism did not withdraw into religio-ethnic enclaves because of Irish leadership, which was intensely patriotic. Herberg explains:

Perhaps the most distinctive feature of Irish Catholicism, and a feature that has proved most influential in the development of Catholicism in America, was the fusion of religion and nationalism in the Irish mind. In the centuries of struggle against an alien and Protestant master, national loyalty came to take on an intense religious coloring, even a kind of "mystical" quality, utterly unintelligible to the Continental mind. To be a Catholic was to be a true Irishman; to be an Irishman was to be a true Catholic. This equation helped the Irish Catholic to survive and prevail in the New World, but what was perhaps even more important, it enabled the Irish Catholic to become a passionately patriotic American while retaining much of his age-old hostility to Protestantism.[74]

In short, the Irish leaders believed Catholicism would thrive in America, as indeed it did.

James Cardinal Gibbons (1834–1921) was such a leader. Although he did not come to the cardinalate until 1886, long after the bitterest persecution was over, he was able to dampen the fires of passion that continued to surge back and forth between Catholic and Protestant. He was able to assure his own people that America was a good place for their kind of religion to flourish, and at the same time he put to rest in the hearts of all non-Catholics the fear that Catholics wanted to subvert religious liberty in America. In the following article he asks only that freedom of religion be equitably distributed to all, Catholics as well as others.

_____ _Document 20_

From "The Church and the Republic" by James Cardinal Gibbons

Fifteen millions of Catholics live their lives in our land with undisturbed belief in the perfect harmony existing between their religion and their duties as American citizens. It never occurs to their minds to question the truth of a belief which all their experience confirms. Love of religion and love of country burn together in their hearts. They love their Church as the divine spiritual society set up by Jesus Christ through which they are brought into a closer communion with God, learn His revealed truth and His holy law, receive the help they need to lead Christian lives and are inspired with the hope of eternal happiness. They love their country with the spontaneous and ardent love of all patriots, because it is their country and the source to them of untold blessings. They prefer its form of government before any other. They admire its institutions and the spirit of its laws. They accept the Constitution without reserve, with no desire, as Catholics, to see it changed in any feature. They can with a clear conscience swear to uphold it.

With an appreciation, the greater because their fathers or they themselves have known persecution—in the British Isle, in Germany, in Poland and elsewhere—they prize both the liberty they enjoy as citizens and the liberty assured to the Church. The separation of Church and State in this country seems to them the natural, inevitable and best conceivable plan, the one that would work best among us, both for the good of religion and of the State. Any change in their relations they would contemplate with dread. They are well aware, indeed, that the Church here enjoys a larger liberty and a more secure position than in any other country to-day where Church and State are united. They have a deep distrust and strong dislike of the

SOURCE: James Cardinal Gibbons, "The Church and the Republic," _North American Review,_ Vol. 189, No. 640 (March 1909), pp. 321–328.

[74] Herberg, op. cit., p. 146.

intermeddling of the State with the concerns of religion: and such a restriction as
the Church was obliged to endure in France, binding the Pope to choose Catholic
bishops only from among the candidates presented to him by the unbelieving
Government officials, seems to them—not fully appreciating the difficulties of
the situation—a scandal and a shame. They most assuredly desire never to see a like
system introduced into the governing of the Church in America. No establishment
of religion is being dreamed of here, of course, by any one; but, were it to be attempted, it would meet with the united opposition of the Catholic people, priests
and prelates.

Catholics feel at home among their countrymen. They are conscious of an un-
stained record of loyalty, of patriotic self-sacrifice and of law-abiding behavior.
Their dearest ambition is to live in peace with all, to antagonize no class; they are
conscious of no barrier separating them more than any other element of the population into a class apart. Strong in the knowledge that an overwhelming majority
of their fellow-citizens understand and appreciate them, they usually ignore the
occasional insults directed to them by a small and rapidly decreasing section of the
community not yet emancipated from ancestral misconception and prejudices, and
still wedded to the conviction that the Gospel is to be propagated by slander and
the fomentation of religious strife.

This form of religious propaganda Catholics know to be abhorrent to the spirit
of every true American; and on that spirit they rely to nullify the spasmodic efforts
of bigotry; for, though a large proportion of the non-Catholics do not sympathize
with Catholic doctrines, this dissent is not carried over into political or social life.
Men have learned in this country to disagree profoundly without rancor or bitterness. With no compromise of principle on either side, moral worth, sterling character, kindly qualities of mind and heart bind together in good-will, admiration and
friendship the lives of those who do not worship at the same altar. The non-Catholic American would receive with a contemptuous smile or an indignant gesture any
suggestion that his Catholic friend, or business associate, carried hidden in his heart
some sinister tenet that gave the lie to his life, and might at any moment oblige
him to turn traitor to the Republic.

The Catholic himself feels, as he has learned from the lips of his own revered and
trusted teachers of religion, that the more faithful he is to his religion the better
and nobler citizen will he be. That religion and patriotism could ever come into
conflict in his bosom seems to him an utter impossibility; and in the religious principles which he has received in common with his fellow Catholics he sees the surest
defence of the State against the forces of disorder and lawlessness, and the insidious
influences that work for the overthrow of our Christian moral standards in private
and public life.

Of this body of American citizens living such a life and imbued with such sentiments (of which there are almost as many proofs as there are Catholics), two synods of Protestant ministers have deemed it just and wise to proclaim to the country
that Catholics cannot be trusted with political office; that they cannot sincerely
subscribe to the Federal Constitution; that their loyalty is illogical, being contrary
to the teaching of the Church; that their religion is opposed to American liberties;
and that they themselves, kept in the dark by their religious guides, are ignorant of

the true nature of their Church's doctrines. In sounding forth these charges to American Catholics and to the country in general, they declare themselves inspired, not by religious antagonism or the desire to profit by a good opportunity, but solely by patriotic solicitude for the permanence of American institutions.

Charges so contrary to the abiding convictions of American Catholics and so hurtful to their deepest affections are naturally resented; yet they do not appear to have excited any commotion among us. It would indeed be a grave matter if these utterances expressed the judgment of the American nation, indicated its sentiments towards our Catholic citizens and preluded a departure from the national policy of religious liberty and equality before the law. Happily, we know this is very far from the fact. The truth is, we believe, these ministers not only do not represent the American attitude towards us, but would meet with determined opposition if they attempted to carry with them even their own congregations. They have good cause to complain, as they do, of the apathy of their co-religionists. . . .

The Catholic religion, as they understand it, is in conflict with the Federal Constitution, and with the object of our institutions. Catholics, then, ought not to be trusted with political office. Accordingly, Americans should seek to exclude Catholics from the chair of the President who is called upon to enforce the Constitution; from the Supreme Bench, whose duty it is to interpret it; from the Senate and the House of Representatives, which have the power to change it. And as the chief evil dreaded from the Catholics is a modification of the existing relations between Church and State, a power theoretically reserved to our State Governments, no Catholic should be chosen Governor, State legislator or judge of a supreme State court. This is the scope of their meaning, though not all explicitly avowed. It would logically be desirable to deny Catholics the right to vote, and with men in the frame of mind their attitude suggests, the realization of this desire in the statute-books, and of their complete programme, would only be a matter of their possessing sufficient power and judging the act politically expedient.

Now this proposal to exclude Catholics from office—for it is no mere theory, but a practical programme earnestly recommended to the American public by two solemn assemblies—is advocated expressly in the interest of religious liberty and for the sake of preserving the Federal Constitution. That document says: "no religious test shall ever be required as a qualification to any office or public trust under the United States." Just understand here, however, remark these Lutheran Baptist synods, an amendment or rather, let us say, a little clause which brings out the sense with admirable clearness: "provided, of course, that this provision be not understood to apply to Roman Catholics."

That Americans in general do not believe in these synodical principles is shown at every election, when . . .districts predominantly Catholic have repeatedly elected Protestants to office, and, *vice versa*, Catholics have been chosen by several strongly Protestant States as their Chief Magistrates or as their representatives in the Senate. Presidents of the United States have shown no lack of confidence in them, calling them into their cabinet, elevating them to the bench of the Supreme Court, one of whose Chief Justices was a Catholic, and charging them with important posts at home and abroad. Religious issues have sometimes been injected into campaigns, never, however, by Catholics so far as I can recall; but every one has a feeling that it is unfortunate and un-American. It has been done mostly in secret, for its authors were ashamed of the light.

It is a new thing, for the present generation at least, to see the chief authorities of important religious bodies advocating the exclusion of loyal American citizens from office on the sole ground of their religious allegiance. This act will be writ indelibly in the annals of our country in the chapter entitled "Religious Intolerance." And in the same chapter, history ought to record that the action, entirely clerical in origin, received no manifestations of sympathy with its aim or spirit from the laity, who thus earned the blame of their leaders (in things spiritual, but not in politics), and the approbation of the American people.

There must be no tampering with the delicate machinery by which religious liberty and equality are secured, and no fostering of any spirit which would tend to destroy that machinery. Religious passions are deep and strong; and any man in his senses who knows human nature or knows the history of Europe, and has at heart the future peace and happiness of our country, whatever his belief, will do nothing to introduce religious strife into the politics of America. Religious tolerance is not the easy superficial virtue it seems in these placid days; intolerance in the dominating party tends to produce intolerance in the injured party. Then religious peace is near an end, unless strong restraints be used. The spirit of the country has changed much in half a century, and it would be very difficult to arouse such fanaticism as I saw in the Know-Nothing days. Prudent men, men who are far-sighted, especially if they are in positions of responsibility, will work for peace and harmony. Such has always been the attitude of our Catholic hierarchy, and, with few exceptions, of our priesthood. I know not what to think of men, putting themselves forward as the leaders of large religious bodies, who counsel the American people to depart from that policy which has promoted peace and good-will among us and made us illustrious among nations for our spirit of liberty and liberality. What good can they hope to accomplish?

I am speaking in no tone of deprecation. We have nothing to fear for ourselves. We are strong, not only in our union and strength, but in the broad American spirit of fair play and love of liberty; and, I may be permitted to add, in our confidence that God destines the Catholic Church in this country to be the bulwark of law and order, of liberty, of social justice and purity. But I speak that I may put forth whatever strength I have to crush this detestable spirit of intolerance which, if it gained strength, would wreck the peace of the country and root out charity from the hearts of men. . . .

Although the first Jews in America came to New Amsterdam in 1624, the Jewish population was not a significant factor in the nation's life until the end of the nineteenth century, when massive numbers of eastern Europeans began to migrate to the New World. Among them were Jews. For the most part they settled in the great urban centers of the Northeast and Midwest and the majority have stayed there. Gaustad points out that today "one half of the nation's Jews reside in five counties in New York and eight in New Jersey."[75]

[75] Gaustad, op. cit., p. 844.

The Jews' problem vis-à-vis the religious consensus in America is somewhat different from that of the Catholics. Jews constitute less than 4 per cent of a predominantly Christian nation, whereas Catholics and Protestants can at least claim to be part of the same religious family, Christianity, but Jews are a distinct and separate religious family. This has not meant, however, that they are pariahs in America. Under the provision of the First Amendment they are guaranteed freedom of worship and belief. Although they were subject to vicious harrassment and intense persecution in the Know-Nothing days of the nineteenth century and from the Ku Klux Klan during the 1920s and although one occasionally reads of a blatant incident of anti-Semitism today, Jews have nevertheless found a permanent and distinct place in the American situation. Indeed, they have been able to exercise a disproportionate amount of influence in a number of fields.

Richard L. Rubenstein (1924–   ), whose own roots are in the Conservative tradition, examines from a Jewish perspective the meaning of religious liberty for Jews today. One should keep in mind, as Rubenstein reminds us in *After Auschwitz,* that the Nazi horror radically altered the way in which any Jew can think about religion in relation to the power of the state.

_____ *Document 21*

From "Church and State: The Jewish Posture"
by Richard L. Rubenstein

The history of Judaism has been more decisively determined by its external relations than that of any other major Western religious community. In view of the tragic events of Jewish history, it is impossible for Jews to enter discussion, dialogue, or competition with men of other faiths without concern for the eventual entailments of that encounter. No other American faith group devotes as much of its organizational energies to interfaith and community relations activities. This is understandable in terms of Jewish history.

It is impossible to understand Jewish reactions within the domain of intergroup relations, especially the highly sensitive and volatile area of church-state problems, apart from the Jewish experience that Jewish relations with non-Jews have led, and can again lead, to genocide on a vast and inhuman scale. It is also impossible to divorce the Jewish posture on church-state issues from the two-thousand-year-old history of the Judeo-Christian conflict. The rival faiths have never been entirely independent and distinct religious movements. The church has always regarded itself as the fulfillment and true successor of the synagogue rather than as an entirely separate movement. For Christians, Jesus as the Christ is the promised Messiah of Israel, foretold and anticipated in the Old Testament. For Jews, Jesus is no more than one

SOURCE: Richard L. Rubenstein, "Church and State: The Jewish Posture" from *Religion and the Public Order,* edited by Donald A. Gianella (Chicago: University of Chicago Press, 1964). Reprinted by permission of the University of Chicago Press.

Jew among many. To the extent that he has significance, it is only because of the misfortunes which have befallen Israel as a result of his career. Attempts on the part of liberal Jews to see him as a continuation of the prophetic tradition, or as a teacher bearing revelation to the non-Jewish world, are clearly contrary to normative Jewish sentiment.

The two religious positions cannot be mediated. Only one of them can conceivably be true. Furthermore, there is far more at stake than mere verbal debate. Since the Christian's eternal salvation is ultimately dependent upon his relationship to the Christ, he cannot be unconcerned with the denials of the Jewish community, the very community upon which revelation was originally bestowed and to whom the promise of the Messiah was given.

One of the most important difficulties faced by Jews in their contacts with believing Christians is that they are seldom, if ever, regarded as commonplace human beings rather than as actors in the divine drama of heaven and hell, salvation and damnation. In reality, Jews simply do not live primarily in the religious dimension in their day-to-day lives despite the meta-historical interpretation given to Jewish existence in normative Jewish faith. Were it possible to construct a phenomenology of Jewish self-discovery, it would be seen that, for the contemporary Jew, the theological dimension is the last to become operative. For the vast majority of Jews, as for Christians, it lies forever dormant. One trauma, however, is experienced by all Jews as they discover the meaning of their being-in-the-world-as Jews. They are struck with horror at the realization of the peculiar significance placed by Christianity on their rather commonplace existence. Even the special Jewish proclivity for cultural and intellectual attainment no longer elicits the sense of pride it once did. The contemporary Jew is likely to be all too well aware of the sociocultural forces which compel him to an excellence he would under normal circumstances forego.

In the Christian scheme, Jews are God bearers and God-murderers. Neither role is especially welcome to ordinary men, and Jews are simply very ordinary men compelled to live in a continuously abnormal life-situation. The Jewish reaction has been by and large both understandable and predictable. Wherever possible Jews have sought to extricate themselves from Christian influence and especially its theological concern for Jewish existence. This is not primarily because of any polemic attitude toward Christianity, but out of a conviction that life and dignity were at stake. Jews have entered modern life most comfortably in those areas in which Christian culture has not been privileged or dominant. Every major Jewish attempt to adjust to modernity has involved withdrawal from overt Christian religious influence. I want to stress the word *withdrawal*. There have been private attempts on the part of the Jews actively to surrender to or to combat Christianity. Neither alternative has ever been the intention or the program of responsible Jews, affirmatively identified with Jewish life. The very act of identification normally implied a perspective on history and social order which understood the inevitability of the continuing presence and influence of Christianity in the culture of the West.

In modern times, Jewish equality of status within the political order has been possible only when and where official Christianity has ceased to be privileged. Where the special pre-eminence of the Christian church remained a relevant political fact, Jews have never been able to attain genuine equality of condition within that community. Jews have also fared best in multi-national and multi-ethnic political communities such as the old Austro-Hungarian Empire or contemporary America.

Jews basically want nothing more than the opportunity to participate in American life under conditions of maximum equality with their fellow citizens. This is the simple practical basis for Jewish sentiment favoring separation of church and state in the United States. The Jewish community has had the experience of living as a minority for a very long time. Out of this experience, it has come to understand the incompatibility of any position other than absolute political neutrality in any religious matters with the demands of equality. As has been indicated, nothing within Jewish tradition favors the separation of the religious and political orders. Nevertheless, everything within Jewish experience does. Were there none but Jews in America and were there a unanimity of Jewish assent on religious matters, there would probably be no such separation. Theologically speaking, one might describe the current situation as a concomitant of the confusion of tongues. I believe most responsible Jewish leaders would agree with Martin Marty's comment that "pluralism is a ground rule and not an altar." It is called for, not by our ideologies, but by the facticity of our concrete, limited situations. As long as America remains a multi-ethnic and multi-religious community, there can be no equitable alternative to political neutrality in religious affairs. . . .

I would go further and suggest that one of the worst aspects of the current debate on church and state is the frequent repetition of some thoroughly specious arguments about the indispensability of religious training for the promotion of virtue. I would not dispute the contention that insightful religious training can and frequently does lead to a life in which the moral dimension is taken seriously in act as well as in thought. But to assert the indispensability of a religious background for morality is to fail to do justice to countless men and women who, while unable to believe in a personal God, have led just and decent lives.

Modernity has known few men of the moral stature of Albert Camus. He was, in his writings and in his person, a thoroughgoing pagan. Camus elected paganism and rejected the Judeo-Christian heritage because he found paganism more consistent with the demands of a moral order and human solidarity than either Judaism or Christianity. His own life was certainly testament to the quality of a life lived very well and very decently without God.

One of the most precious fruits of the religious life is the heightened affirmation of fellow men in the meeting of *I* and *Thou.* Let no man, however, insist upon the *necessity* of religion for this precious gift. The rights of secularists, atheists, and pagans are as deserving of protection as the rights of the most pious. I do not think I err when I suggest that such rights are very much the concern of Jewish religious leaders, though I must emphatically repeat that such ideologies are normally incompatible with Jewish religious sentiment.

What I am suggesting is that Jewish concern for the individual goes beyond securing for him the opportunity to follow his own beliefs. It insists, particularly in a pluralistic society, that as far as possible his right to participate fully in the life of the community be recognized. Neutrality of the state toward religion is the only way to avoid excluding from full participation in community life the many secular humanists who share with the most devoted followers of any Western religion respect for human dignity and the worth of the individual. Recognition of this helps explain the position taken by Jews on many church-state issues.

Thus, while few rabbis objected to the actual content of the Regents' Prayer, most approved of the Supreme Court decision forbidding it in *Engel* v. *Vitale*. Few, if any, in their ranks could feel comfortable with Chief Judge Desmond's defense of the prayer when it was upheld by the New York Court of Appeals. Chief Judge Desmond declared:

> Belief in a Supreme Being is as essential and permanent a feature of the American governmental system as is freedom of worship, equality under the law and due process of law. Like them, it is an American absolute, an application of the natural law beliefs on which the Republic was founded, and which in turn presuppose an Omnipotent Being.

The implication in Chief Judge Desmond's statement that atheists and agnostics are ultimately enemies of the Republic naturally recalls to the Jewish mind its own experience with persecution and disenfranchisement and evokes sympathy for the secular humanist.

On the issue of Bible reading and the Lord's Prayer in the schools the opposition of the Jewish community is certainly understandable. More than prinicple is involved in these cases. These practices naturally tend to exclude Jews from full participation in the community. Apart from all questions of version and translation to be employed, Christians and Jews do not mean the same thing when they speak of the Bible. There can be no doubt that the New Testament cannot but divide Christian and Jew. This is going to happen in any event, but equity demands that institutions such as the public school, to which both Christian and Jew are committed and which both support, not be used as instruments of such division.

The Lord's Prayer is a very special case. The prayer itself is among the most beautiful, simple, and moving ever uttered. Jews, however, find it utterly impossible both to be true to their own traditions and to recite it. In its context, it is very clearly a prayer for the disciples and followers of Jesus. As such, it is one of the most precious possessions of Christendom, but Jews are neither disciples nor followers of Jesus. It thus becomes impossible for Jews to utter the Lord's Prayer without a rejection of their own traditions.

I believe that Mr. Walter Lippmann's comments on the 1963 Supreme Court decision unintentionally reflect a perspective most Jewish leaders would endorse:

> Those who are concerned with the content of secularized public education (and much private education as well) should look upon the decision of the court as having closed a blind alley that led nowhere. The forbidden religious exercises would not and could not have dealt with the great moral and intellectual deficiencies of American education. The exercises were harmless and negligible. But had they been allowed to evolve, they could have led only to religious quarrels. . . .

America represents a new experiment for Jews. It offers the promise of an equality of condition which Jews have never known, even in the most advanced European nations. Like every human ideal, this promise cannot be extricated from the human context in which it is offered. The ideals implicit in law can never entirely be fulfilled. At best, they can be reasonably approximated. Jews do not really expect that the separation of the religious and political orders will ever be completely achieved. This would be possible only if human beings who constitute the raw material of both orders were capable of an almost schizophrenic act of self-division. The absolute application of logic to human affairs leads not to justice but to murder, as the terror of the French Revolution and the rational terror of communism and nazism demonstrate. Nevertheless, historical Jewish experience has taught us that the ideal of a government neutral in religious matters offers the only hope for equality of condition for all men in a multi-ethnic and multi-religious community. Historical experience has also taught us that nothing is gained by the failure of the Jew to seek his rights under law when and where it is possible so to do. Finally, Jews are absolutely convinced that the decisions of our courts must be obeyed and respected. No insight is as deeply or as persistently present in Judaism as the conviction that society is radically imperiled when men assert a priority of personal inclination over the majesty of the law, for in Judaism God Himself is the Bestower and Teacher of the Law.

It is perhaps not inappropriate to end this section of readings on religious liberty with a statement issued by the direct descendants of the Protestant groups who, back in colonial days, enjoyed the privilege of establishment in one or more of the colonies. Today these same groups, who once enjoyed that privilege, want to make sure that disestablishment sticks. The National Council of Churches is, after all, made up of the major American Protestant denominations whose antecedents were, among others, the Congregationalists in New England, the Anglicans in the South, the Swedish Church in Delaware, and the Dutch Reformed in New York. The Council of Churches has, of course, no binding power over its constitutive group; it is, rather, a loose confederation of Protestant churches that cooperate on many programs that will in no way impair the identity of any denominational group. The Council has been particularly conscious of social, economic, and political issues and has provided instruments for cooperation on missionary and educational programs.

When the Supreme Court issued its rulings on prayer and Bible reading in the public schools, a storm of protest broke that has not yet abated. At every session of Congress since then, bills have been introduced to adopt a Constitutional amendment making prayer and Bible reading permissible as a school function. The Council of Churches, sensitive to the delicate and complex nature of religious freedom, has systematically opposed such moves and has sought to give support to the rulings by the Court. The following "policy statement" was adopted in

1963 and presents in lucid and compelling fashion a "Christian" position on religious liberty, which guarantees equal rights and protection for all groups and individuals.

Document 22 _____

From *Pronouncement on the Churches and the Public Schools*

As Americans we are firmly committed to the right of freedom of conscience and freedom of religion, that is, the freedom of each citizen in the determination of his religious allegiance, and the freedom of religious groups and institutions in the exercise and declaration of their beliefs.

The American tradition with respect to the relations of government and religion, often described as "separation of church and state" does not mean that the state is hostile toward, or indifferent to, religion. On the contrary, governments—national, state and local—have prevailingly acknowledged the importance as well as the autonomy of religion and have given expression to this principle in many ways.

In present-day American society, with its diversity of religious conviction and affiliations, the place of religion in public education must be worked out within this recognition of the prevailing positive attitude of the American people as a whole toward religion and safeguarding of religious liberty. . . .

Concern for the Public Schools

We reaffirm our support of the system of public education in the United States of America. It provides a context in which all individuals may share in an education which contributes to the full development of their capacities. It serves as a major cohesive force in our pluralistic society. We also recognize that significant value derives from the fact that this system is financed by public funds, is responsive to the community as a whole, and is open to all without distinctions as to race, creed, national origin, or economic status.

Definition of Roles

Religious ideas, beliefs, values, and the contributions of churches are an integral part of our cultural heritage as a people. The public schools have an obligation to help individuals develop an intelligent understanding and appreciation of the role of religion in the life of the people of this nation. Teaching for religious commitment is the responsibility of the home and the community of faith (such as the church or synagogue) rather than the public schools.

We support the right of religious groups to establish and maintain schools at their own expense provided they meet prescribed education standards.

We support also the right of parents to decide whether their children shall attend public or non-public schools. The parent who chooses to send his children to a non-

SOURCE: *Pronouncement on the Churches and the Public Schools,* adopted by the General Board of the National Council of the Churches of Christ in the United States of America (June 7, 1963).

public school is not excused from the responsibility of the citizen to support and seek to improve the public schools.

Neither the church nor the state should use the public school to compel acceptance of any creed or conformity to any specific religious practice.

It is an essential task of the churches to provide adequate religious instruction through every means at their disposal. These include both those activities which individual churches provide within their own walls and also various joint ventures of churches involving cooperation with the public schools. Christian nurture and the development and practice of Christian worship are inescapable obligations of the congregation and the family. We warn the churches against the all-too-human tendency to look to the state and its agencies for support in fulfilling the churches' mission. Such a tendency endangers both true religion and civil liberties. At the same time, we call the churches to renewed worship, study, work and sacrifice to fulfill their mission as God's people in the world.

Place of Religion in the Public Schools

No person is truly educated for life in the modern world who is not aware of the vital part played by religion in the shaping of our history and culture, and of its contemporary expressions. Information about religion is an essential part of many school subjects such as social studies, literature and the arts. The contributions of religious leaders, movements, and ideas should be treated objectively and broadly in any presentation of these subjects. Public school administrators and textbook producers are to be commended for the progress made to date in including objective information about religion in various subject matter fields. Teachers should be trained to deal with the history, practices, and characteristics of the various religious groups with competence and respect for diverse religious convictions. Their greatest influence will be through the life and attitudes they reflect in the classroom. They should be free as persons to express their own convictions in answer to direct questions from pupils when appropriate to the subject matter under study.

The full treatment of some regular school subjects requires the use of the Bible as a source book. In such studies—including those related to character development—the use of the Bible has a valid educational purpose. But neither true religion nor good education is dependent upon the devotional use of the Bible in the public school program.

The Supreme Court of the United States in the Regents' Prayer case has ruled that "in this country it is no part of the business of government to compose official prayers for any group of the American people to recite as part of a religious program carried on by the government." We recognize the wisdom as well as the authority of this ruling. But whether prayers may be offered at special occasions in the public schools may well be left to the judgment of the board responsible for the program of the public schools in the local community.

While both our tradition and the present temper of our nation reflect a preponderant belief in God as our Source and our Destiny, nevertheless attempts to establish a "common core" of religious beliefs to be taught in public schools have usually proven unrealistic and unwise. Major faith groups have not agreed on a formulation of religious beliefs common to all. Even if they had done so, such a body of religious doctrine would tend to become a substitute for the more demanding commitments of historic faiths.

Some religious holidays have become so much a part of American culture that the public school can scarcely ignore them. Any recognition of such holidays in the public schools should contribute to better community understanding and should in no way divert the attention of pupils and the community from the celebration of these holidays in synagogues and churches.

We express the conviction that the First Amendment to our Constitution in its present wording has provided the framework within which responsible citizens and our courts have been able to afford maximum protection for the religious liberty of all our citizens.

Church Support of Public Schools

American public education should have the full and conscientious support of Christians and Christian churches. Therefore, we urge our constituency to continue efforts to strengthen and improve the American system of public education through positive steps such as the following:

1. Providing intelligent appraisal and responsible criticism of programs of public education;
2. Keeping informed about the needs of the public schools and studying issues related to public education as a basis for intelligent action as citizens;
3. Supporting able candidates for boards of education and being willing to serve as members of such boards;
4. Working at local, state, and national levels for improved legislative and financial support of public schools;
5. Emphasizing to prospective and present teachers the profession of public school teaching as a vocation that is worthy of the best service a Christian can give;
6. Exploring cooperative arrangements of the churches and schools whereby the church's teaching of religion may be improved.

In American education, there is a substantial inter-relation between primary, secondary and higher education.

It needs to be stressed that, in a substantial majority of publicly-maintained institutions of Higher Education, provision is offered for the voluntary election of courses in religion on a parity with all other subjects of the curriculum, and not infrequently for publicly-supported chaplains and other services of religion.

The question should be explored whether these arrangements through which religious instruction and services are provided within state institutions of Higher Education without infringement of law or offense to individual conscience may not offer suggestion for more adequate provision within the public schools of opportunities for the study of religion where desired, fully within the constitutional guarantees of freedom of conscience and of religious expression.

Summary

The American experiment with religious liberty continues. Almost daily we hear or read about the conflict between those who try to impose religious uniformity on others and those who resist it. The battle-grounds are familiar: religious programs in public schools, tax support for sectarian schools, tax exemption on church-owned property, and so on. In the quest for equity in religious disputes, the American people have, in the main, relied on the courts to settle the conflict between competing claims. Admittedly, some of the more extreme believers have refused to acknowledge the authority of the courts, but most people have accepted the judicial wisdom.

Aside from its role as an arbitrator in settling disputes about religious matters, we would be remiss without commenting on the Supreme Court as a civil religious entity. Although Americans ordinarily think of the court as a secular institution, it is clear that it is an important religious institution as well. In the context of Chapter 1 and civil religion, it can be argued that the members of the Court play significant roles as hierarchs of the civil faith. Indeed, Max Lerner has so argued: "the constitution is our Scripture, the Court building is our Temple, and the judges are our high priests." [76]

Because the ultimate religious authority in America rests with the Court, which has refused to favor one ecclesial group over another, the religious bodies have not been able to call on the power of the government to enforce religious uniformity. Instead, the religious groups have become purely voluntary societies that have had to employ the power of persuasion to enlist and keep their constituencies. Thus, revivalism in its various mutations and forms has become the method and device by which some American ecclesial religious groups have attempted to maintain their memberships. The next chapter will explore revivalism as a principal motif in American religion.

[76] See Max Lerner "The Constitution and the Court as Symbols," *Yale Law Journal,* Vol. 46 (1937), pp. 1290–1319.

Revivalism

Whitfield
Frelinghuysen

J. Edwards
Gil + Wm Tennent

American religious patterns are always in flux, never static, and in our present technological era the changes seem to come more rapidly than ever before. Following the end of World War II, in 1945, the country experienced an upsurge in religious interest and involvement. Most observers characterized what was happening as a religious revival, utilizing a familiar descriptive category, though some doubted the depth and permanence of the phenomenon.[1] The decade of the 1960s witnessed a drastic change as the religious prosperity of the previous years began to fade and many churches and religious leaders became preoccupied with political and social issues. But by 1970 a further change had begun to take place as the religious community began to react against the social and political activism of the 1960s and renewed indication of religious revival, albeit in significantly different forms, appeared on the scene. A brief look at these successive changes is instructive.

In the decade and a half following World War II, religion in America rode an unprecedented wave of popularity. Church attendance soared to new heights, contributions to religious causes broke all records, and more than $1 billion annually was spent on church building. Theological seminaries were crowded with young men, many of them veterans of World War II and the Korean war, training for the ministry. Even radio disc jockeys "got religion," and the motion pictures made popular heroes of men like U.S. Senate Chaplain Peter Marshall.[2] At least one religious volume could usually be found on the national best-seller list, and Congress amended the pledge of allegiance to the flag to include the phrase *under God.* Never had religion been held in greater public esteem.

The religious upsurge of the 1950s was a multifaceted phenomenon, drawing on many sources and permeating almost every area of American life. But perhaps its most striking feature was the renewed popularity of the traditional revival meeting or evangelistic crusade, a distinctive American contribution to religious life. The revival meeting is a mode of spiritual outreach designed to reawaken the faith of believers and to reach and persuade large numbers of unbelievers in a relatively short and concentrated period. Many specific individuals and events were central in the postwar revival, but the most representative figure was Billy Graham (1918–   ), a popular Baptist evangelist whose citywide

[1] See, for example, Will Herberg, *Protestant-Catholic-Jew: An Essay in American Religious Sociology* (Garden City, N.Y.: Doubleday, 1960), pp. 2ff.

[2] The filmed story of Marshall's career, *A Man Called Peter*, was a popular hit in movie theaters during the 1950s, along with many other films with religious themes.

crusades in major American population centers, radio and television productions, motion pictures, and books combined to give a new lease on life to "mass evangelism," once thought to be on the verge of disappearing from the religious scene. Graham represented a distinctive American tradition as a legitimate descendant of the great revivalists of the past—Charles G. Finney, Dwight L. Moody, Billy Sunday, and others of like talent—who have played important roles in shaping American religion.

But Graham was not the only striking figure in the postwar revival. Using approaches consistent with their own theological commitments and personal styles, such men as Norman Vincent Peale (1898–   ), minister of the Marble Collegiate (Reformed) Church in New York; Rabbi Joshua L. Liebman (1907–1948), author of the best-selling *Peace of Mind* (1946); and Oral Roberts (1917–   ), a traveling Pentecostal evangelist who emphasized faith healing, drew large followings. Monsignor Fulton J. Sheen's (1895–1979) popular television programs and publications supplied a type of Catholic counterpart to Graham's Protestant thrust and Liebman's Jewish appeal. To some it may seem incongruous to lump together in this way men so different in theological outlook and method. Obviously, Graham, Roberts, and their colleagues represented revivalism in the more traditional sense, whereas Peale, Liebman, and Sheen functioned as religious evangelists with more unique styles and methods. Yet each in his own way contributed to the remarkable mass appeal of religion in the 1950s. Obviously, enthusiasm was not confined to any restricted sector of America's churches and faith traditions.

Another significant facet of the revival was its appeal to American intellectuals. Robert Maynard Hutchins, then president of the University of Chicago, could refer somewhat cynically to the religious message as "the good news of damnation,"[3] but secular leaders of thought did listen, particularly to theologians like Reinhold Niebuhr (1892–1971) and Paul Tillich (1886–1965). A considerable number of intellectuals were drawn into deep religious commitment, including men like Episcopal Bishop James A. Pike (1913–1970), who before his "conversion" was a brilliant lawyer and a professed agnostic. Another example was Will Herberg, noted Jewish teacher and writer, who, interestingly enough, attributed his return to the Jewish faith to his reading of the theology of Protestant Reinhold Niebuhr.

Not so obviously affected by the revival were the alienated groups in American society: the blacks, the Latin Americans of the Southwest, the ghetto dwellers in the big cities. Black Christians, of course, had long used the revival technique as an integral part of their worship and church life. But to many younger, rebellious blacks the whole procedure appeared to be simply another way of avoiding more pressing social issues—of shoring up the status quo. Men like Martin Luther King, Jr.

[3] See Hudson, op. cit., p. 383.

(1929–1968), who might well have been charismatic revivalists in another day, turned their energies instead to the civil rights movement, bypassing the white-oriented evangelistic campaigns. Latins, Catholic by tradition, were virtually untouched by the mainstream revival excitement. And in the ghettos, aside from the continuing efforts of groups such as the Salvation Army and the perennial presence of small, struggling "storefront" churches, little religious change was evidenced.

As the decade of the 1950s drew to a close, however, signs indicated that the excitement was waning. Martin Marty, associate editor of the influential religious weekly *The Christian Century*, believed that the beginning of the end of the revival occurred as early as 1957 and that the downward pace merely accelerated in the following decade.[4] Church attendance leveled off and then began a gradual decline. Many local churches and denominational organizations found themselves in financial difficulty as contributions began to fall off. Overseas missionary efforts had to be curtailed. Many young people felt themselves alienated from the traditonal churches, and their religious interests centered in such nontraditional developments as the "Jesus people," along with new movements with roots in Eastern or Oriental religion— such as the Hare Krishna sect and Zen Buddhist groups. American old-line religious groups faced a new challenge, not only to recruit members but also to hold the loyalties of those already involved, especially the masses of restless young.

Marty characterized the 1960s as a time of religious revolution, contrasting it with the revival of the 1950s.[5] A dramatic cultural and religious shift occurred. Graham and others like him were more and more regarded by a considerable segment of Americans as representative of another age, battling stubbornly to maintain the traditional religious "establishment." Attacks on familiar, long-established institutions, including the churches, were widespread.

The shift in religion was, as always, part of a larger cultural change. The Russian Sputnik had shot into the heavens and the Space Age had dawned. A movement for racial integration was sweeping the nation and the churches could not ignore its implications, either for themselves or for society as a whole. In southeast Asia, the war in Vietnam involved more and more American material, technical aid, and, eventually, American soldiers. An increasing number of Americans, including many religious leaders, came to see the war as morally wrong and militarily pointless. Latin America verged on revolution, and Cuba went Communist. Religion and the churches faced a new kind of world with new focal points of controversy, and the old institutions and time-honored techniques—such as revivalism—seemed useless and irrelevant to many.

[4] Martin E. Marty, *The New Shape of American Religion* (New York: Harper & Row, 1958), p. 11.
[5] See Marty, "The Revival and the Revolution," in *Religion American Style*, edited by Patrick H. McNamara (New York: Harper & Row, 1974), p. 107.

The result was argument and tension within the churches. Often this conflict was characterized as a division between the pulpit and the pew, between clergy and laity, but actually it arose out of the friction between a certain kind of clergy, and many lay people banded together against another kind of clergy-lay coalition. The conservatives held to the old ways and the old attitudes, accusing their more radical opponents of meddling in political and social issues while neglecting the gospel and the spiritual mission of the church. The radicals sought to push the churches into the arena of social conflict, opposing the Vietnam war and the military draft, supporting racial integration in the churches and in society, and coming to the aid of "Third World" forces struggling for economic and political independence.

This schism in religious ranks was inevitably reflected in the churches' attitude toward evangelism. Although many conservative groups continued to embrace revivalism as a central evangelistic technique, response to most of their efforts was limited. Though Graham's personal popularity continued, no clear successors to him in the field of evangelism arose. Fewer local congregations sponsored revival meetings, and on college campuses the denominational student ministries, highly successful in the years following World War II, found themselves in contact with fewer and fewer students. Even those highly conservative youth movements that continued to enjoy considerable popularity, such as Campus Crusade for Christ and Young Life, moved away from traditional revival methods. Once again, as in the past, revivalism, at least in its historically recognizable forms, appeared on its way out as a significant American religious phenomenon.

The decade of the 1970s brought new shifts in the American religious situation. Once again, Martin Marty detected the beginnings of the change as early as 1965 or 1966.[6] A backlash against the religious social activism of the era began to take form, even among more progressive elements in the churches. The Vietnam war ended, leaving a legacy of disillusionment. The racial revolution took a new turn, once it had achieved notable success in altering racially discriminatory laws, and began to emphasize black pride and ethnic political and economic power. As black militants became increasingly assertive, many religious leaders who had advocated racial integration in the churches, for instance, began to endorse segregation, so long as it was voluntary and what blacks seemed to want. Watergate oozed across the political stage, and millions of Americans were repelled by what they perceived as a drama of moral rot and corruption in high places.

The decline in church membership and attendance stopped, leveled off, and then began to climb, though slowly. And the stirrings of revival were felt once again, as so often before in American religious history. The new stirrings, however, took on distinctively different forms. No new Moody, Finney, or Graham appeared on the horizon.

[6] Ibid., p. 113.

Instead, there was an upsurge of charismatic and "Pentecostal" enthusiasm, emphasizing spiritual gifts such as "speaking in tongues" and faith healing. The new revivalism was not confined, however, to the pentecostal and holiness churches, which have played an increasingly important role in American religion since their emergence at the beginning of this century. Rather, it penetrated the ranks of virtually every Protestant denomination as well as American Catholicism. Once an object of derision, in the 1970s Pentecostal religion became almost fashionable. One observer has estimated that by 1975 more than 5 million Americans were part of the charismatic revival, and its influence stretched all the way from staid and decorous Episcopal congregations to storefront churches in the urban slums.[7]

Revival was breaking out in other forms as well. One of the most significant developments of the 1970s was the emergence of the "media church." Building on the groundwork laid by the radio evangelists of the 1950s and the more solid foundations established by men such as Billy Graham, who had demonstrated how effectively modern communication media can be used for religious purposes, a spate of television ministries and organizations began to play a more and more influential role. These spread their own brands of religious revival, usually extremely conservative and often charismatic. Receiving most attention was the PTL ("Praise The Lord") Club, a polished production using the television talk-show format. By the end of the 1970s, it was appearing almost daily on hundreds of television stations across the nation. But there were many others—television personalities like Rex Humbard, Robert Shuler, and Jerry Falwell, to mention only a few. The "media church" became the primary religious commitment of millions of Americans. Instead of attending local church services, many sat by their television sets, and they poured their prayers, money, and support into these ministries.

Once again, the obituaries for revivalism as an integral feature of American religion seem, as so often in the past, to have been premature. Perhaps the major lesson for the student of American religion to learn is that it is impossible to understand American religion without paying attention to the phenomenon of revivalism. One cannot ignore the strong and definitive influences that revivalism has exerted on the historical development of American religion, just as one must not overlook its continuing power today.

Revivalism, of course, is only one aspect of the evangelistic outreach of religious organizations. *Evangelism* is the more general term used to describe the total attempt of churches, by whatever method, to enlist new members or make converts. Revivalism, strictly speaking, as has been indicated earlier, is that particular kind of evangelism in which people, usually in a mass situation, are exhorted to make an immediate

---

[7]David Edwin Harrell, Jr., *All Things Are Possible* (Bloomington: Indiana University Press, 1975), p. 3. Harrell's book is a comprehensive survey of the healing and charismatic revival.

religious decision. They are urged, for instance, "to accept Christ as savior." What is aimed for in the revival meeting is an act of will on the part of the individual. This voluntary decision is often though not always accompanied by considerable emotional excitement.

Revivalism in colonial New England, on the American frontier, and in the developing urban and industrial centers, took varying forms. One aid to understanding the background of contemporary American religion is to apply the interpretative model of challenge and response. From this perspective revivalism is seen to have emerged as part of a response to the challenge of a growing system of American free churches competing for members in a religious pluralism. The disestablishment of state churches after the American Revolution and the spelling out of religious liberty in the First Amendment to the Constitution made voluntarism—the free choice of church affiliation—a permanent feature of the American scene. Such a condition made it imperative that churches actively recruit new members and that they develop effective methods for the persuasion of individuals to make voluntary commitments and to remain faithful to those commitments. Only in this manner could the churches gain and hold their membership.

Thus, the contemporary alterations in the mode of traditional revivalism can be partially understood as a function of the search for a different, more effective type of evangelistic response to the challenges of a changing cultural situation. Revivalism proved itself a successful means by which to deal with the religious needs of a frontier, agrarian America. With modifications it functioned well in the early stages of urbanization. But the social, cultural, and intellectual patterns of today's technological society have forced religious groups to search for more imaginative means of religious recruitment and enthusiasm. Evangelism is not only the extension of earnest concern for people's souls, but also the impulse toward survival for religious institutions and movements.

To gain some appreciation of the indelible marks left on the mainstream of American religious life by revivalism, it is convenient to analyze historical revivalism in three segments: the Great Awakening (roughly 1735–1760), the Second Awakening (1790–1820), and developing urban revivalism (1840–1965).

The Great Awakening

In the first decades of the eighteenth century, the vigorous drive and intense spirituality characteristic of much earlier New England Puritanism had begun to dissipate. Anglicanism in the colonies, except in isolated instances, had never possessed an overabundance of vitality. The steady influx of new settlers, attracted far more because of economic than religious reasons, added to the general religious apathy, whereas troublesome sectarian groups like the Quakers and the Baptists, drawn by the relative religious freedom of the New World, disturbed the orthodoxy of the established churches.

In retrospect it can be seen that there had been a steady movement in colonial life, almost from the beginning, toward a new and radical pattern of religious organization: a system of free and voluntaristic churches existing side by side in equality and in competition with each other. This important development has already been discussed at some length in Chapter 2, and its effects are one essential clue to the rise of revivalism.

Many factors contributed to the gradual breakdown of the Puritan establishment in the New England colonies. Conservative Puritans strongly resisted the erosion of their favored position. Nathaniel Ward, in *The Simple Cobbler of Aggawan in America* (1647), objected to the presence of non-Congregationalists in New England. He argued: "God doth no where in his word tolerate Christian States to give Tolerations to such adversaries of his Truth, if they have power in their hands to prevent them. . . ." But all such arguments were ultimately ineffective, for the Puritan churches themselves were caught in the tide of religious indifference.

A general colonial cultural ethos emphasizing individual initiative and voluntaristic freedom in every area of life further weakened the hold of the established churches on the populace. The availability of seemingly unlimited space provided a freedom of movement undreamed of in the Old World.[8] If one did not agree with the prevailing patterns of religion, there always existed the possibility of moving on to new, unsettled areas. Economic opportunity encouraged a high degree of economic self-determinism: a man literally had the opportunity to "pull himself up by his own bootstraps." And the American frontier nourished the kind of political individualism that flowered into Jeffersonian and, later, Jacksonian democracy. Inevitably, these voluntaristic, individualistic emphases in economics and politics influenced, and were influenced by, the same strains in religion.

The deterioration of established religion and the rise of voluntarism quite naturally weakened the strength of organized religion as a whole. Although such basic religious convictions as the existence of a benevolent God and the overall validity of the Christian revelation were actually challenged by only a comparative few, the great majority of colonial Americans were not formally affiliated with any religious organization. The widespread popularity of rationalism in the eighteenth century further watered down orthodoxy in religious thought and led to the steady growth of so-called Arminianism in much religious thinking. *Arminianism* is the name given to a general type of theology that

---

[8] For a full and perceptive discussion of the importance of space in the development of the American religious pattern, see Sidney E. Mead, *The Lively Experiment* (New York: Harper & Row, 1963).

puts strong emphasis on the individual's own role in working out his or her eternal destiny. It insists that people must not only cooperate with God by seeking and accepting salvation but that they must also help to insure their salvation by leading good moral lives. The Arminian flavor in religion, in contrast to early Calvinism, with its insistence on the total helplessness of depraved humanity to do anything at all about its sinful state, was congenial to a New World frontier culture.

The response of the churches to the challenges of religious apathy and the erosion of their own favored position in the colonies took several forms. One type of response involved a steady relaxation, particularly in many Puritan congregations, of the requirements for church membership. Originally Puritan piety had conceived of full membership in a church as dependent on two factors: a clear and credible testimony of religious conversion and the maintenance of a moral and blameless life in the community. Congregational or Puritan churches believed also that church membership for believing adults included their infant children, who were incorporated into God's saving covenant with their parents and therefore entitled to receive baptism. Upon attaining the age of discretion or "accountability," however, the child was expected to be able to give an account of his or her own repentance and faith and thus become qualified for full participation in the life of the church, including the right to take the Lord's Supper and to vote in church elections. This policy posed no real problem in a time of relative religious fervor, but when many baptized children grew to adulthood without ever giving evidence of any personal experience of God's grace, the situation became more serious. What was to be done with the infant children of these "half-way" church members? Were they, like their parents, entitled to be baptized and to become church members? Would not the result of this practice drastically increase the number of "unregenerate" members of the church? Further complicating the problem was the requirement in the New England colonies that voters or officeholders in the civil government should be church members. Church affiliation was, therefore, an important attribute to status and political power in the community.

Controversy over the matter was vigorous. Finally, in 1662, a position prevailed that came to be called the Half-Way Covenant. Children of the half-way members were to be baptized and brought into the church. For a time the churches insisted on barring such individuals from the Lord's Supper and church elections, though not from civic affairs. But gradually even this restriction was abandoned. Ministers like Solomon Stoddard (1643–1729), pastor of the church at Northampton, Mass- achusetts, argued that the "germ of grace" was present in all who had been baptized into the covenant and that this germ should be nourished and cultivated by partaking of the Lord's Supper. He thought of Com- munion as "a converting ordinance," a device by which the nonbelievers might be converted to Christianity. Although a number of more conservative Congregational churches refused to accept this position, it became more and more widespread. Such a membership grew not only out of theological convictions like those of Stoddard but also out of the need to retain individuals as members of the churches in a time of increasing religious indifference.

The Congregational church's experience in New England was typical of what was taking place in different forms within most of the American religious denominations in the first decades of the eighteenth century. Earlier dedication, springing from a deep conviction on the part of individuals that they had experienced a direct encounter with the redeeming grace of God, had been replaced in many quarters by rational or merely intellectual assent to a collection of orthodox beliefs and dogmas. Stress was more and more placed on the leading of a moral and "decent" life as the essence of religion. Such emphases, even when devoutly pursued, often tended to end in indifference to the churches.

Against this background the American colonies experienced in the middle years of the eighteenth century what H. Richard Niebuhr (1894–1962) has called a national conversion.[9] The Great Awakening, as it came to be known, drastically altered the shape of American religion, and it centered on an outbreak of spiritual fervor whose predominant form was revivalism. Whatever the causes of the Awakening, and they are both diverse and difficult to identify, it can be partly understood as a response by the colonial churches to the challenges of religious apathy and the decline of spiritual concern.

In terms of personalities and events it is customary to trace the beginnings of the Awakening to a series of local revivals that developed in northern New Jersey under the leadership of a Dutch Reformed[10] minister, Theodore Frelinghuysen (1691–1748?). Frelinghuysen began his ministry in the Raritan Valley in 1720. Disturbed by the perfunctory orthodoxy[11] of his parishioners, who seemed more concerned with maintaining their Dutch identity in the New World than with practicing their religious faith, he began to preach an evangelical gospel with fervor and audacity. He called for a return to strict church discipline, especially with regard to admission to the Lord's Supper. He admonished his hearers concerning the necessity of a "holy life" and demanded public acknowledgment and penance for sin.[12] Such preaching predictably aroused strong opposition, particularly from many of Frelinghuysen's fellow ministers, who branded his conduct scandalous and unbecoming to a minister of the gospel. But his people responded in such numbers as to draw attention from other sections of the country, and

---

[9] H. Richard Niebuhr, *The Kingdom of God in America* (New York: Harper & Row, 1959), p. 126.
[10] The Dutch Reformed Church was a strongly Calvinistic body. In the colonies its strength was in New York and New Jersey, where Dutch immigrants had settled. After the Revolution it became the Reformed Church in America.
[11] Literally, "right opinion." In other words, Frelinghuysen thought his parishioners recited all the right beliefs but without conviction.
[12] Showing sorrow and remorse for wrongdoing.

it became clear that religious excitement of a high order was being generated.

Among those who saw and were influenced by the Frelinghuysen revivals was a representative of a notable family of colonial Presbyterian ministers, Gilbert Tennent (1703–1764). Gilbert's father, William Tennent, had arrived in Philadelphia in 1718, where he began to educate young men for the ministry in his own home. In 1735 he built a log cabin to serve as a school for ministers, the so-called Log College, which can be considered an academic ancestor of Princeton University. Here were trained at least eighteen ministers who became widely influential in the evangelical awakenings in the Middle Colonies. Three of the eighteen were William Tennent's own sons: Gilbert, John, and William, Jr.

In 1726 Gilbert Tennent became pastor of the Presbyterian church at New Brunswick, New Jersey, located in the same area as the Dutch Reformed congregations touched by Frelinghuysen's preaching. Tennent and Frelinghuysen became fast friends, and Tennent, inspired by Frelinghuysen's example, soon began to preach in a similar vein to his Presbyterian flock. Inveighing against what he termed the "presumptuous security" of those who professed to be Christians, he accused church members of paying lip service to orthodox doctrine but of giving little or no evidence of any transforming personal power of the Christian gospel in their lives. Tennent called for "conviction," that is, for a personal recognition of sinfulness, and for the making of a decisive choice between everlasting damnation without God's grace or eternal joy through salvation by faith. He insisted that no person could become a Christian without first undergoing the terrible experience of fully realizing that he or she was *not* a Christian and was, in fact, "lost." Only then, proclaimed Tennent, could that person, aware of his or her own sinful helplessness, receive and appropriate God's merciful forgiveness.

In the next decade the Awakening spread rapidly among the Presbyterians of the Middle Colonies. Joined by his brother, John (1723–1764), and other "alumni" of the Log College such as Samuel Blair (1712–1751), Gilbert Tennent carried the fervor of the revival to numerous churches in New Jersey, Pennsylvania, and New York. The response was striking, as numbers of people, many of them already church members, professed conversion to the Christian faith. Apathetic congregations were revitalized and new ones organized. The revival gained additional impetus when, in 1735, Tennent's sermons began to be widely published, along with accounts of the revivals.

A third outbreak of evangelical excitement occurred in the Connecticut Valley, centering in the remarkable figure of Jonathan Edwards, a Puritan Congregationalist educated at Yale, who became pastor at Northampton, Massachusetts, in 1729. First and foremost a scholar, he composed sermons that, when studied today, impress one as closely reasoned and difficult expositions of theological doctrine. His voice and delivery were unimpressive, and he habitually read his lengthy discourses from the pulpit. Nevertheless, despite all apparent difficulties, extraordinary manifestations of revivalism were provoked by his preaching.

In 1737 Edwards's account of the revival in Northampton was published, first in London, then in Boston. Widely read throughout the colonies, the document was instrumental in spreading the fame of the awakening. For example, George Whitefield (1714–1770), the great English preacher who was to become the single most important figure in the Great Awakening, read it during his first visit to this country in 1738 and was profoundly influenced by it. The narrative was especially useful in its day because it gave a detailed description of exactly how the revival had taken place. This description became the pattern for similar efforts in other churches. Not surprisingly, a tendency developed for the revivals to become stereotyped, closely following the Edwards pattern, an effect that extended to the experience of personal religious conversion itself. Thus to be a "true" Christian came to mean, at least in circles influenced by the Awakening, to undergo a particular kind of spiritual experience. In Edwards's thought the desired experience blended both intellectual and emotional elements, both belief and feeling. In this way he sought to preserve the traditional Puritan emphasis on the necessity for a clear understanding of and assent to the basic structures of Christian doctrine, as well as to insist on the reality of personal commitment. But as revival fervor increased, more and more emphasis was placed on feeling and emotion, less and less on intellectual content and understanding. The change had long-term influences on the development of that large segment of American religion given formative shape by the revival phenomena.

Edwards's narrative was written in the form of a letter to an inquiring friend and began with a description of the "extraordinary dullness in religion" that pervaded the town of Northampton at the time he became pastor. The following excerpts from the document throw great light on this seminal development in American revivalism.

Document 23

From *A Faithful Narrative of the Surprising Work of God in the Conversion of Many Hundred Souls in Northampton and the Neighboring Towns and Villages* by Jonathan Edwards

The town of Northampton is about 82 years standing, and has now about 200 families; which mostly dwell more compactly together than any town of such a size in these parts of the country. This probably has been an occasion, that both our corruptions and reformations have been, from time to time, the more swiftly

SOURCE: Sereno D. Dwight (ed.), *The Works of President Edwards with a Memoir of His Life* (New York: B. Franklin, 1847), 10 vols.

propagated from one to another through the town. Take the town in general, and so far as I can judge they are as rational and intelligent a people as most I have been acquainted with . . . .

Just after my grandfather's death,[13] it seemed to be a time of extraordinary dullness in religion. Licentiousness for some years greatly prevailed among the youth of the town; they were many of them very much addicted to night-walking, and frequenting the tavern, and lewd practices, wherein some, by their example, exceedingly corrupted others. It was their manner very frequently to get together, in conventions of both sexes, for mirth and jollity, which they called frolics; and they would often spend the greater part of the night in them, without regard to any order in the families they belonged to; and indeed family government did too much fail in the town. It was become very customary with many of our young people to be indecent in their carriage at meeting, . . . There had also prevailed in the town a spirit of contention between two parties, into which they had for many years been divided; . . .

And then it was, in the latter part of December (1734) that the spirit of God began extraordinarily to set in, and wonderfully to work amongst us; and there were very suddenly, one after another, five or six persons, who were all savingly converted, and some of them wrought upon in a very remarkable manner. . . .

Presently upon this, a great and earnest concern about the great things of religion and the eternal world became universal in all parts of the town, and among persons of all degrees and all ages. The noise amongst the dry bones waxed louder and louder; all other talk but about spiritual and eternal things was soon thrown by; all the conversation, in all companies and upon all occasions, was upon these things only, unless so much as was necessary for people carrying on their ordinary secular business. Other discourse than of the things of religion would scarcely be tolerated in any company. The minds of people were wonderfully taken off from the world, it was treated amongst us as a thing of very little consequence. . . .

Religion was with all sorts the great concern, and the world was a thing only by the bye. The only thing in their view was to get the kingdom of heaven, and every one appeared pressing into it. . . . It then was a dreadful thing amongst us to lie out of Christ, in danger every day of dropping into hell; and what persons' minds were intent upon was to escape for their lives and to fly from the wrath to come. All would eagerly lay hold of opportunities for their souls; and were wont very often to meet together in private houses for religious purposes: and such meetings when appointed were greatly thronged.

There was scarcely a single person in the town, old or young, left unconcerned about the great things of the eternal world. Those who were wont to be the vainest and loosest; and those who had been most disposed to think and speak slightly of vital and experimental religion,[14] were now generally subject to great awakenings. And the work of conversion was carried on in a most astonishing manner, and increased more and more; souls did as it were come by flocks to Jesus Christ. From

---

[13] Edwards's grandfather, Solomon Stoddard (1643–1729), preceded him as pastor at Northampton.

[14] Edwards's use of the term *experimental* is consistent with eighteenth-century usage. It meant roughly what we mean by "experiential" today.

day to day, for many months together, might be seen evident instances of sinners brought out of darkness into marvellous light, and delivered out of a horrible pit and from the miry clay and set upon a rock with a new song of praise to God in their mouths.

This work of God, as it was carried on, and the number of true saints multiplied, soon made a glorious alteration in the town; so that in the spring and summer following, anno 1735, the town seemed to be full of the presence of God: it never was so full of love, nor of joy, and yet so full of distress, as it was then. It was a time of joy in families on account of salvation being brought into them; parents rejoicing over their children as new born, and husbands over their wives, and wives over their husbands. . . . Our public assemblies were then beautiful; the congregation was alive in God's service, every one earnestly intent on the public worship, every hearer eager to drink in the words of the minister as they came from his mouth; the assembly in general were, from time to time, in tears while the word was preached; some weeping with sorrow and distress, others with joy and love, others with pity and concern for the souls of their neighbors. . . .

On whatever occasions persons met together, Christ was to be heard and seen in the midst of them. Our young people when they met, were wont to spend the time in talking of the excellency and dying love of Jesus Christ, the glory of the way of salvation, the wonderful, free, and sovereign grace of God, his glorious works in the conversions of a soul, the truth and certainty of the great things of God's word. . . . Those among us who had been formerly converted were greatly enlivened and renewed with fresh and extraordinary incomes of the spirit of God; . . . Many who before had laboured under difficulties about their own state had now their doubts removed by more satisfying experience and more clear discoveries of God's love.

When this work first appeared and was so extraordinarily carried on amongst us in the winter, others round about us seemed not to know what to make of it. Many scoffed at and ridiculed it; and some compared what we called conversion to certain distempers. But it was very observable of many, who occasionally came amongst us from abroad with disregardful hearts, that what they saw here cured them of such a temper of mind. Strangers were generally surprised to find things so much beyond what they had heard, and were wont to tell others that the state of the town could not be conceived of by those who had not seen it. . . . Many who came to town on one occasion or other had their consciences smitten and awakened; and went home with wounded hearts, and with those impressions that never wore off till they had hopefully a saving issue; and those who had before had serious thoughts, had their awakenings and convictions greatly increased. There were many instances of persons who came from abroad on visits or on business, who had not been long here before, to all appearance, they were savingly wrought upon and partook of that shower of divine blessing which God rained down here, and went home rejoicing; til at length the same work began evidently to appear and prevail in several other towns in the country, . . .

[Edwards then proceeded to recount how the awakening spread to surrounding towns in Massachusetts: South Hadley, Deerfield, Hatfield, West Springfield, Enfield, etc. It then moved beyond the immediate area into Connecticut and New Jersey, where Edwards mentions William and Gilbert Tennent, along with "a very pious young gentleman, a Dutch minister, whose name as I remember was Freelinghousa," as having been involved.]

This seems to have been a very extraordinary dispensation of providence. God has in many respects gone out of and much beyond his usual and ordinary way. The work in this town, and some others about us, has been extraordinary on account of the universality of it, affecting all sorts, sober and vicious, high and low, rich and poor, wise and unwise. It reached the most considerable families and persons, to all appearance, as much as others. In former stirrings of this nature, the bulk of the young people have been greatly affected; but old men and little children have been so now. . . .

This dispensation has also appeared very extraordinary in the numbers of those on whom we have reason to hope it has had a saving effect. We have about six hundred and twenty communicants, which include almost all our adult persons. The church was very large before: but persons never thronged into it, as they did in the late extraordinary time.—Our sacraments are eight weeks [apart], and I received into our communion about a hundred before one sacrament, fourscore of them at one time, whose appearance when they presented themselves together to make an open explicit profession of Christianity, was very affecting to the congregation. I took in near sixty before the next sacrament day: and I had very sufficient evidence of the conversion of their souls through divine grace, though it is not the custom here, as it is in many other churches in this country, to make a credible relation of their inward experience the ground of admission to the Lord's supper.

I am far from pretending to be able to determine how many have lately been the subjects of such mercy; but if I may be allowed to declare anything that appears to me probable in a thing of this nature, I hope that more than 300 souls were savingly brought home to Christ, in this town, in the space of half a year, and about the same number of males as females.

God has also seemed to have gone out of his usual way, in the quickness of his work and the swift progress his Spirit has made in operations on the hearts of many. It is wonderful that persons should be so suddenly and yet so greatly changed. Many have been taken from a loose and careless way of living and seized with strong convictions of their guilt and misery, and in a very little time old things have passed away, and all things have become new with them. . . .

These awakenings when they have first seized on persons have had two effects: one way, that they have brought them immediately to quit their sinful practices; and the looser sort have been brought to forsake and dread their former vices and extravagances. When once the spirit of God began to be so wonderfully poured out in a general way through the two, people had soon done with their old quarrels, backbitings, and intermeddling with other men's matters. The tavern was soon left empty, and persons kept very much at home; . . . The other effect was, that it put them on earnest application to the means of salvation, reading, prayer, meditation, the ordinances of God's house, and private conference; their cry was, What shall we do to be saved?

As to those in whom awakenings seem to have a saving issue, commonly the first thing that appears is a conviction of the justice of God in their condemnation, appearing in a sense of their own exceeding sinfulness, and the vileness of all their performances. . . .

It has been very wonderful to see how personal affections were sometimes moved— when God did as it were suddenly open their eyes and let into their minds a sense of the greatness of his grace, the fullness of Christ, and his readiness to save—after having been broken with apprehension of divine wrath, and sunk into an abyss under a sense of guilt which they were ready to think was beyond the mercy of God. Their joyful surprise has caused their hearts as it were to leap, so that they have been ready to break forth into laughter, tears often at the same time issuing forth like a flood, and intermingling a loud weeping. Sometimes they have not been able to forbear crying out with a loud voice, expressing their great admiration. . . .

Wherever revivals broke out they produced not only new spiritual interest and concern but also dissension and opposition. Part of the dynamic of revival preaching involved a condemnation of the deadness and coldness of the churches, and it was inevitable that much of this condition would be blamed on the ministers, who had somehow failed in their responsibilities. Such attacks became specific in the preaching of Gilbert Tennent and, later, in comments made by Whitefield. In 1740 Tennent delivered a fiery sermon at Nottingham, Pennsylvania, that was then published in Philadelphia. The discourse, entitled "The Danger of an Unconverted Ministry," incensed many clergymen who saw themselves among those whom Tennent labeled as "unconverted." The sermon illustrates the schisms and controversies inherent in the revival movement, factors that helped in a decisive reshaping of American denominational patterns.

Also important to note is the focus of Tennent's attacks, for he was disturbed both by the lack of evangelistic fervor and plain gospel in most of the preaching of his day and by the failure of established schools to train ministers adequately. Such concern about the lack of enthusiasm and "heart power" in the pulpit, joined with the charge that theological schools and seminaries are unorthodox and spiritually unreliable, are continuing characteristics of conservative, revival-oriented dissatisfaction with so-called liberal trends in American Protestantism. A contemporary church leader like Carl McIntire (1906–   ), founder of the dissident American Council of Christian Churches, makes much the same accusations, albeit in somewhat different language, against the current religious establishment in this country. The following document is an excerpt from Tennent's tract.

Document 24

From "The Danger of an Unconverted Ministry" by Gilbert Tennent

. . . My Brethren, we should mourn over those, that are destitute of faithful ministers, and sympathize with them. Our bowels should be moved with the most compassionate tenderness, over these dear fainting souls, that are as sheep having no shepherd; and that after the example of our blessed Lord.

SOURCE: Gilbert Tennent, "The Danger of an Unconverted Ministry" (Boston, 1742).

Dear Sirs! We should also most earnestly pray for them, that the compassionate Saviour may preserve them, by his mighty power, through faith unto salvation; support their sinking spirits, under the melancholy uneasiness of a dead ministry; sanctify and sweeten to them the dry morsels they get under such blind men, when they have none better to repair to. . . .

And indeed, my Brethren, we should join our endeavours to our prayers. The most likely method to stock the church with a faithful ministry, in the present situation of things, the public academies being so much corrupted and abused generally, is to encourage private schools, or seminaries of learning, which are under the care of skillful and experienced Christians; in which those only should be admitted, who upon strict examination, have in the judgment of a reasonable charity, the plain evidences of experimental religion. Pious and experienced youths, who have a good natural capacity, and great desires after the ministerial work, from good motives, might be sought for, and found up and down in the country, and put to private Schools of the Prophets; especially in such places where the public ones are not. This method, in my opinion, has a noble tendency, to build up the Church of God. . . . Don't think it much, if the Pharisees should be offended at such a proposal; . . . If they could help it, they wouldn't let one faithful man come into the ministry; and therefore their opposition is an encouraging sign. Let all the followers of the Lamb stand up and act for God against all opposers: Who is upon God's side?

The improvement of this subject remains. And

1.   If it be so, that the case of those, who have no other or no better than Pharisee-teacher, is to be pitied: then what a scroll and scene of mourning and lamentation, and woe, is opened, because of the swarms of locusts, the crowds of Pharisees, that have as covetously as cruelly crept into the ministry, in this adulterous generation, who as nearly resemble the character given of the old Pharisees, as one crow's egg does another. It is true that some of the modern Pharisees have learned to prate a little more orthodoxly about the new birth than their predecessor Nicodemus, who are, in the meantime, as great strangers to the feeling experience of it, as he. They are blind who see not this to be the case of the body of the clergy of this generation. . . .

2.   From what has been said, we may learn that such who are contented under a dead ministry have not in them the temper of that Saviour they profess. It's an awful sign that they are as blind as moles and as dead as stones, without any spiritual taste and relish. And alas! isn't this the case of multitudes? If they can get one that has the name of a minister, with a . . . black coat or gown to carry on a Sabbathday among them, although never so coldly and insuccessfully; if he is free from gross crimes in practice and takes good care to keep at a due distance from their consciences, and is never troubled about his insuccessfulness; O! think the poor fools, that is a fine man indeed; our minister is a prudent charitable man, he is not always harping upon terror, and sounding damnation in our ear, like some rash-headed preachers, who by their uncharitable methods, are ready to put poor people out of their wits, or to run them into despair. O! how terrible a thing is that despair! Ay, our minister, honest man, gives us good caution against it. Poor silly souls! . . .

3.   We may learn the mercy and duty of those that enjoy a faithful ministry. Let such glorify God for so distinguishing a privilege and labor to walk worthy of it,

to all well-pleasing; lest for their abuse thereof, they be exposed to a greater damnation.

4.   If the ministry of natural men be as it has been represented, then it is both lawful and expedient to go from them to hear godly persons; yea, it's so far from being sinful to do this, that one who lives under a pious minister of lesser gifts, after having honestly endeavored to get benefit by his ministry and yet gets a little or none, but does find real benefit and more benefit elsewhere; I say, he may lawfully go, and that frequently, where he gets most good to his precious soul. . . .

Is not the visible Church composed of persons of the most contrary characters? While some are sincere servants of God, are not many servants of Satan, under a religious mask? And have not these a fixed enmity against the other? How is it then possible that a harmony should subsist between such, till their nature be changed? Can Light dwell with Darkness? . . .

And let those who live under the ministry of dead men, whether they have got the form of religion or not, repair to the living, where they may be edified. Let who will, oppose it. . . . But though your neighbors growl against you and reproach you for doing your duty in seeking your soul's good, bear their unjust censures with Christian meekness and persevere.

The evangelistic efforts of men like Frelinghuysen, Tennent, and Edwards prepared the way of the central catalyst of the Awakening, the remarkable George Whitefield. Naturally gifted with a strong, effective voice and a striking, dramatic delivery, Whitefield was an Oxford graduate, an ordained Anglican minister, and a close associate of John Wesley, the founder of Methodism. Early in his ministry he adopted the practice of preaching in the open air, and the response to his sermons was astonishing. Persuaded by William Tennent (1673–1746) and others to embark on a preaching tour of the colonies, Whitefield arrived in Newport, Rhode Island, on September 14, 1740. During the next 73 days he traveled over 800 miles, delivering more than 130 sermons. Everywhere he was met by huge throngs of people. His Boston visit was described by a local newspaper:

Last Thursday Evening the Rev'd Mr. Whitefield arrived from Rhode Island, being met on the road and conducted to town by several gentlemen. The next day in the forenoon he attended prayers in the King's Chapel, and in the afternoon he preached to a vast congregation in the Rev'd Dr. Colman's meeting house. The next day he preached in the forenoon at the South Church to a crowded audience, and in the afternoon to about 5000 people on the Common; and Lord's Day in the afternoon having preached to a great number of people at the old Brick Church, the house not being large enough to hold those that crowded to hear him, when the exercise was over, he went and preached in the field to at least 8000 persons. . . . [15]

[15] Boston Weekly News-Letter (September 25, 1740), cited in Edwin Scott Gaustad, *The Great Awakening in New England* (New York: Quadrangle, 1957), p. 26. Gaustad's book gives the fullest account of the Great Awakening and its effect on New England.

Whitefield needed no invitations from pastors to preach from their pulpits, for his sermons were delivered wherever and whenever there were those to listen. Not only did the cities and towns gladly hear him, but colleges such as Harvard and Yale received him enthusiastically on their campuses, at least on his initial visit. The fervor of spiritual revival was generated wherever he went.

Whitefield's sermons were models of revival preaching: simple, straightforward, emotional, and eloquent. A not entirely sympathetic observer such as Benjamin Franklin has given us a valuable firsthand description of the evangelist:

> He had a loud and clear voice, and articulated his words so perfectly that he might be heard and understood at a great distance, especially as his auditories observed the most perfect silence. . . . By hearing him often, I came to distinguish easily between sermons newly composed and those which he had often preached in the course of his travels. His delivery of the latter was so improved by frequent repetition, that every accent, every emphasis, every modulation of the voice, was so perfectly well turned and well placed, that, without being interested in the subject, one could not help being pleased with the discourse.[16]

Before Whitefield died in 1770 he made three other preaching tours of the colonies. None was as successful as the first, but Whitefield continued to be a crucial leader in the Awakening. Much of the controversy and division produced by the revivals centered around him. In 1741 Whitefield's *Journal,* in which he described the first New England evangelistic tour, was printed. His comments on the New England ministers and the universities aroused widespread resentment from those two sources. Whitefield wrote:

> Many, nay most that preach, I fear do not experimentally know Christ. . . . God has remarkably in sundry times and diverse manners, poured out his Spirit. . . . The ministers and people of Connecticut seemed to be more simple than those that live near Boston, especially in those parts where I went. But I think the ministers' preaching almost universally by note, is a certain mark they have, in a great measure, lost the old spirit of preaching . . . it is a sad symptom of decay of vital religion, when reading sermons becomes fashionable where extempore preaching did once almost universally prevail. . . . As for the Universities, I believe it may be said, their light is become darkness that may be felt, and is complained of by the most godly ministers. . . . The Church of England is at a low ebb, and, as far as I can find, had people kept their primitive purity, it would scarce have got a footing in New England. . . . [17]

Not surprisingly, many of the ministers and faculties of the universities reacted strongly to these observations. When Whitefield returned to New England in 1744, a number of churches barred him from their pulpits. The Harvard faculty, joined later by the Yale professors, issued a

---

16 Quoted in Gaustad, op. cit., p. 29.
17 Gaustad, op. cit., pp. 54–55.

statement condemning his ministry as harmful to the peace and purity of the churches.

Most prominent in the opposition to the Awakening was Charles Chauncy (1705–1787), minister of the influential First Church (Congregational) of Boston. Moderately sympathetic to the movement at its beginning, Chauncy became increasingly doubtful as to the lasting effects of the revivals. Thus he wrote to a minister friend in Edinburgh concerning Whitefield:

> In answer whereto, I freely acknowledge, wherever he went he generally moved the passions, especially of the younger people, and the females among them; the effect whereof was a great talk about religion, together with a disposition to be perpetually hearing sermons, to neglect of all other business. . . . [18]

Chauncy's doubts about the Awakening, like those of many others, were hardened into overt opposition by the emotional excesses that arose as the revival progressed. Much of the controversy centered around the ministry of James Davenport (1716–1757), whose services were often characterized by weeping, swooning, and other physical reactions. Pretending to be able to distinguish with certainty the saved from the damned, Davenport vehemently and publicly attacked his opponents. He encouraged his hearers to burn their worldly possessions, and they responded by throwing into a great fire their rings, necklaces, fine clothing, and even books written by "unregenerate" pastors. Eventually Davenport, influenced by more level heads among his colleagues, repented of his excesses and retreated to a more sober position. But the damage had already been done. Such happenings fractured almost totally any remaining relationship between those who supported the revivals and those who opposed them.

The Awakening reached its zenith in 1741–1742. Most of the actual work was carried out by little-known men, ministers and laymen, laboring in every section of the colonies. Among the more prominent leaders, in addition to Edwards, Whitefield, and Tennent, were Eleazar Wheelock (1711–1779), who strove mightily in Connecticut, and Benjamin Colman (1673–1747), the respected senior pastor of the Brattle Street Congregational Church in Boston. Revival fervor gripped the imagination of a considerable majority of colonial religious people. As Edwin S. Gaustad has pointed out, "the Awakening was 'Great' because it was general." [19] But the spiritual peaks of excitement could not be long maintained. By 1747 reaction had begun to set in. The "divine showers of blessing" were evidently being withdrawn. But "in 1741–1742, nearly everyone got wet." [20]

The Great Awakening is a striking historical phenomenon, fascinating in its own right. For the contemporary student, however, its continuing

---

[18] Quoted in Gaustad, op. cit., p. 31.
[19] Gaustad, op. cit., p. 42.
[20] Ibid., p. 41.

effects on American religion are most important. *First and foremost, the revival materially affected the strength and disposition of churches in the colonies.* Obviously the overall number of church members was increased, though not perhaps in the proportions one might expect.[21] Many new churches were established, and old, established congregations gained new vigor. But the greater effect by far was on those already counted as members of the churches, especially young people, who were brought in large numbers to inquire as to the state of their souls. Such spiritual anxiety was widespread, reaching into every stratum of society. The contention of some later historians that the Awakening was limited to a particular area or to special social or economic classes has been effectively disproved.[22] It knew no boundaries, either social or geographical. In this regard the Awakening was one factor helping to prepare the way for the American Revolution in that it drew many of the colonies together across political lines in a common religious experience.[23]

But it must not be concluded that the total result was a unifying one. As indicated earlier, the efforts of the evangelists produced not only excitement but also inevitable opposition and hostility. Divisions and schisms within the ranks of the established denominations resulted both in the multiplication of the total number of churches and in the eventual reshaping of American denominational patterns.

Most seriously shaken by the revival was the Congregational Church. Although many Congregationalists were enthusiastic supporters of the Awakening and despite the fact that the denomination benefited in terms of growth from it, the seeds of serious fragmentation were sown. Charles Chauncy became the leader of the "Old Lights," a group comprising roughly one third of New England Congregationalists. He and like-minded clergymen took their stand for what was pragmatically reasonable in religion, over against the revivalists' penchant for the inscrutably supernatural. Chauncy sought truth in common sense and natural philosophy, rather than in special biblical revelation or religious experience. He and others moved steadily toward ever more rigorous religious rationalism, and this dissident Congregational group eventually became the nucleus of American Unitarianism.

The "New Lights," on the other hand, supported the revival and cooperated in its evangelistic efforts. Within the Congregational Church this meant that large groups of revival-oriented members eventually broke away, many of them becoming Baptists. In a number of cases entire church congregations, pastor and all, changed their affiliation from Congregational to Baptist. More than one hundred new Baptist

---

[21] See ibid., pp. 103–104, for a discussion of the actual figures.

[22] See, e.g., ibid, pp. 42–44.

[23] For a comprehensive presentation of this viewpoint, see Alan Heimert, *Religion and the American Mind: From the Great Awakening to the Revolution* (Cambridge, Mass.: Harvard University Press, 1966).

churches sprang up in the New England area during the Awakening. Partly as a result of such schisms, Congregationalists, once the largest and most powerful religious force in America, began to lose ground.

Presbyterians were also divided, though not permanently, by the revival. Gilbert Tennent was expelled by the Synod of Philadelphia in 1741, but he and his sympathizers organized the rival Synod of New York, which rapidly became larger and more powerful than the original group. By the time the two organizations reunited in 1758, the antirevivalists forces had declined drastically in strength. The revival spirit of Tennent and his followers had triumphed. "New Side" Presbyterians worked closely with "New Light" Congregationalists, and in spite of deep differences of opinion within its ranks Presbyterianism in this country held together, gaining considerable strength as a result of the Awakening.

Anglicans tended, by and large, to be hostile to the revival, with notable exceptions such as Devereux Jarratt (1733–1801). Jarratt was a Church of England rector in Dinwiddie County, Virginia, who had been influenced by both Whitefield and John Wesley. In 1763 he was instrumental in bringing about a late-blooming aftereffect of the Awakening among his Anglican congregation. In most cases, however, Anglicans remained aloof and disdainful of the evangelistic fervor. In New England this stance served to attract some people, offended by the extravagances of the Awakening, into Anglican ranks. But in other sections of the country Church of England hostility to the revivals resulted in its relative stagnation in terms of growth. Baptists in the southern colonies multiplied at an astonishing rate, and the first trickle of what was to become a flood of Methodists (followers of John Wesley) began to pull away from the Church of England parishes. But it was the American Revolution that subjected the Anglican church in this country to almost unbearable tensions. It was forced to sever its organizational ties with the English church in a struggle to overcome the stigma of "Toryism." In a sense Anglicanism in the United States had to begin almost anew after the success of the fight for independence, seeking to establish itself as a distinctively American denomination—the Protestant Episcopal Church.

If one compares figures on denominational strength in the colonies in 1780, after the Awakening, with those at the beginning of the century, the revival effects are clearly seen. Considered from the standpoint of the number of churches, the Congregationalists and the Anglicans were by far the largest groups in 1700; lagging far behind were the Baptists, Presbyterians, Dutch Reformed, and Lutherans, in that order. By 1780 the picture was changing. The Congregationalists still had the largest number of churches but, as we have seen, that denomination was seriously divided. Anglicans had slipped back to fourth place, and Presbyterians, Baptists, Reformed, and Lutherans had all made substantial gains. A new American denominational pattern was taking shape, one that was to be solidified for years to come by the Second Awakening.[24]

A second major result of the Great Awakening was its influence in helping to give the great majority of American Christians a basic common understanding of the Christian life and faith. L. J. Trinterud[25] estimates that perhaps 80 per cent of all church people participated in this understanding. The revival crossed denominational lines, producing broad general agreement on what it meant to be a Christian. Denominational differences in doctrine and practice (and there continued to be many) were not considered unimportant but were relegated to a secondary status.

Such a development was perhaps essential for the development of a functioning American pluralism. The various religious groups came to see themselves not as sects, claiming to be sole possessors of religious truth, but as parts of the larger church. Each denomination was named, or "denominated," in its own traditional manner, but all together made up the Christian community. Trinterud quotes Gilbert Tennent in this respect: "All societies who profess Chrisitanity and retain the foundational principles thereof, notwithstanding their different denominations and diversity of sentiments in smaller things, are in reality but one Church of Christ, but several branches (more or less pure in minuter points) of one visible kingdom of the Messiah." [26]

Obviously, the importance of this agreement can be overemphasized. It is certainly true that before the contemporary consensus of American pluralism, embracing Protestants, Catholics, Jews, and others, could take form, other significant developments had to occur. But the Great Awakening did provide a kind of "Protestant consensus" on which to build.

A third and final major result of the Awakening can be found in its permanent influence on the patterns of revival practice and theology. It has already been pointed out that many of the revival efforts tended to be stereotyped according to Edwards's description. The appeal for a definite decision of will, based not only on intellectual assent to doctrine but also on a total personal response to God's free grace, was a standard feature of Awakening preaching. Sermon style, by the examples of Whitefield and others, was altered to a looser, more informal, more extemporaneous delivery. The content of the sermon was concerned primarily with the meaning and method of religious conversion, whose nature received its definitive summary in Jonathan Edwards's careful

[24] See Edwin Scott Gaustad, *Historical Atlas of Religion in America* (New York: Harper & Row, 1962), for comprehensive statistical information.

[25] L. J. Trinterud, *The Forming of an American Tradition* (New York: Books for Libraries, 1949), p. 26.

[26] Quoted in ibid., p. 132.

expositions, many of them produced in response to the work of revival critics like Chauncy. Edwards wrote:

> there is indeed such a thing as true experimental religion, arising from an imme-
> diate divine influence, supernaturally enlightening and convincing the mind, and
> powerfully impressing, quickening, sanctifying, and governing the heart; which
> religion is indeed an amiable thing, of happy tendency, and of no hurtful conse-
> quence to human society. . . . [27]

The overriding aim of the revivalists was to preach the gospel in such a way as to bring men to the place of conversion, a matter of the head but also of the heart. Most of them had no desire, and this was especially true of Edwards, to eliminate a clear, rational understanding and acceptance of the doctrines of the faith. Indeed, Perry Miller, a leading scholar in the field of New England colonial religion, has paid tribute to Edwards's use of reason, acclaiming him as "intellectually the most modern man of his time" and indeed "much ahead of his time." [28] But Edwards's use of reason rested on what he considered its only solid foundation, revelation revived by religious experience. The "affections," as he termed them, played a vital role in salvation.

The religious "coldness" against which the revivalists protested seemed to many of them to arise from a lack of fervent emotional commitment on the part of those who classed themselves as Christians. They stressed the fact that a man's testimony or witness to his conversion must normally include an account of his reception of "experimental" grace. Thus religious conversion—becoming a Christian—was a life-transforming experience that touched the total human personality: mind, heart, and will.

As the revival spread it was perhaps inevitable that preaching "for a decision" tended to emphasize more and more the emotions and will, less and less the mind and reason. Experience in terms of religious feeling became far more crucial than rational understanding. But, with the exception of extremists like Davenport, most Great Awakening preachers retained a strong secondary emphasis on the intellectual content of religious faith. It remained for the Second Awakening, the next great wave of American revivalism, to advance almost purely emotional Christianity to a central position in popular American religion.

Certainly there were other important results of the Awakening, in addition to what has already been listed. For instance, the institutional effects were significant. Such colleges and universities as Hampden-Sydney (1776), Princeton (1746), Brown (1764), Queen's College, later Rutgers (1766), and others largely owe their founding to the impetus of the revival and the felt need to provide places where ministers sympathetic to the new evangelism could be schooled. Missionary efforts among the Indians received renewed attention through the efforts of

[27] Jonathan Edwards, *Works* (New York, 1829), Vol. 10, p. 430.
[28] Perry Miller, *Jonathan Edwards* (New York, 1949), pp. 305, viii.

men like Congregationalist Eleazar Wheelock and Presbyterian David Brainerd (1718–1747). It can also be pointed out that the development of the kind of consensus already discussed, plus the increased strength of nonestablished groups like the Baptists and Methodists, helped to speed the development of religious liberty and the disestablishment of state churches. In summary, however, the Great Awakening supplied energy and fervor that were necessary if the American churches were to confront the gigantic task of Christianizing a whole new continent.

The Second Awakening

It is noteworthy that Alexis de Tocqueville's memorable visit to America occurred in the 1830s. Very probably his discovery that "there is no country in the world in which the Christian religion retains a greater influence over the souls of men" could not have been made thirty years earlier, for by 1800 the excitement and effects of the Great Awakening had deteriorated into apathy and indifference. Full-scale attacks on orthodox Christianity had been leveled during and after the Revolution by spokesmen for a stringently rational religion—men like Thomas Paine (1737–1809), Ethan Allen (1738–1789), and Elihu Palmer (1764–1806). Aggressive deism, which involved a rejection of scriptural revelation, had numerous adherents on college campuses and in intellectual circles. Moral conditions generally were at a low ebb.

A significant new factor in the religious situation involved the problems occasioned by the rapid western expansion of the new nation. The early trickle of settlers into the fertile areas west of the Alleghenies and south of the Ohio River had rapidly become a flood. In the three decades between 1792 and 1822 Kentucky, Tennessee, Ohio, Louisiana, Indiana, Alabama, Illinois, Mississippi, and Missouri were admitted to the Union. By 1829 more than a third of the nation's population lived west of the Allegheny Mountains.

The churches were well aware of the challenge of the developing frontier but their difficulties in dealing with such a challenge were compounded by their own internal lethargy. Gaustad has pointed out that during the first half of the nineteenth century the churches were faced with a double-barreled task: the "conquest of the West" and the "reconquest of the East."[29] The upsurge of religious activity and revivalism associated with the Second Awakening constituted a major part of the dynamic response of America's religious forces to this double challenge.

As with the Great Awakening, the exact beginnings of the new revivalsim are difficult to pinpoint. Baptists and many Presbyterians had, of course, continued some of the revival emphases of the earlier Awakening. Methodists, constituting only a small factor in the earlier revival, had grown steadily, partly as a result of the separation of many Meth-

---

[29] Gaustad, *Historical Atlas of Religion in America,* op. cit., pp. 37, 42.

odist societies from the Anglican churches at the time of the Revolution and partly through their own industry and dedication. Among the specific early events, however, were outbreaks of revival fervor, in 1787, at two small Virginia colleges, Hampden-Sydney and Washington. As a result of the evangelistic excitement on these campuses, thirty to forty young men entered the Presbyterian ministry, many of them dedicating themselves to service on the frontier. Over the next decade scattered intances of such revival stirrings occurred in Maine, Massachusetts, Connecticut, and in central and western New York, as well as in Kentucky and Tennessee on the frontier. These events presaged the phenomena that were to come.

In 1802 remarkable religious activities took place at Yale College, under the leadership of its president, Timothy Dwight (1752–1817). Dwight, a Congregational minister, preached a series of chapel sermons, resulting in the profession of conversion by more than a third of the Yale student body. Out of this experience came such men as Lyman Beecher, destined to become the most prominent leader of the Second New England Awakening, and Nathaniel W. Taylor (1786–1858), the preeminent theologian of the revival movement. The campus revival phenomenon was repeated in subsequent years at Yale and spread also to Amherst, Dartmouth, and Williams. Young ministers moved out from the colleges both to eastern towns and villages and to the wilderness areas of the country, carrying the revival with them as they went.

The frontier revival did not differ from that in the East in terms of basic theology. In both East and West the religious emphases reflected the total cultural ethos of a young and expanding democratic nation. Men like Dwight and Beecher still proclaimed the sovereignty of God, as had Edwards and others before them, but now much more stress was placed on the part each Christian must play in his or her own salvation. The time-honored doctrine of election (the insistence that God alone chose who was to be saved and that the individual could do nothing but await His choice) was pushed into the background. The promise was made that all who earnestly sought reconciliation with God could find it. It was only necessary that people should actively repent of their sins and believe in Jesus Christ as the way of salvation. If they sincerely did these things, God's grace would come in an experience of redemption. Having been saved, Christians were then responsible for living a righteous and godly life, full of good works.

What happened on the frontier to distinguish its religious excitement from that of the eastern seaboard was not unpredictable, given the cultural context in which it took place. In the West the revivalists were dealing with a migrant population, largely unlettered and untutored. Opportunities for the presentation of the gospel were limited, and preachers learned quickly to press for immediate and catastrophic decisions. Most Presbyterian and Congregational evangelists attempted to

30 Hudson, op. cit., p. 137.

conduct their services and make their appeals in the same manner as in the more settled and civilized East, but the masses of the frontier had little taste for such tame religion. Many of them were, as Winthrop Hudson describes it, "like Augustus Longstreet's 'honest Georgian' who preferred his whiskey straight and his politics and religion red hot." [30]

Under these circumstances it was the Baptist and Methodist frontier preachers who were most ready, willing, and able to serve up "red hot" religion. In Kentucky it is estimated that in three years (1800–1803) the Baptists gained more than ten thousand members, and the Methodists had approximately equal success. Some Presbyterians entertained an initial concern for frontier revivalism but most became disenchanted with the strange emotional aspects of the movement and withdrew, leaving the field to other, more flexible groups.

Baptist growth since the Revolution had been phenomenal. By 1800 Baptists were the largest single denomination in the country. They had made great gains in settled areas of the East and South, where generally their ministers were well educated and not given to overly emotional sermonic appeals. But their lack of any centralized denominational organization and their willingness to allow itinerant and relatively unlearned ministers to evangelize the frontier areas made them prime candidates both to lead and to benefit from the new outbreaks of revival interest.

The chief partner of Baptists in evangelizing the West was the relatively new Methodist Episcopal Church. Prior to the American Revolution Methodists were not actually a denomination but rather a group of societies within the Church of England. Devereux Jarratt, the Anglican revivalist, though never himself a Methodist, had assisted greatly in the organization of Methodist societies in Virginia and North Carolina. Lay preachers, such as Robert Strawbridge (d. 1781) and Philip Embury (1728–1773) had been sent to the colonies by Wesley as early as 1765, and in 1772 Robert Williams, another of Wesley's lay preachers, arrived in Virginia to assist Jarratt. With the success of the Revolution, the societies were encouraged to break away from the Church of England to form their own denominational group.

In the beginning many contemporary observers felt that Methodism had no real future in the United States. One estimate of their prospects was expressed in reaction to the building of a fairly large Methodist church building in Delaware during the war years: "It's no use putting up so large a dwelling for the Methodists, for after the war a corncrib will hold them all." [31] But these observers were badly mistaken. Under the vigorous leadership of men like Francis Asbury (1745–1816) Methodist membership doubled during the period of the Revolution. Their reliance on lay preachers and "circuit riders," or traveling ministers, qualified them, along with the Baptists, to play a major role on the

---

[31] J. M. Buckley, *A History of Methodists in the United States* (New York, 1896), p. 186. Quoted in Hudson, op. cit., p. 120.

frontier. In 1800 they were already the third largest American denomination, after the Baptists and Congregationalists, and by 1820 they had overtaken the other two groups to become the largest of all.

Typical of the itinerant Methodist evangelists was Peter Cartwright (1785–1872), a rough-hewn frontier preacher who claimed to have baptized some twelve thousand persons and to have preached over fourteen thousand sermons during his ministry in Kentucky and southern Illinois. Cartwright published his *Autobiography* in 1856, and his account presents a vivid firsthand view of the power and effects of the Second Awakening.

Document 25 _____

From *Autobiography* by Peter Cartwright

The Great Revival

From 1801 for years a blessed revival of religion spread through almost the entire inhabited parts of the West, Kentucky, Tennessee, the Carolinas, and many other parts, especially through the Cumberland country, which was so called from the Cumberland River, which headed and mounted in Kentucky, but in its great bend circled south through Tennessee, near Nashville. The Presbyterians and Methodists in a great measure united in this work, met together, prayed together and preached together.

In this revival originated our camp-meetings, and in both these denominations they were held every year, and, indeed, have been ever since, more or less. They would erect their camps with logs or frame them, and cover them with clapboards or shingles. They would also erect a shed, sufficiently large to protect five thousand people from wind and rain, and cover it with boards or shingles; build a large stand, seat the shed, and here they would collect together from forty to fifty miles around, sometimes further than that. Ten, twenty, and sometimes thirty ministers, of different denominations, would come together and preach night and day, four or five days together; and indeed, I have known these camp-meetings to last three or four weeks, and great good resulted from them. I have seen more than a hundred sinners fall like dead men under one powerful sermon, and I have seen and heard more than five hundred Christians all shouting aloud the high praises of God at once; and I will venture to assert that many happy thousands were awakened and converted to God at these camp-meetings. Some sinners mocked, some of the old dry professors opposed, some of the old starched Presbyterian preachers preached against these exercises, but still the work went on and spread almost in every direction, gathering additional force, until our country seemed all coming home to God.

In this great revival the Methodists kept moderately balanced; for we had excellent preachers to steer the ship or guide the flock. But some of our members ran wild, and indulged in some extravagancies that were hard to control.

SOURCE: From *Autobiography of Peter Cartwright*. Copyright © 1956 by Pierce & Washabaugh (Abingdon Press).

The Presbyterian preachers and members, not being accustomed to much noise or shouting, when they yielded to it went into great extremes and downright wildness, to the great injury of the cause of God. Their old preachers licensed a great many young men to preach, contrary to their Confession of Faith. That Confession of Faith required their ministers to believe in unconditional election and reprobation, and the unconditional and final perseverance of the saints. But in this revival they, almost to a man, gave up these points of high Calvinism, and preached a free salvation to all mankind. The Westminster Confession required every man, before he could be licensed to preach, to have a liberal education; but this qualification was dispensed with, and a great many fine men were licensed to preach without this literary qualification or subscribing to those high-toned doctrines of Calvinism.

This state of things produced great dissatisfaction in the Synod of Kentucky, and messenger after messenger was sent to wait on the Presbytery to get them to desist from their erratic course, but without success. Finally they were cited to trial before the constituted authorities of the Church. Some were censured, some were suspended, some retraced their steps, while others surrendered their credentials of ordination, and the rest were cut off from the Church.

While in this amputated condition, they called a general meeting of all their licentiates. They met our presiding elder, J. Page, and a number of Methodist ministers at a quarterly meeting in Logan County, and proposed to join the Methodist Episcopal Church as a body; but our aged ministers declined this offer, and persuaded them to rise up and embody themselves together, and constitute a Church. They reluctantly yielded to this advice, and, in due time and form, constituted what they denominated the "Cumberland Presbyterian Church"; and in their confession of faith split, as they supposed, the difference between the Predestinarians and the Methodists, rejecting a partial atonement or special election and reprobation, but retaining the doctrine of the final unconditional perseverance of the saints.

What an absurdity! While a man remains a sinner he may come, as a free agent, to Christ, if he will, and if he does not come his damnation will be just, because he refused offered mercy; but as soon as he gets converted his free agency is destroyed, the best boon of Heaven is then lost, and although he may backslide, wander away from Christ, yet he *shall* be brought in. He cannot finally be lost if he has ever been really converted to God.

In this revival, usually termed in the West the Cumberland revival, many joined the different Churches, especially the Methodist and Cumberland Presbyterians. The Baptists also came in for a share of the converts, but not to any great extent. Infidelity quailed before the mighty power of God, which was displayed among the people. Universalism was almost driven from the land. The Predestinarians of almost all sorts put forth a mighty effort to stop the work of God.

Just in the midst of our controversies on the subject of the powerful exercises among the people under preaching, a new exercise broke out among us, called the *jerks,* which was overwhelming in its effects upon the bodies and minds of the people. No matter whether they were saints or sinners, they would be taken under a warm song or sermon, and seized with a convulsive jerking all over, which they could not by any possibility avoid, and the more they resisted the more they jerked. If they would not strive against it and pray in good earnest, the jerking would usually abate. I have seen more than five hundred persons jerking at one time in my large congregations. Most usually persons taken with the jerks, to obtain relief, as they said, would rise up and dance. Some would run, but could not get away. Some would resist; on such the jerks were generally very severe.

To see those proud young gentlemen and young ladies, dressed in their silks, jewelry, and prunella, from top to toe, take the *jerks,* would often excite my risibilities. The first jerk or so, you would see their fine bonnets, caps, and combs fly; and so sudden would be the jerking of the head that their long loose hair would crack almost as loud as a wagoner's whip.

I always looked upon the jerks as a judgment sent from God, first, to bring sinners to repentance; and, secondly, to show professors that God could work with or without means, and that he could work over and above means, and do whatsoever seemeth him good, to the glory of his grace and salvation of the world.

There is no doubt in my mind that, with weak-minded, ignorant, and superstitious persons, there was a great deal of sympathetic feeling with a man that claimed to be under the influence of this jerking exercise; and yet, with many, it was perfectly involuntary. It was, on all occasions, my practice to recommend fervent prayer as a remedy, and it almost universally proved an effectual antidote.

There were many other strange and wild exercises into which the subjects of this revival fell; such, for instance, as what was called the running, jumping, barking exercise. The Methodist preachers generally preached against this extravagant wildness. I did it uniformly in my little ministrations, and sometimes gave great offense; but I feared no consequences when I felt my awful responsibilities to God. From these wild exercises, another great evil arose from the heated and wild imaginations of some. They professed to fall into trances and see visions; they would fall at meetings and sometimes at home, and lay apparently powerless and motionless for days, sometimes for a week at a time, without food or drink; and when they came to, they professed to have seen heaven and hell, to have seen God, angels, the devil and the damned; they would prophesy, and, under the pretense of Divine inspiration, predict the time of the end of the world, and the ushering of the great millennium.

This was the most troublesome delusion of all; it made such an appeal to the ignorance, superstition, and credulity of all the people, even saint as well as sinner. I watched this matter with a vigilant eye. If I opposed it, I would have to meet the clamor of the multitude; and if any one opposed it, these very visionists would single him out, and denounce the dreadful judgments of God against him. They would even set the very day that God was to burn the world, like the self-deceived modern Millerites. They would prophesy, that if any one did oppose them, God would send fire down from heaven and consume him, like the blasphemous Shakers. They would proclaim that they could heal all manner of diseases, and raise the dead, just like the diabolical Mormons. They professed to have converse with spirits of the dead in heaven and hell, like the modern spirit rappers. Such a state of things I never saw before, and I hope in God I shall never see again.

Dozens of men like Peter Cartwright helped to evangelize the American frontier, but the real father of the Second Awakening in the West was James McGready (1758–1817), a Presbyterian minister who became pastor of three congregations located in Logan County, Kentucky, in 1796. McGready developed the technique of the "camp meeting," which became the most distinctive feature of frontier religious life.[32] In the sparsely settled new areas people gathered not just for one religious service on Sunday, but for days and sometimes weeks of services, carried on while the worshippers camped in their tents and wagons. McGready conducted such a meeting at Red River, Kentucky, in June 1800. So successful was the revival that it was repeated in July, and similar camp meetings began to be held in the surrounding counties. Barton W. Stone (1772–1844), another Presbyterian minister who had been converted under McGready's earlier ministry in North Carolina, visited the meetings in 1801 and was strongly impressed. His description conveys some of the excitement that was beginning to sweep the territories:

> There, on the edge of a prairie in Logan County, Kentucky, the multitudes came together and continued a number of days and nights encamped on the ground, during which time worship was carried on in some part of the encampment. The scene was new to me and passing strange. It baffled description. Many, very many fell down as men slain in battle, and continued for hours together in an apparently breathless and motionless state, sometimes for a few moments reviving and exhibiting symptoms of life by a deep groan or piercing shriek, or by a prayer for mercy fervently uttered. After lying there for hours they obtained deliverance. The gloomy cloud that had covered their faces seemed gradually and visibly to disappear, and hope, in smiles, brightened into joy. They would rise, shouting deliverance, and then would address the surrounding multitude in language truly eloquent and impressive. With astonishment did I hear men, women, and children declaring the wonderful works of God and the glorious mysteries of the gospel. Their appeals were solemn, heart-penetrating, bold, and free. Under such circumstances many others would fall down into the same state from which the speakers had just been delivered.[33]

Stone himself soon became a central figure in the Awakening. Under his direction a camp meeting at Cane Ridge, Kentucky, in August 1801, became the most famous of all the revival gatherings. Estimates of those in attendance ran as high as twenty thousand. Denominational distinctions were laid aside as Presbyterians, Baptists, and Methodists alike participated. If one remembers that the largest community in Kentucky at this time, Lexington, had less than two thousand inhabitants, one can sense the impact of such a meeting. Hundreds of men, women, and children professed conversion, and the services were marked by much of the wild emotionalism and physical manifestations to which Peter Cartwright refers in the previously quoted section from his *Autobiography.*

As was the case with the Great Awakening, the Second Awakening

---

[32] For a comprehensive treatment of this phenomenon, see Charles A. Johnson, *The Frontier Camp Meeting* (Dallas: Southern Methodist University Press, 1950).

[33] Quoted in L. W. Bacon, *A History of American Christianity* (New York: Plenum Publishing, 1900), p. 234.

also produced hostility and antagonism. Most Presbyterian leaders rapidly became upset with the revivals. Barton Stone engaged in a running controversy with the Presbyterian Synod of Kentucky, and in 1804 he and his followers withdrew from the Synod to form a group that they designated simply as the "Christian Church." The movement grew rapidly, claiming more than thirteen thousand adherents by 1827. In 1832 the group combined with a similar movement that had begun in Pennsylvania under the leadership of another Presbyterian minister, Alexander Campbell (1788–1866). The new denomination became known as the Disciples of Christ, or simply as "Christians." In the next few decades it enjoyed phenomenal growth in the frontier areas, and the Disciples became the third major American frontier religious group, along with the Baptists and Methodists.

By 1840 the revival had passed the peak of its popularity and was entering a time of decline. The camp meetings continued for many years but they were increasingly institutionalized and programmed, lacking the spontaneity and unpredictability of the original meetings. Eventually many of the camp meetings sites became the location of denominational assembly grounds or summer resorts. Some of them, such as those at Chautauqua, New York, and Lake Junaluska, North Carolina, are still in operation today.

What were the lasting results of the Second Awakening? To assess them in any kind of statistical form is difficult. The emergence of Baptists, Methodists, and Disciples of Christ as the major "people's" churches in this country certainly owes much to the frontier revival spirit. The rapid spread of the churches in the western pioneer areas laid a strong foundation for the solid entrenchment of Protestant Christianity in the midwestern and southern sections of the nation. In addition, some remarkable moral effects were produced. Dr. George A. Baxter, president of Washington College in Virginia, returned from a trip to Kentucky in 1801 to write:

> A profane expression was hardly ever heard. A religious awe seemed to pervade the country. Upon the whole I think the revival in Kentucky the most extraordinary that has ever visited the church of Christ; and, all things considered, it was peculiarly adapted to the circumstances of the country into which it came. Infidelity was triumphant and religion was on the point of expiring. Something extraordinary seemed necessary to arrest the attention of giddy people who were ready to conclude that Christianity was a fable and futurity a delusion. This revival has done it. It has confounded infidelity and brought numbers beyond calculation under serious impressions.[34]

Whether such results were permanent or not is, of course, another question. More clearly evident is that the Awakening incorporated certain general characteristics that have had a profound effect on the continuing patterns of religion in America.

[34] Quoted in ibid., p. 237.

The most important of these characteristics can be listed as pietism, individualism, and reductionism.[35] _Pietism_ emphasizes the personal and subjective experiences of religion. Immediate religious experience takes precedence over all else, so that the authority of a person's own encounter with the divine sweeps away all merely human or traditional authorities. Thus the way is open for novelty in religion. If each person's experience is his or her only final source of authority, who can dispute the validity of that experience? No priest or theologian, not even a college-trained minister, is required by the pietist. Under the leadership of God's Spirit, pietists believe that they can adequately understand and interpret their Bible. This strong emphasis on subjective religion carries over into religious practice. Personal religious exercises— such as prayer, private devotions, and regular Bible reading—are of central importance. Individual virtues included in the cultivation of piety become the external signs of a right relationship with God. On the frontier those who were Christians were expected to show by their lives that they were a separate and peculiar people. Obviously this meant that they must abstain from those activities and practices, such as drinking, gambling, and sexual looseness, that marked the lives of most non-Christian persons. Thus a pietistic "frontier ethic" gradually developed, one that has left its mark on the mainstream of American religion.

Individualism is closely connected with pietism. Of course, the entire atmosphere of frontier life was individualistic. In the new, unsettled lands men had to be self-reliant if they were to survive. Religiously, the emphasis was almost altogether on the individual's salvation rather than on the transformation of society as a whole. If enough individuals could be redeemed by the grace of God, the evils of society would take care of themselves. When people had been converted, the shaping of their specific religious beliefs became very much their own business. Such religious privatism, the insistence that religion is solely between each person and his or her God, was thoroughly consistent with the political individualism of the day.

Reductionism is a natural consequence of pietism plus individualism. If every individual is his or her own priest, then there is no need for elaborate institutional creeds or complex theologies. Religion is within the intellectual reach of every person, which in practice means that theology is reduced to simple, basic convictions easily preached and easily understood. Because education was largely unavailable on the frontier, the need for it in religion was dismissed. The revival preacher's sermons consisted mostly of a recounting of his own conversion experience, plus the repeating of selected verses of scripture, or "proof texts," to support his plea that men and women should repent of their sins and trust in Jesus. In the unlettered atmosphere of the new West, it

---

[35] In E. S. Gaustad's _A Religious History of America_ (New York: Harper & Row, 1966), p. 144, these three characteristics are specifically used to describe Methodism as both a denomination and a movement. They are equally applicable to Second Awakening religion as a whole.

was to this kind of preaching that most people could and did respond, but the resulting distrust of theological training and education has given to much American religion, even to the present day, a distinctly anti-intellectual flavor.

Developing Urban Revivalism

While the Second Awakening was spreading like wildfire in the pioneer areas of the country, revival efforts were moving in a distinctly different direction in the more thickly populated areas, especially in the incipiently urban sections of New England. In Connecticut Lyman Beecher, who was among those students influenced by Timothy Dwight's Yale preaching, turned revivalism into a powerful weapon by which conservative Christianity defended itself against the harassment of liberal doctrines and declining spiritual concern. Another Congregational revivalist, Asahel Nettleton (1783–1844), labored with small-town New England congregations in ways reminiscent of Jonathan Edwards. But it was an omen of the future when Nettleton attempted to bring revival to a city like New York; there he was a signal failure. It remained for another evangelist of greater talent and imagination to make the necessary adaptation in revival techniques demanded by the urban situation.

Charles Grandison Finney (1792–1875) can be seen as the transitional figure between the rural and small-town revivalism typical of the period before 1830 and the new style of revivalism in the cities. Indeed, he is the first of the great professional evangelists of whom Billy Graham is a direct descendant. Reared in that area of New York state known as the "Burned-over District," because it had experienced so many successive waves of revival excitement, Finney was trained and practiced as a lawyer. His religious conversion came in 1821, when he was almost thirty years old. Ordained as a Presbyterian minister in 1824, he was eventually unable to accept the Calvinist doctrines of predestination and election. In 1836 he withdrew from Presbyterianism and became a Congregationalist.

Finney's work was done almost exclusively in the rising urban centers of the day. In his campaigns in Philadelphia (1827), New York (1829), and Boston (1831), he argued the case for Christianity in the manner of a lawyer before a jury, holding large audiences spellbound with his eloquence and producing numerous converts, especially from the ranks of laborers and white-collar workers, to whom he especially appealed.

The most controversial and influential aspect of Finney's revivals was his use of what came to be called "new measures." Essentially these were innovative techniques devised by Finney for the urban situation. So successful was their use that, despite vigorous attacks on their propriety, even by men like Beecher and Nettleton, they became standard features of American revivalism for decades. Included among the new measures were the "anxious bench," a pew or seat at the front of the assembly to which concerned men and women were urged to come so that they might work out their struggle with religious conviction. In addition, Finney mobilized the entire community in the revival effort. Organized groups visited people, inviting them to the services. So-called cottage prayer meetings were held in the homes, sometimes for many days prior to the actual beginning of the revival. The traditional routine of Sunday services and an additional weekday lecture or two was displaced by the "protracted meeting," a series of preaching services held every day or evening for several weeks. Public invitations to come forward at the end of the sermon were given, and interested people were directed to the "inquiry room," there to be counseled by ministers and others trained to help them settle their spiritual problems.

In 1834 Finney delivered a lecture to the congregation of the New York Presbyterian church, where he served for a time as pastor, entitled "What a Revival of Religion Is." Widely reprinted, it became a "how-to-do-it" handbook on professional revivalism. The following excerpts are taken from this lecture.

_____ *Document 26*

From "What a Revival of Religion Is" by Charles Grandison Finney

Religion is the work of man. It is something for man to do. It consists in obeying God. It is man's duty. It is true, God induces him to do it. He influences him by his Spirit, because of his great wickedness and reluctance to obey. If it were not necessary for God to influence men—if men were disposed to obey God, there would be no occasion to pray, "O Lord, revive thy work." The ground of necessity for such a prayer is, that men are wholly indisposed to obey; and unless God interpose the influence of his Spirit, not a man on earth will ever obey the commands of God.

A "Revival of Religion" presupposes a declension. Almost all the religion in the world has been produced by revivals. God has found it necessary to take advantage of the excitability there is in mankind, to produce powerful excitements among them, before he can lead them to obey. Men are so sluggish, there are so many things to lead their minds off from religion, and to oppose the influence of the gospel, that it is necessary to raise an excitement among them, till the tide rises so high as to sweep away the opposing obstacles. They must be so excited that they will break over these counteracting influences, before they will obey God.

There is so little *principle* in the church, so little firmness and stability of purpose, that unless they are greatly excited, they will not obey God. They have so little knowledge, and their principles are so weak, that unless they are excited, they will go back from the path of duty, and do nothing to promote the glory of God. The state of the world is still such, and probably will be till the millennium

SOURCE: Charles G. Finney, "What a Revival of Religion Is" (New York, 1835).

is fully come, that religion must be mainly promoted by these excitements. How long and how often has the experiment been tried, to bring the church to act steadily for God, without these periodical excitements! Many good men have supposed, and still suppose, that the best way to promote religion, is to go along *uniformly*, and gather in the ungodly gradually, and without excitement. But however such reasoning may appear in the abstract, *facts* demonstrate its futility. If the church were far enough advanced in knowledge, and had stability of principle enough to *keep awake*, such a course would do; but the church is so little enlightened, and there are so many counteracting causes, that the church will not go steadily to work without a special excitement.

It is altogether improbable that religion will ever make progress among *heathen* nations except through the influence of revivals. The attempt is now making to do it by education, and other cautious and gradual improvements. But so long as the laws of mind remain what they are, it cannot be done in this way. There must be excitement sufficient to wake up the dormant moral powers, and roll back the tide of degradation and sin. And precisely so far as our own land approximates to heathenism, it is impossible for God or man to promote religion in such a state of things but by powerful excitements. This is evident from the fact that this has always been the way in which God has done it. God does not create these excitements, and choose this method to promote religion for nothing, or without reason. Where mankind are so reluctant to obey God, they will not act until they are excited. For instance, how many there are who know that they ought to be religious, but they are afraid if they become pious they shall be laughed at by their companions. Many are wedded to idols, others are procastinating repentance, until they are settled in life, or until they have secured some favorite worldly interest. Such persons never will give up their false shame, or relinquish their ambitious schemes, till they are so excited that they cannot contain themselves any longer.

These remarks are designed only as an introduction to the discourse. I shall now proceed with the main design, to show,

    I. What a revival of religion is not;
    II. What it is; and
    III. The agencies employed in promoting it.

I. A Revival of Religion Is Not a Miracle

1. A miracle has been generally defined to be, a Divine interference, setting aside or suspending the laws of nature. It is not a miracle, in this sense. All the laws of matter and mind remain in force. They are neither suspended nor set aside in a revival.

2. It is not a miracle according to another definition of the term miracle—*something above the powers of nature*. There is nothing in religion beyond the ordinary powers of nature. It consists entirely in the *right exercise* of the powers of nature. It is just that, and nothing else. When mankind becomes religious, they are not *enabled* to put forth exertions which they were unable before to put forth. They only exert the powers they had before in a different way, and use them for the glory of God.

3. It is not a miracle, or dependent on a miracle, in any sense. It is a purely philosophical result of the right use of the constituted means—as much as any other effect produced by the application of means. There may be a miracle among its antecedent causes, or there may not. The apostles employed miracles, simply as a means by which they arrested attention to their message, and established its Divine authority. But the miracle was not the revival. The miracle was one thing; the revival that followed it was quite another thing. The revivals in the apostles' days were connected with miracles, but they were not miracles.

I said that a revival is the result of the *right* use of the appropriate means. The means which God has enjoyed for the production of a revival, doubtless have a natural tendency to produce a revival. Otherwise God would not have enjoined them. But means will not produce a revival, we all know, without the blessing of God. No more will grain, when it is sowed, produce a crop without the blessing of God. It is impossible for us to say that there is not as direct an influence or agency from God, to produce a crop of grain, as there is to produce a revival. What are the laws of nature, according to which, it is supposed, that grain yields a crop? They are nothing but the constituted manner of the operations of God. In the Bible, the word of God is compared to grain, and preaching is compared to sowing seed, and the results to the springing up and growth of the crop. And the result is just as philosophical in the one case, as in the other, and is as naturally connected with the cause.

II. I Am to Show What a Revival Is

It presupposes that the church is sunk down in a backslidden state, and a revival consists in the return of the church from her backslidings, and in the conversion of sinners.

1. A revival always includes conviction of sin on the part of the church. Backslidden professors cannot wake up and begin right away in the service of God, without deep searchings of heart. The fountains of sin need to be broken up. In a true revival, Christians are always brought under such convictions; they see their sins in such a light, that often they find it impossible to maintain a hope of their acceptance with God. It does not always go to that extent; but there are always, in a genuine revival, deep convictions of sin, and often cases of abandoning all hope.

2. Backslidden Christians will be brought to repentance. A revival is nothing else than a new beginning of obedience to God. Just as in the case of a converted sinner, the first step is a deep repentance, a breaking down of heart, a getting down into the dust before God, with deep humility, and forsaking of sin.

3. Christians will have their faith renewed. While they are in their backslidden state they are blind to the state of sinners. Their hearts are as hard as marble. The truths of the Bible only appear like a dream. They admit it to be all true; their conscience and their judgment assent to it; but their faith does not see it standing out in bold relief; in all the burning realities of eternity. But when they enter into a revival, they no longer will renew the love of God in their hearts. . . .

4. A revival breaks the power of the world and of sin over Christians. It brings them to such vantage ground that they get a fresh impulse towards heaven. They have a new foretaste of heaven, and new desires after union to God; and the charm of the world is broken, and the power of sin overcome.

5. When the churches are thus awakened and reformed, the reformation and salvation of sinners will follow, going through the same stages of conviction, repentance, and reformation. Their hearts will be broken down and changed. Very often the most abandoned profligates are among the subjects. Harlots, and drunkards, and infidels, and all sorts of abandoned characters, are awakened and converted. The worst part of human society are softened, and reclaimed, and made to appear as lovely specimens of the beauty of holiness.

III. I Am To Consider the Agencies Employed in Carrying Forward a Revival of Religion

Ordinarily, there are three agents employed in the work of conversion, and one instrument. The agents are God—some person who brings the truth to bear on the mind,—and the sinner himself. The instrument is the truth. There are *always two* agents, God and the sinner, employed and active in every case of genuine conversion.

1. The agency of God is two-fold; by his Providence and by his Spirit.

(1.) By his providential government, he so arranges events as to bring the sinner's mind and the truth in contact. He brings the sinner where the truth reaches his ears or his eyes. It is often interesting to trace the manner in which God arranges events so as to bring this about, and how he sometimes makes everything seem to favor a revival. The state of the weather, and of the public health, and other circumstances concur to make every thing just right to favor the application of truth with the greatest possible efficacy. How he sometimes sends a minister along, just at the time he is wanted! How he brings out a particular truth, just at the particular time when the individual it is fitted to reach is in the way to hear!

(2.) God's special agency by his Holy Spirit. Having direct access to the mind, and knowing infinitely well the whole history and state of each individual sinner, he employs that truth which is best adapted to his particular case, and then sets it home with Divine power. He gives it such vividness, strength, and power, that the sinner quails and throws down his weapons of rebellion, and turns to the Lord. Under his influence, the truth burns and cuts its way like fire. He makes the truth stand out in such aspects, that it crushes the proudest man down with the weight of a mountain. . . .

2. The agency of men is commonly employed. Men are not mere *instruments* in the hands of God. Truth is the instrument. The preacher is a moral agent in the work; he acts; he is not a mere passive instrument; he is voluntary in promoting the conversion of sinners.

3. The agency of the sinner himself. The conversion of a sinner consists in his obeying the truth. It is therefore impossible it should take place without his agency, for it consists in *his* acting right. He is influenced to this by the agency of God, and by the agency of men. Men act on their fellow-men, not only by language, but by their looks, their tears, their daily deportment. See that impenitent man there, who has a pious wife. Her very looks, her tenderness, her solemn, compassionate dignity, softened and moulded into the image of Christ, are a sermon to him all the time. He has to turn his mind away, because it is such a reproach to him. He feels a sermon ringing in his ears all day long.

If Christians have deep feeling on the subject of religion themselves, they will produce deep feeling wherever they go. And if they are cold, or light and trifling, they inevitably destroy all deep feeling, even in awakened sinners.

The church is required to use the means for the conversion of sinners. Sinners cannot properly be said to use the means for their own conversion. The church uses the means. What sinners do is to submit to the truth, or to resist it. It is a mistake of sinners, to think they are using means for their own conversion. The whole drift of a revival, and every thing about it, is designed to present the truth *to* your mind, for your obedience or resistance.

Finney was the most widely known but not the only successful revivalist of the pre-Civil War period. Numerous Baptists, Methodists, and Presbyterians were active in similar campaigns. What is more significant is that revivalism made inroads on many groups traditionally unsympathetic to such methods. Lutheran and Reformed ministers copied Finney's methods, and even some Quakers adopted a general pattern of revivalism. Most surprising of all developments along this line was the rise of an evangelistic group among Unitarians, sparked by the leadership of George E. Ellis and Frederic Dan Huntington. Clearly, by the middle of the nineteenth century, revivalism had become the predominant style of most American Christianity. Indeed, one of the first great historians of American religion, Robert Baird, commented that revivals had become so much a part of the religious system that "he who should oppose himself to revivals, as such, would be regarded by most of our evangelical Christians as, *ipso facto*, an enemy to spiritual religion itself."[36]

The Civil War's ravages left behind a nation ripe for a new upsurge of evangelistic zeal. The pace of urbanization steadily increased, and more and more the big cities became the area of major activity for the churches. Building on the foundations laid by Finney, another major figure further organized and systematized urban evangelism. Dwight Lyman Moody (1837–1899) represented a new dimension in professional revivalism because he was not an ordained minister but a Congregational layman. Originally a shoe salesman, Moody organized revival campaigns in the style of a successful business venture. Such an approach was thoroughly congenial to the ethos of the country in the last half of the nineteenth century, the era of the rise of many major American industrial and manufacturing enterprises. Not surprisingly, much of Moody's support came from the business community, and much of his appeal was to middle- and upper-class business and professional people. He employed every technique of modern business promotion—planning, organization, publicity, efficient executive direction, the expenditure of immense sums of money. Operating with his headquarters in Chicago, Moody was at first primarily involved in such tasks as the organization of Sunday

[36] Quoted by S. E. Mead in H. Richard Niebuhr and D. D. Williams (eds.), *The Ministry in Historical Perspectives* (New York: Harper & Row, 1956), pp. 226–227.

schools and the promotion of the Young Men's Christian Association (Y.M.C.A.). In 1873, however, a two-year tour of the British Isles projected him into international prominence. Thereafter, in association with Ira D. Sankey (1840–1908), the first of the great revival song leaders and musicians, he conducted highly successful campaigns in all the major cities of this country, from New York to San Francisco.

Moody's theology illustrated pietistic reductionism in its clearest form. Never claiming to be anything but a layman and having no formal training in theology, he preached a straightforward, simple version of the gospel, sticking to what he called the "three R's:" "Ruin by sin, Redemption by Christ, and Regeneration by the Holy Ghost." Hundreds of "decision cards" were distributed to his hearers and, when signed, these cards were used by the local ministers to follow up the revival services by enlisting the new converts into the churches of the city.

Moody's revival campaigns were successful not only in securing Christian converts but also in raising huge sums of money. As a result, Moody made a fortune, but he gave it all away, particularly for the establishment of schools and seminaries. Large student conferences were held regularly at Northfield, Massachusetts, under Moody's supervision, and in this manner college and university leaders were brought under his influence. He established a women's school at Northfield as well as the large Bible Institute in Chicago that still bears his name.

By 1880 Dwight L. Moody so completely dominated the American religious scene that, for almost the next three quarters of a century, revivalism was patterned after his example. A series of other evangelists— Gypsy Smith, Sam Jones, R. A. Torrey, and J. Wilbur Chapman—followed in his footsteps. When, however, Moody's methods in the hands of lesser men failed to produce sufficient results, many of the revival preachers turned to more flamboyant and sensational approaches. Perhaps the most accomplished showman of all was William (Billy) Sunday (1863–1935), a converted professional baseball player who reached the zenith of his career between 1914 and 1919, conducting evangelistic campaigns in Pittsburgh, Philadelphia, Boston, Los Angeles, Washington, and most successfully, New York, where he claimed 98,000 converts. Sunday's antics in the pulpit were eccentric, to say the least, and did as much as anything to discredit professional revivalism. Rolling up his sleeves and shaking his fists, he demolished chairs and slid across the stage in imitation of a reprobate sinner trying to reach heaven in the same way a baseball player steals home. A theologically conservative Presbyterian, he preached a simplistic gospel of sin and salvation, mixing his revival pleas with energetic attacks on "booze," dancing, and tobacco. During the crisis period of World War I, he adapted his preaching to emphasize "100 per cent Americanism," insisting that "Christianity and patriotism are synonymous terms" just as "hell and traitors are synonymous."[37]

[37] See Hudson, op. cit., pp. 366–367.

Opposition to revivalism had been steadily gaining ground in many religious quarters since the turn of the century, and the tactics of Sunday and others stimulated the hostility. Such opposition came not only from the traditional liberal and rationalistic antirevival forces but from the ranks of evangelical Protestantism as well. Many churches and pastors preferred to rely on such evangelistic outreaches as the Sunday school rather than on the sporadic excitement of revivals.

Originating in England in the latter part of the eighteenth century, the Sunday school movement, emphasizing Christian education for children, mushroomed in the United States, particularly after the Civil War. Dwight L. Moody, among others, played a prime role in encouraging such schools, and he enlisted an energetic Chicago wholesale grocer, B. F. Jacobs (1834–1902), to head up a nationwide, interdenominational organization with the goal of multiplying the number of Sunday schools in the country. Encouraged by the support of Moody as well as by that of such evangelical liberals as Horace Bushnell, a leading Congregational pastor and theologian, the enthusiasm for organized Christian education grew by leaps and bounds. Bushnell himself was highly critical of revivals, reacting against what he called their "artificial fireworks" and "jump and stir." Religious education for children, he argued, provided a healthier, more natural, and more constant means of grace. It was in this direction that the Sunday school movement as a whole tended to develop.

The Sunday schools gradually replaced revivalism as the primary recruiting device of most American churches. Even today Sunday schools remain a major part of the program of most denominations, and in 1960 over 40 million people were enrolled, including large numbers of adults. In spite of such impressive figures Sunday school leaders admit that the movement continues to incorporate many of the weaknesses characteristic of a purely voluntary, nonprofessional endeavor. Attendance of those enrolled is often poor, teachers are generally not well trained, and pupil preparation is virtually nonexistent. Nevertheless, the educational efforts of the churches continue to play a vital role in contemporary evangelism.

By the beginning of World War II, the popularity of revivalism had reached a low ebb. Some minority church groups, such as the Fundamentalists, a hyperconservative group stretching across several denominations, continued to sponsor revival meetings, as did many "main-line" Baptist, Methodist, Presbyterian, and Disciple churches in the "Bible Belt," the strongly Protestant southern region of the country. But the days of mass evangelism appeared to be numbered. Only certain off-center movements, such as the Foursquare Gospel of the glamorous woman evangelist, Aimee Semple McPherson (1890–1944), and the Moral Rearmament movement led by Frank N. D. Buchman (1878–1960) achieved any large-scale success. Buchman modified traditional revival techniques in order to appeal not to the "down and out" but to the "up and out." In 1939 he filled the Hollywood Bowl in California with thirty thousand people who came to hear his emphases upon the "four absolutes" of honesty, purity, unselfishness, and love, and the "five C's" of confidence, confession, conviction, conversion, and continuance. McPherson, on the other hand, represented an extreme type of Pentecostalism, the label applied to a coalition of church groups emphasizing faith healing and ecstatic manifestations of the presence of the Holy Spirit. Although the Foursquare Gospel movement faded into obscurity after her death, Pentecostalism continued to develop and is today a vigorous, fast-growing segment of American Christianity. By 1960 the Pentecostal and Holiness groups counted more than 1.5 million adherents.

With the close of World War II in 1945, the time was ripe for another general upsurge of revivalism. The twenty years between World Wars I and II had seen a steady decline in religious interest and involvement. Relatively speaking, the churches had lost much of their moral force. The pulpit and church press had ceased to exercise preeminence among the mass media, and the hunger and unemployment of the Great Depression had failed to stimulate any mass return to the faith of the fathers.

With the advent of a war against Hitler and the forces of Nazism, however, the nation was united in a new crusade. The collapse of the European order and the rise of threatening ideologies led Americans to a new concern for their own national heritage, including its religious tradition. Sidney E. Ahlstrom, the religious historian, observed: " 'There are no atheists in foxholes,' was the word from the theatres of military action. In millions of blue-star and gold-star households and in thousands of home churches the same could be said. In this sense, the 'postwar revival' began long before the fighting ceased." [38]

Following the war, as has been indicated, there was a remarkable upsurge in religious activity and affiliation. The trend affected religious communities of all kinds—Protestant, Catholic, and Jewish. According to the statistics of church membership, 49 per cent of the American people had been affiliated with some church or religious organization in 1940. By 1960, the percentage had risen to 69 per cent.

Many reasons were suggested for the postwar revival. Martin Marty theorized that the American people, victorious in war and prosperous in peace, wanted to settle down. They needed to soothe their anxieties, have their way of life sanctified by divine blessing, justify their complacencies, and organize their reality around them.[39] Millions turned to religion for their answers. Ahlstrom speaks of a "surge of piety" that grew partially out of a search for peace of mind and confident living in an "age of anxiety." He goes on to characterize the religion of that time as a generalized "faith in faith," based on pious utilitarianism.[40]

Two prominent public figures—one a politician, the other a preacher—can be used as symbols of the era. President Dwight D. Eisenhower was

[38] Ahlstrom, Sidney E., *A Religious History of the American People* (Garden City, N.Y.: Doubleday, 1975), Vol. 2, p. 445.
[39] Marty, "The Revival and the Revolution," op. cit., p. 107.
[40] Ahlstrom, op. cit., Vol. 2, p. 451.

a prestigious symbol of generalized religiosity and America's smug and patriotic moralism. Eisenhower, who became a member of the Presbyterian church only after his presidential inauguration, tied religion and Americanism together with such public declarations as "America is the mightiest power which God has as yet seen fit to put upon his footstool," and "America is great because she is good." And he provided a classic justification for the new religious outlook. "Our government," he said in 1954, "makes no sense unless it is founded on a deeply felt religious faith—and I don't care what it is."[41]

The second significant personality of the period illustrates the continuing persistence of the revivalistic motif in American religion. It remained for Billy Graham to restore mass evangelism, at least for a time, to a position of prominence. Born in North Carolina, Graham grew up as a Presbyterian but became a Southern Baptist after he began to achieve success as a revivalist. He started his ministry in association with Youth for Christ, a postwar revival-oriented youth movement. In 1949 a tent revival in Los Angeles was given wide publicity, especially by the Hearst chain of newspapers. Three thousand people, including a number of celebrated public figures, made new or renewed commitments in the campaign, and Graham was projected into national prominence. Major evangelistic campaigns in such metropolitan centers as Boston and New York followed. In 1950 Graham and his highly organized team of coworkers began a popular radio program, the Hour of Decision, and by 1956 the Billy Graham Evangelistic Association was effectively using almost all available mass media—advertising, television, radio, cinema, and paperback books—and working with an annual budget of $2 million. In writing his book on revivalism during the early 1940s, William Warren Sweet, the veteran Methodist historian, titled his final chapter, "Revivalism on the Wane"[42]; but Graham was proof that the urban revival tradition in America was anything but dead.

Graham's sincerity has seldom been questioned, and his success in drawing large crowds to hear him preach is undoubted. For many years national polls have established him as one of the country's most admired personalities. But many people have raised serious questions about the nature and results of his evangelistic approach. How "real" and lasting are the decisions made in his services? What effect has Graham's theologically conservative message had on the pressing problems of the nation—issues such as race relations, war and peace, the tensions of the inner-city areas?[43] As Graham became a national religious leader, his stature was reflected in his close friendships with American presidents from Eisenhower to Nixon, but this relationship has also been questioned

[41] Cited in Ahlstrom, op. cit., Vol. 2, p. 450.
[42] W. W. Sweet, *Revivalism in America* (Nashville: Abingdon, 1944).
[43] It should be noted that, early in his career, Graham began to refuse to speak to racially segregated audiences in his revival meetings. This stance drew considerable criticism in the South. For example, in 1957 the governor of South Carolina refused to let Graham speak in the state.

by those who see Graham as a somewhat politically naive supporter of the status quo "establishment" rather than as a prophetic spokesman for the radical claims of Christianity.[44]

Graham's crusades across the country undoubtedly have inspired renewed interest in religion among vast numbers. People respond to the easily understood, Bible-centered messages he preaches, in which religious faith is presented as an all-embracing remedy for the ills of the world. Like Moody and Finney before him, Graham believes that Christian conversion radically transforms human nature. Because the corruption of human nature lies at the root of all human problems, becoming a Christian is regarded as the key not only to peace and human happiness but also to the solution of every social issue. Some observers have felt that Graham's appeal has been largely "to those unsophisticated people who seek a return to the imagined simplicity of the past."[45] Whether this is true or not, the revivals have clearly touched a responsive chord in many Americans who feel a deep spiritual need and sense of frustration in the modern world.

The following excerpts are taken from a chapter entitled "Turning On" in Graham's *The Jesus Generation*, published in 1971. The book was intended primarily for young people, and though not actually a sermon, this chapter is illustrative of Graham's preaching style. He presents his conviction that only a personal commitment to Christ can bring the answer to humanity's salvation; typically, the chapter closes with an appeal for an immediate, personal decision for Christ.

Document 27 _____

From *The Jesus Generation* by Billy Graham

We get dirt off our bodies by turning on the water in the shower. We get the darkness out of a room by turning on the light. We get our automobiles to run by turning on the switch. The "hip" generation popularized the phrase "turning on" to describe the drug experience. Smoking pot, dropping acid, or shooting heroin, they turned on for a high and got into their trip.

To become a Christian, you must "turn on" to God by placing your full faith in

SOURCE: From *The Jesus Generation* by Billy Graham. Copyright 1971 by Billy Graham. Reprinted by permission of Billy Graham Evangelistic Association.

[44] As evidence of Graham's naivete, critics point to his continuing public support of Richard Nixon long after damaging evidence had surfaced against the former president. Additionally, charges were leveled in the press in 1979 that the Billy Graham Association had concealed the exact size of the large reserves of funds in its treasury, a charge later admitted by the Association. Graham's personal integrity was not impugned, however, nor was there any evidence of misuse of the funds. [For a searching and controversial study of Graham and his career, see Marshall Frady, *Billy Graham* (Boston: Little, Brown, 1979).]

[45] Gerald N. Grob and Robert N. Beck (eds.), *American Ideas* (New York: The Free Press, 1963), Vol. 2, pp. 326–327.

Christ as Savior and confessing Him as Lord. And the wonderful thing about it is that it works.

I once conducted a crusade in a city that was having one crisis after another with its restless young people. One night I disguised myself and attended a rock festival in order to discover what attracted so many—thousands. Next day, I reported that I had been present and publicly invited the entire hippie set to attend our services. They responded by the hundreds, and when I invited them to receive Christ, scores came forward. Recently, one of them wrote to me.

"I came to the crusade because I thought you were a regular guy," he said. "To those of us who attended it was to be just another experience, something to relieve our boredom. But as you spoke, I began to hear another voice, and I knew that what you were saying was 'truth.' When you asked us to come forward if we wanted to receive Christ, I rose almost spontaneously and walked down the aisle! Standing there, I felt more alive than I'd ever felt in my life. Everything I had searched for or longed for seemed to materialize in that one moment. I stayed on with my old friends a few more weeks, but presently I gravitated to those who had shared my spiritual experience. All of us began to pray regularly and to study the Bible. I am now attending seminary, studying for the ministry. I expect to spend the rest of my life spreading the thrilling news of God's love and forgiveness with all that will listen."

This young man had been "born again." He had been "turned on" spiritually. Jesus Christ works like that, channeling His revolutionary power into the lives of those who put their faith in Him. He talked frequently about drastic changes, but always they had to start in the heart. This is why He insisted on conversion and new birth. "Verily I say unto you, Except ye be converted, and become as little children," He said, "ye shall not enter into the kingdom of heaven" (Matthew 18:3).

The shape of things to come has been apparent in our crusades for several years now, as a vast majority of our audiences included more and more young people, and as many thousands of them have marched across football stadiums and down the aisles of great indoor arenas to discover a new life. Their identity crisis is over! They have found what they were looking for by turning on to Jesus . . . .

Not long after my own conversion, I read a tract entitled "Four Things God Wants You to Know." Campus Crusade for Christ, which has played a major role in sparking the new "Jesus Revolution," has expanded these four items into a beautiful little booklet and given them away by the hundreds of thousands. Literally, it has helped countless young people to get "turned on" spiritually.

The first law is that God loves you and has a wonderful plan for your life. God loves you! Most young people have heard or perhaps memorized John 3:16, the most familiar verse in the Bible. In one modern version it reads: "For God loved the world so much that He gave His only Son so that everyone who believes in Him should not be lost, but should have eternal life."

Young people talk a lot about love. Most of their songs are about love. "All You Need is Love," "I Can't Live in a World Without Love," "The Glory of Love," "Man Without Love," "Love Can Make the Poorest Man a Millionaire" are recent examples.

"The supreme happiness of life," Victor Hugo said long ago, "is the conviction that we are loved." "Love is the first requirement for mental health," declared

Sigmund Freud. The Bible teaches that "God is love" and that God loves you. To realize that is of paramount importance. Nothing else matters so much.

And loving you, God has a wonderful plan for your life. Who else could plan and guide your life so well? He, the Shepherd; you, one of His sheep. A young woman who came forward in one our meetings told us how God had once seemed so far away; but now in Jesus Christ, He was always near at hand in every situation. "The will of Christ for me," she explained, "is wonderfully simple and simply wonderful."

*The second spiritual law is that you must acknowledge you are a sinner—*by nature and by practice. This sinful nature separates you from God and makes it impossible for you to experience either His love or His plan for your life. David, the great king of Israel, once wrote: "I was shaped in iniquity and in sin did my mother conceive me." Isaiah the prophet expressed the same idea, "All we like sheep have gone astray. We have turned everyone to his own way." Solomon, one of the wisest men who ever lived, explained that man's instinctive behavior, when he excludes God, is invariably disastrous. "There is a way that seemeth right unto man, but the end thereof are the ways of death." Jesus made it clear that the easy, popular way is the wrong way, "Wide is the gate and broad is the way that leadeth to destruction and many (the majority) there be that go in thereat." But "straight is the gate and narrow is the way that leadeth into life and few there are that find it" (Matthew 7:13,14). Paul argued to the Romans that the defilement of the human race was universal. "They have all gone out of the way" and "the way of peace have they not known . . . for all have sinned and come short of the glory of God." Not only does our sin make us come short of God's expectations, but it separates us from God. Isaiah taught, "Your sins have separated His face from you."

Youth senses this guilt, this alienation, this separation from God, and wonders what causes it. A reader wrote to "Dear Abby": "When a kid goes wrong, which factor is more responsible, his heredity or his environment?" Abby replied, "It's a toss-up." The Bible says exactly that! We are sinners both by heredity and environment; both by nature and by nurture; both by instinct and by practice. . . .

Because we *are* sinners, we often feel lonely, and unloved. A social scientist once polled the people of this country and discovered that at any time during the day about 135,000 Americans are saying "I'm sick and tired of everything!" In his first chapter, the prophet Isaiah described the sins of ancient Israel and noted the results: "The whole head is sick and the whole heart is faint." Look around! Listen to youth today. The Rolling Stones have made "I Can't Get No Satisfaction!" one of the most popular modern songs. The title speaks for itself. Sin brings no satisfaction. Inger Stevens won the Golden Globe Award as the best televised actress during the sixties and began the seventies by taking her own life. "Sometime I get so lonely I could scream," she had said. That's alienation! The feeling is shared by the youth of every country in the world.

So why not quit beating around the bush! Why not call our problem by its real name, which is "sin." Sin is selfishness—it's a transgression of God's laws—it's coming short of God's moral requirements—and of these we are *all guilty*. Let's face it, admit it, and forsake it! That is called repentance. Jesus said, "Except ye repent, ye shall all likewise perish." That word repentance is used in the New Testament more than seventy times.

The third spiritual law is that Jesus Christ is God's only provision for man's sin.

Only through Him can you know and experience God's love, forgiveness, salvation, and plan for you. "For at the very time when we were still sinners, then Christ died for the wicked," wrote Paul. John said, "In this was manifest the love of God toward us that the Father sent the Son to be the Saviour of the world." Jesus did not say that he was *a* way. He said: I am *the* Way, *the* Truth, and *the* Life; no man comes to the Father but by me!"

Sometimes we miss the significance of the cross on which Jesus died, stumbling over its simplicity. Its uncomplicated meaning is that Jesus Christ has paid the price of our sins. By taking our place and our punishment, He gave us the gift of forgiveness, cleansing, and everlasting life.

All the religions of the world are simply men looking for God. But Christianity is not merely one more religion. In Christianity, God is searching *for* man—and revealing Himself *to* man. That is why God has placed in man's heart a restlessness and a frustration—until he finds God! God's search for man led to the cross where His only Son suffered and died—died for you. This sounds foolish to modern ears. And to the ancients as well. When Paul went to the pagan city of Corinth, he said: "The proclamation of the cross is foolishness unto them that perish." But then he added: "The foolishness of God is wiser than men and the weakness of God is stronger than men" (1 Corinthians 1:25). In that ancient city, the cross of Christ was a stumbling block to the Jews, and to the Gentiles it was idiocy. Intellectual Corinthians preferred a system of philosophy predicated on the ability of man's mind to unravel the divine. They wanted something their minds could grasp. So Paul tells us that "the natural man receiveth not (cannot understand) the things of God" (1 Corinthians 2:14). Nor must you understand all God's mysteries in order to find Him and receive Him and know Him. A doctor writes a prescription which we cannot read for the treatment of a disease that we do not understand, and we gladly pay a sum which may seem unreasonable because we rely on his knowledge and have faith that he will make us well. Before the cross can have any meaning at all, the Spirit of God must open the mind. So long as we remain separated from God, the Scriptures teach, our minds are covered by a veil. To such a one—to an "outsider"—the cross must appear as a ridiculous symbol. To those of us who have experienced its transforming power, however, it represents the only cure for sin—the basic ill of humanity. The cross is the focal point of the life and ministry of Jesus Christ. His death upon it was no afterthought with God. When Christ took our places, our sin was laid on Him—and sin cannot be in two places at the same time. My sin was laid on Christ and, therefore, I have no sin charged to me. My sin is now Christ's burden. He has taken its load off me. He has become the sin bearer. Though I was indebted to God, Jesus paid off my debts. I will never suffer the shame of judgment or the terrors of hell. "As far as the east is from the west, "said the psalmist, "so far hath he removed our transgressions from us" (Psalm 103:12) . . . .

Are you saying, "I don't understand any of this. It sounds ridiculous! Listen! If a man were drowning and I threw him a life belt, would he say, "I'll not put this belt on until I know whether it's made of rubber or cork or if the material is strong enough to hold me"? No man in danger of drowning talks like that. No man who is ignorant of Christ is capable of comprehending the mystery of the cross as long as he is separated from God.

The Bible says that God was in Christ reconciling the world unto Himself. You are a part of that world. God wants you to be reconciled to Him—and He has provided a way in the person of Jesus.

The fourth spiritual law requires that you must openly accept Christ as your Savior and Lord. Only then can you know and experience God's love and plan for you.

Throughout one's youth, one struggles constantly to be "accepted." We want to be accepted by our parents, by our teachers, by our peers, and by our girl friend or boyfriend. To gain this acceptance, you will do almost anything. In the beginning of the letter written to the Ephesians, Paul exults in the fact that, as believers, God has "destined us—such is His will and pleasure—to be accepted as His sons through Jesus Christ." Think of it—sinners such as you and I *accepted* by God! No wonder John Newton, the slave trader, after his conversion wrote, "Amazing grace, that could save a wretch like me."

To "turn on" spiritually, you need only to open your heart to Jesus Christ and ask Him to come in. He says: "Here I stand knocking at the door; if anyone hears My voice and opens the door, I will come in and sit down to supper with him and he with Me." How beautiful! How simple! How thrilling!. . .

We are supposed to do more than admire Jesus. We are to "put Him on." As Paul wrote to the Ephesians, "Put on the new nature . . . created after the likeness of God in true righteousness and holiness! The likeness to God that we had at the first, the likeness that we lost by sin, is created again in us when our lives are joined to Christ."

Paul the apostle often spoke of the Christian as being "in Christ."

That is a Christian person's true identity.

Having done this, now I know my past—it is sinful but forgiven—and where I come from; I came from God. I know what went wrong; I tried to play God instead of being satisfied to be a real man. I know my future; my destiny is Heaven. And I know the present; I live in the here and now having Jesus always within me, His Holy Spirit to guide, teach, and lead . . . .

Right now, thousands of young people are confronting the living Christ. You can too. Would you like to pray the short prayer we pray in our crusades with those who come forward to receive Christ?

> Oh Lord, I am a sinner. I am sorry for my sins. I am willing to turn from my sins. I receive Jesus Christ as my Lord and Savior. I confess Him as Lord. I want to serve Him from this moment on in the fellowship of His Church. In Christ's name, Amen.

In other sections of this volume Graham adds another frequent emphasis of his preaching: judgment and the possibility that the end of the world may be very near. The urgency of such a conviction has often played a prominent part in revival preaching, as has its companion expectation of the dawning of a golden age, the so-called millennium.[46]

[46] The term *millennium* refers to a thousand-year period of peace and plenty under the direct rule of Christ after his Second Coming. The age is described in the book of Revelation.

Finney, for instance, often employed this theme in his sermons, as did Dwight L. Moody. After World War I the millennial theme assumed an increasingly central role in the doctrines of the Fundamentalists, [47] the most conservative branch of American Protestantism, and also in the beliefs of many of the Pentecostal and Holiness groups. In all these cases the expectation of a catastrophic end of the present age and the millennial hope served as a powerful stimulus to revival preaching.

Graham represents the only significant contemporary exponent of traditional mass evangelism. In fact, revivalism appears to have lost most of its appeal to the mainline church groups in this country, and many religious organizations are actively engaged in the search for something to take the place of the "old-time" revivals. This search has led the churches in several different directions.

First, increased emphasis has been placed on the *educational efforts* of the churches. Sunday Schools, of course, are still widely used, but in recent years more attempts have been made to expand religious education into week-day programs. Often this has taken the form of after-school or "released-time" religious instruction, but legal problems and other difficulties have led many churches and denominations to organize full-scale parochial schools, where religious training is combined with secular education. Obviously, the mushrooming growth of Protestant parochial schools in the last few years, especially in the South, is partially a reaction to the integration of the public schools, but it also reflects the desires of many parents to give their children more religious training than is available in the Sunday School. Catholics, of course, have long relied on parochial schools for indoctrination of their members. Indeed, the energetic Catholic parochial school movement of the nineteenth century can be understood partially as an answer to the threat of Protestant revivalism. Today, however, both Catholics and Protestants are relying on parochial schools, despite the skyrocketing costs of maintaining such institutions.

Efforts have also been made to revise and improve Sunday School curricular materials to make them more appealing and relevant. The Episcopal "Seabury Series" and the "Faith and Work" materials of Southern Baptists are only two examples of new approaches to learning aids. In addition, much attention has been given to the use of group dynamics, encounter groups, and sensitivity training by pastors and other church leaders. Each of these innovations represents an attempt to find new evangelistic and indoctrinational methods suitable to the shape of contemporary culture.

A second area of experimentation is that of *liturgy and worship.* New approaches have been tried, for instance, in the field of church arch-

---

[47]Protestants who rigidly upheld the "fundamentals" of the faith—including the virgin birth, inerrancy of Scripture, and the literal return of Christ on clouds of glory. Fundamentalism enjoyed its greatest popularity after World War I but has had something of a resurgence in the last few years.

itecture, involving the design of the location in which worship takes place. Martin E. Marty comments on these developments:

> Instead of providing lecture halls for prancing preachers or borrowing outworn forms to evoke a false sense of security in worshippers, they [church architects] . . . are asking basic questions. They begin at the beginning by striving to suggest the setting for the human-divine dialogue, the sacred converse. Reminiscence of the cave is in their buildings, enclosures of space which suggest temporary withdrawal for renewed resource. They imply "the Difference" between church and world. The tent is there too, to allow for the perfect parable: the People of God are on the march, and the roofs over the light, wide-open airy churches overarching provide symbolic shelter.[48]

More immediate in effect than architectural changes have been the alterations in liturgy and worship forms. Many historically nonliturgical Protestant churches, for instance, have begun to experiment with stylized forms of worship. In addition, traditional liturgical patterns have been drastically modified, particularly through the use in both Protestant and Catholic congregations of "folk masses," jazz and rock music, drama, and multimedia presentations involving visual and audio aids. Such popular secularized religious entertainment as the "rock-oratorio" *Jesus Christ, Superstar* have been influential in many of these changes.

In the Catholic Church, of course, radical modifications in liturgy followed Vatican II, the ecumenical church council that ended its work in 1963. The use of the vernacular of native language in the Mass, in place of Latin; increased participation of lay Catholics in worship; and relaxation of such traditional disciplines as the ban against eating meat on Fridays are only a few of the changes introduced into Catholic worship and practice.

A third area of search has involved *new ecclesiastical forms*, that is, new ways of church organization and function. Many modern church leaders have been profoundly influenced by the theological writings of men like Karl Barth (1886–1968) and others, who emphasized the concept of the "servant church," arguing on biblical grounds that the primary mission of the church is to identify with the needs of the world about it. Such a picture of the church has far-reaching implications in the area of evangelism. It means that the church is not obliged to be a salesman or a "huckster" of the gospel, intent on persuading people by almost any means possible to join its ranks. Its main concern should be that of ministering to the problems, sufferings, and sorrows of men and women. From this perspective evangelism becomes a secondary emphasis, arising naturally out of the church's service to others.

In the attempt to make the servant image of the church concrete, many experiments in new church forms have been undertaken. These include the Church of the Savior in Washington, D.C., a highly dis-

[48] Marty, *The New Shape of American Religion*, op. cit., pp. 144–145.

ciplined congregation of limited numbers in which every member is required to render a specific number of hours of community service each week. Another type of organizational structure is represented by the Ecumenical Institute in Chicago, whose members live in semi-communal style in an urban ghetto area, identifying themselves as completely as possible with the ghetto residents and their problems. Judson Memorial Baptist Church in Greenwich Village, New York City, is yet a third form of structure, attracting wide attention through its unique ministry to the artists, entertainers, and transient "hippies" of the "Village."

Catholic and Jewish Responses

Although the traditional forms of Protestant revivalism have not been typical of Catholics and Jews in America, certain important influences of revivalism and coordinate efforts among these groups should be mentioned.

Perhaps the most interesting and direct influence of revivalism upon Catholics was the development of the parish mission movement, especially in the last half of the nineteenth century. The kinship of this movement with Protestant revivalism was not widely noticed by scholars until 1978, when a comprehensive study of the movement by Jay P. Dolan took as its thesis that "the religion of revivalism was not exclusively a Protestant enterprise, but it also swept through Catholic America in the second half of the nineteenth century and, in the process, shaped the piety of the people and strengthened the institutional church."[49]

Dolan began his discussion by quoting a passage from the memoirs of Charles G. Finney, referring to a convert at his 1842 revival in Rochester, New York:

Several of the lawyers that were at this time converted in Rochester, gave up their profession and went into the ministry. Among these was one of Chancellor W——'s sons, at that time a young lawyer in Rochester, and who appeared at the time to be soundly converted. For some reason, with which I am not acquainted, he went to Europe and to Rome, and finally became a Roman Catholic priest. He has been for years laboring zealously to promote revivals of religion among them, holding protracted meetings; and, as he told me himself, . . . trying to accomplish in the Roman Catholic church what I was endeavoring to accomplish in the Protestant church. . . .[50]

The person to whom Finney referred was Clarence Walworth, who became one of the foremost parish mission preachers in America.

[49] Jay P. Dolan, *Catholic Revivalism: The American Experience, 1830–1900* (Notre Dame, Ind.: University of Notre Dame Press, 1978), pp. xv–xvi.
[50] Ibid., p. xv.

In his thoroughly documented study Dolan traces the development of the parish mission in American Catholicism, using the terms *parish mission* and *Catholic revival meeting* interchangeably. He justifies this for two reasons: First, nineteenth-century observers, Finney included, were quick to see the similarity between the two phenomena; and second, the parish mission fostered a type of religion, evangelicalism, that has long been associated with the technique of mass evangelism known as revivalism. He points out that in the early part of the nineteenth century the "widespread neglect of religion and the competitive spirit of the American religious environment demanded something more than ritual and ceremony. People had to be converted to religion before they could practice it. The key to the renewal of piety was the Catholic revival."[51]

The parish mission was built around a series of special meetings, sponsored by a Catholic church, usually conducted by a visiting speaker or evangelist, and designed to renew the commitments of the faithful and to convert unbelievers. Dolan stresses many of the similarities between a Protestant revival and a mission. Of particular interest was the content of the sermons. Dolan quotes from a sermon on "Hell" delivered by Walter Elliott, a priest of the Paulist order:

> And so tonight it is that same dire necessity which makes it my miserable business to concentrate in a single sermon all the threatenings of an angry God, to bring forward what has so far been the dark background of every picture for your sole consideration by a more particular description of the torments of the lost. And brethren, if we knew of no hell to preach of, if we had only the sentiment of honor, of gratitude to appeal to, we should never give any missions: they would all be failures. Ah! but when the sinner hears of a fire which is never going to be quenched, of a gnawing worm which shall never die, it strikes terror to his soul, you will see his face turn pale, you will see the tears start unbidden to his eyes.[52]

Obviously, despite great doctrinal differences, there was more than coincidental kinship between preachers like Elliott and the line of Protestant revivalists from Edwards to Graham. Even the newspapers were aware of the similarities. The March 15, 1861, edition of the Newburyport, Massachusetts, *Daily Herald* described the closing night of a Paulist mission:

> We are not unacquainted with revival meetings, and we have before seen people at camp meetings and other excited gatherings, stand up and vow; but we never before saw such a scene. The multitude looked as though they would have sunk into the earth or been burned together at the stake, before one of them would in the slightest manner have denied the faith . . . .
> During some parts of the service, especially at the farewell, the people were greatly moved. The speaker held them as by a sort of electrical influence, and the whole audience quivered like the leaves of a tree in the breeze. Now they sunk; and now the rising tide found vents in sobs and moans.[53]

[51] Ibid., pp. 186–187.
[52] Cited in ibid., p. 98.
[53] Cited in ibid., pp. 84–85.

Dolan concludes that by the end of the century the revival meeting was one of the dominant features of Catholic life. He writes: "Through the revival, evangelicalism became a national religion which united the American people more than has been previously imagined . . . . Revivalism has demonstrated that Catholics were nurtured in a piety that was also strikingly American, fiercely evangelical, and deeply individualistic."[54]

Modifications in Catholic liturgy following Vatican II have already been referred to. Since Vatican II had as a primary purpose the reshaping of the Catholic Church to relate more effectively to the modern world, these changes can, in some sense, be seen as parallel in purpose to that of contemporary modifications of Protestant revivalism. In addition, the extensive use of "retreats" is a popular contemporary practice that had its beginnings in the expansion of the Catholic monastic movement in this country during and after World War II. No important changes in church form or operation were involved, only a new emphasis on a very old facet of religious life. Although Catholics had maintained a few monasteries in the United States for many years, they had never been especially popular. Following the war, however, a large number of young men, many of them veterans, entered the monastic orders, seeking lives of contemplation, discipline, and service. The Catholic orders, particularly the Trappists, a reformed branch of the Cistercians, grew rapidly, and many new monasteries were founded. Most noted of the men who chose this path was Thomas Merton (1905–1969), a highly educated sophisticate who became a Trappist and, later, the author of a number of best-selling books—including his influential autobiography *The Seven Storey Mountain* (1948)—which inspired many others to follow his example.

The Catholic revival of interest in the contemplative life reached far beyond those who actually took monastic vows. Lay people in Catholic churches were also affected, and several large organizations, such as the Christophers, founded by Father James G. Keller, encouraged the practice of prayer and meditation. As part of the general religious shift of the 1960s and early 1970s, however, interest and participation in these groups suffered a decline.

Throughout this discussion of revivalism little has been said about American Judaism. The omission is inevitable, because the Jews in this country have traditionally had little direct involvement with the cyclical revivalistic outbreaks that so profoundly affected Protestants and to a significant extent, as we have just seen, Catholics. Yet it is important to recognize that Judaism has had its own brand of revival, especially since the terrible events associated with Nazi Germany and World War II.

Jewish immigration to this country from Europe, especially that which took place between the Civil War and World War I, was accompanied by large-scale defection from the synagogue. Many Jews (especially, as Will Herberg has pointed out, *second-generation* American

[54] Ibid., p. 203.

Jews,)[55] were eager to blend into the American scene. Certainly other factors also played a part, but whatever the reasons, by the period immediately preceding the outbreak of World War II, far more Jews were unaffiliated with any synagogue than were actively involved. Surveys taken in New York City in the 1930s revealed that more than three fourths of Jewish young people between the ages of fifteen and twenty-five had attended no religious service at all during the previous year.[56]

One attempted answer to this growing Jewish apathy was formulated by Mordecai M. Kaplan (1881–   ), a professor at Jewish Theological Seminary in New York. Kaplan projected an approach to Judaism known as Reconstructionism, which emphasized the importance of the Jewish community as a center of "Jewishness" rather than as a religious entity. He argued that Judaism was not just a religion but a special civilization or culture in which all Jews should share, whether they were religious or not. All Jews should participate in the synagogue, for it is the institution that can best preserve the values of Jewish life and the Jewish heritage. Kaplan's views have been especially influential among Conservative Jews, and many heretofore unaffiliated Jews returned to the synagogue as a result.

More powerful than Reconstructionism in drawing Jews back to the synagogue, however, was Zionism, the movement to establish a national state as a homeland for the Jews of the world. The Zionist movement was shaped in its definite form by Theodor Herzl (1860–1914), a Viennese Jew whose pamphlet *The Jewish State* became its manifesto. After the beginning of Hitler's persecution, which forced thousands of Jews to emigrate from Germany, Zionism gained new impetus. Zionist hopes culminated in 1948 in the establishment of the new state of Israel, and American Jews rallied to the support of Israel by raising millions of dollars to aid in resettling refugees in the young nation. Through succeeding years the cause of Israel has continued to be a unifying force for Judaism. Many young American Jews spend time each year in Israel, working to assist in various Israeli projects.

The World War II holocaust in which more than 6 million European Jews were murdered combined with Zionism to strengthen dramatically the sense of Jewish identity, precipitating a widespread Jewish revival in the United States. Whereas in 1937 the synagogues claimed less than one fourth of all Jews in this country, by 1956 phenomenal growth had taken place. Reform congregations, the most liberal branch of Judaism, had increased their membership fivefold, and Conservative allegiance had more then tripled. Every element of Jewish life, including synagogue attendance, contributions, weekday and Sunday schools, and so on, was revitalized. Although the Jewish revival, like that among Protestants and Catholics, tended to level off in the late 1960s, Judaism

[55] See Herberg's comprehensive discussion of this phenomenon in his *Protestant-Catholic-Jew*, op. cit.

[56] See Nathan Glazer, *American Judaism* (Chicago: University of Chicago Press, 1957), p. 85.

today is still a flourishing segment of the religious community. And to the extent, and this is considerable, that it has been assimilated into the American middle-class culture, Judaism, like all other American religions, has been influenced by revivalism.

Summary

The continuing effects of revivalism remain important even though its traditional forms are no longer in widespread use. Indeed, Perry Miller has described revivalism as the basic and abiding influence on the total American experience.[57] Perhaps the best summary statement of the far-reaching effects of revivalism has been made by H. Richard Niebuhr in his classic study *The Kingdom of God in America.* Niebuhr was speaking specifically of the Great and Second Awakenings, but his words apply equally well to the broader effects of revivalism as a whole.

When the final history of America's "golden day" is written it may appear that its brightness was due in no small part to the rule of the kingdom of Christ . . . the extent and meaning of that rule cannot be measured by counting up the number of converts at camp meetings or by psychological analysis of the mass hysterias which were connected with the revivals. They can be discovered only if the invisible kingdom, the reign of a spirit and a life communicated and effective in a social body by other means than the very tangible ones, is taken into account.

Such in briefest outline seems to be the story of the great renewal of Christ's kingdom which . . . , came upon the land like the sun and rain of spring, refreshing life and promising abundant harvests. It cannot be related as an isolated chapter. Its meaning cannot be retained without ever fresh experience of the life which was manifest in it. But there it stands, a chapter in the past which reaches into the present. In other lands of Christendom it may be possible to ignore the Christian revival of the eighteenth and nineteenth centuries and to see today the re-establishment of Christianity as it was in or before the Reformation. . . . For America, however—the land of Edwards, Whitefield, the Tennents, Backus, Hopkins, Asbury, Alexander, Woolman, Finney and all their company—such an attempt is impossible. It cannot eradicate if it would the marks left upon its social memory, upon its institutions and habits, by an awakening to God that was simultaneous with its awakening to national self-consciousness. It was no wholly new beginning, for the Christianity expressed in it was a more venerable thing than the American nation. Yet for America it was a new beginning; it was our national conversion.[58]

[57] Perry Miller, *Life of the Mind in America from the Revolution to the Civil War* (New York: Harcourt Brace Jovanovich, 1965), Vol. 1.
[58] Niebuhr, op. cit., pp. 125–126.

4 Indigenous American Religious Movements

It is still true that most religiously affiliated Americans belong to churches with a European background and tradition. American Catholics, Jews, and most Protestants trace their religious lineage back through European predecessors, having incorporated their own distinctive developments into a long history. There are other Americans who are associated with certain indigenous movements; that is, movements that have their origins in this country. These Americans are among those who worship at what Robert S. Ellwood has called alternative altars.[1] Although the majority of these religious experiments blossomed and then faded into an early oblivion, a few prospered, enlisting the loyalty and commitment of sizable numbers in the United States and even spreading, through missionary endeavors, into other parts of the world.

Most of these movements began in the early nineteenth century, a period of enthusiasm and ferment in American culture. Commenting on this period, Winthrop Hudson has observed, "While European visitors were impressed by the popularity and vigor of conventional religion, they were also struck by the many new ways to heaven that were being fashioned in the American environment and by the strenuous efforts of others to give the heavenly existence earthly embodiment."[2]

Many factors combined to produce the atmosphere in which new faiths could be born and nourished, but two are worthy of special emphasis. One was the development of the free churches and religious pluralism, providing a context in which any type of religious belief, however strange or disturbing, could obtain a hearing and, if it attracted converts, function on a relatively equal basis with the more venerable religious traditions. Even if it faced hostility and persecution, the religious group could always move on to new territory in search of its freedom to exist, as the Mormons did again and again.

The second major factor was the influence of revivalism, which has been discussed in Chapter 3. After 1800, the tidal wave of the Second Awakening swept across America, especially in the frontier areas, opening channels for diverse kinds of religious innovation. Revivalism emphasized personal and individual religious experience, thus undermining traditional doctrinal moorings. No longer were the trappings of formal education, seminary training, or official church sanction required for the assumption of religious authority. As Sidney Ahlstrom observes,

---

[1] Robert S. Ellwood, *Alternative Altars* (Chicago: University of Chicago Press, 1979).
[2] Winthrop S. Hudson, *Religion in America,* 2d ed. (New York: Scribner, 1973), p. 181.

"Farmers became theologians, offbeat village youths became bishops, odd girls became prophets."[3] Or, as A. Leland Jamison has said,

> The real impact of revivalism . . . lies in . . . the ideas, attitudes, feelings, dreams, and hopes which revivalism helped to disseminate and to be expressed among the American people . . . . Here [in America], as probably nowhere else or ever in Christendom, people had the opportunity of implementing and institutionalizing various particular religious emphases, most of which were as ancient as the Bible itself.[4]

Jamison identified two of the particular emphases that served to stimulate the initiative and imagination of many Christians touched by the revivals: *perfectionism,* the doctrine that "perfect sanctification" or complete holiness was attainable and even necessary to the salvation of the converted Christian; and *millennialism,* a doctrine of "last things," often based on precise and extremely individualistic interpretations of the Book of Revelation and other apocalyptic scriptures[5] urging Christians to prepare themselves and the world for the imminent coming of the Kingdom, or Christ's return. Blended with the millennial vision was the expectation of a "golden age" to be established either by the direct intervention of God or by the preaching and application of the gospel and its teachings. Such an expectation fostered utopian dreams and revolutionary schemes for the remaking of human existence and society.

Perfectionist and Utopian Movements

Before considering the larger and more lasting indigenous movements, we should look briefly at a number of smaller groups that did not survive for long but nevertheless left their mark on the American religious experience. In the early nineteenth century an epidemic of perfectionist and utopian communal societies arose, many of them with a strongly religious emphasis. The atmosphere of the time was described in often quoted words from a letter from Ralph Waldo Emerson, the American essayist, to Thomas Carlyle, the British author, written in the autumn of 1840: "We are all a little wild here with numberless projects of social reform. Not a reading man but has a draft of a new community in his waistcoat pocket." Among the new communities that made an impact upon the American scene were the Shakers, the Oneida Community,

---

[3]Sidney E. Ahlstrom, *A Religious History of the American People* (Garden City, N.Y.: Doubleday, 1975), Vol. 1, p. 575.

[4]A. Leland Jamison, "Religion on the American Perimeter," in *The Shaping of American Religion,* edited by A. Leland Jamison and James Ward Smith (Princeton, N.J.:Princeton University Press, 1969), pp. 197–198.

[5]Writings that envision a cataclysmic end of the age and the destruction of evil forces by the powers of God.

and—out of a somewhat different mold—the various transcendentalist ventures to which Emerson specifically referred, especially those at Brook Farm and Hopedale.

The Shakers (officially called the United Society of Believers in Christ's Second Coming) were followers of Ann Lee (1736–1784), an English prophetess who came to this country with eight followers in 1774. They settled in upper New York and made virtually no converts until 1779, when a group of Baptists who had been stirred by a revival joined the group. Included among the new converts was Joseph Meacham (1742–1796), who soon became the leader of the group, second only to Ann Lee. Through a series of visions, "Mother Ann," as she was called, had become convinced that the source of all human sin and depravity was the sex act, that Christ's Second Coming would be in the form of a woman, and that she was that woman. The end of the age was therefore at hand, and faithful Christians were summoned to a communal and celibate life, destined to usher in the golden age of blessedness for all humanity in the millennial kingdom.

Under Meacham's leadership, the Shakers experienced considerable growth, particularly as a result of the revival excitement of the Second Awakening. Twelve communities were organized in the New England states and New York, with more than two thousand members. In 1805 missionaries were sent to the western frontier, especially Kentucky, where more converts were won and new communities established. By 1825 the Shakers had more than six thousand members, gathered in at least twenty communities.

With the slackening of the Second Awakening, the Shakers began to decline. Economically prosperous at first, they had difficulties as the years went by and steadily lost members. By the end of the century they had virtually disappeared.

The most distinctive feature of Shaker worship was the group dance, accompanied by lively singing. This practice gave them their popular nickname. Communication with the dead, speaking in tongues, and personal testimonies were also important parts of their communal religious life. Because the Kingdom was actually at hand, procreation was unnecessary, and their rule of celibacy freed them from the basic sin of sexual union, as Mother Ann taught. At their height, the Shaker communities were almost idyllic in style and attracted the attention not only of Americans but also of many visitors from Europe.[6]

Another type of perfectionism was illustrated by the Oneida Community, which took a very different view of sexual behavior. Founded by John Humphrey Noyes (1811–1886) in 1848, the community established itself at Oneida, New York, where it functioned in its original form for more than thirty years. Noyes was a protege of Charles G. Finney, the evangelist, who sponsored him in his seminary studies at

---

[6]For further information on the Shakers, see Edward Di Andrews, *The People Called Shakers: A Search for the Perfect Society* (New York: Oxford University Press, 1953).

Andover and Yale. When Noyes began to preach that conversion to Christianity brought with it the possibility of complete freedom from sin, he had a decisive break with Finney. Noyes argued that God wanted men to create a new kind of society in which conditions would be favorable to the attainment of Christian perfection. In such a society the believers, or saints, would not need to be bound by the laws that regulate the conduct of nonbelievers. Thus the community at Oneida included communal ownership of property. But Noyes also preached that because the believers were spiritually bound together in dedication to the faith, their communal relationships should include marriage as well as property. In what was called "complex marriage," every woman in the group was regarded as the wife of every man and every man was the husband of every woman. Children were looked upon as belonging to the whole community and, therefore, as the joint responsibility of all. Although Noyes did not regard such an arrangement as sexual promiscuity, it aroused widespread hostility from outside the community.

Like the Shakers, the Oneida Community flourished economically for a considerable time, with its chief industry being the manufacture of silver plate. But outside pressures combined with a decline of fervency and devotion to destroy it. In 1897 the practice of "complex marriage" was abandoned, and a year later the communal property arrangment was ended. A joint stock company was formed to continue the manufacture of Oneida silverware, and the religious community went out of existence.[7]

Of a much different theological stripe from the more extreme belief systems of the Shakers and Noyes was transcendentalism.[8] But, like the movements already discussed, transcendentalism issued forth in a series of short-lived utopian communities dedicated to achieving perfection in human life and society.

The intellectual fountainhead of transcendentalism was Ralph Waldo Emerson (1803–1882), though he himself remained skeptical about the success of the utopian ventures initiated by his friends and disciples. Emerson was educated at Harvard and became a Unitarian minister, but in 1832 he left the pastorate in Boston because of increasing doubts and dissatisfactions with the prevailing theology of the churches. In 1838 he delivered his now-famous address to the Harvard Divinity School, outlining his religious convictions. The ideas advanced by Emerson so shocked the clergy and faculty, Unitarian though they were, that he was not again invited to speak at Harvard for twenty-seven years. In his address, Emerson expressed his distaste for the orthodox religious tradition and announced his faith in an almost unbounded human capacity to move toward the highest ideals and aspirations of life. The fol-

[7]For a comprehensive description of the community, see Robert A. Parker, *A Yankee Saint: John Humphrey Noyes and the Oneida Community* (New York: Putnam, 1935).

[8]The term *transcendentalist* is of uncertain origin and ambiguous in meaning. Basically, it refers to a concern for the higher use of reason and its objects: the good, the true, the beautiful, and the divine. (See Ahlstrom, op. cit., pp. 34–36).

lowing excerpts from the address give some of the flavor of Emerson's teachings and illustrate how his ideas could become the inspiration for attempts to establish utopian communities in which human beings might reach their destined potential.

Document 28

From "An Address" by Ralph Waldo Emerson

The world is not the product of manifold power, but of one will, of one mind; and that one mind is everywhere active, in each ray of the star, in each wavelet of the pool; and whatever opposes that will is everywhere balked and baffled, because things are made so, and not otherwise. Good is positive, Evil is merely privative, not absolute: it is like cold, which is the privation of heat. All evil is so much death or nonentity . . . . For all things proceed out of this same spirit, which is differently named love, justice, temperance, in its different applications . . . and all things conspire with it . . . .

The perception of this law of laws awakens in the mind a sentiment which we call the religious sentiment, and which makes our highest happiness . . . . By it the universe is made safe and habitable . . . .

This sentiment is divine and deifying. It is the beatitude of man. It makes him illimitable. Through it, the soul first knows itself. It corrects the capital mistake of the infant man, who seeks to be great by following the great, and hopes to derive advantages *from another*—by showing the fountain of all good to be in himself, and that he, equally with every man, is an inlet into the depths of Reason.

The expressions of this sentiment affect us more than all other compositions. The sentences of the oldest time, which ejaculate this piety, are still fresh and fragrant. This thought dwelled always deepest in the minds of men in the devout and contemplative East; not alone in Palestine, where it reached its purest expression, but in Egypt, in Persia, in India, in China. Europe has always owed to oriental genius its divine impulses. What these holy bards said, all sane men found agreeable and true. And the unique impression of Jesus upon mankind, whose name is not so much written as ploughed into the history of this world, is proof of the subtle virtue of this infusion . . . .

Jesus Christ belonged to the true race of prophets. He saw with open eye the mystery of the soul . . . . Alone in all history he estimated the greatness of man. One man was true to what is in you and me. He saw that God incarnates himself in man, and evermore goes forth anew to take possession of his World. He said, in this jubilee of sublime emotion, "I am divine. Through me, God acts; through me, speaks. Would you see God, see me; or see thee, when thou also thinkest as I now think." But what a distortion did his doctrine and message suffer in the same, in the next, and in the following ages! There is no doctrine of the Reason which will bear to be taught by the Understanding. The understanding caught this high chant from the poet's lips, and said, in the next age, "This was Jehovah come down out of

SOURCE: Ralph Waldo Emerson, "An Address," in *The Selected Writings of Ralph Waldo Emerson,* Brooks Atkinson, ed. (New York: Modern Library, 1950), pp. 67–84).

heaven. I will kill you, if you say he was a man." The idioms of his language and the figures of his rhetoric have usurped the place of his truth; and churches are not built on his principles . . . . He spoke of miracles; for he felt that man's life was a miracle, and all that man doth, and he knew that this daily miracle shines as the character ascends. But the word Miracle, as pronounced by Christian churches, gives a false impression; it is Monster . . . .

In this point of view we become sensible of the first defect of historical Christianity. Historical Christianity has fallen into the error that corrupts all attempts to communicate religion. As it appears to us, and as it has appeared for ages, it is not the doctrine of the soul, but an exaggeration of the personal, the positive, the ritual. It has dwelt, it dwells, with noxious exaggeration about the *person* of Jesus. The soul knows no persons. It invites every man to expand to the full circle of the universe, and will have no preferences but those of spontaneous love . . . .

Men have come to speak of the revelation as somewhat long ago given and done, as if God were dead . . . .

The Church seems to totter to its fall, almost all life extinct . . . .

The prayers and even the dogmas of our church are like the zodiac of Denderah and the astronomical monuments of the Hindoos, wholly insulated from anything now extant in the life and business of the people . . . . In a large portion of the community, the religious service gives rise to quite other thoughts and emotions.

Historical Christianity destroys the power of preaching, by withdrawing from it the exploration of the moral nature of man; where the sublime is, where are the resources of astonishment and power . . . .

And now, my brothers, you will ask, What in these desponding days can be done by us? The remedy is already declared in the ground of our complaint of the Church. We have contrasted the Church with the Soul. In the soul then let the redemption be sought. Wherever a man comes, there comes revolution. The old is for slaves. When a man comes, all books are legible, all things transparent, all religions are forms. He is religious. Man is the wonderworker. He is seen amid miracles . . . .

I look for the hour when that Supreme Beauty which ravished the souls of those Eastern men, and chiefly of those Hebrews, and through their lips spoke oracles to all time, shall speak in the West also. The Hebrew and Greek Scriptures contain immortal sentences, that have been bread of life to millions. But they have no epical integrity; are fragmentary; are not shown in their order to the intellect. I look for the new Teacher that shall follow so far those shining laws that he shall see them come full circle; shall see their rounding complete grace; shall see the world to be the mirror of the soul; shall see the identity of the law of gravitation with purity of heart; and shall show that the Ought, the Duty, is one thing with Science, with Beauty, and with Joy.

Emerson's emphasis upon the compatibility of spiritual law with the laws of nature and his call for humanity to work out the potential divinity of their own natures set the stage for those whom he influenced to try their hands at the building of the Kingdom here on earth. The experimental communities at Hopedale and Brook Farm, expressions of what Louisa May Alcott called the "wild oats" of transcendentalism[9] were launched in the early 1840s. George Ripley (1802–1880), a leading transcendentalist and Unitarian minister, organized Brook Farm in 1840. Supported for a time by many of the leading intellectuals of the day, the farm went out of existence in 1847 after a series of disastrous failures to cope with disagreements and divisions among its members. Hopedale, established near Milford, Massachusetts, in 1841 by Adin Ballou (1803–1890), a Universalist minister, represented a more serious attempt to establish the Kingdom of God on earth. Ballou believed that a successful enterprise at Hopedale would trigger a world movement. More than 200 people dedicated themselves to the task, and for over a decade the community flourished, winning considerable fame as a "Christian republic." But in 1856, two of the members who had bought up three fourths of the stock (the community was organized on a joint-stock basis) decided to liquidate the enterprise.

Each of these movements, varied as they were, represented a response to the challenge of a perfect life in a utopian community, organized in accordance with the perceived or revealed will of God and in conformity with the spiritual laws of the universe. All of them reflected the individualism, the optimism, and the confidence of the American frontier. In the American world of the nineteenth century, with its unlimited opportunities, anything seemed possible. The perfectionists carried the American Dream to its ultimate conclusion. Although it cannot be said that the transcendentalists owed much to the atmosphere of revivalism, it is evident that the Shakers and the Oneida community had roots in the enthusiasm of the Second Awakening. In that atmosphere it was easy to believe that God had chosen this country for a special work, and that it was here that he was going to bring about the establishment of his Kingdom. Bronson Alcott spoke for many when he declared that only in America could "the second Eden . . . be planted in which the divine seed is to bruise the head of Evil and restore Man to his rightful communion with God in the Paradise of Good."

The Mormons

Much more substantial and influential than any of the movements discussed thus far was the Mormon group, which survived and prospered to become an important and growing segment of contemporary American religion. The Church of Jesus Christ of Latter-Day Saints (the official designation of the Mormons) had its origin in the work of Joseph Smith (1805–1844), who grew up in the vicinity of Palmyra, New York. Smith's childhood and teenage years were spent in the ferment-

---

[9] Louisa May Alcott, the novelist and daughter of Bronson Alcott, who began a community at Fruitlands, Massachusetts, which lasted only a few weeks, wrote a fictionalized account of Fruitlands, entitled, *The Transcendental Wild Oats.*

ing atmosphere of the frontier revivals, in which his family was deeply involved. Smith later reported that he was greatly confused by the conflicting religious claims made by the various revival preachers and that he finally went away by himself in the woods to seek an answer directly from God. According to Smith, his prayers were answered by a vision of God and of Jesus Christ, who instructed him to await a further revelation of a special task for which he had been divinely chosen. Later he was guided by the angel Moroni to a site near Palmyra, where he discovered some golden plates, long buried. The plates contained the history of groups of people called the Nephites and the Lamanites, descendants of the lost tribes of ancient Israel, who had migrated to the North American continent long before the birth of Christ. The plates also recorded, according to Smith, that Christ had appeared to these people following his resurrection and had established the true church here in America. But the Lamanites, ancestors of the American Indians, had become unfaithful and had eventually defeated the faithful Nephites, killing all of them except their leader, Mormon, and his son, Moroni. Mormon wrote their history upon the plates and instructed Moroni to bury them until a prophet should be appointed to bring the truth of God once again to his people. Smith was given translating spectacles by the angel and deciphered the writing on the plates, which was written down in English and published in 1830 as the Book of Mormon.

The Book of Mormon, accepted in addition to the Bible as scripture by Smith and his followers, answered all of the contemporary religious questions, settling every doctrinal question then in dispute among the revivalist sects. The Book of Mormon stresses human free will, the free grace of God, and baptism as necessary for the forgiveness of sins. It rejects the baptism of infants and sets out a complex system of church government. But a most interesting facet is its portrayal of America as the Promised Land, that area in which God will work out the establishment of His Kingdom. The Mormons understand themselves as called by God to build the "city of Zion," much as the early Puritans felt constrained to establish here in the New World a "Holy Commonwealth." Thus, as with movements already discussed, the locus or center of God's activity is transferred from Palestine to the American continent, as an American prophet is chosen to bring the full and complete revelation of God's truth to all people.

In a series of additional visions Smith was designated the first elder of the restored true church, with power to legislate its doctrines through the reception of continuing revelations from God. The church grew with amazing rapidity, but its growth inevitably aroused opposition in the surrounding communities. As a result, the Mormons were forced to begin a series of westward movements in their attempt to establish Zion. Soon after 1830 they migrated to Kirtland, Ohio, and in 1837 they moved on to Independence and Far West, Missouri. Meanwhile, Smith had set out additional doctrines of the church, many of which divided the group more and more from its surrounding society. The doctrine of a plurality of gods was introduced, as well as the practice of polygamy. Smith taught that marriage was contracted both for time and for eternity, and a series of rituals, including baptism for the dead, was instituted. The resulting increase in antagonism pushed the Mormons on to Nauvoo, Illinois, a thriving city that they founded and that was for a time the largest community in Illinois.

In 1844 Smith was murdered by an angry mob while he was confined in jail in Carthage, Illinois. Under the leadership of Brigham Young, who succeeded Smith, the majority of the Mormons journeyed on to the basin of the Great Salt Lake in Utah, where they found at last a resting place. They established Salt Lake City, and by 1870 their numbers had reached over 140,000.[10]

Under strong pressure from the United States government and as a necessary prerequisite for Utah to become a state, the Mormons abandoned polygamy in 1890 and Utah was accepted into the union in 1896. Missionaries were sent throughout the United States and into foreign countries.[11] By 1980 about 2½ million people counted themselves as Latter-Day Saints. The church has become a prosperous and influential segment of American religion.

The birth and development of Mormonism as a religious and sociological phenomenon has attracted students of American religion for decades. The following article by one of the most astute observers of the Mormons, Thomas F. O'Dea, is valuable for two reasons: First, it provides insights into the development of the Latter Day Saints; second, it illustrates the use in religio-sociological analysis of the important categories of "sect" and "church," defining them and clarifying the difference between them.

Document 29 _____

From "Mormonism and the Avoidance of Sectarian Stagnation" by Thomas F. O'Dea

... This selection attempts to answer two questions: (1) What enabled the Mormon Church to avoid sectarianism? (2) If the Mormon Church did not become a sect, is it, then, an ecclesiastical body or "church" in the sense in which that term has been understood in the sociology of religion since Ernst Troeltsch?

SOURCE: Reprinted from *The Mormons* by Thomas F. O'Dea, by permission of the University of Chicago Press. © 1957 by the University of Chicago, as edited by Patrick H. McNamara in *Religion American Style* (New York: Harper & Row, 1974).

[10] Comprehensive studies of the Mormons are available in Fawn Brodie, *No Man Knows My History: The Life of Joseph Smith* (New York: Knopf, 1946) and Thomas F. O'Dea, *The Mormons* (Chicago: University of Chicago Press, 1957).
[11] Missionary work began very early in Mormon history, and a major source of the church's numerical growth in the first decades of its existence were British and Scandinavian converts, who immigrated from their homes to join the LDS community.

Church and Sect

Ernst Troeltsch and Max Weber define a sect as a body of believers based on contracted or freely elected membership in contrast to the institutional ecclesiastical
body or church in which membership is ascribed. "Born into" and "freely chosen"
signify the vital distinction. For them a church or *ecclesia* is characterized by the
following: (1) membership on the basis of birth; (2) administration of the means
of grace and its sociological and theological concomitants—hierarchy and dogma;
(3) inclusiveness of social structure, often coinciding with ethnic or geographical
boundaries; (4) orientation to the conversion of all; and (5) a tendency to compromise with and adjust to the world. The sect, on the contrary, is characterized by
(1) separatism and defiance of or withdrawal from the demands of the secular
sphere, preferring isolation to compromise; (2) exclusiveness, expressed in attitude
and social structure; (3) emphasis on conversion prior to membership; and (4) voluntary election or joining.

    The sect is often persecuted and is always ascetic. It usually rejects hierarchy and
endeavors to implement the "priesthood of believers" in an egalitarian if narrow
social organization. As H. Richard Niebuhr has observed, sectarianism, strictly
defined, cannot outlast the founding generation and, as Liston Pope has shown,
often does not last it out. The birth of children to the freely electing sectaries and
the worldly success which so often crowns sectarian frugality and industry result
in that adjustment to the world which Weber has called "the routinization of
charisma."

The Avoidance of Sectarianism

The Mormon Church claimed to be a divine restoration of the Apostolic Church
after centuries of apostasy. The mark of the new dispensation was contemporary
revelation. Through the prophet Joseph Smith, the Lord was believed to have
called the elect. The result was the church which was founded in western New York,
at the time a near frontier and the scene of a great religious enthusiasm. To its converts it offered security—a resolution of the outer conflict and inner turmoil of
denominational confusion and one which claimed the sanction of divine revelation.
Convinced of a covenant to build the Kingdom of God on earth, the Latter-day
Saints attempted to establish their settlements on the basis of the Law of Consecration, or United Order of Enoch, a plan announced by the prophet-founder
which reconciled Christian socialism with private initiative and management. This
law was withdrawn in 1838 after some seven years of experiment marked by conten-
tions and jealousies, and tithing was substituted for it.

    The Mormon Church placed great emphasis on the restoration of Hebrew ideals
and on the revival of Old Testament practices and institutions. The Saints were,
they believed, a modern Israel: called by God, party to the covenant, and about to
be gathered unto Zion. Polygamy was but one, although the most notorious, example of such revivals. In restoration and peculiarity, two important aspects of the
Mormon gospel, the attitudes of renewal and exclusiveness characteristic of sects,
were palpably present.

    While commitment to building the Kingdom was sectarian insofar as it required
withdrawal from the world and refusal to accommodate to the routine demands

of secular life, it certainly had other possible implications. The idea of a Christian commonwealth was capable of quite nonsectarian interpretation. Moreover, the withdrawal from "Babylon" did not involve a repudiation of worldly pursuits, for in the City of God, the New Jerusalem, business, family life, government, and even armed defense would be acceptable and accepted. Nature was not seen as corrupted, and the vitiating effect of original sin on preternatural virtue was denied—a most unsectarian doctrine. Work and recreation were both accepted and sanctified. Against the sectarian notions of renewal and exclusiveness must be placed the non-sectarian possibilities of building a Christian society and the doctrine of human goodness—of total "undepravity."

Yet other groups had set out to build the Kingdom, and whatever nonsectarian possibilities lie hidden in the idea of a Christian commonwealth were never made apparent. How many sects built isolated little communities where prosperity followed upon the sectarian ascetic of work and thrift? Such settlements often reached a membership of a thousand and then stopped growing. Others experienced "swarming"; that is, excess numbers, usually in excess of a thousand, migrated and established a new settlement emulating the mother community but independent of its authority. This was the common sectarian fate. How were the Mormons to avoid it and realize the nonsectarian possibilities of their vision?

The Kirtland attempt to build the Kingdom failed because of internal dissent, external opposition, and economic distress—the last the most important. The Saints then migrated to Missouri and there at two points—Jackson County and Far West—endeavored to construct the New Jerusalem. Their strange doctrines claiming contemporary converse with God, their frugality and industry and consequent prosperity, their talk of making the region a "promised land," and their northern manners accentuated by rumors of abolition sentiments aroused the animosity of their neighbors. Consequently, they were driven from the land, and, crossing the Mississippi, the only eastward move in their long wanderings, they entered Illinois, where they built another city. Nauvoo, on the east bank of the river, saw the arrival of converts in great numbers, the first fruits of the European harvest. But there, too, hostility followed the Saints, and rumors that the leaders were practicing polygamy—rumors that turned out to be true—and a more defiant attitude from the Mormon leadership increased gentile antagonism. In 1844 Joseph Smith was murdered at Carthage jail, and in the next three years the Saints were driven from Nauvoo. In 1847, after a period of disorganization and hardship, they migrated to Utah under the leadership of Brigham Young.

In the West the church gained the respite needed for its internal recovery and at the same time the relative isolation required for establishing a civilization whose institutions would be informed by Mormon conceptions and Mormon values. In the 1880's and 1890's, however, the Mormon—gentile conflict broke out anew with considerable acuteness, the issues now being polygamy and the admission of Utah to the Union. After harsh federal legislation and prosecution of Mormon leaders, the church abandoned polygamy and accommodated itself to the demands of the larger American community into which it was reintegrated. Yet relative isolation had done its work: Utah and the surrounding region remained a Mormon culture area, although the implicit claim to it as an exclusive homeland was given up. Moreover, Mormon peculiarity and self-consciousness remained.

In this early period of Mormon history many marks of sectarianism were present: not only the attitude of renewal and exclusiveness but voluntary election as the basis of membership, withdrawal from the secular community, asceticism which placed a high value on hard work, persecution which increased in-group cohesion and the conception of the priesthood of believers. The last doctrine, however, was not interpreted in terms of an egalitarian congregationalism. Rather it found expression in a hierarchial priesthood organization, authoritarian in structure and function. As the church grew, as its early charismatic leadership became more institutionalized in the leading offices, and as it had to stand against external threats, the early congregationalism gave way more and more to authoritarian rule.

What factors militated against the development of a typical sect in this situation? Two have already been mentioned: 1. *the nonsectarian possibilities of building the Kingdom which could require so much subtle accommodation and* 2. *the doctrine of natural goodness, by way of which nineteenth-century American optimism entered Mormon religious consciousness to blend there with the chiliastic expectations of a restorationist movement.* Yet the former alone could not effect the avoidance of sectarianism, as the record of many other groups makes clear; nor could the latter; although, when combined with other factors effective in the concrete situation, both could affect the issue in a powerful and pervasive manner. These two factors combined with the following eight to effect the issue:

3. *Universal missionary understanding of the notion of "gathering the elect."* The Mormon notion of peculiarity was exclusive, but it was not necessarily sectarian in the strictest sense. It was rather committed to missionary work: to calling the elect from the world. . . .

4. *The temporal appropriateness of the doctrine in the late 1830s.* A generation before, the "gathering of the elect" might have been understood in terms of calling the elect from the neighboring counties. But in the second decade of the nineteenth century, American Protestantism had discovered a bigger world. The Mormons came upon the scene in time to inherit the newer and broader definition. The universal understanding of calling the elect, combined with the new worldwide definition of the mission field, worked against a sectarian issue.

5. *The success of missionary work.* The ability of the Mormon gospel to bring meaning and hope to many, in America and in Europe, especially England and Scandinavia, resulted in thousands of conversions. With increased numbers, the notion of the holy city which the Saints were called to build now took on dimensions hardly compatible with sectarianism. Nauvoo had a population of 20,000 when Chicago had 5,000.

6. *The withdrawal of the Law of Consecration.* Had the Law of Consecration worked, the Mormons might have built another one of the successful communitarian settlements of which our history has seen so many. The failure of the Law, on the other hand, deprived them of a blueprint, rigid conformity to which could have been interpreted as the only permissible economic ethic, thereby lending a sectarian narrowness to their activities and inhibiting growth. Moreover, the Law was withdrawn by Joseph Smith in a revelation which still held up its ideals as the will of God. As a result, the flexibility of charismatic leadership was transmitted to the institutionalized church in economic matters, and its spirit vivified economic experiment for the next century, while a killing economic literalism was successfully

eschewed. This is all the more striking, since in scriptural interpretation Mormons have generally been literalists.

7. *The failures and consequent necessity of starting again.* The need to start over again four times in sixteen years also contributed to flexibility, preventing a set routine from developing which could then have been imposed on new problems, thereby limiting growth and contributing to a sectarian atmosphere and structure. Combined with the withdrawal of the Law of Consecration, this made a dogmatism of minutiae impossible.

8. *The expulsion from the Middle West.* The Middle West, the continent's most attractive ecological area, was destined to draw large numbers of non-Mormon settlers. In such a situation it would have been quite impossible for the Mormon Church to maintain any hegemony, spiritual, political, or economic. Instead, it would in all likelihood have become one of a number of denominations accommodating to each other and to the secular world and thus would be reintegrated into the general American community with which it shared many common roots as another small and unimportant Protestant group.

9. *The choice and the existence of a large, unattractive expanse of land in the West.* The Mormon leadership deliberately chose an unattractive region to gain the necessary respite that isolation would give and resisted the seductions of more pleasant prospects. The existence of this arid region was something over which they had no control. It was unquestionably a prerequisite for the future form of their community. The result was the opening up of a huge area waiting to be converted from desert, supporting a scant nomadic population, to a Mormon culture area based on irrigation farming. This also gave the necessary time in isolation for Mormon social institutions to emerge and to "set."

10. *The authoritarian structure of the church and the central government which it made possible.* The existence of a charismatic leader in the early stages of Mormon Church history whose right to rule was believed to be based on divine election and the consequent authoritarian and hierarchical structure of church government permitted scattered settlement in the West under central direction. Such authoritarian characteristics were strengthened by the external conditions of conflict and hardship. Centrifugal tendencies in the West were restrained when not completely inhibited. The priesthood structure and the routinization of prophetic rule might in other circumstances have been completely compatible with sectarianism; yet in the western settlement they combined with open and relatively empty and isolated land, and missionary success and consequent emigration, to make large-scale settlement possible under central government. This combination ruled out the last chance of sectarianism.

These last eight factors, then, combined to militate against a sectarian issue to the Mormon experiment and to bring into existence the Mormon Church of the present day. Instead of becoming a sect, the church became the core of a large culture area. In these eight factors and their combination we have the answer to our first question.

Neither Church nor Sect

The Mormon Church is excluded by definition from the category of church or *ecclesia*, unless it has become one in the course of its development. . . . The question is, then: Has the Mormon Church become an ecclesiastical body in the course of its evolution?

Despite the avoidance of typical sectarian structure and isolation, the Mormon Church has displayed and retained many sectarian characteristics. Most important are: 1. a sense of peculiarity, of election, and of covenant, which is reinforced by explicit theological doctrine; 2. a tendency to withdrawal from the gentile world (this is now most frequently expressed in admonition and symbolic practices; yet it found large-scale expression in the Church Welfare Plan with which the Mormon Church sought to meet the Great Depression as a separate body capable of considerable autarchy); 3. a commitment to "warning the world" and "gathering the elect," the implications of which have been more routine and less dramatic since the accommodation which followed the defeat of the church on the polygamy issue; and 4. chiliastic expectations, still important not only among rural groups but in the writings of some leaders of the church.

While the Mormons have never identified group membership with peculiarity of dress as sectarists have frequently, the strict interpretation of Joseph Smith's no-liquor, no-tobacco counsel serves an analogous function today and has become the focus of the expression of exclusivist sentiments. Moreover, although persecution has stopped, the memory of it preserves ingroup solidarity and strengthens loyalty.

Yet despite the *notae* of the sect, the basic fact in Mormon history since 1890 has been the accommodation of the church to the demands of the larger gentile community. The abandonment of polygamy—that camel at which many strained but which became so identified with loyalty that all were willing to suffer in its defense—was the surrender of what had become the typical Mormon institution. Economic experimentation—the communism of the United Order, for example—became less characteristic of Mormon activities, and, in general, the secular demands of Babylon displaced the earlier enthusiasm for the New Jerusalem. Even the successes of earlier fervor strengthened the trend to accommodation. Having become the dominant group over a large culture area, the Mormon Church experienced the conservatism of the successful, which was not likely to upset a working equilibrium. The involvement of church leadership in established political, economic, and educational institutions, the education of children, the comparatively long-established hierarchy and dogma—all display ecclesiastical features of Mormon organization. The demand for conversion and the aversion to the ecclesiastical practice of infant baptism were soon institutionally compromised in the baptism of the eight-year-old children of Mormon families.

This combination of sectarian characteristics with structure, policy, and circumstances similar to many *ecclesias* suggests that the Mormon Church is a mixture of the pure categories outlined on our typology. Joachim Wach, recognizing this problem—specifically about the Mormons and generally in such typologies—has characterized the Mormon Church as an independent group with semi-ecclesiastical organization. It is, for Wach, neither church nor sect; it is an independent group through whose organization its members have access to the necessary means of salvation.

In terms of theology and group structure there is considerable justification for Wach's classification. Yet, in larger terms, there is more to be said. The Mormon restoration was not only a Christian renewal; it was a Hebrew revival. Mormondom conceived itself as a modern Israel. This alone is not uncommon in Christian experience, and we are likely to take it for granted. Yet in the Mormon case, contemporary conditions of life were to give the revival of Hebrew ideals a more genuine content than would have been possible in smaller groups in less demanding circumstances. The acceptance of a model is always important in the patterning of subsequent behavior, and in the Mormon case the model of the chosen people could not but affect Mormon belief and behavior: polygamy is but the most notorious example.

Guided by this model, the Saints withdrew from the modern Babylon to build the modern Zion. Owing to circumstances over which they had little control, they found themselves wandering in the wilderness. They had sought but part of the Israelitish parallel; circumstances had provided the rest. For sixteen years they were driven about, attempting four times to build their city. Their size, the extent and duration of their suffering, and the way in which defeat several times crowned the most palpable successes combined to transform the bread and water of sectarian affliction into the real presence of national potentiality. Common effort in success and in failure, common suffering from elemental and human adversaries, even common struggle with arms against common enemies—all these lent to the symbolic emulation of ancient Israel an existential reality which devoted sectaries in more (or less) fortunate circumstances could hardly surmise. Mormonism lived its Exodus and Chronicles, not once but many times. It had its Moses and its Joshua. Circumstances had given it a stage on which its re-enactment of biblical history was neither farce nor symbolic pageant.

Throughout this intense group experience—an experience which produced a genuine folk tradition in a decade and a half—Mormon family life and Mormon economic and political activity continued. During this time the Mormons courted and married, begat children and reared them, and established ties of consanguinity and affinity—made more numerous and complex by polygamy—which reinforced and impenetrated those of membership in the church. Economic activity, both cooperative and private, and political necessities established further bonds. Moreover, in the years of wandering the Saints spent their lives in largely Mormon surroundings. This was even more true in the years that followed 1847, when geographical reinforced social isolation.

Fellowship in the Gospel became—and remains today—supported by and imbedded in a matrix of kinship. The circumstance of enforced nomadism and of successive resettlement, brought about by no design of the Saints and yet in close emulation of their Hebraic model, was experienced in a manner that would guarantee its transmission as informal family history as well as the more formally taught church history. In each attempt at settlement a group increasingly conscious of itself as a chosen vessel established its holy city—its spiritual and temporal homeland—only to be driven out under circumstances that strengthened in-group loyalty and increased self-consciousness. In Utah a homeland was finally found where "the desert would blossom as the rose," and all previous Mormon history was reinterpreted as precursory of this final fruition in "the place which God for us prepared." The death of Joseph on the eastern side of the Mississippi was the final act of the first stage, as was that of Moses on the borders of the land of Canaan. It was the first

stage in the development of incipient nationhood. The members of the Church of
Jesus Christ of Latter-day Saints had become—to use the significant term often used
most casually by the Mormons themselves—the "Mormon people." Moreover, the
Mormon people had found a homeland. The ties of religious faith were reinforced
by those of blood and marriage, of common group memories often involving
suffering and heroism, of common economic and cultural aspirations—and now by a
region whose very physiognomy would become symbolic of another and perhaps
greater group achievement, the successful settlement in the desert.

The Mormons were not completely unaware of what they had become. It is true
that their American patriotism, which was an article of faith with them, inhibited
any movement for national independence, and they tended to see their own religious
homeland as part of a secular manifest destiny. Yet the latter was certainly subordinate to a religious conception of Zion in the mountaintops. In 1850 the Mormons established the state of Deseret—much larger than present-day Utah—and
applied for admission to the Union. The covenant people would become an American state rather than an independent nation. In Nauvoo they had been virtually a
state within a state through grant of a special charter from the Illinois legislature,
and all previous attempts to build the city were characterized by considerable autonomy. The Civil War had not yet settled certain limitations of autonomy, nor had
postwar developments in politics, economics, and technology made autonomy
seem so far-fetched as one might imagine in today's conditions. Moreover, it must
be recalled that, in moments of passion in the Mormon—gentile conflict, separatism
and secession were openly considered and that armed, if inconclusive, conflict with
federal forces did take place.

The Mormons had gone from near sect to near nation. The Zionism of the
nineteenth-century Mormons stopped short of the national fulfillment of the Jewish
Zionism of the twentieth century. Yet the Saints had in large part realized the implications of the model which had guided them in such auspicious circumstances.
If their own patriotism combined with their defeat in the Mormon–gentile conflict
to inhibit the full fruition of national sovereignty, Mormondom, nevertheless,
became a subculture with its own peculiar conceptions and values, its own self-
consciousness, and its own culture area. The Mormons, in a word, had become a
people, with their own subculture within the larger American culture and their own
homeland as part of the American homeland.

Conclusion

We have now answered the first two questions. A peculiar concatenation of ten
factors—ideal, matters of conceptions and values; historical, matters of unique
concomitance or convergence in time; and structural, matters of social structure—
combine to explain how the Mormon Church escaped sectarianism. In avoiding the
fate of an isolated sect which had been the nemesis of so many other restorationist
religious groupings, it did not become either a denomination or a church in the sense
of the accepted definitions, although it displayed characteristics of both. Rather,
the emulation of the Old Testament Hebrews in the unsettled conditions of the
nineteenth-century Middle and Far West resulted in the emergence of a Mormon
people—a phenomenon not unlike the emergence of nations and empires from re-

ligious groups in the past or in our own day. The development of nationhood, such as we have seen in contemporary Jewish Zionism, or in the fulfillment of the aspirations of Indian Islam, was inhibited by American patriotic convictions on the part of the Latter-day Saints themselves and by the integrating power of the larger American community; yet the flare-up of separatist sentiment in the heat of conflict suggests the possibilities of development, had circumstances been different. . . .

The Adventists

The most widely publicized religious excitement of the first half of the nineteenth century came as a result of emphasis upon the expected Second Advent, the return of Christ to the earth to establish a material kingdom. The so-called millennial hope—termed this because Christ was expected, according to scriptural prophecy, to reign for a thousand years—was a central part of most revivalistic preaching, and the widespread religious awakening in the first decades of the nineteenth century encouraged many fervent Christians to believe that the long-awaited advent of Christ was near. When the financial panic of 1837 brought about an economic depression in most areas of the country, additional men and women turned to the expectation of Christ's return as a compensation for their financial disappointments. Whereas the utopians and early perfectionists had hoped to build gradually the Kingdom of God on earth in their communal experiments, the Adventists looked for a sudden and cataclysmic event that would establish the Kingdom in the twinkling of an eye, thereby solving all the world's problems.

The central figure in the Adventist excitement was William Miller (1782–1849), a devout Baptist lay preacher and farmer from Low Hampton, New York. His biblical studies led him to a preoccupation with scriptural prophecies, and his calculations led him to predict that Christ would return "about 1843." In 1828 he felt divinely compelled to tell the world of his discovery. According to his testimony he resisted this call, feeling himself unworthy and unqualified for the task, but beginning in 1831 he told a few friends and neighbors of his prophecy. In 1836 he published his computations in book form, entitled *Evidence from Scripture and History of the Second Coming of Christ, About the Year 1843.* The previously mentioned panic of 1837 created a propitious atmosphere for the reception of his volume, and in 1839 Miller was joined by Joshua V. Himes (1805–1895), a Boston minister who attached himself to Miller as a kind of manager and publicity agent. Miller toured the country, speaking in a large tent. Two journals were established, the *Midnight Cry* (New York) and the *Signs of the Times* (Boston), and soon Miller was gathering thousands of converts. His followers came from a diverse denominational background, for his movement was nonsectarian and noncreedal. Winthrop Hudson estimates that at the height of the movement there were more than 50,000 convinced believers and perhaps a million others who were "skeptically expectant."[12]

Until January 1843 Miller was hesitant to be more specific about the Advent date, but he announced then that the event would take place sometime between March 21, 1843 and March 21, 1844. As the year progressed a comet appeared, heightening the excitement. More and more converts joined the ranks of the Millerites. But March 21, 1844, came and went, and the Advent did not take place. At first Miller confessed himself mistaken, but some of his disciples managed to find evidence in the scriptural prophecies that allowed them to assume a minor error in calculation. The new, and certain, date was October 22, 1844. Again the expectancy and excitement mounted, but when there was a second disappointment, most of the converts became disillusioned and even bitter. Miller died in 1849, discredited and almost forgotten.

A nucleus of the Millerite movement remained faithful to the hope of an Advent, however, and in Albany, New York, in 1845 a conference was held that resulted in the organization of a new Adventist movement, a forerunner of the contemporary Advent Christian Church. Destined to be even more significant was the organization of a group under the leadership of Ellen Gould White (1827–1915), who believed that the promised Advent had been delayed because of the failure of Christians to observe properly the Sabbath, the Old Testament seventh day of the week. Mrs. White's group eventually became the Seventh-Day Adventist church. In the 1920s this group experienced a surge of vitality and from 62,000 members in 1906, they grew to 111,000 in 1926, and to about 318,000 in 1960. In addition, their dedicated missionary efforts had earned more than twice this number of converts outside the United States.[13]

Jehovah's Witnesses

Another vigorous Adventist group on the contemporary American scene is the Jehovah's Witnesses, with whom most Americans have had some contact as they visit from house to house or sell their literature on city street corners. Although Jehovah's Witnesses is the official name of the group, they have been known at various times by several other designations: Millennial Dawnists, members of the Watchtower Bible and Tract Society, Russellites, International Bible Students, and Ruth-

[12] See Winthrop S. Hudson, op. cit. p. 196.

[13] The most recent study of the Millerite movement is Francis D. Nichol, *The Midnight Cry* (Washington: Review and Herald Publishing Association, 1944). For full studies of the Seventh-Day Adventists, see M. E. Olsen, *History of the Origin and Progress of Seventh-Day Adventists* (New York: AMS Press, 1932) and David Mitchell, *Seventh-Day Adventists: Faith in Action* (New York: Vantage, 1956).

erfordites. The movement was begun by Charles Taze Russell (1852–1916), known to his followers as Pastor Russell. As a member of a Congregational church in Allentown, Pennsylvania, Russell was troubled, as he recounted his story, by doubts about the authority of the Bible and especially about the doctrine of eternal punishment of the damned. He found his answers in Adventist teaching, and in 1872 he began meeting with a group of other Christians to study the prophecies of the scripture. He soon developed his own understanding of the millennial promise, and in 1879 he began to publish a magazine. In 1880 he published his first book, *Food for Thinking Christians*, and in 1884 he organized his followers into the Zion's Watch Tower Society. Russell began to teach that 1914 was the year of the promised return of Christ, the time when the Kingdom of God would be fully established. When the promised event did not take place as predicted, Russell and his followers re-examined the biblical prophecies and discovered that the return of Christ had indeed taken place in 1914, but only "in spirit." The visible return of Christ to the earth to bring about the final conquest of evil was to take place within a short time.

Russell died in 1916, and his place of leadership was filled by Joseph Franklin Rutherford (1869–1942), usually known as "Judge" Rutherford. Rutherford had been the attorney for Pastor Russell, and he introduced many changes in the movement, including the introduction of the name Jehovah's Witnesses in 1931. Rutherford also popularized the slogan, "Millions now living will never die," and sent his followers on missions of intensive house-to-house visitation. When Rutherford died in 1942, leadership of the Witnesses was assumed by a board of directors, with Nathan H. Knorr (1903–   ) its president.

World War II initiated the greatest period of growth for the Witnesses. Between 1942 and 1947 the membership approximately doubled, increasing from 115,000 to 207,000. By 1960 the figure was about 1 million, with almost three quarters of that number being outside the United States.

Jehovah's Witnesses believe that the entire religious, economic, and political structure of the world is controlled by Satan, employed by him to oppress the righteous believers. All churches and religious organizations (except, of course, for the Witnesses themselves) are tools of the Devil, and the clergy are willing allies of the wealthy, commercial interests in the exploitation of the poor. All governments are structures of evil and must be so regarded by the faithful. The Witnesses find hope in the expectation that the visible return of Christ will soon take place, at which time he will defeat the forces of Satan in the battle of Armageddon, prophesied in the Scripture. Jesus, together with the living Witnesses and the resurrected saints, will then rule the world for a thousand years.

The attitude of the Witnesses toward government has most often brought them into the public eye. Their refusal to salute the flag, to register for the military draft, or to permit their children to receive blood transfusions has often resulted in their arrest and trial. In some cases the courts have upheld their right to hold some of these views, but some popular hostility has been engendered by their attitudes.[14]

Other Groups

Only brief mention can be made of a number of other religious movements of varying degrees of importance that arose in the nineteenth century. These include the Society for Ethical Culture, founded by Felix Adler (1851–1933), a Jewish rabbi who rebelled against his own religious heritage; the Theosophical Society, originated by Madame Helena P. Blavatsky (1831–1891), who claimed that her wisdom had been imparted to her during a visit to Tibet; New Thought, based on the writings of Julius A. Dresser (1838–1893) and Warren Felt Evans (1817–1889); and the Unity School of Practical Christianity, founded at Kansas City in 1886 by Charles and Myrtle Fillmore.[15]

Christian Science

In the period following the Civil War great interest developed in the United States in the subject of "mental healing." A number of religious developments mirrored this interest, the most prominent of which was Christian Science. Because Christian Science, like Mormonism, has grown and prospered in the American climate, it is worthwhile to take a more detailed look at it, as an example of distinctively American religion.

Much of the American interest in mental healing grew out of the European work of Franz Anton Mesmer (1733?–1815), a German physician who taught that one person could exercise hypnotic power over another because of a mysterious magnetic fluid. From him we draw the word *mesmerism*, or hypnotism. One of his American followers was Phineas Parkhurst Quimby (1802–1866) of Portland, Maine, who became convinced that physical disease could be healed by the changing of mental attitudes through suggestion. Among his patients was Mary Baker Eddy (1821–1910), the founder of Christian Science. Although

---

[14] For a comprehensive study of the Witnesses, see H. H. Stroup, *The Jehovah's Witnesses* (New York: Russell & Russell, 1945).

[15] For additional material concerning these various movements, see the following—for Ethical Culture: Stow Persons, *Free Religion: An American Faith* (New Haven: Peter Smith, 1947); for Theosophy: A. B. Kuhn, *Theosophy* (New York: Henry Holt and Co., 1931); for New Thought: C. S. Braden, *Spirits in Rebellion: The Rise and Development of New Thought* (Dallas: Southern Methodist University Press, 1963); and for Unity: J. D. Freeman, *The Household of Faith: The Story of Unity* (Lee's Summit, Mo: Unity Books, 1951).

Mrs. Eddy was treated by Quimby in 1862 and again in 1864, she and her followers have insisted that her teaching arose out of her own spiritual experiences, not under Quimby's tutelage.

As a child and all through her early adult life, Mrs. Eddy suffered from a series of physical and nervous disorders. When she experienced relief from these problems, she attributed her healing to the discovery that God, or Eternal Mind, is the source of all being. All reality is spiritual and, therefore, matter is nonexistent. Because God is totally good and because he has created all that really is, all reality is good. It follows that evil, suffering, and disease are caused by erroneous thought. Through the power released by Christian Science, which is what Mrs. Eddy entitled her new teaching, one can overcome all the illusions that trouble mankind.

One distinctive characteristic of Christian Science is its pragmatism, as is indicated by the inclusion of the term *Science* in its designation. People are invited to practice and believe in Christian Science on the basis of its practicability, a peculiarly American kind of emphasis. "The control mind holds over matter," Mrs. Eddy wrote, "becomes no longer a question when with mathematical certainty we gain its proof and can demonstrate the facts assumed."[16] From the beginning Christian Science has made its most powerful appeal on the basis of its claims to promote the healing of physical infirmity and disease.

Mrs. Eddy formed her first group of followers in Lynn, Massachusetts, her home town, in 1865. That same year she also published what was to become the authoritative textbook of Christian Science, *Science and Health with Key to Scriptures.* When the center of the movement was shifted to Boston, rapid growth ensued, and in 1892 control was vested in a self-perpetuating board of trustees of the First Church of Christ, Scientist, in Boston, known to Christian Scientists as the "Mother Church." All other Christian Science groups, wherever located, are actually branches of the Mother Church. By the time of Mrs. Eddy's death in 1910, her movement had multiplied to almost one hundred thousand members.

Christian Science continued to grow rapidly until about 1940, when its membership figures appeared to level off. In the preceeding three decades, the number of Christian Science churches had approximately tripled. Today there are some thirty-three hundred branches in fifty-eight countries of the world, as well as some five hundred organizations at universities and colleges.

The following article, composed of excerpts from Christian Science publications, sets forth the basic beliefs of the movement and also includes what has become a distinctive feature of its operation, two testimonies of physical healing.

[16]Mary Baker Eddy, *Science and Health with Key to the Scriptures* (Boston: Christian Science Publishing Society, 1875), p. 9.

"What Is Christian Science?"

Christian Science is a religion based on the words and works of Christ Jesus. It draws its authority from the Bible, and its teachings are set forth in *Science and Health with Key to the Scriptures* by Mary Baker Eddy, the discoverer and founder of Christian Science.

The Church of Christ, Scientist, was founded in 1879 when 15 students of Mrs. Eddy met with their teacher and voted to "organize a church designed to commemorate the word and works of our Master, which should reinstate primitive Christianity and its lost element of healing." (*Manual of The Mother Church* by Mary Baker Eddy, p. 17).

A few years later the church took its present and permanent form as The Mother Church, The First Church of Christ, Scientist, in Boston Massachusetts, which together with its branch churches and societies throughout the world, constitutes the Christian Science denomination.

The tenets of Christian Science are found on page 497 of *Science and Health* and read as follows:

1. As adherents of Truth, we take the inspired Word of the Bible as our sufficient guide to eternal life.
2. We acknowledge and adore one supreme and infinite God. We acknowledge His Son, one Christ; the Holy Ghost or divine Comforter; and man in God's image and likeness.
3. We acknowledge God's forgiveness of sin in the destruction of sin and the spiritual understanding that casts out evil as unreal. But the belief in sin is punished so long as the belief lasts.
4. We acknowledge Jesus' atonement as the evidence of divine, efficacious Love, unfolding man's unity with God through Christ Jesus the Way-shower; and we acknowledge that man is saved through Christ, through Truth, Life, and Love as demonstrated by the Galilean Prophet in healing the sick and overcoming sin and death.
5. We acknowledge that the crucifixion of Jesus and his resurrection served to uplift faith to understand eternal Life, even the allness of Soul, Spirit, and the nothingness of matter.
6. And we solemnly promise to watch, and pray for that Mind to be in us which was also in Christ Jesus; to do unto others as we would have them do unto us; and to be merciful, just, and pure.

The first chapter of Genesis states that God created man in His own image and likeness, and that He pronounced all that He had made "very good." Man in the image of God, Spirit, must be wholly spiritual and as perfect as his creator. Then it follows that the sick and sinning mortal man who appears to the physical sense is a false representation of man as he really is.

The Apostle Paul in the fourth chapter of Ephesians writes of the need to "put off the old man" or imperfect material sense of man and to "put on the new man, which after God is created in righteousness and true holiness." To exchange the false concept for the true is to bring healing and regeneration into human experience.

Christian Science does not rest on a blind faith in the unknown but on an understanding of God as infinite, divine Mind, Spirit, Soul, Principle, Life, Truth, and Love. It recognizes God as acting through universal, immutable, spiritual law, an understanding of which constitutes the Science of Christianity.

This Science draws an absolute distinction between the divine Mind, God, and the false mentality of which Paul declared, "The carnal mind is enmity against God" (Rom. 8:7). On the basis of this distinction it repudiates the use of suggestion, will power, hypnotism, and all those forms of psychotherapy which employ the human mind as a curative agent. Instead Christian Science turns thought to the enlightening and saving power of divine Truth. . . .

The aim of Christian Science is a full salvation for mankind, and this includes salvation from every phase of evil—from all that denies the perfection of God and of man in His image and likeness. Thus sin, sickness, lack, sorrow, selfishness, ignorance, fear, and all material-mindedness are included within the range of mortal errors to be corrected and overcome by a scientific understanding of God.

To a Christian Scientist the real importance of a healing is the light it lets through. The change in physical condition or personal circumstance is only the outward and visible evidence of an inward and spiritual grace—a hint of a perceived spiritual fact. In looking back on a healing, the Christian Scientist is likely to think, not "That was the time I was healed of pneumonia," but "That was the time I learned what real humility is," or "That was the time I saw so clearly that all power belongs to God."

The purpose of spiritual healing is never simply to produce physical ease. It is rather to put off the limited, physical concept of man which binds thought to matter, and thus bring to light Paul's "new" man. This is the man whom Christian Scientists understand to be the "real" man, created by God in His own image, spiritual and whole.

When due allowance has been made for the inevitable imperfections in the human practice of Christian Science and for the abuses of it by those who may claim its name without accepting its spirit or its discipline, the fact remains that it has restored the healing of primitive Christianity to a recognized place in modern society. What seemed to most people like a preposterous claim when it was made by a single Christian woman one hundred years ago has been accepted since then by increasing numbers, many of them professional people trained in modern scientific method and the critical examination of evidence. Whole families have relied exclusively on Christian Science for healing through several generations.

Today the legality of the practice of Christian Science is firmly established in the United States and in many other countries. Increasingly, its practice has won recognition as an acceptable alternative to medical treatment in the eyes of public and private agencies concerned with health, despite the natural preference of these agencies for orthodox methods.

In addition to this pragmatic recognition, based on actual long-term experience with Christian Scientists, there is of course the more basic acknowledgment by law of the constitutional right of Christian Scientists to practice healing as part of their religion. On this more fundamental ground, Christian Science practitioners in the United States are exempted by statute from the provisions of the medical practice acts of the various states, since they are engaged not in the practice of medicine but of a religious ministry including healing. This is also the basis of their practice in other countries.

Christian Science healing is in fact one way of worshiping God. It is an integral part of a deeply felt and closely reasoned view of ultimate reality. This very fact sometimes causes its use of the words "real" and "unreal" to be misunderstood. For when Christian Scientists speak of sickness as unreal, they do not mean that humanly it is to be ignored. They mean rather that it is no part of man's true essential being but comes from a mortal misconception of being, without validity, necessity, or legitimacy. Like a mathematical error which has no substance and no principle to support it, sickness is not to be ignored but to be conscientiously wiped out by a correct understanding of the divine Principle of being. This is the metaphysical basis of Christian Science practice.

The Christian Scientist constantly distinguishes between what he calls the absolute and the relative—the absolute facts of spiritual being and the relative needs of human existence. On the one hand Mrs. Eddy writes, "The Christlike understanding of scientific being and divine healing includes a perfect Principle and idea—perfect God and perfect man—as the basis of thought and demonstration" (*Science and Health,* p. 259). On the other hand she writes, "Imperfect mortals grasp the ultimate of spiritual perfection slowly, but to begin aright and to continue the strife of demonstrating the great problem of being, is doing much" (ibid., p. 254).

[The following accounts are typical of testimonials published in the Christian Science periodicals. They are reprinted here from *A Century of Christian Science Healing*—Eds.]

A number of years ago I very suddenly lost my sight. My husband took me to all the local specialists and they pronounced my beyond help. Then I was taken to a large clinic in Chicago. I stayed there for 6 weeks under the observation of 20 eye specialists. They told me I couldn't possibly regain my vision because the sight film had been destroyed. The eye difficulty was attributed to a condition I had before our second child was born, and I was advised not to have any more children. Also, they reported evidence of tuberculosis and I was told I'd better return home for treatment. They gave me only two years, at the most, to live.

I might say here that I was brought up by devout Christian parents who were both students of the Bible. It was through my love of the Bible that I found the way out of my troubles. Things seemed to be as bad as they could be. I was totally blind and growing weaker. We were in desperate circumstances. My husband had spent all his earnings to help me and the firm he was with had gone bankrupt and he was out of a job. He went to another state to look for work. The children and I went to stay with my mother, and later on we went to my sister's. I prayed frequently but I usually finished by thinking that ours surely was a lost cause.

One day my sister was reading the Bible to me and she came to the verse in Matthew, "And all things, whatsoever ye shall ask in prayer, believing, ye shall receive" (21:22). I asked my sister to read this passage over again two or three times. This was an awakening to me for I saw that I had been denying that this statement was true every time I finished praying. Now something changed in me and I began praying with confidence.

My husband had been out of work for three months. But just a few days later he found a job. When he wrote me this I knew my prayer had been answered.

Then a wonderful thing happened. My husband found a nice apartment for us and sent for us on Easter Sunday. It was in the home of a college professor whose entire family were Christian Scientists. I have never known such kindness and consideration as these people expressed to us. As a result of this, the prejudice and resentment which I'd had for years towards Christian Science disappeared. I finally decided to try this religion. I soon had two proofs that I could be helped. One was the solving of a very serious business problem and the other was the healing of an intestinal condition that had bothered me since I was 16 years old.

My husband and daughter read to me from *Science and Health with Key to the Scriptures* and Mary Baker Eddy's other writings and from the Christian Science periodicals. I also had regular help from a Christian Science practitioner.

The first indication that my sight was returning came when I began to recognize the difference between dark and light. I didn't tell anyone for fear this was just an illusion. But then I gradually began to see forms. Of course, we were overjoyed at this progress. This continued for about a year when I began to make out some letters on billboards along the highways—then full sentences. For the next three years progress was slow and gradual, but steady.

There were many changes in my thinking that had to take place. Through Christian Science I got rid of fear, shame, resentment, condemnation, criticism, hatred, and a sense of inferiority.

I learned that God is good and that He loves all His creation and that we must love each other. I learned that God's law is the only true law and entirely good, and I learned to be obedient to it. I learned gratitude. I learned patience, and to think constructively in my opinions of man and the universe. And most of all I learned that man, spiritual man—the man of God's creation—is complete and perfect now. You might say I had to reconstruct my concept of what man is, including myself. I learned most of all that sight or vision is spiritual and cannot be lost, decayed, carried away, or dimmed.

My sight kept on improving and later I was able to read. For many years now, I have been able to see very well and I do all that I want to do, even to driving a car at night with perfect ease. Being able to see, after four years of total blindness, is indeed quite wonderful to me. The tuberculosis disappeared years ago along with the blindness. And you remember, I told you that I was advised not to have another child, but since then I have had two more lovely children without any ill effects.

This happened during my senior year in high school. I'd been pole vaulting for three years and I was having one of my best seasons. I hadn't lost a meet and I'd broken a few school records. The league and the city finals were coming up and a lot of pressure was being put on me to win. I was practicing four and five hours a day. Then two days before our big meet, while I was vaulting, I slipped and fell from a height of about twelve feet. I missed the sawdust pit and came down on the metal box at the end of the runway. I sprained my ankle very badly. The coach took me to the school doctor and he taped it up. He said I'd have to stay off it quite a while and I wouldn't be able to pole vault for the rest of the season.

Well, the coach was feeling quite low. But I'd called a practitioner before going to the doctor's office, and I felt absolutely confident.

I guess the best way to explain it is to go back to when I first started pole vaulting. One day I'd be good and then next I'd be just terrible. It seemed that every day there'd be a new problem. This went on until I began getting rid of the thought of self-glory and started realizing my true goal should be to glorify God, by expressing man's God-given dominion. Not until I really found my goal did I begin to improve. You see, I believe that our purpose in doing things such as athletics is to express divine qualities as best we can—qualities like intelligence, exactness, control.

So when this problem with my ankle came up, I knew it was just another opportunity for me to prove God's care. It wasn't a case of wishful thinking—or trying to use will power. I went to that meet with a feeling of confidence even though the ankle was still quite painful. I felt I'd be taken care of, and that there could not be a cause or effect apart from God that could touch me.

I didn't do any warming up that day, and I by-passed the first jumps until I felt I was perfectly ready. And when I decided to go, I walked out on the runway and prayed for God's guidance. I jumped and I never jumped better in my life. I vaulted all afternoon without any feeling of pain or hindrance, and I had no more trouble with the ankle after that. I took second in the event—but it was because of a minor difference in form. It had nothing to do with my ankle. And even though I didn't win that day, I had a tremendous feeling of satisfaction. To me this proof of God's care was a far better victory than just winning a medal. I felt it was a true victory because it showed me how we can rely on God in everything.

Conservative Judaism

American Judaism includes three major groupings—Reform, Orthodox, and Conservative—that roughly correspond to the denominational "families" within Protestantism. Of these three, conservative Judaism had its organizational genesis in the United States and displays some singularly American characteristics. While it cannot be classified as strictly indigenous in the way the other movments discussed in this chapter have been—it is, after all, an integral part of "main-line" Judaism rather than a radical departure from it—Conservative Judaism does deserve some special consideration. To understand it, one must first look briefly at Jewish history in this country.

The story begins in 1654 with the arrival in New Amsterdam (now
New York) of a small group of *Sephardim*—Jews who had originally
fled Spain because of persecution. In the ensuing years other small
groups of Jews, also mostly Sephardim, made their way to places such
as New Haven, Charleston, Savannah, Richmond, and Philadelphia. As
late as 1800, however, the total number of Jews in the United States did
not exceed two or three thousand.

The Sephardim were by and large a cultured group who blended well
into American life. Religiously, they maintained what they called "dignified orthodoxy" and tended, therefore, to be fairly conservative in
their traditions and beliefs.

The nineteenth century brought drastic changes in the character of
Judaism in America, as successive waves of immigration from Europe
introduced divisive elements along with greatly increased numbers. The
first major wave of immigration, which reached its height in the period
from 1840 to 1880, was largely made up of *Ashkenazim,* mostly German-speaking Jews from northern Europe. *Ashkenazim* was a term originally used in medieval rabbinic literature to describe all Jews living in
northern Europe. Through the centuries, persecution and economic
problems forced many of the Ashkenazim to move eastward into Poland and Russia, where they maintained a fervent piety and strict Orthodox faith. The western Ashkenazim, centered in Germany, did not
develop in precisely the same way; still, at the beginning of the wave of
American immigration in 1840, western Ashkenazic Judaism was at
once deeper, narrower, and less cosmopolitan than that of the original
Sephardic Jews in America.

Some 200,000 Jews came into the United States from 1840 to 1880,
and although the Judaism they brought with them was distinguished by
intense commitment to the Jewish law and the Jewish community, the
new Americans found their faith and traditional way of life severely
tested and strained by life in the new world. For the most part, these
Jews did not withdraw into enclaves in the large cities but scattered out
across the nation, settling in small towns and fledgling urban areas.
Many of them were well educated, coming as they did from the economic middle class, and they adapted rapidly to American patterns of
life. The old forms of religious observance came under great pressure,
and the group was ripe for influences from the movement of Reform
Judaism, which had taken shape in Germany later on during the nineteenth century. Reform Judaism represented an attempt to modify
orthodox rabbinic Judaism in such a way that Jews could more fully
participate in the cultural and social life of the whole community. It
involved revisions in the ancient ceremonies of Judaism, slackening of
the rigid ritual and dietary requirements of Orthodoxy, and an accommodation to the theological and philosophical liberalism of the day.
This movement brought a large number of able, Reform-minded rabbis
from Germany to this country, and they ministered to an American
constituency composed largely of middle-class Jews of German origin.

Thus Reform Judaism in America grew rapidly. By 1880, under the leadership of rabbis like Isaac Meyer Wise (1819–1900) and David Einhorn (1809–1879), Reform Judaism, as Sidney Ahlstrom comments, "had almost come to *be* American Judaism."[17]

But changes in the pattern of immigration were destined, once again, to reshape the nature of American Judaism. Nearly 2 million Jews arrived in this country between 1870 and the beginning of World War I, and the overwhelming majority of them came from eastern Europe, bringing with them the religious commitments of eastern Ashkenazic Orthodoxy. Many of these new immigrants spoke Yiddish; they tended to congregate in the large industrial cities where they could establish their own neighborhoods and observe traditional Jewish customs with a minimum of outside interference. By 1927 probably 80 per cent of the Jews in America were of eastern European ancestry and Orthodox background.

The process of Americanization soon began to affect these Orthodox Jews, however, especially as their children grew up in the American environment, received a secular education, and took their places in the American economic and political systems. Multitudes of them drifted away from the synagogues. A survey of New York city Jewish youth in 1935 indicated that 72 per cent of the young men and 78 per cent of the women had not attended religious services in at least a year. As we saw in the chapter on revivalism, this trend was to be reversed after World War II by many factors, including the Nazi persecution, but one important religious response to the problem was the rise of Conservative Judaism as a new and vital segment of American Judaism.

Conservative Judaism began as an attempt to find a "middle ground" between the Orthodoxy of the eastern European immigrants and the liberalism of the Reform movement. A minority of Jews within the Reform camp became dissatisfied with the extent of Reform accommodation to American life, and matters were brought to a head in 1885 by the serving of shrimp (a violation of Jewish dietary laws) at a Reform banquet honoring graduates of Hebrew Union College. Led by Sebato Morais (1823–1897), the dissidents founded the Jewish Theological Seminary in New York in 1886. The movement did not prosper until 1902, when Solomon Schechter (1850–1915), a Romanian-born intellectual and profound religious thinker, became the president of the seminary. In 1913 Schechter was a leading founder of the United Synagogues of American, an organization of congregations sympathetic to Conservative viewpoints. By 1952 Conservatism embraced 450 rabbis and over 500 synagogues with more than 200,000 member families, and it benefited greatly from the postwar Jewish revival.

Conservatism thus represents in its own way a distinctive American response to the problems faced by an ancient faith struggling to maintain its identity and vitality in the American context. In contrast to Re-

[17]Ahlstrom, op. cit., Vol. 1, p. 696.

form Judaism's more extensive assimilation into American culture, Conservatives include among their objectives:

1. Loyalty to the Torah.[18]
2. Observance of the Sabbath and dietary laws.
3. Preservation in the liturgy of references to Israel's past and the hopes for Israel's restoration.
4. Maintenance of the traditional character of the liturgy, with Hebrew as the language of prayer.[19]

These concerns indicate the desire of Conservatives to maintain a distinctive Jewish tradition and identity. On the other hand, Conservatism has also evidenced the openness to scientific knowledge so characteristic of Reform, along with a willingness to reinterpret its fundamental loyalty to Judaism in terms of changing historical and cultural circumstances. Conservative public worship services have often incorporated such new elements as mixed choirs, family pews, organ music, and the like—all practices burrowed from the surrounding non-Jewish culture. In short, Conservative Judaism has proved itself a workable form of Judaism, well adapted to American religious needs. Although many Orthodox and Reform Jews would obviously disagree, Conservatives like to claim that they represent "authentic American Judaism."[20]

The Holiness-Pentecostal Movements

Like the adherents of Conservative Judaism, the Holiness-Pentecostal groups in the United States have strong roots in their own historic tradition. Their development in this country, however, has been a distinctive one, entitling them to consideration in the study of indigenous American faiths. Indeed, Sidney Ahlstrom judges that Pentecostalism is "one of at least five large and easily differentiated religious movements that bear the stamp 'made in America.'"[21]

The search for holiness, or spiritual perfection, is as ancient as Christianity itself, but in nineteenth-century America that search received powerful impetus from the generally optimistic and self-reliant atmosphere of an expanding frontier culture as well as from the religious excitement of the revivals. The strong Methodist influence in the revivals was an especially important factor, since the founder of Methodism, John Wesley, was a prime exponent of the doctrine of sanctification, or Christian perfectionism. Wesley distinguished between justification, or

[18] The Torah is the traditional compilation of Jewish law and ritual, including the Pentateuch (the first five books of the Hebrew Scriptures).

[19] See Rufus Learsi, *Israel: A History of the Jewish People* (Cleveland: Meridian, 1968), p. 206.

[20] See Ahlstrom, op. cit., Vol. 2, p. 477.

[21] See Ahlstrom, op. cit., Vol. 2, p. 530. The other four movements mentioned by Ahlstrom are Christian Science, Mormonism, Seventh-Day Adventism, and Jehovah's Witnesses.

conversion, and sanctification, insisting that "justified persons are to go on unto perfection." For Wesley, the experience of sanctification was a distinctly different experience from conversion—one that imparted perfect love of God and liberation from sin.[22] Later exponents of perfectionism came to call sanctification the "second blessing."

American Methodism remained faithful to and indeed enthusiastic about the holiness doctrines in the period prior to the Civil War and for several decades after the war. What more staid and dignified leaders in the church considered dangerous excesses and extreme emphases on sanctification gradually led, however, to serious rifts within Methodist ranks, and by the end of the century a number of significant defections had occurred. This resulted in the establishment of several new holiness-oriented denominations, such as the Wesleyan Methodist Church, the Free Methodist Church, and the Church of the Nazarene. Other groups more independent of Methodist roots began to form also. The Church of God, with headquarters in Anderson, Indiana, was organized in 1881, and the Christian and Missionary Alliance was founded by A. B. Simpson, a former Presbyterian minister, in 1887.

In terms of numbers and influence, however, the most significant new religious groups growing out of the Holiness movement were represented by the diverse variety of Pentecostal churches. One historian of the movement observes that they introduced "a new element . . . . into the religious life *of the world.*"[23] Pentecostalism finds its biblical basis in such passages as Joel 2:21–32, which speaks of the "latter rain," interpreted as a promise of the coming of the spiritual gifts of sanctification, and the classic Pentecostal passage, Acts 2:1–20, which describes the events of the first Pentecost. Historians of American Pentecostalism usually trace its beginnings to one of two events. The first of these was the coming of the "gift of the spirit" to Agnes N. Ozman, a student in Bethel Bible College, Topeka, Kansas, on January 1, 1901. Bethel had recently been founded by Charles F. Parham, a prominent Holiness evangelist, and Ozman received the power to speak in tongues (technically known as "glossolalia"). Soon most of the other Bethel students began to speak in tongues which they could not understand, and the movement spread rapidly. The second widely cited cause is the 1906 revival at Azusa Street Mission in Los Angeles, conducted by Parham's student, W. J. Seymour, a young black preacher. Out of the Azusa Street revival came several Pentecostal leaders who established a number of church organizations. Most important were the Church of God in Christ, the largest black Pentecostal group, and several Church of God organizations, the largest of which is the Church of God, headquartered in Cleveland, Tennessee. By 1970, Pentecostals claimed a worldwide membership of over 8 million. Most Pentecostal denominations belong to

---

[22] For a full exposition of Wesley's views on holiness, see John L. Peters, *Christian Perfection and American Methodism* (Nashville, Tenn.: Abingdon, 1956).

[23] Irwin Winehouse, *The Assemblies of God* (New York: Vantage, 1959), p. 11. The italics are the author's.

the Pentecostal Fellowship of North America, organized in 1914 in Little Rock, Arkansas. Among the more prominent groups are the Assemblies of God, the United Pentecostal Church, and the Pentecostal Church of God in America.

Pentecostalism has other distinctive doctrinal emphases in addition to the practice of speaking in tongues. These include a strong belief in divine healing, a distrust of medical care, and a rigid code of personal conduct. Pentecostalists are, of course, strongly conservative in their biblical interpretations and share a doctrinal closeness in this regard to Fundamentalists.

Among recent American religious developments, perhaps the most interesting single phenomenon is the upsurge of what has been called neo-Pentecostalism, a movement that reaches far beyond the Pentecostal churches and includes believers from most major Protestant denominations as well as Roman Catholics. Neo-Pentecostalism—with its emphasis on the gift of the spirit, speaking in tongues, and divine healing—has caused considerable dissension, but it has not produced any new denominations. Beginning originally as a lay movement within the main-line churches, the movement soon enlisted considerable support from clergy. The Full Gospel Businessmen's Fellowship, founded in 1951 by Demos Shakarian, a wealthy California dairyman, promotes interdenominational meetings to spread the experience of the "baptism of the Spirit"; by 1972 the Fellowship had 300,000 members in 900 chapters, with an annual operating budget in excess of a million dollars. Another powerful force in neo-Pentecostalism was Oral Roberts, originally a Pentecostal Holiness preacher, whose nationwide radio and television programs popularized the movement. Although Roberts became an ordained Methodist minister in 1968, his influence was and continues to be widespread.

Other important events in the spread of neo-Pentecostalism included the announcement in 1960 by Dennis J. Bennett, pastor of a two-thousand-member Van Nuys, California, Episcopal church, that he had had a "Pentecostal experience." Eventually Presbyterian, Lutheran, Baptist, Methodist, Dutch Reformed, and United Brethren congregations were also involved. The Pentecostal penetration of major denominational groups grew by leaps and bounds in the 1960s.

Neo-Pentecostalism has not, however, confined itself to Protestant ranks. In some ways, the movement appeared to spread even more rapidly among Catholics than among Protestants. Beginning with the "Duquesne weekend" in mid-Feburary 1967, at which a number of Duquesne University faculty members and students reported the reception of the "baptism of the Spirit," neo-Pentecostalism spread to Catholic centers such as Notre Dame and Fordham universities. A National Conference on Charismatic Renewal in the Catholic Church was organized in 1968 at Notre Dame; by 1972 the annual meeting of the organization drew more than 12,000 participants.

The following chapter is taken from an influential volume by John L.

Sherrill, an Episcopal layman and magazine writer, who set out to write a description of the charismatic movement and ended by himself experiencing the gift of the Spirit.

_____ *Document 31*

From *They Speak with Other Tongues* by John L. Sherrill

There seems to be a strange link between taking a seemingly foolish step—which God specifies—and receiving spiritual power. Moses stretched his rod over the water at Jehovah's command and the Red Sea divided. The penniless widow was instructed, through Elisha, to collect many vessels and to start pouring oil into them from her small jar: when the widow had finished obeying she had collected enough oil to pay all her debts. Elijah had to strike the water with his mantle before it would part.

I once had occasion to talk about this phenomenon with Billy Graham. He had noticed it for years, and was of the opinion that the secret lay in overcoming self-consciousness and self-will sufficiently to perform the task. It was extremely difficult, he had found, for most people to get out of their seats and walk forward to the altar rail at one of his meetings. But he had also observed that the seemingly foolish gesture brought power with it.

For many people speaking in tongues falls into the same category. It seems to them pointless and embarrassing. In these people, no doubt, the final yielding of their tongues produces a deep religious experience. But this was not the point at which my own resistance came. I could see by now some of the logic behind tongues: I could imagine myself praising God in a language I could not understand; I could imagine myself praying for someone in tongues if I could not imagine how to pray for them with my understanding. By now, in fact, I was becoming increasingly eager to receive the Baptism in the Holy Spirit and it seemed fairly likely to me that tongues would be a part of it.

No, the point of resistance for me lay in a different quarter. There was one act which many of the Pentecostals performed which I was *not* going to do. They would stand up, raise both hands toward heaven, and shout "Praise the Lord!" . . . .

I knew that "Praise the Lord" was a favorite phrase of the psalmists, and was even part of the liturgy of my own well-mannered Episcopal service.

Nevertheless, the practice as the Pentecostals did it was objectionable to me. No doubt each person draws the line somewhere . . . .

December 2, 1960. It was the date of the opening of the Full Gospel Business Men's convention in Atlantic City to which Tib [the author's wife] and I had agreed to go, back in the spring, so many months ago. The meetings were being held at The President, one of the large on-the-water hotels. Friday night we registered, went for a walk on the cold, moonlit beach and turned in early.

I don't know why I was so unprepared for the emotions of the breakfast meeting next morning. I'd been to many Pentecostal gatherings by now, but never to such a

SOURCE: John L. Sherrill, *They Speak with Other Tongues* (New York: Pyramid Publications, 1965), pp. 117–119, 121–123.

large one: early in the morning, several hundred men and woman crowded into The President's grand ballroom. They ate rapidly, then pushed their chairs back in obvious anticipation of something to follow.

On the platform at the end of the room sat two dozen business and professional men. Some, I was told, had flown across the country to attend the meetings; one had come in his own private plane.

While we were finishing our coffee, one of these men stood up and called out the name of a song. Everyone joined in, loud, lusty and wonderful as I'd heard it before among Pentecostals. By the middle of the second song a woman at the next table was weeping. There was nothing especially emotional about the song itself, it was one of the standard old Gospel hymms, "When I Survey the Wondrous Cross." But crying seems to be as infectious as laughter. Soon some of the men on the platform were unabashedly bringing out their handkerchiefs. What was it that swept a room this way? I felt it too; so did Tib sitting next to me. Both of us were studiously avoiding looking the other one in the eye.

As the music continued, several people at the tables began to sing "in the Spirit." Soon the whole room was singing a complicated harmony-without-score, created spontaneously. It was eerie but extraordinarily beautiful. The song leader was no longer trying to direct the music, but let the melodies create themselves; without prompting one quarter of the room would suddenly start to sing very loudly while others subsided. Harmonies and counterharmonies wove in and out of each other.

By now tears were flowing without restraint all around the room. A weathered, stonefaced man near us raised calloused hands and sang out, "Praise the Lord!" An elderly woman two tables away stood up and began to dance a little jig. She looked like a great-grandmother, dressed in black with her white hair in a bun. No one paid her the slightest attention. Except me, that is; I couldn't take my eyes off her. And as I watched, a phenomenon occurred which I have still not been able to explain. It was very hot in the ballroom, perhaps 85 degrees. Yet while grandmother danced I distinctly saw, against the dark velvet curtains of the room, soft billows of visible "breath" coming from her mouth as if she were standing outside in the cold.

The effect on me of watching these manifestations is hard to describe. Instead of being embarrassed or feeling that I was watching something unseemly, I had the overall feeling that this was wholesome and good. . . .

And then suddenly it was all over. The singing stopped; the mood of the meeting shifted. People brought out handkerchiefs and dried their eyes. A California dairyman named Demos Shakarian, who is the Fellowship's president, stepped to the center of the platform and conducted the business end of the meeting . . . .

A prayer followed. The "breakfast" meeting lasted for four hours. There was preaching and more singing. There was a period during which people from the floor could tell about some experience with the Holy Spirit. I noticed that several in the audience, when introducing themselves, confirmed what Charles Maurice had told us: there were others in the ballroom who were not Pentecostals by denomination, they were Episcopalians, Methodists, Baptists, Presbyterians, Lutherans. When at last the meeting adjourned for lunch, Dr. William Reed, a surgeon and an Episcopal lay reader whom we'd known for some years, came over to Tib and me and asked us to join a group who were having sandwiches sent to one of the rooms upstairs. The room they had chosen was to become strangely important to me: Room 405.

The door to Room 405 was slightly ajar when we arrived fifteen minutes later, so I knocked and we walked in, wondering who would be there. Sitting with his back to the window which framed the rolling, pounding Atlantic Ocean, was Jim Brown, a Presbyterian minister from Pennsylvania. Bill Reed was on the sofa, talking to a Methodist woman minister from Philadelphia, Olivia Henry. And out in the kitchen making coffee were an Episcopalian social worker named Dorothy Randall and Jim's wife, Marianne. There was not, I noted, a Pentecostal among us.

Tib sat down beside Jim with her back to the Atlantic. The conversation centered on the morning's meeting, the different people who had spoken, the points of view expressed. It was several minutes before I noticed that Tib was not joining in.

Sandwiches arrived from the coffee shop downstairs, and the talk turned to more personal subjects: the needs and hopes that each of us there in the room had brought to the convention. From time to time I looked across at Tib. She sat withdrawn and silent, the sandwich on her plate untouched. She'd said nothing about feeling bad that morning, but there was a weariness about her posture now—as though she held a tremendous weight on her shoulders, all alone.

All at once she stood up. She murmured something about having to make a phone call and before I could stop her, she was gone. . . .

In 405 there was a certain air of expectancy. There were six of us now, seated in a casual circle about the room. Several people had related instances of the power of Spirit-filled prayer, and someone now suggested that we pray this way for the problems on our minds.

Partly in an effort to overcome self-consciousness, I shut my eyes. Soon I'd lost track of who was talking in the room. Someone began to pray in the Spirit. It was a woman's voice, but I did not know whose. In fact, from that moment on I lost contact with individuals. It was as if the separate personalities had disappeared and a single individual, talking in various timbres and accents had taken their place. Minds seemed to work together: a sentence would be started by one person and finished by another.

Now someone else began to pray in tongues. Another started to sing very softly in the Spirit. I felt my throat tighten, as it had downstairs at the height of the singing. I suppose I was crying, deeply, silently. Slowly I began to lose my own identity too, until finally self-awareness disappeared.

This is quite an experience, losing consciousness of self. And I was helped by gaining, at the same time, the awareness that another Presence was in the room. And suddenly He was there . . . the light blazed through my closed lids, blinding, dizzying, fearful. I was afraid of this approaching contact. I tried to pull my mind away from it, to concentrate on the solid room around me and the human beings in it.

"Look neither to the right nor to the left, but only straight ahead."

The voice came from behind me. I thought it was Olivia Henry's but I have never been sure. Just at the moment when I was about to take refuge in self-consciousness, it pulled me back to the center. Several times more, in the next hour, the command was repeated, always just in time to prevent my attention from being sidetracked. I never knew whether the words were meant for me or not, but they performed an immeasurable service. They kept me from being distracted by what was going on to either side, from being conscious of how I looked and what other people thought of me; they brought me back always to the blinding light directly ahead.

There was a lull in the praying and singing. The voices around me receded into a quiet murmur.

A man's voice: "I believe John wants the Baptism in the Spirit."

I felt, more than saw, the five people rise and form a circle around me. . . .

The group moved closer around me. It was almost as if they were forming with their bodies a funnel through which was concentrated the flow of the Spirit that was pulsing through that room. It flowed into me as I sat there, listening to the Spirit-song around me. Now the tongues swelled to a crescendo, musical and lovely. I opened my mouth, wondering if I too could join in, but nothing happened.

I felt a numbness in my lips and a constriction in my throat.

And suddenly I had the impression that in order to speak in tongues I had only to look up. But this was a joyful gesture. All my training and inclination was to approach God with head bowed.

Strange that such a simple gesture as lifting the head should become a battleground. And soon—perhaps because I did not obey quick enough—another directive came clear: not only was I to lift my head but I was to lift my hands too, and I was to cry out with all the feeling in me a great shout of praise to God. A hot, angry flush rose and flooded me. It was the thing above all things that I didn't want to do.

Perhaps because it was so very repugnant to me the issue was clearly drawn as one of sheer obedience.

What other possible significance could there be in my raising my hands high and mouthing some words of praise? But that was what I had to do, and I knew it. Foolish as it seemed. Or maybe because it seemed foolish. I heard E. Stanley Jones saying, "I had to become God's fool."

With a sudden burst of will I thrust my hands into the air, turned my face full upward, and at the top of my voice I shouted:

"Praise the Lord!"

It was the floodgate opened. From deep inside me, deeper than I knew voice could go, came a torrent of joyful sound. It was not beautiful, like the tongues around me. I had the impression that it was ugly: explosive and grunting. I didn't care. It was healing it was forgiveness, it was love too deep for words and it burst from me in wordless sound. After that one shattering effort of will, my will was released, freed to soar into union with Him. No further conscious effort was required of me at all, not even choosing the syllables with which to express my joy. The syllables were all there, ready-formed for my use, more abundant than my earthbound lips and tongue could give shape to.

It was not that I felt out of control of the situation: I had never felt more truly master of myself, more integrated and at peace with warring factions inside myself. I could stop the tongues at any instant, but who would? I wanted them never to stop. And so I prayed on, laughing and free, while the setting sun shone through the window, and the stars came out.

Summary

America has provided a rich breeding ground for many religious movements, most of which have flourished for a short period and then disappeared. Those indigenous movements that have survived and prospered continue to contribute their unique characteristics to the contemporary scene. Although such groups as Conservative Judaism and the Holiness-Pentecostals have clear roots and doctrinal connections with the historic faiths out of which they come, they have nevertheless been shaped profoundly by the American context. And today millions of Americans organize their religious lives around the teachings and practices of obviously indigenous faiths of such groups as the Christian Scientists, the Latter-day Saints, the Seventh-Day Adventists, and Jehovah's Witnesses.

From the perspective of a student of American religion, such movements are noteworthy not only because they are taken seriously by their adherents but also because they exhibit the unmistakable signs of having grown up in the matrix of a distinctive American historical experience. In the case of the four "made in America" religions mentioned above, each derives from revelations that are claimed to have come from God to an American prophet or prophetess. The movements tend to exalt and inculcate the peculiarly American Puritan virtues, suh as diligence, thrift, a high degree of asceticism, and honesty. But perhaps their most remarkable common trait is that each in its own way has shifted the locus of God's primary activity to the American continent. All of these movements teach that God has chosen to given a final and full revelation of His truth to Americans, and there is something of this same flavor even in a movement like Pentecostalism. In one way or another, the eventual triumph of God's purpose is to occur here in the New World. Thus the old Puritan dream of a "New Israel," a Promised Land in which the Holy Commonwealth could at last be built and perfected, has been transformed into a basic tenet of belief. In a secularized form, the Puritan hope helped supply the seeds for the doctrine of Manifest Destiny and the challenge to "make the world safe for democracy." In a more specifically religious sense, that Puritan concept helped to give rise to new and sometimes vital indigenous religious movements. In either case, the creative power of the "American dream" was undeniably at work.

5 Liberalism and Conservatism

The almost unbelievably broad spectrum of American religion, ranging from the most conservative to the most liberal—if we may use these terms—is a striking fact. Surprisingly, both extremes in the spectrum appear, even today, to possess vitality and to attract both interest and adherence. Far-right conservatism—the so-called fundamentalist churches, for example—still claims the allegiance of many Americans, and only a few years ago the "death of God" theology, an extremely liberal movement, stimulated wide interest, receiving front-page coverage in major periodicals and newspapers.[1]

Although it is true that European theology also has both liberal and conservative facets, the relationship between these two streams of thought has never operated in the same way in the United States as in the parent European culture. For several decades, for instance, scholars have been speaking of European culture as "post-Christian," a situation in which atheists, agnostics, secularists, and others outnumber religious believers. Such a description is probably not accurate when applied to the American scene, even when recent shifts have been taken into account. Pure atheists are still relatively hard to find,[2] and American agnostics, as William G. McLoughlin has pointed out, tend to have their own brand of religion to substitute for the traditional faiths.[3]

William A. Clebsch has developed a conception of American religion that he calls "polypolitan." He contends that Americans have lived within a religious "city" or *polis* (the Greek word for *city*) very unlike that of their forebears in Europe. The Americans' religious city has not been their only city, not even their dominant one. Americans live in many cities—economic, political, intellectual, vocational, recreational—and their citizenship in these varied communities helps to form the character of their religious outlook just as profoundly as does their life in the religious polis. Dwelling in this plural universe makes the American a "polypolitan" ("many citied") person.[4]

But not only does the typical American (if such a specimen exists) live

---

[1] Thomas Altizer and William Hamilton from Protestant ranks, and Richard Rubenstein, from a background of Judaism, are typical of this school of thought, which attracted attention in the latter part of the 1960s. For a description of this general movement, see Kenneth Hamilton, *What's New in Religion: A Critical Study of New Theology, New Morality, and Secular Christianity* (Grand Rapids: Eerdmans, 1968).

[2] In recent Gallup polls, less than 2 per cent of those questioned claimed to believe in the nonexistence of God.

[3] See William G. McLoughlin, "How Is America Religious?" in *Religion in America,* edited by William G. McLoughlin and Robert N. Bellah (Boston: Beacon Press, 1968), p. xvi.

[4] See the detailed discussion of this viewpoint in William A. Clebsch, *From Sacred to Profane America* (New York: Harper & Row, 1968), pp. 16–21.

in this multiple environment, he or she is also conditioned thereby to a corresponding pluralism within each of the cities, including the religious one. Americans are sociologically, psychologically, and culturally accustomed to accommodate a diverse variety of viewpoints, even on fundamental issues. That means, among other things, that the pluralism that we have already noted in the American religious pattern is reflected not only in organizations and denominations but also in styles of thinking and believing.

In an earlier section we saw how and why this country originally developed a pattern of organizational religious pluralism. Toleration and, eventually, religious freedom emerged primarily in reaction to the church establishment that prevailed almost everywhere in Europe and that some groups had sought to perpetuate in the New World. And as this country matured, pluralism not only in religious organizations but also in religious thought, or theology, even within the various religious groups, became the approved "American way" of doing things. Sidney E. Mead has noted "a largely neglected strand in the Protestant tradition" that construed this pluralism as a positive good.[5] And Clebsch points out that "precisely those groups most concerned for the finality of their own teachings knew best of all that they must grant to others the very toleration which was the condition of their own existence." He continues:

> In the first national decades the pattern of religious pluralism proved itself almost too well by eliciting the broadly Protestant consensus. Against that unofficial "establishment" arose sectarian protests ranging from the indigenous Mormon religion through the imported Anglo-Catholicism espoused by Episcopalian partisans to the transplanted Roman Catholicism of the Irish—and other nationally identified—Catholic immigrants. Each denounced Protestantism as false; with equal vigor each found the others' protests to be spurious. But each demanded the right to exist, and each granted the same right to all other denominations.[6]

Eventually the strongest argument supporting a polypolitan religious culture is that the agreement to disagree agreeably, on which religion in America has seemed to thrive, has produced a situation inculcating mutual understanding and self-correction by the various religious faiths. Through tolerant rivalry the different denominations compete for the faith of Americans and for the right to help shape the common life of the people. Of course, there are some glaring exceptions in this pattern. Intolerance and bigotry have not by any means been absent from the relationship of American religious groups, but Leo Pfeffer, leading Jewish constitutional lawyer, has summed up the general situation:

> The objective of competition [between religious groups] is not to capture the state but to convince the community. The religious groups wish to translate

[5] Sidney E. Mead, "The Post-Protestant Concept and America's Two Religions, *Religion in Life*, Vol. 33 (Spring 1964), p. 204.
[6] Clebsch, op. cit., pp. 212–213.

their values into communal values mainly through the operation of law. . . .
They seek to achieve it by convincing the master of the state in a democracy—
the people—that the values they urge are the best for the community and should
be adopted by the political representatives of the community.[7]

Competition among the denominations had involved far more, however, than a simple struggle to convince the community of certain political and moral values. It has extended to the whole range of religious beliefs and doctrines. The relative importance of theology[8] has fluctuated,
but it has always been a part of the religious phenomenon. As recently
as 1955 Will Herberg, in *Protestant-Catholic-Jew*, could make a strong
case for the view that most Americans cared little or nothing about
theological problems and convictions. Rather, he argued, there is an
agreement among most adherents to the three major American religious
communities that "faith in faith"—the importance of believing something, no matter what—is the important thing. Today, three decades later,
that case is not nearly so strong. Apparently, something of a theological
revival has taken place. It may not endure for long, and it is problematic
as to how widespread it is, but if one is to judge from the material in
the communications media, the discussions in local church congregations,
and the remarkable interest shown in theology and religious studies on
major public university campuses in the last decade,[9] to mention only
a few selected factors, it would appear that theology is once again a
respectable subject for conversation. William McLoughlin has summed
up his impression of the contemporary mood:

I sense . . . the mood of "New Lights" in all American Awakenings—the conviction that God has yet further light to reveal to his followers in this world
and yet new ways of expressing himself. There is more than faith in faith underlying this revival and more than Kierkegaardian despair in the theology of crisis
which undergirds this generation's search for values. Underneath the querulous
searching . . . stirs a faith more nearly like that of Job facing the whirlwind, anxious but ready to believe. . . .[10]

The freedom inherent in American religious pluralism—this "polypolitan" religious city—seems to serve today as an incentive to theological exploration and controversy, just as it always has. True, in earlier
years the anti-intellectualism that we have noted in the Second Awakening and in later revival movements acted so as to isolate much religion
from the vital social and intellectual currents of the surrounding culture.

[7] Leo Pfeffer, *Creeds in Competition: A Creative Force in Culture* (New York: Harper &
Row, 1958), p. 18.
   [8] Edwin Gaustad has reminded us that the word *theology* consists of two Greek words: *theos*
(God) and *logos* (reason). One word thus combines "the infinite mystery of the universe with
the finite exploration of that universe." See Edwin Scott Gaustad, *A Religious History of
America* (New York: Harper & Row, 1966), p. 272.
   [9] See Claude Welch, *Religion in the Undergraduate Curriculum: An Analysis and Interpretation* (Washington, D.C.: Association of American Colleges, 1972), pp. 49f.
   [10] "Introduction: How Is America Religious?" McLoughlin and Bellah, op. cit., p. xviii.

The result was a set of theological beliefs familiar to those within the closed circle of a particular church or denomination but largely irrelevant and often incomprehensible to most of those outside that circle. But in the latter part of the nineteenth century and all through the twentieth century steady efforts have been made to batter down the barriers between church and culture.

Gaustad points out that most contemporary theology in this country is of the experimental and exploratory type, seeking "not so much to rewrite the ancient creeds as to infuse them with new understanding." And he further observes that

> Americans, when asked what they believe, rarely answer in traditional forms. Something more than a mere recitation of the Apostles' Creed, or Maimonides' Principles, or the Augsburg Confession. And that something is the anticipation that deepest convictions arise from and reflect personal experiences and private hopes. The result is still theology . . . but the American experience and the American dream are unmistakably stamped upon it.[11]

From the beginning the American dream and the American experience have included both conservative and liberal facets. It is not surprising, therefore, that the kind of religious patterns that have developed under the influence of those historical factors have included both liberal and conservative elements.

Liberalism and Conservatism: General Descriptions

In the attempt to classify varying theological beliefs, we have already employed two terms: *liberal* and *conservative*. Often these words have been used as mere labels to be applied as weapons in arguments and controversy meaning virtually nothing. Any serious effort to summarize contemporary religious thought must obviously avoid such name calling. If one understands, however, that these terms can be employed simply as broad general descriptions, without implying value judgments, they can be useful. Perhaps it will be helpful to list a number of significant characteristics that ordinarily distinguish religious liberals from their conservative counterparts.

Conservatives can be described by some of the following terms:

1. *Theocentric*—that is, God-centered. Conservative theology tends to start from God, ascribing all power, sovereignty, and wisdom to Him. Religious conservatives often taken a "low" view of humanity, stressing human sinfulness and weakness.

2. *Otherworldly*—that is, emphasizing the reality and importance of a

---

[11] Gaustad, op. cit., p. 273. The three traditional statements of faith to which Gaustad refers are ancient summaries of Christian and Jewish beliefs. The Apostles' Creed is used in many Catholic and Protestant liturgies of worship. Maimonides' Principles sum up Jewish doctrine, and the Augsburg Confession is the standard statement of Lutheran Reformation teachings.

realm above and beyond the natural, tangible world in which people live. Thus conservatives speak unself-consciously of heaven, hell, life after death, the end of the world and so on.

3. *Revelational*—that is, accepting and understanding of religious truth as derived not from human reason but from some type of special communication from God. This communication may be thought of as coming primarily through sacred writings or scriptures, or through a sacred institution, such as the church, or through some type of personal religious experience, but it always originates in God.

4. *Traditional*—that is, highly valuing religious understandings handed down from previous generations. Some important exceptions to this characteristic exist, particularly among those conservatives who rely on personal religious experience as the prime medium of revelation, a concept that opens the way for religious novelty, as in the Second Awakening. Even in these cases, however, once the truth has been revealed through religious experience, it tends to take on a traditional importance that must be maintained by succeeding generations of believers. Religious conservatism believes it is important to be orthodox, to hold on to "the faith once delivered."

5. *Dogmatic*—that is, committed to certain indisputable beliefs. It is not for men to argue, question, or modify these truths, because they have been supernaturally revealed; rather, human responsibility is to accept and live by them. Obviously all who disagree with these teachings are heretical and in error, because God himself has stamped his approval on them. Religious doctrines must be adhered to faithfully and without compromise.

By contrast, *liberals* can be described by some of these terms:

1. *Anthropocentric*—that is, centered on humanity. Liberal theology generally begins with people and their world, placing a higher value than does most conservative thought on human ability and goodness. Liberalism tends to be inherently optimistic about human capabilities.

2. *Naturalistic*—that is, putting its primary emphasis on the observable world around us, concerned with the "here and now" more than with the hereafter. Liberals are generally more occupied with immediate, present problems than with the future spiritual destiny of mankind.

3. *Rationalistic*—that is, understanding truth to be the product of human rational capacity. Instead of relying on the type of revelation that most conservatives accept, the liberal believes truth is best discovered or "revealed" through the use of human logic and "moral feeling." The liberal rejects the idea of a totally authoritative book or organization.

4. *Revisionist*—that is, accepting the necessity for consistent change and updating of religious teachings. Because people must rely upon their reason and practical experience in order to learn spiritual truths, religious doctrines must be constantly changed as more and more is

learned. Liberals are less impressed than conservatives with the sacredness of tradition. They are reluctant to claim infallibility or finality for any doctrine.

5. *Pragmatic*—that is, impressed with the practical consequences of religious belief. The liberal is interested in whether religion "works," whether it solves human problems and meets human needs and aspirations.

If we look at particular thinkers or religious groups, we will often find them difficult to classify. Each incorporates a mixture of tendencies and characteristics, and whether we call the individual or group "liberal" or "conservative" depends on the quality of the mixture. The classification may also depend partly on one's own theological stance, for we usually see ourselves at the dividing point, calling all those to the right of us "conservatives" and all those to our left "liberals." A small minority of American religious believers can be accurately placed at either end of the liberal-conservative spectrum, but most fall in between those extremes. Nevertheless, the tension caused by differences of viewpoint has been a part of American religious history from the beginning, and it has affected all sectors of religion—Protestant, Catholic, and Jewish. We shall look briefly at developments in all these areas.

Early American Protestantism

Until at least 1840 the American religious situation was overwhelmingly Protestant in character. Although small groups of Jews and Catholics lived in this country prior to that date, their influence was overshadowed by the vast numerical superiority of the Protestants. Within early Protestantism three main kinds of churches can be distinguished, all basically conservative: those of the right (taking *right* as a symbol of the aristocratic, established, "churchly" traditions); those of the left, who opposed the established churches and were strongly individualistic in their religious emphasis; and a large majority group that saw itself as the "middle way." Among those who can be classified as right-wing were the Anglicans—later to become the Protestant Episcopal Church—the Lutherans, and the Reformed Churches of the continental Calvinistic tradition. For these groups Christianity involved an elaborate creedal theology and liturgy. In addition, they tended to support close ties between church and state.

The left-wing groups included the Baptists, the Quakers, and a number of sectarian groups of German origin, such as the Mennonites, the Moravians, and the Schwenkfelders. Stressing the centrality of individual religious experience, they saw the church primarily as a "gathered community," made up only of those who voluntarily chose to be identified with it. Rejecting any ties between church and state, they played down creedal theology and formal liturgies or worship, emphasizing instead the personal freedom of each believer to act according to the leadership of his own conscience. Despite these distinctions, however, their basic theology was in most ways as conservative as, or even more conservative than, that of the right.

The middle way was primarily represented in early America by the Puritans, or Congregationalists, and a closely related group with their roots in Scotland, the Presbyterians. For a considerable time the Congregationalists were the largest and most influential of all American denominations. The middle way combined elements of both the right and the left. Like the churches of the left, they stressed a regenerate, or "saved" membership. At the same time, however, they accepted many views and practices of the right, including the baptism of infants and a close tie between the government and an established church. Once again, in spite of significant differences from the two other groups, the basic Puritan theological position was strongly conservative.

Congregationalism's middle-ground position and the tension involved in maintaining it was a contributing cause to the rise of the first important American liberal movements. Puritanism historically affirmed that genuine religious faith involved both rational and emotional elements. As the original colonists moved off the scene, however, their fervor was replaced by a more conventional religious commitment—one that relied strongly on mere assent to orthodox beliefs and the reasonable character of the Christian faith. Winthrop Hudson has observed, "At best the successors of the Puritans tended to appeal to the head without captivating the heart; at worst they promoted a spirit of rationalism (an attempt to validate the Christian faith by human reason) that frequently ended in indifference."[12]

The Great Awakening, America's first widespread revival phenomenon, constituted a reaction against this loss of fervor and feeling in religion. The revival put great emphasis on the emotional aspects of religious commitment, an emphasis that rapidly affected the majority of Christians of virtually all denominations. As we saw earlier, strong pockets of resistance to the revivals developed. Attacks such as Charles Chauncy's sermon "Enthusiasm Described and Cautioned Against," delivered in the First Church, Boston, in 1743, became more and more frequent. Congregationalism split into the "Old Lights," under the leadership of Chauncy, and the "New Lights," who supported and participated in the revivals. In similar fashion the Presbyterians were divided into the "Old Side" and the "New Side." The Old Light Congregationalists included about a third of the ministers in New England, and it was from this group that Unitarianism was eventually to emerge, as the rational basis for religion was stressed more and more strongly. Prior to the development of the Unitarians, however, another liberal movement, deism, had its effect.

---

[12] Winthrop S. Hudson, *Religion in America*, rev. ed. (New York: Scribner, 1973), p. 60.

Deism represented an elitist development, exercising an influence out of all proportion to its size. It counted among its number many of the leaders of the American Revolution and the founders of the American Republic, with Thomas Jefferson and Benjamin Franklin as prominent examples. The aim of deism was to reduce religious faith to its essentials— that is, to doctrines that the deists felt could be accepted and understood by any rational man. Its creed consisted of the belief that God exists, that he is to be worshipped, that the true worship of God consists of the practice of virtue, that people should repent of their wrongdoing, and that there are future rewards and penalties for all. The deists did not see any necessity for these truths to have been revealed supernaturally in the Bible or through a church; all were clear and logical. This "natural religion" eliminated the miraculous elements in Christianity, contending that a rational God had established a world that operated according to reasonable "laws of nature." Just as human reason was in the process of discovering the secrets of the physical universe, so it could also uncover the secrets of the spiritual universe. The deist faith was consistent with the principles of the Enlightenment, that period of rapid intellectual and scientific advance that dominated the eighteenth century in Europe.

So long as deism remained the province of a limited number of intellectual and social aristocrats, it aroused little reaction from conservatives. In fact, most early deists opposed attempts to disseminate their views on any widespread basis, because they felt that only the intellectually qualified could understand religion rationally. Thus the "superstitions" of traditional Christianity actually had a beneficial effect on the masses of people, providing them with something they could believe and helping to make them more moral. But during and immediately after the American Revolution, more aggressive men of deist persuasion began to arouse concern and opposition. The success of the French Revolution, with its flamboyant hostility to traditional religion, inspired Americans like Thomas Paine (1737–1809), Ethan Allen (1738–1789), and Elihu Palmer (1764–1806) to launch wholesale attacks on revealed religion. Deism became a more popular movement, deist societies were formed on several college campuses, and pamphlets attacking the churches as enemies of progress were widely distributed. For a time conservatives saw deism as a genuine threat. But the excesses of the French Revolution, generally viewed by most Americans as shocking and depraved, along with the lack of any real popular appeal in deist thought, soon combined to eliminate deism as a major force. By the end of the first decade of the nineteenth century it had faded from the scene.

More enduring evidences of the liberal facet in American religion were Unitarianism and Universalism, both having their roots in adverse reactions to the enthusiasm of the Great Awakening, as well as to such orthodox Calvinist doctrines as the teaching of eternal punishment for lost sinners. A steady trend away from conservative theology's insistence upon the sovereignty of God and human helplessness developed among the Old Light Congregationalists. Increasing emphasis was given to mankind and its potential, especially the power of reason.[13] Seemingly irreconcilable differences in the ranks of congregationalism became apparent when Henry Ware (1764–1845), a man known for his liberal doctrines, was elected to the Hollis Professorship of Divinity at Harvard, the most important New England position in theological education. Ware's election was in part responsible for the organization of a rival and more conservative theological school, Andover Seminary, 1808.

During the next twenty years the doctrinal split became an organizational division. In 1825 the American Unitarian Association was formed by one hundred and twenty-five churches, most of which had previously been Congregational.[14] More than one hundred of these churches were in Massachusetts, mostly located in Boston or the vicinity.

The outstanding leader of early Unitarianism was William Ellery Channing (1780–1842), who delivered a classic exposition of the group's doctrines in a sermon preached in Baltimore in 1819 entitled "Unitarian Christianity." Though Channing insisted that the basis of his faith was still the Bible, as the Word of God, he went on to declare that the Scriptures were written by men for men. Their meaning, therefore, should be sought in the same way in which one seeks for meaning in any other book, that is, through the use of reason. Although he did not deny that Jesus was the Savior of men, he refused to accept the orthodox doctrine that Jesus was God. He stressed the oneness or unity of God, rejecting the idea of the Trinity (the belief that God is in three persons—the Father, the Son, and the Holy Spirit). Jesus is the savior in that he is the model for all men. Channing asserted that all men have the capacity to be like Jesus, if they will but respond to his example and leadership. This optimistic view of human nature differed drastically from the traditional Puritan conception of human sinfulness, depravity, and helplessness apart from God's grace.

Document 32 _Liberalism_ _____

From "Unitarian Christianity" by William Ellery Channing

There are two natural divisions under which my thoughts will be arranged. I shall endeavor to unfold, lst, The principle which we adopt in interpreting the

SOURCE: William Ellery Channing, "Unitarian Christianity" (Baltimore, 1819).

[13] A reliable source for this development is Conrad Wright, *The Beginnings of Unitarianism in America* (Boston: Beacon Press, 1955).

[14] A notable exception was King's Chapel in Boston, the former church of the royal governor. This Anglican church had become Unitarian in sentiment under the leadership of James Freeman (1759–1835), who had become the Reader of the church in 1782.

Jesus as an example only Not the things he said

Scriptures, And 2dly, Some of the doctrines, which the Scriptures, so interpreted, seem to us clearly to express.

I. We regard the Scriptures as the records of God's successive revelations to mankind, and particularly of the last and most perfect revelation of his will by Jesus Christ. Whatever doctrines seem to us to be clearly taught in the Scriptures, we receive without reserve or exception. We do not, however, attach equal importance to all the books in this collection. Our religion, we believe, lies chiefly in the New Testament. The dispensation of Moses, compared with that of Jesus, we consider as adapted to the childhood of the human race, a preparation for a nobler system, and chiefly useful now as serving to confirm and illustrate the Christian Scriptures. Jesus Christ is the only master of Christians, and whatever he taught, either during his personal ministry, or by his inspired Apostles, we regard as of divine authority, and profess to make the rule of our lives.

This authority, which we give to the Scriptures, is a reason, we conceive, for studying them with peculiar care, and for inquiring anxiously into the principles of interpretation, by which their true meaning may be ascertained. The principles adopted by the class of Christians in whose name I speak, need to be explained, because they are often misunderstood. We are particularly accused of making an unwarrantable use of reason in the interpretation of Scripture. We are said to exalt reason above revelation, to prefer our own wisdom to God's. Loose and undefined charges of this kind are circulating so freely, that we think it due to ourselves, and to the cause of truth, to express our views with some particularity.

Our leading principle in interpreting Scripture is this, that the Bible is a book written for men, in the language of men, and that its meaning is to be sought in the same manner as that of other books. We believe that God, when he speaks to the human race, conforms, if we may so say, to the established rules of speaking and writing. How else would the Scriptures avail us more, than if communicated in an unknown tongue?

. . . Say what we may, God has given us a rational nature, and will call us to account for it. We may let it sleep, but we do so at our peril. Revelation is addressed to us as rational beings. We may wish, in our sloth, that God has given us a system, demanding no labor of comparing, limiting, and inferring. But such a system would be at variance with the whole character of our present existence; and it is part of wisdom to take revelation as it is given to us, and to interpret it by the help of the faculties, which it everywhere supposes, and on which it is founded.

II. Having thus stated the principle according to which we interpret Scripture, I now proceed to the second great head of this discourse, which is, to state some of the views which we derive from that sacred book, particularly those which distinguish us from other Christians.

1. In the first place, we believe in the doctrine of God's UNITY, or that there is one God, and one only. To this truth we give infinite importance, and we feel ourselves bound to take heed, lest any man spoil us of it by vain philosophy. The proposition, that there is one God, seems to us exceedingly plain. We understand by it, that there is one being, one mind, one person, one intelligent agent, and one only, to whom underived and infinite perfection and dominion belong. . . .

We object to the doctrine of the Trinity, that, whilst acknowledging in words, it subverts in effect, the unity of God. According to this doctrine, there are three infinite and equal persons, possessing supreme divinity, called the Father, Son, and Holy Ghost. Each of these persons, as described by theologians, has his own particular consciousness, will, and perceptions. They love each other, converse with each other, and delight in each other's society. They perform different parts in man's redemption, each having his appropriate office, and neither doing the work of the other. The Son is mediator and not the Father. The Father sends the Son, and is not himself sent; nor is he conscious, like the Son, of taking flesh. Here, then, we have three intelligent agents, possessed of different consciousnesses, different wills, and different perceptions, performing different acts, and sustaining different relations; and if these things do not imply and constitute three minds or beings, we are utterly at a loss to know how three minds or beings are to be formed. . . .When we attempt to conceive of three Gods, we can do nothing more than represent to ourselves three agents, distinguished from each other by similar marks and peculiarities to those which separate the persons of the Trinity; and when common Christians hear these persons spoken of as conversing with each other, loving each other, and performing different acts, how can they help regarding them as different beings, different minds?

We do, then, with all earnestness, though without reproaching our brethren, protest against the irrational and unscriptural doctrine of the Trinity. "To us," as to the Apostle and the primitive Christians, "there is one God, even the Father." With Jesus, we worship the Father, as the only living and true God. We are astonished, that any man can read the New Testament, and avoid the conviction, that the Father alone is God. We hear our Saviour continually appropriating this character to the Father. We find the Father continually distinguished from Jesus by this title. "God sent his Son." "God anointed Jesus." Now, how singular and inexplicable is this phraseology, which fills the New Testament, if this title belong equally to Jesus, and if a principal object of this book is to reveal him as God, as partaking equally with the Father in supreme divinity! We challenge our opponents to adduce one passage in the New Testament, where the word God means three persons, where it is not limited to one person, and where, unless turned from its usual sense by the connexion, it does not mean the Father. . . .

2. Having thus given our views of the unity of God, I proceed in the second place to observe, that we believe in the unity of Jesus Christ. We believe that Jesus is one mind, one soul, one being, as truly one as we are, and equally distinct from the one God. We complain of the doctrine of the Trinity, that, not satisfied with making God three beings, it makes Jesus Christ two beings, and this introduces infinite confusion into our conceptions of his character. This corruption of Christianity, alike repugnant to common sense and to the general strain of Scripture, is a remarkable proof of the power of a false philosophy in disfiguring the simple truth of Jesus.

According to this doctrine, Jesus Christ, instead of being one mind, one conscious intelligent principle, whom we can understand, consists of two souls, two minds; the one divine, the other human; the one weak, the other almighty; the one ignorant, the other omniscient. Now we maintain, that this is to make Christ two beings. To denominate him one person, one being, and yet to suppose him made up of two minds, infinitely different from each other, is to abuse and confound language, and to throw darkness over all our conceptions of intelligent natures. According to the common doctrine, each of these two minds in Christ has its own consciousness, its own will, its own perceptions. They have, in fact, no common properties. The divine mind feels none of the wants and sorrows of the human, and the human is infinitely removed from the perfection and happiness of the divine. Can you conceive of two beings in the universe more distinct? We have always thought that one person was constituted and distinguished by one consciousness. The doctrine, that one and the same person should have two consciousnesses, two wills, two souls, infinitely different from each other, this we think an enormous tax on human credulity.

We say, that if a doctrine, so strange, so difficult, so remote from all previous conceptions of men, be indeed a part and an essential part of revelation, it must be taught with great distinctness, and we ask our brethren to point to some plain, direct passage, where Christ is said to be composed of two minds infinitely different, yet constituting one person. We find none. . . .

3. Having thus given our belief on two great points, namely, that there is one God, and that Jesus Christ is a being distinct from, and inferior to, God, I now proceed to another point, on which we lay still greater stress. We believe in the *moral perfection of God*. We consider no part of theology so important as that which treats of God's moral character; and we value our views of Christianity chiefly as they assert his amiable and venerable attributes.

We conceive that Christians have generally leaned towards a very injurious view of the Supreme Being. They have too often felt, as if he were raised, by his greatness and sovereignty, above the principles of morality, above those eternal laws of equity and rectitude, to which all other beings are subjected. We believe, that in no being is the sense of right so strong, so omnipotent, as in God. We believe that his almighty power is entirely submitted to his perceptions of rectitudes; and this is the ground of our piety. It is not because he is our Creator merely, but because he created us for good and holy purposes; it is not because his will is irresistible, but because his will is the perfection of virtue, that we pay him allegiance. We cannot bow before a being, however great and powerful, who governs tyrannically. We respect nothing but excellence, whether on earth or in heaven. We venerate not the loftiness of God's throne, but the equity and goodness in which it is established. . . .

4. Having thus spoken of the unity of God; of the unity of Jesus, and his ininferiority to God; and of the perfections of the Divine character; I now proceed to give our views of the mediation of Christ, and of the purposes of his mission. With regard to the great object which Jesus came to accomplish, there seems to be no possibility of mistake. We believe, that he was sent by the Father to effect a moral, or spiritual deliverance of mankind; that is, to rescue men from sin and its consequences, and to bring them to a state of everlasting purity and happiness. We believe, too, that he accomplishes this sublime purpose by a variety of methods; by his instructions respecting God's unity, parental character, and moral government, which are admirably fitted to reclaim the world from idolatry and impiety, to the knowledge, love, and obedience of the Creator; by his promises of pardon to the penitent, and of divine assistance to those who labor for progress in moral excel-

lence; by the light which he has thrown on the path of duty; by his own spotless example, in which the loveliness and sublimity of virtue shine forth to warm and quicken, as well as guide us to perfection; by his threatenings against incorrigible guilt; by his glorious discoveries of immortality; by his sufferings and death; by that signal event, the resurrection, which powerfully bore witness to his divine mission, and brought down to men's senses a future life; by his continual intercession, which obtains for us spiritual aid and blessings; and by the power with which he is invested of raising the dead, judging the world, and conferring the everlasting rewards promised to the faithful.

. . . The idea, which is conveyed to common minds by the popular system, that Christ's death has an influence in making God placable, or merciful, in awakening his kindness towards men, we reject with strong disapprobation. We are happy to find, that this very dishonorable notion is disowned by intelligent Christians of that class from which we differ. We recollect, however, that, not long ago, it was common to hear of Christ, as having died to appease God's wrath, and to pay the debt of sinners to his inflexible justice; and we have a strong persuasion, that the language of popular religious books, and the common mode of stating the doctrine of Christ's mediation, still communicate very degrading views of God's character. They give to multitudes the impression, that the death of Jesus produces a change in the mind of God towards man, and that in this its efficacy chiefly consists. No error seems to us more pernicious. We can endure no shade over the pure goodness of God. We earnestly maintain, that Jesus, instead of calling forth, in any way or degree, the mercy of the Father, was sent by that mercy to be our Saviour; that he is nothing to the human race, but what he is by God's appointment; that he communicates nothing but what God empowers him to bestow; that our Father in heaven is originally, essentially, and eternally placable, and disposed to forgive; and that his unborrowed, underived, and unchangeable love is the only fountain of what flows to us through his Son. We conceive, that Jesus is dishonored, not glorified, by ascribing to him an influence, which clouds the splendor of Divine benevolence.

We farther agree in rejecting, as unscriptural and absurd, the explanation given by the popular system, of the manner in which Christ's death procures forgiveness for men. This system used to teach as its fundamental principle, that man, having sinned against an infinite Being, has contracted infinite guilt, and is consequently exposed to an infinite penalty. We believe, however, that this reasoning, if reasoning it may be called, which overlooks the obvious maxim, that the guilt of a being must be proportioned to his nature and powers, has fallen into disuse. Still the system teaches, that sin, of whatever degree, exposes to endless punishment, and that the whole human race, being infallibly involved by their nature in sin, owe this awful penalty to the justice of their Creator. It teaches, that this penalty cannot be remitted, in consistency with the honor of the divine law, unless a substitute be found to endure it or to suffer an equivalent. It also teaches, that, from the nature of the case, no substitute is adequate to this work, save the infinite God himself; and accordingly, God, in his second person, took on him human nature, that he might pay to his own justice the debt of punishment incurred by men, and might thus reconcile forgiveness with the claims and threatenings of his law. Such is the prevalent system. Now, to us, this doctrine seems to carry on its front strong marks of absurdity; and we maintain that Christianity ought not to be encumbered with it, unless it be laid down in the New Testament fully and expressly. We ask our adversaries, then, to point to some plain passages where it is taught. We ask for one text, in which we are told, that God took human nature that he might make an infinite satisfaction to his own injustice; for one text, which tells us, that human guilt requires an infinite substitute; that Christ's sufferings owe their efficacy to their being borne by an infinite being; or that his divine nature gives infinite value to the sufferings of the human. Not *one word* of this description can we find in the Scriptures; not a text, which even hints at these strange doctrines. They are altogether, we believe, the fictions of theologians. . . .

5. Having thus stated our views of the highest object of Christ's mission, that it is the recovery of men to virtue, or holiness, I shall now, in the last place, give our views of the nature of Christian virtue, or true holiness. We believe that all virtue has its foundation in the moral nature of man, that is, in conscience, or his sense of duty, and in the power of forming his temper and life according to conscience. We believe that these moral faculties are the grounds of responsibility, and the highest distinctions of human nature, and that no act is praiseworthy, any farther than it springs from their exertion. We believe, that no dispositions infused into us without our moral activity, are of the nature of virtue, and therefore, we reject the doctrine of irresistible divine influence on the human mind, moulding it into goodness, as marble is hewn into a statue. Such goodness, if this word may be used, would not be the object of moral approbation, any more than the instinctive affections of inferior animals, or the constitutional amiableness of human beings.

By these remarks, we do not mean to deny the importance of God's aid or Spirit; but by his Spirit, we mean a moral, illuminating, and persuasive influence, not physical, not compulsory, not involving a necessity of virtue. We object, strongly, to the idea of many Christians respecting man's impotence and God's irresistible agency on the heart, believing that they subvert our responsibility and the laws of our moral nature, that they make men machines, that they cast on God the blame of all evil deeds, that they discourage good minds, and inflate the fanatical with wild conceits of immediate and sensible inspiration.

I have thus given the distinguishing views of those Christians in whose names I have spoken. We have embraced this system, not hastily or lightly, but after much deliberation; and we hold it fast, not merely because we believe it to be true, but because we regard it as purifying truth, as a doctrine according to godliness, as able to "work mightily" and to "bring forth fruit" in them who believe. That we wish to spread it, we have no desire to conceal; but we think, that we wish its diffusion, because we regard it as more friendly to practical piety and pure morals than the opposite doctrines, because it gives clearer and nobler views of duty, and stronger motives to its performance, because it recommends religion at once to the understanding and the heart, because it asserts the lovely and venerable attributes of God, because it tends to restore the benevolent spirit of Jesus to his divided and afflicted church, and because it cuts off every hope of God's favor, except that which springs from practical conformity to the life and precepts of Christ. We see nothing in our views to give offence, save their purity, and it is their purity, which makes us seek and hope their extension through the world.

Somewhat parallel in doctrine to the Unitarians were the Universalists, who usually came from a lower social and economic class. Whereas most Unitarians were middle-or-upper-class urban New Englanders, Universalists came from the less affluent rural population. Under the leadership of Elhanan Winchester (1751–1797), a former Baptist minister, and Hosea Ballou (1771–1852), Universalism spread more rapidly than did Unitarianism, especially in rural and frontier areas. Originally, Universalism centered on a rejection of the conservative belief in Hell, affirming instead that all humanity would eventually be saved. This rejection of the doctrine of eternal punishment was shared with most Unitarians, although for somewhat different reasons.[15] As years went by, the Universalists became almost indistinguishable in belief from the Unitarians. Not until 1961, however, did the two groups finally unite into the Unitarian-Universalist Association.

Just as the Great Awakening produced liberal reactions, so also did the sweeping revivalism of the Second Awakening. As would be expected, the Unitarians and Universalists were unalterably opposed to the revivals, along with such traditionally staid groups as the Episcopalians and some Presbyterians. Thinkers such as Ralph Waldo Emerson and Theodore Parker (1810–1860) viewed the emotional excesses of revivalism with distaste, but they found even Unitarianism too rigid and lifeless. They and other like-minded thinkers developed the loose patterns of transcendentalism, discussed in the previous chapter. Perhaps even more influential in his opposition to the revivals was Congregational minister Horace Bushnell, whose work is discussed in the next section of this chapter.

The revivals not only spurred new directions in liberal thought but also divided the conservatives. Many conservative leaders were alarmed by what they felt was an overemphasis in the revivals upon human works to the neglect of God's sovereign grace. They felt that the revival leaders were manipulating people through the use of special techniques, such as Charles Finney's "new measures," instead of waiting on the work of the Holy Spirit. Other conservatives were upset by what appeared to them to be an increasing neglect of the traditional, historic church, its liturgy, and its sacraments.

One conservative reaction, both to revivalism and to the growing liberalism of the times, was the effort to draw up clear, specific confessions, or creeds, restating the orthodox position. Often these creeds were formulated as specific attempts to prevent conservative theological schools from being infiltrated and subverted by liberal faculty members, thus ensuring that young conservative ministers were firmly indoctrinated. As early as 1834, Hartford (Connecticut) Seminary was founded as a conservative counterforce to Yale, which old-line Congregationalists

---

[15] It has been said, for instance, that Universalists believed that God was too kind to send people to eternal damnation, whereas Unitarians believed that God was too rational to do so.

felt had surrendered to the Arminian (human-centered) tendencies of revivalism. All professors at Hartford were required to sign Articles of Agreement, restating the traditional Calvinist position.

Presbyterians were also beset by controversy and dissent. The bastion of old-time conservatism became Princeton Theological Seminary in New Jersey, where Charles Hodge (1797–1878) was appointed a professorship in 1822, and where he was to remain as the prime champion and spokesman of Presbyterian orthodoxy for fifty years. Hodge was a man of acute intellectual insight and great personal integrity, but a clue to his theological outlook was his boast that "a new idea never originated" at Princeton as long as he was there.

Other denominations had parallel problems. A group known as the Primitive Baptists defected from the larger Baptist group in the 1830s, protesting not only against Arminian revivalism but also against organized missionary endeavors.[16] In 1857 the Christian Reformed church was organized by old-line Calvinists who withdrew from the Dutch Reformed church. Conservative Lutheran groups of somewhat similar persuasion sprang up in various sections of the country, the most important of which was the Missouri Synod Lutherans, formed in 1847 and still today a large and influential conservative denomination.

A different kind of conservative reaction to the double threat of emotional revivalism and emerging liberalism was the "high church" movement, an emphasis upon the preservation in purity of the "true church," with its proper liturgy, sacraments, and ministry. This movement took different directions in different denominational groups, but all the participants shared a central concern for the corporate body of Christianity—the church—as the guardian of truth. John W. Nevin, a German Reformed theological professor at Mercersburg, Pennsylvania, and Episcopal Bishop John H. Hobart (1775–1830) were influential in their respective denominations, and a group of Baptists called Landmarkists argued that Baptists were heirs of an unbroken line of New Testament churches that had preserved the true faith and order of the Christian church from the days of Jesus to the present time.

Protestantism: Later Nineteenth and Twentieth Centuries

The second half of the nineteenth century saw the rise of a succession of new intellectual developments that decisively challenged orthodoxy, compelling the conservatives to rethink and restate their traditional doctrines. Charles Darwin's watershed volume *Origin of Species* appeared in 1859. Within a decade after the Civil War, most important

---

[16] Primitive Baptists argued that when God wished to save the elect among the heathen, he would do it in his own way, without human organizations. Primitive Baptists still exist as a small denomination today.

American scientists had been converted to the "new biology," with its theories of "natural selection" and the "survival of the fittest." Darwin's even more controversial volume *The Descent of Man* (1871), which specifically applied his theories to the origin of the human race, was seen by many conservatives as a frontal attack on the biblical version of the creation.

The religious problems precipitated by Darwin's work were not confined simply to the dispute over whether the story of Genesis should be interpreted literally; in fact, they extended into almost every intellectual area. By the end of the eighteenth century—in response to the challenges of deism, rationalism, Newtonian physics, and Enlightenment philosopy—Christian thinkers had developed a grand conception of the entire natural universe as an orderly, purposeful world that testified to the creative work of the rational mind of God. According to one popular analogy, the universe was a giant watch, ticking away, and its existence proved that somewhere there was a divine Watchmaker who put it together and made it work. But after Darwin, the picture of the natural world was drastically revised. The world was a tooth-and-nail battlefield, a war of all against all, with only the fittest surviving. The Darwinian world view was unacceptable to many Christians.

Evolutionary thinking permeated other intellectual areas as well as biology. Two Englishmen—Herbert Spencer, a philospher, and Thomas Henry Huxley, a biologist—along with two Americans—John Fiske (1842–1901), a historian, and Edward Livingstone Youmans, a journalist—did much to popularize the implications of "social Darwinism."[17] Not only had biological life evolved on the planet, they argued, but society itself and all its institutions, including organized religions, were the result of similar evolutionary processes. The new disciplines of psychology and sociology rapidly became important forces in academic life, and each field of study had crucial and, to many people, frightening implications for the understanding of religion. If humanity's religious experiences could be understood and, even more important, "explained" in purely psychological or sociological terms, what remained of any distinctively spiritual dimension in life? William James's *The Varieties of Religious Experience* (1902), an early classic in the psychology of religion, and William Graham Sumner's *Folkways* (1906), a seminal work in sociology, raised disturbing questions about any notion of absolute or transcendent religious truth.

Even the study of the Bible was not exempt from the inroads of the new intellectual climate. The techniques of "higher criticism," originating mainly in German universities, were applied to the Scriptures, so that the Bible was studied with the same attitude and the same objective scientific methods as those applied to any ancient document. What appeared to the critics to be errors and contradictions in the biblical

[17]See Richard Hofstadter, *Social Darwinism in American Thought* (New York: Braziller, 1959).

text were pointed out; questions of the dates and authorship of the various books of the Bible were raised. Time-honored beliefs, such as the conservative assumption that Moses had written the Pentateuch (the first books of the Old Testament), were denied. The critics concluded that the biblical documents were written by many different authors, edited, and re-edited across the centuries. Books like Isaiah were classified as having two or more authors whose works had been combined by yet another hand. From the perspective of the new sciences, the belief that the Bible enjoyed a unique status as a reliable, authoritative, divinely revealed source of truth was challenged by men like J. W. Draper in his *History of the Conflict Between Religion and Science* (1874) and, on a less scholarly level, by Robert G. Ingersoll (1833–1899), the agnostic son of a Congregational minister, who lectured across the country, questioning and ridiculing the beliefs of orthodox Christians.

These developments and others—such as the comparative study of the world's major religious traditions and the application of secular historical methods to the history of Israel, Jesus, and the Christian church —helped to create an atmosphere of intellectual ferment that put conservative religion on the defensive, encouraging the further spread of religious liberalism. Among Protestant Christians, three broad positions of response to the new intellectual climate emerged. First, some Christians tried to find an intermediate position, somewhere between the extremes of total acceptance or total rejection of the new sciences, hoping that the essentials of the Christian faith and science could be reconciled. A second group resisted the new developments strongly, insisting on the retention of the traditional orthodox doctrines in a virtually unchanged form and without compromise. Finally, and at a somewhat later date, some Christians, accepting wholeheartedly the discoveries and theories of science as well as the findings of the higher critics, sought to modify the faith drastically in order to make it conform to the new scientific world view. It is important to look at these three responses in some detail, for the problems with which they dealt remain a part of the contemporary religious pattern.

A MEDIATING RESPONSE

The first type of response to the new intellectual climate was a mediating one. Typical was the movement sometimes referred to as "evangelical liberalism" and sometimes as "Christocentric liberalism." Beginning with the work of Horace Bushnell (1802–1876), a Connecticut Congregationalist minister and one of the most original American theologians, the movment was an attempt to save the authority and credibility of the Christian faith without reliance on the Bible as an inerrant document whose every word is directly inspired by God.

While later exponents of this position were prepared to accept Darwinian evolution as "God's method of creation," Bushnell himself was more conservative in the area of the "new geology" and the Darwinian views. Interestingly, however, he applied many of the new scientific methods in his interpretation of religious experience and the meaning of the Scriptures. As a pastor-theologian in the early days of the controversies (most of his important works were written before the Civil War), he attempted to mediate between the mechanics of revivalism, on the one hand, and what he considered the errors of Unitarianism on the other. Still, his views influenced many of those who, at a later date, sought to reconcile the growing liberal-conservative rifts of the late nineteenth century. Men like Congregationalists Henry Ward Beecher (1813–1887), Theodore T. Munger (1830–1910), and Newman Smyth (1843–1925); Episcopalian Phillips Brooks (1835–1893); Baptist William Newton Clarke (1840–1912); and especially Washington Gladden (1836–1918), minister of the First Congregational Church of Columbus, Ohio, were deeply influenced by Bushnell. All of them grounded their faith in internal religious experience rather than on external dogmatic authority. They could accept with little difficulty the conclusions of the higher critics that the Bible was neither a geological record nor a textbook of doctrine but a story of religious experience, centering about the disclosure of Jesus Christ, who lived in perfect communion with God. In this way the Christocentric liberals were able to bridge the gap between what they believed to be the essential truths of religion and the claims of the new scientific method.

In his works, Bushnell sought to find a way of fitting the Christian message to the dominant intellectual and social presuppositions of his time. He was open to the increasing knowledge provided by scholars, repulsed by what he considered the excesses of revivalism, uncomfortable with such doctrinal bastions of orthodoxy as original sin,[18] and suspicious of the instantaneous conversion demanded by the traditionalists.

Bushnell developed a sophisticated analysis of language, which was the basis for his work.[19] In exploring the way in which linguistic structure emerges in human relations, Bushnell maintained that there are two dimensions to language: the literal dimension and the symbolic dimension. He further observed that the problem in so much theological discourse is that theologians accept words "not as signs or images, but as absolute measures and equivalents of truth." But, he said, the truths of religion are actually more akin to poetry than to other forms of language.

Bushnell was led to occupy a theological position between the right and the left, between the orthodox and the Unitarians. He was convinced that both groups have a naive faith in the power of theological language. The orthodox identify truth with their verbal theological statements. Unitarians are just as naive in their attack; that is, they take

18 The Calvinist teaching that all people are born into the world as sinners, inheriting the guilt of their forebears as a result of the sin of Adam.

19 Horace Bushnell, "Preliminary Dissertation on Language," *God in Christ* (New York: AMS Press, 1907), pp. 9–117.

orthodoxy too literally. Both parties fail to see that our thinking is no more precise than our language.

Bushnell had a strong belief in the contextual nature of reality. His understanding of human life was organic in scope. He rejected, for the most part, the traditional trust in a single, traumatic religious conversion, insisting that the Christian experience is a process of "becoming," of growing. Today, Bushnell is acknowledged to have been one of the most supple and subtle American theologians since Jonathan Edwards. In an extraordinary way, his theological thought anticipated many of the problems of contemporary theology.

Bushnell's most famous and influential work was *Christian Nurture,* published in 1847. In this volume he denied that children were lost in sin until regenerated by the Holy Spirit in a conversion experience, affirming that a person need never know a time when he was not a Christian. He placed strong reliance on the power of Christian education, an obvious reflection of the increasing intellectual demand for reliable knowledge as the ground of all belief, and his theories became the foundation of new approaches in the field of religious education.

Bushnell's work in the area of language anticipated what both later liberals and conservatives were to realize was the central issue between them: the authority of the Bible as the revealed Word of God. If the Scriptures were interpreted literally and with a conviction that there could be no error of any kind in them, hard-line conservatives could see no way to accept the findings of the new sciences. Men such as William Newton Clarke (1841–1912), a professor at Colgate Seminary (Baptist), felt that traditional views of the inspiration of the Bible should be rethought and reformulated. The following excerpts from an article by Clarke describe his own changes in this regard.

_____ *Document 33*

From *Sixty Years with the Bible: A Record of Experience* by William Newton Clarke

I looked upon the Bible as so inspired by God that its writers were not capable of error. I did not feel myself at liberty to dissent from its teachings, to doubt the accuracy of its statements, or to question the validity of its reasonings. This was not the result of a theory of the manner of inspiration: it was my working principle in use of the Bible, inherited from earlier times. Anywhere else, I should not have taken seriously the great age of the patriarchs; but since it was written in the Bible I thought that nothing but skepticism would doubt it. If I doubted that, I might doubt anything that was written there. So I believed that Methuselah lived his nine hundred and sixty-nine years. The hand of Paul, I saw, lay heavily upon the activi-

SOURCE: William Newton Clarke, *Sixty Years with the Bible: A Record of Experience* (New York, 1909), pp. 42–48, 102–108. Reprinted in *Religion in the American Experience,* Robert T. Handy (New York: Harper & Row, 1972), pp. 122–129.

ties of Christian women, but I distrusted the arguments by which some were endeavoring to lift it off—or rather, I distrusted the entire business of tampering with such matters. Paul was an inspired man, and his prohibitions were not to be set aside. As a witness to truth, Paul, or any other inspired writer, was the same as God. Hence the presumption was that his commands were universal and permanent in their scope, and to argue these prohibitions down to a local and temporary application in Corinth seemed to me to belittle the Bible and degrade it from its high estate. God's written requirements were presumably universal. And of this reasoning I do not think so badly, even now. If I still held the same premises, I am inclined to think that I should be compelled to hold the same conclusions.

As to the character of inspiration, however, I remember the rising of one rather startling question. No one heard it but myself, but I heard it and it went far into my mind. In the sixties the famous book called "Essays and Reviews, by Clergymen of the Church of England," created a stir that now seems incredible. At present it would seem gentle as a summer's breeze, but then it was a veritable storm-center in English theology. I did not read the book, but I picked it up one day in the library, and read the statement, in effect, that any theory of inspiration, or divine influence in writing, that can be true of the Bible must be true of all parts of the Bible: it must account for the qualities of Judges as well as of John, of Esther as well as of Isaiah, of the Song of Solomon as well as of the Epistle to the Romans, of the Apocalypse as well as of the Gospel of Luke. That startled me, and I laid down the book with the feeling that I had read enough for once. "Of course that is true," I said to myself, for there was nothing else to say. The statement proved itself. A good theory of inspiration must be good all round, fitting all the inspired writings. But before I had closed the book the conviction had flashed upon me that I knew no theory of inspiration that could stand this reasonable test. The theories that I had studied might account for some books, but were transparently impossible for others. They were framed to account for the highest quality of the Bible in its noblest parts, and assume that that high quality ran through the whole—which it does not. I felt pretty certain also that it would be impossible to construct a theory of inspiration that would meet this reasonable demand, if inspiration was to bear anything more than a very general and indefinite meaning. I was not able to imagine a divine influence in writing that would equally account for the composition of Galatians, Proverbs, Job, and the Gospels, to say nothing of other books. I went away from the library "under conviction" that these things were so. No immediate results followed upon this silent episode, but it had its lasting influence upon my life. Strong confidence in definite theories of inspiration was not to be expected of me after that.

Although I did not in my student days depart from my inherited manner of dealing with the Scriptures, I can now see plainly that suggestions of the historical method, unnamed and unrecognized, were creeping in. My studies in theology and history were preparing me for larger methods though I did not know it yet, and so was my work upon the Bible itself. Textual criticism is a revolutionary thing: I have often wondered that advocates of verbal inspiration were so tolerant of it. If we cannot be perfectly sure of the very words that first were written, we cannot claim that any text in our possession is verbally inspired; and as for the idea that there was a verbally inspired and faultless text whose faultlessness was lost as soon as it was copied, the wonder is that any one ever took it seriously at all. Exegesis is revolutionary, too, and quite incompatible with permanent confidence in verbal inspiration. The practice of tracing out each writer's thought, with earnest endeavor to do justice to all his peculiarities of every kind, is enough to bring other ideas of inspiration into view. . . .

During the seventies I was usually in attendance upon a weekly conference of ministers living in and about a city, at which all sorts of religious and theological topics were discussed. More than once in the decade the advent question was taken up, being a question that men were interested in discussing as they are not now, and on both sides of it I heard as able advocates as our denomination contained. The premillennial and postmillennial views of the advent were presented, elaborated, and defended, sometimes with conspicuous power. It was not in vain, though the results were not such as the disputants were seeking. In consequence of the discussion several things became clear to me, some at once and some on further reflection.

The first thing that I observed was that neither of the two theories could be better defended from the Bible than the other. Either could be defended perfectly well, by making proper selection of proof texts. The Bible contained the confident prediction of an early advent, and at the same time it contained an outlook upon the future that neither included an early advent nor had place for one. I observed that both doctrines were obtainable from the Bible, but was impressed by the fact that neither one was the doctrine of the Bible as a whole. In the sense of being found in the Scriptures, both were scriptural; but in the better sense of rightly representing the Scriptures, neither was scriptural. The contesting theories had been too successful in debate: each by its very success had destroyed not only the other but itself.

At first I did not see how much this meant, but gradually it came to me, and a very important change in my convictions was a necessary result. It was borne in upon me that the Bible contains material for two opposite and irreconcilable doctrines about the early return of Christ to this world. Both doctrines cannot be true: one of them at least must rest upon misjudgment. Since this is the fact, it certainly cannot be that I am required to believe all that the Bible says because the Bible says it. If either one of the theories is true, no matter which, I certainly am not bound by the testimony that the Bible bears in favor of the other. Whatever its nature may be, the book in which these facts are found cannot have been given me by God as a good that bears his own authority in support of all its statements. The book from which these two theories can be drawn is of necessity a different book from that. Thus the Bible itself, upon examination, shows me that it is not a book infallible throughout, in which error does not exist, and that I am not required to say that it is. This negative statement followed plainly from the discussion.

Of course the corresponding positive statement was just as evidently true. The discussion showed that upon one point at least the early Christians, including apostles and writers of the New Testament, were mistaken—not only could be mistaken, but were. They believed that their Lord was soon to return to this world in visible glory. He did not so return: hence they cherished an expectation that was wrong.

This I was required to affirm on the authority of facts, even though the disappointed expectations stand recorded on the pages of the Bible. I was required to affirm it in fact; on the authority of the Bible itself. Of this I could have no doubt. It is true that I heard some of the best men I knew laboring hard to show that the expectation did not exist, but their labor was in vain. I saw that it did exist, and that it proved to be a false expectation. Arguments to the contrary were quibbles, well-meant though they were. At present, of course, the intense vitality of the advent hope is one of the commonplaces of New Testament knowledge. No one who professes scholarship at all ever thinks of doubting it. At that time, however, understanding of the matter was less advanced, and it is less surprising than it would be now that the fact could be argued against. Nevertheless, upon me the truth was dawning: how could it fail to dawn? I perceived that writers in the Bible had recorded unquestioning expectation of the almost immediate occurrence of an event that has never occurred at all. Certainly they were in error on that point. Their inspiration, of whatever kind it was, was not a safeguard against this error, but allowed them, or rather perhaps impelled them, to work their mistaken view of the immediate future into our holy book.

From all this it followed that I was not obliged to agree with these writers in all that they had written, or to look upon them as infallible guides. It did not follow that therefore I ought to throw the Bible away, and I am thankful that that foolish suggestion so often supposed to attend upon such discoveries did not occur to me. But it did follow that I was not required to accept all statements in the Bible as true and all views that it contained as correct. Apparently I was a free reader, not a reader upon whom assent was obligatory. Apparently I might judge its statements in view of facts. And it was not some outside heretic or unbeliever that was persuading me to this conclusion: I was led to it by examination of the book itself. Its own contents bore witness to its errancy—to use a word with which I afterward became familiar. In coming to this judgment I was simply going whither the Bible led me. As I look back I wonder on what ground I ought to have proceeded if I was to judge otherwise. What would any friend advise? How, starting from the facts that I first encountered, should I have reached the conclusion that all statements in the Bible were binding upon me?

I have said that I moved slowly and unevenly in the change that I am now recording. I have dated this conviction against the inerrancy of the Bible here in the seventies, and here it belongs, for at this time it was planted in my mind and I began to be aware of its presence and its importance. But its growth was gradual, and its victory over my thinking was slow in coming—surer perhaps for being slow. Years passed before it came to its own. This is no wonder, in view of my early training. Nevertheless, when the new conception had made so valid an entrance it deserved well of the future, and was sure to do its work. . . .

A REASSERTION OF ORTHODOXY

The second type of response was that of the rigid conservatives, who insisted that the orthodox doctrines of the Christian faith must remain unchanged despite the assertions of the scientists and critics. Any modification of these doctrines was viewed as heresy, to be resisted at all costs. Unimpressed by the intellectual stature of their adversaries, the conservatives relied on an unquestioning faith. Charles Hodge, a leading defender of orthodoxy, said of his foes in 1857: "We can even afford to acknowledge our incompetence to meet them in argument, or to answer their objections; and yet our faith remains unshaken and rational."[20]

Like Clarke, operating from a more liberal perspective, the conservatives also saw the crucial question as that of Biblical authority. If the Bible contains errors, then it cannot, they argued, be an infallible guide to faith. And if the Bible is not dependable, then what solid basis is left for the Christian religion? Protestants had historically admitted no other authority but the Bible. If that foundation crumbled, the whole structure collapsed.

This position was cogently set out by Archibald Alexander Hodge (1823–1886), son of Charles Hodge (1797–1878), the distinguished Princeton theologian, and himself a noted Presbyterian thinker. The following statement describes a view of the Bible that is still held by many Americans.

Conservatism ————— *Document 34*

From "The Inspiration of the Bible" by Archibald Alexander Hodge

Necessary Presuppositions

1. *What are the necessary presuppositions, as to principles, and matters of fact, which must be admitted before the possibility of inspiration of any particular book can be affirmed?*

1st. The existence of a personal God, possessing the attributes of power, intelligence, and moral excellence in absolute perfection.

2d. That in his relation to the universe he is at once immanent and transcendant. Above all, and freely acting upon all from without. Within all, and acting through the whole and every part from within, in the exercise of all his perfections, and according to the laws and modes of action he has established for his creatures, sustaining and governing them, and all their actions.

3d. His moral government over mankind and other intelligent creatures, whereby he governs them by truth and motives addressed to their reason and will, rewards and punishes them according to their moral characters and actions, and benevolently educates them for their high destiny in his communion and service.

4th. The fact that mankind, instead of advancing along a line of natural development from a lower to a higher moral condition, have fallen from their original state and relation, and are now lost in a condition involving corruption and guilt, and incapable of recovery without supernatural intervention. *needed conversion*

SOURCE: Archibald Alexander Hodge, *Outlines of Theology* (Grand Rapids: Wm. B. Erdsman Publishing Company, 1928), pp. 65–69. Used by permission.

[20] See *Princeton Review*, Vol. 29 (1857), p. 662.

handwritten note top: truthfulness ↓

handwritten note lower left: thinking Gods thoughts after Him

5th. The historical integrity of the Christian Scriptures, their veracity as history, and the genuineness and authenticity of the several books.

6th. The truth of Christianity in the sense in which it is set forth in the sacred record.

All of these necessary presuppositions, the truth of which is involved in the doctrine that the Scriptures are inspired, fall under one of two classes—

1. Those which rest upon intuition and the moral and spiritual evidences of divine truth, such as the being and attributes of God, and his relations to world and to mankind, such as the testimony of conscience and the moral consciousness of men as sinners justly condemned, and impotent.
2. Those which rest upon matters of fact, depending upon historical and critical evidence as to the true origin and contents of the sacred books.

If any of these principles or facts are doubted, the evidence substantiating them should be sought in their appropriate sources, *e.g.,* the department of Apologetics—the Theistic argument and Natural Theology, the evidences of Christianity, the Historic Origin of the Scriptures, the Canon, and Criticism and Exegesis of the Sacred Text.

Statement of the Church Doctrine of Inspiration

2. *In what sense and to what extent has the Church universally held the Bible to be inspired?*

That the sacred writers were so influenced by the Holy Spirit that their writings are as a whole and in every part God's word to us—an authoritative revelation to us from God, indorsed by him, and sent to us as a rule of faith and practice, the original autographs of which are absolutely infallible when interpreted in the sense intended, and hence are clothed with absolute divine authority.

3. *What is meant by "plenary inspiration"?*

A divine influence full and sufficient to secure its end. The end in this case secured is the perfect infallibility of the Scriptures in every part, as a record of fact and doctrine both in thought and verbal expression. So that although they come to us through the instrumentality of the minds, hearts, imaginations, consciences, and wills of men, they are nevertheless in strictest sense the word of God.

4. *What is meant by the phrase "verbal inspiration," and how can it be proved that the words of the Bible were inspired?*

It is meant that the divine influence, of whatever kind it may have been, which accompanied the sacred writers in what they wrote, extends to their expression of their thoughts in language, as well as to the thoughts themselves. The effect being that in the original autograph copies the language expresses the thought God intended to convey with infallible accuracy, so that the words as well as the thoughts are God's revelation to us.

That this influence did extend to the words appears—1st, from the very design of inspiration, which is, not to secure the infallible correctness of the opinions of the inspired men themselves (Paul and Peter differed, Gal. ii. 11, and sometimes the prophet knew not what he wrote), but to secure an infallible record of the truth. But a record consists of language.

2d. Men think in words, and the more definitely they think the more are their thoughts immediately associated with an exactly appropriate verbal expression. Infallibility of thought can not be secured or preserved independently of an infallible verbal rendering.

5. By what means does the Church hold that God has effected the result above defined?

The Church doctrine recognizes the fact that every part of Scripture is at once a product of God's and of man's agency. The human writers have produced each his part in the free and natural exercise of his personal faculties under his historical conditions. God has also acted concurrently in and through them that the whole organism of Scripture and every part therefore is his word to us, infallibly true in the sense intended and absolutely authoritative.

God's agency includes the three following elements:

1st. His PROVIDENTIAL agency in producing the Scriptures. The whole course of redemption, of which revelation and inspiration are special functions, was a special providence directing the evolution of a specially providential history. Here the natural and the supernatural continually interpenetrate. But, as is of necessity the case, the natural was always the rule and the supernatural the exception; yet as little subject to accident, and as much the subject of rational design as the natural itself. Thus God providentially produced the very man for the precise occasion, with the faculties, qualities, education, and gracious experience needed for the production of the intended writing. Moses, David, Isaiah, Paul, or John, genius and character, nature and grace, peasant, philospher, or prince, the man, and with him each subtle personal accident, was providentially prepared at the proper moment as the necessary instrumental precondition of the work to be done.

2d. REVELATION of truth not otherwise attainable. Whenever the writer was not possessed, or could not naturally become possessed, of the knowledge God intended to communicate, it was supernaturally revealed to him by vision or language. This revelation was supernatural, objective to the recipient, and assured to him to be truth of divine origin by appropriate evidence. This direct revelation applies to a large element of the sacred Scriptures, such as prophecies of future events, the peculiar doctrines of Christianity, the promises and threatenings of God's word, etc., but it applies by no means to all the contents of Scripture.

3d. INSPIRATION. The writers were the subjects of a plenary divine influence, called inspiration, which acted upon and through their natural faculties in all they wrote, directing them in the choice of subject and the whole course of thought and verbal expression, so as while not interfering with the natural exercise of their faculties, they freely and spontaneously produced the very writing which God designed, and which thus possesses the attributes of infallibility and authority as above defined.

This inspiration differs, therefore, from revelation—1. In that it was a constant experience of the sacred writers in all they wrote, and affects the equal infallibility of all the elements of the writings they produced. While, as before said, revelation was supernaturally vouchsafed only when it was needed. 2. In that revelation communicated objectively to the mind of the writer truth otherwise unknown. While Inspiration was a divine influence flowing into the sacred writer subjectively, communicating nothing, but guiding their faculties in their natural exercise to the producing an infallible record of the matters of history, doctrine, prophecy, etc., which God designed to send through them to his Church.

It differs from spiritual illumination, in that spiritual illumination is an essential element in the sanctifying work of the Holy Spirit common to all Christians. It never leads to the knowledge of new truth, but only to the personal discernment of the spiritual beauty and power of truth already revealed in the Scriptures.

Inspiration is special influence of the Holy Spirit peculiar to the prophets and apostles, and attending them only in the exercise of their functions as accredited teachers. Most of them were the subjects both of inspiration and spiritual illumination. Some, as Balaam, being unregenerate were inspired, though destitute of spiritual illumination.

The Proof of the Church Doctrine of Inspiration

6. *From what sources of evidence is the question as to the nature and extent of the Inspiration of the Scriptures to be determined?*

1st. From the statements of the Scriptures themselves.
2d. From the phenomena of Scripture when critically examined.

The Statements of the Scriptures as to the Nature of Their Own Inspiration

7. *How can the propriety of proving the Inspiration of the Scriptures* from their own assertions be vindicated?

We do not reason in a circle when we rest the truth of the inspiration of the Scriptures on their own assertions. We come to this question already believing in their credibility as histories, and in that of their writers as witnesses of facts, and in the truth of Christianity and in the divinity of Christ. Whatever Christ affirms of the Old Testament, and whatever he promises to the Apostles, and whatever they assert as to the divine influence acting in and through themselves, or as to the infallibility and authority of their writings, must be true. Especially as all their claims were endorsed by God working with them by signs and wonders and gifts of the Holy Ghost. It is evident that if their claims to Inspiration and to the infallibility and authority of their writings are denied, they are consequently charged with fanatical presumption and gross misrepresentation, and the validity of their testimony on all points is denied. When plenary inspiration is denied all Christian faith is undermined.

8. *How may the Inspiration of the apostles be fairly inferred from the fact that they wrought miracles?*

A miracle is a divine sign ($\sigma\eta\mu\varepsilon\iota o\nu$) accrediting the person to whom the power is delegated as a divinely commissioned agent, Matt. xvi, 1, 4; Acts xiv. 3; Heb. ii. 4. This divine testimony not only encourages, but absolutely renders belief obligatory.

Where the sign is God commands us to believe. But he could not unconditionally command us to believe any other than unmixed truth infallibly conveyed.

As in the earlier days, conservatives in this period were greatly concerned about the orthodoxy of teachers in their theological seminaries. One result of this concern was a series of heresy trials, in which attempts were made to oust liberal professors. Most notable of the trials was that of Presbyterian Charles A. Briggs (1841–1913) of Union Theological Seminary in New York. In public addresses Briggs had vigorously condemned the doctrine of verbal inspiration (the belief that each word of the Bible is divinely inspired). As a consequence he was tried for heresy by the presbytery of New York, the governing body of the Presbyterians and became an Episcopalian. Another outcome of the trial was that Union Seminary eventually severed its connections with the Presbyterian church and became interdenominational. Today Union is still among the outstanding theological schools in the country and generally associated with the more liberal elements in American Christianity.

Among other notable heresy trials were those of Algernon S. Crapsey (1847–1927) in the Protestant Episcopal church and Henry Preserved Smith (1847–1929) in the Presbyterian church. In addition, a number of other teachers were forced to resign their positions in denominational theological schools because of their alleged liberal views. These included Alexander Winchell (1824–1891) at Vanderbilt, Crawford H. Toy (1836–1919) at Southern Baptist Theological Seminary in Louisville, Kentucky, and James Woodrow (1828–1907) at Columbia Theological Seminary in Decatur, Georgia.

A DEPENDENCE ON SCIENCE

Scientific modernism is typical of a third kind of response, one that accepted almost wholly and uncritically the new discoveries of science. Early representatives of this position, who must be classified as predecessors of the movement rather than full members of it, were enthusiastic in their agreement with scientific theories like evolution; however, they retained many conservative religious beliefs. For instance, John Fiske, the author of *Outline of Cosmic Philosophy* (1974), saw evolution as "God's way of doing things," and/even Henry Ward Beecher, whom we have already described as a mediator, classed himself as "a cordial Christian evolutionist." Later liberals, however, reacted more radically and completely against orthodoxy. Shailer Matthews of the University of Chicago, although an active Baptist, accepted as totally valid the methodologies of science, classifying himself unabashedly as a modernist. In the following excerpts from *The Faith of Modernism*, published in 1924, Matthews sets out a clear definition of the Modernist approach.

Document 35 _____

From *the Faith of Modernism* by Shailer Matthews

What then is Modernism? A heresy? An infidelity? A denial of truth? A new religion? So its ecclesiastical opponents have called it. But it is none of these. To describe it is like describing that science which has made our modern intellectual world so creative. It is not a denomination or a theology. *It is the use of the methods of modern science to find, state and use the permanent and central values of inherited orthodoxy in meeting the needs of a modern world.* The needs themselves point the way to formulas. Modernists endeavor to reach beliefs and their application in the same way that chemists or historians reach and apply their conclusions. They do not vote in conventions and do not enforce beliefs by discipline. Modernism has no Confession. Its theological affirmations are the formulations of results of investigation both of human needs and the Christian religion. The Dogmatist starts with doctrines, the Modernist with the religion that gave rise to doctrines. The Dogmatist relies on conformity through group authority; the Modernist upon inductive method and action in accord with group loyalty.

An examination of the Modernist movement will disclose distinct aspects of these characteristics.

1. The Modernist movement is a phase of the scientific struggle for freedom in thought and belief.

The dogmatic mind found its natural and most effective expression in the Roman Catholic Church and in the Protestantism of the sixteenth and seventeenth centuries. Because it developed under the influences of Roman law, its possessors were trained in the methods of the lawyer and the schoolman, and dominated by deductive logic. It regarded doctrine as of the nature of law and church-membership as an obedience to theological statutes passed by church authorities. Its range of interest in philosophy was practically limited to Aristotle, and its theological method was to organize texts of the Bible and bring about the adoption of the resulting formulas or dogmas as authoritative statements comparable with a legal code. Protestantism preserved most of these dogmas while setting up new authority for accepting them. It was not interested in the church as an historical movement, but in the literature of the first stages of that movement. It detached the Bible from history and declared it to be the sole and divinely given basis of revealed truth. Yet the Bible it accepted was determined by authority, and biblical truth was authoritatively said to be expressed in creeds and catechisms and Confessions adopted and enforced by authority. The dogmatic mind has always sought to express its beliefs sharply and clearly and with condemnatory clauses. Its century-long anathematizing of heretics shows that it is quite as truly interested in keeping nonconformists out of the church as in expressing truth held by the church. Naturally it has never been primarily interested in science, international peace, or social justice. It has often attacked scientists; it has never thought of abolishing war; and it has preferred charity and heaven to economic readjustment. One of its most bitter controversies has been over the relation of "works" to faith. . . .

SOURCE: From Shailer Matthews, *The Faith of Modernism* (New York: AMS Press, 1924), pp. 29–36. Reprinted by permission.

2. Modernists are Christians who accept every scientific theory as material for theological thinking. But the Modernist starts with the assumption that scientists know more about nature and man than did the theologians who drew up the Creeds and Confessions. He is open-minded in regard to scientific discovery. Believing that all facts, whether they be those of religious experience or those of the laboratory, can fit into the general scheme of things, he welcomes new facts as rapidly as they can be discovered.

When, therefore, he finds experts in all fields of scientific investigation accepting the general principle of evolution, he makes it a part of his intellectual apparatus. He does this not because he has a theology to be supported, but because he accepts modern science. He has no illusions as to the finality of this or that theory, which, like Darwinism, attempts, though imperfectly, to describe an evolutionary process, but he is convinced that scientists have discovered that there is continuity of development in the physical world, and that, therefore, such continuity must be recognized by religious thinkers. He is cautious about appropriating philosophies, but he is frankly and hopefully an evolutionist because of facts furnished by experts. . . .

3. Modernists are Christians who adopt the methods of historical and literary science in the study of the Bible and religion.

From some points of view, this, although not the most fundamental, is their most obvious characteristic. It was the critical study of the Scriptures with which the movement started in the Roman Catholic Church and it has laid the foundation for theological discussion in Protestantism. The Modernist is a critic and an historian before he is a theologian. His interest in method precedes his interest in results . . . in general the Modernist may be said to be first of all a Christian who implicitly trusts the historical method of an approach to Christian truth.

4. The Modernist Christian believes the Christian religion will help men meet social as well as individual needs.

Any acquaintance with social facts makes plain how responsive the individual is to social influences. Any intelligent religious program must take such facts into account. But programs differ. Some emphasize rescue and others emphasize salvation. The dogmatic mind has always preferred rescue. In practice it has varied from the asceticism of the monk to the rejection of social idealism. In theology it has limited salvation to elect individuals. On the other hand, students of society know that the relation of the individual to the social order involves him in responsibility for social actions as well as liability to social influences. Therefore, they undertake to transform social forces for the benefit of the individual. Such a policy is furthest possible from a belief that humanity needs only better physical conditions. It is a solemn affirmation that the Christian cannot hold himself guiltless if he permits the existence of economic, political and recreational evils, and that he will be the victim of such evils if he does not undertake to correct or destroy them. . . .

But when the Modernist speaks of saving society he does not believe that society will save itself. He believes that the constant need of God's gracious help is to be understood as clearly through the laws given him by the sociologist as by the psychologist. He, therefore, hopefully undertakes to apply the Golden Rule to group-action as truly as to individuals. He could carry Christian attitudes and convictions into our entire life. He urges the duty of sacrifice on the part of nations and of classes, whether they be employers or employees, as truly as on that of individuals. He is the savior of men in society.

This is one reason why the Modernist is an object of suspicion. The dogmatic mind is almost always to be found among social reactionaries. To no small degree Modernism in theology is opposed because Modernists urge reform in economic matters. In the struggle over economic privilege the Modernist is properly feared as one who takes Jesus seriously and believes implicitly that his Gospel applies to wages and war as truly as to oaths, charity and respectability.

5. The Modernist is a Christian who believes that the spiritual and moral needs of the world can be met because they are intellectually convinced that Christian attitudes and faiths are consistent with other realities.

In so far as by trustworthy methods he reaches intellectual conclusions not in accord with those reached by deduction or by major premises given by authority, the Modernist knows himself as emancipator. Christianity is under suspicion in so far as it refuses to submit any tenet to impartial scrutiny. Each intellectual epoch has made that scrutiny. Modernism as a scientific method is for today what scholasticism and legal methods were to the past. It is no more negative than is chemistry. If all its conclusions are not the same as those previously held, it is because some things are established beyond question and the perspective of the importance of beliefs has been determined. A scientific method cannot start with authority because it cannot assume conclusions at the beginning of its investigation. . . .

In brief, then, *the use of scientific, historical, social method in understanding and applying evangelical Christianity to the needs of living persons, is Modernism.* Its interests are not those of theological controversy or appeal to authority. They do not involve the rejection of the supernatural when rightly defined. Modernists believe that they can discover the ideals and directions needed for Christian living by the application of critical and historical methods to the study of the Bible; that they can discover by similar methods the permanent attitudes and convictions of Christians constituting a continuous and developing group; and that these permanent elements will help and inspire the intelligent and sympathetic organization of life under modern conditions. Modernists are thus evangelical Christians who use modern methods to meet modern needs. Confessionalism is the evangelicalism of the dogmatic mind. Modernism is the evangelicalism of the scientific mind.

The conflict between liberals and conservatives that raged in the nineteenth century erupted in its most virulent form in the Fundamentalist-Modernist struggle of the early twentieth century. As the Modernists steadily gained strength, particularly in the northern sections of the United States, conservatives were placed more and more on the defensive. In an attempt to consolidate their position, conservatives identified certain central doctrines of their faith as the essential or fundamental tests of orthodoxy. At the Niagara Bible Conference of 1895, for instance, a group of extreme conservatives listed five basic doctrines:

1. The inerrancy of scripture.
2. The virgin birth and divinity of Christ.

3. The belief that Christ took the place of sinners in his death on the cross, thus providing a "substitutionary atonement."[21]
4. The physical resurrection of Christ from the tomb.
5. The bodily return of Christ to the earth in his Second Coming.

Anyone who did not accept these five dogmas was marked as a heretic. Essentially the same five "fundamentals" were endorsed by the Presbyterian General Assembly of 1910 as well as by some other conservative groups, and they came to be popularly accepted as a summary of genuine conservative Christianity. Those who held vigorously to these doctrines came to be known as Fundamentalists.

Between 1909 and 1912 Reuben A. Torrey (1856–1928) and Amzi C. Dixon (1854–1925), both connected with the Moody Bible Institute in Chicago, a school founded by Dwight L. Moody and a stronghold of Fundamentalist belief, published ten small volumes called *The Fundamentals*, in which they endeavored to reduce traditional orthodoxy to its bare but necessary bones. Through the help of wealthy California businessmen, these volumes were distributed to millions of pastors and church members throughout the country, and they were influential in helping to shape a Fundamentalist bias among church members of most Protestant denominations.

Briefly interrupted by World War I, the doctrinal controversies within Protestantism flared up again at the close of the fighting. Billy Sunday hammered away from his platform against the twin enemies of religious liberalism and "godless socialism," virtually equating true Christianity with American patriotism and the free enterprise system. William Jennings Bryan, three times an unsuccessful Democratic candidate for the presidency, entered the struggle in 1920 as a spokesman for Fundamentalism. Almost every denomination in every section of the country became involved in the controversy in one way or another.

The liberals did not hesitate to strike back. A leading champion of the Modernist cause was Harry Emerson Fosdick (1878–1969), at that time pastor of the First Presbyterian Church of New York City. His famous sermon entitled "Shall the Fundamentalists Win?," preached in 1922, attracted wide attention and succeeded in thoroughly infuriating the Fundamentalists.

_____ *Document 36*

"Shall the Fundamentalists Win?" by Harry Emerson Fosdick

This morning we are to think of the Fundamentalist controversy which threatens to divide the American churches, as though already they were not sufficiently split

SOURCE: Harry Emerson Fosdick, "Shall the Fundamentalists Win?" *The Christian Work*, Vol. 102 (June 10, 1922), pp. 716–719, 722.

[21]This understanding of the work of Christ stresses a penal element, that is, Christ is believed to have taken upon himself punishment properly due humanity and thus has satisfied God's just demands.

and riven. A scene, suggestive for our thought, is depicted in the fifth chapter of the Book of Acts, where the Jewish leaders had before them Peter and other of the apostles because they had been preaching Jesus as the Messiah. Moreover, the Jewish leaders propose to slay them, when in opposition Gamaliel speaks: "Refrain from these men, and let them alone; for if this counsel or this work be of men, it will be overthrown; but if it is of God ye will not be able to overthrow them; lest haply ye be found even to be fighting against God." . . .

Already all of us must have heard about the people who call themselves the Fundamentalists. Their apparent intention is to drive out of the evangelical churches men and women of liberal opinions. I speak of them the more freely because there are no two denominations more affected by them than the Baptist and the Presbyterian. We should not identify the Fundamentalists with the conservatives. All Fundamentalists are conservatives, but not all conservatives are Fundamentalists. The best conservatives can often give lessons to the liberals in true liberality of spirit, but the Fundamentalist program is essentially illiberal and intolerant. The Fundamentalists see, and they see truly, that in this last generation there have been strange new movements in Christian thought. A great mass of new knowledge has come into man's possession: new knowledge about the physical universe, its origin, its forces, its laws; new knowledge about human history and in particular about the ways in which the ancient peoples used to think in matters of religion and the methods by which they phrased and explained their spiritual experiences; and new knowledge, also, about other religions and the strangely similar ways in which men's faiths and religious practices have developed everywhere. . . . The new knowledge and the old faith cannot be left antagonistic or even disparate, as though a man on Saturday could use one set of regulative ideas for his life and on Sunday could change gear to another altogether. We must be able to think our modern life clear through in Christian terms, and to do that we also must be able to think our Christian faith clear through in modern terms.

There is nothing new about the situation. It has happened again and again in history, as, for example, when the stationary earth suddenly began to move and the universe that had been centered in this planet was centered in the sun around which the planets whirled. Whenever such a situation has arisen, there has been only one way out: the new knowledge and the old faith had to be blended in a new combination. Now, the people in this generation who are trying to do this are the liberals, and the Fundamentalists are out on a campaign to shut against them the doors of the Christian fellowship. Shall they be allowed to succeed?

It is interesting to note where the Fundamentalists are driving in their stakes to mark out the deadline of doctrine around the Church, across which no one is to pass except on terms of agreement. They insist that we must all believe in the historicity of certain special miracles, pre-eminently the virgin birth of our Lord; that we must believe in a special theory of inspiration—that the original documents of the Scripture, which of course we no longer possess, were inerrantly dictated to men a good deal as a man might dictate to a stenographer; that we must believe in a special theory of the atonement—that the blood of our Lord, shed in a substitutionary death, placates an alienated Deity and makes possible welcome for the returning sinner; and that we must believe in the second coming of our Lord upon the clouds of heaven to set up a millennium here, as the only way in which God can bring history to a worthy denouement. Such are some of the stakes which are being driven to mark a deadline of doctrine around the Church.

If the man is a genuine liberal, his primary protest is not against holding these opinions, although he may well protest against their being considered the fundamentals of Christianity. . . . The question is, Has anybody a right to deny the Christian name to those who differ with him on such points and to shut against them the doors of the Christian fellowship? The Fundamentalists say that this must be done. In this country and on the foreign field they are trying to do it. They have actually endeavored to put on the statute books of a whole State binding laws against teaching modern biology. If they had their way, within the Church, they would set up in Protestantism a doctrinal tribunal more rigid than the Pope's. In such an hour, delicate and dangerous, when feelings are bound to run high, I plead this morning the cause of magnanimity and liberality and tolerance of spirit. I would, if I could reach their ears, say to the Fundamentalists about the liberals what Gamaliel said to the Jews, "Refrain from these men, and let them alone; for if this counsel or this work be of men, it will be overthrown; but if it is of God ye will not be able to overthrow them; lest haply ye be found even to be fighting against God."

That we may be entirely candid and concrete and may not lose ourselves in any fog of generalities, let us this morning take two or three of these Fundamentalist items and see with reference to them what the situation is in the Christian churches. . . .

We may well begin with the vexed and mooted question of the virgin birth of our Lord. I know people in the Christian churches, ministers, missionaries, laymen, devoted lovers of the Lord and servants of the Gospel, who, alike as they are in their personal devotion to the Master, hold quite different points of view about a matter like the virgin birth. Here, for example, is one point of view: that the virgin birth is to be accepted as historical fact; it actually happened; there was no other way for a personality like the Master to come into this world except by a special biological miracle. This is one point of view, and many are the gracious and beautiful souls who hold it. But, side by side with them in the evangelical churches is a group of equally loyal and reverent people who would say that the virgin birth is not to be accepted as an historic fact. . . . So far from thinking that they have given up anything vital in the New Testament's attitude toward Jesus, these Christians remember that the two men who contributed most to the Church's thought of the divine meaning of the Christ were Paul and John, who never even distantly allude to the virgin birth.

Consider another matter on which there is a sincere difference of opinion between evangelical Christians: the inspiration of the Bible. One point of view is that the original documents of the Scripture were inerrantly dictated by God to men. Whether we deal with the story of creation or the list of the dukes of Edom or the narratives of Solomon's reign or the Sermon on the Mount or the thirteenth chapter of the First Corinthians, they all came in the same way, and they all came as no other book ever came. They were inerrantly dictated; everything there—scientific opinions, medical theories, historical judgments, as well as spiritual insight—is infallible. That is one idea of the Bible's inspiration. But side by side with those who hold it, lovers of the Book as much as they, are multitudes of people who never think about the Bible so. Indeed, that static and mechanical theory of inspiration seems to them a positive peril to the spiritual life.

Consider another matter upon which there is a serious and sincere difference of opinion between evangelical Christians: the second coming of our Lord. The second coming was the early Christian phrasing of hope. No one in the ancient world had ever thought, as we do, of development, progress, gradual change, as God's way of working out His will in human life and institutions. They thought of human history as a series of ages succeeding one another with abrupt suddennesss. The Graeco-Roman world gave the names of metals to the ages—gold, silver, bronze, iron. The Hebrews had their ages, too—the original Paradise in which man began, the cursed world in which man now lives, the blessed Messianic Kindgom some day suddenly to appear on the clouds of heaven. It was the Hebrew way of expressing hope for the victory of God and righteousness. When the Christians came they took over that phrasing of expectancy and the New Testament is aglow with it. The preaching of the apostles thrills with the glad announcement, "Christ is coming!"

In the evangelical churches to-day there are differing views of this matter. One view is that Christ is literally coming, externally, on the clouds of heaven, to set up His Kingdom here. I never heard that teaching in my youth at all. It has always had a new resurrection when desperate circumstances came and man's only hope seemed to lie in divine intervention. It is not strange, then, that during these cha-otic, catastrophic years there has been a fresh rebirth of this old phrasing of expec-tancy. "Christ is coming!" seems to many Christians the central message of the Gos-pel. In the strength of it some of them are doing great service for the world. But, unhappily, many so overemphasize it that they outdo anything the ancient Hebrews or the ancient Christians ever did. They sit still and do nothing and expect the world to grow worse and worse until He comes.

Side by side with these to whom the second coming is a literal expectation, another group exists in the evangelical churches. They, too, say, "Christ is coming!" They say it with all their hearts; but they are not thinking of an external arrival on the clouds. They have assimilated as part of the divine revelation the exhilarating insight which these recent generations have given to us, that development is God's way of working out His will. . . . And these Christians, when they say that Christ is coming, mean that, slowly it may be, but surely, His will and principles will be worked out by God's grace in human life in institutions, until "He shall see of the travail of His soul and shall be satisfied."

These two groups exist in the Christian churches and the question raised by the Fundamentalists is, Shall one of them drive the other out? Will that get us anywhere?

The first element that is necessary is a spirit of tolerance and Christian liberty. When will the world learn that intolerance solves no problems? This is not a lesson which the Fundamentalists alone need to learn; the liberals also need to learn it. Speaking, as I do, from the viewpoint of liberal opinions, let me say that if some young, fresh mind here this morning is holding new ideas, has fought his way through, it may be by intellectual and spiritual struggle, to novel positions, and is tempted to be intolerant about old opinions, offensively to condescend to those who hold them and to be harsh in judgment on them, he may well remember that people who held those old opinions have given the world some of the noblest character and the most rememberable service that it ever has been blessed with, and that we of the younger generation will prove our case best, not by controversial intolerance, but by producing, with our new opinions, something of the depth and strength, nobility and beauty of character that in other times were associated with other thoughts. It was a wise liberal, the most adventurous man of his day—Paul the Apostle—who said, "Knowledge puffeth up, but love buildeth up."

Nevertheless, it is true that just now the Fundamentalists are giving us one of the worst exhibitions of bitter intolerance that the churches of this country have ever seen. As one watches them and listens to them he remembers the remark of General Armstrong of Hampton Institute, "Cantankerousness is worse than heterodoxy." There are many opinions in the field of modern controversy concerning which I am not sure whether they are right or wrong, but there is one thing I am sure of: courtesy and kindliness and tolerance and humility and fairness are right. Opinions may be mistaken; love never is. . . .

The second element which is needed, if we are to reach a happy solution of this problem, is a clear insight into the main issues of modern Christianity and a sense of penitent shame that the Christian Church should be quarreling over little matters when the world is dying of great needs. If, during the war, when the nations were wrestling upon the very brink of hell and at times all seemed lost, you chanced to hear two men in an altercation about some minor matter of sectarian denominationalism, could you restrain your indignation? You said, "What can you do with folks like this who, in the face of colossal issues, play with the tiddledywinks and peccadillos of religion?" So, now, when from the terrific questions of this generation one is called away by the noise of this Fundamentalist controversy, he thinks it almost unforgivable that men should tithe mint and anise and cummin, and quarrel over them, when the world is perishing for lack of the weightier matters of the law, justice, and mercy, and faith. . . .

The present world situation smells to heaven! And now, in the presence of colossal problems, which must be solved in Christ's name and for Christ's sake, the Fundamentalists propose to drive out from the Christian churches all the consecrated souls who do not agree with their theory of inspiration. What immeasurable folly!

Well, they are not going to do it; certainly not in this vicinity. I do not even know in this congregation whether anybody has been tempted to be a Fundamentalist. Never in this church have I caught one accent of intolerance. God keep us always so and ever increasing areas of the Christian fellowship; intellectually hospitable, open-minded, liberty-loving, fair, tolerant, not with the tolerance of indifference, as though we did not care about the faith, but because always our major emphasis is upon the weightier matters of the law.

The Fundamentalist-Modernist conflict reached its somewhat ludicrous climax at the famous Scopes trial in Dayton, Tennessee. The actual issue—whether a high school biology teacher had violated a Ten-

nessee law prohibiting the teaching of evolution in the public schools—
was virtually forgotten as the trial became a debate between William
Jennings Bryan, who served as a special prosecutor, and Clarence
Darrow, the famed criminal lawyer, who was also a bitter foe of
Fundamentalism.

It must not be assumed, however, that all or even most Protestants
were firmly located in either the Fundamentalist or Modernist camps.
The great majority attempted once more to find a middle way—a resting place between the two extremes. Theologians like Augustus H.
Strong (1836–1921) of Rochester Theological Seminary and John A.
Faulkner (1857–1931) of Drew Theological Seminary were concerned
to maintain the Bible as a normative standard of Christian faith, but
they were not interested in debating evolution, verbal inspiration, or
the details of the Second Coming. They believed that scientific methods
of studying the Scriptures were acceptable but that the most productive
results would come when these methods were used by people of deep
Christian faith. As Strong put it, the point was "not how man made the
Scripture for himself, but how God made the Scripture through the imperfect agency of man."[22] He and others argued that Christians could
study the Bible critically and honestly without abandoning it as the
authoritative basis of their beliefs.

Such moderate approaches were overshadowed in the public eye,
however, by the belligerence and intolerance of the extremists on both
sides. In reaction, middle-of-the-road conservatives were often pushed
into alliance with moderate liberals. Princeton Theological Seminary,
long a bastion of orthodoxy, was torn by dissension when one of its
professors, J. Gresham Machen (1881–1937), took the side of the Fundamentalists. Though he was an eloquent spokesman for his position,
Machen succeeded in alienating most of his conservative colleagues.
Finally there was a reorganization of Princeton, and Machen departed
to found Westminster Seminary in Philadelphia, along with the Orthodox Presbyterian church, both strongly Fundamentalist in orientation.
Among the Baptists the extremists also succeeded in creating division
and dissension. In 1932 Fundamentalist dissidents withdrew from the
American (Northern) Baptists to organize the General Association of
Regular Baptists; later another such group, the Conservative Baptist
Association, was formed. Other denominational groups were similarly
splintered, and a large number of small Fundamentalist organizations
came into being. The long-run results of the controversy were tragically
divisive and are still being felt.

Though the liberalism of the early twentieth century was able vigorously to combat the Fundamentalist attacks, it began to falter in the
1930s. The impact of the Great Depression, followed in 1941 by the
outbreak of World War II, played havoc with much of the idealistic

[22]See Augustus H. Strong, *Outlines of Systematic Theology* (Philadelphia: American Baptist
Publication Society, 1903), p. 62.

optimism of the earlier liberals about human nature. A chorus of voices began to announce the collapse of liberal theology,[23] especially those theologians somewhat indiscriminately linked together as "neo-ortho-dox": Karl Barth (1886–1968) and Emil Brunner (1889–1965) in Europe and Reinhold Niebuhr (1892–1970) and his brother H. Richard Niebuhr (1894–1962) in this country. Distrusting the liberal doctrine of evolutionary progress in human affairs, these thinkers reasserted the sovereignty of God, the centrality of biblical revelation, and the necessity for salvation by grace. They consciously harked back to the major themes of the Protestant Reformation for their theological sources, taking with great seriousness the sinful condition of humanity. Indeed, in perhaps his most important work, *Moral Man and Immoral Society* (1932), Reinhold Niebuhr emphasized in bold terms the manifold possibilities for evil inherent not only in individual man but even more so in social structures such as corporations, labor unions, and governments. At one and the same time he called Christians to a more radical political orientation aimed at drastically changing society and to a more conservative religious stance. From the standpoint of neo-orthodoxy, American liberalism, with its optimistic views of human and societal potential, was weighed and found wanting.

Neo-orthodoxy was profoundly influential in American theology, but its reception was mixed. The Niebuhr brothers and others of like mind did not call for any return to the literal acceptance of scripture or the time-honored dogmas as did the Fundamentalists. Sidney Ahlstrom has described the reactions to neo-orthodoxy in these words:

> Neo-orthodoxy was not greeted with joy in every quarter. To countless liberal preachers and theologians it seemed merely an erudite form of the very Fundamentalism that they had shaken off in the bolder days of their youth. To the more learned Fundamentalists, on the other hand, Karl Barth's theology (not to speak of American Neo-orthodoxy) was but a confusing form of modernism, especially dangerous because it had cut itself loose from religious experience, natural theology, philosophical rationalism, and a propositional view.[24]

Neo-orthodoxy was not the only response to traditional liberalism during the period immediately before and after World War II. Conservative thinkers such as Carl F. H. Henry (1912–   ), editor of *Christianity Today*, a fortnightly magazine that rapidly became the voice of "neo-evangelicalism," sought to restate the old orthodoxy in ways that would counter both liberalism and neo-orthodoxy. And, within the liberal camp itself, Paul Tillich (1881–1965), who left Germany in the

[23]See, e.g., John Bennett, "After Liberalism—What?" *The Christian Century* (November 8, 1933), pp. 1403–1406; and Walter Marshall Horton, *Realistic Theology* (New York: Harper & Row, 1934).

[24]By "propositional view" Ahlstrom is referring to the belief that religious truth has been revealed in clear-cut, literal statements or propositions in the Bible. See Sidney E. Ahlstrom, *A Religious History of the American People* (Garden City, N.Y.: Doubleday, 1975), Vol. 2, pp. 438–439.

early 1930s to do his most effective work in the United States, developed a complex theology based on the hotly debated movement of existentialism. In Europe, Rudolf Bultmann and Dietrich Bonhoeffer, who was executed in a Nazi prison camp in 1945, pursued a similar path. Drawing heavily upon the line of thought begun by the nineteenth-century Danish writer Søren Kierkegaard, these thinkers were preoccupied with the introspective human problems of guilt, alienation, and anxiety. Like the neo-orthodox theologians, they prescribed a return to the biblical message of justification by faith alone, but their understanding of that message was shaped by categories of internal human experience.

It was at this point that most of the neo-orthodox and Barthian thinkers demurred. They claimed that Tillich's method was basically flawed because he began his theology at approximately the same point the liberals did—by asking, "What is the question at the center of human existence to which God is the answer?" Tillich resisted the notion that he had sold out to liberalism, but it is clear that he could not be cast in the same general camp as his neo-orthodox critics. His position was, in a sense, one of mediation between liberalism and neo-orthodoxy. Nevertheless, his broad interests in art and culture enabled Tillich to speak to theological problems in a language that attracted intellectuals from many disciplines.

Although both neo-orthodoxy and existentialism had great influence in theological schools and among some members of the clergy, they never attained large popular followings in the churches and some of their lasting effects were swallowed up in the religious revival that came after World War II. The work of Billy Graham and others of his type represented a return to a modified Fundamentalism, though without the belligerence and virulence of the earlier version. Allegiance to the literal teachings of Scripture on the basis of its direct inspiration by God continues clearly to be a major ingredient in the religious commitment of large numbers of American Protestants.

The slackening of the postwar revival in the mid-1960s, together with considerable criticism of the nature of that revival, led to new developments in American religious thinking, some of which served to intensify the historical tension between liberals and conservatives. On the conservative side, a resurgence of interest in biblical studies and the excitement of the charismatic movement (see Chapter 4, pp. 218–222) injected considerable energy. Churches with a decided conservative theological bias continued to grow, despite the general overall decline in religious interest. A revealing study by Dean M. Kelley, published in 1972, concluded that "while most of the mainline Protestant denominations are trying to survive what they hope will be but a temporary adversity, other denominations are overflowing with vitality, such as the Southern Baptist Convention, the Assemblies of God, the Churches of God, the

Pentecostal and Holiness groups, the Evangelicals. . . ."[25] Kelley theorized that the liberal churches were too preoccupied with matters such as fellowship, entertainment, and social issues, thus competing in these areas with many secular organizations. He notes that conservative churches, by contrast, "offer an incentive (or commodity?) that is not as widely available—salvation—and offer it persistently."[26] Conservatives, of course, were quick to seize upon such data as renewed justification for their theological position.

On the liberal side, the existentialist insistence on interpreting religious belief and experience primarily in terms of human-centered categories produced eventually such radical movements as the "death of God" movement, which rejected traditional religious language as meaningless in terms of any transcendental or supernatural significance. Human experience, argued thinkers like William Hamilton and Thomas J. J. Altizer, demonstrated that if God ever lived, he is now dead, and "man come of age" (a phrase used by Dietrich Bonhoeffer) is on his own.[27] In the age of the mass media, such radical views received widespread attention, though the attention was not matched by depth of understanding. The most significant result of the movement, which proved to be something of a short-lived theological fad, was that "a massive credibility gap in matters of faith and religion opened up."[28]

Another important trend in liberal theology was an increasing criticism of the organized church, largely based on sociological approaches. Such studies as Peter Berger's *The Noise of Solemn Assemblies* (1961), Gibson Winter's *The Suburban Captivity of the Churches* (1961), and Martin Marty's *The Second Chance for American Protestants* (1963) described the churches as prisoners of the culture, stubbornly seeking to perpetuate structures and strategies no longer relevant to the modern world. To these critics, the traditional theology of the churches appeared meaningless and outmoded. It needed to be rethought and restated in a way that could blend faith and everyday life in a technological society.

In the late 1960s and throughout the 1970s, it became increasingly clear that there was a good deal of such rethinking occurring, sometimes with painful results. In the area of theological ethics, for example, the so-called new morality stirred widespread popular interest and bitter controversy, especially as it dealt with changing standards of sexual conduct. Almost every church group in America decided that the time had come to appoint study commissions to reexamine positions on sex-

---

[25] Dean M. Kelley, *Why Conservative Churches Are Growing* (New York: Harper & Row, 1972), p. 20.
[26] Ibid., p. 137.
[27] See Thomas J. J. Altizer and William Hamilton, *Radical Theology and the Death of God* (New York: Macmillan, 1966).
[28] Ahlstrom, op. cit., Vol. 2, p. 604.

ual ethics that had gone virtually unchallenged and unchanged for centuries. Conservatives branded the new morality a pseudonym for permissiveness and moral laxity, while more liberal church leaders felt a need for readjustment in religious attitudes.[29]

The argument over sexual morality, however, was only one part of a wider questioning of values and institutions long revered in American culture. Distrust and criticism of the institutional church was part of a broader distrust of and disillusionment with almost all established structures. The argument over sexual morality eventually involved many churches in controversy over issues such as those posed by "gay liberation"—questions about the spiritual standing and rights within the churches of homosexuals.

Most explosive of all issues, perhaps, were those raised by the women's liberation movement. Pressure was exerted within the various denominations for the ordination of women to the ministry, and feminist theologians entered their protests against what they perceived as the traditional male orientation of Christian theology.

Thus, American Protestantism in the 1970s, while experiencing some reaction within its ranks against the earlier activist involvement in civil rights and Vietnam war protests, continued to be faced with social and political problems. Indeed, an unexpected change of heart occurred among some conservatives. Historically, as we have seen, conservatives and liberals have in most cases assumed contrasting attitudes toward religious participation in the social and political process. Liberals have favored active intervention while conservatives have urged that "religion and politics don't mix." Many—perhaps most—contemporary conservatives continue to affirm this position, but in the last decade an increasingly vocal minority of evangelical Protestants has sought to develop an activist social policy alongside a conservative, Bible-centered theology. A vigorous statement from a proponent of this viewpoint is found in these excerpts from an article by William Pannell, a professor at Fuller Theological Seminary, one of the country's most influential "neo-evangelical" institutions.

Document 37

From "Evangelicals and the Social Crisis" by William Pannell

Some years ago Harry Golden spole of a phenomenon in the South which he claimed was unique in our country's history . . . the emergence of a different revolu-

SOURCE: "Evangelicals and the Social Crisis," by William Pannell, in *Seeds of the Kingdom*, Sojourners Magazine, 1029 Vermont Avenue, NW, Washington, D.C. 20005. Copyright: 1977, Peoples Christian Coalition.

[29] An influential presentation of the new morality was Joseph Fletcher's *Situation Ethics: The New Morality* (Philadephia: Westminster, 1966). See also Paul Lehmann, *Ethics in a Christian Context* (New York: Harper & Row, 1963).

tionary, the black man. Golden identified two weapons used by black men to force communication and recognition. "One is the writ, the brief, the court argument . . . the law, the oldest complex in our Anglo-Saxon civilization. The second weapon is even more remarkable. It is Christianity, the oldest complex in our Western civilization". . . .

This celebrated author, editor of the *Carolina Israelite*, . . . concluded: "If Christianity is saving the Negro, so is he saving Christianity." Interesting insight. And yet evangelicals were conspicuous by their absence in that struggle precisely because they did not perceive it as being evangelical . . . .

Why? In the first place, we seem to have an inadequate theology of sin. We have dwelled so long on the gross sins of individuals that we have very little understanding of the corporate nature of sin. We can only speak meaningfully of evangelical social concern if we understand the relationship between individual sin and its corporate consequences. Rosemary Reuther is helpful when she writes . . . :

. . . A prophetic sense of sin might indeed acknowledge that sin begins in the personal . . . but its expression is corporate, social, and even cosmic. Sin builds up a corporate structure of alienation and oppression which man, individually, cannot overcome. This corporate structure of sin distorts the character of man in community and in creation so fundamentally that it can be visualized as a false world.

Now we evangelicals know this. We teach this in the schools we sponsor. The people who write our journals know this. But this reality is treated as an abstraction. Sin is real, but slums are not; we have not shown the ethical and moral connection between sin and slums. Greed is real, but excessive profiteering in the name of free enterprise in not; lust is real, but we prefer to inveigh against the swivel-hipped secretary who ambles seductively down the office aisle rather than the callous manipulation of the Justice Department to re-elect a president.

We fail to acknowldege that as members of the community of fallen humanity, we are responsible for the misery of others; we have not only practiced sin, but have also rejoiced with others who did likewise. The fruit of that corporate sin now provides the economic base for our evangelical institutions.

Secondly, we have preached . . . a privatistic application of the Cross, which is inadequate. The Cross, in the minds of most American Christians, is either an historical artifact upon which Jesus died or else a bad case of lumbago. But in the experience of our Lord, it was "the judgment of this world" (John 12:31). We have called men to repent on issues that God is not the least bit concerned about. Rather, conversion requires a proclamation of the Cross that awakens the individual to his need for a radical change. The individual must be confronted by a demand that illumines not only his responsibility for his own sin, but also his culpability for the creation and perpetuation of society's corporate sins . . . .

Thirdly, we suffer from what Helmut Thielicke calls a "false conservatism"—an attitude which fails to perceive the political implications of the Church's prophetic and pastoral role in society. Says Thielicke . . . :

False conservatism expresses itself in the inclination to accept world conditions as they are. Under this pseudo-conservative banner, a corrupt social order, which

keeps part of humanity living at substandard economic levels while allowing
another class to exploit and profiteer, is regarded as a matter of divine providence—or visitation—calling for simple acceptance and submission. . . . If everything that takes place is regarded as God's doing, then it is obviously sanctioned
by what is assumed to be the will of God. Logically, then, it can never be opposed. Even though child labor, malnutrition, and the oppression and humiliation of millions cry out to heaven, they must simply be accepted.

It is a terrible judgment on Christianity and on false theology that the decisive
social movements of the last hundred years have not originated in any will on the
part of the Church to play the good Samaritan. The Church has not taken the
Lord's command to "love thy neighbor" as a concrete commission to change a
blatantly unjust social situation. . . . To be sure, Christians have helped the needy.
Think of the Church's many works of mercy and of the countless acts of private
charity. But these were bound to be regarded as alms, and hence as humiliating to
the recipients, a cover-up for an unjust situation, so long as the proletariat were
given the impression that the Church actually tolerated the unjust situation as a
whole—and did so in the name of that evil conservatism which even dared to claim
sanction for itself in the will of God. . . .

But what about the future? The question is not whether the evangelical has a
future. Given the self-perpetuating nature of institutions, it is probable that we shall
see most of our organizations prosper "till Jesus comes." Beyond that, the ball gets
cloudy. The question is rather: is there any future for evangelicals in social action?

There is, of course, without question now a mood among a new breed of evangelicals which can make significant breakthroughs. Some of this new leadership had
its sensitivities honed to razor edge in the '60s as part of the student protest movement. What many older evangelicals do not admit is that much of the current ag-
gravation about social concerns owes it life to these and other civil-rights movements. Now older, and recovering from the shock induced by the collapse of the
New Left, many of these people are also discovering in the New Testament a more
radical discipleship than their fathers knew. Some of these people have made their
way into evangelical seminaries and will be exerting significant leadership in the
near future. . . .

To complement this evangelical mood is a profoundly significant change of attitude in America, particularly in intellectual circles. Robert Heilbroner puts it like
this:

We are experiencing the onset of a new mood in the 70s. This new mood is conservative, although not in the usual sense in which the word is used in political
debate. I would describe it as the rediscovery of a perspecitve on human events
that highlights certain aspects of history, of "human nature ," . . . This new
mood dwells on the persistence of human folly in the face of heroic efforts to enlighten it with reason; on the perversity and cruelty that provide an insistent
basso ostinato to the melodies of progress; on the extraordinary ease with which
human sacrifice can be marshalled for war and the tremendous difficulties of
adducing it for the tasks of peace; . . .

Heilbroner calls this mood "radical conservatism" and cites as one of its key features its willingness to ask terrible questions "that go to the root of things."

Why does mankind refuse to make the changes, often within easy grasp, that might rid it of the oppression it has known from earliest times? Why do human beings display the laziness, the cowardice, the stupidity, inertia, or indifference that allows things to go on as they are?

These will be acknowledged by evangelicals as root questions, and if Heilbroner is correct, then it is possible to take advantage of this conservative frame of mind. The scriptures supply the answer to this moral and ethical dilemma of man. But the evangelical church will need to overcome serious deficiencies in order to seize the moment for God. . . .

What are the trends and factors that help to make contemporary American Protestant theology an area of continuing flux and liberal-conservative tension? The sociological analyses referred to earlier have helped us to understand how inextricably religion and culture are intertwined, mutually interacting in dialectical fashion. Sidney Ahlstrom has discerned three elements in the current religio-cultural patterns showing that a profound shift has occurred in "the presuppositional substructures of the American mind":

1. A growing commitment to a naturalism or "secularism" and corresponding doubts about the supernatural and the sacral.
2. A creeping (or galloping) awareness of vast contradictions in American life between profession and performance, the ideal and the actual.
3. Increasing doubt as to the capacity of present-day ecclesiastical, political, social, and educational institutions to rectify the country's deep-seated woes.[30]

These elements may be partial clues as to why American Protestantism in the 1980s appears to be in such widespread disarray. We live in an era of radical transition, and neither conservative nor liberal theology can escape modification and drastic reshaping.

Catholicism

By the nature of its organizational unity and hierarchical structure, Roman Catholicism historically has had less diversity within its ranks than has Protestantism. This is not to say, however, that Catholicism is

[30] Ahlstrom, op. cit., Vol. 2, p. 609.

monolithic, because as we shall see, tensions and controversies have existed within the Catholic Church almost from the beginning of its experience in America.

Catholicism became a major force in the United States in the years of massive immigration following the Civil War. True, Catholic ranks had earlier been swelled by the acquisition of the French settlements along the Mississippi River, and at least a million immigrants of Roman Catholic background had arrived in the United States between 1790 and 1850. But the real flood of Catholic immigration came later. By 1870 there were 4 million American Catholics; in 1880 6 million. By 1920 every sixth American and every third church member was a Catholic.[31]

The first major evidence of liberal-conservative tensions in American Catholicism came in connection with arguments over the place and the authority of laypeople in the church. American Catholics participated in the general emphasis upon individual rights and liberties that characterized the period immediately following the American revolution and the establishment of the Republic. In 1818 Archbishop Ambrose Marechal (1764–1828) of Baltimore explained the problem:

> The American people pursue with a most ardent love the civil liberties which they enjoy. For the principle of civil liberty is paramount with them, so that absolutely all the magistrates from the highest to the lowest are elected by popular vote. . . . Likewise all the Protestant sects . . . are governed by these same principles, and as a result they elect and dismiss their pastors at will. Catholics, in turn, living in their midst, are . . . exposed to the danger of admitting the same principles of ecclesiastical government.[32]

A sizable number of Catholic congregations asserted their rights to choose their own pastor, in disobedience to church rules and regulations. Not until the custody and ownership of all church property was transferred from the congregations to the Catholic bishops was the church able to assert its authority clearly.

A second problem for American Catholics arose in connection with arguments over the importance of "Americanizing" the church. Many conservative Catholics were suspicious of the "melting pot" influences of life in the United States, bringing together as it did people of many national backgrounds and diverse religious faiths. After the Civil War tension between German and Irish immigrant Catholics added fuel to the fire. It was the contention of many that the church in America should be organized along ethnic lines; that is, there should be a German diocese, an Italian diocese, an Irish diocese,[33] and so on. A leading spokesman for this view was Peter Paul Cahensley, who declared in a

---

[31] A concise and helpful account of the American Catholic experience is given in John Tracy Ellis, *American Catholicism* (Chicago: University of Chicago Press, 1956).

[32] John T. Ellis (ed.), *Documents of American Catholic History* (Milwaukee: Bruce Publishing Co., 1956), p. 219.

[33] The diocese is a geographic area over which a bishop rules.

petition to the Pope (1891) that in the United States the Catholic Church had lost 10 million souls through its failure to make provision for them in their own languages. This viewpoint incorporated the belief that the way to keep an immigrant a good Catholic was to keep him isolated insofar as possible from American life.

An opposite opinion quickly emerged. Father Isaac Hecker and the Paulist Fathers, an order of missionary priests that had been founded in 1859, urged that the way to win more converts and to strengthen the church was not to impede Americanization but to speed it. This position found strong support from leading members of the American Catholic hierarchy, notably James Cardinal Gibbons (1834-1921), Archbishop John Ireland (1838-1918), and Bishop John J. Keane (1839-1918). These three men represented a relatively liberal American Catholicism, and in time their view was to prevail. Gibbons's *The Faith of Our Father* (1876), widely read in the United States, has been called "one of the most successful Catholic apologetics ever written in English."[34] In it Gibbons emphasized the necessity of Americanizing the church, and his views were apparently supported by the papacy, for the Pope rejected the Cahensley petition.

Gibbons, Ireland, and Keane felt that there should be no conflict between Catholic beliefs and American ideals. They favored greater lay participation in the life of the church and encouraged cooperative Catholic relationships with other church bodies. In the sphere of education they preferred to work out an accommodation with the public schools, rather than following the policy of attempting to establish a complete system of Catholic parochial schools, parallel to the public system. But the liberals were vigorously opposed at every point, especially by the great mass of German Catholic immigrants and by conservative church leaders such as Archbishop Michael A. Corrigan (1839-1902) of New York and Bishop Bernard McQuaid (1823-1909) of Rochester. McQuaid called the public school system "a huge conspiracy against religion, individual liberty, and enterprise."[35] Eventually the conservatives were victorious, as papal intervention supported a complete system of parochial education. And Pope Leo XIII became increasingly conservative in the later years of his papacy, so that, in 1899, he issued a strong condemnation of liberal tendencies in a letter entitled *Testem Benevolentiae*, addressed to Cardinal Gibbons. After that communication, traditional conservatives were able to consolidate their control of the American church.

So complete was the conservative domination in the church during the first decades of the twentieth century that the stringent controversies over the nature of biblical authority, which helped to rip Protestantism asunder, hardly affected the American Catholic Church. Thus

---

[34] Hudson, op. cit., p. 252. See also Document 18, "The Church and the Republic," pp. 117-121.

[35] Ibid., p. 243.

few Catholic reactions were generated in the United States when Pope Leo XIII set forth a rigidly traditional view of biblical inspiration and denounced liberal theology. His successor, Pius X (1903–1914), issued in 1907 the now famous encyclical or teaching letter entitled *Pascendi Dominici Gregis*, in which he roundly condemned Modernism. He later summarized the official position in another decree, entitled *Lamentabili*. By adhering to a strong conservative position, he apparently thought he could save the church from the acrimony and division that had afflicted Protestantism. The following selected propositions are from *Lamentabili* —propositions the Pope found to be erroneous.

Document 38 _____

From "Errors of the Modernists Concerning the Church, Revelation, Christ, and the Sacraments" by Pope Pius X

11. Divine Inspiration does not extend to every part of Holy Scripture in a manner that safeguards all and each single part of the Bible from error.

16. The narratives in the Gospel of John are not truly historical but a mystical meditation on the Gospel; the speeches in the Gospel of John are theological meditations on the mystery of salvation, devoid of historical veracity.

19. Heterodox commentators more faithfully explain the sense of the Scriptures than do Catholic commentators.

20. Revelation is nothing else but the acquired consciousness of man's own relationship to God.

27. The divinity of Jesus Christ is not provable from the Gospels themselves but a deduction from the notion of a messiah and from the Christian conscience itself.

29. It is permissible to say that the historical Christ is inferior to the Christ of Faith.

35. Christ was not always conscious of his messianic dignity.

45. Not everything which St. Paul wrote about the institution of the Eucharist (cf. I Cor. 11:23–25) needs to be understood as historical fact.

56. The Roman Church, because of political conditions and not because of any divine commission, became the head of the other Churches.

58. Truth is no more immutable than man himself since, through man, with man, and in man, truth itself evolves.

60. Christian doctrine, in its beginnings, was Jewish, but later, through successive stages, it was Pauline, Johannine, then, Hellenistic, and finally universal.

64. The progress of human learning demands that the concepts of Christian doctrine about God, creation, revelation, the person of the Incarnate Word, and redemption, be completely rethought.

65. Modern Catholicism cannot be reconciled to true learning unless it transforms itself into a non-dogmatic Christianity, which is to say, a liberal and broad church Protestantism.

SOURCE: H. Denziger, C. Bannwart, Karl Rahner (eds.), "Lamentabili," *Enchiridion Symbolorum* (Rome, 1957), pp. 564–569.

Note: His Holiness approves and confirms this decree of the Most Eminent Cardinals, and orders that each and every of the above propositions be rejected and condemned.

The development of a significant liberal movement within American Catholicism was a long, slow process, but as World War I came and went, there were signs and stirrings. The National Catholic Welfare Conference was organized in 1919 as the first national Catholic agency for social reform. In 1924 Michael Williams (1877–1950), a Catholic layman, founded the magazine *Commonweal*, which rapidly became the leading voice of "liberal Catholicism," particularly in the area of social involvement. The Catholic Worker movement, founded by Dorothy Day (1899–1980), a former Socialist who had become a Catholic, was yet another evidence of more liberal social attitudes within the church.

Not until after World War II, however, did liberalism as a *theological* influence begin to have an impact on the American Catholic Church. In the 1950s and 1960s thinkers like John Courtney Murray (1904–1967) and Gustave Weigel (1906–1964) led the way in encouraging active Catholic involvement in the intellectual and theological ferment of the times. The openess of their stances was viewed with alarm by many Catholics, especially the faculty of theology at the Catholic University in Washington, D.C., which was a conservative citadel. Murray and Weigel rejected traditional views that democracy of the type practiced in the United States was less than satisfactory as a political system and argued that political democracy, including the separation of church and state, could be grounded on Catholic, and more important, Christian principles.[36] In the 1960s, largely as a result of the "fresh air" introduced into the church by Pope John XXIII (who had convened the second Vatican Council), the conservatives were pushed into a defensive position and the ranks of liberals swelled considerably.

The accession of John XXIII to the papacy in 1958 coincided with striking new appraisals of the theological state of American Catholicism from within its own ranks. Observers like former President John J. Cavanaugh of Notre Dame and Catholic historian Monsignor John Tracy Ellis pointed out how ill prepared Catholics were for the new developments of the twentieth century. Ellis observed that the so-called heroic age of the American church, when it was preoccupied with absorbing the flood of Catholic immigrants, was over, and he went on to say:

We stand on the threshold of another act in the ceaselessly unfolding drama of the Church's life in this land. . . . Today's world and today's America have a right to expect from the third most numerous body of Catholics in the universal

[36] See, e.g., John Courtney Murray, *We Hold These Truths* (New York: Doubleday, 1960).

Church . . . a positive contribution to a remedy for the ills that beset them in the atomic age.[37]

The General Council of the Roman Catholic Church (popularly known as Vatican II), convened by Pope John in 1962, was probably the most important event in the life of the church in the past four hundred years. Ahlstrom believes that, as a result of the Council, the church "was shaken by forces of change more powerful and fundamental than those which had been advanced by the Protestant Reformation."[38] Scarcely any part of the church's life and doctrine was left untouched. The style and language of worship was modified, the church's relationships to the world and to other religious groups were markedly transformed, church discipline was relaxed at many points, and a host of other changes were set in motion. Not only at the international and national levels but in almost every community in this country, new types of cooperation and dialogue among Catholics and Protestants suddenly became possible. Though some American Catholic prelates, notably Cardinal James McIntyre of Los Angeles, were slow in instituting the reforms called for by the Council, changes inevitably took place. In many cases, younger, liberal priests carried out even more radical changes than the Council itself had stipulated.

The predictable results were dissidence and unrest on both the Catholic right and left. Groups of conservative Catholics organized, for instance, to combat and protest the elimination of the Latin Mass. Among such groups was the Catholic Traditionalist movement, organized in 1965 by Father Gommar A. DePauw. On the other side, liberal priests and nuns openly questioned the authority of their bishops, calling for more changes such as the clerical right to marry. Issues such as birth control, increased lay participation in church affairs, and the rights of women[39] aroused strong feelings and created divisions. Many Catholics differed vehemently and publicly with some of the official policies of the church. It can be persuasively argued that journalist John O'Connor was not exaggerating in the title of his study published in 1969: *The People versus Rome: Radical Split in the American Church.*[40]

Today the Roman Catholic Church is experiencing, perhaps more than ever before, the kind of liberal-conservative tensions that have bedeviled Protestantism throughout its history. These tensions affect the church at every level. At the most profound level of theology, German Catholic scholar Hans Küng, who is widely read and respected in this country, has sought to demonstrate both historically and theologically

[37]John Tracy Ellis, "American Catholicism in 1960: An Historical Perspective," *American Benedictine Review*, Vol. 11 (March–June) 1960, pp. 1–20.
[38]Ahlstrom, op. cit., Vol. 2, pa. 525.
[39]Interestingly, many of the leading crusaders for women's liberation came from Catholic ranks, including Mary Daly, Rosemary Reuther, and Sally Cunneen, among others.
[40]New York, Random House, 1969.

that infallibility cannot be attached to papal teachings.[41] And in popular Catholic belief, a Gallup poll conducted for *Newsweek* magazine indicated that 78 per cent of those Catholics questioned believed that their children would still be saved if they left the church. Even more interestingly, when asked who or what they relied on when they became confused in their religious beliefs, almost as many answered that they relied on Billy Graham as on the teachings of the pope![42]

Sister Elaine M. Prevallet, a member of the Theology Department at Loretto Heights College in Denver, Colorado, cogently sums up some of her reactions as a faithful Roman Catholic in this hectic period.

—————————————————————————————— *Document 39*

From "The Experience of Being a Roman Catholic in a Time of Change" by Sister Elaine M. Prevallet

In this attempt to reflect upon "the experience of being a Roman Catholic in a time of change," I shall try to do two things: First, I shall try to stay in touch with my own experience; and, second, I shall try to relate broader theological issues to that experience. At the outset, I should probably say that my experience is not exactly typical—if indeed there be any such thing as typical. It is conditioned by my profession as a teacher of theology in a college which has very rapidly changed from a rather conservative Catholic college for women to an independent coed institution with a religiously heterogeneous student population . . . . My profession, in any case, demands that I stay in touch with students' questions and perceptions, and hence effectively ensures that my own thinking be consistently challenged and changing. Secondly, my experience is conditioned by the fact that I am a sister, and some groups of sisters have been among the most aggressive and progressive in making the changes we felt were necessary to bring our Christian dedication into the twentieth century. This has been especially challenging for me, because it necessitated a rather thorough rethinking of the tradition of spirituality in which I was reared, a consistent attempt to separate the peripheral and nonessential from the core of my commitment, the accidental trappings from the substance. What went on for me in that context is perhaps a miniature of what is and has been going on in the whole Church—an attempt to distinguish the essential from the peripheral. . . .

My position, then, is only more or less similar to that of other persons within the Roman Catholic community. But precisely here we can note a significant change in the picture—and in the experience—of Roman Catholicism: a shift from a very stable, well-ordered group who all knew and professed the same faith in the same words—the Catholic monolith—to groups of persons who have found or are finding

SOURCE: "The Experience of Being a Roman Catholic in a Time of Change," by Sister Elaine M. Prevallet, in *Religion American Style*, edited by Patrick H. McNamara (New York: Harper & Row, 1974), pp. 205–209.

[41] Hans Küng, *Infallibility? An Inquiry* (Garden City, N.Y.: Doubleday, 1971).
[42] *Newsweek*, October 4, 1971.

communities of support and coming to find their own faith and take their own stand. We have, all of us, I imagine, felt ourselves shaken, our security threatened, our faith called into question. As one might expect, there are different ways of reacting: Some will become impatient with the slowness of change, decide the Church is antiquated and hopeless, and drop out. Some will sever affiliation but for the opposite reason: The Church has changed so fast and so radically as to be unrecognizable as the Church one knew and loved, so radically changed that one feels no identification with it, is disillusioned and disappointed by it—and so drop out. It could, no doubt, be called an identity crisis: It is no longer so easy to know what it means to be a Roman Catholic, no longer easy to say what a Roman Catholic believes or holds on various issues. One is thrown much more upon one's own resources, and one is turned much more toward one's brother and sister in faith. From that standpoint, an identity crisis can be a valuable prelude to a new level of self-consciousness, commitment and community. . . .

Perhaps one can speak with some accuracy of a relativistic perspective as having had great impact upon Catholic consciousness. Contemporary historical consciousness is one factor in the kind of de-absolutizing we have undergone; the experience of plurality is another. Ecumenical awareness is surely part of this perspective: We have had, in the last decade, to admit that the Spirit of God is not bound by the structure of the Roman Catholic or even the Christian churches; we have had to admit that Protestants—and even Jews, Buddhists, and Moslems—may turn up in heaven and that not in spite of but because of their religious beliefs and practice. Experientially, this has meant a modification of many absolutist attitudes among Roman Catholics: from thinking we knew it all, no doubt with some arrogance, to greater humility before the truth; from believing that everyone had to believe it and say it our way to an attitude of openness to one's Christian or non-Christian neighbor as a possible source of insight into truth; . . .

Equally, in the area of morality, focused in the birth control controversy but helped along by changes such as that in the law of Friday abstinence and the possibility of fulfilling one's obligation by going to Mass on Saturday instead of Sunday, there is less trust of ecclesiastical laws as absolutes. It may sound preposterous to equate the issues of birth control or abortion with the issues of whether or not one eats meat on Friday and goes to church on Sunday, but in point of fact, deviations from the Church's stance on all those were taught to us as mortal sins, equally absolute in deserving damnation. It was, of course, a naive and unnuanced moral sensitivity; yet the change has spawned distrust and even cynicism: If a thing could be a mortal sin deserving of hell one day and nothing at all the next, simply by ecclesiastical fiat, then how trusting can we be of any ecclesiastical laws or moral pronouncements at all? And again, there are varieties of responses: those who learn to think through their moral positions and arrive at a more carefully nuanced and personally appropriated moral sense and those who retire into positions of negativism. Experientially, the former has meant bearing the responsibility for much more serious thought and information gathering, making many more decisions, and, of course, living with many more unanswered questions.

Another powerful influence within Roman Catholicism is the movement to find the meaning of the Church and the focus of the gospel in terms of social justice. Roman Catholicism has, even in this country, precedent in radicalism set by persons such as Dorothy Day who spans the last decades as witness to radical concern for the poor and the pacifist movement. The Berrigans can be said to stand in that same tradition. The movement toward a social-gospel interpretation of Christianity, the challenge to radicalism, is now a powerful force—from Vatican II and its document on the Church in the modern world down to the Harrisburg Seven. Many Catholics, of course, are not even conscious of the Berrigans; many regard them as mixed up, as priests gone astray, are embarrassed that they are Catholics, let alone priests. But for others, and among them a growing number of priests, they seem to have effected a kind of consciousness raising, a courageous and challenging summons to be "on the margin," to stand off from the status quo, to criticize one's involvement or implication in the structured evils in our society. I think I am not naive when I say that there is a growing social conscience in the Roman Catholic community which presents yet another challenge to established systems, habits, works, thought patterns. For those who hear the challenge, it often complicates their relationship to the Roman Catholic establishment.

And finally, the most evident, perhaps: the change in Roman Catholic attitudes toward authority. That is, of course, part of the larger picture of a changing world and society. It has been noted that in a stable society, a rigid hierarchical system is adequate, because its task is simply to provide instructions on how to behave in a framework in which the major outlines of conduct are already agreed upon by all. But in a society of rapid social change, it seems clear that a hierarchy will have to assume a different style and role. . . . Clearly, the style of leadership which has characterized the Roman Catholic Church seems out of joint in a society which is undergoing such rapid social changes as we are, and in which participation and intelligent assent must be the keynote of advance. Yet there is an obvious dilemma, for there are those in the Church who hope for an answer-giving kind of leader. These are disappointed, for if Rome or the bishops give some answers, they do not give nearly enough to allay these peoples' fears. For others, they give too many and in areas where their silence would be better appreciated. In short, they can't win. Perhaps it is enough to say here that people do not know what to believe about authority, whether or when to believe if authority does speak. . . .

The task—reform both of society and of the Church—seems so massive as to be paralyzing. And so, if one has to speak of the experience of being a Roman Catholic in a time of change, one necessarily speaks of confusion and uncertainty, unsettledness and doubt, disillusion and frustration. But one can also speak of personal conviction and commitment, challenge and inner growth, courage and hope. All of these are our individual and collective experience. Our theologians say, "Why should we continue to hope? . . . There is hope because we believe that the power of the Gospel of Jesus Christ shows itself time and again as more powerful than all our human failures and foolishness in the church, stronger than all our discouragement." That is where we are.

Judaism

Judaism emerged as a major religious force in this country as the result of successive waves of immigration from Europe. In the process the

Jewish theological climate was profoundly shaped by the differing character of these immigrant groups. The earliest American Jews were Sephardim, Jews of Spanish or Portuguese origin, who settled in the colonies in small numbers prior to the American Revolution. The Sephardim were thoroughly orthodox in their doctrine but had developed their own distinctive rituals.

In the period between 1840 and 1880 large numbers of middle-class, reasonably well-educated Jews immigrated to this country from Germany. Most of these Jews became part of Reform Judaism, a liberal Jewish movement that had originated in Germany. At Frankfurt, Germany, in 1843, the founders of Reform Judaism had issued the following declaration:

> First, we recognize the possibility of unlimited development in the Mosaic religion. Second, the collection of controversies, dissertations, and prescriptions commonly designated by the name Talmud possesses for us no authority from either the doctrinal or practical standpoint. Third, a Messiah who is to lead back the Israelites to the land of Palestine is neither expected nor desired by us—we know no fatherland except that to which we belong by birth citizenship.[43]

Reform Judaism thus rejected most of the central beliefs of traditional orthodoxy, including the authority of the Talmud, the sacred summary of the biblical interpretations and wise commentaries of the ancient rabbis.

Under the leadership of Issac M. Wise (1819–1900), who arrived in this country in 1846, Reform Judaism rapidly became the major stream in American Jewish life in the middle years of the nineteenth century. Wise succeeded in uniting the growing number of Reform synagogues into the Union of American Hebrew Congregations, formed in 1873; in 1875, he founded Hebrew Union College in Cincinnati to train rabbis.

Wise's own theological position was representative of most Jewish liberal thought. He rejected the traditional beliefs in a personal Messiah and the resurrection of the dead. Although he accepted the authority of the "Torah of God" (the Ten Commandments), he taught that the "Torah of Moses" (the rest of the Pentateuch, or first five books of the Hebrew scripture) was the application of the divine law to a particular historical situation and should be constantly updated as conditions in the culture changed. He modernized the synagogue service by introducing the use of English into the ritual and by revising the prayer book.

Other Reform leaders went even further than did Wise, embracing such radical innovations as the substitution of Sunday morning services in place of the traditional Sabbath or Saturday services. Wise himself urged as a compromise the shifting of the service to Friday evening, the beginning of the Sabbath, a suggestion that received little support in

[43]Cited in David Philipson, *The Reform Movement in Judaism* (New York: KTAV Publishing House, 1931), p. 122.

the nineteenth century but that has become the general practice of Reform synagogues today. Such eagerness to accommodate Jewish patterns to a predominantly Protestant religious situation and to "Americanize" Judaism created internal Jewish dissension, culminating in the withdrawal of more conservative elements from Reform in 1883 to organize themselves into Conservative Judaism, a movement discussed in the previous chapter.

By 1880 there were an estimated quarter of a million Jews in the United States. But a second wave of immigration was to change drastically the character of American Judaism. The new immigrants came in great numbers, not from middle-class Germany but from eastern Europe. With a few notable exceptions, they were poverty-stricken, largely uneducated, and unskilled in trades or professions. Unlike the earlier immigrants, who had scattered across the country, these new arrivals huddled together in the great cities of the eastern part of the United States. Most of them were fleeing anti-Semitic persecution, and the majority had reacted to their persecution by retreating into a rigid and suspicious Jewish orthodoxy which they transported to this country. But among the immigrants were also some whose response to their troubles had been to abandon Judaism, associating themselves instead with radical antireligious movements for social reform. The established American Jewish community found it difficult to identify with either of these two new groups: either the strenuously conservative religious Jews or the antireligious social radicals. Consequently, tension arose within American Judaism.

By 1920 more than four fifths of all American Jews had an east European background; as a result, the number of Orthodox synagogues far outnumbered Reform and Conservative. Jews unaffiliated with any synagogue, however, were even more numerous than the combined total of all affiliated Jews, and their proportion steadily grew, creating a dangerous situation. One attempt to respond to this "flight from Judaism" was the Reconstructionist movement, led by Mordecai M. Kaplan (1881–   ) of the Jewish Theological Seminary. Kaplan sought to make the synagogue once more the center of Jewish life, largely by transforming it from a religious institution into an institution for the cultivation and maintenance of "Jewishness." His central affirmation was that Judaism was not a religion but a civilization or culture in which both religious and nonreligious Jews could share. For Kaplan, the traditional rituals and ceremonies were important as symbolic "cement" serving primarily to bind the Jewish people together. Conservative Judaism was most responsive to Kaplan's ideas and adopted many of them as a program for action.

Yet another and even more significant movement in Judaism helped to reverse the decline in affiliation with the synagogue. This was Zionism, given its modern shape by Theodor Herzl, who argued in his pamphlet *The Jewish State* (1896) that the only hope for Jews lay in a national rebirth. Such a rebirth included the necessity for a Jewish homeland, preferably in Palestine. Zionism spread rapidly, particulary among Conservative Jews. In addition, some Orthodox, who linked Zionism with the ancient expectation of the restoration of Israel, were sympathetic. Reform Jews generally opposed the movement, at least in the beginning, because they viewed Judaism primarily as a religion and favored cultural and social assimilation into the national ethos in which they lived. But the German Nazi horror of the 1930s, with its creation of a gigantic Jewish refugee problem, transformed the Zionist issue from a theoretical into a practical one. Some place was needed to resettle the refugees. Jews of all persuasions were drawn closer together by their common opposition to Hitler and their sympathy for and indentification with their persecuted brethren. By 1935 a majority of Reform Jews, as well as others, had moved into the Zionist camp. When the state of Israel was finally established in 1948, it drew enthusiastic support from American Jews, who contributed tremendous sums of money through the United Jewish Appeal in order to insure the viability of the new Jewish state.

In the post-World War II period American Judaism underwent a remarkable revival. Winthrop Hudson has compiled significant figures that show that in 1937 the combined synagogue membership in the United States was about a million and a half, barely more than one fourth of all American Jews. Orthodox Judaism was the largest, with about 200,000 families; Conservatives claimed about 75,000 families; the Reform group consisted of about 50,000 families. But by 1956 the situation had changed decisively. Reform membership, for example, had increased fivefold, counting more than 255,000 families. Conservatives had tripled in number, and Orthodox Judaism was exhibiting a new and fervent vitality, particularly in connection with its flourishing university, Yeshiva.[44]

Undoubtedly, many factors contributed to this resurgence, not all of them clearly discernible. The Nazi holocaust and the establishment of Israel made their contributions. It is possible, however, that the special experience of the Jews in America, which contributed originally to the abandonment by many of Judaism as a religion, also paradoxically provided the necessary background for the revival. Such is the contention of Arthur A. Cohen, who has argued that the American pluralistic tradition and the American environment "made it possible for the Jew to become an American without ceasing to be a Jew." In the process, however, many Jews felt it necessary to divest themselves of that portion of their Jewishness that they deemed most likely to prevent their full assimilation as Americans: their Jewish religious faith. "America was tolerant of the Jew," Cohen wrote. "The Jew was conspicuously intolerant of himself. He did more than the environment demanded—he paid a higher price

[44] See Hudson, op. cit., p. 336.

than was asked."[45] The result was empty synagogues and declining religious affiliation. In these circumstances, as we have seen, most Jewish religious leaders responded by stressing Judaism as a cultural way of life or a nationalistic center, rather than as a matter of faith, belief, and religious tradition.

This predominance of secularized Judaism appeared to create a spiritual vacuum for many Jews. Winthrop Hudson describes the situation in the decade of the 1950s, commenting on the Jewish resurgence of religious vitality:

> The same spiritual hunger that was leading other Americans into a quest for personal religious experience was present in the Jewish community. By 1970 rabbis on campuses and in synagogues were surprised to discover widespread interest in discussions of Jewish mysticism, spiritual disciplines, and personal religious faith. Some younger Jews, having become disenchanted with what seemed to them to be the spiritual void of conventional Judaism, sought to develop a renewed or "parallel" Judaism of their own in communes or "covenanted" communities committed to strict religious discipline. . . . With astonishing rapidity after 1970 Jewish scholars began to mine the rich resources of Jewish mystical piety, producing a flood of articles dealing with the Jewish mystical tradition. Younger Jews were especially drawn to the mystical enthusiasm of the Hasidim which had its beginnings in eighteenth-century eastern Europe, being attracted partly by the countercultural aspects of Hasidic communal life, but more interested in the Hasidic experience of ecstatic encounter with God than in rituals and customs.[46]

The twentieth-century Jewish experience in America, culminating in the revival following World War II, has produced a great diversity in Jewish theology, running the full gamut from very conservative to very liberal. In Europe, Jewish thinkers such as Leo S. Baeck (1873–1956), a profound spokesman for Reform ideas; Franz Rosenzweig (1886–1923), a more conservative theologian; and Martin Buber (1878–1965), whose thought influenced Christians even more, perhaps, than it did Jews, have all made distinctive contributions to American Jewish thought. In the United States Abraham Heschel, who came to this country in 1940 from Europe, combined rigorous scholarship with a fervent and somewhat mystical affirmation of traditional Judaism, encouraging modern Jews to seek a new confrontation with their own classic heritage.

But at least in one respect Judaism is not different from American Protestantism and Catholicism, and that is in the wide gulf between the work of serious religious thinkers and what happens at the local congregational level, where much of the emphasis is on practicality and social activity. True, there were significant theological aspects of the revival of the 1950s, but by the 1970s Jews, like many other Americans,

[45] Arthur A. Cohen, *The Natural and the Supernatural Jew* (New York: McGraw-Hill, 1962), pp. 193–194, 202.
[46] Hudson, op. cit., pp. 438–439.

were discovering that the revival had provided inadequate preparation for the social and spiritual crises the country and its churches were called on to face. As with its two partners in the tripartite American religious situation, Judaism is currently having to deal with the erosion of secularity and the disruptions of increased social mobility. The rate of interfaith marriage, for example, has risen markedly. Radical thinkers have attacked the central facets of the ancient faith, and a theologican like Rabbi Richard Rubenstein, one of the original "death of God" thinkers, can argue that there is no longer any real possibility of theological inquiry, in the traditional sense, "after Auschwitz"—after the terrible Jewish experience of the Holocaust of World War II.[47]

Much of the uniqueness of Judaism within the total American religious ambience lies in its continuing struggle to live in two worlds at the same time: the secular world of a non-Jewish culture and the sacred world of the Jewish religious commitment. Such a dual allegiance has never been easy to maintain, but by and large the Jews have succeeded remarkably well in preserving their own identity while at the same time blending into the surrounding cultural ethos. The gradual disappearance of the Jewish ghettos in the large cities, together with the decline of anti-Semitism, has relieved some of the outside pressure on Jews, but this, paradoxically, is making it increasingly difficult for Jews to hold on to a distinctive ethnic and religious heritage. Nathan Glazer of Harvard University has addressed this problem; the following excerpts are taken from his article.

Document 40 ─────────────────────────────────────

From "The Crisis in American Jewry" by Nathan Glazer

If one hears the term, "crisis," in connection with the Jewish community, I believe most Jews will think of two things: one, the threat of anti-Semitism, and two, the threat of assimilation. Now in the last two decades we have been hardly concerned with the level of anti-Semitism, which is quite low, even though there have been some disturbing signs and portents in recent years. We have been considerably more concerned with the possibility of assimilation. But it is neither of these two possible senses of crisis that concern me in this lecture. When I consider the position of the American Jewish community today, I rather think of an internal crisis, a crisis of identity and self-conception, and if you will—I think the term is not too extravagant—a spiritual crisis. . . .

The major unanswered question as to American Judaism—and this is a question that by its nature is not easily to be settled by social surveys—remains, what is

SOURCE: Nathan Glazer, "The Crisis in American Jewry" in *Religion American Style*, edited by Patrick H. McNamara (New York: Harper & Row, 1974), pp. 238–244. Used by permission.

[47]Richard Rubenstein, *After Auschwitz: Radical Theology and Contemporary Judaism* (Indianapolis: Bobbs Merrill, 1966).

Judaism to be? Here I think we can begin to discern an emerging dilemma that to my mind affects Judaism in a special way, and that makes its problems distinct from the crises of religion in America in general. American Judaism, as it has moved further and further away from traditional Judaism, has moved in two directions. One direction has been to make Jewish ethnicity—peoplehood and nationality—in larger and larger degree the major content of Jewish religion. This is not a movement in complete contradiction to traditional religion. Judaism has always emphasized the chosen and distinctiveness of the Jewish people. But there is no question in my mind that American Judaism has emphasized this much more strongly than was ever the case in traditional Judaism.

There were various reasons for this. As Will Herberg pointed out almost twenty years ago, American society tolerantly left room for Jewish religion but was somewhat less tolerant toward long-sustained, long-maintained ethnic, national differences. You could be a member of a religion and a full American. It was somewhat harder to be a member of another national group and a full American, though there were many tendencies in American thinking and practice which argued for this.

More significant perhaps than this general American tendency to encourage religion at the expense of ethnicity or nationality was the specific impact on American Jewish life of the rise of Israel. The permanent danger to the state of Israel and the close personal, emotional, and historical ties between American Jews and Israelis have made it impossible to create a non-national, non-ethnic form of Judaism. There have been a number of such efforts, which have gained some intellectual respectability—in particular of course classical Reform Judaism and its various later developments such as those represented by the American Council for Judaism. We know what reputation that now has among most Jews. And yet we should recall that the idea of non-national Judaism—Judaism as a humanist religion increasingly divorced from a people with a specific social character and interests—once seemed to make sense to a good number of intelligent Jews.

There has been a second strand in the development of a new content for American Judaism. This is liberalism—liberalism in the form of political and social ideals that emphasized the equality of men, the importance of nondiscrimination, freedom of opportunity, and the like. While on the one hand the anti-national side of Reform Judaism failed utterly, the liberal side has been, if anything, continually strengthened. One of the most intriguing parts of Marshall Sklare's study of Lakeville is the section where he asks Lakeville Jews to give him their conception of a good Jew. Various formulations are suggested to the respondents. Obeying the precepts of traditional Judaism is far down on the list. Supporting Israel is higher. But at the very top is to be fair and honest to one's fellow men, not to discriminate, to protect civil liberties, civil rights, and liberal ideals. The result is quite clear—when you ask American Jews what it is to be a good Jew, the answer is, to be a liberal.

My thesis is: the major problems facing Judaism and Jews today lie in the development of certain contradictions, certain dilemmas, inherent in the effort to combine these two tendencies that make up modern American Judaism, the ethnic and the national on the one hand, and the liberal on the other, and the development of these ideals themselves.

Let me explore some of these emerging dilemmas.

First: the main subject of liberal social ideals for twenty-five years has been the condition of the Negro. If we go back and review the various commissions on social justice of the Reform and Conservative denominations, we will see that, alongside the major issue of peace, has been the major issue of the status of the Negro. We are all aware of what a fantastic change has occurred in the thinking and outlook of the Negro—or black man as he now prefers to be known—in the past five years, changes which have seriously damaged the capacity of liberals and liberal ideals to play a major role in the development of a more satisfactory social position for the Negro in the United States. At one time—only four or five years ago—we saw no contradiction, indeed there was none, between liberal ideals—non-discrimination, equal opportunity, civil liberties and civil rights—and the desires of Negroes. Indeed, in those days all agreed that it was only through the realization of liberal ideals that the desires of Negroes could be fulfilled.

Today, almost all liberal ideals are challenged by the more militant black leaders and their white allies. The dependence on democratic processes and on non-violence; the importance of equal opportunity and fairness to individuals; the hope for integration; tolerance of a variety of viewpoints—all these are anathema to most young blacks, and indeed most black leaders are forced to act as if they agree with them. Five years ago few of us saw any contradiction in being a Jew, in the sense in which so many Jews saw themselves as Jews, and the achievement of equality for Negroes. Today the word liberal is a dirty word among black militants and their white allies. Judaism finds that its kind of liberalism, instead of allying it with the oppressed and deprived and their hopes for a better life, cuts it off from them. This is deeply troubling to Jews, and Judaism.

There is a second reason, aside from the challenge to the value of liberalism, why Judaism is troubled by the radical shift in Negro political attitudes. It is that Judaism's other side, its ethnic-national side, also brings it into conflict with current political attitudes among black and white radicals. Concretely, there is the conflict between the interests of Jews and Negroes in many cities. Here liberal ideals seem to come into conflict with ethnic interests. Perhaps ultimately more dangerous, there is the conflict between Israel and the Arabs, and the way it is reflected in black political attitudes in this country. The Arabs, to blacks, are "Africans," "oppressed," "colonized," victimized by "American Imperialism"—just as the blacks are, in militant eyes. Israel is cast as the imperialist, western, white oppressor.

There are some special and accidental reasons for this black militant view which places Israel in the camp of the enemy of the blacks. After all, Israel in reality has strong links with many black states, and good relations with them. To unravel the image of Israel in black militant eyes would be a task that involves history, myth, and interests in some inextricable mixture. Israel is seen as mirroring the American Jewish landlord, storekeeper, lawyer, doctor, social worker, teacher, who in the past and even today play such a large role in the ghetto.

Thus the liberal side of Judaism and the ethnic side of Judaism both place Judaism in the dilemma of finding that it is in opposition to the group that has been for so long the chief subject and object of domestic liberalism. This is a dilemma and a troubling one.

Perhaps the most serious dilemma relates to the safety of Israel. You will recall that many doves on Vietnam became hawks on Israel. But many Jews must be concerned over recent polls that have shown that Americans are less willing to send troops to defend Israel than many other countries. Even India scored better on this item. The connection between Israel's security and the American military is closer than many of us would like to think. Thus, Israel gets supplies from the United States, and in return provides captured Migs and radar installations for American inspection. It is not only in Arab eyes that the United states is the principal and only military ally of Israel—in many respects the U.S. in reality is, even if rather unwillingly, and even if, as I suspect, our diplomats and military men would prefer to be tied up with the Arabs. . . .

Under the present circumstances in American Judaism one is torn between an effort fo find a more contemporary, a more "relevant" content to Judaism, and an effort to shore up the old content. I must say, I am not sanguine about the effort to remodel the content of Judaism as it has emerged in the United States. On the one hand, I do not see the strength of a religion of pure traditionalism, strong as tradition is in many respects. Nor do I believe Judaism can be strong as a religion of disembodied humanism, strong as that ideal was in the past.

There is strength in the ethnic-liberal mixture. It is tied to tradition and it is tied to contemporary Jewish reality. The new amalgam gave renewed content, viability, validity, to an old faith for millions.

And on the other hand, the association of ethnic-national feeling and liberalism with religion aided these tendencies too. It prevented the national-ethnic trend from becoming pure chauvinism. I believe Jewish nationalism is still far from chauvinism and protected from getting there by its links to religion. Thus, I am deeply impressed by how Israel's defense has not become infected with hatred of others.

Religion does something for liberalism, too. Liberalism, in some of its tendencies, can become an inhuman kind of scientific and rational concern with simply material matters. The religious component makes this harder.

I end up with no ringing call to replace the inadequate and false idols of ethnicity and liberalism with some new sounder content—internationalism and radicalism, for example, I do not believe that liberalism and ethnic attachment *are* false idols. Rather, our task is to deepen our understanding of what Judaism has in practice become. We must try to give new validity to ethnic attachment and to liberalism, both humanized, or spiritualized, if you will, by association with an old religion. We must become critics and analysts of our beliefs, so we can understand their implications better, hold to them with greater strength, and hope that we can communicate them more effectively to our children. We must be able to convince our children that we hold to these commitments not because we have simply, flaccidly accepted them from our past, or because they serve our interests, but because they do indeed provide the best patterns to organize our lives on earth.

Summary

Because of the pragmatic quality of American life, the "doing of theology" has not often occupied center stage among religious folk in this country. This pragmatism does not mean, however, that Americans lack conviction about religious doctrine. Quite the contrary. The debate has been vigorous, sometimes even vicious, between what we have called, for lack of more precise terms, liberals and conservatives in American theology. From the beginning, the bracing winds of the Enlightenment and its progeny have gradually moved the main-line church groups toward a more "rational" theology. Yet one cannot say, in all fairness, that conservatives were or are more irrational—only that they are much more likely to base their argument on a supernatural foundation that deliberately goes beyond rationalism. Once having moved beyond their initial presuppositions of faith, many conservative theologians have made their arguments on a rigorously rational basis.

Whether conservative or liberal, however, pragmatic Americans have insisted on putting their theology to work. Religious thought has seldom been the master; rather, it has been the servant of a remarkable variety of programs that have had as their aim the improvement of the human lot. And since these programs and the theological enterprise itself must take place in interaction with the culture, decisive cultural changes have inevitably meant modifications in both the forms of faith and the shape of religious good works. In the next chapter we shall see how faith has served good works among religious people in America.

Missions, Humanitarianism, and the Social Gospel 6

Missions, humanitarianism, and the social gospel are three closely related movements, all of which made their American appearance during the nineteenth century. All three grew out of the same ideological soil, a fruitful combination of revivalism with the boundless optimism about humanity and the world that characterized so much of the period. Moreover, all three movements illustrate the pragmatic and activistic quality of American religion. Being the sort of creatures they were, nineteenth-century American religious believers were more likely to express their faith by mounting a campaign to improve the lot of humanity than by performing some sort of ritual or liturgy. "Deeds, not creeds" was their motto.

Clearly the social gospel was the most revolutionary of the three movements. Its appearance after the Civil War dramatically altered the direction for American Christianity, especially for Protestantism.[1] It was not that everyone agreed to the policies proposed by the social gospelers, but from then on, all American churchgoers would have to decide what position they would take toward the churches' involvement with social and political issues. As the name implies, the movement sought to make religion relevant to the problems of society. But large numbers of sincere churchmen were opposed to the movement; they believed that the churches' primary objective could only be salvation for the individual person. All of which meant that many denominations were torn by bitter debate about the social gospel. Businessmen and industrialists, who also happened to be church members, reacted negatively when their economic interests were challenged. They believed that the concept of rugged individualism, so precious in the eyes of the young nation, was in danger of being subverted. To them the infant labor movement was especially suspect.

The missions movement, on the other hand, sought primarily to save individual souls, one by one, until the entire world was conquered. But even this seemingly noncontroversial movement had its problems. What, exactly, was the quality of the new life to which the world was to be converted? It has seemed to some critics that American Protestant missionaries were often animated by a zeal to convert the "pagan" to the American way of life as well as to Christ. The doctrine of Manifest Destiny so dominated the era that many missionaries actually believed that

---

[1] Judaism was not much affected at first. Toward the end of the century, large numbers of eastern European Jews who emigrated to America were caught up in movements directed toward achieving social justice, but many of those who did so no longer thought of themselves as religious Jews. The labor movement was especially attractive to them.

their specially ordained society and religion, Anglo-Saxon Protestantism, should be adopted by everyone else.

Humanitarianism may be further differentiated from the other two. Its function was not so much to save souls as to be the helping instrument of destitute men, women, and children. If by their charitable acts, others were converted to religion, well and good, but that was not always the humanitarian's primary aim.

Christian Missions Today

With the notable exception of the burgeoning fundamentalist and Pentecostal groups, main-line Christian denominations began to lose their enthusiasm for sending missionaries to other lands during the 1960s. At the end of 1976, the United Presbyterians reported that their overseas staff had been reduced by a half in a twenty-year span. The Episcopal Church's cut was even more dramatic. By the early 1970s it was supporting only one third as many missionaries to other lands as it had in the late 1950s, and by 1976 a further decline of 14 per cent had taken place.[2]

The reasons for the growing disenchantment with foreign missions can only be guessed at, but there are certain facts that will not disappear when the question is asked. For example, the fact that financial support for national denominational agencies had declined during recent years obviously meant that there was less money for foreign missionary activity—especially in view of rising costs and inflation. It simply took far more money to fund a missionary program in the 1970s than it had in prior decades.[3] In addition, mission funds were relatively easy to cut back; missionaries do not have much power at the budget committee table when funds are being allocated. But probably the most debilitating factor of all was the nation's response to American intervention in armed conflicts abroad. More than at any time in the history of the republic, people began to question the rationale for exporting *anything* American, whether military, economic, political, or religious. "How can people of one culture," asked Charles West, "intervene in the life of another to establish there a new concept of justice and law, a new vision of humanity, or a new perception of saving truth? How can a missionary movement, whatever its creed or program, avoid ending in imperialist domination, frustration, or both?"[4] In spite of these somber notes, the decline in missionary activity was not universal.

[2] See "Foreign Mission Programs Are Decreasing," *St. Petersburg Times Magazine of Religion* (December 25, 1971), p. 7, and "The Employment Situation for Ordained Protestant Clergy," *Yearbook of American and Canadian Churches* (Nashville, Tenn.: Abingdon, 1978), pp. 248–251.

[3] See Constant H. Jacquet, Jr., "Effects of Inflation on Per Capita Giving: 1961–76," *Yearbook of American and Canadian Churches* (Nashville, Tenn.: Abingdon, 1978), p. 244.

[4] Charles C. West, "Missions and Revolutions," *Christianity and Crisis*, Vol. 10, No. 1 (February 2, 1970), p. 6.

Though clearly there were some problems with main-line Protestant missions, there were, at the same time, pockets of vigorous activity among the fringe groups or among what Henry Van P. Dusen once called "the third force in Christendom"—sects such as the Churches of God, Adventist groups, Assemblies of God, Pentecostal and Holiness churches, Jehovah's Witnesses, and the Churches of Christ.[5] Leaders of this loosely defined "third force" alongside Catholicism and Protestantism believed the older churches were incapable of winning the world for Christ and believed themselves to be specially ordained for that important task. Although the major denominations began cutbacks in overseas operations in the 1950s and 1960s, third-force groups, fervently convinced of their task, supported their overseas operations with more money and more personnel than ever before. Third-force missionary efforts more than offset the economies of the mainline denominations; they accounted for the increase in actual dollars spent abroad during the 1970s.

The crisis of confidence in the older missionary efforts led many ecclesiastical leaders to reassess their strategies. David M. Stowe, executive head of America's oldest interdenominational missionary society, has argued that, because traditional methods seem to have failed, more imaginative strategies would have to be devised for the years ahead. He said that a new kind of missionary would be required for the "radically new world." Such a missionary would have to abandon the comfort and prestige of clerical identification, assume the role of servant rather than priest or king, and direct his or her energies toward improving the standard of living rather than advancing ecclesiastical interests. And, most important of all, the new breed of missionaries would have to take a humbler, more appreciative attitude toward the so-called foreign culture in which they work. Indeed, they might have to be willing to concede that the foreign culture is nobler, more humane, and more sophisticated than their own native culture in some important respects.[6]

Only time will tell whether the adjustments in strategy will save missions from eventual extinction. J. M. Bonino wrote in 1968 that the churches "should work for total withdrawal or separation," if they could not find a way to neutralize the incipient imperialism and colonialism in missions. Some observers even went so far as to suggest that the very idea behind missions is fallacious and forecast the demise of missionary activity altogether. They pointed to the growing pressure among the nations of Africa and Asia against any product originating in the United States, religion included. Cultural domination and proselytism, as such, were not only outmoded but reprehensible for non-Western nations.

Most of those responsible for deciding mission strategy agree that the

---

[5] "The Third Force's Lessons for Others," *Life*, June 9, 1958, pp. 122–123.

[6] George W. Cornell, "Foreign Missions Said Facing Drastic Change," *Tallahassee Democrat* (February 5, 1971), p. 6.

old approach is as defunct and unrealistic as colonialism. But they point out that missionaries, by and large, have in fact ceased to be purveyors of American imperialism. Indeed, one executive holds that Christian missions have often fostered the sense of national self-esteem in the emerging nations: "There isn't a revolution in the nonwestern world that can't be traced to missionary efforts."[7] Rather than obstructing political independence, the ideology behind missions has implicitly, if not explicitly, supported egalitarianism and national self-determination.

The executive in question, Ralph Winter, is a Presbyterian missionary-scholar. He has sought to explode what he considers to be popular misconceptions about Christian missions. Although some authorities on the subject have claimed that Christian missions have often been a conservative sociopolitical force, dedicated to preserving the status quo, Winter argues otherwise. He readily admits that there have been, from time to time, outrageous abuses and holds no brief for missionaries who have force-fed Western ideas to unsuspecting people in other lands. But he points out that the basic posture of missions has historically been a liberating one: they have helped to end slave trading, put a stop to tribal warfare, and altered debilitating caste systems. They have often checked the unscrupulous activities of white settlers. Moreover, says Winter, much of the leadership in the emerging nations has been provided by native Christians: "After World War II, when more and more African and Asian governments run by Western nations were toppled and replaced by national leadership, everybody assumed that 'Yankee go home' meant 'missionary go home.' But that's just not so." After the chaos subsided in the Congo, hundreds of missionaries were encouraged to return. When Jomo Kenyatta established his revolutionary government in Kenya, for example, 75 per cent of his cabinet were Christian. In Guatemala, Winter himself discovered that those missionaries who had some contribution to make were highly sought after by local authorities.[8]

A profoundly disturbing exception to this general trend was discovered in the fall of 1975 when the White House and the Central Intelligence Agency admitted that missionaries had been used to gather information at overseas locations. A U.S. Senate investigation revealed the existence of fourteen "covert arrangements" involving the "direct operational use" of twenty-one American missionaries and members of the clergy. Although it did turn out that some of the missionaries were unaware that they had been co-opted by the CIA, the damage was nonetheless severe. Under prodding by Senator Mark O. Hatfield, the CIA

[7]Ralph Winter as quoted by Ken Briggs, "Missionaries Have Earned Status Abroad," St. Petersburg Times Magazine of Religion, September 11, 1971, p. 5.
[8]See The New York Times, June 8, 1976, p. 12. See also Arthur J. Moore, "Render Unto Caesar: Missionaries and the CIA," Christianity and Crisis, Vol. 31, No. 5 (March 29, 1976), pp. 54–56.

soon agreed that it would no longer seek to use American missionaries for intelligence purposes and expanded the definition of "missionary" to include all Americans abroad who perform tasks involving preaching, teaching, healing, and proselytizing, even if they are not controlled by denominational or ecumenical agencies, "provided their ultimate sponsorship comes from religious organizations." The incident provoked an outcry from rank-and-file church members as well as denominational leaders.

Despite this appalling development, there have been positive signs in recent decades, the most significant of which is the important shift in missionary personnel policy. Top priority has been given to developing indigenous leadership to replace Americans abroad. Most denominational executives no longer want to be accused of having sent "enlightened" Americans to the "benighted masses" abroad. But by developing an indigenous ministry, the churches in foreign cultures can find ways of adapting Christianity to new and different situations. There will, of course, be risks involved, but most missionary strategies believe the risks are worth taking. For example, one well-known theologian of missions has noted:

> A Church of India which is truly indigenous will be exposed to the dangers of syncretism, nationalism, racialism and cultural absorption to a very much greater degree than one which continues to bear the heavy stamp of its foreign origin. The fact remains that the Church of India can properly fulfil her calling only when she meets the challenge and the risk in the freedom of her faith and not under the shelter of any Western defences.[9]

But creating an indigenous ministry and church means much more than simple identification with an alien culture:

> There is a real danger that a Church beset with too tender a conscience about her foreign origin and character may waste her energies in adapting herself to aspects of an indigenous culture already consigned to the past and doomed to become out of date. The critical question that in our time faces the worldwide Church is whether she is able and ready to serve her Lord amidst the needs of such a rapidly changing world as ours. The problems which the Church has to face in Tokyo or Hong Kong are vastly different from, say, the concerns of a village congregation in South India or the question of what missionary approach should be adopted towards a recently discovered Papuan tribe in the interior of New Guinea.[10]

Creating an indigenous church, then, means not only making Christianity relevant to a different place but also to another time, a time and a place not "ours." Only one who indwells that situation can do the job properly.

[9] Arend Th. Van Leeuwen, *Christianity in World History* (New York: Scribner, 1964), p. 423.
[10] Ibid., p. 424.

The experience of denominations which have moved toward formation of native churches has been impressive and instructive. Waldo A.
Cesar described the Protestant experience in Brazil:

> From 1949 to 1961 the number of missionaries doubled from 700 to 1,400, but
> the number of Brazilian pastors rose from 1,400 to 20,000! There were only 15
> or 20 centers of preparation (Bible schools, Bible institutes, and seminaries or
> colleges of theology) in 1916; there were 126 in 1961. Despite this growth, the
> marks of missionary *implantation* continue strong enough to prohibit true au-
> tonomy. All of the major efforts—new movements, publications, and even the
> construction of churches—almost always depend on resources from outside the
> country.

So long as that remains true, he says, the church in Brazil or in any
other place will never be free and strong.[11]

It is precisely at this point that the Pentecostalists have broken the
mould. Their success overseas may be directly attributable to the fact
that they have cut themselves free from the sending church in America
or Europe. They have become truly native because they did not have to
rely on a trained ministry in order to carry on their work:

> This was a real revolution and an important key to the future expansion of the
> movement: *the administrative functions were no longer the exclusive province of
> foreign missionaries or of a national elite educated in theological seminaries.*
>   Pentecostalism breaks the barrier of theological education which separated
> the layman from the pastor. Each convert participates from the beginning in the
> missionary work of the community and knows that, God willing, he can one day
> be pastor . . . .
>   The elimination of a body of pastors with an abstract theological training
> favors a rapprochement between the community and its leader. The latter is no
> longer imposed on the congregation by a hierarchical decision: he is the natural
> leader of the group. He belongs to the same social class and has similar problems
> of existence and subsistence; he thinks as his flock thinks. Much has been said
> and written about the advantages of education and the necessity for theological
> education. Without wishing to deny these advantages, one ought to take into
> consideration the fact that the years spent in high school and college create
> thought processes and needs which are different from those of the urban or rural
> working class member of a community. There exists between the traditional
> Protestant pastor (or the Catholic priest) and his congregation a cultural and so-
> cial distance—frequently an abyss—with no possibility of dialogue.[12]

Whether or not one agrees with this assessment is beside the point. It
is clear that the major denominations will continue to make an impact
on other cultures only insofar as they will be able to "go native." But
curiously enough, it has not been just the unsophisticated wisdom of the
Pentecostalists that has helped induce change among main-line Protes-

[11]Waldo A. Cesar, "The Condition of Protestantism in Latin America," *The Religious Situation: 1969*, edited by Donald R. Cutler (Boston: Beacon Press, 1969), p. 154.

[12]Christian Lalive D'Epinay, "The Pentecostal 'Conquest' of Chile," ibid., p. 181. One
should note the parallel arguments mounted here by D'Epinay and some of the arguments put
forth by revivalists during the Great Awakening in America two hundred years earlier.

tants. They have also learned much from some of their own more sophisticated minds. Paul Tillich, one of modern Protestantism's great theologians, helped contemporary strategists reassess missions. He called for
dialogue with alien peoples in place of seeking their conversion: "It
would be a tremendous step forward if Christianity were to accept
this!"[13] Tillich was convinced that Christians had much to learn from
the religious experience of others. Conflict is, of course, endemic to
such intercultural encounters. The people of one culture always believe
they possess "the truth," which necessarily implies that all others, to
some degree, dwell in error. Tillich writes:

> Consequently the encounter of Christianity with religions . . . implies a rejec-
> tion of their claims insofar as they contradict the Christian principle, implicitly
> or explicitly. But the problem is not the right of rejecting that which rejects us;
> rather it is the nature of this rejection. It can be the rejection of everything for
> which the opposite group stands; it can be a partial rejection together with a par-
> tial acceptance of assertions of the opposite group; or it can be a dialectical union
> of rejection and acceptance in the relation of these two groups. In the first case
> the rejected religion is considered false, so that no communication between the
> two contradictory positions is possible. The negation is complete and under cer-
> tain circumstances deadly for the one or the other side. In the second case some
> assertions and actions of the one or the other side are considered false, others
> true. This is more tolerant than the attitude of total negation, and it is certainly
> an adequate response to a statement of facts or ideas some of which may be true,
> some false . . . . The third way of rejecting other religions is a dialectical union of
> acceptance and rejection, with all the tensions, uncertainties, and changes which
> such dialectics implies.[14]

Tillich then uses an illustration that most Americans can understand,
the Jewish–Christian encounter: "Many Christians feel that it is a questionable thing . . . to try to convert Jews. They have lived and spoken
with their Jewish friends for decades. They have not converted them,
but they have created a community of conversation which has changed
both sides of the dialogue."[15] The pluralistic character of the American
situation requires that a citizen adopt such an attitude toward all persons no matter what their religious persuasion might be.
    Judaism itself seems devoid of any missionary impulse. Why this is so
is not altogether clear. Robert Gordis has suggested that the Jews' "deep-
seated reluctance" to seek converts stems from "the long centuries of
medieval intolerance and oppression," which, he said, as recently as
1955, hardly makes it worth the risk to attempt to win others to Judaism. The days of intolerance are far from over, he noted.[16]
    Some observers have suggested that Judaism lacks any missionary im-

[13] Paul Tillich. *Christianity and the Encounter of the World Religions* (New York: Columbia
University Press, 1963), p. 95.
[14] Ibid., pp. 28–30.
[15] Ibid., pp. 94–95.
[16] Robert Gordis, "Missionary Activity and Religious Tolerance," *Judaism for the Modern
Age* (New York: Farrar, Straus & Giroux, 1955), p. 339.

pulse because the faith of Israel is built on the doctrine of election. Because God has already chosen or elected the nation of Israel, the idea of missions to convert other nations *or* individuals never seriously occurs to the Jews. Missions in a Jewish context is a theological anomaly.

Not so, says Arthur Hertzberg, the distinguished rabbi and scholar. In the first place, missionary groups have been recently established in Judaism, one in Jerusalem and a second in Chicago. The question of conversion to Judaism is therefore a real one. However, as Tillich does, Hertzberg argues for tolerance and understanding between religious groups: "It is obvious that American society and the world need theologies that are at once true to themselves and yet make possible a reasonable peace among religions." Though he acknowledges that Judaism is the truth and possesses ultimate validity *for him*, he still accedes that, because all people share a common humanity, forbearance and tolerance are absolutely necessary. Although Jews may regard themselves "as the bearers of special responsibilities, they claim no monopoly on salvation. All people are under certain obligations, and the righteous among them 'have a share in the life to come.' " Thus, argues Hertzberg, Christians and Jews must learn "to live together, with mutual regard for the other's faith, but *not to engage in active efforts at conversion.*" In the end, he pleads, "let us stand separately for our various truths. Let us stand together for the peace of society. Let us not do to one another that which is hateful to any of us. And let us await the judgment of God."[17]

The Origin and Development of Missions in America

The Christian church, by definition, is a mission. At least that has been the "conventional wisdom" up until recently. Christ's last words to his disciples were to preach the good news to all the nations and baptize them. So central has this injunction been to the life of the churches that no period of Christian history has been devoid of evangelism. One could argue quite convincingly that the church has been most robust when it has obeyed the so-called Great Commission and has been most stagnant when it has forgotten the commission and become self-serving.

The settlement of America was no exception. As soon as the first colonists came to the New World, the church turned its attention to converting the Indians, who, to the colonists, were simply another "nation" to be converted. The Spanish missions to Florida and New Mexico, as well as the Puritans in New England, thought of the natives as new candidates for evangelism. Even the scrupulously tolerant Quak-

---

[17]Emphasis added. Arthur Hertzberg, "Conversion: The Jewish Approach," *The Jewish Heritage Reader*, edited by Morris Adler and Lily Edelman (New York: Taplinger, 1965), pp. 201, 199, 202. For a further discussion of Jewish–Christian relations, see Chapter 8.

ers of the Middle Colonies were zealous in their mission to the Indians. Accordingly, every Royal Charter contained some reference to saving the "savages" from their dark and fallen state. Spain's Charles V, in issuing the 1523 patent for Florida, claimed that the "principal intent in the discovery of new lands is that the inhabitants thereof, who are without the light or knowledge of faith, may be brought to understand the truths of our holy Catholic faith, that they may come to a knowledge thereof and become Christians and be saved."[18] Plymouth's charter called for "the conversion of such savages as yet remain wandering in desolation and distress to civil society and the Christian religion." And the Massachusetts Bay patent enjoined every citizen of that colony to win the Indians "to the knowledge and obedience of the only true God and Savior of mankind," which, to say the least, gave short shrift to native deities.[19] Though it is clear that motives for emigrating to the New World were not always unambiguously religious (there were economic and political motives as well), there is no denying that a very strong missionary impulse lay behind most colonization projects. Schools were established to educate the "savage," and mission posts were often established next to Indian settlements. The subsequent history of the whites' harsh treatment of the natives is, of course, a long and dreary chapter in American history. But one must recall that the Christians sincerely believed they were merely fulfilling the biblical injunction by sharing their "superior" culture and religion with the "ignorant" Indians. Though this kind of rationalization does not serve as an excuse, it does explain how and why certain decisions were made. As they attempted to form the model community for themselves, the Christians also sought to impose the same model upon the Indians. Cotton Mather (1663–1728), in his *Magnalia Christi Americana*, recorded how John Eliot founded and helped to structure the Indian town of Natick along biblical lines:

> Here it was that in the year 1651 those that had heretofore lived like wild beasts in the wilderness now compacted themselves into a town; and they first applied themselves to forming of their civil government . . . Mr. Eliot on a solemn fast, made a public vow; that seeing these Indians were not prepossessed with any forms of government, he would instruct them into such a form, as we had written in the word of God, that so they might be a people in all things ruled by the Lord. Accordingly he expounded unto them the eighteenth chapter of Exoxus; and then they chose rulers of hundreds, of fifties, of tens. . . .
> The little towns of these Indians being pitched upon this foundation, they utterly abandoned that polygamy which had heretofore been common among them; they made severe laws against fornication, drunkenness, and sabbath-breaking, and other immoralities. . . .
> At length was a church-state settled among them; they entered as our churches do, into an holy convenant, wherein they gave themselves, first unto the Lord,

[18]Quoted by Edwin Scott Gaustad, *A Religious History of America* (New York: Harper & Row, 1966), p. 10.
[19]William Warren Sweet. *The Story of Religion in America* (New York: Harper & Row, 1950), p. 156.

and then unto one another, to attend the rules, and helps, and expect the blessing of the everlasting gospel. . . .[20]

Throughout the rest of the Colonial period, extensive work was carried on among blacks as well as Indians, but with a familiar result: separate religious establishments for them. The denominations, with the exception of Quakers, continued to remain "racially" exclusive. In the
seventeenth century, slaveholders asked whether or not, under English
common law, the status of a slave would be altered by baptism. By answering in the negative, the courts allowed the churches to persist in
their segregated paths. Even so, nearly all blacks and many Indians were
"converted" to Christianity. It was not long, however, before counter-
vailing forces set in. Toward the end of the eighteenth century, two of
the major black denominations had already come into being: the African
Methodist Episcopal Church in 1787 and the African Methodist Episcopal Zion Church in 1796.

At the beginning of the nineteenth century, the first massive missionary effort began. Important as the Colonial era projects had been, they
could not compare in scope or effect with the missions to the frontier
during the National period. Edwin Scott Gaustad writes, "The spiritual
needs of both retreating Indian and advancing white tested the mettle
of every minister and every church. Where it seemed appropriate denominations worked together; where it seemed necessary, they worked
alone."[21] There was now a sense in which the missionary effort could
really be called American for the first time. The nation was a fact. During the Colonial period the Society for the Propagation of the Gospel
and other groups from England supported and actually continued to
supervise missionary activities in the New World. But after the Revolution, there would be no more help from abroad. The American denominations were on their own.

It is also pertinent to note that this great burst of missionary activity
was a direct outgrowth of the Great Awakening. Much of the enthusiasm generated in that surge of religious fervor was directed toward
evangelizing the West. Soon missionary societies were organized along
denominational lines: Congregationalists in Connecticut, Massachusetts,
and New Hampshire; Baptists in Massachusetts, Pennsylvania, Maine,
and New York. These groups not only sent missionaries to the frontier
but frequently sent along enough money to construct schools and
churches. It was common for the parson to be the sole teacher in the
frontier town. Those communities that were not large enough to support a clergyman by themselves would have to share him with nearby
communities. Thus the circuit rider or touring minister became a familiar figure in the West.

As the nation grew and the magnitude of the challenge presented by

[20]Ibid., p. 157.
[21]Gaustad, op. cit., p. 165.

the frontier came to be appreciated, some of the missionary groups consolidated their efforts in order to have a more efficient operation. Denominational leaders were also struck by the contradiction of churches competing for the salvation of souls—a basic conflict with the Christian conviction that the Body of Christ is one and indivisible.

In 1801 a Plan of Union was entered into by Congregationalists and Presbyterians, with the hope that their combined resources could make a greater impact on the new settlements in the West. This step opened the way for other mergers, and a number of new groups were soon formed: the American Bible Society (1816), the American Sunday School Union (1824), and the American Home Mission Society (1826). These and other organizations, which had local groups as predecessors, were effective structures for more concentrated action on the frontier. Sectarian divisiveness was mitigated and a national missionary strategy adopted. In 1825 one theological student noted that America needed a missionary system "which shall have no sectional interests, no local prejudices, no sectarian views; a system which shall bring the most remote parts of our nation into cordial cooperation, awaken mutual interest in the same grand and harmonious design, produce a new feeling of brotherhood, and thus bind us all together by a new cord of union."[22] The nonsectarian character of the missionary societies was entirely consistent with the nonsectarian character expressed by the leaders of the First and Second Awakenings.

It soon became evident that the missionary activity of the churches could not be confined to the national boundaries. New England whalers had fished in the great waters of the South Pacific, and clipper ships brought back news from the Orient.

In 1810 the American Board of Commissioners for Foreign Missions (A.B.C.F.M.) was established when a group of students at Andover Theological Seminary decided to offer themselves for Christian service in India. Among them was Adoniram Judson (1788–1850), who subsequently worked on a translation of the Bible into Burmese, and Luther Rice (1783–1836), who eventually returned to America and raised large sums of money for Baptist work in Asia.

In 1817 Episcopalians and others under the leadership of William Holland Wilmer (1782–1827) of Alexandria formed the American Colonization Society, one of the more unusual groups in the history of missions. Their plan was to repatriate manumitted slaves to Africa where they could create a Christian state from which the rest of the so-called dark continent would be converted to Christ. The first freedman arrived in Africa in 1822, and by 1860 over 11,000 had been repatriated.

The result of this effort was the establishment of the modern nation of Liberia, which remains nominally Christian to this day. In 1832 the project was dealt a severe blow when William Lloyd Garrison denounced

<hr />

[22] Ibid., p. 167.

it as a device to strengthen the institution of slavery. Only the more conservative members of the churches continued to support it.

In 1819 seven young Congregational families under the leadership of Hiram Bingham left Boston for the Hawaiian Islands, where they erected a highly successful mission to the Polynesian tribes. By 1850 the New Englanders were joined by a group of Mormons, whose religion grew rapidly in the Islands.[23] English soon became the dominant language, and by 1863 Hawaii was considered "home missions" by the A.B.C.F.M.

Essentially the same story could be repeated for many other locales. American missionaries fanned out over the globe and established themselves in the remotest outposts in order to save the "heathen" from their errors. Sidney Mead has commented,

> It was the idea of destiny which added "the inducements of philanthropy to those of patriotism" in the American mind and broadened the idea of progress and its laws to include all of humanity. America's destiny came to be seen as her call to spread the amazing benefits of the American democratic faith and its free-enterprise system throughout the world, gradually transforming the world into its own image.[24]

The American overseas effort did not reach its peak, however, until the end of the century. As soon as the guns of the Civil War were silenced, the reunited nation threw itself headlong into industrial and commercial development. The war itself had spurred technological change. American entrepreneurs established markets in Latin America, Africa, and the Far East. Successive national administrations worked diligently to negotiate trade agreements favorable to the burgeoning American economy. As always, military support followed commercial interest, and the nation soon found itself embroiled in political disputes that erupted in various parts of the world. Spanish policies in the Caribbean and the Philippines were particularly odious and led the United States to engage in a brief but successful war with Spain. As a result of the conflict, Cuba was freed from Spanish domination, but Guam, the Philippines, and Puerto Rico were claimed as possessions by the United States. Hawaii was also annexed at this time, so that what had begun primarily as a religious "conquest" in the Pacific ended in territorial acquisition. During the same period, American military power was exerted in order to pry open the business door to China and other parts of the Far East. Justification for American intervention was explained by President McKinley:

> I am not ashamed to tell you, gentlemen, that I went down on my knees and prayed Almighty God for light and guidance more than one night. And one night late it came to me this way. . . . There was nothing left for us to do but to take

[23] See Chapter 4 for a sketch of the Church of Jesus Christ of Latter-day Saints.
[24] Sidney E. Mead, *The Lively Experiment* (New York: Harper & Row, 1963), p. 152.

them all and to educate the Filipinos and uplift and civilize and Christianize them, and by God's grace do the very best we could by them, as our fellow men for whom Christ also died.[25]

There were segments of the American ecclesial establishment that opposed the expansionist policies of the government, but there were few who could tolerate reports of the cruel policies of the Spanish. It was fairly easy, then, to rationalize the war once it got underway. The *Christian Advocate* published a fairly typical editorial in the spring of 1898 that said, in part,

> As long as the war was not declared, any citizen without exposing himself to just imputation of his patriotism, could oppose it and urge strenuously in favor of a favorable use of peaceful arts of diplomacy. But war having been resolved upon . . . loyalty to the country now requires every citizen to support "the powers that be.". . . Public attempts to show that the war was ill-advised and unnecessary are now out of place.[26]

At the same time, Catholic bishops issued a pastoral letter that decried war but pledged to help "liberate the suffering Cubans and Filipinos":

> We, the members of the Catholic Church, are true Americans and as such are loyal to our country and our flag, and obedient to the highest degrees and the supreme authority of the nation, and it calls upon the faithful to beg the God of battles to crown their arms on land and sea with victory and triumph, to stay unnecessary effusion of blood, and speedily to restore peace by glorious victory for our flag.[27]

During this period, when the nation flexed its military muscle on the international scene, religious leaders were sending more men and material into the foreign mission field. As we have seen, many religious leaders agreed with the sentiments expressed by Josiah Strong in his tract for the times, *Our Country* (1885): America's duty to other peoples throughout the world was to share its "superior" Anglo-Saxon brand of religion.

In the summer of 1886, Dwight L. Moody, the prominent urban evangelist of the nineteenth century, called a meeting of college students at his conference center in Northfield, Massachusetts. Stirred by Moody's challenge, the students left Northfield in a great state of excitement, returned to their own colleges, and within two years had enlisted more than two thousand volunteers for overseas work. Two years later, the Student Volunteer Movement was officially established. This remarkable organization grew rapidly and within a fifty-year span sent sixteen thousand volunteers into the foreign mission field.

Among those who responded to Moody's call was John Raleigh Mott

---

[25] Quoted by Winthrop S. Hudson, *Religion in America* (New York: Scribner, 1965), p. 318.
[26] Quoted by Sweet, op. cit., p. 357.
[27] Ibid., pp. 357–358.

(1865–1955), a young man who soon became one of the most gifted leaders of the foreign missions movement. His interest in overseas work was of long standing. After graduating from Cornell, he became secretary of the International Committee of the Y.M.C.A. and later became general secretary of the World Student Christian Federation, an organization for which he was largely responsible. He is best known, however, for his lifelong leadership in the Student Volunteer Movement. Throughout his life, he propagandized on behalf of missions, wrote a number of books on the subject, and made popular one of the more memorable slogans for foreign work: "The Evangelization of the World in Our Generation." He was convinced that, as Christ had come in the fullness of time, so the twentieth century was also a providentially significant time. Modern technology offered the churches the tools of communication with which the entire world could be Christianized. The following selection amply illustrates his enthusiasm for his subject and the sparkling optimism that infused the nation prior to World War I.

Document 41

From *The Decisive Hour of Christian Missions* by John R. Mott

Possibilities of the Present Situation

It is apparent that the situation in the non-Christian world is of such an urgent and critical character as to demand far greater consecration and effort on the part of the Christian Church. It is also clear, that the Church, with the assured manifestation of the power of God, can, by adequate planning, by the creation of a strong home base, and by the development of efficient forces on the mission field, meet the present unique situation. The possibilities of triumphant success resulting from a worthy advance by the Church, and the possibilities of grave consequences which would result from a failure to improve the wonderful opportunity, are such as to demand the most serious consideration.

In the first place, there is the possibility of carrying the Gospel to all the non-Christian world. It is possible so far as the accessibility and open-mindedness of the inhabitants of the non-Christian world are concerned. The non-Christian world is known to-day as it never has been before. The work of exploration has been comprehensive, thorough, and, so far as the inhabited parts of the world are concerned, is practically completed. The whole world is remarkably accessible. Improved means of communication have within the past two decades been spread like a network over nearly all the great spaces of the unevangelized world, or are to-day being projected over these regions. For example, railway lines are being rapidly extended in different sections of Africa, in the Levant, in Central Asia, in the Chinese Empire, and in the more populous parts of the East Indies, giving missionaries easy access to hundreds of millions of people who could not have been readily reached even one

SOURCE: John R. Mott, *The Decisive Hour of Christian Missions* (New York: Student Volunteer Movement for Foreign Missions, 1910), pp. 221–239.

generation ago. One of the most significant and hopeful facts with reference to
world evangelization is that the vast majority of the people of the non-Christian
nations and races are under the sway, either of Christian governments or of those
not antagonistic to Christian missions. This should greatly facilitate the carrying
out of a comprehensive campaign to make Christ known.

The minds of the people in most countries are more open and favorable to the
wise and friendly approach of the Christian missionaries than at any time in the
past. In Japan . . . there is almost everywhere a readiness to hear and to consider
the Gospel message. . . . The leaders of the nation and other thoughtful men of
Japan are feeling the need of a new moral basis, and many of them are looking to
Christianity to furnish it. Within a half generation ex-territoriality has been done
away with in Japan as a result of the revision of her treaties with Western nations,
thus permitting missionaries to travel, work, and reside in any part of the country.

Almost the whole population of Korea is now ready to listen to the Gospel. The
troubles through which these people are passing are causing them to turn in great
numbers to Christianity for comfort and strength. Contact with the outside world
and the progress of education, as well as the teaching of the missionaries, have
swept away many deep-seated superstitions. The authorities are conciliatory, and in
some cases directly helpful, to the Christian movement.

It is said that in no part of Manchuria is there open hostility to the Gospel. On
the contrary there seems to be marked readiness and willingness to hear and to understand the Christian doctrine. Even in Mongolia the people are more open and responsive to the Gospel appeal than they were a decade ago. In nearly every part of
China there are signs that the solid indifference and the proud aloofness of the past
are giving way. . . . This does not necessarily imply that there is a higher valuation
put upon Christianity, but it does mean that there is certainly less hostility manifested toward its representatives. This is due chiefly to the removal of ignorance,
prejudice and superstition by the dissemination of knowledge, and to the influence
of the lives and teaching of the missionaries.

Owing to the great complexity of the situation on the Indian continent it is difficult to express concisely the situation throughout the whole field. By common consent the masses of outcastes and lower castes are more receptive to-day than ever.
There is scarcely a limit to the numbers who would place themselves under instruction of properly qualified Christian teachers. . . . Here and there thoughtful, earnest,
spiritually-minded Hindus are reading the words of Christ and seeking to understand
Him. If Christian intercourse with these important men could now be multiplied,
large numbers of them would be led into full and open discipleship.

Workers among Moslems in India all testify that their attitude toward Christ and
His people is more friendly and favorable than it was in the last generation. The
Parsees, owing to the increase of education and the friendly work of missionaries,
are more accessible and responsive than they were a few years ago. . . . Notwithstanding the many adverse influences and the more pronounced hostility and opposition in certain quarters, it is undoubtedly true that, taking India as a whole, the
field is more open than it was twenty, or even ten years ago.

Throughout the larger part of the vast African continent there is a great and
pressing opportunity for the presentation of the claims of Christ. In Mohammedan

Africa indeed there is considerable hindrance from government opposition or restrictions. Moslem intolerance has still to be reckoned with among the people, but this intolerance is weakening, and, as the missionaries wisely adapt themselves to the conditions, the way is becoming more and more open. In pagan Africa not only is the way open, but those to whom the way leads are awaiting the arrival of the messengers. We have been unable to learn of any extensive field throughout the great Island World which is absolutely closed to the wise and devoted ambassador of Jesus Christ.

There are multiplied evidences of larger access and freedom for the proclamation of the Gospel to classes of people in Russia and in many parts of Latin Europe and Latin America who hitherto have been without faith in the living Christ.

When has the Christian Church been confronted with such a wide opportunity as the one now before her in the non-Christian world as a whole? As always, opportunity spells responsibility, and this unparalleled openness comes to the Church as a great test and trial of the reality and the living strength of its faith, and of its capacity for comprehensive Christian statesmanship and generalship.

There is the possibility of grave consequences to the Church in Christian lands resulting from its failure to perform its missionary duty. If the Church does not rise to the present situation and meet the present opportunity there will result a hardening of the minds and hearts of its members which will make them unresponsive to God. If the situation now confronting the Church throughout the world does not lead men to larger consecration, and to prompt and aggressive effort, it is difficult to imagine what more God can do to move the Church to perform its missionary duty unless it be to bring upon it some general calamity.

The only thing which will save the Church from the imminent perils of growing luxury and materialism is the putting forth of all its powers on behalf of the world without Christ. Times of material prosperity have ever been the times of greatest danger to Christianity. The Church needs a supreme world-purpose—a gigantic task, something which will call out its energies, something which will throw it back upon God. This desideratum is afforded by the present world-wide missionary opportunity and responsibility. To be able to lay hold in particular of the lives of the strongest young men and women, the Church must offer them a task of such magnitude as will call forth their heroism. May it not be that God designs that the baffling problem which confronts Christianity in the non-Christian world shall constitute the school for disciplining the faith and strengthening the character of His followers? To preserve the pure faith of Christianity, a world-wide plan and conquest are necessary. This lesson is convincingly taught on the pages of Church history. The concern of Christians to-day should not be lest non-Christian people refuse to receive Christ, but lest they, in failing to communicate Him, will themselves lose Him.

Above all there is the possibility of the enrichment of the Church. The movement to carry forward an enterprise to make Christ known to all mankind will inevitably widen the horizon and sympathies of the Church. It will be impossible to plan and wage a world-wide campaign without being enlarged by the enterprise itself. The life of the Church depends upon its being missionary. Revivals of missionary devotion and of spiritual life have ever gone hand in hand. The missionary activities of the Church are the circulation of its blood, which would lose its vital power if it never flowed to the extremities. The missionary problem of the Church to-day is not primarily a financial problem, but is that of ensuring a vitality equal to the imperial expansion of the missionary programme. The only hope of this is for Christians to avail themselves of the more abundant life through Christ bestowed in the pathway of obedience to Him.

It is a decisive hour for the non-Christian nations. Far-reaching movements—national, racial, social, economic, religious—are shaking them to their foundations. These nations are still plastic. Shall they set in Christian or pagan molds? Their ancient faiths, ethical restraints, and social orders are being weakened or abandoned. Shall our sufficient faith fill the void?

It is a decisive hour for the Christian Church. If it neglects to meet successfully the present world crisis by failing to discharge its responsibility to the whole world, it will lose its power both on the home and on the foreign fields and will be seriously hindered in its mission to the coming generation. Nothing less than the adequacy of Christianity as a world religion is on trial.

It is indeed the decisive hour of Christian missions. It is the time of all times for Christians of every name to unite and with quickened loyalty and with reliance upon the living God, to undertake to make Christ known to all men, and to bring His power to bear upon all nations. It is high time to face this duty and with serious purpose to discharge it. . . .

After several decades of feverish activity in the foreign mission field, the nation was drawn into the European conflict of 1914–1918, which, according to President Wilson, was fought to make the world safe for democracy. As Nelson Burr aptly notes, "enthusiam for bringing American democracy to the world in association with missions rose to the character of a crusade in the period of World War I."[28] But after the war, a general malaise set in and people in important places began to question America's involvement in international politics. As isolationism grew in the political sphere, laymen began to wonder about foreign missions. Were they appropriate? Were they even economically viable? Missionary giving steadily declined during this period, and the number of persons taking overseas assignments dropped from 2,700 in 1920 to 252 in 1928.[29] In 1930 the Laymen's Foreign Missions Inquiry was called to investigate the matter, and two years later a report was issued. Financed by John D. Rockefeller, Jr., and chaired by Harvard Philosophy Professor William E. Hocking (1873–1966), the committee members attempted, insofar as possible, to make what they considered to be an objective report. They acknowledged that missions had served a worthy purpose in the past and that they should by all means be continued. But they called for a shift in basic strategy. The churches should not attempt so much to convert others as to provide technical support of

[28] Nelson Burr, *A Critical Bibliography of Religion in America* (Princeton, N.J.: Princeton University Press, 1961), Vol. 4, p. 408.
[29] Hudson, op. cit., p. 373.

various kinds—medical, educational, agricultural. Any sort of charitable act, whether it had specifically religious overtones or not, would be considered a fundamentally Christian act. In its basic presuppositions, the report was a logical expression of the popular liberal theology of the day. Indeed, the committee looked forward to the day when a new worldwide religion would emerge from the amalgamation of the existing great religious traditions.

For the greater part of the nineteenth century, the Catholic Church was so busy attempting to integrate its own immigrants into the mainstream of American life that it had little time for consideration of missions to other lands. Only a handful of American Catholic missionaries had found their way overseas. Besides, America itself had long been the object of missionary efforts by the Congregation for the Propagation of the Faith, the official missionary arm of the Vatican. Indeed, it was not until 1908 that the American Church was removed from the Congregation's jurisdiction.

By the second decade of this century, American Catholics began seriously to turn their interest to overseas work. It is reported that there were an estimated 16 million Catholics in America by 1910 and that financial contributions for overseas work had well passed the $1 million mark. In 1911 two American priests, James Anthony Walsh and Thomas Frederick Price, secured permission from the American archbishops to establish the Catholic Foreign Mission Society and a seminary (Maryknoll) for the purpose of training missionary clergy. In 1918 the first group of missionaries was sent out and it was not long before Maryknoll fathers were found in all parts of the globe. By 1960 over one ninth of all Catholic missionaries, of whatever stripe, in whatever part of the world, were sent out by the American Church, and U.S. Catholic dollars made up the major financial backing for worldwide Catholic missions. The author of the letter below was James Cardinal Gibbons, whose contribution to the proposition that Roman Catholic communicants can be good American citizens was noted in Chapter 2.

Document 42 _____

From "The Launching of the Catholic Foreign Mission Society of America (Maryknoll), March 25, 1911"

To the Most Reverend Archbishops of the United States:
VENERABLE BRETHREN:

I submit to your consideration a plan to establish an American Foreign Mission Seminary.

That such a Seminary is needed, and urgently, seems daily more evident. The

SOURCE: *Documents of American Catholic History*, edited by John Tracy Ellis (Milwaukee, Wis.: Bruce, 1956), pp. 293–296.

prestige of our country has become wide-spread; and Protestants, especially in the Far East, are profiting by it, to the positive hindrance of Catholic missioners. I understand that even the educated classes in China, misled by the almost complete abscence of American Catholic priests, believe that the Church of Rome has no standing in America.

The priests of the United States number more than 17,000 but I am informed that there are hardly sixteen on the foreign missions. This fact recalls a warning which the late Cardinal Vaughan gave in a kindly and brotherly letter addressed to me twenty-two years ago, urging us American Catholics not to delay participation in foreign missions, LEST OUR OWN FAITH SHOULD SUFFER.

We must confess that as a Catholic body we have only begun, while our Protestant fellow-countrymen have passed the century mark in foreign mission work and are represented today in the heathen world by some thousands of missioners, who are backed by yearly contributions running up into the millions.

A seminary, such as that contemplated, if established with the good-will of the entire American Hierarchy, can hardly fail to draw, emphatically, the attention of American Catholics. . . .

With pleasure, therefore . . . I submit the following outline of the plan, secured after conference with those immediately interested:

It is proposed to establish an American Foreign Mission Seminary for the training of secular priests.

This Seminary, like those of Paris, London (Mill Hill), Milan, et al., would necessarily be independent of any diocese, and directly under Propaganda, which would control its status, rules, etc., and apportion its fields of labor.

It would be national in its character, organized and sustained by priests of the United States, guided, of course, by the best traditions of similar institutions abroad. It would appeal to young men reared in this country.

It is proposed to begin the work on a small scale, near some established house of Catholic philosophy and theology. It would seek its PERMANENT home, well removed from the heart of city life, gradually securing its own professors, and developing an exclusively apostolic atmosphere. No definite location is suggested, although a preference has been expressed by the organizers for a center reasonably convenient to the more populous Catholic zones and, if possible, not too far removed from those states in which a knowledge of foreign missions has already been cultivated.

It is expected that Preparatory Colleges will be needed, to serve later as feeders to the Seminary.

Two priests are immediately concerned in this undertaking, to which they are willing to devote their lives—Rev. James Anthony Walsh of Boston and Rev. Thomas F. Price of North Carolina.

Fr. Walsh is a priest of the Boston Archdiocese. He was ordained in 1892, and the late revered Archbishop Williams appointed him, more than eight years ago,

Diocesan Director for the Propagation of the Faith. . . . He also directs the Catholic Foreign Mission Bureau, editing THE FIELD AFAR and issuing other publications bearing on the subject of foreign missions.

Fr. Price has spent twenty-five years in difficult mission work. He is the Superior of the Apostolate of Secular Priests of North Carolina and editor of the magazine, TRUTH.

. . . these two priests, having secured the encouragement of the Hierarchy, shall, with the permission of their Bishops, visit without delay the most important foreign mission Seminaries and apply in person to Rome for the authorization necessary to start.

Returned with proper credentials, they would aim to carry out, with the approval of the individual Bishops, the following plan:

a) To secure spiritual aid, asking prayers and Communions from seminaries, religious houses of men and women, institutions, etc., etc.

b) To spread a knowledge of the missions, by means of conference and illustrated talks and by an output of mission literature.

c) To seek material support, chiefly by increasing the subscription list of THE FIELD AFAR, which has already a wide circle of interested and generous readers among the clergy and laity.

It is my purpose to ask the Most Reverend Archbishops at our next meetings:

1. If they will commend the proposed idea.
2. In the event of their favorable consideration, if they will fix, or at least suggest, one or more desirable locations from which a choice might be made, both for a provisional and for a permanent Seminary.

I would, therefore, ask the Most Reverend Archbishops to discuss with their suffragans this proposed schema, that the views and suggestions of all the Bishops of the country may be obtained and common understanding arrived at, and our common desire and the united commendation of the Hierarchy be made known to Rome and to the Catholic body of the United States.

Faithfully yours in Christ,
J. Card Gibbons

Feast of the Annunciation [March 25], 1911.

Humanitarianism Today

Lord Bryce wrote of the American people:

In works of active beneficence no country has surpassed, perhaps none equalled, the United States. Not only are the sums collected for all sorts of philanthropic purposes larger relatively to the wealth of America than in any European country, but the amount of personal interest shown in good works and personal effort devoted to them seems to a European visitor to exceed what he knows at home.[30]

There is, of course, no way to prove or disapprove what Lord Bryce said, but it is a fact that philanthropy is one of the biggest industries in the country, much of it either church-connected or having religious impulses at its roots. In 1959 it was estimated that Americans gave over $8 billion for philanthropic projects: to churches, schools, hospitals, and humanitarian enterprises of all descriptions. Of this amount, about $3.96 billion was given directly to church-related agencies. Americans *have* given away a great deal of money. The motives for such giving might be subject to inquiry, but the fact of giving is incontestable.[31] By 1976 the total philanthropic giving had grown from $8 billion to an astonishing $29.42 billion, of which $12.84 billion was given to church-related agencies.[32]

It is extremely difficult, if not impossible, to separate the purely religious from the purely secular in any discussion of American humanitarianism. At no place do the terms *religion* and *secular* seem to be more elastic or more indistinguishable than in the field of philanthropy. There are, it is true, some projects that have begun as broadly "humanitarian" enterprises, with no visible "religious" purpose in mind, such as museums and libraries, but these institutions are lumped together in the popular mind with churches and hospitals as causes worthy of support. Americans have had no difficulty in seeing the Hand of God at work in the most common, ordinary, "secular" places. As long as they improve the lot of mankind, humanitarian projects seem vaguely religious to a good many Americans. As one observer notes, "Those agencies furnish a channel of Christian benevolence and also a vocational outlet for the ideals of a service that Christianity has fostered."[33]

William Clebsch has pointed out that many projects begun under religious auspices later on break all *official* connections with the founding agency. One has only to think of many of the nation's institutions of higher education. According to Clebsch's thesis, they have become "profane"; that is, they have literally gone *pro fanum,* or outside the temple of religion. They no longer exist under the direct supervision or with the sponsorship of the churches; they are on their own, out in the world.[34] But that really does not matter, because Americans by and large do not distinguish carefully between the two realms.

There are, however, many humanitarian programs that a local congregation performs simply by reason of its existence. Some of these

---

[30] James Bryce, *The American Commonwealth* (New York: Macmillan, 1901), p. 723.

[31] Alfred de Grazia and Ted Gurr, *American Philanthropy* (New York: New York University Press, 1961), pp. 95, 99.

[32] Coustant H. Jacquet (ed.), *Yearbook of American Churches 1978* (New York: Council Press, 1978), p. 238.

[33] F. Ernest Johnson, as quoted by de Grazia and Gurr, op. cit., p. 105.

[34] See William A. Clebsch, *From Sacred to Profane America* (New York: Harper & Row, 1968), for a detailed examination of this thesis.

services are rendered informally and without a great deal of planning. For example, the clergy, as professionals—be they priests, rabbis, pastors—often act as psychological counselors or clinicians. Sometimes they have received training for these purposes, but more often they act as therapists, quite unself-consciously, in the casual day-to-day contacts they have with their flock. Just how successful these professionals are is open to debate and has been the subject of considerable study in recent years, but the fact remains that the shepherd of the flock, by virtue of his position in the congregation, is charged to care for the people.

Local parish churches and synagogues may also operate in a variety of social service capacities—as travelers' aid stations, recreation centers, educational institutions, and so on. They may sponsor scout troops and other programs for young people. They look after the sick, the aging, the destitute, and provide vocational guidance for those who request it. They sometimes operate half-way houses for those returning to society after confinement in hospitals, prisons, or other types of rehabilitation centers. Some of the more socially conscious congregations will support programs for relief from drug addiction. During the latter part of the nineteenth century and the early part of the present century, local congregations even went so far as to build gymnasiums, swimming pools, and other recreational facilities in order to "get the children off the streets."

There are, of course, the more centralized offices to which the local congregations contribute support. Every denomination has its own synodical, district, or diocesan agencies that extend services not only to their own members, but frequently to the public at large. One thinks immediately of Catholic hospitals run by religious orders, located in many cities throughout the country, whose policies open their doors to all sick people, irrespective of their religious persuasion—or lack of it. One also thinks of the Anti-Defamation League of B'nai B'rith, originally chartered for the purpose of protecting Jews from prejudice, which has now taken on the cause of Afro-Americans, Chicanos, and any other minority group that suffers prejudice and ill treatment. Many of the denominations, with the help of federal money, now build retirement homes and geriatric ciinics. There are not denominational restrictions at these institutions. The list of projects is almost inexhaustible—summer camps, schools, day-care centers—programs of all kinds, which much of the time cannot be supported by one congregation alone but can be adequately funded and staffed by regional or national ecclesial organizations.

In addition to the exclusively denominational programs, there are many quasireligious programs that receive wide support from churchpersons. The YMCA and YMHA fall into this category. The United Fund, United Jewish Appeal, Community Chest, and Red Feather Agencies, health-related foundations, the Salvation Army, and the

American Red Cross are among the numerous groups to which the average American gives his support year by year.

But the largest single philanthropic agency in America today is the federal government, which in the early 1970s was spending nearly half its better than $200 billion annual budget on various welfare programs. The significance of this fact can be appreciated only when we take into account that the first permanent welfare program was not adopted by the federal government until 1935, when Congress passed the Social Security Act, and that only $8.7 million was being spent on public welfare programs of various sorts in 1940.[35] By fiscal year 1978 the federal budget had more than doubled—to $458 billion. In that budget, it was estimated that 38 cents out of every dollar would go to "direct benefit payments to individuals." Add to this massive federal program those programs developed by state and local governments, and one can gain an appreciation for the magnitude of America's dedication to assisting those in need.

Although many would argue about the effectiveness of governmental aid, the principle point to note here is that philanthropy has not been left to the churches or private secular agencies to perform by themselves. The federal government today is handling many of the programs that were at one time administered almost exclusively by the churches.

Some of the most ardent supporters of social legislation during the last several decades have been religious leaders who have looked on the New and Fair Deal social legislation as secularized versions of the biblical injunction to love and care for one's neighbor.

Catholics, for example, were told by the redoubtable John Ryan in the 1930s that the New Deal was entirely consistent with the Church's teaching because it promoted the general welfare:

> The general policy of greatly increased governmental regulation and assistance is constitutionally justifiable and morally right. The particular policies are on the whole ethically sound: they are morally right. . . . Never before in our history have the policies of the federal government embodied so much legislation that is of a highly ethical order. Never before in our history have government policies been so deliberately, formally and consciously based upon conceptions and convictions of moral right and social justice.[36]

Among more politically conservative religious leaders today, however, a reaction has set in against philanthropy by government. William G. McLoughlin tells how some popular Protestant leaders have sought to "curtail" and even "dismantle" governmental welfare projects:

> These Protestants abetted attacks upon the TVA ("creeping socialism"), the social security act (taxing the provident to aid the improvident), and the income

---

[35] Robert Morris (ed.), *Encyclopedia of Social Work* (New York: National Association of Social Workers, 1971), Vol. II, p. 1584.

[36] Quoted by David J. O'Brien, *American Catholics and Social Reform: The New Deal Years* (New York: Oxford University Press, 1968), p. 136.

tax (which denied Andrew Carnegie's claim that the men who made millions were the men best able to distribute them as God's stewards). Norman Vincent Peale's best-selling books rephrased the American success myth in pseudopsychological and sociological terms. . . . Equating Protestantism with laissez faire economics. . . . Peale joined Billy Graham and other conservative ministers in writing for *Christian Economics,* a magazine subsidized by wealthy Protestant laymen and devoted to returning the United States to free enterprise of the Manchester School. "Let the churches speak up for capitalism," said Peale in a typical essay reprinted for millions in *The Reader's Digest* in 1953.

. . . Graham's Sunday afternoon broadcasts stridently denounced the deficit spending of the Roosevelt administration and the "giveaway" foreign aid programs of the Truman administration. In reference to American aid to underdeveloped nations, he declared. "Their greatest need is not more money, food, or even medicine, it is Christ. . . Give them the Gospel of love and grace first and they will clean themselves up, educate themselves, and better their economic condition." Graham insisted that one CARE package did more good than millions spent on the Marshall Plan or Point Four Programs because it represented voluntary, person-to-person charity rather than bureaucratic government assistance.[37]

But today's liberal and conservative, if we may use these elusive labels for a moment, did not suddenly appear on the scene; they are descendants of distinguished forerunners in American religion, dating back to the earliest colonial days.

The Origin and Development of Humanitarianism

John Winthrop, in his *Model for Christian Charity* (1630), set forth two basic principles for the new society he founded at Massachusetts Bay: covenant and stewardship. Though these principles were by no means peculiar to Winthrop, his essay does provide a striking glimpse into the colonial attitude toward philanthropy.

By "covenant," Winthrop meant that citizens of New England were bound to one another because they were first bound to God. The covenant was a compact made and cemented by the action of God. It was *not* a kind of social contract that could be entered into at will, as the eighteenth-century rationalists were later to theorize. Rather, the Puritans believed that God had deliberately called them out of the decaying Old World into a new relationship with Him in the New World, a relationship in which He was to be their God and they His people. The model was the Israel of old.

Within the covenantal community, there were no clear distinctions between church and society. All who were members of the church were thereby fully enfranchised citizens of the civil order, but insofar as the Puritans did make a distinction between church and state, the church was assigned the responsibility for seeing that the First Table of the Ten Commandments was obeyed. Those commandments define man's rela-

[37]William G. McLoughlin, "Changing Patterns of Protestant Philanthropy," *The Religious Situation: 1969,* edited by Donald R. Cutler (Boston: Beacon Press, 1969), pp. 599–600.

tionship to God. The state was charged with overseeing the Second Table, the commandments that define man's relationship with man. And in their reading of the Second Table, the Puritans believed that no one, except possibly the heretic, was unworthy of community support in time of need.

This form of government naturally turned out to be a socially conservative system in that the various strata of society were assumed to have been divinely ordered. Although everyone might ultimately be equal in the eyes of God, He nevertheless assigned each person to his station according to a preconceived plan. The Puritan Fathers therefore naturally developed a sense of *noblesse oblige,* because their positions required them to care for those persons less fortunate than they. It also encouraged a spirit of submission to authority among the less fortunate: because God had placed them in a subservient position, they should be satisfied to follow the wisdom of their rulers. Rich and poor, learned and unlearned, male and female, ruler and ruled were all bound together in the well-structured convenantal community, which meant that early on in American life, certain men were the divinely appointed philanthropists for their fellow citizens who, because of a quirk in God's plan, happened to be in need of some kind of assistance.

It is well known, as McLoughlin points out, "that the Puritans very soon after their arrival in the wilderness passed laws requiring each town to establish public schools paid for by taxation and open to all inhabitants."[38] They believed education to be but one more means of opposing Satan's wily devices. Through education one would be much better equipped to understand God's plan for the holy community. Accordingly, John Harvard (1607–1638) in 1638 bequeathed his library and half his estate to a newly founded school in the town of Cambridge.

In the Puritan mind the biblical idea of stewardship was coupled with the idea of the covenant. The doctrine of stewardship held that God had given to His faithful servants a special charge to oversee not just their own material possessions, but the Lord's vineyard (in their case, New England) in its entirety. In other words, the Puritans believed themselves to be responsible for the well-being of the whole commonwealth. It comes as no surprise, then, to learn that they designed for themselves a highly regulated society. Wages and prices were set, production quotas assigned, commerce carefully managed, interest rates controlled. Thus, the Puritans, in the earliest days of the nation's history, wrote two basic themes into the script of American philanthropy: covenant and stewardship. They have been reiterated countless times.

The next stage in the development of American philanthropy grew out of the two major movements that swept America during the eighteenth century, the Great Awakening and the Enlightenment: the two figures who best represent these movements for our present discussion are George Whitefield and Benjamin Franklin.

[38] Ibid., p. 553. Much of this section is indebted to McLoughlin's very fine essay.

Whitefield, it will be recalled, set fire to thousands of cold hearts up and down the Atlantic seaboard in his 1739 trip to the colonies. For decades the churches had been gradually losing touch with the people. Then, as we all know, Whitefield and others, through their spectacularly successful preaching, were able to correct the deteriorating situation. But in our eagerness to tell the story of revivalism, we sometimes forget one of the most important ingredients in Whitefield's program: the orphanage in Georgia. Along with his first aim of converting human souls to Christ, the fiery young preacher solicited monies for a school in Savannah. He repeatedly appealed to his bearers for their support, and his *Journals* are filled with accounts of their generosity. Rich and poor alike supported his projects.

But the orphanage itself was not nearly so important as the principle it represented. A fundamental premise of revivalism was that there must be some outward expression of the sinner's inward experience. That is why the tears and the moaning and shouting were accepted as "proof" that something had occurred within the hearts and minds of the newly converted sinners. Jonathan Edwards and other theologians of the movement explained in their treatises on the subject that the great value of "experimental" or experiential religion lay precisely in the fact that one could literally *see* the effects of conversion. Thus, philanthropy or sharing one's material wealth with others was accepted as tangible evidence that one had been touched by the appeals of the preacher.

A second and correlative principle at work in revivalism may be filed under the heading of voluntarism. Whereas the seventeenth-century Puritans of Massachusetts Bay had legislated philanthropy, Whitefield and the Awakeners made it a voluntary matter. It is too pat, of course, to attribute the origins of voluntary giving solely to the Great Awakening, but it is not too much to say that voluntarism became permanently institutionalized in American life through the Awakening. Privilege and establishment were dealt a blow from which they could never recover, and voluntary association became the pattern for American religious institutional membership. Indeed, the whole idea of church *membership* originated at this time. Prior to the eighteenth century, one did not choose to belong to one denomination or another, because there were not any. Nor did one choose, prior to this time, to support financially one voluntary group or another. One simply functioned as an English citizen who also supported the church (through taxes) because one was English. There were, of course, dissenters, but even they were compelled, by law, to support the establishment.

The Great Awakening changed all that. Though Whitefield was ostensibly a Calvinist, admittedly a conservative brand of Christianity, his Calvinism functioned only insofar as it convinced him that all people were sinners and in dire need of the Gospel. But he was also convinced that all could receive the good news, *if* they would but repent. No one, by virtue of church membership, was assured of salvation. Indeed, the nominal and lukewarm character of institutionalized religion worried Whitefield more than anything else. A great democratic streak ran through his preaching as he called upon people of all ranks and stations in life to turn back and be saved. Thus, the aristocracy inherent in Calvinism gave way to the democracy implicit in the voluntary religion that he preached, for *anyone* could prove the sincerity of his or her conviction simply by a voluntary act.

At the same time the Awakeners called for philanthropy as a proof of religious conversion, rationalists like Benjamin Franklin were busy soliciting funds from the general public on other grounds. Franklin held that one person's duty to another was based on natural law, that all men are brothers and hence must share in the *common*wealth. He appealed to common sense and to what he thought was the innate good in everyone. It is prudent, he would say, to repair the social fabric by caring for the destitute and the down and out, for it indirectly improves one's own lot. Accordingly, McLoughlin correctly observes that Whitefield's approach was basically "theocratic, otherworldly, spiritual," and Franklin's was "anthropocentric, utilitarian, rational." This does not mean that Franklin's approach was radically secular. A kind of attenuated Calvinism lurked in his background, which gave his kind of benevolence a religious cast, even if it was a Calvinsim in which "pietism and fervor [had been] replaced by utility and prudence." [39]

Typical of the humanitarian project of the rationalist was the Pennsylvania Hospital, founded in 1751–1752 by Franklin and a Philadelphia physician, Thomas Bond. The first general hospital in America, the story of its beginning is also an appropriate illustration of the cooperative effort of public and private funding, a pattern that has extended to the present day. When Bond was not able to raise enough money among voluntary subscribers, he turned for help to Franklin and the Pennsylvania Assembly. Rural legislators were reluctant at first to support a project that was designed primarily to benefit the city but finally agreed to contibute £2,000 if Franklin could match the sum with voluntary subscriptions. Franklin accepted the challenge and succeeded in raising the additional £2,000 voluntarily and the project was under way. The example was followed in other cities eventually, the most notable of which was Massachusetts General in Boston (1811).

The type of humanitarianism embraced by Franklin and other eighteenth-century rationalists flourished during the next century and has persisted until today. However, the greater portions of nineteenth-century humanitarian projects were begun and carried on by the descendants of Whitefield—the "evangelicals," [40] as they were called. Leaders of the Second Awakening, men like Charles Grandison Finney and Ly-

[39] Ibid., pp. 560–561.
[40] *Evangelical* is a technical term that refers roughly to the tradition in Protestantism that places great emphasis on personal religious experience. It is closely identified with revivalism in American religious history.

man Beecher, operated on the premise that a sincere faith must issue in some kind of voluntary good work. As one scholar has explained,

> the revival campaigns of the Second Awakening stressed a doctrine of "disinterested benevolence" . . . as the key to Christian social responsibility. Sin was defined as including "selfishness," and the effect of conversion was to shift "the controlling preference of the mind" from a "preference of self interest" to a "preference for disinterested benevolence." If one's conversion was genuine, it was insisted, this shift in the preference of the mind would express itself in action. The conversion experience, therefore, was not the end of the Christian life but only its beginning. Working was quite as necessary as believing and working meant participating fully in every good cause.[41]

The committed Christian was therefore challenged by the preaching of the day to prove his conversion by supporting any of the great voluntary societies that surfaced during the nineteenth century: the American Education Society (1815), the American Tract Society (1825), the American Society for the Promotion of Temperance (1826), the American Peace Society (1828), the American Anti-Slavery Society (1833), and others. Redemption was no longer God's business alone; He required, and got from the evangelicals, human assistance.[42]

The Unitarian William Ellery Channing explained the importance of the voluntary way to American life:

> In truth, one of the most remarkable circumstances or features of our age, is the energy with which the principle of combination, or of action by joint forces, by associated numbers, is manifesting itself. It may be said, without much exaggeration, that every thing is done now by societies. Men have learned what wonders can be accomplished in certain cases by union, and seem to think that union is competent to every thing. You can scarcely name an object for which some institution has not been formed. Would men spread one set of opinions, or crush another? They make a society. Would they improve the penal code, or relieve poor debtors? They make societies. Would they encourage agriculture, or manufactures, or science? They make societies. Would one class encourage horse-racing, and another discourage traveling on Sunday? They form societies. We have immense institutions spreading over the country, combining hosts for particular objects. We have minute ramifications of these societies, penetrating everywhere except through the poorhouse, and conveying resources from the domestic, the laborer, and even the child, to the central treasury. The principle of association is worthy the attention of the philosopher, who simply aims to understand society, and its most powerful springs. To the philanthropist and the Christian it is interesting, for it is a mighty engine, and must act either for good or for evil, to an extent which no man can foresee or comprehend.[43]

[41] Hudson, op. cit., p. 152.

[42] Though one could by no stretch of the imagination include Catholics as participants in the Second Awakening, they were not unaffected by the mood of the era. In 1809 Mother Elizabeth Bayley Seton established the order of the Sisters of Charity of St. Joseph, and in 1845 Catholic laymen called the first American conference of the Society of St. Vincent de Paul.

[43] Quoted by Robert T. Handy, "The Voluntary Principle in Religion and Religious Freedom in America." *Voluntary Associations: A Study of Groups in Free Societies*, edited by D. B. Robertson (Richmond: John Knox Press, 1966), p. 133.

Thus early-nineteenth-century Americans looked with great confidence toward the nation's future because they believed so strongly in the power of benevolence. Finney not only called for the conversion of individual men and women but also fervently proclaimed the imminent transformation of the nation as a whole. In 1835 he declared, "If the Church will do her duty, the millennium may come in this country in three years."[44] In short, God would create a world without poverty, crime, illness, or war—with the help of the faithful. Needless to say, traditional Calvinism was being significantly modified when a religious leader could attribute such power to men.

Lyman Beecher was skeptical at first of Finney's sensational revival methods, but he changed his mind when he began to appreciate the magnitude of Finney's accomplishments. Beecher readily adopted the "new measures" for himself and became an exceedingly effective revivalist. Like Finney, he had great hopes for transforming the young nation, which was, "in the providence of God, destined to lead the way in the moral and political emancipation of the world."[45] So convinced was Beecher that he left Connecticut and a highly successful ministry there to become president of the newly founded Lane Theological Seminary in Cincinnati, where he hoped to raise up an indigenous ministry for the frontier. But Lane was only one of dozens of colleges and seminaries formed as a result of the Second Awakening, some of which still operate today: Washington & Jefferson (1802), Centre (1823), Wabash (1824), Lafayette (1826), Davidson (1837), [Case-] Western Reserve (1826), Colgate (1817), George Washington (1821), Furman (1826), Mercer (1833), Wake Forest (1834), DePauw (1837), Emory (1836), Gettysburg (1832), Franklin & Marshall (1836), Hobart (1822), Trinity (1833), and Kenyon (1824).

These institutions could be formed because voluntarism had attained full maturity by this time. Men like Lyman Beecher during the first several decades of the nineteenth century were able to channel the converted good wills of thousands of Americans into benevolent projects. Winthrop Hudson, in writing about the voluntary societies, notes that they came into their own when Congregationalism was finally disestablished in New England:

> This was particularly true after 1818 when the fight to save the establishment in Connecticut was lost, thus permitting Lyman Beecher—the real architect of the voluntary system in America—to devote his full attention to transforming the societies into a "a gigantic religious power," thoroughly "systematized" and "compact" in organization.[46]

Beecher's eloquence and genius, his millennial hopes and personal aspirations, are nowhere more graphically displayed than in his *Plea for*

[44] Quoted by Gaustad, op. cit., p. 151.
[45] Ibid.
[46] Hudson, op. cit., p. 152.

the West, a euphoric plan for channeling the entire humanitarian impulse of America into the frontier. Here was another new opportunity for creating the ideal Christian society, and Lane Theological Seminary was to show the way.

Document 43

From *A Plea for the West* by Lyman Beecher

It was the opinion of Edwards, that the millennium would commence in America. When I first encountered this opinion, I thought it chimerical: but all providential developments since, and all the existing signs of the times, lend corroboration to it. But if it is by the march of revolution and civil liberty, that the way of the Lord is to be prepared, where shall the central energy be found, and from what nation shall the renovating power go forth? What nation is blessed with such experimental knowledge of free institutions, with such facilities and rescources of communication, obstructed by so few obstacles, as our own? There is not a nation upon earth which, in fifty years, can by all possible reformation place itself in circumstances so favorable as our own for the free unembarrassed application of physical effort and pecuniary and moral power to evangelize the world. . . .

It is equally plain that the religious and political destiny of our nation is to be decided in the West. There is the territory, and there soon will be the population, the wealth, and the political power. The Atlantic commerce and manufactures may confer always some peculiar advantage on the East. But the West is destined to be the great central power of the nation, and under heaven, must affect powerfully the cause of free institutions and the liberty of the world.

The West is a young empire of mind, and power, and wealth, and free institutions, rushing up to giant manhood, with a rapidity and a power never before witnessed below the sun. And if she carries with her the elements of her preservation, the experiment will be glorious—the joy of the nation—the joy of the whole earth, as she rises in the majesty of her intelligence and benevolence, and enterprise, for the emancipation of the world.

It is equally clear, that the conflict which is to decide the destiny of the West, will be a conflict of institutions for the education of her sons, for purposes of superstition, or evangelical light; of despotism, or liberty. . . .[47]

1. The thing required for the civil and religious prosperity of the West, is universal education, and moral culture, by institutions commensurate to that result—the all-pervading influence of schools, and colleges, and seminaries, and pastors and churches. When the West is well supplied in this respect, though there may be great relative defects there will be, as we believe, the stamina and the vitality of a perpetual civil and religious prosperity.

SOURCE: Lyman Beecher, *A Plea for the West* (Cincinnati: Truman and Smith, 1835), pp. 9–23.

[47] "Superstition" and "despotism" were marks of the Roman Catholic Church in Beecher's mind.

2. By whom shall the work of rearing the literary and religious institutions of the West be done?

Not by the West alone.

The West is able to do this great work for herself—and would do it, provided the exigencies of her condition allowed to her the requisite time. The subject of education is nowhere more appreciated; and no people in the same time ever performed so great a work as has already been performed in the West. Such extent of forest never fell before the arm of man in forty years, and gave place, as by enchantment, to such an empire of cities, and towns, and villages, and agriculture, and merchandise, and manufactures, and roads, and rapid navigation, and schools, and colleges, and libraries, and literary enterprise, with such a relative amount of religious influence, as has been produced by the spontaneous effort of the religious denominations of the West. . . .

But this work of self-supply is not completed, and by no human possibility could have been completed by the West, in her past condition.

No people ever did, in the first generation . . . New England did not. Her colleges were endowed exclusively by foreign munificence, and her churches of the first generation were supplied chiefly from the mother country;—and yet the colonists of New England were few in number, compact in territory, homogeneous in origin, language, manners, and doctrines; and were coerced to unity by common perils and necessities; and could be acted upon by immediate legislation; and could wait also for their institutions to grow with their growth and strengthen with their strength. But the population of the great West is not so, but is assembled from all the states of the Union, and from all the nations of Europe, and is rushing in like waters of the flood, demanding for its moral preservation the immediate universal action of those institutions which discipline the mind, and arm the conscience and the heart. . . . A nation is being "born in a day," and all the nurture of schools and literary institutions is needed, constantly and universally, to rear it up to a glorious and unperverted manhood. . . .

Whence, then, shall the aid come, but from those portions of the Union where the work of rearing these institutions has been most nearly accomplished, and their blessings most eminently enjoyed? And by whom, but by those who in their infancy were aided; and who, having freely received, are now called upon freely to give, and who, by a hard soil and habits of industry and economy, and by experience are qualified to endure hardness as good soldiers and pioneers in this great work? And be assured that those who go to the West with unostentatious benevolence, to identify themselves with the people and interests of that vast community, will be adopted with a warm heart and an unwavering right hand of fellowship.

But how shall this aid be extended to our brethren of the West in the manner most acceptable and efficacious?

Not by prayers and supplications only, nor by charities alone, nor by colonial emigrations: for these, though they might cultivate their own garden, would for obvious reasons be fenced in, and exert but a feeble general influence beyond their own inclosures. Those who go out to do good at the West, should go out to mingle with the people of the West, and be absorbed in their multitude, as rain drops fall on the bosom of the ocean and mingle with the world of waters.

Nor is it by tracts, or Bibles, or itinerating missions, that the requisite intellectual and moral power can be applied. There must be permanent powerful literary and moral institutions, which, like the great orbs of attraction and light, shall send forth at once their power and their illumination, without them all else will be inconstant and ephemeral. Let it not, however, for a moment be supposed, that the schools of the West are to be sustained by the emigration of an army of instructors from the East. For through the present *necessity,* the aid of qualified instructors is not to be repelled, but invited; yet for any permanent reliance, it is but a drop of the bucket to the ocean.

Nothing is more certain, than that the great body of teachers of the West must be educated at the West. It is by her own sons chiefly, that the great work is to be consummated which her civil and literary and religious prosperity demands.

But how shall the requisite supply of teachers for the sons and daughters of the West be raised up? It can be accomplished by the instrumentality of a learned and pious ministry, educated at the West.

Experience has evinced, that schools and popular education, in their best estate, go not far beyond the suburbs of the city of God. All attempts to legislate prosperous colleges and schools into being without the intervening influence of religious education and moral principle and habits of intellectual culture which spring up in alliance with evangelical institutions, have failed. Schools wane, invariably, in those towns where the evangelical ministry is neglected, and the Sabbath is profaned, and the tavern supplants the worship of God. Thrift and knowledge in such places go out, while vice and irreligion come in.

But the ministry is a central luminary in each sphere, and soon sends out schools and seminaries as its satellites by the hands of sons and daughters of its own training. A land supplied with able and faithful ministers, will of course be filled with schools, academies, libraries, colleges, and all the apparatus for the perpetuity of republican institutions. It has always been so—it always will be.

Although their language was liberally sprinkled with millennialist terms, Beecher and other more conservative evangelicals tended to think of Christianity as a means of maintaining social control. For them the benevolent groups—the Bible and tract societies, the education societies, the Sunday school societies—were all means of inculcating the proper values among the masses, especially the more benighted segments of the population. From our perspective, their actions may appear to have been a cynical attempt to manipulate the poor and needy. Such a charge, however, is not altogether fair. Their aims and motives were laudably Christian, if we start with their premises. They simply believed that Christianity, when properly practiced throughout the nation, would lead to God's kingdom on earth. They also believed as firmly as anyone else in a democratic America. They were committed as anyone else to equal opportunity of employment and readily condemned any attempt to exploit working people. But the point is, according to McLoughlin, "they were so firmly convinced that a pious, thrifty, hard-working, honest, frugal man would work his way to the top that they could only assume that those who failed to do so were somehow at fault themselves."[48]

Following the Civil War, three humanitarian movements were imported from England and were assimilated by the great wave of voluntarism that had washed across America. They were the YMCA, the Salvation Army, and the settlement house movement.

The YMCA, established to provide a "home away from home" for rural boys who found their way to the cities, was an offshoot of evangelical Protestantism. Representatives of evangelical churches were usually represented on the boards of directors. Room and board, libraries, game rooms, athletic facilities, lectures, and other "wholesome activities" were provided for the young men in order to protect them from the potentially irreligious and immoral influences of urban life. Sunday school and gospel meetings were regularly scheduled events. Dwight L. Moody raised millions of dollars for the construction of YMCA buildings throughout the country. The Association, as he called it, was influential in his own life as a young man: "I believe in the Young Men's Christian Assocation with all my heart. Under God it has done more in developing me for Christian work than any other agency."[49] Toward the end of the century, at the time when Protestants began their exodus to the suburbs, the mission of the YMCA changed. YMCA centers maintained a tenuous link with evangelical Christianity, but they became less specifically religious and turned their efforts to welfare and education, while maintaining inexpensive hotel and athletic facilities in the midst of the cities.[50]

Jane Addams established Hull House in Chicago in 1889. Because she believed so intensely, as she said, in "the solidarity of the human race," she thought it necessary to expose the college-educated and privileged classes to the deprivations suffered by slum dwellers. In her mind, the problems of poverty, ignorance, and want were not just the problems of the poor but were shared by all members of society. Only as people from all walks of life could learn to live "quietly side by side" would the problems be overcome. Though Hull House supported no particular brand of Protestantism, Miss Addams saw Christianity as "a simple and natural expression in the social organism itself." In keeping with the Quakerism handed down to her by her father, she perceived "a spark of divinity" in each individual and was thereby enabled to give her attention unstintingly to each needy person she met. Edwin Gaustad has written, "Her energies as wide as her sympathies, she threw herself into the battle of social justice, women's rights, civil

---

[48]McLoughlin, op. cit., p. 575.
[49]William R. Moody, *The Life of Dwight L. Moody* (New York: Fleming H. Revell Company, 1900), p. 115.
[50]McLoughlin, op. cit., pp. 586–587.

liberties, child welfare, and international peace—all with unstinted dedication."[51]

General William C. Booth's Salvation Army arrived in America from England as a full-blown movement in the 1880s. The Army's principal aim was to carry the gospel to the "down-and-out" people in the inner city—those who had been abandoned by the standard brand denominations when they fled to the more comfortable suburbs. Unlike the YMCA, which gradually lost its ties with evangelical Christianity, the Salvation Army eventually became one among the myriad sects on the American denominational landscape. As McLoughlin notes, "its theology was no different from evangelicalism though its pietism and fervor were more intense and more dramatic." Although many late-nineteenth-century Americans believed that giving assistance directly to the needy was the height of indiscretion, the Army was always ready to give "food, clothing, and shelter to the poor without trying to ascertain whether they were deserving or the underserving poor." They operated on the twin assumptions that a hungry man had difficulty in hearing any sort of gospel and that "an act of charity was often the best form of evangelism."[52]

At the turn of the century, there were few Americans who believed that certain persons were poor because they deserved to be. Instead, the general supposition was that the poor could be relieved of their suffering and find respectability if they were converted and given a fair opportunity to improve their lot. Moody put it this way:

> It is a wonderful fact that men and women saved by the blood of Jesus rarely remain subjects of charity but rise at once to comfort and respectability. . . . I don't see how a man can follow Christ and not be successful. . . . A heart that is right with God and man seldom constitutes a social problem, and by seeking first the kingdom of God and His righteousness, nine-tenths of social betterment is effected by the convert himself and the other tenth by Christian sympathy.[53]

At the time that Moody and others were making such pronouncements, great industrial fortunes were being amassed and "the captains of industry"—those who had learned successfully to manipulate the massive mechanisms of the economy—appropriated for themselves the rationale put forth by the evangelicals. The John D. Rockefellers and the Andrew Carnegies found what they perceived to be a ready-made explanation for their own successes. They simply took the gospel as preached by the conservative evangelicals, changed its emphasis slightly, and justified their own prodigious accumulations of wealth while devising ways of sharing some of it with others. Although these men were generous in their support of various benevolent causes, they were properly criticized for not grasping the fact that their success was largely re-

[51] Gaustad, op. cit., p. 248.
[52] McLoughlin, op. cit., pp. 587–588.
[53] Quoted in ibid., p. 588.

sponsible for great pockets of poverty throughout the country. Ironically, their gifts were often aimed at alleviating the suffering of the very people at whose expense their great fortunes were made. Carnegie (1835–1919) and Rockefeller, however, gave little direct aid to the poverty-striken masses, because they held that most needy people simply did not know how to help themselves. They furthermore thought that most humanitarian agencies were inefficiently managed. What the agencies required was hardheaded business practice to counter the sentimentality that reigned in the hearts of those who ministered to the poor. As McLoughlin correctly notes, the policies of Rockefeller and Carnegie "constituted a serious reaction from social reform to self help. Or as Carnegie put it more positively, it was a shift from ameliorative reform to preventive reform."[54] They were, however, the architects and founders of the first great American trusts, which to this day play such a significant role in our national life.

Andrew Carnegie, born in Scotland, the child of poverty-striken parents, worked his way up through the Pennsylvania Railroad and after the Civil War entered the steel business. His organization was the forerunner of the giant U.S. Steel Corporation. His ideas on wealth and its management were first published in *The North American Review* in 1889 and later revised for publication in book form as *The Gospel of Wealth*.

_____ *Document 44*

From "Wealth" by Andrew Carnegie

The problem of our age is the proper administration of wealth, so that the ties of brotherhood may still bind together the rich and poor in harmonious relationship. The conditions of human life have not only been changed, but revolutionized, within the past few hundred years. In former days there was little difference between the dwelling, dress, food, and environment of the chief and those of his retainers. The Indians are to-day where civilized man then was. When visiting the Sioux, I was led to the wigwam of the chief. It was just like the others in external appearance, and even within the difference was trifling between it and those of the poorest of his braves. The contrast between the palace of the millionaire and the cottage of the laborer with us to-day measures the change which has come with civilization.

This change, however, is not to be deplored, but welcomed as highly beneficial. It is well, nay, essential for the progress of the race, that the houses of some should be homes for all that is highest and best in literature and the arts, and for all the refinements of civilization, rather than that none should be so. Much better this great

SOURCE: Andrew Carnegie, "Wealth," *The North American Review*, Vol. 391 (June 1889), pp. 653–664.

[54] Ibid., p. 585.

irregularity than universal squalor. . . . The "good old times" were not good old
times. Neither master nor servant was as well situated then as to-day. A relapse to
old conditions would be disastrous to both—not the least so to him who serves—and
would sweep away civilization with it. But whether the change be for good or ill, it
is upon us, beyond our power to alter, and therefore to be accepted and made the
best of. It is a waste of time to criticise the inevitable.

It is easy to see how the change has come. One illustration will serve for almost
every phase of the cause. In the manufacture of products we have the whole story.
It applies to all combinations of human industry, as stimulated and enlarged by the
inventions of this scientific age. Formerly articles were manufactured at the domestic hearth or in small shops which formed part of the household. The master and his
apprentices worked side by side, the latter living with the master, and therefore subject to the same conditions. When these apprentices rose to be masters, there was
little or no change in their mode of life, and they, in turn, educated in the same
routine succeeding apprentices. There was, substantially, social equality, and even
political equality, for those engaged in industrial pursuits had then little or no political voice in the State.

But the inevitable result of such a mode of manufacture was crude articles at high
prices. To-day the world obtains commodities of excellent quality at prices which
even the generation preceeding this would have deemed incredible. In the commercial world similar causes have produced similar results, and the race is benefited
thereby. The poor enjoy what the rich could not before afford. What were the luxuries have become the necessaries of life. The laborer has now more comforts than
the farmer had a few generations ago. The farmer has more luxuries than the landlord had, and is more richly clad and better housed. The landlord has books and
pictures rarer, and appointments more artistic, than the King could then obtain.

The price we pay for this salutary change, is no doubt, great. We assemble
thousands of operatives in the factory, in the mine, and in the counting-house, of
whom the employer can know little or nothing, and to whom the employer is little
better than a myth. All intercourse between them is at an end. Rigid Castes are
formed, and, as usual, mutual ignorance breeds mutual distrust. Each Caste is without sympathy for the other, and ready to credit anything disparaging in regard to it.
Under the law of competition, the employer of thousands is forced into strictest
economics, among which the rates paid to labor figure prominently, and often there
is friction between the employer and the employed, between capital and labor, between rich and poor. Human society loses homogeneity.

The price which society pays for the law of competition, like the price it pays for
cheap comforts and luxuries, is also great; but the advantages of this law are also
greater still, for it is to this law that we owe our wonderful material development,
which brings improved conditions in its train. But, whether the law be benign or
not, we must say of it, as we say of the change in the conditions of men to which
we have referred: It is here; we cannot evade it; no substitutes for it have been
found; and while the law may be sometimes hard for the individual, it is best for
the race, because it insures the survival of the fittest in every department. We accept
and welcome, therefore, as conditions to which we must accommodate ourselves,
great inequality of environment, the concentration of business, industrial and com-

mercial, in the hands of a few, and the law of competition between these, as being not only beneficial, but essential for the future progress of the race. Having accepted these, it follows that there must be great scope for the exercise of special ability in the merchant and in the manufacturer who has to conduct affairs upon a great scale. That this talent for organization and management is rare among men is proved by the fact that it invariably secures for its possessor enormous rewards, no matter where or under what laws or conditions. The experienced in affairs always rate the MAN whose services can be obtained as a partner as not only the first consideration, but such as to render the question of his capital scarcely worth considering, for such men soon create capital; while, without the special talent required, capital soon takes wings. Such men become interested in firms or corporations using millions; and estimating only simple interest to be made upon the capital invested, it is inevitable that their income must exceed their expenditures, and that they must accumulate wealth. Nor is there any middle ground which such men can occupy, because the great manufacturing or commercial concern which does not earn at least interest upon its capital soon becomes bankrupt. It must either go forward or fall behind: to stand still is impossible. It is a condition essential for its successful operation that it should be thus far profitable, and even that, in addition to interest on capital, it should make profit. It is a law, as certain as any of the others named, that men possessed of this peculair talent for affairs, under the free play of economic forces, must, of necessity, soon be in receipt of more revenue than can be judiciously expended upon themselves; and this law is as beneficial for the race as the others.

We start, then, with a condition of affairs under which the best interests of the race are promoted, but which inevitably gives wealth to the few. Thus far, accepting conditions as they exist, the situation can be surveyed and pronounced good. The question then arises—and, if the foregoing be correct, it is the only question with which we have to deal,—What is the proper mode of administering wealth after the laws upon which civilization is founded have thrown it into the hands of the few? And it is of this great question that I believe I offer the true solution. It will be understood that *fortunes* are here spoken of, not moderate sums saved by many years of effort, the returns from which are required for the comfortable maintenance and education of families. This is not *wealth*, but only *competence*, which it should be the aim of all to acquire.

There are but three modes in which surplus wealth can be disposed of. It can be left to the families of the descendents; or it can be bequeathed for public purposes; or, finally, it can be administered during their lives by its possessors. Under the first and second modes most of the wealth of the world that has reached the few has hitherto been applied. Let us in turn consider each of these modes. The first is the most injudicious. In monarchical countries, the estates and the greatest portion of the wealth are left to the first son, that the vanity of the parent may be gratified by the thought that his name and title are to descend to succeeding generations unimpaired. The condition of this class in Europe to-day teaches the futility of such hopes or ambitions. The successors have become impoverished through their follies or from the fall in the value of land. . . . Why should men leave great fortunes to their children? If this is done from affection, is it not misguided affection? Observation teaches that, generally speaking, it is not well for the children that they should be so burdened. . . . Wise men will soon conclude that, for the best interests of the members of their families and of the state, such bequests are an improper use of their means.

As to the second mode, that of leaving wealth at death for public uses, it may be said that this is only a means for the disposal of wealth, provided a man is content to wait until he is dead before it becomes of much good in the world. Knowledge of the results of legacies bequeathed is not calculated to inspire the brightest hopes of much posthumous good being accomplished. . . . Men who leave vast sums in this way may fairly be thought men who would not have left it at all, had they been able to take it with them. The memories of such cannot be held in grateful remembrance, for there is no grace in their gifts. It is not to be wondered at that such bequests seem so generally to lack the blessing.

There remains, then, only one mode of using great fortunes. . . . Under its sway we shall have an ideal state, in which the surplus wealth of the few will become, in the best sense, the property of the many, because administered for the common good, and this wealth, passing through the hands of the few, can be made a much more potent force for the elevation of our race than if it had been distributed in small sums to the people themselves. Even the poorest can be made to see this, and to agree that great sums gathered by some of their fellow-citizens and spent for public purposes, from which the masses reap the principal benefit, are more valuable to them than if scattered among them through the course of many years in trifling amounts.

Poor and restricted are our opportunities in this life; narrow our horizon; our best work most imperfect; but rich men should be thankful for one inestimable boon. They have it in their power during their lives to busy themselves in organizing benefactions from which the masses of their fellows will derive lasting advantage, and thus dignify their own lives.

This, then, is held to be the duty of the man of Wealth: First, to set an example of modest, unostentatious living, shunning display or extravagance; to provide moderately for the legitimate wants of those dependent upon him; and after doing so to consider all surplus revenues which come to him simply as trust funds, which he is called upon to administer, and strictly bound as a matter of duty to administer in the manner which, in his judgment, is best calculated to produce the most beneficial results for the community—the man of wealth thus becoming the mere agent and trustee for his poorer brethren, bringing to their service his superior wisdom, experience, and ability to administer, doing for them better than they would or could do for themselves.

. . . Those who would administer wisely must, indeed, be wise, for one of the serious obstacles to the improvement of our race is indiscriminate charity. It were better for mankind that the millions of the rich were thrown into the sea than so spent as to encourage the slothful, the drunken, the unworthy. Of every thousand dollars spent in so-called charity to-day, it is probable that $950 is unwisely spent: so spent, indeed, as to produce the very evils which it proposes to mitigate or cure. . . .

In bestowing charity, the main consideration should be to help those who will

help themselves; to provide part of the means by which those who desire to improve may do so; to give those who desire to rise the aids by which they may rise;
to assist, but rarely or never to do all. Neither the individual nor the race is improved by almsgiving. Those worthy of assistance, except in rare cases, seldom require assistance. The really valuable men of the race never do, except in cases of
accident or sudden change. Every one has, of course, cases of individuals brought
to his own knowledge where temporary assistance can do genuine good, and these
he will not overlook. But the amount which can be wisely given by the individual
for individuals is necessarily limited by his lack of knowledge of the circumstances
connected with each. He is the only true reformer who is as careful and as anxious
not to aid the unworthy as he is to aid the worthy, and, perhaps, even more so, for
in almsgiving more injury is probably done by rewarding vice than by relieving
virtue.

Thus is the problem of Rich and Poor to be solved. The laws of accumulation
will be left free; the laws of distribution free. Individualism will continue, but the
millionaire will be but a trustee for the poor; intrusted for a season with a great part
of the increased wealth of the community, but administering it for the community
far better than it could or would have done for itself. . . .

Such, in my opinion, is the true Gospel concerning Wealth, obedience to which
is destined some day to solve the problem of the Rich and the Poor, and to bring
"Peace on earth, among men Good-Will."

The attitudes of men like Carnegie were in large measure responsible
for the origin of the social gospel, which took precisely the opposite
tack from the gospel of wealth. Rather than seeking to reform the individual, the leaders of the social gospel sought to reform the society or
environment that had created poverty.

The Social Gospel Today

"Should the churches engage in partisan politics?" "Should they encourage economic boycotts?" "Should they participate in social protests?" Questions such as these are calculated to evoke a hurricane of
feelings among American churchmen today. The debate is a perennial
one and even makes good copy for newspapers and popular magazine
articles. Not too long ago, *U.S. News & World Report* carried a story
entitled, "Should Churches Use Their Funds to Force Social Change?"
The unsigned article detailed the controversy that has been gradually
building up in denominational circles concerning the billions of dollars
in securities and bank accounts owned by the churches. Over the years
dividends from invested capital have helped to operate hospitals,
schools, orphanages, and other social service projects. Well and good.
But now, "activist" clergy and laymen have begun to question the

morality of investing in companies that may directly or indirectly contribute to war efforts, racism, or environmental pollution. They demand that the money be reinvested in so-called clean enterprises or
that the assets even be liquidated and given away. In the four-year period from 1967 to 1971,

Chase Manhattan
- The Mission Board of the United Methodist Church withdrew a
  $10 million investment portfolio from a New York bank that re-
  fused to stop doing business with the Union of South Africa,
  where racial apartheid was practiced.

Kodak
- The leadership of five denominations joined black militants in demanding that a large photographic equipment company change its
  policy in hiring minority workers.

Exxon
- Leaders of the United Presbyterian Church and the United Church
  of Christ lobbied the shareholders and customers of a large oil
  company to cease operations in Angola and Mozambique, where
  colonialism was still practiced by the Portuguese.
- The National Council of the Episcopal Church attempted to persuade a large automobile manufacturer to stop making cars in
  South Africa.

In addition to these, church leaders have raised questions before
stockholders' meetings concerning environmental pollution, the racial
composition of boards of directors, and other issues that might reflect
on what has come to be called "corporate responsibility."

Investments held by Catholic and Jewish bodies have also come in
for close scrutiny by members of those two religious traditions. The
magazine article points out that the Archdiocese of Chicago is reported
to have sold about $30 million worth of shares in a utility that became
involved in an environmental controversy.

Although some of the actions of the churches and synagogues could
only be considered a "nuisance" in the eyes of corporate management,
the potential for making their influence felt is impressive. Authorities
estimated that religious groups in the United States owned between $11
billion and $20 billion of investments of one kind or another.[55] *Should*
the churches use their funds to force social change? In two articles that
appeared in *The Reader's Digest*, Clarence W. Hall argued not. What the
"activists" promote, he said, is not justice but terrorism. He took as his
primary target the World Council of Churches, the large ecumenical
agency that came into being shortly after the end of World War II. The
WCC, according to Hall, "is using church power and church funds to
back insurrection in the United States and Africa." He then asked
rhetorically, "Is this what Christ taught?" To substantiate his claim that
the WCC is fomenting revolution, he cited the WCC's "Programs to
Combat Racism." Although the casual observer might consider it laud-

[55] *U.S. News & World Report*, September 20, 1971, pp. 71-72.

able that black majorities are attempting to "wrest power" from white minorities in Africa, the program is in fact sinister, he said: "Of the 19 beneficiaries, 14 were known to be engaged in guerrilla activities, many of them terrorist. Worse, four of the most generously financed groups are avowedly communist." Hall then enumerated other WCC actions that, in his mind, were of dubious judgement:

- A campaign to raise money for support of American conscientious objectors [then] in Sweden and Canada, or, as Hall calls them, "draft dodgers and deserters."
- A "World Conference on Church and Society," which called for a radical redistribution of wealth and people, styled by the author as "world socialism."
- A consultation on race in London in which it was held that, "if the church is to attack racism significantly, then it must be willing to be not only an institution of love but an institution of power"— perhaps even "the power of violence."

Hall also reminded the reader that the United Presbyterian Church gave money to the Angela Davis defense fund, and the Episcopalians gave $50,000 to the "Alianza of New Mexico," which he said is "an organization dedicated to virtual guerilla war aimed at establishing a separate Chicano nation in the southwestern United States." The point is that the churches are engaged in activities that many people, Clarence Hall among them, consider to be inimical to the true course of Christianity. The reaction was swift and sure: significant cuts in financial contributions.[56]

Conservative Protestants have generally maintained that regenerating the individual takes precedence over changing the society. Indeed, most of the time they have looked with disfavor on the churches' slightest involvement with social and political problems. One of their most prominent spokesmen, Carl F. H. Henry, has said, "The dignity of the Church is damaged when ecclesiastical leaders appear before political bodies to plead special cases in areas where churchmen obviously lack the information necessary to reach a sound political judgement."[57]

Recent studies on the subject indicate that most laymen do not want the church to become too deeply involved in trying to change society by "direct action." In a recent volume, in which he assembles much of the available data on the matter, Jeffrey K. Hadden points out that although 82 per cent of the laity in America concede that "clergymen have a responsibility to speak out as the moral conscience of this nation," they are about equally divided on whether "clergy should speak

[56]Clarence W. Hall, "Must Our Churches Finance Revolution?" *The Reader's Digest* (October, 1971), pp. 95–100.

[57]Quoted by Roy E. Branson, "Time to Meet the Evangelicals?" *The Christian Century* (December 21, 1969), p. 1642, an excellent discussion of the possible rapprochement between conservatives or "Evangelicals" and the "liberal" wing of Protestantism.

out on social, economic, and political issues." In other words, clergy may enunciate broad general moral principles from the pulpit, but they should avoid specific strategies for changing society. Moreover, 72 per cent of the laity believe that "clergymen who participate in demonstrations and picketing do more harm than good for the cause they support" and reported that they would "be upset" if their minister, priest, or rabbi " were to participate in a picket line or a demonstration." It should be noted, however, that Jews are much more prone to accept social activism among the clergy than either Catholics or Protestants.

Though one cannot logically equate "clergy" and "church," and least of all Protestants, this is precisely what happens in the popular mind. Lay people do equate clergy and church and are opposed to activist clergy representing institutional religion in any official way.[58]

On the other hand, some of the apologists for "conservative" Protestantism do admit that "Christians have a duty to bring their Christian ethic to bear on society."[59] Others point out that Christianity "is not limited to regenerative action. Once having established the primacy of its redemptive function it should not hesitate to be a critical voice when moral issues and human rights are at stake."[60]

Probably the most noteworthy advocate of social activism in recent years has been Harvey Cox (1929–   ) of Harvard. His paperback bestseller, *The Secular City*, catapulted him into national visibility in 1965. Many regarded him as a successor to Walter Rauschenbusch (1861–1918), whose writing established him as the prime expositor of the social gospel when it first appeared in America at the turn of the century, but Cox argued that what he was describing was more than a return to the old themes of the social gospel. Certain events in the intervening years make that impossible. The "new breed" of socially activist clergy possesses a much tougher and more realistic attitude toward the world than did Rauschenbusch and his contemporaries.[61] According to Cox, the "new breed" has come to see that moral solutions to urban problems of poverty and deprivation must of necessity employ political strategies: "They speak unapologetically of the struggle for power in the city and the churches' responsibility to enter into the struggle on the side of the exploited and powerless."[62] Moreover, the "new breed" cuts across social classes, race, and denominational background; Jews and Catholics have joined disinherited whites and the black poor.

[58] Jeffrey K. Hadden, *The Gathering Storm in the Churches* (Garden City, N.Y.: Doubleday, 1970), pp. 148–151.

[59] Hall, op. cit., p. 95.

[60] David McKenna, quoted by Bransom, op. cit., p. 1642.

[61] For a discussion comparing the two, see "The Social Gospel Old & New: Walter Rauschenbusch and Harvey Cox," *Religion in Life*, Vol. 36 (Winter 1967), pp. 516–533.

[62] See Harvey Cox, "The 'New Breed' in American Churches: Sources of Social Activism in American Religion," *Religion in America*, edited by William G. McLoughlin and Robert N. Bellah (Boston: Beacon Press, 1968), pp. 371ff.

Cox found himself embroiled in a new but familiar controversy in the mid-1970s as he and a group of twenty colleagues in the Boston area felt compelled to issue a sweeping theological statement attacking what they considered to be the escapist tendencies of the contemporary church. The group called on present-day believers to recognize that God is actively concerned about the state of the world and challenged the church to become more heavily involved with the plight of the dispossessed. The way to spiritual renewal, they said, is not to retreat from the world's struggles but to join the poor and the oppressed in their suffering. The group was made up of six Episcopalians, four Presbyterians, two Baptists, a Methodist, three Roman Catholics, three members of the United Church of Christ, and two Lutherans. Five were women. Many of them were connected with the Boston Industrial Mission.

Drawing heavily on "liberation" theology—a type of religious thought which originated primarily in response to the needs and condition of Christianity as found in the Third World nations—The Boston Affirmations, as the statement was called, poured fuel on a dispute between those who defend the social gospel tradition and those who argue for a more disciplined and more spiritual approach to Christianity. The latter view had been adopted by another group, meeting in Hartford, Connecticut, a year earlier, that had issued what they called, "An Appeal for Theological Affirmation."[63]

The Hartford appeal urged the church to reject "false and debilitating" secular ideas that had allegedly crept into the thinking of contemporary believers. Though it did not take aim directly at Cox, the type of theology he had espoused over the years was one of its primary targets.

The Hartford group was convened by Richard John Neuhaus, a Lutheran pastor in Brooklyn, and Peter Berger, a sociologist at Rutgers. The participants were, for the most part, theologians drawn principally from the conservative wings of Protestantism and Catholicism. Ironically, Neuhaus had been a founder of Clergy and Laity Concerned about Viet Nam and in the forefront of activist causes during the late 1960s and early 1970s. He claimed that the Hartford appeal was not a repudiation of his earlier position. Rather, history's agenda had changed, which meant that the church's agenda must change. He told a reporter that there are periods of history "when evil is so clearly defined that all Christians are called to come to witness. The 60s was one of those times. But we are concerned with re-examining some of the excesses and mistakes of the movement."[64]

In June of 1975, the Faith and Order Commission of the National Council of Churches sponsored a debate in New York City between

---

[63]For a complete treatment of the controversy, see Francine du Plessix Gray, "To March or Not to March," *The New York Times*, June 27, 1975, Section VI, p. 6.

[64]Ibid., p. 31.

speakers for the opposing forces. There, Neuhaus explained the motive for the Hartford meeting and the document which came out of it:

> We [were] saying that an awful lot of contemporary theology—right, left, and center—has . . . become anthropology, that it is no longer in tension with, in a dialectical relationship to the referent which we call God, the Transcendent which keeps it under judgment. God is irretrievably committed to the human struggle—of course as Christians we believe that—but God is not to be equated with the human struggle.
>
> And it is this that Hartford is protesting against—the equation of God with our programs, again whether our programs be the advancement of the "great American way of life" or Marxist revolution or the attainment of peace of mind or some kind of human potential as salvation. . . .
>
> It is precisely the emphasis, in short, upon *transcendence*, upon the over-againstness of God bringing also our programs under judgment, that can restore the credibility of the kind of nexus we are both trying to build between theology and social change, that can restore that credibility and can restore to the tasks to which we would call the church a good many churchpeople who have been profoundly alienated from theology, from what is viewed as progressive religious thought, because they believed you did have to make a choice between being prophetic and priestly, between comfort and challenge, between church and worldliness.[65]

Furthermore, said Neuhaus on another occasion, the Hartford appeal reflected the wisdom of the ordinary layperson: "After all, what do most people see as the function of religion? . . . They see prayer, worship, transcendence, eternal life. . . . And they're right!"[66]

So the lines were clearly drawn: on the one hand were the Hartford pietists who emphasized transcendence, correct doctrine, and personal salvation; on the other hand were the Boston social activists who held that faith develops out of the struggle for justice.

The Hartford appeal, its authors were eager to make clear, was not offered as a creed or complete statement of the Christian faith. Rather, its purpose was to call attention to some of the themes prevalent among religious thinkers and others during the mid-1970s which threatened to undermine the integrity of the faith. As a consequence, the appeal will appear to some to be fragmentary and incomplete. Nonetheless, it is a valuable addition to the tradition out of which it springs. It and the successor document, the Boston Affirmation, received widespread comment in the secular press as well as in religious publications here and abroad.[67] The Appeal was issued January 26, 1975.

[65]See "The Hartford Debate," *Christianity and Crisis*, Vol. 35, No. 12 (July 21, 1975), p. 174.

[66]Gray, op. cit., p. 7.

[67]Martin Marty of the University of Chicago and *The Christian Century* considered the debate between the two groups "a media event." See *The Christian Century*, Vol. XCIII, No. 1 (January 7-14, 1976), pp. 6 and 135. He also told Francine de Plessix Gray, "Neuhaus and Cox are very clever with the press; they wanted an event and they created one. But it's a pseudo-event, because Hartford sets up straw men modernisms that I haven't heard anyone in the Church ever say, and Boston is so nostalgic for the '60s it's regressive. . . . They've done a media hype because there's nothing else to write about." See Gray, op. cit., p. 34.

"An Appeal for Theological Affirmation"

The renewal of Christian witness and mission requires constant examination of the assumptions shaping the Church's life. Today an apparent loss of a sense of the transcendent is undermining the Church's ability to address with clarity and courage the urgent tasks to which God calls it in the world. This loss is manifest in a number of pervasive themes. Many are superficially attractive, but upon closer examination we find these themes false and debilitating to the Church's life and work. Among such themes are:

Theme 1: Modern thought is superior to all past forms of understanding reality, and is therefore normative for Christian faith and life.

In repudiating this theme we are protesting the captivity to the prevailing thought structures not only of the twentieth century but of any historical period. We favor using any helpful means of understanding, ancient or modern, and insist that the Christian proclamation must be related to the idiom of the culture. At the same time, we affirm the need for Christian thought to confront and be confronted by other worldviews, all of which are necessarily provisional.

Theme 2: Religious statements are totally independent of reasonable discourse.

The capitulation to the alleged primacy of modern thought takes two forms: one is the subordination of religious statements to the canons of scientific rationality; the other, equating reason with scientific rationality, would remove religious statements from the realm of reasonable discourse altogether. A religion of pure subjectivity and nonrationality results in treating faith statements as being, at best, statements about the believer. We repudiate both forms of capitulation.

Theme 3: Religious language refers to human experience and nothing else, God being humanity's noblest creation.

Religion is also a set of symbols and even of human projections. We repudiate the assumption that it is nothing but that. What is here at stake is nothing less than the reality of God: *We did not invent God; God invented us.*

Theme 4: Jesus can only be understood in terms of contemporary models of humanity.

This theme suggests a reversal of "the imitation of Christ"; that is, the image of Jesus is made to reflect cultural and countercultural notions of human excellence. We do not deny that all aspects of humanity are illumined by Jesus. Indeed, it is necessary to the universality of the Christ that he be perceived in relation to the particularities of the believers' world. We do repudiate the captivity to such metaphors, which are necessarily inadequate, relative, transitory, and frequently idolatrous. Jesus, together with the Scriptures and the whole of the Christian tradition, cannot be arbitrarily interpreted without reference to the history of which they are

SOURCE: *Worldview*, Vol. 18, No. 4 (April 1975), pp. 39–40.

part. The danger is in the attempt to exploit the tradition without taking the tradition seriously.

Theme 5: All religions are equally valid; the choice among them is not a matter of conviction about truth but only of personal preference or lifestyle.

We affirm our common humanity. We affirm the importance of exploring and confronting all manifestations of the religious quest and of learning from the riches of other religions. But we repudiate this theme because it flattens diversities and ignores contradictions. In doing so, it not only obscures the meaning of Christian faith, but also fails to respect the integrity of other faiths. Truth matters; therefore differences among religions are deeply significant.

Theme 6: To realize one's potential and to be true to oneself is the whole meaning of salvation.

Salvation contains a promise of human fulfillment, but to identify salvation with human fulfillment can trivialize the promise. We affirm that salvation cannot be found apart from God.

Theme 7: Since what is human is good, evil can adequately be understood as failure to realize potential.

This theme invites false understanding of the ambivalence of human existence and underestimates the pervasiveness of sin. Paradoxically, by minimizing the enormity of evil, it undermines serious and sustained attacks on particular social or individual evils.

Theme 8: The sole purpose of worship is to promote individual self-realization and human community.

Worship promotes individual and communal values, but it is above all a response to the reality of God and arises out of the fundamental need and desire to know, love, and adore God. We worship God because God is to be worshipped.

Theme 9: Institutions and historical traditions are oppressive and inimical to our being truly human; liberation from them is required for authentic existence and authentic religion.

Institutions and traditions are often oppressive. For this reason they must be subjected to relentless criticism. But human community inescapably requires institutions and traditions. Without them life would degenerate into chaos and new forms of bondage. The modern pursuit of liberation from all social and historical restraints is finally dehumanizing.

Theme 10: The world must set the agenda for the Church. Social, political, and economic programs to improve the quality of life are ultimately normative for the Church's mission in the world.

This theme cuts across the political and ideological spectrum. Its form remains the same, no matter whether the content is defined as upholding the values of the American way of life, promoting socialism, or raising human consciousness. The

Church must denounce oppressors, help liberate the oppressed, and seek to heal human misery. Sometimes the Church's mission coincides with the world's programs. But the norms for the Church's activity derive from its own perception of God's will for the world.

Theme 11: An emphasis on God's transcendence is at least a hindrance to, and perhaps incompatible with, Christian social concern and action.

This supposition leads some to denigrate God's transcendence. Others, holding to a false transcendence, withdraw into religious privatism or individualism and neglect the personal and communal responsibility of Christians for the earthly city. From a biblical perspective, it is precisely because of confidence in God's reign over all aspects of life that Christians must participate fully in the struggle against oppressive and dehumanizing structures and their manifestations in racism, war, and economic exploitation.

Theme 12: The struggle for a better humanity will bring about the Kingdom of God.

The struggle for a better humanity is essential to Christian faith and can be informed and inspired by the biblical promise of the Kingdom of God. But imperfect human beings cannot create a perfect society. The Kingdom of God surpasses any conceivable utopia. God has his own designs which confront ours, surprising us with judgment and redemption.

Theme 13: The question of hope beyond death is irrelevant or at best marginal to the Christian understanding of human fulfillment.

This is the final capitulation to modern thought. If death is the last word, then Christianity has nothing to say to the final question of life. We believe that God raised Jesus from the dead and are ". . . convinced that there is nothing in death or life, in the realm of spirits or superhuman powers, in the world as it is or in the world as it shall be, in the forces of the universe, in heights or depths—nothing in all creation that can separate us from the love of God in Christ Jesus our Lord" (Romans 8:38 f.).

The Boston Affirmations, issued January 6, 1976, state the classical position of the social gospel—that there is often a false separation between thought and action, faith and works, doctrine and deeds. They further rest on the premise that salvation is not simply a personal matter between the individual and God but requires active involvement in solving such problems as poverty, disease, illiteracy, and discrimination. Cox said in an interview the day the Affirmations were issued, "Our main concern was to anchor social concern in the Biblical message and in the central tradition of the Church."[68]

[68]*The New York Times*, January 6, 1976, p. 21.

Document 46 _____

"The Boston Affirmations"

The living God is active in current struggles to bring a Reign of Justice, Righteousness, Love, and Peace. The Judeo-Christian traditions are pertinent to the dilemmas of our world. All believers are called to preach the good news to the poor, to proclaim release to the captives and recovery of sight to the blind, to set at liberty those who are oppressed, and to proclaim the acceptable year of the Lord. Yet we are concerned about what we discern to be present trends in our churches, in religious thought, and in our society. We see struggles in every arena of human life, but in too many parts of the church and theology we find retreat from these struggles. Still, we are not without hope nor warrants for our hope. Hopeful participation in these struggles is at once action in faith, the primary occasion for personal spiritual growth, the development of viable structures for the common life, and the vocation of the people of God. To sustain such participation, we have searched the past and the present to find the signs of God's future and of ours. Thus, we make the following affirmations.

Affirmations

Creation: God brings into being all life, all resources, all genuine meanings.

Humanity is of one source and is not ultimately governed by nature or history, by the fabric of societies or the depths of the self, by knowledge or belief. God's triune activity sustains creative order, evokes personal identity and is embodied in the dynamic movements of human history in an ever more inclusive community of persons responsibly engaged in all aspects of the ecosphere, history, and thought.

Fall: Humanity is estranged from the source of life.

We try to ignore or transcend the source and end of life. Or we try to place God in a transcendent realm divorced from life. Thereby we give license to domination, indulgence, pretense, triviality, and evasion. We endanger creative order, we destroy personal identity, and we corrupt inspired communities. We allow tyranny, anarchy, and death to dominate the gift of life.

Exodus and Covenant: God delivers from oppression and chaos. God chooses strangers, servants, and outcasts to be witnesses and to become a community of righteousness and mercy.

Beyond domination and conflict God hears the cry of the oppressed and works vindication for all. God forms "nobodies" into a people of "somebodies" and makes known the laws of life. The liberation experience calls forth celebrative response, demands responsibility in community, and opens people and nations for a common global history.

Prophecy: In compassion God speaks to the human community through prophets.

Those who authentically represent God have interpreted—and will interpret—the

SOURCE: *Worldview*, Vol. 18, No. 3 (March 1976), pp. 45–46.

activity of God in social history. They announce the presence of God in the midst
of political and economic life; they foretell the judgment and hope that are implicit
in the loyalties and practices of the common life; and they set forth the vision of
covenantal renewal.

Wisdom: The cultural insights and memories of many peoples and ages illuminate
the human condition.

The experience and lore of all cultures and groups bear within them values that
are of wider meaning. Racism, genocide, imperialism, sexism are thus contrary to
God's purpose and impoverish us all. Yet all wisdom must also be tested for its
capacity to reveal the human dependence on the source of life, to grasp the depths
of sin, to liberate, to evoke prophecy, and to form genuine covenant.

The New Covenant: God is known to us in Jesus Christ. The source and end of life
is disclosed in that suffering love which breaks the power of sin and death, which
renders hope in the action of God to reconcile and transform the world, which
shatters the barriers of ethnic, class, familial, national, and caste restrictions. Meaning and divine activity are incarnate in history and human particularity.

Church Traditions: God calls those who trust the power of suffering love to form
into communities of celebration, care, and involvement.

Those called together enact renewing forms of association and movement to the
ends of the earth, responding by word and deed to the implications of faith for
each age and for us today:

- The early Eastern church celebrated the dependence of humanity upon the
  cosmos, and of the cosmos upon God, demanding a sacramental attitude toward the whole of creation.
- The Formers of doctrine set forth the meanings of faith in the face of cultured despisers, exposed the frail foundations of various secularisms, and gave
  new directions to both the faithful and civilization.
- The Monastics assumed vows to exemplify life-styles beyond preoccupation
  with gain, freedom from familial and sexual stereotyping, and disciplined lives
  of service.
- The Scholastics engaged secular culture, demanding of each generation critical
  and synthetic reappropriation of tradition.
- The Reformers preached the work of protest against religious pretense and demanded reliance upon the gifts of divine empowerment.
- The Sectarians nurtured the spirit that cannot be contained by priesthood,
  dogma, hierarchy, authoritative word, or any established power, and demanded democracy, freedom, toleration, and the redistribution of authority,
  power, and wealth.
- And today many reach out for wider fellowships, demanding ecumenical en-
  gagements and a witness which frees and unites.

Wherever the heirs of these movements are authentic, they confess their sins, worship the power that sustains them, form a company of the committed, and struggle for justice and love against the powers and principalities of evil.

Present Witnesses: The question today is whether the heritage of this past can be sustained, preserved, and extended into the future. Society as presently structured, piety as presently practiced, and the churches as presently preoccupied evoke profound doubts about the prospects. Yet we are surrounded by a cloud of witnesses who prophetically exemplify or discern the activity of God. The transforming reality of God's reign is found today:

- In the struggles of the poor to gain a share of the world's wealth, to become creative participants in the common economic life, and to move our world toward an economic democracy of equity and accountability.
- In the transforming drive for ethnic dignity against the persistent racism of human hearts and social institutions.
- In the endeavor by women to overcome sexist subordination in the church's ministry, in society at large, and in the images that bind our minds and bodies.
- In the attempts within families to overcome prideful domination and degrading passivity and to establish genuine covenants of mutuality and joyous fidelity.
- In the efforts by many groups to develop for modern humanity a love for its cities as centers of civility, culture, and human interdependence.
- In the demands of the sick and the elderly for inexpensive, accessible health care administered with concern, advised consent, and sensitivity.
- In the voices of citizens and political leaders who demand honesty and openness, who challenge the misplaced trust of the nation in might, and who resist the temptations to make a nation and its institutions objects of religious loyalty.
- In the research of science when it warns of dangers to humanity and quests for those forms of technology which can sustain human well-being and preserve ecological resources.
- In the humanities and social sciences when the depths of human meanings are opened to inquiry and are allowed to open our horizons, especially whenever there is protest against the subordination of religion to scientific rationality or against the removal of religion from realms of rational discourse.
- In the arts where beauty and meaning are explored, lifted up, and represented in ways that call us to deeper sensibilities.
- In the halls of justice when righteousness is touched with mercy, when the prisoner and the wrongdoer are treated with dignity and fairness.
- And especially in those branches and divisions of the church where the truth is spoken in love, where transforming social commitments are nurtured and persons are brought to informed conviction, where piety is renewed and recast in concert with the heritage, and where such struggles as those here identified are seen as the action of the living God who alone is worshipped.

On these grounds, we cannot stand with those secular cynics and religious spiritualizers who see in such witnesses no theology, no eschatological urgency, and no

Godly promise or judgment. In such spiritual blindness, secular or religious, the world as God's creation is abandoned, sin rules, liberation is frustrated, covenant is broken, prophecy is stilled, wisdom is betrayed, suffering love is transformed into triviality, and the church is transmuted into a club for self- or transcendental awareness. The struggle is now joined for the future of faith and the common life. We call all who believe in the living God to affirm, to sustain, and to extend these witnesses.

Although the Hartford and Boston pronouncements received widespread treatment in the press, another statement had gone virtually unnoticed when published in Chicago on Thanksgiving Day of 1973. A group of evangelicals, concerned that they and the whole evangelical wing of Christianity had fallen short in meeting their social obligations, issued the Chicago Declaration. Written in confessional form, it is notable in the context of this chapter because of the evangelical tendency to slight social involvement in the desire to show the preeminence of personal salvation. The group listed nine areas in which they believed they had erred. It was a widely representative gathering, ranging from the conservative elder statesman Carl Henry to Richard Mouw, a young philosopher who had headed Evangelicals for McGovern. The declaration reads in part:

> We acknowledge that we have failed to condemn the exploitation of racism at home and abroad by our economic system . . . . Before God and a billion hungry neighbors, we must rethink our values regarding our present standard of living and promote more just acquisition and distribution of the world's resources . . . . We must challenge the misplaced trust of the nation in economic and military might—a proud trust that promotes a national pathology of war and violence which victimizes our neighbors at home and abroad. We must resist the temptation to make the nation and its institutions objects of near-religious loyalty. . . . We acknowledge that we have encouraged men to prideful domination and women to irresponsible passivity.[69]

With this type of statement, evangelicals had begun to sound very much like direct descendants of Walter Rauschenbusch and first cousins to Harvey Cox.

The Origin and Development of the Social Gospel

> The social-gospel movement cannot be defined theologically or institutionally. It was never incorporated in any new organizations; it did not result in any new denominations. The theologies associated with the movement were many and as diverse as the diverse and individualistic religious pattern in America could provide.[70]

Sidney Mead is correct. About the most that one can say about the

[69] See Gray, op. cit., p. 38.
[70] Mead, op. cit., p. 178.

social gospel without fear of immediate contradiction is that it has been a self-conscious attempt by some Christians to recover and make relevant to urban-industrial America the social teachings of the Christian tradition. Generally speaking, those who have been associated with the movement have come from the "liberal" wing of Protestantism and, if we can say that there was a social gospel among Catholics, from the "liberal" wing of Catholicism.

It is also correct to say that the social teachings, in themselves, were not particularly new. There was a long and venerable tradition in Christianity that understood the gospel in social terms. What was new were the conditions to which the social gospel movement addressed itself in late nineteenth-century America. But prior to that some of the most important works in the history of Christianity dealt with social or political problems: St. Augustine sketched a plan for a Christian social order in his *City of God*; Calvin designed a Protestant society in *The Institutes*; and John Winthrop drew the outline for the Puritan commonwealth in New England. Why, then, give so much attention to the social gospel? Because at the end of the nineteenth century there were some fairly serious problems connected with the rise of industrialism that cried out for attention, and certain people within the churches responded. As a result, the direction of modern Christianity was changed.

We have already seen how great numbers of eighteenth-and nineteenth-century church people attempted to redress the ills of the day through organized philanthropy. Improvements in the living conditions of the poor were obtained by the efforts of numerous churchmen who gave generously to one cause or another. But a number of thoughtful people came to believe that philanthropy was not the ultimate answer. More radical measures were needed. "Charity," explained one observer in 1893, "whether public or private, mainly deals with results, to mitigate effects; public action must be applied to the industrial system itself in order to prevent a continuation of the causes."[71] This comment did not mean that philanthropy had failed; only that it dealt with symptoms rather than the disease itself.

Following the Civil War more and more economic power was concentrated in the hands of a few people and a few corporations, which did not always bode well for the worker and the consumer. America's economy ran hot and cold: there were several severe economic recessions and adjustments before the turn of the century, but industrialization of the nation continued uninterrupted. People by the thousands left the farm yearly to find a place in business or industry. The free enterprise system was running full blast, with little, if any, restraint, as competition between businesses became more acute. Darwin's law, the survival of the fittest, was applied to the social order and invoked to justify one's success in business. In this brutally competitive situation,

---

[71] Charles Worcester Clark, quoted by Mead, ibid., p. 167.

where the rich got richer and the poor poorer, many people felt that a complete restructuring of the system was a necessity. The labor movement became the principal tool used by the working man to gain some kind of leverage.

During this period both sides made use of religion. The "captains of industry" were quick to claim the gospel for their cause. Andrew Carnegie, as we have already seen, believed that his accumulation of wealth signified that he had been providentially selected to solve the problems of the poor. God had given him talent, power, and the wherewithal to correct a bad situation. Moreover, the free enterprise system was the best ever devised, because it entrusted wealth to the kind of people who could discriminate between worthwhile philanthropy and unrealistic programs that would simply perpetuate poverty. The cardinal rule, for Carnegie, was to help those who helped themselves. Any other method would only foster laziness, sloth, and indifference.

Toward the end of "Wealth" Carnegie wrote, "Neither the individual nor the race is improved by alms-giving."[72] Instead, they are both improved when wise and benevolent men are able to distribute wealth to those who, through frugality and hard work, are willing to lift themselves out of poverty. One earnest professor of the period even went so far as to bless the free enterprise system with the stature of natural law. He objected to proposed legislation mandating an eight-hour workday on the ground that to enact such legislation would have substituted civil law for natural law. Neither justice nor economic stability would be served by such a move, he said.[73] In effect, working conditions, no matter how sorry, were an expression of the divine plan. Here we see that *laissez faire* economics, in which no controls of any kind are placed on business, was joined with social Darwinism, in which the most vigorous economic operators will survive, and both received the benediction of evangelical religion.

It is interesting to note in this connection that whereas the power elite justified its position in society with the logic of providential selection, it blamed poverty on the inherent laziness and worthlessness of the poor. Henry Ward Beecher, son of the illustrious Lyman and brother to Harriet Beecher Stowe (1811–1896), admitted that poverty was not *always* the result of wrongdoing, but, generally speaking, people were poor because they deserved to be. They had sinned.[74] Beecher's younger contemporary Phillips Brooks urged his hearers to turn their backs on "idleness, intemperance, and selfishness" in order to become "consecrated, manly, noble, lofty-minded." Any man has it within himself to overcome the poverty of his own situation.[75]

[72] Andrew Carnegie, "Wealth," *The North American Review*, Vol. 391 (June 1889), p. 663.
[73] Mead, op. cit., p. 158.
[74] Quoted in ibid., p. 160.
[75] Phillips Brooks, "Address at the Laying of Corner Stone . . . ." *Religious Issues in American History*, edited by Edwin Scott Gaustad (New York: Harper & Row, 1968), p. 196.

The proponents of the social gospel demurred. How could anyone so easily requisition religion on behalf of greed? One contributor to an 1886 number of *The Methodist Review* complained:

> A civilization that permits man to be the greatest enemy of man, and allows the hardest and most repugnant toil to draw the lowest pay, is a cheat and a sham; the political economy that permits it is a falsehood and a fraud; and a religion that allows it without constant, earnest, and persistent protest is a humbug.[76]

In that same year Washington Gladden, pastor of the First Congregational Church in Columbus, Ohio, and one of the giants of the social gospel movement, sent a questionnaire to a large number of workers in 1886 in order to determine why they did not attend church. Two principal reasons were given: the inability to dress as the average churchgoer did and a feeling of not being wanted. The churches seemed to be in the control of capitalists. One of Gladden's respondents wrote:

> Of course the manufacturers can and should dress better than the laborer; but when we see them so full of religion on Sunday, and then grinding the faces of the poor on the other six days, we are apt to think they are insincere. . . . When the capitalist prays for us one day in the week, and preys on us the other six, it can't be expected that we will have much respect for his Christianity.[77]

Proponents of the social gospel then began to develop ways in which the church could bring pressure to bear on the system. They worked with the fundamental assumptions that Christianity is not otherworldly but this-worldly and that it is the mission of the churches to bring the Kingdom of God into being on this earth. They understood the law of love to mean that the old individualism of evangelical Christianity was no longer satisfactory. Not just individuals but the entire society would have to experience salvation. One author wrote in 1892:

> The Christian conception of life and its supreme good rests on this fundamental fact which Jesus announced, that the kingdom of God is not something wholly future, or remote from our present participation in it, but it is a real power and an actual reign of God already begun on earth—a kingdom of heaven into which we may now enter, and which offers through citizenship in it some immediate possession of the highest good and present part in the eternal life.[78]

In order for the Kingdom of God to come into being, leaders of the social gospel believed that all social, political, and economic relations between people had to be transformed in such a way that all persons would have equal opportunity, fair wages, good health services, a chance

---

[76] Quoted by Charles Howard Hopkins, *The Rise of the Social Gospel in American Protestantism, 1865-1915* (New Haven, Conn.: Yale University Press, 1940), p. 84.

[77] Quoted in ibid., p. 85.

[78] Newman Smyth, quoted in ibid., p. 128.

at education, freedom from unfair labor practices, representation at city hall, and so on. They framed and sought legislation that would redress the balance of power between rich and poor. They attacked the problems of urban living, especially tenement abuses, and supported the infant labor movement with great vigor.

Strikes throughout the last quarter of the nineteenth century brought everything to a head. During the 1870s and 1880s labor unrest swept the nation's railroads. At Pittsburgh alone, twenty-six people were killed in 1877. In 1886 the McCormick Harvester strike occurred. Six of the workers were killed one day, and on the following, a riot occurred in Chicago's Haymarket Square that claimed the lives of seven policemen; seventy persons were injured. The Carnegie Corporation's Homestead plant was struck in 1892. Several hundred Pinkerton detectives and the state militia were summoned to break it up. Seven were killed. In 1894 the Pullman strike was called. Railroads in a number of states were halted. Rioting, looting, burning, and shooting occurred throughout the country. And so it went.

The country's religious leaders were divided. Over the 1877 railroad strike, *The Independent* was hysterical:

> If the club of the policemen, knocking out the brains of the rioter, will answer, then well and good; but if it does not promptly meet the exigency, then bullets and bayonets, canister and grape—with no sham or pretense, in order to frighten men, but with fearful and destructive reality—constitute the one remedy and the one duty of the hour. . . .Napoleon was right when he said that the way to deal with a mob was to exterminate it.[79]

Of the Homestead incident, a number of professors at the liberal Andover seminary held that "law and order" would not solve the problem: "the maintenance of order in congested labor districts is not the settlement of the labor question." The issue at hand, in their estimation, was that of the "personal rights in equity in the plant, which the men had contributed so much to build up by their skill and character." To give credit for the growth of the business merely to Carnegie's shrewdness without recognizing the contribution made by the men in the shop was the height of injustice. Although it might be legal, it is plainly unfair "whenever a question of work or wages arises, for the management to say, if you don't like the place you can quit."[80]

Throughout the period, various spokesmen came forward to speak on the behalf of the workers. Washington Gladden asked, following the stormy events of 1866, "Is It Peace or War?" He saw concentrations of power building up on both sides of the issue. Though he struck hardest at "conscienceless" corporations (they were the most flagrant offenders),

[79] Quoted by Mead, op. cit., p. 165.
[80] Quoted in ibid., p. 166.

in the end he passionately called for understanding from labor as well
as management:

> Over all this wretched strife one can imagine those "better angels of our
> nature," whose ministry Abraham Lincoln once pathetically but vainly invoked,
> bending with divine compassion and crying to the embattled hosts with solemn
> rebuke and benignant appeal: Is it well, brother men, is it well to fight? Is it
> not better to be friends? Are you not all children of one Father? Nay, are you
> not, as the great apostle said, members one of another? Your war is not only
> wholesale fratricide, it is social suicide. It is little to say that you cannot afford
> to fight; you cannot live apart; you must live for one another. That is the way
> you were made to live; and you will never have anything but trouble and sorrow
> till you learn that way and walk in it. The stars in their courses will fight against
> you until you make peace with one another. Have we not had more than enough
> of war and its dismal noises and its spectral train of woes; more than enough of
> silent looms and fireless forges; of children's faces pale with hunger, and women's
> sunken eyes; of hearts made fierce and hard by long-cherished enmities; of class
> arrayed against class and neighbor against neighbor? Oh, put it all away from
> you—the hate, the suspicion, the scorn; stand here together, brethren as you are,
> helpers of one another as you must be, and promise one another that you will
> do what you can, everyone of you, to bring the day when between Labor and
> Capital there shall be no longer war, but peace for evermore.[81]

Gladden and his ilk were dogged optimists.

The most formidable mind among writers in the social gospel movement was Walter Rauschenbusch. After an active parish ministry in
Hell's Kitchen in New York City, he went back to teach at his own
seminary in Rochester. In 1907 he published *Christianity and the
Social Crisis*, which established him as a new champion of the working
people. The book's instantaneous success drew him into public discussion, where a number of people asked him what actions they should
take to make his program effective. In 1910–1911 he delivered a series
of lectures that embodied his response, and they were soon gathered in
a volume entitled, *Christianizing the Social Order* (1912). Five years
later he published *A Theology for the Social Gospel*.

Martin Luther King, Jr. (1929–1968), a later proponent of the social
gospel said of Rauschenbusch's first book that it

> left an indelible imprint on my thinking. Of course there were points at which
> I differed with Rauschenbusch. I felt that he had fallen victim to the nineteenth
> century "cult of inevitable progress," which led him to an unwarranted optimism
> concerning human nature. Moreover, he came perilously close to identifying the
> kingdom of God with a particular social and economic system—a temptation
> which the church should never give in to. But in spite of these shortcomings
> Rauschenbusch gave to American Protestantism a sense of social responsibility
> that it should never lose.[82]

---

[81] Washington Gladden, "Is It Peace or War?" *The Social Gospel in America, 1870-1920*,
edited by Robert T. Handy (New York: Oxford University Press, 1966), p. 71.
[82] Quoted by Handy, ibid., p. 259.

/av~

From "Wanted—A Faith for a Task" by Walter Rauschenbusch

Our entire generation needs a faith, for it is confronting the mightiest task ever undertaken consciously by any generation of men. Our civilization is passing through a great historic transition. We are at the parting of the ways. The final outcome may be the decay and extinction of Western civilization, or it may be a new epoch in the evolution of the race, compared with which our present era will seem like a modified barbarism. We now have such scientific knowledge of social laws and forces, of economics, of history that we can intelligently mold and guide the evolution in which we take part. Our fathers cowered before the lightning; we have subdued it to our will. Former generations were swept along more or less blindly toward a hidden destiny; we have reached the point where we can make history make us. Have we the will to match our knowledge? Can we marshal the moral forces capable of breaking what must be broken, and then building what must be built? . . .

Our moral efficiency depends on our religious faith. The force of will, of courage, of self-sacrifice liberated by a living religious faith is so incalculable, so invincible, that nothing is impossible when that power enters the field. The author of the greatest revolution in history made the proposition that even the slightest amount of faith is competent to do the unbelievable; faith as tiny as a mustard seed can blast away mountains.

The chief purpose of the Christian Church in the past has been the salvation of individuals. But the most pressing task of the present is not individualistic. Our business is to make over an antiquated and immoral economic system; to get rid of laws, customs, maxims, and philosophies inherited from an evil and despotic past; to create just and brotherly relations between great groups and classes of society; and thus to lay a social foundation on which modern men individually can live and work in a fashion that will not outrage all the better elements in them. Our inherited Christian faith dealt with individuals: our present task deals with society.

The Christian Church in the past has taught us to do our work with our eyes fixed on another world and a life to come. But the business before us is concerned with refashioning this present world, making this earth clean and sweet and habitable.

Here is the problem for all religious minds: we need a great faith to serve as a spiritual basis for the tremendous social task before us, and the working creed of our religion in the form in which it has come down to us, has none. Its theology is silent or stammers where we most need a ringing and dogmatic message. It has no adequate answer to the fundamental moral questions of our day. It has manifestly furnished no sufficient religious motives to bring the unregenerate portions of our social order under the control of the Christian law. Its hymns, its ritual, its prayers, its books of devotion, are so devoid of social thought that the most thrilling passions of our generation lie in us half stifled for lack of religious utterance. The whole scheme of religion which tradition has handed down to us was not devised for such ends as we now have in hand and is inadequate for them. We need a new foundation for Christian thought.

Twenty-five years ago the social wealth of the Bible was almost undiscovered to most of us. We used to plow it six inches deep for crops and never dreamed that mines of anthracite were hidden down below. Even Jesus talked like an individualist in those days and seemed to repudiate the social interest when we interrogated him. He said his kingdom was not of this world: the things of God had nothing to do with the things of Caesar: the poor we would always have with us: and his ministers must not be judges and dividers when Labor argued with Capital about the division of inheritance. To-day he has resumed the spiritual leadership of social Christianity, of which he was the founder. It is a new tribute to his mastership that the social message of Jesus was the first great possession which social Christianity rediscovered. A course of lectures on the social teachings of Jesus is usually the earliest symptom that the social awakening has arrived. Is it another compliment to the undischarged force of his thoughts that we handle them so gingerly, as if they were boxed explosives? We have also worked out the social ideas of the Old Testament prophets. But that is about as far as the popular comprehension of the Bible has gone. We have let Paul severely alone. The Apocalypse is not yet printed in red, as it might be. Few commentaries show any streaks of social insight. We have no literature that introduces the ordinary reader to the whole Bible from the social point of view.

In its systematic doctrinal teaching the Church is similarly handicapped. It is trying old tools to see if they will fit the new job. It has done splendidly in broadening certain principles developed under religious individualism and giving them a social application. But more is needed.

With true Christian instinct men have turned to the Christian law of love as the key to the situation. If we all loved our neighbor, we should "treat him right," pay him a living wage, give sixteen ounces to the pound, and not charge so much for beef. But this appeal assumes that we are still living in the simple personal relations of the good old times, and that every man can do the right thing when he wants to do it. But suppose a business man would be glad indeed to pay his young women the $12 a week which they need for a decent living, but all his competitors are paying from $7 down to $5. Shall he love himself into bankruptcy? In a time of industrial depression shall he employ men whom he does not need? And if he does, will his five loaves feed the five thousand unemployed that break his heart with their hungry eyes? If a man owns a hundred shares of stock in a great corporation, how can his love influence its wage scale with that puny stick? The old advice of love breaks down before the hugeness of modern relations. We might as well try to start a stranded ocean liner with the oar which poled our old dory from the mud banks many a time. It is indeed love that we want, but it is socialized love. Blessed be the love that holds the cup of water to thirsty lips. We can never do without the plain affection of man to man. But what we most need to-day is not the love that will break its back drawing water for a growing factory town from a well that was meant to supply a village, but a love so large and intelligent that it will persuade an ignorant people to build a system of waterworks up in the hills, and that will get after the thoughtless farmers who contaminate the brooks with typhoid bacilli,

protection for environment

and after the lumber concern that is denuding the watershed of its forests. We want a new avatar of love.

The Church has also put a new stress on the doctrine of stewardship, hoping to cure the hard selfishness of our commercial life by quickening the sense of responsibility in men of wealth. This also is wholly in the right direction, but here, too, the Church is still occupying the mental position of the old régime. The word "stewardship" itself comes down to us from an age of great landed proprietors. It has an antique dignity that guarantees it as harmless. The modern equivalent would be trusteeship. But a trustee does not own; he merely manages. If he mismanages or diverts trust funds to his own use, he is legally liable. If that is what we mean when we preach stewardship, we should be denying the private property rights on which capitalism rests, and, morally expropriating the owners. In that case we ought to see to it that this moral conception of property was embodied in the laws, and that the people would get orderly legal redress against stewards who have misused their trusteeship. That would mean a sort of Recall for business men. But in fact the Church puts no such cutting edge on the doctrine. It uses it to appeal to the conscience of powerful individuals to make them realize that they are accountable to God for the way they spend their money. The doctrine is not yet based on modern democratic feeling and on economic knowledge about the sources of modern wealth. It calls for no fundamental change in economic distribution, but simply encourages faithful disbursement of funds. That is not enough for our modern needs.

The Golden Rule is often held up as a sufficient solution of the social problem. "If only all men would act on the Golden Rule!" But curiously enough men find it hard to act on it, even when they indorse and praise it. There seem to be temptations of gain or of fear in our modern life before which our good intentions collapse. But even as a standard to guide our moral intelligence the Golden Rule is not really adequate for our needs. It is a wonderfully practical guide in all simple, personal relations. It appeals to our imagination to put ourselves in the other man's place and thus discover how we ought to treat him. It turns the flank of our selfishness, and compels that highly developed instinct in us to put itself into the service of love. Like the span measure of our right hand we can carry this rule about with us wherever we go, but it is hardly long enough to survey and lay out the building site of the New Jerusalem. Jesus probably did not intend it for more than an elementary method of figuring our duty.

The Church has also revived the thought of following Jesus in daily conduct, living over again the life of Christ, and doing in all things as he would do in our place. That has been an exceedingly influential thought in Christian history. In the life of Saint Francis and his brotherhood, in the radical sects, and in single radiant lives it has produced social forces of immense power. In our own time . . . we have seen thousands of young people trying for a week to live as Jesus would. But it is so high a law that only consecrated individuals can follow it permanently and intelligently, and even they may submit to it only in the high tide of their spiritual life. To most men the demand to live as Jesus would, is mainly useful to bring home the fact that it is hard to live a Christlike life in a mammonistic society. It convicts our social order of sin, but it does not reconstruct it.

These are all truly religious ideas, drawn from the teachings of Jesus himself, and very effective in sweetening and ennobling our personal relations. But they set up no ideal of human society, demand no transformation of social institutions, create no collective enthusiasms, and furnish no doctrinal basis for a public morality. They have not grown antiquated, and never will. But every step in the evolution of modern society makes them less adequate for its religious needs. The fact that the Church is leaning so hard on them at present shows how earnestly it is trying to meet the present need, and also how scanty is the equipment with which it confronts the new social task.

So we return to the question: What is the religious basis for the task of Christianizing and regenerating the social order? Suppose that a Christian man feels a throbbing compassion and fellow-feeling for the people, and a holy anger against the institutionalized wrong that is stunting and brutalizing their lives, converting the children of God into slaves of Mammon. Suppose that he feels this so strongly that he hardly cares what becomes of his own soul if only he can help his nation and race. Suppose that a whole generation is coming vaguely to feel that way. What great word of faith does historic Christianity offer to express and hallow and quicken this spiritual passion which is so evidently begotten of the spirit of Christ? Must he go to materialistic Socialism to find a dogmatic faith large enough to house him, and intellectual food nutritious enough to feed his hunger? Thousands have left the Church and have gone to Socialism, not to shake off a faith, but to get a faith.

I raise this challenge because I believe Christianity can meet it. My purpose is not critical, but wholly constructive. If I did not believe in the vitality and adaptability of the Christian faith, I should sit down with Job on the ashes and keep silence.

But let no one take the challenge lightly. It points to no superficial flaw in the working machinery of the Church, but to the failure of our religious ideas to connect with our religious needs, and that is fundamental. Religion, to have power over an age, must satisfy the highest moral and religious desires of that age. If it lags behind, and presents outgrown conceptions of life and duty, it is no longer in the full sense the Gospel.

Catholics were not inactive during the crises that attended the rise of industrialism. Of the millions of Catholics who immigrated to America after the Civil War, most of them found their way into the factories, mines, and shops of the nation. The Knights of Labor, the major labor group, attracted many church people to its ranks. When there was a move within the hierarchy to condemn the union, James Cardinal Gibbons stepped forward to defend it. The Knights of Labor had earlier been condemned in Canada, and he wanted to avoid a similar development in the United States. He called attention to the "grave and threatening social evils" and "public injustices" perpetrated by the cynical manipulators of the mammoth corporations. The labor union movement he termed "altogether natural and just" in response to the wrongs done to working people. That they could freely assemble to protect themselves he cited as a symbol of "the genius of our country." He warned that to deny Catholics this legitimate form of power would more than likely alienate millions of them from the Church. Cardinal Gibbons won his point, and the subject was dropped.[83]

Other Catholic prelates stepped forward to take the side of labor—most notably John Ireland, John J. Keane, and John L. Spaulding. In 1891 Pope Leo XIII issued the historic encyclical *Rerum novarum*. This document upheld the right of workers to join together in associations and even suggested that the government could intervene in order to correct the imbalance that existed between labor and management. Though a basically conservative instrument, it put the Church squarely on the side of progress in the industrial crisis.

One of the most significant developments of American Catholicism was the formation in 1917 of the National Catholic Welfare Conference (NCWC), an organization of American bishops which serves as a mechanism for providing the church with coordinated action on a national scale in educational and social matters. Headquartered in Washington, it keeps the church in close touch with policy issues that arise within the federal government. Its four departments cover the Catholic press, education, lay organizations, and social action. The last department was headed for years by John A. Ryan (1869–1945) and is responsible for acquainting Catholics with the church's teaching on social issues and for presenting the church's position to governmental figures. Ryan, one of the longtime and great leaders among Catholics in the fight for social justice, spent most of his career at the Catholic University of America in Washington. For over four decades he devoted his considerable talent and restless energy to publishing books and tracts that sharpened the conscience of the nation and the church. His favorite topic was "a living wage." It appears in most of his writings in one way or another and was the title of a chapter in *The Church and Labor* (1920), a book he helped to edit.

_____ *Document 48*

From "A Living Wage" by John A. Ryan

Although the idea of a living wage goes back at least to the early Middle Ages, it received its first systematic and authoritative expression in the Encyclical of Pope Leo XIII, "On the Condition of Labor." . . . In that document the great pontiff flatly rejected the prevailing doctrine that wages fixed by free consent were always fair and just. This theory, he said, leaves out of account certain important considerations. It ignores the fundamental fact that the laborer is morally bound to preserve

SOURCE: John A. Ryan and Joseph Husslein (eds.), *The Church and Labor* (New York: Macmillan, 1920), pp. 259–267.

[83] "Cardinal Gibbons' Defense of the Knights of Labor, February 20, 1887," *Documents of American Catholic History*, edited by John Tracy Ellis (Milwaukee, Wis.: The Bruce Publishing Company, 1956), pp. 460–473.

his life, and that his only means of fulfilling this duty is to be found in his wages. Therefore, concluded Pope Leo, "a workman's wages ought to be sufficient to maintain him in reasonable and frugal comfort." This proposition, he declared, is a "dictate of natural justice."

What is "reasonable comfort"? Evidently, it is something more than the conditions and essentials of mere existence. To have merely the means of continuing to live and to work is not to be in comfort. What degree of comfort is reasonable? To this question we could get a hundred different answers from as many different persons. Each of the one hundred might conceive reasonable comfort as that to which he had become accustomed, or that to which he aspired because it seemed to bring happiness to others. The reasonable comfort that the Pope had in mind is merely the reasonable minimum. It is that smallest amount which will satisfy right reason. . . .

Like every other human being, the wage-earner is a person, not a thing, nor a mere animal. Because he is a person, he has certain needs that are not felt by animals, and his needs and his welfare have a certain sacredness that does not belong to any other species of creatures. . . . He has intrinsic worth and dignity. He is made in the image and likeness of God. He is an end in himself. He was not created for the pleasure, or utility, or aggrandizement of any other human being or group of human beings. His worth and his place in the universe are to be measured with reference to himself, not with reference to other men, or to institutions, or to states. He is worth while for his own sake.

What, then, are the needs to which are attached this prerogative of intrinsic worth and sacredness? How much of the good things of life must a man have in order that he may live in a manner worthy of a person? In general, he must have sufficient goods and opportunities for the exercise of all his faculties and the development of his personality. On the physical side, this means food, clothing and housing adequate to maintain him in health and working efficiency. If he is underfed, or insufficiently clothed, or improperly housed, he is treated with even less consideration than wise and humane men extend to their beasts of burden. Since the worker is not merely an animal and an instrument of production, but an intellectual and moral person, he requires the means of exercising and developing the faculties of his soul. Therefore he needs some education, some facilities for reading and study, the means of practicing religion, an environment that will not make unreasonably difficult the leading of a moral life, and sufficient opportunities of social intercourse and recreation to maintain him in efficiency and to give him that degree of contentment that is essential to a healthy outlook on life. As regards the future, the worker requires a certain minimum amount of security against sickness, accident, and old age. Finally, all these goods should be available to the worker, not as a single man, but as the head of a family; for marriage is among the essential needs of the great majority.

All the foregoing goods and opportunities are included in the concept of reasonable comfort. Within the last few years, many groups of persons have attempted to translate these requisites into more concrete symbols. They have tried to describe reasonable comfort or a decent livelihood in terms of food, housing, insurance, etc. Their statements and estimates have shown a remarkable measure of agreement. This substantial uniformity proves that "reasonable comfort," is not only a practical and tangible conception, but one that springs from the deepest intuitions of reason and morality.

When we consider man's position in relation to the bounty of nature, we are led to accept three fundamental principles. The first may be thus stated: Since the earth was intended by God for the support of all persons, all have essentially equal claims upon it, and essentially equal rights of access to its benefits. On the one hand, God has not declared that any of His children have superior or exceptional claims to the earth. On the other hand, all persons are made in the image and likeness of God, composed of the same kind of body and soul, affected by the same needs, and destined for the same end. Therefore they are all equally important in His sight. They are all equally persons, endowed with intrinsic worth and dignity, ends in themselves, not instruments to the welfare of others. Hence they stand upon an essentially equal footing with regard to the animal, plant, and mineral bounty of the earth. This bounty is a common gift, possession, heritage. The moral claims upon it held by these equal human persons are essentially equal. No man can vindicate for himself a superior claim on the basis of anything that he finds in himself, in nature or in the designs of nature's God.

Nevertheless, this equal right of access to the earth is not absolute. It is conditioned upon labor, upon the expenditure of useful and fruitful energy. As a rule, the good things of the earth are obtained in adequate form and quantity only at the cost of considerable exertion. And this exertion is for the most part irksome, of such a nature that men will not perform it except under the compulsion of some less agreeable alternative. The labor to which the earth yields up her treasures is not put forth spontaneously and automatically. Therefore, the equal and inherent right of men to possess the earth and utilize its benefits becomes actually valid only when they are willing to expend productive energy and labor. This is the second fundamental principle.

From the two principles of equal right of access to the earth, and universal obligation to perform a reasonable amount of useful labor, follows a third fundamental principle. It is that men who at any time or in any way control the resources of the earth are morally bound to permit others to have access thereto on reasonable terms. Men who are willing to work must be enabled to make real and actual their original and equal right of access to the common bounty of nature. For the right to subsist from the earth implies the right actually to participate in its benefits on reasonable conditions and through reasonable arrangements. Otherwise the former right is a delusion. To refuse any man reasonable facilities to exercise his basic right of living from the common bounty by his labor is to treat this right as nonexistent. Such conduct by the men who are in possession implies a belief that their rights to the gifts of God are inherently superior to the right of the person whom they exclude. This position is utterly untenable. It is on exactly the same basis as would be the claim of a strong man to deprive a weak one of liberty. The right to freedom of movement is not more certain nor more indestructible than the right of access on reasonable terms to the bounty of the earth. Were a community to imprison an innocent man it would not violate his rights more vitally than does the proprietor or the corporation that deprives him of reasonable access to the resources of nature. In both cases the good that he seeks is a common gift of God.

This, then, is the moral basis underlying the laborer's right to a living wage. Like all other men, he has an indestructible right of access to the goods of the earth on reasonable terms. Obviously, the conditional clause, "on reasonable terms," is of very great importance. Neither the laborer nor anyone else has a right of direct and unconditional access to those portions of the earth that have rightly become the property of others. Such a claim would be the height of unreason. The laborer's right to participate in the common heritage must be actualized in such a way as not to interfere with the equally valid rights of others. The laborer's right must be satisfied with due regard to existing acquired rights and the existing form of industrial organization.

For the wage-earner of to-day, therefore, access to the resources of nature can be had only through wages. The men who have appropriated the goods and opportunities of the earth have shut him out from any other way of entering upon his natural heritage. Therefore they are morally bound to use and administer these goods in such a way that his right shall not be violated and his access to the resources of nature not rendered unreasonably difficult. This means that the industrial community in which he lives, and for which he labors, shall provide him with the requisites of a decent livelihood in the form of living wages. On the one hand, the worker has performed a reasonable amount of labor; on the other hand, the industrial community is the beneficiary of his services. In the product which he has created the community has the wherewith to pay him living wages. To refuse him this amount of remuneration is surely to deprive him of access to the earth and to a livelihood on reasonable terms.

Though wracked by panics and economic instability during the nineteenth century, the single greatest economic crisis in American history was, of course, the Great Depression of the 1930s. During that period millions of Americans suffered severe economic deprivation. Frederick Lewis Allen has described the scene:

The major phenomena of the Depression were mostly negative and did not assail the eye.
But if you knew where to look, some of them would begin to appear. First, the breadlines in the poorer districts. Second, those bleak settlements ironically known as "Hoovervilles" in the outskirts of the cities and on vacant lots—groups of makeshift shacks constructed out of packing boxes, scrap iron, anything that could be picked up free in a diligent combing of the city dumps: shacks in which men and sometimes whole families of evicted people were sleeping on automobile seats carried from auto-graveyards, warming themselves before fires of rubbish in grease drums. Third, the homeless people sleeping in doorways or on park benches, and going the rounds of the restaurants for left-over half-eaten biscuits, piecrusts, anything to keep the fires of life burning. Fourth, the vastly increased number of thumbers on the highways, and particularly of freight-car transients on the railroads: a huge army of drifters ever on the move, searching half-aimlessly for a place where there might be a job. According to Jonathan Norton Leonard, the Missouri Pacific Railroad in 1929 had "taken official cognizance" of 13,745 migrants; by 1931 the figure had already jumped to 186,028. It was estimated that by the beginning of 1933, the country over, there were a million of these transients on the move. Forty-five thousand had passed through El Paso

in the space of six months; 1,500 were passing through Kansas City every day. Among them were large numbers of young boys, and girls disguised as boys. According to the Children's Bureau, there were 200,000 children thus drifting about the United States. So huge was the number of freight-car hoppers in the Southwest that in a number of places the railroad police simply had to give up trying to remove them from the trains: there were far too many of them.[84]

Even many of those who had been prosperous lost everything they had. Bankruptcy was a common event. Wall Street financiers jumped out of office windows. Times were hard.

The nation responded to the crisis by turning out of office a president who was later judged to have been one of the more competent individuals to occupy the office. Nearly everyone now agrees that Herbert Hoover was the victim of circumstance. Perhaps no one could have handled it. In his place they elected Franklin D. Roosevelt, who had forced a coalition between the incipient power of the labor movement, big-city bosses, the Eastern liberal establishment, and the residual populist voters in the South. The black population, insofar as it could make its power felt (poll taxes were still the rule in the South), lost practically all identification with the party of Lincoln and cast its lot with the patrician Roosevelt. Those blacks who had moved to the big industrial centers acquired a relationship with the big-city bosses.

Notable in both the labor movement and the big-city machines were the large ethnic groups. Most had migrated to the United States around the turn of the century and most were Catholic. Democratic candidates in the heavily industrialized areas began to recognize the significance of the "Catholic" vote. F.D.R. was particularly attentive to this fact. Prominent laymen served in his administration—Joe Kennedy, Jim Farley, and Frank Murphy among others. They, in turn, became a vital link to the hierarchy. Roosevelt even found clerics to be helpful. Chief among his counselors was John Ryan. So unblinking was he in his support of the president that he was affectionately known as "the Right Reverend New Dealer."

One of the most unusual responses to the economic crisis of the 1930s arose within Catholicism itself. Indeed, so naive was the Catholic Worker Movement that it was reminscent of a much earlier period. Perhaps the fact that its witness is so radical is what gives the movement its staying power. In quite another sense, however, the Catholic Worker Movement (CWM) seems very up-to-date. Its communitarian base is not too different from that of similar movements which grew out of the protests of the 1960s and the counterculture.

The two central figures in the movement were Peter Maurin and Dorothy Day. Maurin, a Frenchman who had made his way to the United States by way of Canada, became the chief theoretician of the movement, while Miss Day became the chief polemicist and guiding

[84]Frederick Lews Allen, *Since Yesterday: The Nineteen-Thirties in America* (New York: Harper, 1940), pp. 60–61.

hand behind *The Catholic Worker*, a publication obviously designed to offer a Christian alternative to *The Daily Worker*, an official organ of the Communist party in the United States. The CWM was not about to concede the territory to the Communists, whose program—confrontation and violence—was no more acceptable than that of unbridled capitalism. For the CWM, the only answer was what has been described as "voluntary socialism," voluntary solidarity with the poor.

The chief concern for Maurin and Day was the prevailing secularism of the period. The believed that the church as an institution had become so insulated from the principal issues of the day that it had lost its relevance. It did not reach people in their despair. Indeed, they could see no significant action by the church to deal with the increasingly impersonal nature of modern society, where mass production dehumanized the workers, where big government forgot its role as servant of the people, where even the labor movement had succumbed to bigness and failed to deal with individuals and their needs. The CWM envisioned a new, integrated world in which each person will be seen as a creature of God, redeemed by Christ, and consequently of incalculable worth. David J. O'Brien has written of Maurin:

> His program differed markedly from the usual Catholic social outline. Although believing strongly in the dignity of labor, Maurin had little use for unions, since in selling their labor, workers were equally guilty with capitalists of treating it as a commodity. Maurin feared that as long as men accepted the assembly line and the abundance of the factory system, they would not think in terms of personality or community. . . . Maurin called for decentralization, voluntary cooperation, mutual aid, and rural handicrafts, free from state control, centralized power and commercialization.
>
> He saw no hope of achieving these objectives through politics because politicians were forced to follow rather than form public opinion. . . . Reform began with the individual's acceptance of solidarity with the poor and personal responsibility for the reconstruction of his own life and the life of society.[85]

It is instructive to note how the venerable tradition of poverty informed the Catholic Worker Movement. By holding to the ideal of voluntary poverty, the movement stood in radical contrast to the major reform proposals suggested by the politicians and technocrats of the day. The movement rejected the socialist concept of class struggle and held that the primary causes of the economic crisis were avarice and greed. By identifying with the plight of the worker and practicing charity, said the CWM, the true Christian solution was to be found. They formed "houses of hospitality" in the urban centers where Cath-

---

[85] David J. O'Brien, *American Catholics and Social Reform: The New Deal Years* (New York: Oxford, 1968), p. 196. Much of this section is indebted to O'Brien's excellent essay. See also William D. Miller's very fine treatment of the movement in *A Harsh and Dreadful Love: Dorothy Day and the Catholic Worker Movement* (New York: Liveright, 1973). One should also consult Dorothy Day, *House of Hospitality* (New York: Sheed, 1939), *From Union Square to Rome* (Silver Spring, Md.: Preservation of the Faith Press, 1938), *Loaves and Fishes* (Garden City, N.Y.: Doubleday, 1952), and *The Long Loneliness* (New York: Harper, 1952).

olics could actually practice voluntary poverty and share the lot of those who had nothing. They felt that to possess a surplus of anything —as long as there were those in need—was unthinkable and wished not to convert those who came to the houses for help but only to join them in their suffering. The hope was that by assuming solidarity with the poor, they might influence others to follow their example. In 1936, the movement formed its first farming commune in Pennsylvania, which had essentially the same goal as the urban houses of hospitality.

Miss Day, one of the great women in the history of American religion, was born in Illinois and attended the University of Illinois. She was converted to Catholicism after a brief sojourn as an Episcopalian. Early in her life, she was overwhelmed with the condition of the average American worker and first turned to the programs espoused by the "far left." She was a member of the Socialist party and became involved with the Industrial Workers of the World—popularly known as the "Wobblies." Her practice of solidarity is therefore traceable back to these early days. However, O'Brien points out that, after her conversion to Catholicism, she found a natural theoretical or theological basis for her belief in the communitarian approach, for each individual is part of the Mystical Body of Christ.[86]

The interests of the Catholic Worker Movement were not confined to the plight of the poor, however. It also turned its energies to causes such as pacifism, racial injustice, and anti-Semitism. In recent years, the movement has been vehement in its opposition to America's involvement in war and was a rallying point for many who conscientiously objected to forced military service. In the beginning, the movement had almost universal support from the Catholic press and the hierarchy, but the more it became involved with issues beyond concern for the poor and the ideal of voluntary poverty, the less support there was.

It is difficult to assess the long-term effects of the movement. Its leaders' confidence in the power of the average layperson to contribute directly to solving widespread social problems was a hint of the laicism that was to become popular under the leadership of Pope John XXIII. It inculcated among the laity an independence of thought and action rarely before seen in the history of American Catholicism. When there was a conflict, the members of the movement simply refused to let the authority of the church be substituted for their own consciences. A whole generation of younger Catholics have therefore found in the movement a model for Christian witness in a world they believe to have become increasingly more inhumane.

Some have considered the movement so naive as to have been impractical and ineffective over the long haul. Perhaps it did tend to oversimplify issues by polarizing them into a conflict between the person and the state or between the individual and the organization. Perhaps it

[86]*Ibid.*, p. 201.

did err when it underestimated the capacity of government to correct the evils of the day. As O'Brien says, however,

> if they erred, they did so on the side of freedom and human dignity and they stirred the American Catholic conscience as no one had done before. In the days of abundance that followed World War II the issues of income distribution, union organization, and industrial government which dominated Catholic social thought during the Depression seemed increasingly irrelevant. The problems that disturbed Peter Maurin and Dorothy Day—depersonalization, bureaucracy, racism, and war—became the great issues confronting the American people. Desspite the weaknesses of their thought, the Catholic Workers, far more than their contemporaries, were true prophets of American Catholicism.[87]

Prophets indeed. For later generations who lived through the crises of the Cold War, Little Rock, Watts, Vietnam, and Watergate, the analysis offered by the Catholic Worker Movement was deadly. Martin Luther King, Jr., and Harvey Cox, if they were not in the direct line of descent from Dorothy Day and Peter Maurin, would find much to their liking in the movement. But, then, they would also find the work of John Ryan compatible.

The social gospel, by whatever tag it is identified, then, has become a permanent feature of the American religious environment; though initially a Protestant phenomenon, it has had its Catholic expression as well.

Summary

And so the debate continues. What should the ecclesial religious groups of America have to do with the social and economic problems of the nation? Should they intervene directly in order to force change of some kind? Or should they be content to concern themselves primarily with the private lives and consciences of their members? This question, of course, has tremendous implications for the morally sensitive person. For those who accept any version of Western monotheism, there has to be only *one* absolute answer to such a question.

But the genius of American religion inheres in the fact that we are likely to recieve a plurality of answers to such a question, for before the law and before the American society generally, there can be no single answer. We are dedicated to the value of many answers.

It is not unimportant to note, in this connection, that it is precisely in a culture within which pluralism is the order of the day and where a religious establishment is forbidden that some of the most active and longstanding social gospel efforts have been achieved. *Because* religion is purely a voluntary matter, the social gospel could thrive in the first place.

[87]*Ibid.*, p. 210.

The question of missions is a bit more complicated, as we have seen. Indeed, there is now a fundamental quandary about the purpose of "foreign missions"—whether American religious groups can still defend themselves as "sending" churches. While some of the Pentecostal and Adventists groups—the "Third Force"—continue to justify the traditional methods of mission in foreign lands, main-line Protestants have severe doubts about the old strategies. Technical assistance can be offered the indigenous churches in other lands, but that is about the extent of what should be done, they say. Further, the churches "over there" have much to tell churches in America by sending their word to us.

Now is a pivotal moment in missions. With the shocks of the Southeast Asian conflict still very much in mind, it will probably take American religious groups some time to sort out the question of missions. The rhetoric of a John Mott seems quite dated.

7 Black and White in the American Religious Pattern

The religious experience of the Afro-American minority population demonstrates anew the intricate and inextricable way in which religion and culture are related. As H. Richard Niebuhr stressed over fifty years ago, one cannot interpret the "black and white" religious experience in America without recourse to the sociological principle of racial caste.[1] Both black and white religious consciousness and institutional forms have been shaped by the pattern of interplay between master and slave populations and between economically and culturally "superior" and "inferior" social groupings. Yet even though secular social structures have determined the religious patterns of "black and white" Americans, the religious experience has, in turn, influenced American culture in the secular realms of the arts, the sciences, and politics.

The Dilemma

In his classic study the Swedish sociologist Gunnar Myrdal characterized the racial problem in America as a "dilemma."[2] The dilemma, Myrdal maintained, arises out of the disparity between the American "creed" of equality and the actual status of black Americans. A dilemma is a special kind of problem that cannot be resolved within the structure in which it is posed. The original slave and the later racial caste status has been the overwhelming reality for the black religious experience in particular as well as for the Afro-American experience in general. In much of the "official" version of the general religious experience in America, there has been a "concealment" or an unconscious repression of the very reality of black religion. Similar to the way in which the novelist Ralph Ellison could speak, in writing of the black experience in America, of the "invisible man,"[3] so the antebellum black church has often been referred to as an "invisible" institution and much of the black religious experience has gone unacknowledged and unchron-

---

[1] H. Richard Niebuhr, *The Social Sources of Denominationalism* (New York: World Publishing, 1929), pp. 236–263.

[2] Gunnar Myrdal, *An American Dilemma* (New York: Harper & Row, 1944).

[3] See Ralph Ellison, *Invisible Man* (New York: Random House, 1947), p. 3: "I am an invisible man. No, I am not a spook like those who haunted Edgar Allan Poe; nor am I one of your Hollywood-movie ectoplasms. I am a man of substance, of flesh and bone, fiber and liquids— and I might even be said to possess a mind. I am invisible, understand, simply because people refuse to see me."

354

icled.[4] Although Afro-Americans were brought to Colonial America as early as 1619 and although the slave and free black populations continued to increase, the black experience is not reflected in the original documents of the American civil religion. In the beginning of the American civil religious tradition the primary conceptual framework was provided by the language of Puritanism and the Enlightenment. As the Puritans finally excluded the American Indians as candidates for admission to the covenant, so the Jeffersonians compromised on the issue of the inclusion of slaves in the national covenant of those "men created equal." This decision rendered "invisible" those peoples not in the original act of "founding." The horns of the national dilemma were set from the beginning.

It is an interesting fact that responses to the original omission have occurred dramatically in approximately hundred year cycles. Thus in the 1860s there was a tragic engagement of the issues of the exclusion that had occurred in 1776 and 1787. In the decades of the 1950s and 1960s there was another movement that had as its goal the bringing to visibility of the "invisible people."

"BLACK AND WHITE TOGETHER": THE CIVIL RIGHTS MOVEMENT, 1954-1966

In the decade 1954-1966 there emerged a "freedom movement" for full equality on the part of "Negro" people and for their complete integration into all structures of American life. The beginning of the movement usually is dated May 17, 1954, when the United States Supreme Court, in the case *Brown* v. *Board of Education*, judged that the "separate but equal" doctrine on which the segregation of school facilities had been based was unconstitutional.[5] The Court ordered the desegregation of public schools with all deliberate speed. This decision by the Court probably encouraged a belief in faster progress toward racial justice and integration. For the first time since Reconstruction it seemed possible that the governmental institutions of the nation might be mobilized to bring decisive changes toward racial justice.

The next dramatic event occurred in the form of the Montgomery bus boycott in December 1955. A black seamstress, Rosa Parks, decided that she was too tired to move to the back of the bus at the driver's direction, and she thereby triggered the boycott. The leadership of the boycott fell upon the new young minister of Montgomery's Dexter Avenue Baptist Church, Martin Luther King, Jr. In the wake of the effectiveness of

[4] See E. Franklin Frazier, *The Negro Church in America* (New York: Schocken Books, 1964), pp. 16ff.
[5] *Brown*, et al. v. *Board of Education of Topeka*, et al. See George Ducas and Charles Van Doren (eds.), *Great Documents in Black American History* (New York: Praeger, 1970), pp. 253-261.

the boycott there came bombings, legal harassments, and the spreading of bus boycotts to other cities.

Encouraged by Dr. King's example of Gandhian nonviolent tactics, students in Greensboro, North Carolina, devised the tactic of the "sit-ins" at the segregated lunch counters in local five-and-dime stores. This student movement, beginning in 1958 and 1959, spread to other cities. On May 4, 1961, the first "freedom rides" began, protesting segregated facilities that were regulated by interstate commerce. In 1963 a major breakthrough was won in Birmingham, Alabama, for Negro employment and public accommodations. In Birmingham and in Albany, Georgia, Dr. King went to jail for leading demonstrations. On August 28, 1963, more than 250,000 whites and Negroes staged a peaceful march and demonstration in Washington for civil rights and jobs.

On June 2, 1964, a civil rights bill was enacted that focused on black inclusion in public accommodations. The impact of the religious communities on the influencing of the passage of this bill was great. For the first time in American history a single Protestant, Eastern Orthodox, Roman Catholic, and Jewish testimony was presented to Congress in support of legislation. The consensus of proponents and opponents of the bill was that the legislation passed because of the persistent power of the religious communities. Senator Russell of Georgia purportedly said it had passed because "those damn preachers had got the idea it was a moral issue."[6]

In the summer of 1964 the Council of Federated Organizations developed a summer project working in Mississippi. Hundreds of students recruited by the cooperating organizations were trained by the National Council of Churches and then sent out to do remedial teaching and community organization for citizenship among impoverished blacks of Mississippi.

With the 1964 Civil Rights Act on the books, 1965 became a year of changing focus for the civil rights movement. The objective shifted from desegregating public facilities to political action. Dr. King selected Selma, Alabama, in the heart of the "black belt" region, because Selma was a city that had a potential majority of black voters who were disenfranchised by the white power structure. On Sunday, March 7, several hundred Negroes attempted to march from Selma to the state capitol in Montgomery, which was fifty miles away. Mounted state police and sheriff's deputies unleashed a brutal attack on the men, women, and children as they attempted to cross the bridge that spanned the Alabama river on the east side of the town. The nation's attention focused on Selma as the Department of Justice entered the case and petitioned for an injunction against state officials who had tried to prevent the march.

---

[6] According to Robert W. Spike, *The Freedom Revolution and the Churches* (New York: Association Press, 1965), p. 108.

Members of the clergy and civil rights leaders descended on the Alabama community. Certainly one of the most inspiring and somewhat incongruous sights in American religious history was to see Archbishop Iakovos, primate of the Greek Orthodox Church in the Western Hemisphere; Rabbi Abraham Heschel; Roman priests; and Martin Luther King, Jr., locked arm in arm in Selma's Brown's Chapel, swaying and singing the freedom movement anthem:

> We shall overcome
> We shall overcome
> We shall overcome, someday.
> Oh, deep in my heart,
> I do believe
> We shall overcome someday.
>
> Black and white together
> Black and white together
> Black and white together, someday.
> Oh, deep in my heart,
> I do believe
> We shall overcome someday.

The federal judge in Montgomery issued the injunction and the victorious march from Selma to Montgomery had a festival dimension to it. Nuns, priests, rabbis, seminarians, and celebrities all joined with local blacks in the march to the Alabama capitol building in Montgomery. President Lyndon Johnson had announced he would send a voting rights bill to Congress.

The Selma to Montgomery march constituted the peak of the civil rights movement. Congress passed the Voting Rights Act, August 4, 1965. It was signed on August 6. The act provided new tools to assure the right to vote and supplemented the previous authority granted in the Civil Rights Acts of 1957, 1960, and 1964. But on August 11, a seven-day period of race riots, considered by many the worst in the nation's history, broke out in the Watts area of Los Angeles, California. "Black Power" advocates gained control of civil rights organizations that had previously been committed to nonviolent strategies. After Selma, 1965, the civil rights movement shifted from the South to the great urban centers of the North. When this happened there was a noticeable falling away of white liberal support for civil rights activities. Even before the assassination of Dr. King, April 4, 1968, the momentum of the movement had been significantly reduced and the objective of integration was being exchanged for that of black identity and "black power."

Clearly, Martin Luther King, Jr., provided the inspiration for the civil rights movement, 1954–1966. As founder and president of the Southern Christian Leadership Conference, Dr. King represented the vital center of the movement that had both more conservative and more militant representatives. As a theologian-clergyman, he articulated such a high moral social criticism and advocated nonviolent tactics for social change in such an earnest manner that he aroused the conscience of the nation. In the person and work of Martin Luther King two streams of the American religious tradition converged. One, of course, was southern black religion. The other was the liberal Protestant social ethics to which he was exposed during his doctoral studies at Boston University.[7] King learned of pacifism from representatives of the Social Gospel tradition, rigorous pacifists such as Walter Muelder and Alan Knight Chalmers. From Edgar Sheffield Brightman (1919–1953) and Harold DeWolf (1905–   ) he caught the commitment to the philosophical-theological position of personal idealism, an expression of religious liberalism based on a philosophical theology that emphasized the concept of person as a metaphysical and value orientation. It was the combination of able black Baptist preacher and university scholar that enabled him to lead so effectively.

King's oratory was rich and inspiring. A splendid example of his ability to move a crowd was his climactic articulation of black hopes and aspirations in front of the Lincoln Memorial in the march on Washington, August 28, 1963.

> I have a dream that one day,
> on the red hills of Georgia,
> sons of former slaves and the
> sons of former slaveowners will be able
> to sit down together at the table of brotherhood.
> I have a dream that one day even the
> state of Mississippi, a state sweltering
> with the heat of injustice, sweltering
> with the heat of oppression, will be
> transformed into an oasis of freedom and justice.
> I have a dream that my little children will
> one day live in a nation where they will not
> be judged by the color of their skin
> but by the content of their character. . . .[8]

One of the most eloquent statements that Dr. King ever made was his classic "Letter from Birmingham Jail." The letter was occasioned by the protest of eight clergymen that Dr. King was disturbing the peace of Birmingham by leading civil rights demonstrations. The following was Dr. King's reply.

[7]Martin Luther King, Jr., *Stride Toward Freedom: The Montgomery Story* (New York: Harper & Row, 1958), p. 100.
[8]Quoted in C. Eric Lincoln, *The Negro Pilgrimage in America* (New York: Praeger, 1969), p. 153.

Document 49

"Letter from Birmingham Jail" by Martin Luther King, Jr.[1]

April 16, 1963

My Dear Fellow Clergymen:

While confined here in the Birmingham city jail, I came across your recent statement calling my present activities "unwise and untimely." Seldom do I pause to answer criticism of my work and ideas. If I sought to answer all the criticisms that cross my desk, my secretaries would have little time for anything other than such correspondence in the course of the day, and I would have no time for constructive work. But since I feel that you are men of genuine good will and that your criticisms are sincerely set forth, I want to try to answer your statement in what I hope will be patient and reasonable terms.

I think I should indicate why I am here in Birmingham, since you have been influenced by the view which argues against "outsiders coming in." I have the honor of serving as president of the Southern Christian Leadership Conference, an organization operating in every southern state, with headquarters in Atlanta, Georgia. We have some eighty-five affiliated organizations across the South, and one of them is the Alabama Christian Movement for Human Rights. Frequently we share staff, educational and financial resources with our affiliates. Several months ago the affiliate here in Birmingham asked us to be on call to engage in a nonviolent direct-action program if such were deemed necessary. We readily consented, and when the hour came we lived up to our promise. So I, along with several members of my staff, am here because I was invited here. I am here because I have organizational ties here.

But more basically, I am in Birmingham because injustice is here. Just as the prophets of the eighth century B.C. left their villages and carried their "thus saith the Lord" far beyond the boundaries of their home towns, and just as the Apostle Paul left his village of Tarsus and carried the gospel of Jesus Christ to the far corners of the Greco-Roman world, so am I compelled to carry the gospel of freedom beyond my own home town. Like Paul, I must constantly respond to the Macedonian call for aid.

Moreover, I am cognizant of the interrelatedness of all communities and states. I cannot sit idly by in Atlanta and not be concerned about what happens in Birmingham. Injustice anywhere is a threat to justice everywhere. We are caught in an

[1] AUTHOR'S NOTE: This response to a published statement by eight fellow clergymen from Alabama (Bishop C. C. J. Carpenter, Bishop Joseph A. Durick, Rabbi Hilton L. Grafman, Bishop Paul Hardin, Bishop Nolan B. Harmon, the Reverend George M. Murray, the Reverend Edward V. Ramage and the Reverend Earl Stallings) was composed under somewhat constricting circumstances. Begun on the margins of the newspaper in which the statement appeared while I was in jail, the letter was continued on scraps of writing paper supplied by a friendly Negro trusty, and concluded on a pad my attorneys were eventually permitted to leave me. Although the text remains in substance unaltered, I have indulged in the author's prerogative of polishing it for publication.

inescapable network of mutuality, tied in a single garment of destiny. Whatever affects one directly, affects all indirectly. Never again can we afford to live with the narrow, provincial "outside agitator" idea. Anyone who lives inside the United States can never be considered an outsider anywhere within its bounds.

You deplore the demonstration taking place in Birmingham. But your statement, I am sorry to say, fails to express a similar concern for the conditions that brought about the demonstrations. I am sure that none of you would want to rest content with the superficial kind of social analysis that deals merely with effects and does not grapple with underlying causes. It is unfortunate that demonstrations are taking place in Birmingham, but it is even more unfortunate that the city's white power structure left the Negro community with no alternative.

In any nonviolent campaign there are four basic steps: collection of the facts to determine whether injustices exist; negotiation; self-purification; and direct action. We have gone through all these steps in Birmingham. There can be no gainsaying the fact that racial injustice engulfs this community. Birmingham is probably the most thoroughly segregated city in the United States. Its ugly record of brutality is widely known. Negroes have experienced grossly unjust treatment in the courts. There have been more unsolved bombing of Negro homes and churches in Birmingham than in any other city in the nation. These are the hard brutal facts of the case. On the basis of these conditions, Negro leaders sought to negotiate with the city fathers. But the latter consistently refused to engage in good-faith negotiation.

Then, last September, came the opportunity to talk with leaders of Birmingham's economic community. In the course of the negotiations, certain promises were made by the merchants—for example, to remove the stores' humiliating racial signs. On the basis of these promises, the Reverend Fred Shuttlesworth and the leaders of the Alabama Christian Movement for Human Rights agreed to a moratorium on all demonstrations. As the weeks and months went by, we realized that we were the victims of a broken promise. A few signs, briefly removed, returned; the others remained.

As in so many past experiences, our hopes had been blasted, and the shadow of deep disappointment settled upon us. We had no alternative except to prepare for direct action, whereby we would present our very bodies as a means of laying our case before the conscience of the local and the national community. Mindful of the difficulties involved, we decided to undertake a process of self-purification. We began a series of workshops on nonviolence, and we repeatedly asked ourselves: "Are you able to accept blows without retaliating?" "Are you able to endure the ordeal of jail?" We decided to schedule our direct-action program for the Easter season, realizing that except for Christmas, this is the main shopping period of the year. Knowing that a strong economic-withdrawal program would be the byproduct of direct action, we felt that this would be the best time to bring pressure to bear on the merchants for the needed change.

Then it occurred to us that Birmingham's mayoralty election was coming up in March, and we speedily decided to postpone action until after election day. When we discovered that the Commissioner of Public Safety, Eugene "Bull" Connor, had piled up enough votes to be in the run-off, we decided again to postpone action until the day of the run-off so that the demonstrations could not be used to cloud the issues. Like many others, we waited to see Mr. Connor defeated, and to this end we endured postponement after postponement. Having aided in this community need, we felt that our direct-action program could be delayed no longer.

You may well ask: "Why direct action? Why sit-ins, marches and so forth? Isn't negotiation a better path?" You are quite right in calling for negotiation. Indeed, this is the very purpose of direct action. Nonviolent direct action seeks to create such a crisis and foster such a tension that a community which has constantly refused to negotiate is forced to confront the issue. It seeks so to dramatize the issue that it can no longer be ignored. My citing the creation of tension as part of the work of the nonviolent-register may sound rather shocking. But I must confess that I am not afraid of the word "tension." I have earnestly opposed violent tension, but there is a type of constructive nonviolent tension which is necessary for growth. Just as Socrates felt that it was necessary to create a tension in the mind so that individuals could rise from the bondage of myths and half-truths to the unfettered realm of creative analysis and objective appraisal, so must we see the need for nonviolent gadflies to create the kind of tension in society that will help men rise from the dark depths of prejudice and racism to the majestic heights of understanding and brotherhood.

The purpose of our direct-action program is to create a situation so crisis-packed that it will inevitably open the door to negotiation. I therefore concur with you in your call for negotiation. Too long has our beloved Southland been bogged down in a tragic effort to live in monologue rather than dialogue.

One of the basic points in your statement is that the action that I and my associates have taken in Birmingham is untimely. Some have asked: "Why didn't you give the new city administration time to act?" The only answer that I can give to this query is that the new Birmingham administration must be prodded about as much as the outgoing one, before it will act. We are sadly mistaken if we feel that the election of Albert Boutwell as mayor will bring the millennium to Birmingham. While Mr. Boutwell is a much more gentle person than Mr. Connor, they are both segregationists, dedicated to maintenance of the status quo. I have hope that Mr. Boutwell will be reasonable enough to see the futility of massive resistance to desegregation. But he will not see this without pressure from devotees of civil rights. My friends, I must say to you that we have not made a single gain in civil rights without determined legal and nonviolent pressure. Lamentably, it is an historical fact that privileged groups seldom give up their privileges voluntarily. Individuals may see the moral light and voluntarily give up their unjust posture; but, as Reinhold Niebuhr has reminded us, groups tend to be more immoral than individuals.

We know through painful experience that freedom is never voluntarily given by the oppressor; it must be demanded by the oppressed. Frankly, I have yet to engage in a direct-action campaign that was "well timed" in the view of those who have not suffered unduly from the disease of segregation. For years now I have heard the word "Wait!" It rings in the ear of every Negro with piercing familiarity. This "Wait" has almost always meant "Never." We must come to see, with one of our distinguished jurists, that "justice too long delayed is justice denied."

We have waited for more than 340 years for our constitutional and God-given rights. The nations of Asia and Africa are moving with jetlike speed toward gaining

political independence, but we still creep at horse-and-buggy pace toward gaining a
cup of coffee at a lunch counter. Perhaps it is easy for those who have never felt
the stinging darts of segregation to say, "Wait." But when you have seen vicious
mobs lynch your mothers and fathers at will and drown your sisters and brothers
at whim; when you have seen hate-filled policemen curse, kick and even kill your
black brothers and sisters; when you see the vast majority of your twenty million
Negro brothers smothering in an airtight cage of poverty in the midst of an affluent
society; when you suddenly find your tongue twisted and your speech stammering
as you seek to explain to your six-year-old daughter why she can't go to the public
amusement park that has just been advertised on television, and see tears welling
up in her eyes when she is told that Funtown is closed to colored children, and see
ominous clouds of inferiority beginning to form in her little mental sky, and see her
beginning to distort her personality by developing an unconscious bitterness toward
white people; when you have to concoct an answer for a five-year-old son who is
asking: "Daddy, why do white people treat colored people so mean?"; when you
take a cross-country drive and find it necessary to sleep night after night in the uncomfortable corners of your automobile because no motel will accept you; when
you are humiliated day in and day out by nagging signs reading "white" and "colored"; when your first name becomes "nigger," your middle name becomes "boy"
(however old you are) and your last name becomes "John," and your wife and
mother are never given the respected title "Mrs."; when you are harried by day and
haunted by night by the fact that you are a Negro, living constantly at tiptoe stance,
never quite knowing what to expect next, and are plagued with inner fears and
outer resentments; when you are forever fighting a degenerating sense of "nobodi-
ness"—then you will understand why we find it difficult to wait. There comes a
time when the cup of endurance runs over, and men are no longer willing to be
plunged into the abyss of despair. I hope, sirs, you can understand our legitimate
and unavoidable impatience.

You express a great deal of anxiety over our willingness to break laws. This is
certainly a legitimate concern. Since we so diligently urge people to obey the Supreme Court's decision of 1954 outlawing segregation in the public schools, at first
glance it may seem rather paradoxical for us consciously to break laws. One may
well ask: "How can you advocate breaking some laws and obeying others?" The
answer lies in the fact that there are two types of laws: just and unjust. I would be
the first to advocate obeying just laws. One has not only a legal but a moral responsibility to obey just laws. Conversely, one has a moral responsibility to disobey unjust laws. I would agree with St. Augustine that "an unjust law is no law at all."

Now, what is the difference between the two? How does one determine whether
a law is just or unjust? A just law is a man-made code that squares with the moral
law or the law of God. An unjust law is a code that is out of harmony with the
moral law. To put it in the terms of St. Thomas Aquinas: An unjust law is a human
law that is not rooted in eternal law and natural law. Any law that uplifts human
personality is just. Any law that degrades human personality is unjust. All segregation statutes are unjust because segregation distorts the soul and damages the personality. It gives the segregator a false sense of superiority and the segregated a
false sense of inferiority. Segregation, to use the terminology of the Jewish phi-

losopher Martin Buber, substitutes an "I-it" relationship for an "I-thou" relationship and ends up relegating persons to the status of things. Hence segregation is not only politically, economically and sociologically unsound, it is morally wrong and sinful. Paul Tillich has said that sin is separation. Is not segregation an existential expression of man's tragic separation, his awful estrangement, his terrible sinfulness. Thus it is that I can urge men to obey the 1954 decision of the Supreme Court, for it is morally right; and I can urge them to disobey segregation ordinances, for they are morally wrong.

Let us consider a more concrete example of just and unjust laws. An unjust law is a code that a numerical or power majority group compels a minority group to obey but does not make binding on itself. This is *difference* made legal. By the same token, a just law is a code that a majority compels a minority to follow and that it is willing to follow itself. This is *sameness* made legal.

Let me give another explanation. A law is unjust if it is inflicted on a minority that, as a result of being denied the right to vote, had no part in enacting or devising the law. Who can say that the legislature of Alabama which set up that state's segregation laws was democratically elected? Throughout Alabama all sorts of devious methods are used to prevent Negroes from becoming registered voters, and there are some counties in which even though Negroes constitute a majority of the population, not a single Negro is registered. Can any law enacted under such circumstances be considered democratically structured?

Sometimes a law is just on its face and unjust in its application. For instance, I have been arrested on a charge of parading without a permit. Now, there is nothing wrong in having an ordinance which requires a permit for a parade. But such an ordinance becomes unjust when it is used to maintain segregation and to deny citizens the First-Amendment privilege of peaceful assembly and protest.

I hope you are able to see the distinction I am trying to point out. In no sense do I advocate evading or defying the law, as would the rabid segregationist. That would lead to anarchy. One who breaks an unjust law must do so openly, lovingly, and with a willingness to accept the penalty. I submit that an individual who breaks a law that conscience tells him is unjust, and who willingly accepts the penalty of imprisonment in order to arouse the conscience of the community over its injustice, is in reality expressing the highest respect for law.

Of course, there is nothing new about this kind of civil disobedience. It was experienced sublimely in the refusal of Shadrach, Meshach and Abednego to obey the laws of Nebuchadnezzar, on the ground that a higher moral law was at stake. It was practiced superbly by the early Christians, who were willing to face hungry lions and the excruciating pain of chopping blocks rather than submit to certain unjust laws of the Roman Empire. To a degree, academic freedom is a reality today because Socrates practiced civil disobedience. In our nation, the Boston Tea Party represented a massive act of civil disobedience.

We should never forget that everything that Adolf Hitler did in Germany was "legal" and everything the Hungarian freedom fighters did in Hungary was "illegal." It was "illegal" to aid and comfort a Jew in Hitler's Germany. Even so, I am sure that, had I lived in Germany at the time, I would have aided and comforted my Jewish brothers. If today I lived in a Communist country where certain principles dear to the Christian faith are suppressed I would openly advocate disobeying that country's anti-religious laws.

I must make two honest confessions to you, my Christian and Jewish brothers. First, I must confess that over the past few years I have been gravely disappointed with the white moderate. I have almost reached the regrettable conclusion that the Negro's great stumbling block in his stride toward freedom is not the White Citizen's Counciler or the Ku Klux Klanner, but the white moderate, who is more devoted to "order" than to justice; who prefers a negative peace which is the absence of tension to a positive peace which is the presence of justice; who constantly says: "I agree with you in the goal you seek, but I cannot agree with your methods of direct action"; who paternalistically believes he can set the timetable for another man's freedom; who lives by a mythical concept of time and who constantly advises the Negro to wait for a "more convenient season." Shallow understanding from people of good will is more frustrating than absolute misunderstanding from people of ill will. Luke-warm acceptance is much more bewildering than outright rejection.

I had hoped that the white moderate would understand that law and order exist for the purpose of establishing justice and that when they fail in this purpose they become the dangerously structured dams that block the flow of social progress. I had hoped that the white moderate would understand that the present tension in the South is a necessary phase of the transition from an obnoxious negative peace, in which the Negro passively accepted his unjust plight, to a substantive and positive peace, in which all men will respect the dignity and worth of human personality. Actually, we who engage in nonviolent direct action are not the creators of tension. We merely bring to the surface the hidden tension that is already alive. We bring it out in the open, where it can be seen and dealt with. Like a boil that can never be cured so long as it is covered up but must be opened with all its ugliness to the natural medicines of air and light, injustice must be exposed, with all the tension its exposure creates, to the light of human conscience and the air of national opinion before it can be cured.

In your statement you assert that our actions, even though peaceful, must be condemned because they precipitate violence. But is this a logical assertion? Isn't this like condemning a robbed man because his possession of money precipitated the evil act of robbery? Isn't this like condemning Socrates because his unswerving commitment to truth and his philosophical inquiries precipitated the act by the misguided populace in which they made him drink hemlock? Isn't this like condemning Jesus because his unique God-consciousness and never-ceasing devotion to God's will precipitated the evil act of crucifixion? We must come to see that, as the federal courts have consistently affirmed, it is wrong to urge an individual to cease his efforts to gain his basic constitutional rights because the quest may precipitate violence. Society must protect the robbed and punish the robber.

I had also hoped that the white moderate would reject the myth concerning time in relation to the struggle for freedom. I have just received a letter from a white brother in Texas. He writes: "All Christians know that the colored people will receive equal rights eventually, but it is possible that you are in too great a religious hurry. It has taken Christianity almost two thousand years to accomplish what it has. The teachings of Christ take time to come to earth." Such an attitude stems from a tragic misconception of time, from the strangely irrational notion that there is something in the very flow of time that will inevitably cure all ills. Actually, time itself is neutral; it can be used either destructively or constructively. More and more I feel that the people of ill will have used time much more effectively than have the people of good will. We will have to repent in this generation not merely for the hateful words and actions of the bad people but for the appalling silence of the good people. Human progress never rolls in on wheels of inevitability; it comes through the tireless efforts of men willing to be co-workers with God, and without this hard work, time itself becomes an ally of the forces of social stagnation. We must use time creatively, in the knowledge that the time is always ripe to do right. Now is the time to make real the promise of democracy and transform our pending national elegy into a creative psalm of brotherhood. Now is the time to lift our national policy from the quicksand of racial injustice to the solid rock of human dignity.

You speak of our activity in Birmingham as extreme. At first I was rather disappointed that fellow clergymen would see my nonviolent efforts as those of an extremist. I began thinking about the fact that I stand in the middle of two opposing forces in the Negro community. One is a force of complacency, made up in part of Negroes who, as a result of long years of oppression, are so drained of self-respect and a sense of "somebodiness" that they have adjusted to segregation; and in part of a few middle-class Negroes who, because of a degree of academic and economic security and because in some ways they profit by segregation, have become insensitive to the problems of the masses. The other force is one of bitterness and hatred, and it comes perilously close to advocating violence. It is expressed in the various black nationalist groups that are springing up across the nation, the largest and best-known being Elijah Muhammad's Muslim movement. Nourished by the Negro's frustration over the continued existence of racial discrimination, this movement is made up of people who have lost faith in America, who have absolutely repudiated Christianity, and who have concluded that the white man is an incorrigible "devil."

I have tried to stand between these two forces, saying that we need emulate neither the "do-nothingism" of the complacent nor the hatred and despair of the black nationalist. For there is the more excellent way of love and nonviolent protest. I am grateful to God, that, through the influence of the Negro church, the way of nonviolence became an integral part of our struggle.

If this philosophy had not emerged, by now many streets of the South would, I am convinced, be flowing with blood. And I am further convinced that if our white brothers dismiss as "rabble-rousers" and "outside agitators" those of us who employ nonviolent action, and if they refuse to support our non-violent efforts, millions of Negroes will, out of frustration and despair, seek solace and security in black nationalist ideologies—a development that would inevitably lead to a frightening racial nightmare.

Oppressed people cannot remain oppressed forever. The yearning for freedom eventually manifests itself, and that is what has happened to the American Negro. Something within has reminded him of his birthright of freedom, and something without has reminded him that it can be gained. Consciously or unconsciously, he has been caught up by the *Zeitgeist*, and with his black brothers of Africa and his brown and yellow brothers of Asia, South America and the Caribbean, the United States Negro is moving with a sense of great urgency toward the promised land of racial justice. If one recognizes this vital urge that has engulfed the Negro community, one should readily understand why public demonstrations are taking place. The Negro has many pent-up resentments and latent frustrations, and he must release them. So let him march; let him make prayer pilgrimages to the city hall; let him go on freedom rides—and try to understand why he must do so. If his repressed emotions are not released in nonviolent ways, they will seek expression through violence; this is not a threat but a fact of history. So I have not said to my people: "Get rid of your discontent." Rather, I have tried to say that this normal and healthy discontent can be channeled into the creative outlet of nonviolent direct action. And now this approach is being termed extremist.

But though I was initially disappointed at being categorized as an extremist, as I continued to think about the matter I gradually gained a measure of satisfaction from the label. Was not Jesus an extremist for love: "Love your enemies, bless them that curse you, do good to them that hate you, and pray for them which despitefully use you, and persecute you." Was not Amos an extremist for justice: "Let justice roll down like waters and righteousness like an ever-flowing stream." Was not Paul an extremist for the Christian gospel: "I bear in my body the marks of the Lord Jesus." Was not Martin Luther an extremist: "Here I stand; I cannot do otherwise, so help me God." And John Bunyan: "I will stay in jail to the end of my days before I make a butchery of my conscience." And Abraham Lincoln: "This nation cannot survive half slave and half free." And Thomas Jefferson: "We hold these truths to be self-evident, that all men are created equal. . . ." so the question is not whether we will be extremists, but what kind of extremists we will be. Will we be extremists for hate or for love? Will we be extremists for the preservation of injustice or for the extension of justice? In that dramatic scene on Calvary's hill three men were crucified. We must never forget that all three were crucified for the same crime—the crime of extremism. Two were extremists for immorality, and thus fell below their environment. The other, Jesus Christ, was an extremist for love, truth and goodness, and thereby rose above his environment. Perhaps the South, the nation and the world are in dire need of creative extremists.

I had hoped that the white moderate would see this need. Perhaps I was too optimistic; perhaps I expected too much. I suppose I should have realized that few members of the oppressor race can understand the deep groans and passionate yearnings of the oppressed race, and still fewer have the vision to see that injustice must be rooted out by strong, persistent and determined action. I am thankful, however, that some of our white brothers in the South have grasped the meaning of this social revolution and committed themselves to it. They are still all too few in quantity, but they are big in quality. Some—such as Ralph McGill, Lillian Smith, Harry Golden, James McBride Dabbs, Ann Braden and Sarah Patton Boyle—have written about our struggle in eloquent and prophetic terms. Others have marched with us down nameless streets of the South. They have languished in filthy, roach-infested jails, suffering the abuse and brutality of policemen who view them as "dirty nigger-lovers." Unlike so many of their moderate brothers and sisters, they have recognized the urgency of the moment and sensed the need for powerful "action" antidotes to combat the disease of segregation.

Let me take note of my other major disappointment. I have been so greatly disappointed with the white church and its leadership. Of course, there are some notable exceptions. I am not unmindful of the fact that each of you has taken some significant stands on this issue. I commend you, Reverend Stallings, for your Christian stand on this past Sunday, in welcoming Negroes to your worship service on a nonsegregated basis. I commend the Catholic leaders of this state for integrating Spring Hill College several years ago.

But despite these notable exceptions, I must honestly reiterate that I have been disappointed with the church. I do not say this as one of those negative critics who can always find something wrong with the church. I say this as a minister of the gospel, who loves the church; who was nurtured in its bosom; who has been sustained by its spiritual blessings and who will remain true to it as long as the cord of life shall lengthen.

When I was suddenly catapulted into the leadership of the bus protest in Montgomery, Alabama, a few years ago, I felt we would be supported by the white church. I felt that the white ministers, priests and rabbis of the South would be among our strongest allies. Instead, some have been outright opponents, refusing to understand the freedom movement and misrepresenting its leaders; all too many others have been more cautious than courageous and have remained silent behind the anesthetizing security of stained-glass windows.

In spite of my shattered dreams, I came to Birmingham with the hope that the white religious leadership of this community would see the justice of our cause and, with deep moral concern, would serve as the channel through which our just grievances could reach the power structure. I had hoped that each of you would understand. But again I have been disappointed.

I have heard numerous southern religious leaders admonish their worshipers to comply with a desegregation decision because it is the law, but I have longed to hear white ministers declare: "Follow this decree because integration is morally right and because the Negro is your brother." In the midst of blatant injustices inflected upon the Negro, I have watched white churchmen stand on the sidelines and mouth pious irrelevancies and sanctimonious trivialities. In the midst of a mighty struggle to rid our nation of racial and economic injustice, I have heard many ministers say; "Those are social issues, with which the gospel has no real concern." And I have watched many churches commit themselves to a completely other-worldly religion which makes a strange, un-Biblical distinction between body and soul, between the sacred and the secular.

I have traveled the length and breadth of Alabama, Mississippi and all the other southern states. On sweltering summer days and crisp autumn mornings I have looked at the South's beautiful churches with their lofty spires pointing heavenward. I have beheld impressive outlines of her massive religious-education buildings. Over and over I have found myself asking, "What kind of people worship here? Who is their God? Where were their voices when the lips of Governor Barnett dripped with words of interposition and nullification? Where were they when Governor Wallace gave a clarion call for defiance and hatred? Where were their voices of support when bruised and weary Negro men and women decided to rise from the dark dungeons of complacency to the bright hills of creative protest?"

Yes, these questions are still in my mind. In deep disappointment I have wept over the laxity of the church. But be assured that my tears have been tears of love. There can be no deep disappointment where there is not deep love. Yes, I love the church. How could I do otherwise? I am in the rather unique position of being the son, the grandson and great-grandson of preachers. Yes, I see the church as the body of Christ. But, oh! How we have blemished and scarred that body through social neglect and through fear of being nonconformists.

There was a time when the church was very powerful—in the time when the early Christians rejoiced at being deemed worthy to suffer for what they believed. In those days the church was not merely a thermometer that recorded the ideas and principles of popular opinion; it was a thermometer that was a thermostat that transformed the mores of society. Whenever the early Christians entered a town, the people in power became disturbed and immediately sought to convict the Christians for being "disturbers of the peace" and "outside agitators." But the Christians pressed on, in the conviction that they were a "colony of heaven," called to obey God rather than man. Small in number, they were big in commitment. They were too God-intoxicated to be "astronomically intimidated." By their effort and example they brought an end to such ancient evils as infanticide and gladiatorial contests.

Things are different now. So often the contemporary church is a weak, ineffectual voice with an uncertain sound. So often it is an arch-defender of the status quo. Far from being disturbed by the presence of the church, the power structure of the average community is consoled by the church's silent—and often even vocal—sanction of things as they are.

But the judgment of God is upon the church as never before. If today's church does not recapture the sacrificial spirit of the early church, it will lose its authenticity, forfeit the loyalty of millions, and be dismissed as an irrelevant social club with no meaning for the twentieth century. Every day I meet young people whose disappointment with the church has turned into outright disgust.

Perhaps I have once again been too optimistic. Is organized religion too inextricably bound to the status quo to save our nation and the world? Perhaps I must turn my faith to the inner spiritual church, the church within the church, as the true ekklesia and the hope of the world. But again I am thankful to God that some noble souls from the ranks of organized religion have broken loose from the paralyzing chains of conformity and joined us as active partners in the struggle for freedom. They have left their secure congregations and walked in the streets of Albany, Georgia, with us. They have gone down the highways of the South on tortuous rides for freedom. Yes, they have gone to jail with us. Some have been dismissed from their churches, have lost the support of their bishops and fellow ministers. But they have acted in the faith that right defeated is stronger than evil triumphant. Their witness has been the spiritual salt that has preserved the true meaning of the gospel in these troubled times. They have carved a tunnel of hope through the dark mountain of disappointment.

I hope the church as a whole will meet the challenge of this decisive hour. But even if the church does not come to the aid of justice, I have no despair about the future. I have no fear about the outcome of our struggle in Birmingham even if our motives are at present misunderstood. We will reach the goal of freedom in Birmingham and all over the nation, because the goal of America is freedom. Abused and scorned though we may be our destiny is tied up with America's destiny. Before the pilgrims landed at Plymouth, we were here. Before the pen of Jefferson etched the majestic words of the Declaration of Independence across the pages of history, we were here. For more than two centuries our forebears labored in this country without wages; they made cotton king; they built the homes of their masters while suffering gross injustice and shameful humiliation—and yet out of a bottomless vitality they continued to thrive and develop. If the inexpressible cruelties of slavery could not stop us, the opposition we now face will surely fail. We will win our freedom because the sacred heritage of our nation and the eternal will of God are embodied in our echoing demands.

Before closing I feel impelled to mention one other point in your statement that has troubled me profoundly. You warmly commended the Birmingham police force for keeping "order" and "preventing violence." I doubt that you would have so warmly commended the police if you had seen its dogs sinking their teeth into un-armed, nonviolent Negroes. I doubt that you would so quickly commend the po-licemen if you were to observe their ugly and inhumane treatment of Negroes here in the city jail; if you were to watch them push and curse old Negro women and young Negro girls; if you were to see them slap and kick old Negro men and young boys; if you were to observe them, as they did on two occasions, refuse to give us food because we wanted to sing our grace together. I cannot join you in your praise of the Birmingham police department.

It is true that the police have exercised a degree of discipline in handling the demonstrators. In this sense they have conducted themselves rather "non-violently" in public. But for what purpose? To preserve the evil system of segregation. Over the past few years I have consistently preached that nonviolence demands that the means we must use must be as pure as the ends we seek. I have tried to make clear that it is wrong to use immoral means to attain moral ends. But now I must affirm that it is just as wrong, or perhaps even more so, to use moral means to preserve im-moral ends. Perhaps Mr. Conner and his policemen have been rather nonviolent in public, as was Chief Prichett in Albany, Georgia, but they have used the moral means of nonviolence to maintain the immoral end of racial injustice. As T. S. Eliot has said: "The last temptation is the greatest treason: To do the right deed for the wrong reason."

I wish you had commended the Negro sit-inners and demonstrators of Birming-ham for their sublime courage, their willingness to suffer and their amazing disci-pline in the midst of great provocation. One day the South will recognize its real heroes. They will be the James Merediths, with the noble sense of purpose that en-ables them to face jeering and hostile mobs, and with the agonizing loneliness that characterizes the life of the pioneer. They will be old, oppressed, battered Negro women, symbolized in a seventy-two-year-old woman in Montgomery, Alabama, who rose up with a sense of dignity and with her people decided not to ride segre-gated buses, and who responded with ungrammatical profundity to one who inquired about her weariness: "My feet is tired, but my soul is at rest." They will be the young high school and college students, the young ministers of the gospel and a host of their elders, courageously and nonviolently sitting in at lunch counters and willingly going to jail for conscience' sake. One day the South will know that when these disinherited children of God sat down at lunch counters, they were in reality standing up for what is best in the American dream and for the most sacred values in our Judaeo-Christian heritage, thereby bringing our nation back to those great wells of democracy which were dug deep by the founding fathers in their formulation of the Constitution and the Declaration of Independence.

Never before have I written so long a letter. I'm afraid it is much too long to take your precious time. I can assure you that it would have been much shorter if I had been writing from a comfortable desk, but what else can one do when he is alone in a narrow jail cell, other than write long letters, think long thoughts and pray long prayers?

If I have said anything in this letter that overstates the truth and indicates an unreasonable impatience, I beg you to forgive me. If I have said anything that understates the truth and indicates my having patience that allows me to settle for anything less than brotherhood, I beg God to forgive me.

I hope this letter finds you strong in the faith, I also hope that circumstances will soon make it possible for me to meet each of you, not as an integrationist or a civil-rights leader but as a fellow clergyman and a Christian brother. Let us all hope that the dark clouds of racial prejudice will soon pass away and the deep fog of misunderstanding will be lifted from our fear-drenched communities, and in some not too distant tomorrow the radiant stars of love and brotherhood will shine over our great nation with all their scintillating beauty.

Yours for the cause of Peace and Brotherhood,
Martin Luther King, Jr.

"BLACK POWER" AND THE MOVE TOWARD SEPARATION

Slowly, almost imperceptibly, the civil rights movement for integration was transformed into a different movement. Perhaps a more accurate way of stating it is that the black movement for liberation took a different direction. It is not too difficult to chart its beginning and course of development.

On June 6, 1966, James Meredith, the law student who had previously integrated the University of Mississippi, began a 220-mile voting rights walk from Memphis, Tennessee, to Jackson, Mississippi. Meredith was shot and wounded shortly after beginning his journey and this caused a number of civil rights leaders to carry on the march. Along the route of march Stokely Carmichael and others often led the group in chanting "black power . . . black power." On June 26, in front of the state capitol in Jackson, Carmichael urged the fifteen thousand blacks in attendance to "build a base of power." Earlier in the year Carmichael, as the new president of the Student Nonviolent Coordinating Committee, had announced a new "black power" policy that entailed the removal of whites from leadership and policy-making roles in civil rights, organizations.

What seemed to be happening was the development of a new ethnic spirit on the part of the Afro-American. They discovered that it is impossible to move from slavery to being full Americans without first being "Afro-Americans." In the words of a speaker at a black power forum in Atlanta, "Martin King was trying to get us to love white folks before we learned to love ourselves, and that ain't no good." C. Eric Lincoln wrote:

> The contemporary "black revolution" is the overdue expression of the black man's discovery of himself and his ethnic group. He is not a "Negro" anymore; he is an Afro-American or a Blackamerican. In the rejection of the appellation "Negro" he is trying desperately to communicate something more than a projection of his own self-image. He wants to signify his newly discovered ethnic spirit. He is a *black* man—not necessarily in color, but in affiliation. He belongs to a community of black men—a black sub-culture. Yet he is American, because despite the discrimination which limits his participation in the social process, he logically and properly belongs to (and has made important contributions to) the national culture. His sub-culture is "Blackamerican." His national culture, like his national political status, is "American."[9]

An interesting, though not surprising, development in the latter part of the 1960s was the manner in which Malcolm X (1925–1965), a Black Muslim minister until 1964, rose in stature to become the leading symbol of the meaning of "black power" for the Afro-American.

Malcolm was born Malcolm Little in Omaha, Nebraska, the son of a Baptist minister who was a follower of Marcus Garvey (1887–1940). Later the family moved to Lansing, Michigan. Malcolm was six years old when his home was burned by the Ku Klux Klan. His mother was institutionalized after being judged mentally incompetent by social welfare authorities. From Lansing, Malcolm went to Boston and then to Harlem, where he excelled in the drug trade, the numbers racket, bootlegging whiskey, and other forms of street hustling. At about the age of twenty-three Malcolm was converted to the Nation of Islam while he was serving a ten-year prison sentence for burglary.

After several years of imprisonment, Malcolm joined the Muslim temple in Detroit and then became the minister of the New York temple in 1954. For ten years he served faithfully the cause of "the honorable Elijah Muhammed" (1897–1975) and became the most famous Muslim spokesman in America. Apparently, jealously in the Muslim group and the direction of Malcolm's own personal development began to cause estrangement between the New York minister and the Messenger of Allah. In 1964 Malcolm broke with Mr. Muhammed and established his own Muslim Mosque, Inc. After an important pilgrimage to Mecca and other parts of Africa, Malcolm returned to America with a broader and more open perspective. He founded the Organization of Afro-American

---

[9] Lincoln, op. cit., p. 171.

Unity (OAAU) on a nonsectarian basis. On February 22, 1965, while he was addressing a meeting of the OAAU, Malcolm was murdered by a gunman in a ballroom in Washington Heights in New York City.

Malcolm X was a striking black leader. He was quick witted and sharp tongued. Many who heard him found him almost hypnotic. A man of great energy and obvious intelligence, he always evoked wonder at what he might have been had he known the advantages of formal education. His book *The Autobiography of Malcolm X*[10] is a moving and powerful work that has become something of a classic. Malcolm probably was more feared than loved by black Americans while he lived, but three years after his death the concepts he preached had become the dominant motifs of black consciousness. The concepts that Malcolm expounded on the basis of the religious imagery and the "sacred history" of the Nation of Islam became secularized and placed under the rubric of "black power":

1. Pride in blackness.
2. The necessity to know black history.
3. Black separation.
4. The need for black unity.
5. Black control of the political and economic institutions of the black community.

In *The Autobiography of Malcolm X* Malcolm tells of his transfer to the Norfolk Correctional Institute, a minimum security prison in Massachusetts. In an institution that emphasized rehabilitation and personal development, Malcolm Little becomes acquainted with the Nation of Islam through the efforts of his family and enters into the life of the mind through the prison library. Like so many Black Muslims he is converted while in prison. Note the recitation of the Muslim sacred mythology. Perhaps most poignant of all is Malcolm's awe before the ordered life and dignity in the Muslim home of his brother, Wilfred. In Malcolm's conversion we see what an eloquent minister once termed "the expulsive power of a new affection" as Malcolm finds a focus and purpose in his Muslim commitment that causes a dramatic break with his former patterns of behavior.

Document 50 ___ Look at _____

From *The Autobiography of Malcolm X*

Independently of all this, my sister Ella had been steadily working to get me transferred to the Norfolk, Massachusetts, Prison Colony, which was an experi-

SOURCE: From *The Autobiography of Malcolm X*, by Malcolm X, with the assistance of Alex Haley. Copyright © 1964 by Alex Haley and Malcolm X. Copyright © 1965 by Alex Haley and Betty Shabazz. Reprinted by permission of Random House, Inc.

[10] Malcolm X, *The Autobiography of Malcolm X* (New York: Grove Press, 1964).

mental rehabilitation jail. In other prisons, convicts often said that if you had the right money, or connections, you could get transferred to this Colony whose penal policies sounded almost too good to be true. Somehow, Ella's efforts in my behalf were successful in late 1948, and I was transferred to Norfolk.

The Colony was, comparatively, a heaven, in many respects. It had flushing toilets; there were no bars, only walls—and within the walls, you had far more freedom. There was plenty of fresh air to breathe; it was not in a city.

There were twenty-four "house" units, fifty men living in each unit, if memory serves me correctly. This would mean that the Colony had a total of around 1200 inmates. Each "house" had three floors and, greatest blessing of all, each inmate had his own room.

About fifteen per cent of the inmates were Negroes, distributed about five to nine Negroes in each house.

Norfolk Prison Colony represented the most enlightened form of prison that I have ever heard of. In place of the atmosphere of malicious gossip, perversion, grafting, hateful guards, there was more relative "culture" as "culture" is interpreted in prisons. A high percentage of the Norfolk Prison Colony inmates went in for "intellectual" things, group discussions, debates, and such. Instructors for the educational rehabilitation programs came from Harvard, Boston University, and other educational institutions in the area. The visiting rules, far more lenient than other prisons', permitted visitors almost every day, and allowed them to stay two hours. You had your choice of sitting alongside your visitor, or facing each other.

Norfolk Prison Colony's library was one of its outstanding features. A millionaire named Parkhurst had willed his library there; he had probably been interested in the rehabilitation program. History and religions were his special interests. Thousands of his books were on the shelves, and in the back were boxes and crates full, for which there wasn't space on the shelves. At Norfolk, we could actually go into the library with permission—walk up and down the shelves, pick books. There were hundreds of old volumes, some of them probably quite rare. I read aimlessly, until I learned to read selectively, with a purpose.

I hadn't heard from Reginald in a good while after I got to Norfolk Prison Colony. But I had come in there not smoking cigarettes, or eating pork when it was served. That caused a bit of eyebrow-raising. Then a letter from Reginald telling me when he was coming to see me. By the time he came, I was really keyed up to hear the hype he was going to explain.

Reginald knew how my street-hustler mind operated. That's why his approach was so effective.

He had always dressed well, and now, when he came to visit, was carefully groomed. I was aching with wanting the "no pork and cigarettes" riddle answered. But he talked about the family, what was happening in Detroit, Harlem the last time he was there. I have never pushed anyone to tell me anything before he was ready. The offhand way Reginald talked and acted made me know that something was coming.

He said, finally, as though it had just happened to come into his mind, "Malcolm, if a man knew every imaginable thing that there is to know, who would he be?"

Back in Harlem, he had often liked to get at something through this kind of indirection. It had often irritated me, because my way had always been direct. I looked at him. "Well, he would have to be some kind of a god—"

Reginald said, "There's a *man* who knows everything."

I asked, "Who is that?"

"God is a man," Reginald said. "His real name is Allah."

Allah. That word came back to me from Philbert's letter; it was my first hint of any connection. But Reginald went on. He said that God had 360 degrees of knowledge. He said that 360 degrees represented "the sum total of knowledge."

To say I was confused is an understatement. I don't have to remind you of the background against which I sat hearing my brother Reginald talk like this. I just listened, knowing he was taking his time in putting me onto something. And if somebody is trying to put you onto something, you need to listen.

"The devil has only thirty-three degrees of knowledge—known as Masonry," Reginald said. I can so specifically remember the exact phrases since, later, I was going to teach them so many times to others. "The devil uses his Masonry to rule other people."

He told me that this God had come to America, and that he had made himself known to a man named Elijah—"a black man, just like us." This God had let Elijah know, Reginald said, that the devil's "time was up."

I didn't know what to think, I just listened.

"The devil is also a man," Reginald said.

"What do you mean?"

With a slight movement of his head. Reginald indicated some white inmates and their visitors talking, as we were, across the room.

"Them," he said. "The white man is the devil."

He told me that all whites knew they were devils—"especially Masons."

I never will forget: my mind was involuntarily flashing across the entire spectrum of white people I had ever known; and for some reason it stopped upon Hymie, the Jew, who had been so good to me.

Reginald, a couple of times, had gone out with me to that Long Island bootlegging operation to buy and bottle up the bootleg liquor for Hymie.

I said, "Without any exception?"

"Without any exception."

"What about Hymie?"

"What is it if I let you make five hundred dollars to let me make ten thousand?"

After Reginald left, I thought. I thought. Thought.

I couldn't make of it head, or tail, or middle.

The white people I had known marched before my mind's eye. From the start of my life. The state white people always in our house after the other whites I didn't know had killed my father . . . the white people who kept calling my mother "crazy" to her face and before me and my brothers and sisters, until she finally was taken off by white people to the Kalamazoo asylum . . . the white judge and others who had split up the children . . . the Swerlins, the other whites around Mason . . . white youngsters I was in school there with, and the teachers—the one who told me in the eighth grade to "be a carpenter" because thinking of being a lawyer was foolish for a Negro. . . .

My head swam with the parading faces of white people. The ones in Boston, in the white-only dances at the Roseland Ballroom where I shined their shoes . . . at the Parker House where I took their dirty plates back to the kitchen . . . the railroad crewmen and passengers . . . Sophia. . . .

The whites in New York City—the cops, the white criminals I'd dealt with . . . the whites who piled into the Negro speakeasies for a taste of Negro *soul* . . . the white women who wanted Negro men . . . the men I'd steered to the black "specialty sex" they wanted. . . .

The fence back in Boston, and his ex-con representative . . . Boston cops . . . Sophia's husband's friend, and her husband, whom I'd never seen, but knew so much about . . . Sophia's sister . . . the Jew jeweler who'd helped trap me . . . the social workers . . . the Middlesex County Court people . . . the judge who gave me ten years . . . the prisoners I'd known, the guards and the officials. . . .

A celebrity among the Norfolk Prison Colony inmates was a rich, older fellow, a paralytic, called John. He had killed his baby, one of those "mercy" killings. He was a 33rd-degree Mason, and what power Masons had—that only Masons ever had been U.S. Presidents, that Masons in distress could secretly signal to judges and other Masons in powerful positions.

I kept thinking about what Reginald had said. I wanted to test it with John. He worked in a soft job in the prison's school. I went over there.

"John," I said, "how many degrees in a circle?"

He said, "Three hundred and sixty."

I drew a square. "How many degrees in that?" He said three hundred and sixty.

I asked him was three hundred and sixty degrees, then, the maximum of degrees in anything?

He said "Yes."

I said, "Well, why is it that Masons go only to thirty-three degrees?"

He had no satisfactory answer. But for me, the answer was that Masonry, actually, is only thirty-three degrees of the religion of Islam, which is the full projection, forever denied to Masons, although they know it exists.

Reginald, when he came to visit me again in a few days, could gauge from my attitude the effect that his talking had had upon me. He seemed very pleased. Then, very seriously, he talked for two solid hours about "the devil white man" and "the brainwashed black man."

When Reginald left, he left me rocking with some of the first serious thoughts I had ever had in my life: that the white man was fast losing his power to oppress and exploit the dark world: that the dark world was starting to rise to rule the world again, as it had before; that the white man's world was on the way down, it was on the way out.

"You don't even know who you are," Reginald had said. "You don't even know, the white devil has hidden it from you, that you are of a race of people of ancient civilizations, and riches in gold and kings. You don't even know your true family name, you wouldn't recognize your true language if you heard it. You have been cut off by the devil white man from all true knowledge of your own kind. You have been a victim of the evil of the devil white man ever since he murdered and raped and stole you from your native land in the seeds of your forefathers. . . ."

I began to receive at least two letters every day from my brothers and sisters in Detroit. My oldest brother, Wilfred, wrote, and his first wife, Bertha, the mother of his two children (since her death, Wilfred has met and married his present wife, Ruth). Philbert wrote, and my sister Hilda. And Reginald visited, staying in Boston awhile before he went back to Detroit, where he had been the most recent of them to be converted. They were all Muslims, followers of a man they described to me as "The Honorable Elijah Muhammad," a small, gentle man, whom they sometimes referred to as "The Messenger of Allah." He was, they said, "a black man, like us." He had been born in America on a farm in Georgia. He had moved with his family to Detroit, and there had met a Mr. Wallace D. Fard who he claimed was "God in person." Mr. Wallace D. Fard had given to Elijah Muhammad Allah's message for the black people who were "the Lost-Found Nation of Islam here in this wilderness of North America."

All of them urged me to "accept the teachings of The Honorable Elijah Muhammad." Reginald explained that pork was not eaten by those who worshiped in the religion of Islam, and not smoking cigarettes was a rule of the followers of The Honorable Elijah Muhammad, because they did not take injurious things such as narcotics, tobacco, or liquor into their bodies. Over and over, I read, and heard, "The key to a Muslim is submission, the attunement of one toward Allah."

And what they termed "the true knowledge of the black man" that was possessed by the followers of The Honorable Elijah Muhammad was given shape for me in their lengthy letters, sometimes containing printed literature.

"The true knowledge," reconstructed much more briefly than I received it, was that history had been "whitened" in the white man's history books, and that the black man had been "brainwashed for hundreds of years." Original Man was black, in the continent called Africa where the human race emerged on the planet Earth.

The black man, original man, built great empires and civilizations and cultures while the white man was still living on all fours in caves. "The devil white man," down through history, out of his devilish nature, had pillaged, murdered, raped, and exploited every race of man not white.

Human history's greatest crime was the traffic in black flesh when the devil white man went into Africa and murdered and kipnapped to bring to the West in chains, in slave ships, millions of black men, women, and children, who were worked and beaten and tortured as slaves.

The devil white man cut these black people off from all knowledge of their own kind, and cut them off from any knowledge of their own language, religion, and past culture, until the black man in America was the earth's only race of people who had absolutely no knowledge of his true identity.

In one generation, the black slave women in America had been raped by the slavemaster white man until there had begun to emerge a homemade, handmade, brainwashed race that was no longer even of its true color, that no longer even knew its true family names. The slavemaster forced his family name upon this rape-mixed race, which the slavemaster began to call "the Negro."

This "Negro" was taught of his native Africa that it was peopled by heathen, black savages, swinging like monkeys from trees. This "Negro" accepted this along with every other teaching of the slavemaster that was designed to make him accept and obey and worship the white man.

And where the religion of every other people on earth taught its believers of a God with whom they could identify, a God who at least looked like one of their own kind, the slavemaster injected his Christian religion into this "Negro." This "Negro" was taught to worship an alien God having the same blond hair, pale skin, and blue eyes as the slavemaster.

This religion taught the "Negro" that black was a curse. It taught him to hate everything black, including himself. It taught him that everything white was good, to be admired, respected, and loved. It brainwashed this "Negro" to think he was superior if his complexion showed more of the white pollution of the slavemaster. This white man's Christian religion further deceived and brainwashed this "Negro" to always turn the other cheek, and grin, and scrape, and bow, and be humble, and to sing, and to pray, and to take whatever was dished out by the devilish white man; and to look for his pie in the sky, and for his heaven in the hereafter, while right here on earth the slavemaster white man enjoyed *his* heaven.

Many a time, I have looked back, trying to assess, just for myself, my first reactions to all this. Every instinct of the ghetto jungle streets, every hustling fox and criminal wolf instinct in me, which would have scoffed at and rejected anything else, was struck numb. It was as though all of that life merely was back there, without any remaining effect, or influence. I remember how, some time later, reading the Bible in the Norfolk Prison Colony library, I came upon, then I read, over and over, how Paul on the road to Damascus, upon hearing the voice of Christ, was so smitten that he was knocked off his horse, in a daze. I do not now, and I did not then, liken myself to Paul. But I do understand his experience.

I have since learned—helping me to understand what then began to happen within me—that the truth can be quickly received, or received at all, only by the sinner who knows and admits that he is guilty of having sinned much. Stated another way: only guilt admitted accepts truth. The Bible again: the one people whom Jesus could not help were the Pharisees; they didn't feel they needed any help.

The very enormity of my previous life's guilt prepared me to accept the truth.

Not for weeks yet would I deal with the direct, personal application to myself, as a black man, of the truth. It still was like a blinding light.

Reginald left Boston and went back to Detroit. I would sit in my room and stare. At the dining-room table, I would hardly eat, only drink the water. I nearly starved. Fellow inmates, concerned, and guards, apprehensive, asked what was wrong with me. It was suggested that I visit the doctor, and I didn't. The doctor, advised, visited me. I don't know what his diagnosis was, probably that I was working on some act.

I was going through the hardest thing, also the greatest thing, for any human being to do; to accept that which is already within you, and around you.

I learned later that my brothers and sisters in Detroit put together the money for my sister Hilda to come and visit me. She told me that when The Honorable Elijah Muhammad was in Detroit, he would stay as a guest at my brother Wilfred's home, which was on McKay Street. Hilda kept urging me to write to Mr. Muhammad. He understood what it was to be in the white man's prison, she said, because he, himself, had not long before gotten out of the federal prison at Milan, Michigan, where he had served five years for evading the draft.

Hilda said that The Honorable Elijah Muhammad came to Detroit to reorganize his Temple Number One, which had become disorganized during his prison time; but he lived in Chicago, where he was organizing and building his Temple Number Two.

It was Hilda who said to me, "Would you like to hear how the white man came to this planet Earth?"

And she told me that key lesson of Mr. Elijah Muhammad's teachings, which I later learned was the demonology that every religion has, called "Yacub's History." Elijah Muhammad teaches his followers that first, the moon separated from the earth. Then, the first humans, Original Man, were a black people. They founded the Holy City Mecca.

Among this black race were twenty-four wise scientists. One of the scientists, at odds with the rest, created the especially strong black tribe of Shabazz, from which America's Negroes, so-called, descend.

About sixty-six hundred years ago, when seventy per cent of the people were satisfied, and thirty per cent were dissatisfied, among the dissatisfied was born a "Mr. Yacub." He was born to create trouble, to break the peace, and to kill. His head was unusually large. When he was four years old, he began school. At the age of eighteen. Yacub had finished all of his nation's colleges and universities. He was known as "the big-head scientist." Among many other things, he had learned how to breed races scientifically.

This big-head scientist, Mr. Yacub, began preaching in the streets of Mecca, making such hosts of converts that the authorities, increasingly concerned, finally exiled him with 59,999 followers to the island of Patmos—described in the Bible as the island where John received the message contained in Revelations in the New Testament.

Though he was a black man, Mr. Yacub, embittered toward Allah now, decided, as revenge, to create upon the earth a devil race—a bleached-out, white race of people.

From his studies, the big-head scientist knew that black men contained two germs, black and brown. He knew that the brown germ stayed dormant as, being the lighter of the two germs, it was the weaker. Mr. Yacub, to upset the law of nature, conceived the idea of employing what we today know as the recessive genes structure, to separate from each other the two germs, black and brown, and then grafting the brown germ to progressively lighter, weaker stages. The humans resulting, he knew, would be, as they became lighter, and weaker, progressively also more susceptible to wickedness and evil. And in this way finally he would achieve the intended bleached-out white race of devils.

He knew that it would take him several total colorchange stages to get from black to white. Mr. Yacub began his work by setting up a eugenics law on the island of Patmos.

Among Mr. Yacub's 59,999 all-black followers, every third or so child that was born would show some trace of brown. As these became adult, only brown and brown, or black and brown, were permitted to marry. As their children were born,

Mr. Yacub's law dictated that, if a black child, the attending nurse, or midwife, should stick a needle into its brain and give the body to cremators. The mothers were told it had been an "angel baby," which had gone to heaven, to prepare a place for her.

But a brown child's mother was told to take very good care of it.

Others, assistants, were trained by Mr. Yacub to continue his objective. Mr. Yacub, when he died on the island at the age of one hundred and fifty-two, had left laws, and rules, for them to follow. According to the teachings of Mr. Elijah Muhammad, Mr. Yacub, except in his mind, never saw the bleached-out devil race that his procedures and laws and rules created.

A two-hundred-year span was needed to eliminate on the island of Patmos all of the black people—until only brown people remained.

The next two hundred years were needed to create from the brown race the red race—with no more browns left on the island.

In another two hundred years, from the red race was created the yellow race.

Two hundred years later—the white race had at last been created.

On the island of Patmos was nothing but these blond, pale-skinned, cold-blue-eyed devils—savages, nude and shameless; hairy, like animals, they walked on all fours and they lived in trees.

Six hundred more years passed before this race of people returned to the mainland, among the natural black people.

Mr. Elijah Muhammad teaches his followers that within six months time, through telling lies that set the black men fighting among each other, this devil race had turned what had been a peaceful heaven on earth into a hell torn by quarreling and fighting.

But finally the original black people recognized that their sudden troubles stemmed from this devil white race that Mr. Yacub had made. They rounded them up, put them in chains. With little aprons to cover their nakedness, this devil race was marched off across the Arabian desert to the caves of Europe.

The lambskin and the cable-tow used in Masonry today are symbolic of how the nakedness of the white man was covered when he was chained and driven across the hot sand.

Mr. Elijah Muhammad further teaches that the white devil race in Europe's caves was savage. The animals tried to kill him. He climbed trees outside his cave, made clubs, trying to protect his family from the wild beasts outside trying to get in.

When this devil race had spent two thousand years in the caves, Allah raised up Moses to civilize them, and bring them out of the caves. It was written that this devil white race would rule the world for six thousand years.

The Books of Moses are missing. That's why it is not known that he was in the caves.

When Moses arrived, the first of these devils to accept his teachings, the first he led out, were those we call today the Jews.

According to the teachings of this "Yacub's History," when the Bible says "Moses lifted up the serpent in the wilderness," that serpent is symbolic of the devil white race Moses lifted up out of the caves of Europe, teaching them civilization.

It was written that after Yacub's bleached white race had ruled the world for six thousand years—down to our time—the black original race would give birth to one whose wisdom, knowledge, and power would be infinite.

It was written that some of the original black people should be brought as slaves to North America—to learn to better understand, at first hand, the white devil's true nature, in modern times.

Elijah Muhammad teaches that the greatest and mightiest God who appeared on the earth was Master W. D. Fard. He came from the East to the West, appearing in North America at a time when the history and the prophecy that is written was coming to realization, as the non-white people all over the world began to rise, and as the devil white civilization, condemned by Allah, was, through its devilish nature, destroying itself.

Master W. D. Fard was half black and half white. He was made in this way to enable him to be accepted by the black people in America, and to lead them, while at the same time he was enabled to move undiscovered among the white people, so that he could understand and judge the enemy of the blacks.

Master W. D. Fard, in 1931, posing as a seller of silks, met, in Detroit, Michigan, Elijah Muhammad. Master W. D. Fard gave to Elijah Muhammad Allah's message, and Allah's divine guidance, to save the Lost-Found Nation of Islam, the so-called Negroes, here in "this wilderness of North America."

When my sister, Hilda, had finished telling me this "Yacub's History," she left. I don't know if I was able to open my mouth and say good-bye.

I was to learn later that Elijah Muhammad's tales, like this one of "Yacub," infuriated the Muslims of the East. While at Mecca, I reminded them that it was their fault, since they themselves hadn't done enough to make real Islam known in the West. Their silence left a vacuum into which any religious faker could step and mislead our people. . . .

Hilda, the next morning, gave me some money to put in my pocket. Before I left, I went out and bought three things I remember well. I bought a better-looking pair of eyeglasses than the pair the prison had issued to me; and I bought a suitcase and a wrist watch.

I have thought, since, that without fully knowing it, I was preparing for what my life was about to become. Because those are three things I've used more than anything else. My eyeglasses correct the astigmatism that I got from all the reading in prison. I travel so much now that my wife keeps alternate suitcases packed so that, when necessary, I can just grab one. And you won't find anybody more time-conscious than I am. I live by my watch, keeping appointments. Even when I'm using my car, I drive by my watch, not my speedometer. Time is more important to me than distance.

I caught a bus to Detroit. The furniture store that my brother Wilfred managed was right in the black ghetto of Detroit; I'd better not name the store, if I'm going to tell the way they robbed Negroes. Wilfred introduced me to the Jews who owned the store. And, as agreed, I was put to work, as a salesman.

"Nothing Down" advertisements drew poor Negroes into that store like flypaper. It was a shame, the way they paid three and four times what the furniture had cost, because they could get credit from those Jews. It was the same kind of cheap, gaudy-looking junk that you can see in any of the black ghetto furniture stores today. Fabrics were stapled on the sofas. Imitation "leopard skin" bedspreads, "tiger skin" rugs, such stuff as that. I would see clumsy, work-hardened, calloused hands scrawling and scratching signatures on the contract, agreeing to highway-robbery interest rates in the fine print that never was read.

I was seeing in real life the same point made in a joke that during the 1964 Presidential campaign *Jet* magazine reported that Senator Barry Goldwater had told somewhere. It was that a white man, a Negro, and a Jew were given one wish each. The white man asked for securities; the Negro asked for a lot of money; the Jew asked for imitation jewelry "and that colored boy's address."

In all my years in the streets, I'd been looking at the exploitation that for the first time I really saw and understood. Now I watched brothers entwining themselves in the economic clutches of the white man who went home every night with another bag of money drained out of the ghetto. I saw that the money, instead of helping the black man, was going to help enrich these white merchants, who usually lived in an "exclusive" area where a black man had better not get caught unless he worked there for somebody white.

Wilfred invited me to share his home, and gratefully I accepted. The warmth of a home and a family was a healing change from the prison cage for me. It would deeply move almost any newly freed convict, I think. But especially this Muslim home's atmosphere sent me often to my knees to praise Allah. My family's letters while I was in prison had included a description of the Muslim home routine, but to truly appreciate it, one had to be a part of the routine. Each act, and the significance of that act, was gently, patiently explained to me by my brother Wilfred.

There was none of the morning confusion that exists in most homes. Wilfred, the father, the family protector and provider, was the first to rise. "The father prepares the way for his family," he said. He, then I, performed the morning ablutions. Next came Wilfred's wife, Ruth, and then their children, so that orderliness prevailed in the use of the bathroom.

"In the name of Allah, I perform the ablution," the Muslim said aloud before washing first the right hand, then the left hand. The teeth were thoroughly brushed, followed by three rinsings out of the mouth. The nostrils also were rinsed out thrice. A shower then completed the whole body's purification in readiness for prayer.

Each family member, even children upon meeting each other for that new day's first time, greeted softly and pleasantly, "As-Salaam-Alaikum" (the Arabic for "Peace be unto you"). "Wa-Alaikum-Salaam" ("and unto you be peace") was the other's reply. Over and over again, the Muslim said in his own mind, "Allahu-Akbar, Allahu-Akbar" ("Allah is the greatest").

The prayer rug was spread by Wilfred while the rest of the family purified themselves. It was explained to me that a Muslim family prayed with the sun near the horizon. If that time was missed, the prayer had to be deferred until the sun was beyond the horizon. "Muslims are not sun-worshipers. We pray facing the East to be in unity with the rest of our 725 million brothers and sisters in the entire Muslim world."

All the family, in robes, lined up facing East. In unison, we stepped from our slippers to stand on the prayer rug.

Today, I say with my family in the Arabic tongue the prayer which I first learned in English: "I perform the morning prayer to Allah, the Most High. Allah is the greatest. Glory to Thee Oh Allah, Thine is the praise, Blessed is Thy Name, and Exalted is Thy Majesty. I bear witness that nothing deserves to be served or worshiped besides Thee."

No solid food, only juice and coffee, was taken for our breakfasts. Wilfred and I went off to work. There, at noon and again at around three in the afternoon, unnoticed by others in the furniture store, we would rinse our hands, faces and mouths, and softly meditate.

Muslim children did likewise at school, and Muslim wives and mothers interrupted their chores to join the world's 725 million Muslims in communicating with God.

Wednesdays, Fridays, and Sundays were the meeting days of the relatively small Detroit Temple Number One. Near the temple, which actually was a storefront, were three hogslaughtering pens. The squealing of hogs being slaughtered filtered into our Wednesday and Friday meetings. I'm describing the condition that we Muslims were in back in the early 1950's.

The address of Temple Number One was 1470 Frederick Street, I think. The first Temple to be formed, back in 1931, by Master W. D. Fard, was formed in Detroit, Michigan. I never had seen any Christian-believing Negroes conduct themselves like the Muslims, the individuals and the families alike. The men were quietly, tastefully dressed. The women wore ankle-length gowns, no makeup, and scarves covered their heads. The neat children were mannerly not only to adults but to other children as well.

I had never dreamed of anything like that atmosphere among black people who had learned to be proud they were black, who had learned to love other black people instead of being jealous and suspicious. I thrilled to how we Muslim men used both hands to grasp a black brother's both hands, voicing and smiling our happiness to meet him again. The Muslim sisters, both married and single, were given an honor and respect that I'd never seen black men give to their women, and it felt wonderful to me. The salutations which we all exchanged were warm, filled with mutal respect and dignity: "Brother" . . . "Sister" . . . "Ma'am" . . . "Sir." Even children speaking to other children used these terms. Beautiful!

Lemuel Hassan then was the Minister at Temple Number One. "As-Salaikum," he greeted us. "Wa-Salaikum," we returned. Minister Lemuel stood before us, near a blackboard. The blackboard had fixed upon it in permanent paint, on one side, the United States flag and under it the words "Slavery Suffering and Death," then the word "Christianity" alongisde the sign of the Cross. Beneath the Cross was a painting of a black man hanged from a tree. On the other side was painted what we were taught was the Muslim flag, the crescent and star on a red background with the words "Islam: Freedom, Justice, Equality," and beneath that "Which One Will Survive the War of Armageddon?"

For more than an hour, Minister Lemuel lectured about Elijah Muhammad's teachings. I sat raptly absorbing Minister Lemuel's every syllable and gesture. Frequently, he graphically illustrated points by chalking key words or phrases on the blackboard.

I thought it was outrageous that our small temple still had some empty seats. I complained to my brother Wilfred that there should be no empty seats, with the surrounding streets full of our brainwashed black brothers and sisters, drinking, cursing, fighting, dancing, carousing, and using dope—the very things that Mr. Muhammad taught were helping the black man to stay under the heel of the white man here in America.

From what I could gather, the recruitment attitude at the temple seemed to me to amount to a self-defeating waiting view . . . an assumption that Allah would bring us more Muslims. I felt that Allah would be more inclined to help those who helped themselves. I had lived for years in ghetto streets; I knew the Negroes in those streets. Harlem or Detroit were no different. I said I disagreed, that I thought we should go out into the streets and get more Muslims into the fold.

"Black power" also manifested itself in the circles of organized religion in America; that is, the conventional religious organizations—churches and synagogues. In September 1968, the Interreligious Foundation for Community Organization (IFCO) launched plans for a National Black Economic Development Conference to be held in 1969. The meeting was convened in Detroit on April 20, 1969, and, under the insurgent leadership of James Forman (1929–   ), a "Black Manifesto" was passed by a vote of 187 to 63. The manifesto was addressed "To the White Churches and the Synagogues in the United States of America and to All Other Racist Institutions." For the first time the idea of reparations was injected into contemporary discussion of the race issue. After a preamble that was laced with Marxist interpretations of American racism, the manifesto proper alluded to centuries of Afro-American exploitation in the United States and then laid out its "nonnegotiable" demands:

We are therefore demanding of the white Christian churches and Jewish synagogues, which are part and parcel of the system of capitalism, that they begin to pay reparations to black people in this country. We are demanding $500,000,000 from the Christian white churches and the Jewish synagogues. This total comes to fifteen dollars per nigger. This is a low estimate, for we maintain there are probably more than 30,000,000 black people in this country. Fifteen dollars a nigger is not a large sum of money, and we know that the churches and synagogues have a tremendous wealth and its membership, white America, has profited and still exploits black people. We are also not unaware that the exploitation of colored peoples around the world is aided and abetted by white Christian churches and synagogues. This demand for $500,000,000 is not an idle resolution or empty words. Fifteen dollars for every black brother and sister in the United States is only a beginning of the reparations due as a people who have been exploited and degraded, brutalized, killed and persecuted. Underneath all of this exploitation, the racism of this country has produced a psychological effect upon us that we are beginning to shake off. We are no longer afraid to demand our full rights as a people of this decadent society.[11]

The news media in the United States gave prominent coverage when Forman interrupted a Sunday morning worship service at New York City's Riverside Church, the "cathedral church" of liberal Protestantism (a congregation that is both interdenominational and interracial). Forman presented Black Manifesto demands for that congregation's "share" of the $500 million being demanded of the white religious community. The "manifesto" phenomenon was a major reality at denominational gatherings throughout the summer of 1969. Denominational moderators and presiding officers prepared for "surprise" visits by Forman at their national meetings. The Manifesto, though meeting with much negative reaction, did elicit some degree of new programming and the release of funds for some of the projects it specified. Almost every major religious community now has an organized "black caucus" that tends to continue the emphasis of the Manifesto with regard to black claims on white resources.

For the past decade James H. Cone, African Methodist Episcopal (AME) minister and theologian, has been an articulate and persistent exponent of black theology. Born in Bearden, Arkansas, Cone has written of his struggle to discern what it means to be Christian in a racist society. His earlier books argued that black power was not only compatible with the Old and New Testament teachings but that black liberation is the gospel of Jesus Christ.[12] In these books Cone derived his theology from the white Western—primarily European—theological tradition. Realizing that, even as he was attempting to write black theology, he was still captive to white concepts, Cone turned to a study of black music—the spirituals and the blues.[13]

As was the case with several students of the Afro-American experience, Cone found the spirituals an authentic source of black piety. An interesting aspect of his study is Cone's treatment of the blues as a secularized version of the spiritual. E. Franklin Frazier wrote how, in a similar way, the rise of gospel singers outside the churches was to be interpreted as the secularization of the spirituals: "They must fall back upon the only vital heritage that has meaning for them and that social heritage is the religious heritage represented by the Spirituals which are becoming secularized."[14] In the document that follows we read an excerpt from Cone's chapter "The Meaning of Heaven in the Black Spirituals."

[11] Robert S. Lecky and H. Elliot Wright, *Black Manifesto: Religion, Racism, and Reparations* (New York: Sheed, 1969), pp. 119–120.
[12] See James H. Cone, *Black Theology and Black Power* (New York: Seabury, 1969) and *A Black Theology of Liberation* (Philadelphia: Lippincott, 1970).
[13] James H. Cone, *The Spirituals and the Blues* (New York: Seabury, 1972).
[14] Frazier, op. cit., p. 75.

"The Meaning of Heaven in the Black Spirituals" by James H. Cone

> I am a poor pilgrim of sorrow.
> I'm in this world alone.
> No hope in this world for tomorow.
> I'm trying to make heaven my home.

Related to the experience of suffering and death was the problem of the future, the "last things," which in systematic theology is called eschatology. How was it possible for black slaves to take seriously their pain and suffering in an unfriendly world and *still* believe that God was liberating them from earthly bondage? How could they *really* believe that God was just when they knew only injustice, oppression, and death? What exactly was revealed in their encounter with God that made them know that their humanity was protected from the insanity of white masters and governmental officials? The answer to those questions lies in the concept of heaven, which is the dominant idea in black religious experience as expressed in the black spirituals.

As I have suggested in previous discussions, the concept of heaven in black religion has not been interpreted rightly. Most observers have defined the black religious experience exclusively in terms of slaves longing for heaven, as if that desire was unrelated to their earthly liberation. It has been said that the concept of heaven served as an opiate for black slaves, making for docility and submission. It may be that part of this charge is related to the outmoded cosmology of the spirituals. Their old-fashioned "world pictures" can blind modern critics to the message of a people seeking expression amid the dehumanization of slavery. It is like discarding the Bible and its message as irrelevant because the biblical writers had a three-storied conception of the universe. While not all biblical and systematic theologians agree with Rudolf Bultmann's method of "demythologization" as the way to solve the problem (among others) of biblical cosmology, most would agree that he is correct in his insistence that the gospel message is not invalidated by its pre-scientific world-picture. A similar perspective can illumine the heaven theme in the spirituals.

Let me admit then that the black slaves' picture of the world is not to be defended as a viable scientific analysis of reality; that the language of heaven was a white concept given to black slaves in order to make them obedient and submissive; that the image of the Promised Land, where "the streets are pearl and the gates are gold," is not the best one for communicating with contemporary Black Power advocates, who stress political liberation by any means necessary; that a "new" black theological language is needed if black religion is going to articulate today the historical strivings of black people in America and the Third World. The question nevertheless remains: How was it possible for black people to endure the mental and physical stresses of slavery and still keep their humanity intact? I think the answer is found in black eschatology. Maybe what is needed is not a dismissal of the idea of heaven but a reinterpretation of it, so that oppressed blacks today can develop styles of resistance not unlike those of their grandparents.

Heaven and Black Existence

The place to begin is with Miles Fisher's contention that the spirituals are primarily "historical documents." They tell us about the black movement for historical liberation, the attempt of black people to define their present history in the light of their promised future and not according to their past miseries. Fisher notes that heaven for early black slaves referred not only to a transcendent reality beyond time and space; it designated the earthly places that blacks regarded as lands of freedom. Heaven referred to Africa, Canada, and the northern United States.

Frederick Douglass wrote about the double meanings of these songs:

We were at times remarkably buoyant, singing hymns, and making joyous exclamations, almost as triumphant in their tone as if we had reached a land of freedom and safety. A keen observer might have detected in our repeated singing of

> O Canaan, sweet Canaan,
> I am bound for the land of Canaan,

something more than a hope of reaching heaven. We meant to reach the *North*, and the *North* was our Canaan.

Harriet Tubman also used the spirituals in her struggle to free black people from the bonds of slavery. The spirituals were communicative devices about the possibilities of earthly freedom. Sarah Bradford reported how Tubman used the song in order to let her relatives and friends know that she intended to escape North to freedom.

> When dat ar ole chariot comes,
>   I'm gwine to lebe you,
> I'm boun' for de promised land,
>   Frien's, I'm gwine to lebe you.
> I'm sorry, frien's, to lebe you,
>   Farewell! oh, farewell!
> But I'll meet you in de mornin',
>   Farewell! oh, farewell!
> I'll meet you in de mornin',
>   When you reach de promised land;
> On de oder side of Jordan,
>   For I'm boun' for de promised land.

As with Douglass, Tubman's concept of "de promised land on de oder side of Jordan" was not just a transcendent reality. It was the North and later Canada. Said Harriet, after reaching free territory: "I looked at my hands to see if I was de same person now I was free. Dere was such a glory ober everything, de sun came like gold trou de trees, and ober de fields, and I felt like I was in heaven."

However, she was not content to be free while others remained in bondage.

I had crossed de line of which I had so long been dreaming. I was free; but dere was no one to welcome me to de land of freedom, I was a stranger in a strange land, and my home after all was down in de old cabin quarter, wid de ole folks, and my brudders and sisters. But to dis solemn resolution I came; I was free, and dey should be free also; I would make a home for dem in de North, and de Lord helping me, I would bring dem all dere. Oh, how I prayed den, lying all alone on de cold, damp ground; "Oh, dear Lord," I said, "I hain't got no friend but you. Come to my help, Lord, for I'm in trouble!"

According to Sarah Bradford, Harriet went back South nineteen times and brought with here "over three hundred pieces of living and breathing 'property' " to the promised land.

In this context "Swing Low, Sweet Chariot" referred to the "idea of escape by 'chariot,' that is, by means which a company could employ to proceed northward." When black slaves sang, "I looked over Jordan and what did I see, Coming for to carry me home," they were looking over the Ohio River. "The band of angels was Harriet or another conductor coming for him; and 'home' was a haven in the free states or Canada." "Steal away" meant to sneak into the woods for a secret slave meeting, and "Follow the Drinking Gourd" meant following the Great Dipper to the Ohio River and freedom.

But while it is true that heaven had its this-wordly topographical referents, not all black slaves could hope to make it to Africa, Canada, or even to the northern section of the United States. The ambiguity and failure of the American Colonization Society's experiments crushed the hopes of many black slaves who were expecting to return to their African homeland. And blacks also began to realize that the North was not so significantly different from the South as they had envisioned, particularly in view of the Fugitive Slave Act of 1850 and the Dred Scott Decision in 1858. Black slaves began to realize that their historical freedom could not be assured as long as white racists controlled the governmental processes of America. Thus they found it necessary to develop a style of freedom that *included* but *did not depend upon* historical possibilities. What could freedom mean for black slaves who could never expect to participate in the determination of the laws governing their lives? Must they continue to define freedom in terms of the possibility of escape and insurrection, as if their humanity depended on their willingness to commit suicide? It was in response to this situation that the black concept of heaven developed.

For black slaves, who were condemned to carve out their existence in captivity, heaven meant that the eternal God had made a decision about their humanity that could not be destroyed by white masters. Whites could drive them, beat them, and even kill them; but they believed that God nevertheless had chosen black slaves as his own and that this election bestowed upon them a freedom to be, which could not be measured by what oppressors could do to the physical body. Whites may suppress black history and define Africans as savages, but the words of slave masters do not have to be taken seriously when the oppressed know that they have a *some-*

bodiness that is guaranteed by the heavenly Father who alone is the ultimate sovereign of the universe. This is what heaven meant for black slaves.

The idea of heaven provided ways for black people to affirm their humanity when other people were attempting to define them as nonpersons. It enabled blacks to say yes to their right to be free by affirming God's promise to the oppressed of the freedom to be. That was what they meant when they sang about a "city called heaven."

> I am a poor pilgrim of sorrow.
> I'm in this world alone.
> No hope in this world for tomorrow.
> I'm trying to make heaven my home.
>
> Sometimes I am tossed and driven.
> Sometimes I don't know where to roam.
> I've heard of a city called heaven.
> I've started to make it my home.
>
> My mother's gone on to pure glory.
> My father's still walking in sin.
> My sisters and brothers won't own me
> Because I'm tryin' to get in.

In the midst of economic and political disfranchisement, black slaves held themselves together and did not lose their spiritual composure, because they believed that their worth transcended governmental decisions. That was why they looked forward to "walking in Jerusalem just like John" and longed for the "camp meeting in the promised land."

It is evident that the pre-scientific images of heaven in these songs point to a biblical emphasis usually glossed over by New Testament scholars. Black slaves are expressing the Christian contention that the death and resurrection of Christ bestows upon people a freedom that cannot be taken away by oppressors. They were saying: "We are human beings and not even the slave masters can do anything about that!"

A fuller appreciation of the contemporary situation in black and white religious patterns will be gained by reviewing the historical antecedents to which many of the leaders and much of the content of the documentary material have alluded.

Historical Origins and Expressions of the Dilemma

SLAVERY

All roads lead to slavery when we attempt to understand black culture in the United States. In the 1970s much significant research was carried on concerning the scope and nature of American slavery. Among students of the black experience there had been some difference of opinion concerning the survival of Africanisms during the course of the slave experience in the United States.[15] Frazier had concluded that the destruction of clan and kinship organization was so devastating that in an alien civilization "whatever remained of their religious myths and cults had no meaning whatever."[16] There is an emerging consensus among contemporary scholars that significant Africanisms survived capture, the middle passage, and plantation life.

Today it is recognized that the slaves' proverbs, folk tales, sexual attitudes, material culture, and religious practices came directly from Africa. To be sure, these Africanisms have not been kept in static form. Albert J. Raboteau has observed:

> The fact is that they have continued to develop as living traditions putting down new roots in new soil, bearing new fruit as unique hybrids of American origin. African styles of worship, forms of ritual, systems of belief, and fundamental perspectives have remained vital on this side of the Atlantic, not because they were preserved in a pure orthodoxy but because they were transformed.[17]

In a similar fashion black slaves also transformed Christian traditions to meet their needs.

From the beginning of the slave trade in Colonial America, Africans received Christian baptism. There was anxiety about this practice until the courts established that baptism did not make a black slave free. Throughout the seventeenth century there was concern expressed for the salvation of African slaves. The venerable Richard Baxter (1615–1691), English Puritan leader, published in 1673 his *Christian Directory* for the saints in America. Included in this volume was a chapter titled "Directions to those Masters in Foreign Plantations who have Negroes and other slaves; being a solution of several cases about them." In this chapter Baxter called upon masters to "understand well how far your power over your slaves extendeth and what limits God hath set thereto."[18] Baxter reminded the masters that slaves had immortal souls and that owners were trustees whose power over the slaves carried grave responsibility. Finally, Baxter admonished the slaveholders to "make it your chief end in buying and using slaves to win them to Christ and

---

[15]The first opinion stresses the loss of African elements during the course of the slave experience. A typical example of this position is advanced by Stanley M. Elkins, *Slavery: A Problem in American Institutional and Intellectual Life* (Chicago: University of Chicago Press, 1968). The second school of thought can be seen in Melville J. Herskovits, *The Myth of the Negro Past* (New York: Harper & Row, 1941). Herskovits stresses the continuity and resilience of African culture in the New World.

[16]Frazier, op. cit., p. 6.

[17]Albert J. Raboteau, *Slave Religion: The "Invisible Institution" in the Antebellum South* (New York: Oxford, 1978), p. 4.

[18]Quoted in Charles C. Jones, *The Religious Instruction of the Negroes in the United States* (Savannah: Thomas Purse, 1842), pp. 6–7.

save their souls." The *Directions* apparently had an extensive circulation throughout the colonies.

Although slaves were baptized and taken into the Anglican church during the seventeenth century, it was not until the early eighteenth century that a systematic mission to the Afro-American was attempted. In 1701 The Society for the Propagation of the Gospel in Foreign Parts (S.P.G.) was established. The society considered its threefold mission to be, "The care and instruction of our people settled in the Colonies; the conversion of the Indian savages; and the conversion of the Negroes." In 1727 the Bishop of London, who exercised jurisdiction over the Anglican church in America, became an advocate for the conversion of the Negroes, and wrote two letters on the subject. In the first letter Edmund Gibson (1669–1748) addressed himself "to masters and mistresses of families, in the English Plantation abroad," exhorting them to encourage and promote the instruction of their Negroes in the Christian faith. The second in the same year, addressed the missionaries there, directing them to circulate the general letter, and exhorting them to give their assistance toward the instruction of the Negroes "within their several parishes." The bishop's letters of advocacy on behalf of the black population articulate a genuine concern for the African slaves, and they also frankly acknowledged several of the difficulties encountered in such a mission.

Document 52

Bishop Gibson's Letters for the Promotion of the Instruction of Black Slaves in the Christian Faith

The Bishop of London's Letter to the Masters and Mistresses of Families in the English Plantations abroad; exhorting them to encourage and promote the Instruction of their Negroes in the Christian Faith. London, 1727.

The care of the Plantations abroad being committed to the Bishop of London, as to religious affairs, I have thought it my duty to make particular inquiries into the state of religion in those parts; and to learn, among other things, what number of slaves are employed within the several governments, and what means are used for their instruction in the Christian faith. I find the numbers are prodigiously great; and am not a little troubled to observe how small a progress has been made in a Christian country towards the delivering those poor creatures from the pagan darkness and superstition in which they were bred, and the making them partakers of the light of the Gospel, and of the blessings and benefits belonging to it. And, which is yet more to be lamented, I find there has not only been very little progress made in the work, but that all *attempts* towards it, have been by too many indus-

SOURCE: Charles C. Jones, *The Religious Instruction of the Negroes in the United States* (Savannah: Thomas Purse, 1842), pp. 16–27.

triously discouraged and hindered; partly by magnifying the *difficulties* of the work beyond what they really are: and partly by mistaken suggestions of the change which baptism would make in the condition of the Negroes, to the loss and disadvantage of their masters.

I. *As to the Difficulties*: it may be pleaded that the Negroes are *grown persons* when they come over, and that having been accustomed to the pagan rites and idolatries of their own country, they are prejudiced against all other religions, and more particularly against the Christian, as forbidding all the licentiousness which is usually practiced among the heathens.

But if this were a good argument against attempting the conversion of Negroes, it would follow that the Gospel is never further to be propagated than it is at present, and that no endeavors are to be used for the conversion of heathens at any time, or in any country, whatsoever: because all heathens have been accustomed to pagan rites and idolatries, and to such vicious and licentious living as the Christian religion forbids. But yet, God be thanked, heathens have been converted and Christianity propagated in all ages, and almost all countries, through the zeal and diligence of pious and good men; and this without the help of miracles. And if the present age be as zealous and diligent in pursuing the proper *means* of conversion, we have no reason to doubt, but that the divine assistance is, and will be, the same in all ages.

But a further difficulty is, that they are *utter strangers to our language* and *we to theirs;* and the gift of tongues being now ceased, there is no means left of instructing them in the doctrines of the Christian religion. And this, I own, is a real difficulty, as long as it continues, and as far as it reaches. But if I am rightly informed, many of the Negroes who are grown persons when they come over, do of themselves attain so much of our language as enables them to understand and to be understood, in things which concern the ordinary business of life; and they who can go so far, of their own accord, might doubtless be carried much further, if proper methods and endeavors were used to bring them to a complete knowledge of our language, with a pious view to the instructing them in the doctrines of our religion. At least some of them, who are more capable and more serious than the rest, might be easily instructed both in our language and religion, and then be made use of to convey instruction to the rest in their own language. And this, one would hope, may be done with great ease, wherever there is a hearty and sincere zeal for the work.

But whatever difficulties there may be in instructing those who are *grown up* before they are brought over, there are not the like difficulties in the case of *their children*, who are born and bred in our own Plantations, who have never been accustomed to pagan rites and superstitions, and who may easily be trained up, like all other children, to any language whatsoever, and particularly to our own; if the making them good Christians be sincerely the desire and intention of those who have the property in them and the government over them.

But supposing the difficulties to be much greater than I imagine, they are not such as render the work *impossible*, so as to leave no hope of *any degree* of success; and nothing less than an *impossibility* of doing any good at all, can warrant our giving over and laying aside all means and endeavors, where the propagation of the Gospel and the saving of souls are immediately concerned.

Many undertakings look far more impracticable before trial, than they are afterwards found to be in experience; especially where there is not a good heart to go about them. And it is frequently observed that small beginnings, when pursued with resolution, are attended with great and surprising success. But in no case is the success more great and surprising than when good men engage in the cause of God and religion, out of a just sense of the inestimable value of a soul, and in full and well grounded assurance that their honest designs and endeavors for the promoting religion, will be supported by a special blessing from God.

I am loth to think so hardly of any *Christian* master, as to suppose that he can *deliberately hinder* his Negroes from being instructed in the Christian faith; or which is the same thing, that he can, upon sober and mature consideration of the case, finally resolve to deny them the *means and opportunities* of instruction. Much less may I believe that he can, after he has seriously weighed this matter, permit them to labor on the Lord's day: and least of all, that he can put them under a kind of *necessity* of laboring on that day, to provide themselves with the conveniences of life; since our religion so plainly teaches us that God has given one day in seven, to be a day of rest; not only to man, but to the beasts. That it is a day appointed by him for the improvement of the soul, as well as the refreshment of the body; and that it is a duty incumbent upon masters, to take care that all persons who are under their government, keep this day holy, and employ it to the pious and wise purposes for which God,—our great Lord and Master—intended it. Nor can I think so hardly of any missionary, who shall be desired by the master to direct and assist in the instruction of his Negroes (either on that day or on any other, when he shall be more at leisure,) as to suppose that he will not embrace such invitations with the utmost readiness and cheerfulness, and give all the help that is fairly consistent with the necessary duties of his function, as a parochial minister.

If it be said that no time can be spared from the daily labor and employment of the Negroes, to instruct them in the Christian religion; this is in effect to say that no consideration of propagating the Gospel of God, or saving the souls of men, is to make the *least abatement* from the temporal profit of the masters; and that God cannot or will not make up the little they may lose in that way, by blessing and prospering their undertakings by sea and land, as a just reward of their zeal for his glory and the salvation of men's souls. In this case, I may well reason as St. Paul does in a case not unlike it, that if they make you partakers of their temporal things, (of their strength and spirits, and even of their offspring,) you ought to make them partakers of your spiritual things, though it should abate somewhat from the profit which you might otherwise receive from their labors. And considering the *greatness* of the profit that is received from their labors, it might be hoped that all Christian masters, those especially who are possessed of considerable numbers, should also be at some small *expense* in providing for the instruction of these poor creatures, and that others, whose numbers are less, and who dwell in the same neighborhood, should join in the expense of a common teacher for the Negroes belonging to them. The Society for Propagating the Gospel in Foreign Parts, are sufficiently sensible of the great importance and necessity of such an established and regular provision for the instruction of the Negroes, and earnestly wish and pray, that it may please God to put it into the hearts of good Christians, to enable them to assist in the work, by seasonable contributions for that end: but at present their fund does scarce enable them to answer the many demands of missionaries, for the performance of divine service in the poorer settlements, which are not in a condition to maintain them at their own charge.

II. But it is further pleaded, that the instruction of heathens in the Christian faith, is in order to their baptism: and that not only the *time* to be allowed for instructing them, would be an abatement from the profits of their labour, but also, that the *baptizing* them when instructed would destroy both the property which the masters have in them as slaves bought with their money and the right of selling them again at pleasure, and that the making them Christians, only makes them less diligent and more ungovernable.

To which it may be very truly replied, that Christianity and the embracing of the Gospel does not make the least alteration in civil property, or in any of the duties which belong to civil relations; but in all these respects, it continues persons just in the same state as it found them. The freedom which Christianity gives is a freedom from the bondage of sin and satan, and from the dominion of men's lusts and passions and inordinate desires; but as to their *outward* condition, whatever that was before, whether bond or free, their being baptized and becoming Christians, makes no manner of change in it. As St. Paul has expressly told us, 1 *Cor.* 7: 20, where he is speaking directly to this point, "Let every man abide in the same calling wherein he was called:" and at the 24th verse, "Let every man wherein he is called therein abide with God." And so far is Christianity from discharging men from the duties of the station or condition in which it found them, that it lays them under stronger obligations to perform those duties with the greatest diligence and fidelity, not only from the fear of man but from a sense of duty to God, and the belief and expectation of a future account. So that to say that Christianity tends to make men less observant of their duty in any respect, is a reproach that it is very far from deserving: and a reproach that is confuted *by the whole tenor of the Gospel precepts*, which inculcate upon all, and particularly upon servants (many of whom were then in the condition of slaves,) a faithful and diligent discharge of the duties belonging to their several stations out of conscience towards God. And it is also confuted by *our own reason*, which tells us how much more forcible and constant the restraint of *conscience* is, than the restraint of *fear*; and last of all, it is confuted by *experience*, which teaches us the great value of those servants who are truly religious, compared with those who have no sense of religion.

As to their being more ungovernable after baptism than before, it is certain that the Gospel every where enjoins not only diligence and fidelity, but also *obedience* for conscience sake: and does not deprive masters of any proper methods of enforcing obedience, where they appear to be necessary. Humanity forbids all cruel and barbarous treatment of our fellow-creatures, and will not suffer us to consider a being that is endowed with reason on a level with brutes: and Christianity takes not out of the hands of superiors any degrees of strictness and severity that fairly appear to be necessary for the preserving subjection and government. The general law both of humanity and of Christianity, is kindness, gentleness and compassion towards all mankind, of what nation or condition soever they be; and therefore we are to make the exercise of those amiable virtues our *choice* and *desire*, and to have recourse to severe and vigorous methods unwillingly and only out of necessity. And of this *necessity*, you yourselves remain the judges, as much *after* they receive baptism as *before*; so that you can be in no danger of suffering by the change; and as to *them*, the greatest hardships that the most severe master can inflict upon them is not to be compared to the cruelty of keeping them in the state of heathenism and depriving them of the means of salvation as reached forth to *all mankind* in the Gospel of Christ. And in truth one great reason why severity is at all necessary to maintain government, is the *want* of religion in those who are to be governed, and who therefore are not to be kept to their duty by any thing but *fear and terror;* than which there cannot be a more uneasy state, either to those who govern or those who are governed.

III. That these things may make the greater impression upon you, let me beseech you to consider yourselves not only as masters, but as *Christian* masters, who stand obliged by your profession to do all that your station and condition enable you to do, towards breaking the power of satan and enlarging the kingdom of Christ, and as having a great opportunity put into your hands of helping on this work, by the influence which God has given you over such a number of heathen idolaters, who still continue under the dominion of satan. In the next place let me beseech you to consider *them* not barely as slaves, and upon the same level with laboring beasts, but as *men*-slaves and *women*-slaves, who have the same frame and faculties with yourselves and have souls capable of being made eternally happy, and reason and understanding to receive instruction in order to it. If they came from abroad, let it not be said that they are as far from the knowledge of Christ in a Christian country as when they dwelt among pagan idolaters. If they have been born among you and have never breathed any air but that of a Christian country, let them not be as much strangers to Christ as if they had been transplanted, as soon as born, into a country of pagan idolaters.

Hoping that these and the like considerations will move you to lay this matter seriously to heart, and excite you to use the best means in your power towards so good and pious a work; I cannot omit to suggest to you one of the best motives that can be used for disposing the heathens to embrace Christianity, and that is *the good lives of Christians.* Let them see in you and in your families, examples of sobriety, temperance and chastity, and of all the other virtues and graces of the Christian life. Let them observe how strictly you oblige yourselves and all that belong to you to abstain from cursing and swearing, and to keep the Lord's day and the ordinances which Christ hath appointed in the Gospel. Make them sensible, by the general tenor of your behaviour and conversation, that your inward temper and disposition is such as the Gospel requires, that is to say, mild, gentle and merciful, and that as oft as you exercise vigor and severity, it is wholly owing to their idleness or obstinacy.

By these means you will open their hearts to instruction, and *prepare* them to receive the truths of the Gospel; to which if you add a pious *endeavor and concern* to see them duly instructed, you may become the instrument of saving many souls, and will not only secure a blessing from God upon all your undertakings in this world, but entitle yourselves to that distinguishing reward in the next which will be given to all those who have been zealous in their endeavors to promote the salvation of men and enlarge the kingdom of Christ. And that you may be found in that number, at the great day of accounts, is the sincere desire and earnest prayer of your faithful friend.

EDM. LONDON.
May 19, 1727.

The Bishop of London's Letter to the Missionaries in the
English plantations: exhorting them to give their assistance
toward the Instruction of the Negroes of their several Parishes
in the Christian Faith.

Good Brother:
   Having understood by many letters from the Plantations, and by the accounts of persons who have come from thence, that very little progress hath hitherto been made in the conversion of the Negroes to the Christian faith; I have thought it proper for me to lay before the masters and mistresses the obligations they are under to promote and encourage that pious and necessary work. This I have done in a letter directed to them, of which you will receive several copies in order to be distributed to those who have Negroes in your parish; and I must entreat you, when you put the letter into their hands, to enforce the design of it by any arguments that you shall think proper to be used; and also, to assure them of your own assistance in carrying on the work.
   I am aware that in the Plantations where the parishes are of so large extent, the care and labor of the parochial ministers must be great; but yet I persuaded myself that many vacant hours may be spared from the other pastoral duties to be bestowed on this; and I cannot doubt of the readiness of every missionary, in his own parish, to promote and further a work so charitable to the souls of men, and so agreeable to the great end and design of his mission.
   As to those ministers who have Negroes of their own, I cannot but esteem it their indispensable duty to use their best endeavors to instruct them in the Christian religion in order to their being baptized; both because such Negroes are their proper and immediate care, and because it is in vain to hope that other masters and mistresses will exert themselves in this work, if they see it wholly neglected or but coldly pursued in the families of the clergy; so that any degree of neglect on your part, in the instruction of your own Negroes, would not only be withholding from *them* the inestimable benefits of Christianity, but would evidently tend to the obstructing and defeating the *whole design* in every other family.
   I would also hope that the school masters in the several parishes, part of whose business it is to instruct youth in the principles of Christianity, might contribute somewhat towards the carrying on his work, by being ready to bestow upon it some of their leisure time; and especially upon the Lord's day, when both they and the Negroes are most at liberty, and the clergy are taken up with the public duties of their function.
   And though the assistance they give to this pious design, should not meet with any reward from men, yet their comfort may be that it is the work of God and will assuredly be rewarded by him; and the less they are *obliged* to this on account of any reward they receive from *men*, the greater will their reward be from the

hands of God. I must therefore entreat you to recommend it to them in my name, and to dispose them by all proper arguments and persuasions, to turn their thoughts seriously to it, and to be always ready to offer and lend their assistance at their leisure hours.

And so, not doubting your ready and zealous concurrence in promoting this important work and earnestly begging a blessing from God upon this and all your other pastoral labors, I remain, your affectionate friend and brother.

EDM. LONDON.
May 19, 1727.

Dean Stanhope (or Canterbury) states in his sermon, 1714, that success had attended the efforts of the society, and speaks of "children, servants, and slaves catechised."

Bishop Berkeley was in the Colony of Rhode Island from 1728 till late in 1730, and he also preached a sermon before the society, February 18, 1731, in which he thus speaks of the Negroes: "the Negroes in the government of Rhode Island, are about half as many more than the Indians, and both together scarce amount to a seventh part of the whole Colony. The religion of these people, as is natural to suppose, takes after that of their masters. Some few are baptized: several frequent the different assemblies; and far the greater part, none at all.

We have no accurate records of the number converted to Christianity through the efforts of the S.P.G.. Actually we also know very little about the success of missionaries who were sponsored by the Moravians, Quakers, Presbyterians, and Roman Catholics. Despite the encouraging reports from some of the missionaries, it seems clear that only a relatively small number of slaves in the American colonies could have been even nominally Christian.[19]

THE DAWN OF A NEW DAY

The large-scale conversion of black slaves to Christianity came through the evangelicalism which resulted from the first Great Awakening.[20] When Methodists and Baptists and, to a lesser degree, Presbyterians began their revival efforts in the South, large numbers of slaves responded to this religious expression. The black historian Carter G. Woodson (1875–1950) referred to this development as "The Dawn of a New Day."[21] White evangelicalism was the principal means by which blacks were able to order their experience and define their community, but their own slave status and African culture transformed the received faith. Donald G. Mathews states the relationship succinctly: "Black religion in the Old South was a churning suspension of ideas and behavior patterns fed by African and Christian traditions. The process

[19]Marcus W. Jernegan, "Slavery and Conversion in the American Colonies," *American Historical Review*, Vol. 21 (April 1916), pp. 504–527.
[20]See Chapter 3.
[21]Carter G. Woodson, *The History of the Negro Church* (Washington, D.C.: Associated Publishers, 1921), pp. 23–39.

which throughout the period worked to transform the suspension into a more stable compound unfolded essentially through four channels: folk religion, autonomous black congregations, black constituencies associated with white churches, and black memberships of mixed, white-controlled churches."[22] Mathews believes that the African notion of spirit possession which became identified with the conversion experience made Christianity more attractive to the slaves. The absence of drumming, dancing, and sacrifice would have been felt by Africans. At any rate, slaves found evangelical Christianity emotionally satisfying and a resource for coping with their social condition.

THE INVISIBLE INSTITUTION

There emerged from the Christian religion of the enslaved blacks "the invisible institution."[23] Frazier quotes an ex-slave who wrote:

> Our preachers were usually plantation folks just like the rest of us. Some man who had been taught something about the Bible would be our preacher. The coloured folks had their code of religion, not nearly so complicated as the white man's religion, but more closely observed. . . . When we had our meetings of this kind, we held them in our own way and were not interferred with by the white folks.[24]

The black preacher played a central role in the "invisible institution." He was "called" to his office as preacher and the authority of his call was so much the greater if, in addition to a religious "call experience," he was licensed to preach by the Methodist or Baptist Church. The preacher needed to possess some knowledge of the Bible, and he needed to be able to sing. Because of the free congregational polity of the Baptist churches the black preacher was able to lead his followers in a manner that was not possible in the Methodist polity. To some degree and in accordance with different local situations, the white master would recognize the black preacher's leadership role. But any recognition accorded the slave congregations by the whites was understood as recognition accorded to them as segments of white organizations. White supervision was constant and the black church was not an independent institution until after the Civil War. The antebellum church of the disinherited—that is, the black slave church, was indeed an "invisible institution."

THE INSTITUTIONAL CHURCHES OF THE FREE NEGRO

Another significant phenomenon in the history of the black religion in America was the development of the institutional churches of the free Negroes. The free black population in the colonies and in the

[22] Donald G. Mathews, *Religion in the Old South* (Chicago: University of Chicago Press, 1977), p. 208.
[23] Frazier, op. cit., p. 16.
[24] Ibid.

Republic increased until the time of the Civil War. Frazier lists five sources of this increase: (1) the children born of free black persons; (2) mulatto children born of colored mothers; (3) mulatto children born of white servants or free women; (4) children of free Negro and Indian parentage; (5) slaves who were set free.[25] Although it is impossible to determine the proportions of free blacks that came from each source, it is generally conceded that most blacks became free through manumission, or the freeing of slaves by their white masters.

In the beginning the status of black preachers and black communicants in white church organizations was not at all clear. In the South black Christians joined Methodist and Baptist churches where they worshipped in segregated sections. In many places the Presbyterians and Episcopalians built separate church edifices for their black members.[26] The issue was not limited to the South, as we can see when we consider the person and work of Richard Allen (1760–1831), founder and bishop of the African Methodist Episcopal Church.

Richard Allen was born a slave in the city of Philadelphia in 1760. He was sold to a planter who brought him to Delaware. He was converted in 1777 and was soon thereafter allowed by his master to purchase his freedom. He became a Methodist preacher in 1780 and was permitted to travel with white Methodist ministers and was granted ministerial appointments by Methodist Bishop Francis Asbury. In 1786 he was invited to preach in the St. George Methodist Episcopal Church in Philadelphia. Allen initially petitioned Methodist authorities to permit him to carry on work among the black Methodists in a separate congregation. His petition was denied, but it was not too long before Afro-Americans were removed from seats around the wall and told to sit in the gallery. Allen, Absalom Jones, and William White were requested to leave their seats while they were kneeling in prayer. Allen wrote:

> We had not been long upon our knees before I heard considerable scuffling and low talking. I raised my head up and saw one of the trustees, H——— H———, having hold of the Reverend Absalom Jones, pulling him up off his knees, and saying, "You must get up—you must not kneel here." Mr. Jones replied, "Wait until prayer is over." Mr. H——— H——— said, "No, you must get up now, or I will call for aid and force you away." Mr. Jones said, "Wait until prayer is over, and I will get up and trouble you no more." With that he beckoned to one of the other trustees, Mr. L——— S———, to come to his assistance. He came, and went to William White to pull him up. By this time prayer was over, and we all went out of the Church in a body, and they were no more plagued with us in the Church. This raised a great excitement and inquiry among the citizens, in so much that I believe they were ashamed of their conduct. But my dear Lord was with us, and we were filled with fresh vigor to get a house erected to worship God in.[27]

[25] Ibid., p. 21.
[26] Ibid., p. 25.
[27] Richard Allen, *The Life, Experience and Gospel Labors of the Rt. Rev. Richard Allen* (Philadephia: A.M.E. Book Concern, n.d.), pp. 14–15.

Allen organized the Bethel Church in 1794. Bishop Asbury ordained Allen deacon and then he later received elder's orders. In other cities African Methodist Episcopal churches were established. The representatives of these churches met in 1816 and established the African Methodist Episcopal Church. In this constituting session Allen was elected bishop and a book of discipline was adopted that was essentially a duplication of the same articles of religion and procedures that were contained in the *Discipline* of the Methodist Episcopal Church.[28]

In New York City Peter Williams, Sr., joined with other Afro-Americans in leaving the John Street Church to form the Zion Church, which developed into the African Methodist Episcopal Zion Church. Throughout the country independent Baptist congregations were established, although they were not to organize a national convention until many years later. When the Methodist church divided over the issue of slavery in 1844, some black Methodists continued to worship in the Methodist congregations of their masters. After the Civil War the Negroes who had been in the Methodist Episcopal Church South were permitted to organize into a separate body, which became the Colored Methodist Episcopal Church (C.M.E.). In these various Methodist and Baptist denominations a great proportion of black Christians remain today.

SLAVERY OR FREEDOM

The enduring dilemma about which Myrdal wrote with such analytical thoroughness generated in the mid-nineteenth century an explosive force that left general socioeconomic upheaval in its wake. Sydney Ahlstrom writes of both the inevitability and the essentially "moral" nature of the Civil War:

> It was not "moral" because one side was good and the other evil, nor because purity of motive was more pronounced on one side than on the other. It was a moral war because it sprang from a moral impasse on issues which Americans in the mid-nineteenth century could no longer avoid or escape. Had there been no slavery, there would have been no war. Had there been no moral condemnation of slavery, there would have been no war. Yet slavery had become a massive American institution, and the South, given its racial predicament, could not entertain emancipation: the peculiar institution was worth disunion. By 1860, on the other hand, the nation's always uneasy conscience had been aroused, and in the North it had been shaped into a crusade which could not accept either indefinitely continued compromise or peaceable secession. So war came. Its origins go back at least to Europe's almost simultaneous discovery of the African Gold Coast and the New World. Its aftermath still constitutes the country's chief moral challenge.[29]

Much of the antislavery impulse was linked to the general reform and benevolence measures that were the products of the Second Great

---

[28]Woodson, op. cit., pp. 75–77.
[29]Sydney E. Ahlstrom, *A Religious History of the American People* (New Haven, Conn.: Yale University Press, 1972), p. 649.

Awakening. Among the measures were temperance, education, women's rights, prison and hospital reform, and peace crusades. The decades of the 1830s saw the beginning of the mounting antislavery movement. The abrasive abolitionist crusader William Lloyd Garrison (1805–1879) published his first edition of the *Public Liberator and Journal of the Times* on January 1, 1831. At the Lane Theological Seminary in Cincinnati, a convert of Charles Finney, Dwight Weld, expounded an antislavery point of view. Asa Mahan (1800–1889) and Finney made Oberlin College (Ohio) a center for Finneyite abolition sentiment. In Boston William Ellery Channing and Wendell Phillips (1811–1883) led the antislavery forces. Ahlstrom writes, "In New England, New York, and the Northwest antislavery and evangelicalism had struck a close and powerful alliance that would soon wield great political influence."[30]

The decade of the 1830s was equally decisive in the slave states. In this decade there was a great swing to fervent support of slavery. One source of this reaction was the fear and anger aroused by a Virginia slave revolt led by Nat Turner (1800–1831). "Nat Turner's revolt" is perhaps the most famous of over one hundred recorded slave revolts. Turner led about seventy slaves on a rampage that claimed the lives of at least fifty-seven white persons in twenty-four hours. When the revolt was put down Turner managed somehow to escape and hide for approximately two months before he was caught, tried, and executed.

Turner was a religious mystic who apparently believed that he was chosen of God to lead a revolt that would virtually end the system of slavery. Turner allegedly made a "full and voluntary" confession to Thomas R. Gray. The document that follows is composed of excerpts from Turner's "confession," which was recorded while he was awaiting death.

Document 53

From The Alleged Confession of Nat Turner

Sir,—You have asked me to give a history of the motives which induced me to undertake the late insurrection, as you call it—To do so I must go back to the days of my infancy, and even before I was born. I was thirty-one years of age the 2nd of October last, and born the property of Benj. Turner, of this county. In my childhood a circumstance occurred which made an indelible impression on my mind, and laid the ground work of that enthusiasm, which has terminated so fatally to many, both white and black, and for which I am about to atone at the gallows. It is here necessary to relate this circumstance—trifling as it may seem, it was the commencement of that belief which has grown with time, and even now, sir, in this

SOURCE: Herbert Aptheker, *Nat Turner's Slave Rebellion* (New Jersey: Humanities Press, Inc., 1966), pp. 127–149. Reprinted by permission.

[30] Ibid., p. 653.

dungeon, helpless and forsaken as I am, I cannot divest myself of. Being at play with other children, when three or four years old, I was telling them something, which my mother overhearing, said it had happened before I was born—I stuck to my story, however, and related somethings which went, in her opinion, to confirm it— others being called on were greatly astonished, knowing that these things had happened, and caused them to say in my hearing, I surely would be a prophet, as the Lord had shewn me things that had happened before my birth. And my father and mother strengthened me in this my first impression, saying in my presence, I was intended for some great purpose, which they had always thought from certain marks on my head and breast. . . . My grandmother, who was very religious, and to whom I was much attached—my master, who belonged to the church, and other religious persons who visited the house, and whom I often saw at prayers, noticing the singularity of my manners, I suppose, and my uncommon intelligence for a child, remarked I had too much sense to be raised, and if I was, I would never be of any service to any one as a slave—To a mind like mine, restless, inquisitive and observant of every thing that was passing, it is easy to suppose that religion was the subject to which it would be directed, and although this subject principally occupied my thoughts—there was nothing that I saw or heard of to which my attention was not directed—The manner in which I learned to read and write, not only had great influence on my own mind, as I acquired it with the most perfect ease, so much so, that I have no recollection whatever of learning the alphabet— but to the astonishment of the family, one day, when a book was shewn to me to keep me from crying, I began spelling the names of different objects—this was a source of wonder to all in the neighborhood, particularly the blacks—and this learning was constantly improved at all opportunities—when I got large enough to go to work, while employed, I was reflecting on many things that would present themselves to my imagination, and whenever an opportunity occurred of looking at a book, when the school children were getting their lessons, I would find many things that the fertility of my own imagination had depicted to me before; all my time, not devoted to my master's service, was spent either in prayer, or in making experiments in casting different things in moulds made of earth, in attempting to make paper, gun-powder, and many other experiments, that although I could not perfect, yet convinced me of its practicability if I had the means.* I was not addicted to stealing in my youth, nor have ever been—Yet such was the confidence of the negroes in the neighborhood, even at this early period of my life, in my superior judgment, that they would often carry me with them when they were going on any roguery, to plan for them. Growing up among them, with this confidence in my superior judgment, and when this, in their opinions, was perfected by Divine inspiration, from the circumstances already alluded to in my infancy, and which belief was ever afterwards zealously inculcated by the austerity of my life and manners, which became the subject of remark by white and black.—Having soon discovered to be great, I must appear so, and therefore studiously avoided mixing in society, and wrapped myself in mystery, devoting my time to fasting and prayer— By this time, having arrived to man's estate, and hearing the scriptures commented

---

*When questioned as to the manner of manufacturing those different articles, he was found well informed on the subject.

on at meetings, I was struck with that particular passage which says: "Seek ye the kingdom of Heaven and all things shall be added unto you." I reflected much on this passage, and prayed daily for light on this subject—As I was praying one day at my plough, the spirit spoke to me, saying "Seek ye the kingdom of Heaven and all things shall be added unto you." *Question*—what do you mean by the Spirit? *Ans.* The Spirit that spoke to the prophets in former days—and I was greatly astonished, and for two years prayed continually, whenever my duty would permit—and then again I had the same revelation, which fully confirmed me in the impression that I was ordained for some great purpose in the hands of the Almighty. Several years rolled round, in which many events occurred to strengthen me in this my belief.

At this time I reverted in my mind to the remarks made of me in my childhood, and the things that had been shewn me—and as it had been said of me in my childhood by those by whom I had been taught to pray, both white and black, and in whom I had the greatest confidence, that I had too much sense to be raised, and if I was, I would never be of any use to any one as a slave. Now finding I had arrived to man's estate, and was a slave, and these revelations being made known to me, I began to direct my attention to this great object, to fulfill the purpose for which, by this time, I felt assured I was intended. Knowing the influence I had obtained over the minds of my fellow servants, (not by the means of conjuring and such like tricks— for to them I always spoke of such things with contempt but) by the communion of the Spirit whose revelations I often communicated to them, and they believed and said my wisdom came from God. I now began to prepare them for my purpose, by telling them something was about to happen that would terminate in fulfilling the great promise that had been made to me—About this time I was placed under an overseer, from whom I ran away—and after remaining in the woods thirty days, I returned, to the astonishment of the negroes on the plantation, who thought I had made my escape to some other part of the country, as my father had done before. But the reason of my return was, that the Spirit appeared to me and said I had my wishes directed to the things of this world, and not to the kingdom of Heaven, and that I should return to the service of my earthly master—"For he who knoweth his Master's will, and doeth it not, shall be beaten with many stripes, and thus have I chastened you." And the negroes found fault, and murmured against me, saying if they had my sense they would not serve any master in the world. And about this time I had a vision—and I saw white spirits and black spirits engaged in battle, and the sun was darkened—the thunder rolled in the Heavens, and blood flowed in streams—and I heard a voice saying, "Such is your luck, such you are called to see, and let it come rough or smooth, you must surely bare it." I now withdrew myself as much as my situation would permit, from the intercourse of my fellow servants, for the avowed purpose of serving the Spirit more fully—and it appeared to me, and reminded me of the things it had already shown me, and that it would then reveal to me the knowledge of the elements, the revolution of the planets, the operation of tides, and changes of the seasons. After this revelation in the year of 1825, and the knowledge of the elements being made known to me, I sought more than ever to obtain true holiness before the great day of judgment should appear, and then I began to receive the true knowledge of faith. And from the first steps of righteousness until the last, was I made perfect; and the Holy Ghost was with me, and said, "Behold me as I stand in the Heavens"—and I looked and saw the forms of men in different attitudes—and there were lights in the sky to which the children of darkness gave other names than what they really were—for they were the lights of the Savior's hands, stretched forth from east to west, even as they were extended on the cross on Calvary for the redemption of sinners. And I wondered greatly at these miracles, and prayed to be informed of a certainty of the meaning thereof—and shortly afterwards, while laboring in the field, I discovered drops of blood on the corn as though it were dew from heaven—and I communicated it to many, both white and black, in the neighborhood—and I then found on the leaves in the woods hieroglyphic characters, and numbers, with the forms of men in different attitudes, portrayed in blood, and representing the figures I had seen before in the heavens. And now the Holy Ghost had revealed itself to me, and made plain the miracles it had shown me—For as the blood of Christ had been shed on this earth, and had ascended to heaven for the salvation of sinners, and was now returning to earth again in the form of dew—and as the leaves on the trees bore the impression of the figures I had seen in the heavens, it was plain to me that the Savior was about to lay down the yoke he had borne for the sins of men, and the great day of judgment was at hand. About this time I told these things to a white man, (Etheldred T. Brantley) on whom it had a wonderful effect—and he ceased from his wickedness, and was attacked immediately with a cutaneous eruption, and blood oozed from the pores of his skin, and after praying and fasting nine days, he was healed, and the Spirit appeared to me again, and said, as the Savior had been baptised so should we be also—and when the white people would not let us be baptised by the church, we went down into the water together, in the sight of many who reviled us, and were baptised by the Spirit—After this I rejoiced greatly, and gave thanks to God. And on the 12th of May, 1828, I heard a loud noise in the heavens, and the Spirit instantly appeared to me and said the Serpent was loosened, and Christ had laid down the yoke he had borne for the sins of men, and that I should take it on and fight against the Serpent, for the time was fast approaching when the first should be the last and the last should be first. *Ques.* Do you not find yourself mistaken now? *Ans.* Was not Christ crucified? And by signs in the heavens that it would make known to me when I should commence the great work— and until the first sign appeared, I should conceal it from the knowledge of men— And on the appearance of the sign, (the eclipse of the sun last February) I should arise and prepare myself, and slay my enemies with their own weapons. And immediately on the sign appearing in the heavens, the seal was removed from my lips, and I communicated the great work laid out for me to do, to four in whom I had the greatest confidence, (Henry, Hark, Nelson, and Sam)—It was intended by us to have begun the work of death on the 4th July last—Many were the plans formed and rejected by us, and it affected my mind to such a degree, that I fell sick, and the time passed without our coming to any determination how to commence— Still forming new schemes and rejecting them, when the sign appeared again, which determined me not to wait longer.

Since the commencement of 1830, I had been living with Mr. Joseph Travis, who was to me a kind master, and placed the greatest confidence in me; in fact, I had no cause to complain of his treatment to me. On Saturday evening, the 20th of

August, it was agreed between Henry, Hark and myself, to prepare a dinner the next day for the men we expected, and then to concert a plan, as we had not yet determined on any. Hark, on the following morning, brought a pig, and Henry brandy, and being joined by Sam, Nelson, Will and Jack, they prepared in the woods a dinner, where, about three o'clock, I joined them.

Q. Why were you so backward in joining them?

A. The same reason that had caused me not to mix with them for years before.

I saluted them on coming up, and asked Will how came he there, he answered, his life was worth no more than others, and his liberty as dear to him. I asked him if he thought to obtain it? He said he would, or lose his life. This was enough to put him in full confidence. Jack, I knew, was only a tool in the hands of Hark, it was quickly agreed we should commence at home (Mr. J. Travis') on that night, and until we had armed and equipped ourselves, and gathered sufficient force, neither age nor sex was to be spared (which was invariably adhered to). We remained at the feast, until about two hours in the night, when we went to the house and found Austin; they all went to the cider press and drank, except myself. On returning to the house, Hark went to the door with an axe, for the purpose of breaking it open, as we knew we were strong enough to murder the family, if they were awaked by the noise; but reflecting that it might create an alarm in the nighborhood, we determined to enter the house secretly, and murder them whilst sleeping. Hark got a ladder and set it against the chimney, on which I ascended, and hoisting a window, entered and came down stairs, unbarred the door, and removed the guns from their places. It was then observed that I must spill the first blood. On which, armed with a hatchet, and accompanied by Will, I entered my master's chamber, it being dark, I could not give a death blow, the hatchet glanced from his head, he sprang from the bed and called his wife, it was his last word, Will laid him dead, with a blow of his axe, and Mrs. Travis shared the same fate, as she lay in bed. The murder of this family, five in number, was the work of a moment, not one of them awoke; there was a little infant sleeping in a cradle, that was forgotten, until we had left the house and gone some distance, when Henry and Will returned and killed it; we got here, four guns that would shoot, and several old muskets, with a pound or two of powder. We remained some time at the barn, where we paraded; I formed them in a line as soldiers, and after carrying them through all the manoeuvres I was master of marched them off to Mr. Salathul Francis', about six hundred yards distant. Sam and Will went to the door and knocked. Mr. Francis asked who was there, Sam replied it was him, and he had a letter for him, on which he got up and came to the door; they immediately seized him, and dragging him out a little from the door, he was dispatched by repeated blows on the head; there was no other white person in the family. We started from there for Mrs. Reese's, maintaining the most perfect silence on our march, where finding the door unlocked, we entered, and murdered Mrs. Reese in her bed, while sleeping; her son awoke, but it was only to sleep the sleep of death, he had only time to say who is that, and he was no more. From Mrs. Reese's we went to Mrs. Turner's, a mile distant, which we reached about sunrise, on Monday morning. Henry Austin, and Sam went to the still, where, finding Mr. Peebles, Austin shot him, and the rest of us went to the house; as we approached, the family discovered us, and shut the door. Vain hope! Will, with one stroke of his axe, opened it, and we entered and found Mrs. Turner and Mrs. Newsome in the middle of a room, almost frightened to death. Will immediately killed Mrs. Turner, with one blow of his axe. I took Mrs. Newsome by the hand, and with the sword I had when I was apprehended, I struck her several blows over the head, but not being able to kill her, as the sword was dull. Will turning around and discovering it, dispatched her also. A general destruction of property and search for money and ammunition, always succeded the murders. . . . On this I gave up all hope for the present; and on Thursday night after having supplied myself with provisions from Mr. Travis's, I scratched a hole under a pile of fence rails in a field, where I concealed myself for six weeks, never leaving my hiding place but for a few minutes in the dead of night to get water which was very near; thinking by this time I could venture out, I began to go about in the night and eaves drop the houses in the neighborhood; pursuing this course for about a fortnight and gathering little or no intelligence, afraid of speaking to any human being, and returning every morning to my cave before the dawn of day. I know not how long I might have led this life, if accident had not betrayed me, a dog in the neighborhood passing by my hiding place one night while I was out, was attracted by some meat I had in my cave, and crawled in and stole it, and was coming out just as I returned. A few nights after, two negroes having started to go hunting with the same dog, and passed that way, the dog came again to the place, and having just gone out to walk about, discovered me and barked, on which thinking myself discovered, I spoke to them to beg concealment. On making myself known they fled from me. Knowing then they would betray me, I immediately left my hiding place, and was pursued almost incessantly until I was taken a fortnight afterwards by Mr. Benjamin Phipps, in a little hole I had dug out with my sword, for the purpose of concealment, under the top of a fallen tree. On Mr. Phipps' discovering the place of my concealment, he cocked his gun and aimed at me. I requested him not to shoot and I would give up, upon which he demanded my sword. I delivered it to him, and he brought me to prison. During the time I was pursued, I had many hair breadth escapes, which your time will not permit you to relate. I am here loaded with chains, and willing to suffer the fate that awaits me.

In assessing the effects of Nat Turner's revolt Herbert Aptheker concluded that the rebellion acted as an accelerator of trends already set in motion:

When what appear to be the effects of the Nat Turner Revolt are scrutinized, the generalization that may fairly be drawn is that their tendency was to *accentuate existing trends* and thus to help bring about an open and decisive break between the Northern and Southern civilizations. It is true that such factors as soil exhaustion, rivalry in westward expansion, agrarianism versus industrialism, slave versus free labor, were all-important causes of this break, were, indeed the break itself. But it is also true that such prolonged and objective forces need some overt, subjective, spectacular event to crystallize them.[31]

[31] Herbert Aptheker, *Nat Turner's Slave Rebellion* (New York: Humanities Press, 1966), p. 57.

One result of the Turner rebellion was the virtual disappearance of abolitionist societies in the South and their contrasting appearance by the hundreds in the North.

The gathering storm in American life, which was created by the forces of incompatibility between those who could not live with the institution of slavery and those who could not live without it, continued to grow after 1840. It is not possible here to review the psychological, economic, and political factors that swept the nation toward the agony of Civil War. But we do need to note the religious dimension that was a significant cross current in the turbulence.

In 1835 William Ellery Channing, patriarch of Unitarian Christianity and pastor of the Federal Street Church in Boston, published a series of influential addresses on *Slavery*. Edwin Scott Gaustad offers the following commentary on the structure of Channing's argumentation in the *Addresses:*

> His eight chapters examine slavery from every major angle: man as property, man as a creature with sacred rights, slavery as an intrinsic evil ("An institution so founded in wrong, so imbued with injustice, cannot be made a good."), slavery as removable, and finally "a few reflections on the duties belonging to the times." [32]

In 1844 James Russell Lowell (1819–1891) interpreted the antislavery movement under biblical motifs with his poem "The Present Crisis":

> Once to every man and nation
> Comes the moment to decide
> In the strife of truth with falsehood,
> For the good or evil side;
> Some great cause, God's new Messiah,
> Offering each the bloom or blight,
> And the choice goes by forever
> 'Twixt that darkness and that light.
>
> By the light of burning martyrs
> Jesus' bleeding feet I track,
> Toiling up new Calvaries ever
> With the cross that looks not back;
> New occasions teach new duties
> Time makes ancient good uncouth;
> They must upward still and onward,
> Who could keep abreast of truth.

Eight years later Harriet Beecher Stowe, daughter of Lyman Beecher and sister to Henry Ward Beecher of New York City's famed Plymouth Church, enlisted fiction in the cause of the antislavery movement with

---

[32] Edwin Scott Gaustad (ed.), *Religious Issues in American History* (New York: Harper & Row, 1968), p. 156.

her publication of *Uncle Tom's Cabin*. Ms. Stowe was certain that God wrote the book.

The issue of slavery versus freedom divided America's major church families. The Methodist Episcopal Church, having long since modified John Wesley and Francis Asbury's disciplinary proscriptions regarding slavery, was divided on the issue and, in 1844, separated into two general conferences. On May 1, 1845, the Methodist Episcopal Church, South, came into existence in Louisville, Kentucky. In 1845 the Baptist church was divided into the Southern Convention and what was to become the "American Baptist Missionary Union." The Disciple of Christ churches were not sufficiently organized on a national level to have to confront the divisive force of abolitionism. The same was true of American Judaism, with the Reform leader Issac M. Wise assuming a basically neutral posture. The Congregationalists, Unitarians, and Universalists remained undivided because they did not have significant constituencies in the South. The Lutheran churches did not have a truly national ecclesiastical structure, and although there was general antislavery sentiment in Lutheran circles, each local and ethnic Synod adjusted to the issue on its own terms. The Protestant Episcopal Church, composed largely of communicants who were generally conservative and thus oriented toward the status quo, had a long tradition that provided that ecclesiastical jurisdictional lines should conform to national boundaries. It divided into two "national" churches. The official position of the Roman Catholic Church was that, although the slave trade was to be condemned, slavery as a principle of social organization was not intrinsically sinful.

Of the three great evangelical denominations that divided over the issue of slavery, the Presbyterian church, because of its genuinely national character as well as its serious theological orientation, was the denomination that reflected the national dilemma most graphically.

In 1830, the decade of increasing polarization between proslavery and antislavery forces, Presbyterian church leaders began to divide over "the old orthodoxy and the new metaphysics." The Presbyterian church became sharply and almost evenly separated between the "Old School" and the "New School" partisans. The Old School was composed largely of members with Scotch-Irish background. The New School members tended to have New England or English backgrounds. The issues were (1) doctrinal compromises occasioned by cooperation with the Congregationalists; (2) denominational control of missionary work; and (3) the attitude toward slavery. Antislavery agitation was found chiefly in the New School areas. In 1837, an Old-School-controlled General Assembly cut off four New School synods that comprised 533 churches and more than 100,000 members. More than three-fourths of the southern churches adhered to the Old School Assembly.

For an impressive length of time the Old School Presybterians held off schism by simply avoiding the issue of slavery. In 1845 the General

Assembly, forced to engage the issue by pressure brought from midwestern synods, proclaimed that slavery was biblical and admonished slaveholders to treat their slaves as immortal human beings. The official position adopted by the General Assembly in 1849 was that slavery was essentially a civil institution that was properly to be dealt with by legislatures rather than by churches. This seeming "staying power" led one observer to point out that the Old School Presbyterian Church and the Democratic party remained the two most important links that continued to hold the nation together.[33] The Democratic party divided first!

One of the conceptual weapons that provided for Old School cohesiveness in a time of division was the doctrine, largely developed and articulated by James Henley Thornwell (1812–1862), concerning the "spirituality of the church." Thornwell, Presbyterian clergyman and president of South Carolina College from 1851 to 1855, was perhaps the most influential leader in the southern segment of the Old School Presbyterian Church. Thornwell answered Channing's addresses against slavery, defending the institution on the basis of a Calvinistic interpretation of Providence: "In the inscrutable Providence of God, it is, no doubt, arranged that the circumstances of individuals, and the social and political institutions of communities, are, upon the whole, those which are best adapted to the degree of their moral progress."[34] Thornwell's discussion of the relation of the church to slavery employed an argument concerning the relationship of the church to society, which was anything but traditional Calvinism: "It [the church] has no commission to construct society afresh, to adjust its elements in different proportions, to rearrange the distribution of its classes, or to change the forms of its political constitutions."[35]

The Old School Presbyterian Church did not formally divide until after political secession. In May of 1861, when the General Assembly expressed its loyalty to the Union, schism was the immediate result. Southern churchmen met in Augusta, Georgia, and, acknowledging slavery to be the cause of disunion, published a declaration in an attempt to account for their action. Thornwell authored the address and read it before the assembled delegates. Here we see the South's "peculiar institution" defended by a "peculiar theory" of the "spirituality of the church." The address declared that the provinces of church and state are perfectly distinct and the one has not the right to usurp the other: "They are planets moving in different orbits, and unless each is

[33] As cited by Ernest Trice Thompson, *The Spirituality of the Church* (Richmond, Va.: John Knox Press, 1961), p. 27.

[34] J. B. Adger and J. L. Girardeau (eds.), *The Collected Writings of James Henley Thornwell, D.D., Ll.D.* (Richmond Presbyterian Committee on Publication, 1873), p. 421.

[35] Ibid., p. 383. John Calvin, the sixteenth-century Genevan reformer, had believed that the total life of a culture should be ordered after the insights of the Gospels. Calvinists were traditionally concerned with shaping a Christian civilization—the idea of "the Godly commonwealth."

confined to its own track, the consequences may be as disastrous in the moral world, as the coalition of different spheres in the world of matter." This theory, articulated by the newly formed Presbyterian Church in the Confederate States, was "born in the slavery controversies of the ante-bellum period, was strengthened by the Civil War, and confirmed in the bitter days of reconstruction."[36]

EMANCIPATION AND THE BLACK CHURCH

Out of the physical wreckage and social chaos that the Civil War left in its wake, the "freedmen" organized their churches. Here we see the integration of the "invisible institution" of the slaves into the institutional church. The A.M.E. Church ordained and commissioned those Afro-Americans who as slaves had been called to preach. The Colored Primitive Baptists were organized in 1866. Black Baptist state conventions were organized throughout the country. In 1866 the Southern Methodist Church released its Afro-American members in order that they could establish the Colored Methodist Episcopal Church, founded in 1870. The Northern Methodist Church established a separate conference for its black membership with its own presiding bishop. But the two African Methodist Episcopal Churches were to be the denominations of the majority of black Methodists. By the end of the century there were 2.7 million church members in a black population of 8.3 million.[37]

The role played by the black church in the structuring of Afro-American social life was even more significant than the phenomenon of rapid numerical growth. We have noted how organized social life among blacks had been almost totally destroyed under the institution of slavery. Emancipation did not automatically bring order and structured living for the freedman. Frazier wrote:

> Under slavery the Negro family was essentially an amorphous group gathered around the mother or some female on the plantation. The father was a visitor to the household without any legal or recognized status in family relation. . . . Whatever might be the circumstances of the Negro family life under the slave regime, family and sex relations were constantly under the supervision of the whites.[38]

From this situation the black church was able to shape a pattern of monogamous marriage and a greater degree of stability in family life.

The black church also pioneeered efforts toward economic cooperation among Afro-Americans. The all-important mutual aid societies emerged largely out of the churches. They were organized among the poor, landless free blacks, to meet the major crises of life, namely, sick-

[36] Thompson, op. cit., p. 25.
[37] See Ahlstrom, op. cit., p. 698.
[38] Frazier, op. cit., pp. 31–32.

ness and death, and were therefore known as "sickness" and burial societies. From such societies secular insurance companies had their birth.

The educational work of the southern black churches was built on the foundations laid by northern missionary educators. One of the largely unrecognized chapters in the relation between white and black Christians was the educational crusade carried on by northern white missionaries among the freedmen. The American Missionary Association, established in 1846 by several missionary societies of the Congregational churches, raised millions of dollars and recruited thousands of teachers to work among southern blacks after the Civil War. Their faith in the ability of the Afro-American to respond to educational opportunity was one of the most morally significant aspects of the abolitionist impulse in its constructive expression. Morehouse College in Georgia, Talladega College in Alabama, Tougaloo College in Mississippi, Hampton Institute in Virginia, and Fisk University in Tennessee were founded and supported by northern churches during the period of Reconstruction. In addition, by working with the Freedman's Bureau, which was authorized by Congress in 1865, these teachers and administrators "laid the foundation for a public school system for the newly emancipated Negro. Negroes trained in these schools supported by northern churches and philanthropy became the educated leaders among Negroes." [39] The authors of an authoritative history of higher education in America remind us that, prior to 1900, "practically all of the faculty members of southern Negro colleges were idealistic educational missionaries who had been educated in northern colleges." [40] This chapter of Reconstruction experience should not be forgotten amidst the conventional interpretation of the period, which usually treats Reconstruction as a tragic failure.

Schools and colleges also were established and maintained by the black denominations, but their comparatively narrow focus on religious nurture has meant that they have not often reached degrees of recognized educational excellence. Frazier observed that the attendance of black students at private colleges has reflected the general social stratification of the black community. Upper-class Afro-American youth generally have attended the schools established by the Congregational church and the better schools supported by the white Methodists and Baptists for black Americans. [41]

With the general failure of Reconstruction and the reestablishment of white supremacy the black church became the single political arena open for black Americans. It was the only one of his institutions over which the Afro-American had control. The church was the avenue for

[39] Ibid. p. 39.

[40] John S. Brubacher and Willis Rudy, *Higher Education in Transition* (New York: Harper & Row, 1958), p. 75.

[41] Frazier, op. cit., p. 41.

achievement and social status. It was, as Frazier pointed out, the black person's "refuge in a hostile white world."

Black sociologists and anthropologists are in disagreement over whether or not the black church in the last four decades of the nineteenth century constituted "a retrograde force, a brake on the dignity and political intelligence of the race,"[42] or whether it was a change-oriented institution, which Jerome Holland (1916–   ) characterized as "a protesting organization throughout its history in America."[43] One point on which there is virtual consensus is that the black church was the central institution in the life of the Afro-American. C. Eric Lincoln writes:

> His church was his school, his forum, his political arena, his social club, his art gallery, his conservatory of music. It was lyceum and gymnasium as well as *sanctum sanctorum*. His religion was his fellowship with man, his audience with God. It was the peculiar sustaining force which gave him strength to endure when endurance gave no promise, and the courage to be creative in the face of his own dehumanization.[44]

The black church was not without its protesters such as Bishop Henry M. Turner,[45] but it is difficult to understand how it could be free for greater protest when it had before it the obvious tasks of organizing a social structure for a slave people and providing relief in the face of recalcitrant American racism.

THE BLACK CHURCHES IN THE CITIES

The great migrations of Afro-Americans to the cities, most especially their movement to the northern cities, produced problems of adjustment that were almost as dramatic as the difficulties they faced in their

---

[42] David L. Lewis, *King: A Critical Biography* (New York: Praeger, 1970), p. 1.

[43] Jerome H. Holland, "The Role of the Negro Church As an Organ of Protest," *Journal of Negro Education,* Vol. 11 (April 1942), p. 165.

[44] C. Eric Lincoln, preface in Gayraud S. Wilmore, *Black Religion and Black Nationalism* (Garden City, N.Y.: Doubleday, 1972), p. vi.

[45] Turner (1834–1915) was born of free ancestry in South Carolina and joined the Methodist Church at fourteen years of age. He had acquired some education and became a chaplain in the Union Army during the Civil War. After the war he was transferred to the A.M.E. Church. He became active in Republican Party politics and was elected to the Georgia legislature. He was expelled from the legislature with the advent of white supremacy. He also was forced to resign a postmastership in Macon, Georgia, to which he had been appointed by President Grant. He supported emigration to Africa not long after the war, and as a bishop he actively promoted the cause. His plan for African colonization had little success, but his fiery attacks on American racism were both strong and unremitting. "A man who loves a country that hates him is a human dog and not a man." The Constitution was, in his words, "a dirty rag." He advised his black countrymen "to return to Africa or get ready for extermination." Lawrence D. Reddick writes, "when he felt that his last days on earth were near, he deliberately dragged himself off to Canada, in order not to die on American soil." Turner was a precursor of those twentieth-century black Americans who were to give way to despair over the possibility of Afro-American inclusion into the mainstream of American life. Cf. Ahlstrom, op. cit., pp. 711–712; Frazier, op. cit., p. 42; Lerone Bennett, Jr., *Before the Mayflower: A History of the Negro in America 1619–1964* (Baltimore: Penguin Books, 1970), p. 226.

transition from slavery to emancipation. After emancipation, black people moved into the cities of the South in far greater proportion than did the whites. The great wave of migration to the northern cities occurred during World War I, which created a demand for unskilled industrial workers. Frazier states that until the war nine tenths of the Afro-Americans were still in the South and about four fifths of those still lived in rural areas.[46] As a result of this labor market and the desire of black Americans to escape southern oppression, new "black belts" were established in the metropolitan centers of the North. Later, during World War II, Afro-Americans were attracted to the war industries in western cities. As a result of these migrations, by 1960 two thirds of Afro-Americans in the United States lived in urban environments.

The changes in the black American's mental outlook that accompanied his "urbanization" were reflected in the life of the institutional church. In an important study conducted in the mid-1930s,[47] Benjamin Mays and Joseph W. Nicholson discovered what Frazier termed the significant trend toward the "secularization" of the black churches. Frazier explained, "By secularization we mean that the Negro churches lost their predominantly other worldly outlook and began to focus attention on the Negro's condition in this world."[48] Black preachers in a number of northern cities became influential in politics. Congressman Adam Clayton Powell (1908-1972) began his career as pastor of the Abyssinian Baptist Church in New York City, where he was prominent as an activist leader of black boycotts against business that would not hire Afro-Americans.

In the northern cities churches were much larger than they had been in the South. The average membership of a black northern church was almost 800, whereas in the South black congregations were significantly smaller.[49] The very size of these large congregations tended to provide an unsatisfactory church community for many transplanted rural blacks who desired a more intimate congregational life, similar to what they had known before migration. This need was met by the "storefront churches" in all American cities, both North and South. In their survey Mays and Nicholson found that, out of 2,104 church buildings in twelve cities, 777 were "storefront chruches" or "house churches."[50] These "churches" are usually located in abandoned stores or homes in deteriorating neighborhoods. Often they are gathered by "jack-leg" preachers, that is, preachers who are uneducated and without the clerical authority conveyed by ordination.

In *Go Tell It on the Mountain* the black novelist James Baldwin described a Sunday morning service in a Harlem storefront church. Bald-

---

[46] Frazier, op. cit., p. 47.

[47] Benjamin Elijah Mays and Joseph W. Nicholson, *The Negro's Church* (New York: Institute of Social and Religious Research, 1933).

[48] Frazier, op. cit., p. 51.

[49] Mays and Nicholson, op. cit., p. 107.

[50] Ibid., p. 313.

win had been raised to attend such a church, and his novel is, to a degree, autobiographical. Note how the novelist's narrative bears a striking correspondence to Frazier's sociological characterization of the elements of storefront church religion:

> The sermon by the pastor is of a type to appeal to traditional ideas concerning hell and heaven and the imagery which the Negro has acquired from the Bible. Much emphasis is placed upon sins of the flesh, especially sexual sins. The preacher leads the singing of the Spirituals and other hymns with which the Negroes of a folk background are acquainted. The singing is accompanied by "shouting" or holy dancing which permits the maximum of free religious expression on the part of the participants.[51]

Document 54

Description of Storefront Worship by James Baldwin

On Sunday mornings and Sunday nights the church was always full; on special Sundays it was full all day. The Grimes family arrived in a body, always a little late, usually in the middle of Sunday school, which began at nine o'clock. This lateness was always their mother's fault—at least in the eyes of their father; she could not seem to get herself and the children ready on time, ever, and sometimes she acutally remained behind, not to appear until the morning service. When they all arrived together, they separated upon entering the doors, father and mother going to sit in the Adult Class, which was taught by Sister McCandless, Sarah going to the Infant's Class, John and Roy sitting in the Intermediate, which was taught by Brother Elisha.

When he was young, John had paid no attention in Sunday school, and always forgot the golden text, which earned him the wrath of his father. Around the time of his fourteenth birthday, with all the pressures of church and home uniting to drive him to the altar, he strove to appear more serious and therefore less conspicuous. But he was distracted by his new teacher, Elisha, who was the pastor's nephew and who had but lately arrived from Georgia. He was not much older than John, only seventeen, and he was already saved and was a preacher. John stared at Elisha all during the lesson, admiring the timbre of Elisha's voice, much deeper and manlier than his own, admiring the leanness, and grace, and strength, and darkness of Elisha in his Sunday suit, wondering if he would ever be holy as Elisha was holy. But he did not follow the lesson, and when, sometimes, Elisha paused to ask John a question, John was ashamed and confused, feeling the palms of his hands become wet and his heart pound like a hammer. Elisha would smile and reprimand him gently, and the lesson would go on.

Roy never knew his Sunday school lesson either, but it was different with Roy— no one really expected of Roy what was expected of John. Everyone was always

SOURCE: Excerpted from the book _Go Tell It on the Mountain_ by James Baldwin. Copyright © 1952, 1953 by James Baldwin. Reprinted with permission of The Dial Press.

[51] Frazier, op. cit., p. 54.

praying that the Lord would change Roy's heart, but it was John who was expected to be good, to be a good example.

When Sunday school service ended there was a short pause before morning service began. In this pause, if it was good weather, the old folks might step outside a moment to talk among themselves. The sisters would almost always be dressed in white from crown to toe. The small children, on this day, in this place, and oppressed by their elders, tried hard to play without seeming to be disrespectful of God's house. But sometimes, nervous or perverse, they shouted, or threw hymnbooks, or began to cry, putting their parents, men or women of God, under the necessity of proving—by harsh means or tender—who, in a sanctified household, ruled. The older children, like John or Roy, might wander down the avenue, but not too far. Their father never let John and Roy out of his sight, for Roy had often disappeared between Sunday school and morning service and had not come back all day.

The Sunday morning service began when Brother Elisha sat down at the piano and raised a song. This moment and this music had been with John, so it seemed, since he had first drawn a breath. It seemed that there had never been a time when he had not known this moment of waiting while the packed church paused—the sisters in white, heads raised, the brothers in blue, heads back; the white caps of the women seeming to glow in the charged air like crowns, the kinky, gleaming heads of the men seeming to be lifted up—and the rustling and the whispering ceased and the children were quiet; perhaps someone coughed, or the sound of a car horn, or a curse from the streets came in; then Elisha hit the keys, beginning at once to sing, and everybody joined him, clapping their hands, and rising, and beating the tambourines.

The song might be: *Down at the cross where my Saviour died!*
Or: *Jesus, I'll never forget how you set me free!*
Or: *Lord, hold my hand while I run this race!*

They sang with all the strength that was in them, and clapped their hands for joy. There had never been a time when John had not sat watching the saints rejoice with terror in his heart, and wonder. Their singing caused him to believe in the presence of the Lord; indeed, it was no longer a question of belief, because they made that presence real. He did not feel it himself, the joy they felt, yet he could not doubt that it was, for them, the very bread of life—could not doubt it, that is, until it was too late to doubt. Something happened to their faces and their voices, the rhythm of their bodies, and to the air they breathed; it was as though wherever they might be became the upper room, and the Holy Ghost were riding on the air. His father's face, always awful, became more awful now; his father's daily anger was transformed into prophetic wrath. His mother, her eyes raised to heaven, hands arched before her, moving, made real for John that patience, that endurance, that long suffering, which he had read of in the Bible and found so hard to imagine.

On Sunday mornings the women all seemed patient, all the men seemed mighty. While John watched, the Power struck someone, a man or woman; they cried out, a long, wordless crying, and, arms outstretched like wings, they began the Shout. Someone moved a chair a little to give them room, the rhythm paused, the singing stopped, only the pounding feet and the clapping hands were heard; then another cry, another dancer; then the tambourines began again, and the voices rose again, and the music swept on again, like fire, or flood, or judgment. Then the church seemed to swell with the Power it held, and, like a planet rocking in space, the temple rocked with the Power of God. John watched, watched the faces, and the weightless bodies, and listened to the timeless cries. One day, so everyone said, this Power would possess him; he would sing and cry as they did now, and dance before his King. He watched young Ella Mae Washington, the seventeen-year-old granddaughter of Praying Mother Washington, as she began to dance. And then Elisha danced.

At one moment, head thrown back, eyes closed, sweat standing on his brow, he sat at the piano, singing and playing; and then, like a great black cat in trouble in the jungle, he stiffened and trembled, and cried out. *Jesus Jesus, oh Lord Jesus!* He struck on the piano one last, wild note, and threw up his hands, palms upward, stretched wide apart. The tambourines raced to fill the vacuum left by his silent piano, and his cry drew answering cries. Then he was on his feet, turning, blind, his face congested, contorted with this rage, and the muscles, leaping and swelling in his long, dark neck. It seemed that he could not breathe, that his body could not contain this passion, that he would be, before their eyes, dispersed into the waiting air. His hands, rigid to the very fingertips, moved outward and back against his hips, his sightless eyes looked upward, and he began to dance. Then his hands closed into fists, and his head snapped downward, his sweat loosening the grease that slicked down his hair; and the rhythm of all the others quickened to match Elisha's rhythm; his thighs moved terribly against the cloth of his suit, his heels beat on the floor, and his fists moved beside his body as though he were beating his own drum. And so, for a while, in the center of the dancers, head down, fists beating, on, on, unbearably, until it seemed the walls of the church would fall for very sound; and then, in a moment, with a cry, head up, arms high in the air, sweat pouring from his forehead, and all his body dancing as though it would never stop. Sometimes he did not stop until he fell—until he dropped like some animal felled by a hammer—moaning, on his face. And then a great moaning filled the church.

There was sin among them. One Sunday, when regular service was over, Father James had uncovered sin in the congregation of the righteous. He had uncovered Elisha and Ella Mae. They had been "walking disorderly"; they were in danger of straying from the truth. And as Father James spoke of the sin that he knew they had not committed yet, of the unripe fig plucked too early from the tree—to set the children's teeth on edge—John felt himself grow dizzy in his seat and could not look at Elisha where he stood, beside Ella Mae, before the altar. Elisha hung his head as Father James spoke, and the congregation murmured. And Ella Mae was not so beautiful now as she was when she was singing and testifying, but looked like a sullen, ordinary girl. Her hips were loose and her eyes were black—with shame, or rage, or both. Her grandmother, who had raised her, sat watching quietly, with folded hands. She was one of the pillars of the church, a powerful evangelist and very widely known. She said nothing in Ella Mae's defense, for she must have felt, as the congregation felt, that Father James was only exercising his clear and painful duty; he was responsible, after all, for Elisha, as Praying Mother Washington was responsible for Ella Mae. It was not an easy thing, said Father James, to be the pas-

tor of a flock. It might look easy to just sit up there in the pulpit night after night,
year in, year out, but let them remember the awful responsibility placed on his
shoulders by almighty God—let them remember that the Word was hard, that the
way of holiness was a hard way. There was no room in God's army for the coward
heart, no crown awaiting him who put mother, or father, sister, or brother, sweet-
heart, or friend above God's will. Let the church cry amen to this! And they cried:
"Amen! Amen!"

The Lord had led him, said Father James, looking down on the boy and girl before him, to give them a public warning before it was too late. For he knew them to
be sincere young people, dedicated to the service of the Lord—it was only that,
since they were young, they did not know the pitfalls Satan laid for the unwary. He
knew that sin was not in their minds—not yet; yet sin was in the flesh; and should
they continue with their walking out alone together, their secrets and laughter, and
touching of hands, they would surely sin a sin beyond all forgiveness. And John
wondered what Elisha was thinking—Elisha, who was tall and handsome, who
played basketball, and who had been saved at the age of eleven in the improbable
fields down south. *Had* he sinned? Had he been tempted? And the girl beside him,
whose white robes now seemed the merest, thinnest covering for the nakedness of
breasts and insistent thighs—what was her face like when she was alone with Elisha,
with no singing, when they were not surrounded by the saints? He was afraid to
think it, yet he could think of nothing else; and the fever of which they stood
accused began also to rage in him.

After this Sunday Elisha and Ella Mae no longer met each other each day after
school, no longer spent Saturday afternoons wandering through Central Park, or
lying on the beach. All that was over for them. If they came together again it would
be in wedlock. They would have children and raise them in the church.

This was what was meant by a holy life, this was what the way of the cross demanded. It was somehow on that Sunday, a Sunday shortly before his birthday,
that John first realized that this was the life awaiting him—realized it consciously,
as something no longer far off, but iminent coming closer day by day.

Any discussion of the Afro-American church in the city should take
note of one black ecclesiastical phenomenon that arose out of the "Garvey movement." Marcus Manasseh Garvey was an immigrant from the
British West Indies who succeeded, at the peak of his influence in 1921,
in organizing the largest black movement up to that time in American history. Coming to the United States in 1916, he had within a year organized
the Universal Negro Improvement Association in New York. Garvey
preached black economic independence. In line with his economic program, Garvery founded in 1919 the Black Star Line, a shipping company venture that ultimately led to his prosecution and conviction for
mail fraud. Garvey emphasized a pride in blackness: "Up, you mighty
race, you can accomplish what you will!" He also expounded a "back

to Africa" nationalism in which he promised the Afro-American that his glorious African past augured a brillant future there:

> So Negroes, I say, through the Universal Negro Improvement Association, that there is much to live for. I have a vision of the future, and I see before me a picture of a redeemed Africa, with her dotted cities, with her beautiful civilization, with her millions of happy children, going to and fro.[52]

Garvey's organization had as many as 2 million "active dues-paying members" and 4 million sympathizers scattered throughout the world, though most of the membership was in the Western Hemisphere.

The African Orthodox Church was founded in New York City on September 2, 1921, by the Rev. Dr. George Alexander McGuire (1866–1934), a native of Antigua, a sometime Anglican priest, and one of the leading Negro clergymen of the Protestant Episcopal Church in his day. Previously rector of several prominent Negro Episcopal parishes, McGuire also had served as Archdeacon for Colored Work in the Diocese of Arkansas and from 1911–1913 was Field Secretary of the American Institute for Negroes.

Although it has always welcomed white participation, the purpose of the new denomination was "to cast off forever the yoke of white Ecclesiastical dominance" and to express "the spirit of racial leadership . . . in harmony with the aroused racial consciousness of the Negro people." Constituted primarily by West Indians of Anglican background, the church was, and continues to be, deeply committed to formal liturgy, a hierarchial priesthood, and the validity of its episcopal orders.

McGuire received consecration at the hands of Joseph Rene Villate, Exarch and Metropolitan of the American Catholic Church in the U.S.A. Villate's own consecration is generally considered valid, though irregular, and the African Orthodox Church thus claims apostolic succession from one of the ancient sees in Christendom.

McGuire served as Chaplain General to Marcus Garvey's Universal Negro Improvement Association and was one of the Garvey's most able and trusted lieutenants. As a religious spokesman for Garvey's black nationalism, McGuire urged Negroes to "erase the white gods from your hearts. We must go back to our own native church to our own God." It

---

[52] As quoted by Ducas and Van Doren (eds.), op. cit. p. 212. See also Edmund David Cronon, *Black Moses: The Story of Marcus Garvey and the Universal Negro Improvement Association* (Madison: University of Wisconsin Press, 1955); Elton C. Fax, *Garvey: The Story of a Pioneer Black Nationalist* (New York: Dodd, Mead, 1972); and Theodore G. Vincent, *Black Power and the Garvey Movement* (Berkeley, Calif.: Ramparts Press, 1971). Randall K. Burkett, *Garveyism as a Religious Movement: The Institutionalization of a Black Civil Religion* (Metuchen, N.J.: Scarecrow Press, 1978). Richard Newman, "The Origins of the African Orthodox Church," *The Negro Churchman* (Millwood, N.Y.: Kraus Reprint Co., 1977). Randall K. Burkett, *Black Redemption: Churchmen Speak for the Garvey Movement* (Philadelphia: Temple University Press, 1978).

is the height of self-negation, McGuire asserted, for Negroes to worship a Caucasian deity. Black people should eliminate pictures of a white Christ and white Madonna from their homes: "Then let us start our Negro painters getting busy and supply a black Madonna and a black Christ for the training of our children." These admonitions were never institutionalized within the African Orthodox Church.[53]

BLACK CULTS IN THE CITIES

A new development in the religious life of the Afro-American was the development of black religious cults. A cult is distinguished from both the institutional church and the storefront church in that it constitutes a new religion; new in the sense of an imported religion or in the sense of a mutation from an existing religion. Further, the cult also changes the communicants' conception of themselves. Finally, the cult is built around the leadership of a charismatic figure who is the discoverer and founder of the group and whose authority comes directly from God.[54]

The "Holiness" cults seek to restore a purer state of Christianity through the sanctification of their members. Their worship is characterized by ecstatic frenzy, and they insist that their members abstain from "carnal-minded" activities—the use of tobacco, alcoholic beverages, swearing, dancing, card playing, and adultery. A Holiness church in Philadelphia was founded by a woman, Bishop Ida Robinson.[55] Perhaps the best-known Holiness cult was the Father Divine Peace Mission movement.[56] Still another flamboyant and effective cult leader was Bishop Charles Manuel Grace (1882–1960), popularly known as "Sweet Daddy" Grace. Charles Grace organized a group known as the United House of Prayer for All People with churches in cities along the eastern seaboard. The *Amsterdam News* as late as 1956 carried the following story under the caption "Daddy Grace to Use Fire Hose on 300":

> Some 4,000 followers of Bishop C. M. Grace this week converged on 125th Street and Eighth Avenue for the 30th Annual Convocation of the House of Prayer. The convocation will end Sunday with the Bishop, who is better known as Daddy Grace, presiding over a fire-house baptismal followed by a parade.

[53] Richard Newman, "Marcus Garvey and the African Orthodox Church: Religious Nationalism in Africa and the United States," unpublished paper read at The Amercan Academy of Religion, New England Region, Brown University, April 2, 1970.
  Interestingly, and ironically, the African Orthodox Church's most important impact has been in Africa through the ministry of Daniel William Alexander, Archbishop and Primate of the church's African Province. Alexander ordained the Uganda nationalist Rueben Spartas whose African Orthodox Church was received under the jurisdiction of the Greek Orthodox Patriarchate of Alexandria. In Kenya Alexander ordained leaders of the independent churches and schools that broke away from the Scottish missions following the controversy over female circumcision in 1929. These leaders and their independent organizations formed the base for the Mau Mau movement, and, ultimately, Kenyan freedom.
[54] See Arthur Huff Fauset, *Black Gods of the Metropolis: Negro Cults of the Urban North* (Philadelphia: University of Pennsylvania Press, 1944).
[55] Ibid., chap. II.
[56] See Robert A. Parker, *The Incredible Messiah* (Boston: Little, Brown, 1937); and also Fauset, op. cit., chap. VI.

Starting at 11:00 A.M. Sunday, the mass baptism, at which an estimated 300 persons will officially become followers of Daddy Grace, will be held at 20 West 115th Street. Elder Price said a fire hose was being used at the baptism as "a matter of convenience. In the South," he said, "we have pools to baptize people in. We don't have them here. So, the fire hose is used."[57]

Two other cults are different from the above mentioned groups because they are in discontinuity with the main-line religious tradition of the Afro-American. One of these is the Church of God, or black Jews.[58] This cult was founded by F. S. Cherry. The sacred scripture of the group is the Jewish Talmud. The members of the cult look upon themselves as black Jews, "true" Jews (the "white" Jews) being depicted as frauds. The cult teaches that black persons were the original inhabitants of the earth and that, in the final restoration of all things, black Jews will occupy important places. In this cult God has become black and, through such exercises as the learning of Hebrew, Afro-American identity is transformed.

The second cult is the Moorish Science Temple of America, founded by Timothy Drew (1886–1929), who was born in North Carolina.[59] The scriptural authority in the "Holy Koran of the Moorish Temple of Science" is not to be confused with the Orthodox Mohammedan Koran. Timothy Drew, whose name was changed to Noble Drew Ali, taught that Afro-Americans should not be called Negroes, colored, or black, but rather "Moorish-Americans." Rather than urge actual emigration to Africa, Drew Ali emphasized a "psychological" emigration, stressing that it was enough to identify with an Islamic African nation and to adopt its religion. Drew Ali died under mysterious circumstances in Chicago in 1929.[60]

The Moorish Science Temple disintegrated into several factions, one of which was the Nation of Islam, better known as the Black Muslims. The Nation of Islam was founded by Wallace D. or W. D. Fard in Detroit in 1930. The mysterious Fard told his converts that he had come from the Moslem Holy City of Mecca to bring liberation to his black brethren in North America, who, according to Fard, belonged to the same race as his own.[61] Many of his initial followers had been members of the the Garvey Movement and/or disciples of the Noble Drew Ali. Fard wrote two manuals for the Black Muslim movement: *The Secret Ritual of the Nation of Islam* and *Teaching for the Lost Found Nation of Islam in a Mathematical Way*. He described himself as one who had

---

[57] *Amsterdam News* (July 28, 1956), as quoted by Allan Schoener, *Harlem on My Mind: Cultural Capitol of Black America, 1900–1968* (New York: Random House, 1968), p. 211. See also Fauset, op. cit., p. 26.

[58] See Howard Brotz, *The Black Jews of Harlem: Negro Nationalism and the Dilemmas of Negro Leadership* (New York 1964). See also Fauset, op. cit., chap. IV.

[59] See Fauset, op. cit., chap. V.

[60] Theodore Draper, *The Rediscovery of Black Nationalism* (New York 1969), p. 71.

[61] See C. Eric Lincoln, *The Black Muslims in America* (Boston Beacon Press, 1961; rev. ed. 1973), pp. 10–14.

been sent to wake his "uncle"—that is, the lost black nation in North America—and to inform him of his true identity and of his temporary captivity among "the blue-eyed devils." Within three years Fard had developed an effective organization that included the temple, a University of Islam, a Muslim Girls Training Class, and a military organization called "Fruit of Islam." Elijah Poole, whose family had migrated from Georgia in the 1920s, became identified with the Nation of Islam. Because of his single-minded devotion to the movement, Poole, who had been renamed Elijah Muhammed, was elevated by Fard to be a chief Minister of Islam. On the occasion of Fard's mysterious disappearance in June 1934, Mr. Muhammed assumed the leadership of the Nation of Islam.

Mr. Muhammed moved his headquarters from Detroit to Chicago. There he reshaped the movement into a militant and efficient organization. Fard became identified with the deity Allah and was honored as such in Moslem cultic activities. Mr. Muhammed, who had been the close servant of Allah, then assumed the title "Prophet." He came to be referred to as the Prophet and as the Messenger of Allah. Eric Lincoln wrote, in 1961, of the strength and cohesiveness of the Muslim movement at that time:

> The Black Muslims are an intensely dedicated, tightly disciplined block of more than 100,000 American Negroes, convinced that they have learned the utlimate truth and ready to make any sacrifice it may demand of them. Theirs is not a "Sunday religion": the Muslim temples hold frequent meetings, and every Muslim is required to attend two (and often more) meetings a week. Nor is it a religion which spares the billfold. The mass of Muslims are from the Negro lower class, with relatively low incomes, and they are encouraged to live respectably and provide for their families. But the men are urged to hold steady jobs; and all Muslims are forbidden to gamble, smoke, drink liquor, overeat, indulge in fripperies or buy on credit. As a result most Muslims enjoy a healthy standard of living and still have enough cash left over to swell the movement's coffers.[62]

Throughout the 1940s and 1950s the Nation of Islam slowly grew among the black lower classes and prison inmates. When the movement became visible in the late 1950s, largely through the effectiveness of Malcolm X's ministry, its message espousing complete separation of the races was in vivid contrast to the integrationist approach that characterized the civil rights movement. Tirades against "blue-eyed white devils" characterized the movement's rhetoric.

One of the most interesting developments in the 1970s was the movement from sectarian to main-line religious status by the Black Muslims. After his death in 1975 Elijah Muhammed was succeeded by his son Wallace D. Muhammed. The movement, now called the World Community of Islam in the West, has disbanded its paramilitary organization—The Fruit of Islam—and bases its faith and practice on the

---

[62] Lincoln, op. cit., p. 17.

themes of brotherhood, interfaith cooperation, and efforts to build a peaceful society. The effort of Imam Wallace (the new leader's more modest title) is to bring the movement into doctrinal and liturgical conformity with orthodox Islam. Wallace has said: "There is no superiority in any color. The only superiority is in obedience to God."

The Contemporary Situation

"TWO SOCIETIES—ONE BLACK, ONE WHITE"

Only July 28, 1967, after four summers of racial unrest and disorder, President Lyndon Johnson established the National Advisory Commission on Civil Disorders. The president asked the group to deal with three basic questions concerning the outbreak of urban violence: (1) What happened? (2) Why did it happen? (3) What can be done to prevent it happening again? The composition of the Commission was criticized for its moderate character.[63] Only two members of the panel were black and there were no radicals—white or black. The Commission's published findings, commonly referred to as the Kerner Report, were all the more arresting because they came from establishment moderates. Its basic finding was that white racism was the root cause of racial disorders: ". . . [W]hite society is deeply implicated in the ghetto. White institutions created it, white institutions maintain it, and white society condones it."[64] The Commission concluded, "Our Nation is moving toward two societies, one black, one white—separate and unequal." It recommended massive programs in employment, education, the welfare system and housing.

Ten years later the Kerner Report's prophecy was in some ways fulfilled. The Vietnam war, a national policy of benign neglect, and a waning of interest in racial justice took their toll. The drift toward separate and unequal societies has continued. There is yet another duality in the black economy itself expressed by a slowly growing black middle class and an increasingly jobless lower class.

Jimmy Carter won the presidency in 1976 on the basis of the support of Southern blacks who were empowered to vote by the Civil Rights Act of 1965.[65] Carter could not have been elected in 1976 had there not been a Selma to Montgomery march in 1965. Many black

---

[63] The Commission was composed of Otto Kerner, Governor of Illinois; John Lindsay, Mayor of New York City; Fred R. Harris, Senator, Oklahoma; I. W. Abel, President, United Steelworkers of America; Edward Brooke, Senator, Massachusetts; Charles B. Thornton, Chairman of the Board, Litton Industries; James C. Corman, U.S. Representative, California; Roy Wilkins, Executive Director, NAACP; William M. McCulloch, U.S. Representative from Ohio; Katherine Graham Reden, Commissioner of Commerce, State of Kentucky; Herbert Jenkins, Chief of Police, Atlanta, Ga.

[64] The Report of The National Advisory Commission on Civil Disorders (U.S. Government Printing Office: 1968), p. 1.

[65] The New York Times, Nov. 6, 1976.

leaders, nonetheless, felt they had little political leverage in 1978. The reality of white racism, black unemployment, poor schools, inadequate housing and health care, and discrimination in employment, housing, and educational opportunities, were still a part of the Afro-American experience in 1978. Charles S. Spivey, Jr., a minister in the AME Church, described the black situation as an issue of survival.

Document 55

"A Matter of Survival" by Charles S. Spivey, Jr.

The future for black people in the United States centers on the question of survival. Their future is certain to include more of the struggle, organized pressure, tension, resistance and violence that have marked the past. Any new gains must be won in the context of the mounting global crises of population, energy, food and environmental pollution. The national climate will be marked by scarcity, uncertainty and fear. Organized efforts of blacks to increase their share of the benefits of life in this affluent nation will occur in an atmosphere increasingly hostile to any redistribution of a diminshing supply of advantages. Violence over school integration in some cities has exposed this nation's virulent and endemic racism, which cannot be ignored. Good people, seeing their life style and future eroded by forces outside the power of their national ability to control, may all too easily reinstate models for the management of "disturbing minorities," such as the treatment accorded native and Japanese Americans, the Jews in Nazi Germany or blacks in southern Africa.

Survival will compel a broad range of responses, national and local, including an organized and sustained drive to gain control and direction of institutions and resources serving black communities (schools, health and welfare agencies, community funds, police and political organizations). Their redirection for more effective service to black communities must accompany other tactics.

For example, financial resources of the black communities must be organized and channeled through a Black United Fund or other body to furnish solid, long-term support for black agencies and organizations committed to stiffened black resistance to exclusion, domination and deprivation.

Black churches have a key role in transforming the current mood of despair. Their proclamation of a robust, liberating gospel will nourish, sustain and mobilize black soul and spirit for the struggle. They must challenge individuals and groups to view and use their success in the "system" as points of leverage for wresting relief for the excluded and ignored masses. Their rejection of counsels of accommodation will find a broad base of suport among the masses, but their challenge to prevailing American faith and practice will meet with rejection, resistance and repression.

White churches face a task for which few have much stomach. The conversion of a church and community too often committed to the maintenance of an acquisitive, exploitive society will not be easy. A nation bent on the continued wasteful, dispro-

SOURCE: Charles S. Spivey, Jr., "Prescription for Change: Improving the Future for Black Americans," A symposium in *The Christian Century,* Vol. XCV, No. 2, January 18, 1978.

portionate use of the world's resources will give short shrift to this kind of subversive activity. Who can tell how far white churches will go to identify with black communities and protect them from the violent reaction of whites determined to retain all and yield nothing to those demanding equity and justice? Courageous, daring and determined white leadership may appear in sufficient time and force to stay the heavy hand of repression. The price will no doubt be high.

Whites and blacks have conflicting expectations from government. The increased concentration of power in the national government to exercise strict control and management of national resources and a shaky economy will increase the possibility of a more tightly controlled society with the consequent erosion of the human rights of all. The end result poses danger for all people, black and white. Those who support this lot rather than the more wholesome choice of a society that is open to all people can be expected to use every resource to maintain their brand of domestic tranquility. Blacks and others who dissent may have little success in changing this course.

The stresses and strains of an uncertain future will force drastic changes in the American way of life. For blacks already suffering from exclusion and deprivation, there is neither confidence nor certainty that their lot will improve. Risk and danger are certain. For them, the future demands total commitment of heart, soul, mind and strength to the struggle for liberation in the steadfast confidence that God wills their deliverance, joins them in their struggle and will bless their sacrifice with victory.

THE DILEMMA REVISITED

It is interesting that the author of *An American Dilemma,* the first analytical interpretation of racial injustice in America, has expressed a more hopeful prospect for Afro-American progress. The Swedish economist Gunnar Myrdal wrote that, if we take the broad view, the life and work of Afro-Americans have improved much in the past thirty-five years. It is fitting to conclude our chapter with Myrdal's reflection on the enduring dilemma thirty-five years after the original study was published.

Document 56

'The Dilemma Revisited" by Gunnar Myrdal

Now after more than 30 years I have returned to the problems of race relations in America with *An American Dilemma Revisited: The Racial Crisis in the United States in Perspective.* I have taken the findings in the old book as a firm baseline for the study of the dynamics in more recent decades. I decided to use again the ideals of the American creed as the instrumental value premises. In what meanwhile has happened to race relations in America, I find no reason to surrender my contention that a gradually ever fuller realization of the ideals contained in that national ethos

SOURCE: Gunnar Myrdal, "A Worried America" *The Christian Century,* Vol. XCIV, No. 41, Dec. 14, 1977.

is more than a selected viewpoint when observing and analyzing the facts; it is and will remain the historical trend of change in this country—in a sense the destiny of America, if America is not going to give up its essential national personality.

Certainly, if we take the broad view, the conditions of life and work for black people have improved much during the past 35 years. There have been setbacks, and the advance has been uneven—more pronounced for the professional middle class than for the working class. There has been less advance for the poor masses in the growing urban ghettos and for many blacks still working in southern agriculture. Again in the broad view, their facilities for health and education have been improving. Jim Crow in the south, which at the time of *An American Dilemma* was still a firmly functioning institutional system, has crumpled and disappeared. Legislation and, though less perfectly, its implementation have increasingly awarded blacks their full civil rights. At the same time, public opinion polls demonstrate a continuous improvement in the dominant white population groups' ideas about black people and how they should be treated. In some respects the south is advancing more rapidly than the north.

What has been happening can from one point of view be described as a change in the fundamental purpose of the liberalization process. What was a fight for civil rights has broadened into strivings for equal human rights. The reforms have come to concern all disadvantaged groups, including women. At the same time, blacks have increasingly become actors on the scene who have to consider strategy and tactics. The problem of race relations is no longer merely a "white man's problem," as I could realistically characterize it 35 years ago. Blacks, like whites, are now facing the dilemma, and their own actions have considerable influence on the development of race relations.

The broad view I have hinted at is important. Nonetheless, there is a long way to go before blacks are commonly afforded equal opportunities in the pursuit of happiness. There is still much segregation and discrimination, and even if poverty-stricken blacks are only one-third at most of all the poor in America, poor people are a much larger proportion of the black population than of the white.

The national agenda for the 1980s apparently will not include a priority item for racial justice. The administration of Ronald Reagan, as it moves away from domestic programs aimed at distributive justice, is signaling a change in national priorities as basic as the Great Society programs of President Johnson in the mid-1960s. Whether this direction is of short- or long-term duration remains to be seen. One certainty is that the solution to the "American dilemma" has proved to be elusive and the optimism of the mid-1950s and 1960s has turned to frustration by the 1980s. The depth and scope of the dilemma were underestimated.

Summary

The linkage between past emphasis and contemporary black consciousness is easy to locate at such themes as the rediscovery of African origins, black pride, and black economic development. The black and white communities are now in a period when the hope of reconciliation has dimmed and the goal of integration has faded.

Still the gains of the civil rights movement from 1954 to 1965 were substantial and have had a permanent effect on the political and economic structures that have determined the relations between white and Afro-Americans. This movement, which had its roots in a sporadic history of individual and group protests against slavery and discrimination, ignited fires of protest activity, that expanded the scope of the liberating process to include not only blacks, but also browns, Indians, women, students, rural poor whites, and urban welfare recipients. This movement obviously had a significantly religious dimension to it. In a similar way the recent emphasis on black ethnic consciousness probably contributed to the current renaissance of interest in, and celebration of, ethnicity among whites.[66]

As far as institutional patterns are concerned Richard Niebuhr summarized the cycle of schism succinctly five decades ago:

The series of steps from fellowship to schism includes complete fellowship of white and Negro Christians in the local church, segregation within the local church, segregation into distinctly racial local churches with denomination fellowship, segregation into racially distinct dioceses or conferences with fellowship in the highest judicatories of the denomination, and, finally, separation of the races into distinct denominations.[67]

The white churches and synagogues have projected alternating patterns of concern and indifference, pious platitudes and impressive service, paternalism and cooperative recognition in their relation to black churches. Religious groups remain the most consistently racially segregated institutions in our society.

There is accuracy in the perspective of those scholars who have criticized the Afro-American churches for being escapist and otherwordly, as well as in the opinion of those who have interpreted the churches' role as innovative and change-oriented. The black church emerged as an institution to protect black people from the effects of oppression and to provide them with a vehicle for community. Hence the black church was, and is, both preserving and protesting, accommodative and assertive, pastoral and prophetic.

The inescapable conclusion is that, whether in estrangement or in cooperation, exploitation or justice, oppression or equality, in American religion and culture the reality will be black *and* white because this was the composition from the beginning.

[66]See Michael Novak, *The Rise of the Unmeltable Ethnics* (New York: Macmillan, 1973).
[67]Niebuhr, op. cit., p. 253.

Ecumenism and Interfaith Cooperation

8

From the vantage point of the 1980s, one of the striking character-istics of American religious life in the year 1960 was the almost eu-phoric enthusiasm for the ecumenical movement among Christians and for the increasing cooperation between Christians and Jews. To be sure, the general movement toward religious unity and cooperation had been gaining in momentum and cohesiveness for several decades. In 1928 the National Conference of Christians and Jews had been established to promote interfaith education. In 1948 the World Council of Churches, a council including 212 Protestant and Orthodox churches, came into being. In 1950 the National Council of Churches of Christ in America was organized. But in 1960, and throughout the decade that followed, there was something of a peak in ecumenical and cooperative activity. But first, a definition or "location" of some key terms and basic concepts.

The word *ecumenical* is derived from the Greek word *oikoumene,* which originally meant "the inhabited earth or world." A secondary meaning was the "world" in the sense of its inhabitants, that is, human-kind. At times the word was commonly used to denote the Roman Em-pire. An extraordinary use of the word seems to have meant the *whole* inhabited world.[1] The modern and general use of the term dates from the 1920s, when the Stockholm and Lausanne conferences brought representatives of many churches together. The term *ecumenism* prop-erly applies to the movement toward unity among various Christian bodies. W. A. Visser't Hooft, the first general secretary of the World Council of Churches, writes of the two meanings of ecumenism: "first, the study of the faith, order, life and work of the churches as they are in their relations with each other; second, the study of the nature of the unity and universality of the Church and of the ways and means through which the churches may arrive at a fuller manifestation of that unity and universality."[2]

The term *interfaith* refers to relations between different religious faiths, in America most commonly denoting relations between Chris-tians and Jews. Both *ecumenism* and *interfaith* imply activities of coop-eration and conversation, but the term *ecumenism* further implies the idea of "reunion" among the separated branches of Christianity.

---

[1] William F. Arndt and F. Wilbur Gingrich, *A Greek-English Lexicon of the New Testament and Other Early Christian Writings* (Chicago: University of Chicago Press, 1957), pp. 563–564.
[2] W. A. Visser't Hooft, "Ecumenism," *Handbook of Christian Theology* (Cleveland: World Publishing, 1958), p. 91.

The Decade of Ecumenism

As noted, there occurred in 1960 an extraordinary convergence of events that brought ecumenical endeavors to a peak. Of great importance was the surprising and revolutionary pontificate of Pope John XXIII, which began in 1958. He convened the Second Vatican Council (1962–1965) of the Roman Catholic Church in 1959. In 1960 a Presbyterian theologian, Robert McAfee Brown, and a Jesuit scholar, Gustave Weigel, published a book entitled *An American Dialogue: A Protestant Looks at Catholicism and a Catholic Looks at Protestantism*. The book was undertaken through the initiative of Will Herberg, a Jewish scholar. The spirit of the time is exemplified in this excerpt from the message of the National Council of Churches of Christ to its member churches, issued on December 8, 1960:

> We rejoice in the churches' growing habit of planning their programs in conference with one another. We are thankful that some of these ministries are now carried forward unitedly. We are grateful for the steady advance of understanding and mutual trust among us. We look forward to the time when each member denomination, recognizing the authenticity of Christian discipleship in all the others, will entrust to any of them the care of human souls and responsibility for advancing Christ's mission in the world. And we call upon all churches to continue to pray and labor for the full unity, visible and invisible, of the people of God.[3]

THE CONSULTATION ON CHURCH UNITY

One of the most dramatic proposals on the part of ecumenical leaders was made by the Rev. Dr. Eugene Carson Blake on Sunday, December 4, 1960. At the time Dr. Blake was the stated clerk (the denomination's chief executive officer) of the United Presbyterian Church in the United States and was later to succeed Visser't Hooft as general secretary of the World Council of Churches. At the invitation of James A. Pike, California's colorful Episcopal bishop, Blake climbed into the big pulpit of Grace Cathedral in San Francisco and proposed a merger of his denomination, the Methodist Church, the Protestant Episcopal Church and the United Church of Christ. Immediately after the sermon was delivered, Bishop Pike endorsed the Blake proposal.

The document below is the historic and influential sermon preached by Blake on behalf of Christian reunion. His plea was that participating denominations might transcend their disunity and find a common life in a church "truly catholic, truly evangelical, and truly reformed."

---

[3] "Message to the Member Churches," unanimously adopted by the Fifth General Assembly, National Council of the Churches of Christ in the United States of America, at San Francisco, December 8, 1960. *Christian Century*, Vol. 77, No. 51 (Dec. 20, 1960), p. 1505.

Document 57 _____

"A Proposal Toward the Reunion of Christ's Church"
by Eugene Carson Blake

> Text: Romans: 15:5-7: *"Now the God of patience and consolation grant you to be like-minded one toward another according to Christ Jesus! That ye may with one mind and with one mouth glorify God, even the Father of our Lord Jesus Christ. Wherefore receive ye one another as Christ also received us to the glory of God."*

This is a significant occasion. When I received the gracious invitation from your Dean and Bishop to preach in this pulpit, on this particular morning, it became clear to me at once that the occasion demanded not only as good a sermon as God might enable me to prepare and preach, but also a sermon that would deal with the unity of the Church of Jesus Christ realistically—neither glossing over divisions with politeness nor covering them with optimistic generalities.

Led, I pray by the Holy Spirit, I propose to the Protestant Episcopal Church that it together with the United Presbyterian Church in the United States of America invite the Methodist Church and the United Church of Christ to form with us a plan of church union both catholic and reformed on the basis of the principles I shall later in this sermon suggest. Any other churches which find that they can accept both the principles and plan would also be warmly invited to unite with us.

I hasten to make it clear that at this stage this is not an official proposal. My position as Stated Clerk of my church's General Assembly gives me no authority to make such a proposal officially on behalf of my church. I speak this morning as one of the ministers of my church privileged and required to preach under the Word of God. I speak as a minister especially privileged—and therefore under a special requirement—especially privileged to have represented my communion for the past nine years in many formal and informal relationships with other communions both inside and outside the ecumenical movement. I speak as one minister of Jesus Christ who believes that God requires us to break through the barriers of nearly 500 years of history, to attempt under God to transcend the separate traditions of our churches, and to find a way together to unite them so that manifesting the unity given us by our Lord Jesus Christ, his Church may be renewed for its mission to our nation and to the world "that the world may believe."

Before setting forth the basic principles of the union which I propose, it is, I think, important to make clear the compelling considerations that have moved me to believe that union ought now to be sought by us and to clear away some possible misunderstandings of reasons and motives for seeking it.

I

First of all, I am moved by the conviction that Jesus Christ, whom all of us confess as our divine Lord and Savior, wills that his Church be one. This does not mean that his Church must be uniform, authoritarian or a single mammoth organization. But it does mean that our separate organizations, however much we sincerely try to cooperate in councils, present a tragically divided church to a tragically divided world. Our divided state makes almost unbelievable our common Christian claim that Jesus Christ is Lord and that He is the Prince of Peace. The goal of any unity or union in which we ought to be interested was clearly stated by the Central Committee of the World Council of Churches last summer. The unity sought is primarily a local unity, "one which brings all in each place who confess Jesus Christ as Lord into a fully committed fellowship with one another." The World Council statement emphasized that the unity sought "is not one of uniformity nor a monolithic power structure." The point of church reunion is not to be found chiefly in national or international organization; it is found most fundamentally in local communion and common witness in all the places where men live.

In October, I was at a political dinner at which I had been invited to give the invocation. A gentlemen introduced himself to me as we were waiting to go to the tables and asked me what church I represented. When I told him, he said, "My wife is a Presbyterian. I am an Episcopalian. We go happily to each other's churches. Why don't you church officials do something about bringing our churches together?" Many such ordinary Christians wonder why we continue to be divided.

In The Christian Century last January, Bishop Pike wrote: ". . . of this I am sure: the Holy Ghost is on our side whenever we break through the barriers between Christian bodies. He will increasingly provide guidance to show the ways in which we can defeat the complacent obstinacy of our national church bodies in this regard."

And I am sure that Bishop Pike agrees with me that there are many complacencies in local churches among members and ministers that must be disturbed by the Holy Ghost if Christ's will for his Church is to be accomplished in our time and place. For although many American church members are ready to criticize their church leaders for inaction, I fear that just as many are complacently happy in the divided state of the Church.

Another clear reason for moving toward the union of American churches at this time came home to me with compelling force during the presidential campaign this fall. The religious issue was, you will remember, quite generally discussed even though all the high level politicians attempted to avoid it as much as possible. Now that the election has been decided and nobody really knows how much the religious question figured in the result, I recall the issue to remind you that one result is clear. Every Christian church, Protestant, Orthodox, Anglican and Roman Catholic, has been weakened by it. Never before have so many Americans agreed that the Christian churches, divided as they are, cannot be trusted to bring to the American people an objective and authentic word of God on a political issue. Americans more than ever see the churches of Jesus Christ as competing social groups pulling and hauling, propagandizing and pressuring for their own organizational advantages.

And this is at a time when the United States of America finds itself at a pinnacle of world power and leadership—needing for herself and the whole free world that kind of spiritual vision and inspiration that only the Church of Jesus Christ, renewed and reunited, can give. Our culture, our civilization, our world leadership are under the materialistic threat of Marxist communism. But our culture becomes increasingly secular, our civilization becomes increasingly decadent, and our world leadership becomes increasingly confused precisely because their Christian foundations are undermined and eroded. And our divided churches, all more and more sectarian in fact, are all therefore less and less Christian in influence.

II

Finally, I am moved to propose this step of church union this morning because my proposal grows out of the convictions expressed in 1959 by 34 leaders of Presbyterian and Reformed churches, theologians and administrators, from all over the world in an address to their fellow Christians, made on the occasion of the 400th anniversary of the Calvinist Reformation. We said:

"The occasion we celebrate (i.e., the 400th anniversary of the beginnings of Presbyterianism) makes invitations more appropriate than proclamations. We ourselves are ready to accept all invitations from sister churches to that comparison of opinion and experience in which Christians submit themselves afresh to the Lord of the Church. And we issue our own invitations to all who would, with us, *put their tradition and systems under the judgment of Christ*, seeking his correction, and ready to relinquish what he does not approve.

"All that we claim for the Presbyterian and Reformed Christians we would lay on the altar. We offer it all to our fellow Christians for whatever use it may be to the whole Church. With the whole Church we hold ourselves alert for the surprises with which the Lord of history can alter the tempo of our renewal, and for the *new forms* with which an eternally recreating God can startle us while he secures his Church."

III

In this spirit and out of this conviction, I now propose the principles upon which a church union of the scope I have suggested may be even now possible of achievement under God.

Let me begin by re-emphasizing the requirement that a reunited Church must be both reformed and catholic. If at this time we are to begin to bridge over the chasm of the Reformation, those of us who are of the reformation tradition must recapture an appreciation of all that has been preserved by the catholic parts of the Church, and equally those of the catholic tradition must be willing to accept and take to themselves as of God all that nearly 500 years of reformation has contributed to the renewal of Christ's Church.

Let me pause here to be quite sure that all of you understand exactly the sense in which I am using the word *catholic*. In common parlance in America we often talk about "the Catholic Church" and mean "the Roman Catholic Church." That is not the meaning of *catholic* that I here use. At the other extreme all our churches repeat the Apostles' Creed in which we say, "I believe in the Holy Catholic Church." All of us claim to be catholic in the strict sense of confessing that Jesus Christ has established one universal Church in all ages and in all places and that we are at least part of it. Here, however, I have used the word *catholic* in still a third sense when I speak of the "catholic parts of the Church." I refer to those practices and to those understandings of faith and order, of church and sacraments which are catholic in contrast to the protestant or evangelical practices and understandings. I refer specifically, for example, to the Anglo-Catholic or high church practices and understandings of your own church. When I say then that the proposal I make is to establish a church both catholic and reformed, I mean one which unites catholic and reformed understandings and practices in an even broader and deeper way than that already present in your communion.

Such a union as I now propose must have within it the kind of broad and deep agreement which gives promise of much wider union than seems possible at the present moment, looking ultimately to the reunion of the whole of Christ's Church.

IV

First let me list the principles of reunion that are important to all who are of catholic tradition.

1. The reunited church must have visible and historical continuity with the Church of all ages before and after the Reformation. This will include a ministry which by its orders and ordination is recognized as widely as possible by all other Christian bodies. To this end, I propose that, without adopting any particular theory of historic succession, the reunited church shall provide at its inception for the consecration of all its bishops by bishops and presbyters both in the apostolic succession and out of it from all over the world from all Christian churches which would authorize or permit them to take part.

I propose further that the whole ministry of the uniting churches would then be unified at solemn services at which the bishops and representative ministers from each church would, in humble dependence on God, act and pray that the Holy Spirit would supply to all and through all what each has to contribute and whatever each may need of the fullness of Christ's grace, commission and authority for the exercise of a new larger ministry in this wider visible manifestation of Christ's Holy and Catholic Church. You will note that this proposal implies no questioning of the reality of any previous consecration or ordination, nor any questioning of their having been blessed and used by God. It does imply that a renewal of our obedience to Jesus Christ in this visible uniting of his Church can be the occasion of fresh indwelling of the Holy Spirit and a new *charisma* for us all.

I mention first this principle of visible and historical continuity not because it is necessarily the most important to the catholic Christian but because it it the only basis on which a broad reunion can take place, and because it is and will continue to be the most difficult catholic conviction for evangelicals to understand and to accept. My proposal is simply to cut the Gordian knot of hundreds of years of controversy by establishing in the united church an historic ministry recognized by all without doubt or scruple. The necessary safeguards and controls of such a ministry will become clear when I am listing the principles of reunion that catholic-minded Christians must grant to evangelicals if there is to be reunion between them.

2. The reunited church must clearly confess the historic trinitarian faith received from the Apostles and set forth in the Apostles' and Nicene Creeds. Here there is no real issue between the Presbyterian and Episcopal churches. The difference that must be bridged is the issue between those in all our churches who stand for a corporate confession of historic faith and those who fear that any required confes-

sion is too restrictive. A quarter of a century ago this would have been a sharper issue and more difficult to bridge. The tendency of the Presbyterian Church to be over-legalistic and of the Episcopal Church to be over-traditional have been modified by renewed theological and biblical understanding in our time. Equally the tendency in some of the so-called free churches to suppose that no belief, that no confesssion of faith, was necessary has given way to a general recognition of the necessity of corporate and individual confession of Christian faith as against the secular, humanistic, and atheistic ideologies of our times.

3. The reunited church must administer the two sacraments, instituted by Christ, the Lord's Supper (or Holy Communion, or Eucharist) and Baptism. These must be understood truly as means of grace by which God's grace and presence are made available to his people. It will not be necessary, I trust, for a precise doctrinal agreement to be reached about the mode of operation of the sacraments so long as the proper catholic concern for their reality is protected so that, with the Word, the Sacrament is recognized as a true means of grace and not merely a symbolic memorial.

Much more could be said. Doubtless there are those of catholic tradition who would like even at this stage to add precise points to protect their consciences and convictions. The above, however, are the basic points and seem to be to be enough to be listed as basic principles if we are willing to add one more word. It must be agreed that every attempt will be made by those drawing up an actual plan of union to include within it those essentials of catholic practice and faith that will enable those of that persuasion to worship and witness joyfully and in good conscience within the fellowship of the united church.

V

And now let me list the principles of reunion that are important to all who are of the reformation tradition:

1. The reunited church must accept the principle of continuing reformation under the word of God by the guidance of the Holy Spirit. A few years ago I would have felt that here was an issue on which no possible agreement could be reached. The reformation churches have traditionally found their authority for faith and life in the Scriptures alone. So long as the wording *sola scriptura* is required, no bridge can be made between catholic and evangelical. But it is now clear in ecumenical conversations that Protestants generally have come to recognize the right place of tradition, just as Catholics have generally become aware of the rightness of judging all tradition by the Scriptures as interpreted to the Church by the Holy Spirit.

The point that the reformation tradition does require from a reunited church is that God, speaking through the Scriptures, must be able to reform the Church from age to age. While the Bible is not a law book or a collection of proof texts, it is God's instrument to speak his saving Word to Christians and to the Chruch. If the catholic must insist on taking the sacraments more seriously than some protestants have sometimes done, so protestants in the reunited church must insist on catholics fully accepting the reformation principle that God has revealed and can reveal himself and his will more fully through the Holy Scriptures. The reuinted church must keep Word and Sacrament equally and intimately united in understanding and appreciation.

2. The reunited church must be truly democratic in its government, recognizing that the whole people of God are Christ's Church, that all Christians are Christ's ministers even though some in the church are separated and ordained to the ministry of word and sacrament. You will have noticed that in the first catholic principle which I mentioned I proposed that the traditional three-fold ministry in the apostolic succession be established in the reunited church. If evangelical protestants are to enter such a church with joy and in conscience there are several subsidiary points that must be made clear in the government and ethos of the reunited church.

Episcopal churches should recognize that it will be with great reluctance that Presbyterians and Congregationalists will accept bishops in the structure of the church. I should say, however, that there are many aspects of episcopacy that American Presbyterians and other non-episcopal churches more and more generally recognize as valuable and needed. We Presbyterians, for example, need pastors of pastors quite desperately, and we know it. But we don't need an aristocratic or authoritarian hierarchy, and we don't believe a reunited church does either. Furthermore, Congregationalists and Presbyterians need to recognize how much of democracy is now practiced in American episcopal churches. In this diocese I remind you that presbyteries have been already established.

On the positive side we Presbyterians would offer to the reunited church the office of the ordained ruling elder, elected by the people in their congregations to share fully and equally in the government of the church. It will be important for all entering this union to attempt creatively to develop a new form of government that avoids the monarchical, clerical and authoritarian tendencies that have been historically the dangers of episcopal church government. Equally this new form of government must avoid the bureaucratic dangers that appear to be the chief threat of non-episcopal churches. It is the essence of protestant concern, however, that decisions should generally be made by ordered groups of men under the guidance of the Holy Spirit rather than by a man who has personal authority to impose on others his decision or judgment.

While Protestants more and more recognize that a *catholic* understanding of the sacraments does not necessarily imply a clerical control of the church nor the priestly abuses that introduced fear and magic into the medieval church and chiefly caused the Reformation, nevertheless they hold the conviction as strongly as ever that clericalism and priestly control of the church must be guarded against by a government of the church in which lay people and ministers share equally.

It will be further important to continue to protect in the united Church the responsible freedom of congregations, including the election of their pastors and the responsible freedom of ministers to answer the call of God received through the free action of the people. I may say that this ought to present no great problem since all our churches are largely *congregational* in this respect. At the same time I would hope that all of those entering into such a union as I here propose would be concerned also to find a way in the context of such freedom to preserve the Methodist ability to find some place of employment of his gifts for every minister who is in good and regular standing. If the reunited church is to have a dedicated and competent ministry, we must find a better way than any of us has yet found to recruit, educate and employ a ministry avoiding on the one hand professionalism and on the other that kind of equalitarianism which produces disorder and anarchy in the church.

3. The reunited church must seek in a new way to capture the brotherhood and sense of fellowship of all its members and ministers. Let me illustrate what I mean by a series of suggestions of what might appear on the surface to be minor matters but which if creatively resolved in the reunited church would not only remove many protestant misgivings but would, I believe, strengthen the witness of the Church to the world. Since it appears to be necessary to have certain inequalities in status in the Church as between members and officers, and as among deacons, presbyters and bishops, let us make certain that the more status a member or minister has the more simple be his dress and attitude. Let us seek to make it evident in every possible way that in the Church the greatest is the servant of all. "My brother" is a better form of Christian address than "your grace." A simple cassock is generally a better garb for the highest member of the clergy than cape and miter. And must there be grades of reverends, very, right, most, etc.? Do there even need to be any reverends at all? It is actually provided explicitly in the Union Plan of Ceylon that a bishop shall not be addressed as "My Lord." It would be my hope that those planning for a reunited church would take the occasion to find many ways to exhibit to each other and to the world that we take seriously our Lord's word: "You know that those who are supposed to rule over the Gentiles lord it over them and their great men exercise authority over them. But it shall not be so among you; but whoever would be great among you must be your servant."

Clearly connected with this will be such matters as finding a way to avoid too great inequities in ministers' salaries, in the richness or grandeur of ecclesiastical establishments, lest the poor be alienated or the world conclude that luxury has sapped the soul of the Church. I speak in the full recognition of the spiritual value of this great church and the rightness of completing it in beauty. Yet I speak for simplicity and brotherhood as ever being the requirement of Christ's Church.

4. Finally, the reunited church must find the way to include within its catholicity (and because of it) a wide diversity of theological formulation of the faith and a variety of worship and liturgy including worship that is nonliturgical.

The great confessions of the Reformation must have their place in the confession, teaching and history of the reunited church just as do the ecumenical agreements of the undivided Church. I would hope that such a reformation confession as the Heidelburg Catechism, partly because of its Lutheran elements, might be lifted up in some acceptable formula as having a proper place in the confession of the whole Church. And further, the reunited church should, as led by the Holy Spirit under the Word, from time to time seek to confess its united faith to the world in new formulations appropriate to its place and time. Our two churches, however, need to appreciate better than they have the fact that direct and joyful experience of Jesus Christ as John Wesley knew it can be restricted too much by overreliance on creedal formulas. Our two churches need to appreciate better than they have the liberating and creative inspiration of the Holy Spirit in the theological freedom of the congregational churches at their best.

Thus the united church must avoid that kind of legalistic formulation of doctrine which on the ground of expressing unity of faith in fact produces a sterile uniformity which breeds alternately neglect and schism.

In worship there is great value in a commonly used, loved and recognized liturgy. But such liturgy ought not to be imposed by authority or to be made binding upon the Holy Spirit or the congregations. More and more it would be our hope that in such a church as is here proposed, there would be developed common ways of worship both historic and freshly inspired. But history proves too well that imposed liturgy like imposed formulation of doctrine often destroys the very unity it is designed to strengthen.

Again, there are many more things that those of the evangelical tradition in all our churches would doubtless like at this stage to add as precise points to protect their consciences and convictions. The above, however, seem to be the essential and basic points which such a union as I propose would require if here again we are willing to add one more word. We must agree that every attempt will be made by those drawing up the plan of union to include within it those essentials of reformation faith and practice that will enable those of that persuasion to worship and witness joyfully and with good conscience within the fellowship of the reunited church.

Here I would insert the assumption that all would understand that the reunited church must remain in the ecumenical movement and its councils. It must be no less—it must be even more concerned beyond itself, recognizing that its reunion was but a stage and a step toward that unity which Christ requires his Church to manifest. This means also that the reunited church must provide that such relationships of fellowship, cooperation and intercommunion as the several churches now have will be continued; this despite the difficulty and tension that such ambiguous relationships will continue to cause.

VI

In conclusion, I would remind you that precise ways of formulating such a reunion as I have sketched have been worked out in several ways, particularly in the subcontinent of India in the several plans of union there. One may ask why they have preceded us in this, and alternatively why we should look to their example for light and inspiration toward union here.

The answer to these questions is a simple one. Christians in India recognize themselves to be a small and beleaguered minority in a pagan and secular world. They have realized full well that they could not afford the luxury of their divisions. I submit that even though our numbers and wealth and prestige may be greater than theirs, we too need to recognize that we cannot afford the luxury of our historic divisions. It is because of this conviction that I have felt impelled to preach this sermon.

There are two results that I pray may, under God, come from it. If there is support for what I have said in my own church, any or all of our presbyteries may, if they will, overture the General Assembly which meets next May asking that assembly to make an official proposal. I further hope that the Protestant Episcopal Church, by its own processes, will also take an early action in this direction so that in your General Convention next fall the invitation to the Methodist Church and the United Church of Christ may be jointly issued to proceed to draw up a plan of union to which any other churches of Jesus Christ accepting the bases suggested and the plan developed will be warmly invited to join.

Paul wrote, "Complete my joy by being of the same mind, having the same love, being in full accord and of one mind." The Apostle continued: "Do nothing from selfishness or conceit, but in humility count others better than yourselves. Let each of you look not only to his own interests but also to the interests of others. Have this mind among yourselves which you have in Christ Jesus, who, though he was in the form of God, did not count equality with God a thing to be grasped, but emptied himself, taking the form of a servant, being born in the likeness of men. And being found in human form, he humbled himself and became obedient unto death, even death on the cross. Therefore God has highly exalted him and bestowed on him the name that is above every name, that at the name of Jesus every knee should bow . . . and every tongue confess that Jesus Christ is Lord to the glory of God the father."

If you, dear friends, and all others who consider and discuss this proposal do so in this spirit and from this motive, I have no fear but that the eternally recreative God will find his way to renew and reunite his Church.

Blake's sermon was a media event that captured the attention of churches and secular groups. It got its preacher on the cover of *Time*. The four denominations designated in Blake's sermon committed themselves to consultation and met at Washington, D.C., in April of 1962. The group of denominational representatives constituted itself the Consultation on Church Union (COCU). By 1963 the Disciples of Christ and the United Brethren had become full participants. Between 1965 and 1967 three black denominations—the African Methodist Episcopal, the African Methodist Episcopal Zion, and the Christian Methodist Episcopal churches—entered into the COCU experience. In a surprising vote of its General Assembly, the Presbyterian Church in the United States ("Southern Presbyterian") came into the COCU in 1966. At the meeting in Dayton, Ohio, a Plan of Union Commission was authorized and directed to draft a "plan" to be brought before a plenary session of the union, not later than 1970. In St. Louis, March 1970, the COCU, now composed of nine member churches, focused on a draft text of *A Plan of Union for the Church of Christ Uniting*. The plan was approved for transmittal to "the member churches and to all Christians for study and response, seeking their assistance in the further development of this Plan of Union."[4]

It was at this point that the COCU experienced the ecumenical apathy and disillusionment that seems to have characterized the early 1970s. Little feeling for or against the proposed plan was expressed,

[4] *Digest of the Proceedings of the Consultation on Church Union*, Vol. 9 (1970), p. 89.

with the exception of some Fundamentalists and neo-evangelicals who had habitually opposed most "main-line" ecumenism as a departure from doctrinal standards and as evidence of an erosion of evangelical zeal.[5] As in the case of some other movements, the ecumenical euphoria of the early 1960s gave way to the exhaustion and, in some cases, to the boredom of the 1970s. Paul A. Crow, General Secretary of COCU, summarized the shift in climate in this way: "certain dominant traits characterize the new mood among Christians: a crisis of faith, a polarization over the church's involvement in social action, an anti-institution, anti-establishment spirit, declining membership roles and finances."[6]

In the Eleventh Plenary of the COCU (Memphis, April 1973), after receiving three thousand responses to the plan sent in by local church members, the delegates decided members of the local churches were "unready" for serious discussion of organic union at that time. The revised plan called for a new emphasis on experimental ministries on the local level with the conviction that viable proposals for organization and structure of the projected Church of Christ Uniting (note that the original acronym for the COCU is the same as that designating the name of the proposed church) could only be developed out of the ecumenical experiences gained from living and working together.

The COCU, ironically, reached its highest point of achievement at a time when few seemed to care. Martin Marty writes, "It set out to overcome separation at a time when symbol-makers now set a new premium on at least strategic 'separation' in various racial, sexual, generational, or other movements."[7]

Twenty years after Blake's historic sermon, COCU is still alive if not vigorous. Ten denominations, including three black Methodist churches, now compose it. A new document entitled *In Quest of a Church Uniting* has been sent to member denominations for study and response by December 1981. The COCU's impact on the average member of a COCU denomination has not been great. Church leaders have not been enthusiastic in their response to the organization's overtures. A veteran ecumenical leader, Albert C. Outler, has observed, "COCU has begun to gather a barely discernible momentum, despite the basic apathy toward it on the part of the denominational curia in *all* the member churches." Outler explains the causes for this apathy: "The major failure of COCU is the fact that our most significant forward steps leave our bureaucrats indifferent or even defensive. The origins of our denominations were focused on matters of *conscience*; their continuance, in most cases, has become a matter of *self-interest* to people who would stand to lose—

[5] See Harold Lindsell, "COCU: A Critique," two parts in *Christianity Today*, Vol. 15, No. 1 (October 9, 1970), and Vol. 15, No. 2 (October 23, 1970), pp. 3-5, 8-10.

[6] Paul Crow, "A New Beginning," *Church Union at Midpoint* (New York: Association Press, 1972), p. 34.

[7] Martin E. Marty, "The New Generation," *Church Union at Midpoint* (New York: Association Press, 1972), p. 182.

their jobs or their clout or whatever—if union were ever consummated on any effective basis."[8]

COCU now has a broader base and agenda with more laypersons, women, youth, ethnic and racial minorities. The COCU documents have led more main-line church members to an engagement of the crucial issues regarding church order and missions than any other movement in the history of American Christianity.

VATICAN COUNCIL II

Although there had been "low profile" pioneers who quietly laid the groundwork for the ecumenical spirit in Roman Catholicism as early as the pontificate of Leo XIII (1810–1903), that spirit emerged dramatically in the reign of "good Pope John." When Giuseppe Roncalli (1881–1963) became Pope John XXIII, his spontaneous outreach to the entire human family—the "whole world"—created a new situation. John announced in January of 1959 that he intended to call a council[9] of the Roman Catholic Church, suggesting that the church should open the windows to let in some fresh air. What followed was a breakthrough of great proportions.

The very fact that a council was called was an event of great magnitude. Prior to Vatican II, the dogma of papal infallibility had seemed to be employed toward the increasing centralization of church governance in the office of the Pope. Perceiving what seemed to be an irrevocable direction toward papal monarchy, Protestants had inferred that there would be no more general councils of the Roman Catholic Church.

Beyond this, John created the Secretariat for the Promotion of Christian Unity and gave it a status independent of the Curia, the court of officials that helps the Pope with the administration of the church. As head of the Secretariat, John appointed Augustin Cardinal Bea, S.J. (1881–1968), a German biblical scholar, who became one of the leaders of the council. The Secretariat was noteworthy in that it had the task of drafting the crucial schema *Decree on Ecumenism*. The Secretariat also prepared the various drafts of the statements on Religious Liberty and on the Jews. Finally, the Secretariat provided a means of access between council members and non-Roman Catholic observers (Protestant and Eastern Orthodox Christians).

Probably no other Vatican II document reflects so clearly the church's new attitude toward non-Roman Catholic Christians as does the *Decree on Ecumenism*. In this document there is no discussion of Protestants as "schismatics and heretics," but rather they are referred

---

[8] Albert C. Outler as quoted in Janet Harbison Penfield's article "COCU at 20: An Anniversary Waltz," The *Christian Century*, Vol. XCVII, No. 39 (December 3, 1980), p. 1190.

[9] A council is a formal meeting of bishops and representatives of several churches convened for the purpose of regulating doctrine and/or discipline; general or ecumenical councils are assemblies of the bishops of the entire church; such councils have been held to possess the highest authority that the church can give; for Roman Catholics it is believed that such councils must be summoned and their decrees confirmed by the pope.

to as "separated brethren." Pope John died on June 3, 1963. Pope Paul VI was elected on June 21, 1963, and promptly announced his intention to continue the council. The *Decree of Ecumenism* was promulgated on November 21, 1964, at the close of the third session of Vatican II. The following document is excerpted from the full Decree on Ecumenism.

_____ *Document 58*

From *Decree on Ecumenism* by Pope Paul VI

1. Promoting the restoration of unity among all Christians is one of the chief concerns of the Second Sacred Ecumenical Synod of the Vatican. The Church established by Christ the Lord is, indeed, one and unique. Yet many Christian communions present themselves to men as the true heritage of Jesus Christ. To be sure, all proclaim themselves to be disciples of the Lord, but their convictions clash and their paths diverge, as though Christ Himself were divided (cf. 1 Cor. 1:13). Without doubt, this discord openly contradicts the will of Christ, provides a stumbling block to the world, and inflicts damage on the most holy cause of proclaiming the good news to every creature.

Nevertheless, the Lord of Ages wisely and patiently follows out the plan of His grace on behalf of us sinners. In recent times He has begun to bestow more generously upon divided Christians remorse over their divisions and a longing for unity.

Everywhere, large numbers have felt the impulse of this grace, and among our separated brethren also there increases from day to day a movement, fostered by the grace of the Holy Spirit, for the restoration of unity among all Christians. Taking part in this movement, which is called ecumenical, are those who invoke the Triune God and confess Jesus as Lord and Savior. They join in not merely as individuals but also as members of the corporate groups in which they have heard the gospel, and which each regards as his Church, and, indeed, God's. And yet, almost everyone, though in different ways, longs that there may be one visible Church of God, a Church truly universal and sent forth to the whole world that the world may be converted to the gospel and so be saved, to the glory of God.

This sacred Synod, therefore, gladly notes all these factors. It has already declared its teaching in the Church, and now, moved by a desire for the restoration of unity among all the followers of Christ, it wishes to set before all Catholics certain helps, pathways, and methods by which they too can respond to this divine summons and grace.

Catholic Principles on Ecumenism

2. What has revealed the love of God among us is that the only begotten Son of God has been sent by the Father into the world, so that, being made man, the Son might by His redemption of the entire human race give new life to it and unify it (cf. 1 Jn. 4:9; Col. 1:18-20; Jn. 11:52). Before offering Himself up as a spotless victim upon the altar of the cross, He prayed to His father for those who believe:

SOURCE: Walter M. Abbott, S.J., and Very Rev. Msgr. Joseph Gallagher (eds.), *The Documents of Vatican II* (New York: The American Press, 1966), pp. 341-355.

"That all may be one even as thou, Father, in me, and I in thee; that they also may be one in us, that the world may believe that thou hast sent me" (Jn. 17:21). In His Church He instituted the wonderful sacrament of the Eucharist by which the unity of the Church is both signified and brought about. He gave His followers a new commandment of mutual love (cf. Jn. 13:34), and promised the Spirit, their Advocate (cf. Jn. 16:7), who, as Lord and life-giver, would abide with them forever.

After being lifted up on the cross and glorified, the Lord Jesus poured forth the Spirit whom He had promised, and through whom He has called and gathered together the people of the New Covenant, who comprise the Church, into a unity of faith, hope, and charity. For, as the apostle teaches, the Church is: "one body and one Spirit, even as you were called in one hope of your calling; one Lord, one faith, one baptism" (Eph. 4:4–5). For "all you who have been baptized into Christ, have put on Christ . . . for you are all one in Christ Jesus" (Gal. 3:27–28). It is the Holy Spirit, dwelling in those who believe, pervading and ruling over the entire Church, who brings about that marvelous communion of the faithful and joins them together so intimately in Christ that He is the principle of the Church's unity. By distributing various kinds of spiritual gifts and ministries (cf. 1 Cor. 12: 4–11), He enriches the Church of Jesus Christ with different functions "in order to perfect the saints for a work of ministry, for building up the body of Christ" (Eph. 4:12).

In order to establish this holy Church of His everywhere in the world until the end of time, Christ entrusted to the College of the Twelve the task of teaching, ruling, and sanctifying (cf. Mt. 28:18–20, in conjunction with Jn. 20: 21–23). Among their number He chose Peter. After Peter's profession of faith, He decreed that on him He would build His Church; to Peter He promised the keys of the kingdom of heaven (cf. Mt. 16:19, in conjunction with Mt. 18:18). After Peter's profession of love, Christ entrusted all His sheep to him to be confirmed in faith (cf. Lk. 22:32) and shepherded in perfect unity (cf. Jn. 21: 15–17). Meanwhile, Christ Jesus Himself forever remains the chief cornerstone (cf. Eph. 2:20) and shepherd of our souls (cf. 1 Pet. 2:25).

It is through the faithful preaching of the gospel by the apostles and their successors—the bishops with Peter's successor at their head—through their administration of the sacraments, and through their loving exercise of authority, that Jesus Christ wishes His people to increase under the influence of the Holy Spirit. Thereby too, He perfects His people's fellowship in unity: in the confession of one faith, in the common celebration of divine worship, and in the fraternal harmony of the family of God.

The Church, then, God's only flock, like a standard lifted high for the nations to see (cf. Is. 11:10–12), ministers the gospel of peace to all mankind (cf. Eph. 2: 17–18, in conjunction with Mk. 16:15), as she makes her pilgrim way in hope toward her goal, the fatherland above (cf. 1 Pet. 1:3–9).

This is the sacred mystery of the unity of the Church, in Christ and through Christ, with the Holy Spirit energizing a variety of functions. The highest exemplar and source of this mystery is the unity, in the Trinity of Persons, of one God, the Father and the Son in the Holy Spirit.

3. From her very beginnings there arose in this one and only Church of God certain rifts (cf. 1 Cor. 11:18–19, Gal. 1:6–9; 1 Jn. 2:18–19), which the apostle strongly censures as damnable (cf. 1 Cor. 1:11ff.; 11:22). But in subsequent cen-

turies more widespread disagreements appeared and quite large Communities became separated from full communion with the Catholic Church—developments for which, at times, men of both sides were to blame. However, one cannot impute the sin of separation to those who at present are born into these Communities and are instilled therein with Christ's faith. The Catholic Church accepts them with respect and affection as brothers. For men who believe in Christ and have been properly baptized are brought into a certain, though imperfect, communion with the Catholic Church. Undoubtedly, the differences that exist in varying degrees between them and the Catholic Church—whether in doctrine and sometimes in discipline, or concerning the structure of the Church—do indeed create many and sometimes serious obstacles to full ecclesiastical communion. These the ecumenical movement is striving to overcome. Nevertheless, all those justified by faith through baptism are incorporated into Christ. They therefore have a right to be honored by the title of Christian, and are properly regarded as brothers in the Lord by the sons of the Catholic Church.

Moreover some, even very many, of the most significant elements or endowments which together go to build up and give life to the Church herself can exist outside the visible boundaries of the Catholic Church: the written word of God; the life of grace; faith, hope, and charity, along with other interior gifts of the Holy Spirit and visible elements. All of these, which come from Christ and lead back to Him, belong by right to the one Church of Christ.

The brethren divided from us also carry out many of the sacred actions of the Christian religion. Undoubtedly, in ways that vary according to the condition of each Church or Community, these actions can truly engender a life of grace, and can be rightly described as capable of providing access to the community of salvation.

It follows that these separated Churches and Communities, though we believe they suffer from defects already mentioned, have by no means been deprived of significance and importance in the mystery of salvation. For the Spirit of Christ has not refrained from using them as means of salvation which derive their efficacy from the very fullness of grace and truth entrusted to the Catholic Church.

Nevertheless, our separated brethren, whether considered as individuals or as Communities and Churches, are not blessed with that unity which Jesus Christ wished to bestow on all those whom He has regenerated and vivified into one body and newness of life—that unity which the holy Scriptures and the revered tradition of the Church proclaim. For it is through Christ's Catholic Church alone, which is the all-embracing means of salvation, that the fullness of the means of salvation can be obtained. It was to the apostolic college alone, of which Peter is the head, that we believe our Lord entrusted all the blessings of the New Covenant, in order to establish on earth the one Body of Christ into which all those should be fully incorporated who already belong in any way to God's People. During its pilgrimage on earth, this People, though still in its members liable to sin, is growing in Christ and is being gently guided by God, according to His hidden designs, until it happily arrives at the fullness of eternal glory in the heavenly Jerusalem.

4. Today, in many parts of the world, under the inspiring grace of the Holy Spirit, multiple efforts are being expended through prayer, word, and action to attain that fullness of unity which Jesus Christ desires. This sacred Synod, therefore,

exhorts all the Catholic faithful to recognize the signs of the times and to participate skillfully in the work of ecumenism.

The "ecumenical movement" means those activities and enterprises which, according to various needs of the Church and opportune occasions, are started and
organized for the fostering of unity among Christians. These are: first, every effort
to eliminate words, judgments, and actions which do not respond to the condition
of separated brethren with truth and fairness and so make mutual relations between
them more difficult; then, "dialogue" between competent experts from different
Churches and Communities. In their meetings, which are organized in a religious
spirit, each explains the teaching of his Communion in greater depth and brings out
clearly its distinctive features. Through such dialogue, everyone gains a truer knowledge and more just appreciation of the teaching and religious life of both Communions. In addition, these Communions cooperate more closely in whatever
projects a Christian conscience demands for the common good. They also come together for common prayer, where this is permitted. Finally, all are led to examine
their own faithfulness to Christ's will for the Church and, wherever necessary,
undertake with vigor the task of renewal and reform.

When such actions are carried out by the Catholic faithful with prudence, patience, and the vigilance of their spiritual shepherds, they contribute to the blessings of justice and truth, of concord and collaboration, as well as of the spirit of
brotherly love and unity. The result will be that, little by little, as the obstacles to
perfect ecclesiastical communion are overcome, all Christians will be gathered, in a
common celebration of the Eucharist, into that unity of the one and only Church
which Christ bestowed on His Church from the beginning. This unity, we believe,
dwells in the Catholic Church as something she can never lose, and we hope that it
will continue to increase until the end of time.

However, it is evident that the work of preparing and reconciling those individuals
who wish for full Catholic communion is of its nature distinct from ecumenical
action. But there is no opposition between the two, since both proceed from the
wondrous providence of God.

In ecumenical work, Catholics must assuredly be concerned for their separated
brethren, praying for them, keeping them informed about the Church, making the
first approaches towards them. But their primary duty is to make an honest and
careful appraisal of whatever needs to be renewed and achieved in the Catholic
household itself, in order that its life may bear witness more loyally and luminously
to the teaching and ordinances which have been handed down from Christ through
the apostles.

For although the Catholic Church has been endowed with all divinely revealed
truth and with all means of grace, her members fail to live by them with all the
fervor they should. As a result, the radiance of the Church's face shines less brightly
in the eyes of our separated brethren and of the world at large, and the growth of
God's kingdom is retarded. Every Catholic must therefore aim at Christian perfection (cf. Jas. 1:4; Rom. 12:1-2) and, each according to his station, play his part so
that the Church which bears in her own body the humility of the dying of Jesus (cf.
2 Cor. 4:10; Phil. 2:5-8), may daily be more purified and renewed, against the day

when Christ will present her to Himself in all her glory, without spot or wrinkle (cf. Eph. 5:27).

While preserving unity in essentials, let all members of the Church, according to the office entrusted to each, preserve a proper freedom in the various forms of spiritual life and discipline, in the variety of liturgical rites, and even in the theological elaborations of revealed truth. In all things let charity be exercised. If the faithful are true to this course of action, they will be giving even richer expression to the authentic catholicity of the Church, and, at the same time, to her apostolicity.

On the other hand, Catholics must joyfully acknowledge and esteem the truly Christian endowments from our common heritage which are to be found among our separated brethren. It is right and salutary to recognize the riches of Christ and virtuous works in the lives of others who are bearing witness to Christ, sometimes even to the shedding of their blood. For God is always wonderful in His works and worthy of admiration.

Nor should we forget that whatever is wrought by the grace of the Holy Spirit in the hearts of our separated brethren can contribute to our own edification. Whatever is truly Christian never conflicts with the genuine interests of the faith; indeed, it can always result in a more ample realization of the very mystery of Christ and the Church.

Nevertheless, the divisions among Christians prevent the Church from effecting the fullness of catholicity proper to her in those of her sons who, though joined to her by baptism, are yet separated from full communion with her. Furthermore, the Church herself finds it more difficult to express in actual life her full catholicity in all its aspects.

This sacred Synod is gratified to note that participation by the Catholic faithful in ecumenical work is growing daily. It commends this work to bishops everywhere in the world for their skillfull promotion and prudent guidance.

The Practice of Ecumenism

5. Concern for restoring unity pertains to the whole Church, faithful and clergy alike. It extends to everyone, according to the potential of each, whether it be exercised in daily Christian living or in theological and historical studies. This very concern already reveals to some extent the bond of brotherhood existing among all Christians, and it leads toward that full and perfect unity which God lovingly desires.

6. Every renewal of the Church essentially consists in an increase of fidelity to her own calling. Undoubtedly this explains the dynamism of the movement toward unity.

Christ summons the Church, as she goes her pilgrim way, to that continual reformation of which she always has need, insofar as she is an institution of men here on earth. Therefore, if the influence of events or of the times has led to deficiencies in conduct, in Church discipline, or even in the formulation of doctrine (which must be carefully distinguished from the deposit itself of faith), these should be appropriately rectified at the proper moment.

Church renewal therefore has notable ecumenical importance. Already this renewal is taking place in various spheres of the Church's life: the biblical and liturgical movements, the preaching of the word of God, catechetics, the apostolate of the laity, new forms of religious life and the spirituality of married life, and the Church's social teaching and activity. All these should be considered as favorable pledges and signs of ecumenical progress in the future.

7. There can be no ecumenism worthy of the name without a change of heart. For it is from newness of attitudes (cf. Eph. 4:23), from self-denial and unstinted love, that yearnings for unity take their rise and grow toward maturity. We should therefore pray to the divine Spirit for the grace to be genuinely self-denying, humble, gentle in the service of others, and to have an attitude of brotherly generosity toward them. The Apostle of the Gentiles says: "I, therefore, the prisoner in the Lord, exhort you to walk in a manner worthy of the calling with which you were called, with all humility and meekness, with patience, bearing with one another in love, careful to preserve the unity of the Spirit in the bond of peace" (Eph. 4: 1-3). This exhortation applies especially to those who have been raised to sacred orders so that the mission of Christ may be carried on. He came among us "not to be served but to serve" (Mt. 20:28).

St. John has testified: "If we say that we have not sinned, we make him a liar, and his word is not in us" (1 Jn. 1:10). This holds good for sins against unity. Thus, in humble prayer, we beg pardon of God and of our separated brethren, just as we forgive those who trespass against us.

Let all Christ's faithful remember that the more purely they strive to live according to the gospel, the more they are fostering and even practicing Christian unity. For they can achieve depth and ease in strengthening mutual brotherhood to the degree that they enjoy profound communion with the Father, the Word, and the Spirit.

8. This change of heart and holiness of life, along with public and private prayer for the unity of Christians, should be regarded as the soul of the whole ecumenical movement, and can rightly be called "spiritual ecumenism."

Catholics already have a custom of uniting frequently in that prayer for the unity of the Church with which the Savior Himself, on the eve of His death, appealed so fervently to His Father: "That all may be one" (Jn. 17:21).

In certain special circumstances, such as in prayer services "for unity" and during ecumenical gatherings, it is allowable, indeed desirable, that Catholics should join in prayer with their separated brethren. Such prayers in common are certainly a very effective means of petitioning for the grace of unity, and they are a genuine expression of the ties which even now bind Catholics to their separated brethren. "For where two or three are gathered together for my sake, there am I in the midst of them" (Mt. 18:20).

As for common worship, however, it may not be regarded as a means to be used indiscriminately for the restoration of unity among Christians. Such worship depends chiefly on two principles: it should signify the unity of the Church; it should provide a sharing in the means of grace. The fact that it should signify unity generally rules out common worship. Yet the gaining of a needed grace sometimes commends it.

The practical course to be adopted, after due regard has been given to all the circumstances of time, place, and personage, is left to the prudent decision of the local episcopal authority, unless the Bishops' Conference according to its own statutes, or the Holy See, has determined otherwise.

9. We must come to understand the outlook of our separated brethren. Study is absolutely required for this, and should be pursued with fidelity to truth and in a spirit of good will. When they are properly prepared for this study, Catholics need to acquire a more adequate understanding of the distinctive doctrines of our separated brethren, as well as of their own history, spiritual and liturgical life, their religious psychology and cultural background. Of great value for this purpose are meetings between the two sides, especially for discussion of theological problems, where each can deal with the other on an equal footing. Such meetings require that those who take part in them under authoritative guidance be truly competent. From dialogue of this sort will emerge still more clearly what the true posture of the Catholic Church is. In this way, too, we will better understand the attitude of our separated brethren and more aptly present our own belief.

10. Instruction in sacred theology and other branches of knowledge, especially those of a historical nature, must also be presented from an ecumenical point of view, so that at every point they may more accurately correspond with the facts of the case.

For it is highly important that future bishops and priests should have mastered a theology carefully worked out in this way and not polemically, especially in what concerns the relations of separated brethren with the Catholic Church. For it is upon the formation which priests receive that the necessary instruction and spiritual formation of the faithful and of religious depend so very greatly.

Moreover, Catholics engaged in missionary work, in the same territories as other Christians, ought to know, particularly in these times, the problems and the benefits which affect their apostolate because of the ecumenical movement.

11. The manner and order in which Catholic belief is expressed should in no way become an obstacle to dialogue with our brethren. It is, of course, essential that doctrine be clearly presented in its entirety. Nothing is so foreign to the spirit of ecumenism as a false conciliatory approach which harms the purity of Catholic doctrine and obscures its assured genuine meaning.

At the same time, Catholic belief needs to be explained more profoundly and precisely, in ways and in terminology which our separated brethren too can really understand.

Furthermore, Catholic theologians engaged in ecumenical dialogue, while standing fast by the teaching of the Church and searching together with separated brethren into the divine mysteries, should act with love for truth, with charity, and with humility. When comparing doctrines, they should remember that in Catholic teaching there exists an order or "hierarchy" of truths, since they vary in their relationship to the foundation of the Christian faith. Thus the way will be opened for this kind of fraternal rivalry to incite all to a deeper realization and a clearer expression of the unfathomable riches of Christ (cf. Eph. 3:8).

12. Before the whole world, let all Christians profess their faith in God, one and three, in the incarnate Son of God, our Redeemer and Lord. United in their efforts, and with mutual respect, let them bear witness to our common hope, which does

not play us false. Since in our times cooperation in social matters is very widely practiced, all men without exception are summoned to united effort. Those who believe in God have a stronger summons, but the strongest claims are laid on Christians, since they have been sealed with the name of Christ.

Cooperation among all Christians vividly expresses that bond which already unites them, and it sets in clearer relief the features of Christ the Servant. Such cooperation, which has already begun in many countries, should be ever increasingly developed, particularly in regions where a social and technical evolution is taking place. It should contribute to a just appreciation of the dignity of the human person, the promotion of the blessings of peace, the application of gospel principles to social life, and the advancement of the arts and sciences in a Christian spirit. Christians should also work together in the use of every possible means to relieve the afflictions of our times, such as famine and natural disasters, illiteracy and poverty, lack of housing, and the unequal distribution of wealth. Through such cooperation, all believers in Christ are able to learn easily how they can understand each other better and esteem each other more, and how the road to the unity of Christians may be made smooth.

One of the "American" contributions to Vatican II was the leadership provided by an American Roman Catholic scholar in the development of the *Declaration on Religious Freedom*, promulgated on December 7, 1965. Fr. John Courtney Murray, S.J., was one of the chief drafters of the document. Murray had long been recognized as a leading authority on the issue of the relationship between church and state.[10] Prior to the promulgation of this document many non-Roman Catholic Americans were fearful that the Roman Catholic Church did not really believe in religious freedom and they therefore worried over increasing Catholic power. *The Declaration on Religious Freedom* assured the world that the Roman Catholic Church does not deal with the civil order in terms of a double standard—"freedom for the church when Catholics are a minority, privilege for the church and intolerance for others when Catholics are a majority."[11] With its experience of religious voluntarism, it was fitting that the doctrinal contribution of the American Catholic Church to the council should have been in the area of its understanding of religious freedom.

The Second Vatican Council had a telling effect on American Roman Catholicism. Liturgical renewal proved to be the most obvious reform as American Catholics participated in the English Mass and began to experience the congregational singing of hymns.

Ecumenical relations were transformed as almost every American neighborhood experienced ecumenical fellowship. One of the most far-reaching developments was the conceptualization and development

[10] See Thomas T. Love, John Courtney Murray: *Contemporary Church-State Theory* (Garden City, N.Y.: Doubleday, 1965).

[11] John Courtney Murray, introduction to "Religious Freedom," in Abbott, Walter M. (ed.), *The Documents of Vatican II* (New York: Guild Press, 1966), p. 673.

of "livingroom dialogues," which were lay-sponsored discussion groups for Roman Catholics, Protestants, and Orthodox Christians, organized along guidelines suggested in an available paperback.[12] What is a liturgical commonplace today would have been unthinkable in 1960. A Roman Catholic Mass in New Orleans is not considered innovative when the congregation sings as the opening hymn Martin Luther's Reformation hymn "A Mighty Fortress Is Our God" and as the recessional a hymn by Harry Emerson Fosdick. At the same time Congregationalists, Presbyterians, and other American Protestants often worship along the lines of a Roman Catholic folk Mass!

DEVELOPMENTS AFTER VATICAN II

Much of Paul VI's strategy as Pope seemed designed to assure faithful Catholics that change was not coming too fast. While he did prevent curial conservatives from undoing Vatican II reforms, Paul nevertheless was cautious in his decision making. The doctrine of collegiality in the governance of the church developed by Vatican II was never implemented effectively. The council had decreed that the pope ruled together with the bishops of the world. The Synod of Bishops, created by Pope Paul, actually had little power. The pope and his secretary of state ruled with a firm hand. The synod could not issue its own report, choose the topics for discussion, or even set the agenda. Many liberal Catholics felt that Paul VI had turned against the spirit of Vatican II. There was great resistance to Pope Paul's encyclical *Humanae Vitae* (of Human Life), published in 1968, which reinforced the Catholic taboo against the practice of contraception. Many Roman Catholics chose to continue practicing contraception.

Giovanni Batista Montini, Pope Paul VI, died on August 6, 1978. What happened after Paul VI's death was truly extraordinary: the world witnessed the death of two popes and the election of their successors within two months. Cardinal Albino Luciani of Venice was elected by the College of Cardinals on August 27, 1978. He took the name John Paul. The name signaled the new pope's intention to maintain a balance between John's innovation and Paul's prudence. John Paul died September 29, 1978.

Luciani's surprise successor was Karol Wojtyla, the junior cardinal from Cracow, Poland, who was elected on October 15, 1978. Taking the name John Paul II, Wojtyla was the first non-Italian pope since 1522. At the age of fifty-eight, Wojtyla was young for a pope. He had been trained as a scholar and was known as a pragmatic coalition builder. Now, as John Paul II, he is a vigorous man who has already visited Ireland, Latin America, the United States, the Philippines, Japan, and other nations since succeeding to the papal throne. John Paul has proved to be theologically conservative, reinforcing traditional

---

[12] William B. Greenspun and William A. Nordgren (eds.), *Living Room Dialogues* (New York: National Council of Churches and Paulist Press, 1965), p. 256.

Roman Catholic teachings regarding priestly discipline, sexuality, and the role of women in the church. The pope has also cautioned social activists that they should not get too involved in liberation theology because the church should not become identified with any particular ideology. This conservative posture has disappointed many progressives in the church.

Progressives in the Roman Catholic Church felt that the gauntlet was thrown down by the Vatican in what has come to be called "the Küng affair." On December 18, 1979, the Sacred Congregation for the Doctrine of the Faith (formerly known as the Inquisition) declared that Hans Küng (1928–   ), a progressive Swiss priest and theologian, would no longer be recognized as an official theological representative of the Roman Catholic Church. John Paul II gave his personal approval to the congregation's statement. Küng compared his case with that of Galileo and said: "That same inquisitorial authority has resumed the same inhumane policies." The German Protestant theologian Jürgen Moltmann asked, "Was the 'opening up' of the church through Vatican II but an interlude, not meant to be taken seriously?"

The central issue in the Küng affair has to do with the precise meaning of teaching authority in the church. There is a tension between the role of the Roman magisterium—the teaching authority of pope and bishops—and the role of the church's theologians. Is it possible to synthesize hierarchical authority with free theological criticism? The following document is an address given by Hans Küng at the University of California, Berkeley. His visit to Berkeley was sponsored by the Pacific School of Religion, an interdenominational seminary. In this address Küng asserts that both the pope and hierarchy are busily engaged in subverting Vatican II. Küng's supporters think of him almost as a modern Luther; others view him as an uncooperative troubler of the church. Küng speaks for himself in "Where I Stand."

Document 59 _____

"Where I Stand" by Hans Küng

Ladies and gentlemen, my dear friends, when I was here at Berkeley the first time, it was under John XXIII. Then I was a part of the majority. Now I think I am still in the same church, but as a part (maybe) of the minority—in any case, a part of the loyal opposition to His Holiness.

In this lecture, the first in the United States since the severe measures taken against me in Rome, I would like to begin with a word of thanks to my American friends. The manifestations of solidarity in recent months have been overwhelming, not only in Europe, but also in the United States. And I gladly admit that these

SOURCE: Reprinted by permission of the Pacific School of Religion, 1798 Scenic Avenue, Berkeley, California. The address was first given at PSR, and appeared in *PSR Bulletin*, Vol. LIX, No. 1, January 1981.

signs of fellowship—from universities, theologians, groups of priests and lay-people, and from numerous individuals—Catholics, Protestants, Jews—were what made it possible for me and my colleagues in the Institute for Ecumenical Research in Tübingen to survive those difficult weeks—spiritually, mentally, and also with humor.

This invitation, especially, to the Pacific School of Religion in Berkeley, which arrived in Tübingen at the very climax of the conflict, was for me a supremely encouraging sign of hope and solidarity. I would like to express my heartfelt thanks for it to the president, colleagues and students of the Pacific School of Religion. Because of their extraordinary support, I decided that when I had the time free to come to America, I would go first to Berkeley, California!

A great deal has become clear in recent months. Rome has not only become more Roman—paradoxically, under a Polish pope—but my theology has also remained Catholic. With considerable agreement from my own church, I have left no doubt about my remaining now as formerly in this Catholic Church of mine and about my determination to fight for its renewal. Why? Because I have no intention of abandoning the Catholic Church to a rather conservative clan of Vatican court theologians and curial bureaucrats and their German allies. I say unreservedly "Yes" to a truly Catholic Church, but decidedly "No" to any kind of Roman opposition or repression. I will go at any time to Rome for honest discussions under honest procedures, but I shall never submit to the Roman Inquisition. I must say, too, because I was asked about these matters earlier today at a press conference, that in August I wrote a personal letter to the Pope. I expressed again that I would come to Rome and talk to him whenever he wants. But up to the time of my departure from Germany, I had no answer from Rome. I had no answer. It is that simple.

Even the withdrawal of official approbation (which I still regard as a great wrong and a theological mistake—also, I think, a political mistake) could not leave me in any doubt about my membership in this church. And, as we know, even the Vatican Congregation for the Doctrine of the Faith—formerly called the "Holy Office" or the "Holy Inquisition"—does not dispute the fact that I am still a Catholic, even a Catholic priest, and at the same time a theologian. But how can a Catholic who is a theologian call himself anything but a Catholic theologian?

The conflicts of recent months have cost me my membership in the Department of Catholic Theology, but not in the University of Tubingen where I kept my chair of Ecumenical Theology and where I kept the Institute for Ecumenical Research, now under the direct responsibility of the President and Senate of the university. I have even more freedom than before and I shall certainly use it! I can continue to do research, teach and prepare students for the doctorate. But the focal point of my work has shifted mainly to a systematic treatment of *ecumenical theology*, a *theology of the Oikoumené*. This does not mean that my associates and I claim any monopoly on ecumenical theology, but we would like to be the vanguard of an ecumenical movement which, after more than 450 years of schism, will finally lay open the path toward a reciprocal recognition on the part of the denominations.

An explanation of what I understand by ecumenical theology can perhaps best illustrate where I stand particularly against the background of the present situation, characterized as it is by an ecumenical standstill in both the Catholic and the Protestant churches. I am referring to the standstill that exists, not on the parish or grass roots level where I think there are many ecumenical contacts and the movement is quietly going on, but on the higher levels. This is the subject of the first part of my lecture.

Ecumenical Standstill in the Catholic Church

Ecumenical theology—a daring enterprise? Perhaps it is so again today. Formerly, almost twenty years ago when our Institute for Ecumenical Research was founded, a Catholic theologian concerned with ecumenical theology was not exactly risking his neck. Then there was a pope who *talked* less about the *Oikoumené* and did more for it, who called to Rome theologians like Yves Congar, Henri de Lubac, Karl Rahner and others, who had been dismissed, exiled or otherwise disciplined under his predecessor. This pope was, of course, John XXIII. There was a Council then which, unlike later synods and ecclesiastical gatherings, did not merely issue documents but created ecumenical facts, roused hopes of overcoming the Catholic-Protestant schism which had lasted 450 years, of overcoming also the East-West schism which had lasted twice as long—precisely because of Roman arrogance in policy matters. This was the Second Vatican Council.

More recently, however, the general weather has fundamentally changed and an ecumenical depression, at present stationary, has spread from Rome out across the Alps and across the Atlantic. Previously the ecumenical barometer had stood for a long time at "changeable." But even immediately after the Council, under Paul VI, strong and particularly curial reactions largely brought to a standstill efforts at ecumenical renewal in the more northerly and westerly regions. Curial cardinals of different nationalities but not of a different mentality strengthened Romanity more than ecumenicity. The Holy Office changed its name and also slightly its method, but scarcely its spirit. At the beginning critical voices like those of Cardinal Lercaro (Bologna), Cardinal Suenens (Malines-Brussels), the Dutch Bishops and some Canadians, were heard from the episcopate, but they soon became silent because they were not supported by the other bishops in Germany, especially in France, and I think also in the United States.

In the post-conciliar period, pope, curia and episcopate were not prepared to admit that important council texts represented a compromise, as for example: stressing afresh episcopal collegiality, but at the same time reinforcing certain papal primacy of jurisdiction in the old absolutist form; permitting certain prayers and hymns in the vernacular, but at the same time confirming Latin as *the* liturgical language of the Western Church; bringing out in the main text the importance of a personal decision of conscience for the most intimate questions of marital morality, but at the same time citing in a footnote that paragraph of the encyclical *Casti connubii* which declares so called "artificial" birth control to be a mortal sin. Nor were pope, curia and episcopate prepared in the post-conciliar period to adopt a clear stand in regard to the justified demands of other Christian churches. Ecumenically important questions concerning birth control, celibacy, divorce and other things, on which discussion had not been permitted at the Council, were later decided—with an appeal to that very Council—in a negative sense. Instead of doing something for ecumenical understanding, there was an appeal again and again for prayer and further study, together with an exchange of ecumenical courtesies.

The consequences of this disastrous post-conciliar development was an increasing polarization at the roots of the Catholic Church itself in a way that had not been known at the time of the epoch-making turning point under John XXIII. Nevertheless, the vernacular language was fully established in the liturgy, the practice of dispensations from the law of celibacy facilitated, and some slight progress was achieved in other respects. A good deal remained undecided. "Let my successor decide these things," was often the motto of this temporizing pope, Paul VI, skeptical in regard to himself and suffering under the far too heavy demands of an office that was to crush his immediate successor, John Paul I, after thirty-three days.

With the entry to office of John Paul II, Karol Wojtyla, a new situation emerged. You may understand it is for me a delicate matter. If I express myself in a concrete way, it is not in order to restrict the problems considered here wholly to that of the papacy or to make a personal issue out of the conflict in which I am myself involved, but to point to the significance of the pope in a church that without him would be as little capable of ecumenical action as the American democracy without its president. This I think we have to take seriously. It soon became clear under this pope that the period of hesitation, of reserve, of cautious tactical procedure, was at an end. On the basis of the first encyclical of this in many ways extraordinary personality, it was possible to hope that the new pontificate would be marked by a freshly adopted Christian humanism, by a new openness, by a new dialogue with the Christian sister-churches, and a new dialogue also with the Jews and with the secular world in general.

Instead, the *ambivalence* of this pontificate was soon made manifest. For me personally the journey of the pope, John Paul II, to the United States and all the pronouncements he made in this country had a decisive influence. A lot of friends had urged me very much earlier to speak out, but after what the pope said in the United States it was clear that I must in conscience speak out and not wait longer. And so my interim balance sheet for the first year of the pontificate of John Paul II, published in the *New York Times* and in other papers over the world, provoked a great deal of indignation and, as far as is known, provided the background for the Roman measures against me.

Today, after two years of this pontificate, I find my total, basically critical impression confirmed by many people. I regret to say this because I expected a different kind of pontificate and I was quite happy when I heard about his election. With all his personal charm, his fascination and his public impact—reminding us of Pius IX and Pius XII—with all his marked openness to the world, his sturdy health, bustle and wanderlust, also with all his very justified social and humanitarian appeals to the First, Second, and Third Worlds (on which I can heartily agree, of course), there is a blatant difference between a *foreign* policy progressive at least in its social aspect and a *home* policy that is both theologically and practically conservative, even, I must say, reactionary. Under this pope, who brought with him from his Polish homeland certain convictions and a particular model of a unitary church, *a period of restoration and reaction* has undoubtedly begun that may have ecumenically devastating consequences if we do not have a change in the coming months. Recently Roman and Catholic have been closely identified again; there has been an insistence on juridical primacy, on literal infallibility and on doctrinal orthodoxy.

The demands of the Council for genuine collegiality and plurality, for dialogue and a hierarchy of truths, are repeated as a matter of theory but played down in practice. In Rome, Vatican II is regarded less as the beginning of a new orientation than as representing the maximum possibility of openness in the church, as a Council whose historical influence must now come to an end. It is thought that the best way to achieve this purpose is by quoting the Council's documents selectively in one's own favor—thus violating at least the spirit, and probably the letter, of Vatican II. Centralism, triumphalism, clericalism, Marianism—often criticized and condemned at the Council—are *joyfully* celebrating a revival, even in new forms of their original status. The integralist slogans, destined for the church itself, include "complete truth of the Catholic faith" (meaning agree on everything), "perfect agreement with the Church's hierarchy" (even where you cannot agree), "return to the old teaching and discipline" (when we already know it is worthless to go back to all that went before the Council). These slogans are often welcomed also by those conservative politicians and journalists inside and outside the Catholic Church who have obviously not the slightest intention of submitting themselves to this strict teaching and discipline.

And, while the pope is traveling around, the Curia rules in Rome. One reactionary document after another, concerning doctrine, liturgy and morality is issued by the Vatican. Women especially—on such issues as ordination of women, nuns in lay clothing, young girls as servers at Mass—have incurred Vatican displeasure. After these come the theologians, many of whom have been openly or secretly disciplined in this past year. Fear and silence are widespread. I mean fear to speak out, because it has become dangerous. And I am an example of what that means. Priests, religious, seminarians—Jesuits especially, and I will not exclude the Dominicans at Berkeley—have been called to order; a halt to laicisation faces priests seeking to marry, the essential distinction between clergy and laity has been given new emphasis. The progressive Dutch episcopate, split up by Rome's appointment of two new bishops, was forced by a Vatican pseudo-synod into total capitulation. Despite all protests, the Roman Curia as a whole, supported by the episcopate in many countries and especially in Germany, is pursuing a policy of repression, leading to tremendous tensions and polarizations within the Catholic Church and probably also within Christianity. But criticism of the pope (wholly constructive in intention and perceptible even in Poland) is regarded by some Catholics as *lèse majesté* and provokes angry letters to the editor, even in supposedly liberal newspapers.

In this situation, therefore, we have to consider who has the highest authority within the Catholic Church. And I cannot imagine that he who has the really highest authority in the Catholic Church, he whom Christianity invokes—I mean Jesus of Nazareth—that if he came again he would himself take up the same attitude today as the Roman authorities in controversial questions. I cannot imagine:

• that *he*, who warned the Pharisees against imposing intolerable burdens on
  human beings' shoulders, would today declare all "artificial" contraception to
  be mortal sin;

- that *he*, who invited failures particularly to his table, would forbid all remarried divorced people ever to approach that Table;
- that *he*, who was constantly accompanied by women who provided for his keep, and whose apostles, with the exception of Paul alone, were and remained each and every one married, would today forbid marriage to ordained men and would forbid ordination to all women, and thus increasingly deprive parishes of their pastors;
- that *he*, who took the adulteress and other sinners under his protection, would pass such harsh verdicts on delicate questions requiring, certainly, discriminating and critical judgment, delicate questions like pre-marital sex, homosexuality and other problems.

Nor can I think that, if he came again today, he would agree in the present ecumenical climate that the difference of denomination should be maintained as an impediment to marriage; that the validity of the ordination and the eucharistic celebration of Protestant pastors should be denied even today after 450 years; that open communion and con-celebration of the eucharist, shared church buildings and parish centers, and ecumenical instruction, should be prevented; that without convincing reasons, attempts should be made to take responsible people—theologians, student chaplains, teachers of religion, catechists, functionaries in Catholic associations, journalists—and tame them with decrees and declarations and, whenever possible, disciplinary and financial measures.

If we want to be Christian, we cannot demand freedom and human rights for the church externally and not grant them internally. And we cannot replace urgently needed reforms within the church by fine words at synods and congresses or at papal demonstrations about the Third World and the North-South conflict. Justice and freedom go together and cannot be preached only when it costs the church and its leaders nothing. Furthermore, we cannot fight about matters of secondary importance and allow both the great Christian conception of the future and the clear priorities to be missed. I have to say this again and again, I think, even if they do not like it in Rome. Ultimately, perhaps, they will understand that it is also a real service to the pope and to the Roman Church because I am not against them. I am for them, but I would like them to follow again the path of John XXIII and not of Pius XII.

Is it surprising, therefore, that—contrary to all official denials on the part of Rome and the bishops—there is talk of "putting the Council on ice," of the failure of the National and Roman synods, of the withdrawal of newly discovered dimensions of church attachment, of retreat into the Roman Catholic ghetto, of a suppression of the new creative freedom and joy in the church, and that there also is talk of an ecumenical standstill in the Roman Catholic institutional church? All this is perceptibly in contrast to the ecumenical awareness at the grass roots level, where it is regarded largely as anachronistic to continue mutually to "ex-communicate" one another in the divided churches, particularly in the face of the vast economic, political and social needs of the First, Second and Third Worlds. We need not *excommunicate* each other again and again; instead we must *communicate*.

All these apprehensions, as far as the *Oikoumené* is concerned, are underlined by the fact that the pope always notes the existence of other churches and their leaders merely marginally, giving the impression that this is more the exercise of a papal duty in a so-called ecumenical age than a serious ecumenical encounter. In Constantinople, once again instead of ecumenical action, a new ecumenical commission was set up. We have several of them already. All the pope's meetings with Protestant Church leaders hitherto on his journeys have been disappointing. In Poland, Ireland and the United States, particularly, these meetings did not improve but rather worsened the ecumenical climate. There were no dialogues, only monologues. As for the leaders of the German Protestant churches, in the land of the origin of the Reformation, they needed several weeks of debate behind the scenes in order to get just one hour to talk with the pope. He has a lot of time in other places, but they must be happy with sixty minutes—if the pope is not late.

Critical challenges, as in the United States or in France, were given no notice; often the pope had no time even to listen to the other church leaders. In Ireland the Presbyterians had to hand the address they had prepared to the papal secretary, and received no answer five months later. In America there were similar embarrassing incidents. I say this so clearly because I hope it will also be heard in Rome. And maybe the same mistakes can be avoided in the pope's journey to Germany, which will be more difficult than the other trips, probably, because people are not expecting positive statements anymore.

Even more serious and disastrous in the long run are many of Rome's doctrinal statements which betray an internal conflict by speaking in one way for ecumenical publicity and in another for Catholic home-consumption. Everything that might seem to be an internal matter for the Catholic Church today has direct ecumenical consequences. By the Roman Decree of 18 December 1979 alone, against my humble self, three central ecumenical demands were condemned:

1. The ecumenical clarification of the problems of infallibility. (I asked only for a *clarification* of the problems and nothing more. I have certain doubts and the right to speak out about them—and I am not alone in the Catholic Church with my doubts. But any consideration of the problem of infallibility was condemned.)
2. The recognition of Protestant order, ordinations, and eucharistic celebrations.
3. The possibilities of an ecumenically comprehensive understanding of the eucharist.

The importance of these three points for the ecumenical climate in particular is obvious. Practical concerns like mixed marriage, children's education, ecumenical religious instruction and inter-communion are imposing a strain on millions of people (in American as elsewhere), and their consideration depends on discussion of these three ecumenical key questions. Consequently, I cannot understand how some Protestant church leaders in Germany can be silent in the face of this new trend in the Catholic Church, as if it would have no adverse effect on ecumenical collaboration. The impression is forced upon us that leading Protestants in Germany and elsewhere today prefer to leave protesting to the critical Catholics. That is not very comfortable, as you can imagine. So I turn now to the second part of my lecture.

Ecumenical Standstill in the Protestant Churches

I do not know enough about the situation in America, but in the German-speaking countries—not only Germany but also Austria and my home country, Switzerland—it seems as though, for the sake of church order and ecumenical peace at all costs, an unholy alliance is being organized between Catholic bishops and their Protestant counterparts. Out of fear of conflict, anxiety about changes in one's own denominational camp and possible loss of denominational property, a disastrous ecumenical spiral of silence is burdening the people in our parishes as it tries to protect the denominational status quo on both sides—Catholic and Protestant. This is what I call an alibi-ecumenism in which the ecclesiastical bureaucracy on each side wants to decide alone what denominational frontiers are to be respected. I think the parish priests know quite well what to do, but they are hindered by high commands. In Germany we often have what you do not have in the United States—confidential agreements in ecumenical fields of activity where it is permitted to do something in the social area but not to touch on the questions of inter-communion, acknowledging other ministries and so on. And I think all this prevents individuals and churches from really coming together, especially on the local level, in those concerns that are decisive in Christian faith and life, in worship and religious instruction.

You will understand that, as an ecumenical theologian, I have to speak frankly to both sides, for at present not everything is ecumenically for the best either in Rome or in Geneva and other ecumenical centers. As a matter of fact, the Roman stagnation has had a paralyzing effect in many ways on the World Council of Churches. In addition, there are personal and financial problems, tensions between those who are mainly theologically and ecclesiastically oriented and the more socio-politically oriented, between the Western industrial nations and the developing countries, tensions between Eastern Orthodox and Western Protestant Churches, a "reconciled unreconciledness" between the denominational world federations—the Lutheran World Federation, the Reformed Alliance and so on.

The World Council of Churches itself, which seems to have learned a great deal from the Vatican, has been troubled (like Martha in the gospel) "about many things," without anyone in the church itself getting involved with sufficient energy to accomplish the original aim, which is still, I believe, the unity of Christendom. A symptom of this, observed with the greatest uneasiness in the Catholic Church, is the depreciation and now, it seems to many, the paralysis of the formerly central Commission for Faith and Church Order by the dismissal of Dr. Thomas Vischer, its secretary and inspirer for many years. At the same time the joint theological commission of the World Council of Churches and the Roman Secretariat for unity seems to be condemned to complete passivity, and the joint committee "for society development and peace" of the World Council of Churches and the Roman Church (SODEPAX), will soundlessly give up its work at the end of the present year without anyone complaining. Hence, unfortunately, unless we are completely deceived, precisely as a result of the Roman policy of obstruction there is an ecumenical stagnation in Geneva, which does not augur much good for the immediate future. And this has a tremendous influence in all the different countries. I recently attended a celebration of the 450th Anniversary of the Augsburg Confession by the

Lutheran churches. The same situation existed. The Catholic bishops and the Lutheran bishops all praised each other and exchanged nice greetings. Even Protestant leaders had absolutely no courage to speak out about the present situation. No word of criticism because this could harm ecumenical relations. That is, I think, really a pseudo-ecumenicism. I come to the third part of my lecture.

The Task of the Theologian

What are we to do about all this? Are we as theologians to haul down the sail and drift merely because everything is calm at the moment? Are we to despair for that reason, give up for that reason? This problem has always existed. How many Catholic theologians at the time of Pius IX (First Vatican Council) faced similar difficulties?

In times of depression, of stagnation, of resignation, the important thing is not to give up, but quietly to seize the initiative for a further positive ecumenical development. "Going My Way," according to a very old film some of you may have seen, can be costly. It was about a Catholic curate having some difficulty with conservative parish priests. Nevertheless, there is ground for hope. Maybe the pope after a time will see that we have to change on certain issues, that we have to speak to each other, to listen to each other maybe. . . . And often popes considered conservative at first ended as liberal ones like John XXIII. And others who started as liberals ended as conservatives. It is a little like American politics. This is a time when we cannot make a definitive judgment in all these matters.

What is more important is that without any spectacular public response and and despite all the impediments created from above, ecumenical understanding continues at the roots of our congregations. It depends still to a great extent on the pastors at the local level and on their real situations—how far they go with ecumenical collaboration or what practice they follow in questions of birth control, admitting divorced people and so on. I know that we have great differences all over the world.

In the service of our congregations, the church at the grass roots level, and also in the service of the *Oikoumené*, the theologian has a task that no priest, no pastor in the parish, no bishop and no pope can take from him or her. I am not saying anything against a special apostolic succession of bishops (and to a certain extent also of priests). This sound Catholic view can well be understood in a deep evangelical Protestant sense. I believe that bishops, and also priests, succeed to the apostles in the mission of founding and governing the churches. But I also insist that this is not the main reason for monopolizing and canalizing God's spirit in the church.

First, it is a basic truth of New Testament church order:

- that all believers are the church and form the people of God;
- that all believers are moved by the spirit and not only some;
- that all in the church have their own charism, their own personal vocations and their special ministries;
- that the church may not be split up under any circumstances into the church teaching and the church taught, into a commanding church and an obeying church, into "clergy" and "laity," merely because there is an official succession of ministries of leadership. We all have to be taught, but all of us also have

something to teach. To divide the church is to act as if we were not all brothers
and sisters under the one Lord, who have to listen together, jointly to obey
God and serve one another.

Second, it is a basic truth especially of the Pauline order that, together with the
apostles, there are the prophets and—admittedly in third place—the teachers or
theologians. In addition to the succession of *apostles*, the special official succession
of church leaders (I agree perfectly with this and support it), there is the succession
of *prophets* and the succession of *teachers* or theologians. No theologian, of course,
should claim to belong to the succession of the Old and New Testament prophets;
fortunately, no university department of theology—not even the Pacific School of
Religion—can train a prophet. More seriously, how could anyone aware of the
almost intolerable burden of the prophet's task even aspire to such a vocation? No,
it is not the succession of the apostles nor that of the prophets, but the succession
of the teachers, of the *didaskaloi*, the *doctores*, to which the theologian may claim
to belong. And with Paul the theologian may certainly raise the provocative question,
"Are *all* teachers?" (1 Cor. 12:29) Paul thinks *not*, and says that "there are varieties of gifts" (1 Cor. 12:4) and that "the Spirit apportions to each one individually
as he wills" (12:11). And in fact "God has appointed in the church first apostles,
second prophets, third teachers" (12:28).

Thus throughout the centuries, in the most varied forms and shapes, in congregations and schools, in hermits' cells and in monasteries and convents, in universities and basis-groups, academically and wholly nonacademically, there have always
been teachers of theology. And from New Testament times, in one way or another
as far as it is possible for human beings, they have carried out their special task:
over and over again, with new means and methods, to transmit, interpret and apply
the original message of Christ. Their *didaskalia*, their teaching office, unlike prophecy, is based not immediately on revelation but on tradition; and, unlike prophecy,
it is less a direct address for the concrete situation than a fundamental interpretation
and instruction, less in the form of an intuitive prophetic appeal than a general
systematic explanation.

There *must* be theology, teaching, in the church. "Woe to me if I do not preach
the gospel," says St. Paul in the First Letter to the Corinthians (9:16). "Woe to
me if I do not teach the truth of the gospel," a teacher in the church might say
today.

Or must critical theologians in the church again remain silent, as they were so
often silent or reduced to silence (and not only in the Catholic Church) as late
as the nineteenth century under Pius X and his anti-modernist purge, and in the
middle of the century under Pius XII and his suppression both of the worker
priests and of leading French theologians? Are the only persons allowed to speak
to be once more the court-theologians whose primary task from the time of Constantine and the courtbishop Eusebius of Caesaria has been to supply their masters
with arguments, texts, and ideology?

No, the call must not go out again: *doctores taceant in ecclesia.* "Let teachers
keep silent in the church." Theologians must not be conformist, but critical;
critical first, certainly, in regard to themselves but also in regard to their own
tradition. For what does a church look like where critical theologians are silent?

What happens to a church in which no one takes the trouble to reflect critically in intellectual honesty on the *good* tradition (for there is also a bad tradition), the *authentic* teaching (there is also a false teaching), the *original* message (there is also a message that is not original)—in a word, on the truth of the gospel which must be brought out again and again from the "there and then" to the "here and now?" This is a theology understood, in Gerhard Ebeling's terms, as a "reflective account rendered on the Christian faith," our common Christian faith, whose task and obligation mean *truthfully* seeking and *telling* the Christian truth. Recognizing this need to seek and tell the truth in truthfulness, I come to the fourth part of my lecture.

The Freedom of Theology

Is it not grotesque, my dear friends, that theology today is again in need of an *apologia*? Theology has to be defended, and curiously enough, not primarily in the face of a secular and often secularist world, but within the church itself. There theology has to be defended against propositions approved by the highest authority. It was to an audience of American professors that John Paul II declared what German cardinals said before in Germany: "The faithful have a right not to be made insecure by theories."

Yet there are those who will ask: "Is not the theory of the task of theology and the theologians put forward here by me *un Catholic*, insofar as it excludes a teaching office of pope and bishops?" I would answer quite directly, "By no means."

First, I have always affirmed the justification of a pastoral office of proclamation, and in this sense I affirmed the necessity in our church of a teaching office, a teaching ministry. I have never denied that.

Second, I have also affirmed the justification of the abbreviative summary articles of faith, or professions of faith; and I have also clearly affirmed the justification of defensive and delimiting articles of faith, that is, of definitions of faith or dogmas. My counter question—if you want my serious interrogation of the Roman authorities—has always concerned only the problem of infallibility of certain propositions; that is, whether such articles of faith, the two as given on the pope and the two on Mary, asserted with an invocation of the Holy Spirit, are bound to be *a priori* "infallibly" true propositions or whether, being human words, they might not perhaps occasionally be false. I never said all this is false. I never said there are not true definitions. I am very much for true definitions. I would have been very happy if, for instance, at the time of Nazism in Germany we could have had true propositions for the Jews from the church bishops or from the Roman Pontiff. We didn't get them because they don't like to make any dangerous remarks in dangerous times.

So, as I say, I am not at all against clear words in the church. I just believe it is a question whether you can invoke the Holy Spirit for certain propositions. We are always happy if they are true. And we hope they are true. But I do not think we have an *a priori* guarantee that they are true. That is the *only* question. But it is a question. Whoever disagrees may disagree, but he or she cannot just say there is no question.

Now, as formerly, I stand by the declaration on "Freedom for Theology"

[Published in *Herder Correspondence* (London, February, 1969)] which emerged
in Tübingen in 1968, directed to Rome signed first by Karl Rahner, Yves Congar,
Edward Schillebeeckx and myself, and eventually by 1,360 Catholic professors of
theology from 53 countries. There we read:

> We firmly uphold and affirm a teaching office (magisterium) of the pope and
> the bishops, an office which is under the word of God and which is there in the
> service of the Church and its proclamation.

But we also read there:

> At the same time, we know that this pastoral office cannot and must not super-
> sede, hamper and impede the teaching task of the theologians as scholars.

Here we reach the sore point. Theology can seek and tell the trugh truthfully
only if it is *free theology*. Twelve years ago all these Catholic theologians felt
compelled,

> in complete, genuine and unambiguous loyalty to the Catholic Church . . . in
> real and sober earnest to point out publicly: the freedom of theologians and
> theology in the service of the Church, regained by Vatican II, must not be
> jeopardized again.

At the same time we were concerned, not only about academic freedom of research
and teaching, but also quite decidedly about the theologically-justified freedom of
a Christian and theologian:

> This freedom is one of the fruits and exigencies of the liberating and redeeming
> message of Jesus himself, and remains a fundamental and essential aspect of the
> freedom of the sons of God in the Church, as preached and defended by Paul.
> All the teachers in the Church must therefore preach and proclaim the word,
> pressing it home on all occasions, convenient or inconvenient, welcome or un-
> welcome.

> But some would say, "Are not then theologians infallible? Can not theologians
> err also?" I would answer with the declaration that was signed by most of my
> Catholic colleagues at Tübingen, also by Professor Joseph Ratzinger, now Cardinal
> Archbishop of Munich and Freising, who has become one of the main opponents
> of my position. At that time we all agreed on the following:

> We are fully aware that we theologians can err in our theology. We are convinced,
> however, that erroneous theological conceptions cannot be rooted out by force.
> In our world they can only be put right and corrected by free and unimpeded
> objective argument and debate among scholars, in which the truth can gain the
> victory through and by itself.

If the warning by the 1,360 Catholic theologians, following on this, had been heeded by Rome and the German Bishops' Conference, we would have been spared a great deal during the past year:

> Any form of inquisition, however subtle, not only harms the development of a sound theology, it also causes irreparable damage to the credibility of the Church as a community in the modern world. For that reason we expect from the pastoral teaching office of the pope and the bishops that it will trust as a matter of course our *sensus ecclesiae*, or loyalty to the Church, and that it will support without prejudice whatsoever our work as theologians for the welfare and well-being of humanity in the Church and in the world. We would like to fulfill our duty, which is to seek the truth and speak the truth, without being hampered by administrative measures and sanctions. We expect our freedom to be respected whenever we pronounce or publish, to the best of our knowledge and in conscience, our well-founded theological convictions. . . .

Many Christians in my country, and, I trust also in this country, are convinced that the call for unity—so that the church can make its contribution in the modern world—has been answered by suggesting a way that they regard as false. "It is wrong," leaders of the German Catholic Youth Association have written, "to think that it is possible to survive the dangers of our time only by internal discipline. If Jesus tells his friends 'He who wants to keep his life will lose it and has already lost it. But he who stakes his life and surrenders it will gain it and has already gained it' (according to John 12:25): this is true equally of his church." We do not want churches for their own sake; we want churches that are, in the words of Cardinal Dopfner, a "sign of the unity of human beings with God and of human beings with one another." The German Catholic Youth leaders say further:

> The way of Jesus, the way of freedom which he followed, was not an inculcation of dogmas and laws, it was an invitation: "Be willing to change, to be continually changing: have the courage to be free and to accept responsibility for your own life and the life of your fellow human beings. God is with you." Jesus gave us an example of what such a life, freely accepted, logically implies. Even if we do not match up to this demand, we cannot do otherwise than apply this standard to our action and to that of the Church as a whole.

This is what I want to do particularly in this church, the Catholic Church to which I belong. For the future of this church and of all the churches, in all my working, thinking and praying, I will trust in him who alone is the true Lord of the church and of all churches. And for that, of course, I also need your help. Thank you.

Historical Roots of Ecumenism in America

Ecumenism did not begin with Vatican II or with Hans Küng's statement of his position to American Christians under the sponsorship of a

Protestant seminary. Before assessing the ecumenical movement in the 1980s, we should review some of its antecedents.

CONGREGATIONAL AND PRESBYTERIAN COOPERATION IN THE NINETEENTH CENTURY

After the Revolutionary War, the migration of settlers, especially New Englanders, into the "Old Northwest" (upstate New York, Ohio, Illinois, Indiana, Minnesota, Wisconsin) provided the occasion for one of the first sustained church union efforts in American religious history, the Plan of Union (1801–1852). This was an effort on the part of the two leading denominations of the Northeast, the Presbyterians and the Congregationalists, to cooperate in the cause of western mission work.

As the two denominations began missionary work on the frontier of western New York, they became increasingly interested in the possibilities of cooperation. As early as 1787, Congregationalist Timothy Dwight, the grandson of Jonathan Edwards and president of Yale, worked in behalf of drawing the General Association of Connecticut into a closer union with the Presbyterian General Assembly. Jonathan Edwards, Jr. (1745–1801), a Connecticut Congregationalist who had been educated at Princeton, was a natural mediator between middle colony Presbyterianism and Congregationalism. Edwards became president of Union College in Schenectady, New York, in 1799. The Connecticut General Association appointed Edwards to a committee that was commissioned to "prepare a report" on the subject of the permanent adjustment of the relations between the two denominations. The report was the celebrated Plan of Union of 1801. The essential thrust of the plan was a comity agreement that allowed Congregational and Presbyterian settlers in each community to establish a congregation and to have a pastor of either denomination.

Document 60

The Plan of Union of 1801

Regulations adopted by the General Assembly of the Presbyterian Church in America, and by the General Association of the State of Connecticut (provided said Assocition agree to them), with a view to prevent alienation, and to promote union and harmony in those new settlements which are composed of inhabitants from these bodies.

1. It is strictly enjoined on all their missionaries to the new settlements, to endeavour, by all proper means, to promote mutual forbearance, and a spirit of accommodation between these inhabitants of the new settlements who hold the Presbyterian, and those who hold the Congregational form of church government.

SOURCE: Reprinted with permission from Williston Walker, *The Creeds and Platforms of Congregationalism* (Philadelphia: Pilgrim Press, 1960).

2. If in the new settlements any church of the Congregational order shall settle a minister of the Presbyterian order, that church may, if they choose, still conduct their discipline according to Congregational principles, settling their difficulties among themselves, or by a council mutually agreed upon for that purpose. But if any difficulty shall exist between the minister and the church, or any member of it, it shall be referred to the Presbytery to which the minister shall belong, provided both parties agree to it; if not, to a council consisting of an equal number of Presbyterians and Congregationalists, agreed upon by both parties.

3. If a Presbyterian church shall settle a minister of Congregational principles, that church may still conduct their discipline according to Presbyterian principles, expecting that if a difficulty arise between him and his church, or any member of it, the cause shall be tried by the Association to which the said minister shall belong, provided both parties agree to it; otherwise by a council, one-half Congregationalists and the other Presbyterians, mutually agreed upon by the parties.

4. If any congregation consist partly of those who hold the Congregational form of discipline, and partly of those who hold the Presbyterian form, we recommend to both parties that this be no obstruction to their uniting in one church and settling a minister; and that in this case the church choose a standing committee from the communicants of said church, whose business it shall be to call to account every member of the church who shall conduct himself inconsistently with the laws of Christianity, and to give judgment on such conduct. That if the person condemned by their judgment be a Presbyterian, he shall have liberty to appeal to the Presbytery; if he be a Congregationalist, he shall have liberty to appeal to the body of the male communicants of the church. In the former case, the determination of the Presbytery shall be final, unless the church shall consent to a farther appeal to the Synod, or to the General Assembly; and in the latter case, if the party condemned shall wish for a trial by a mutual council, the cause shall be referred to such a council. And provided the said standing committee of any church shall dispute one of themselves to attend the Presbytery, he may have the same right to sit and act in the Presbytery as a ruling elder of the Presbyterian church.

The plan was approved by the Presbyterian assembly and was submitted to the Connecticut General Association at its meeting in Litchfield, June 16, 1801. It was ratified with alteration. Later the Congregational Associations of Vermont, New Hampshire, and Massachusetts ratified and supported the plan. Williston Walker writes of the idealism and nascent ecumenism that motivated the makers of this covenant:

> The agreement was entered into with perfect good faith and with entire cordiality on both sides. It was intended to affect only the missionary churches on the frontier of civilization, and the framers seem to have little or no thought that those churches would ever grow to be a great factor in American Christian life, and that what was well enough as an expedient in new communities would have a different aspect when these wilderness plantations grew populous.[13]

[13] Williston Walker, *The Creeds and Platforms of Congregationalism* (Boston: Pilgrim Press, 1893), p. 532.

The long-range effect of the plan was to facilitate the absorption of many Congregational churches into Presbyterianism. Walker estimates that by 1828 the plan had added more than six hundred congregations to the Presbyterian churches in New York, Pennsylvania, and the states and territories lying to the west of them. The Plan of Union ultimately may have transformed over two thousand churches, which were in origin and polity Congregational, into Presbyterian churches.[14] One Congregational minister declared, "They have milked our Congregational cows, but have made nothing but Presbyterian butter and cheese."

Actually it is not a justifiable conclusion that Presbyterians are to be blamed for this consequence of the plan. Presbyterian connectionalism[15] naturally tended to absorb independent congregations. Further, although the denominational consciousness of Congregationalism was relatively weak, that of Presbyterianism was strong and assertive. Donald Yoder offers a positive evaluation of the consequences of the plan:

> Despite its rejection in 1837 by the Old School Presbyterians and in 1852 by the Congregationalists, the Plan of Union accomplished much good on the frontier. For half a century it united at least partially the national evangelistic forces of two of the major Churches in the United States, providing an object lesson of what could be done through concerted action. It led to the further cooperation of the two groups, and others, in the great missionary and benevolent societies. And if the Congregationalists lost out in some areas to their Presbyterian brethren, they did it willingly, preferring a more closely integrated system of church polity than their own afforded.[16]

THE DISCIPLES OF CHRIST

Another contribution to religious unity in America grew out of the milieu of revivalism on the early nineteenth-century frontier. The Disciples of Christ or, as it is perhaps more commonly known today, the Christian Church, was established through the convergence of movements largely generated through the efforts of Barton Stone and Alexander Campbell. It was the first indigenous American ecclesial movement, and, until it was surpassed by the growth of the Mormons, the largest of the "native" American religious groups. It is also important to note that, until recently, the Disciples preferred not to think of themselves as merely one more denomination among the many American sects but as an all-encompassing movement that existed above the sectarian spirit.

[14] Walker, op. cit., pp. 532–533.

[15] Connectionalism refers to the fact that in Presbyterian polity there is a system of "courts" from the congregations through the Presbytery made up of a group of congregations, a Synod composed of Presbyteries, and, finally, a General Assembly; each division of government or "court" has its specified powers; this provides a "connectiveness" and cohesiveness that is impossible in a pattern of church government where each local congregation is independent and autonomous.

[16] Donald Yoder, in Ruth Rouse and Stephen Charles Neill (eds.), A History of the Ecumenical Movement 1517–1948 (Philadelphia: Westminster Press, 1954), p. 234.

One of the first contributory developments to what was to become the Disciples' movement coalesced around the person and work of Barton Warren Stone (1772–1844) and the remarkable revival he led in Cane Ridge, Kentucky, in August of 1801. Stone was a New Light Presbyterian, and he, along with other leaders of the Cane Ridge revival, soon came under the suspicion of Presbyterian leadership for reasons of "loose" churchmanship, low educational standards, and the inclination toward heresy. In 1803 they withdrew from the Synod of Kentucky and formed the Springfield Presbytery. It was not long before the members of the Springfield Presbytery realized that their position was such that it was incongruous for them to be in a "presbytery" at all. Accordingly, in 1804 they published the Last Will and Testament of the Springfield Presbytery. In this document we see a commitment to "union with the body of Christ" for all Christians and a voluntary dissolution of their organization.

Document 61

The Last Will and Testament of the Springfield Presbytery

The Presbytery of Springfield, sitting at Cane-ridge, in the county of Bourbon, being, through a gracious Providence, in more than ordinary bodily health, growing in strength and size daily; and in perfect soundness and composure of mind; and knowing that it is appointed for all delegated bodies once to die; and considering that the life of every such body is very uncertain, do make and ordain this our last Will and Testament, in manner and form following, viz:

Imprimis. We *will*, that this body die, be dissolved, and sink into union with the Body of Christ at large; for there is but one Body, and one Spirit, even as we are called in one hope of our calling.

Item. We *will*, that our *name* of distinction, with its *Reverend* title, be forgotten, that there be but one Lord over God's heritage and his name One.

Item. We *will*, that our power of making laws for the government of the church, and executing them by delegated authority, forever cease; that the people may have free course to the Bible, and adopt *the law of the Spirit of life in Christ Jesus.*

Item. We *will* that candidates for the Gospel ministry henceforth study the Holy Scriptures with fervent prayer, and obtain license from God to preach the simple Gospel, *with the Holy Ghost sent down from heaven*, without any mixture of philosophy, vain deceit, traditions of men, or the rudiments of the world. And let none henceforth take *this honor to himself, but he that is called of God, as was Aaron.*

Item. We *will*, that the church of Christ resume her native right of internal government—try her candidates for the ministry, as to their soundness in the faith, acquaintance with experimental religion, gravity and aptness to teach; and admit

SOURCE: Winfred Ernest Garrison and Alfred T. DeBroot, *The Disciples of Christ: A History* (St. Louis: Christian Board of Publication, 1948), pp. 109–110.

no other proof of their authority but Christ speaking in them. We will, that the church of Christ look to the Lord of the harvest to send forth laborers into his harvest; and that she resume her primitive right of trying those *who say they are apostles and are not.*

Item. We *will*, that each particular church, as a body, actuated by the same spirit, choose her own preacher, and support him by a free will offering, without a written *call* or *subscription*—admit members—remove offences; and never henceforth *delegate* her right of government to any man or set of men whatever.

Item. We *will*, that the people henceforth take the Bible as the only sure guide to heaven; and as many as are offended with other books, which stand in competition with it, may cast them into the fire if they choose; for it is better to enter into life having one book, than having many to be cast into hell.

Item. We *will*, that preachers and people, cultivate a spirit of mutual forbearance; pray more and dispute less; and while they behold the signs of the times, look up, and confidently expect that redemption draweth nigh.

Item. We *will*, that our weak brethren, who may have been wishing to make the Presbytery of Springfield their king, and who know not what is now become of it, betake themselves to the Rock of Ages, and follow Jesus for the future.

Item. We *will*, that the Synod of Kentucky examine every member, who may be *suspected* of having departed from the Confession of Faith, and suspend every such suspected heretic immediately; in order that the oppressed may go free, and taste the sweets of gospel liberty.

Item. We *will*, that Ja_____, the author of two letters lately published in Lexington, be encouraged in his zeal to destroy *partyism.* We will, moreover, that our past conduct be examined into by all who may have correct information; but let foreigners beware of speaking evil of things which they know not.

Item. Finally we *will*, that our *sister bodies* read their Bibles carefully, that they may see their fate there determined, and prepare for death before it is too late.

Springfield Presbytery, }L.S.
June 28th, 1804

Thomas Campbell (1763–1854) and his son Alexander Campbell provided an interesting approach to Christian unity that was peculiarly American. Thomas had been very concerned over religious division in his native Northern Ireland, and he brought this concern to the Presbyterian region of western Pennsylvania in 1807. There he gathered a number of followers into a group that called itself the Christian Association of Western Pennsylvania. To explain his program he published in 1809 a document called the *Declaration and Address*. It is considered one of the classic statements on Christian unity. Campbell's plan for the development of Christian unity was based on a "restoration" of primitive New Testament Christianity. Campbell argued that, by uniting on the fundamentals, the divisiveness of frontier Christianity could be overcome. In the conclusion he wrote:

To prepare the way for a permanent scriptural unity amongst Christians, by calling up to their consideration of fundamental truths, directing their attention to first principles, clearing the way before them by removing the stumbling blocks, the rubbish of ages which has been thrown upon it and fencing it on each side, that in advancing towards the desired object, they may not miss the way through mistake, or inadvertency, by turning aside to the right hand or to the left, is, at least, the sincere intention of the above propositions.[17]

Under the catalytic leadership of yet another Scotsman, Walter Scott (1796–1861), the "Campbellites" and the "Stonites" joined to become the Disciples of Christ in 1832. Although the Disciples' movement eventually became another denomination, there has been a persistent ecumenical witness on the part of the Disciples in both the nineteenth and twentieth centuries. This spirit is rooted in the origin and early years of the denomination.

THE EVANGELICAL ALLIANCE

In the latter part of the eighteenth century, American religious life was characterized by a rather high degree of interdenominational acrimony, the first third of the nineteenth century by a moderation of hatred and suspicion, but, in the years immediately preceding the Civil War, by a resurgence of sectarian bitterness. In 1867 a notable effort toward Christian unity in America was realized with the establishment of the American branch of the Evangelical Alliance.

The Alliance had been constituted in August, 1846, at a remarkable gathering of Protestants that was assembled in Freemasons' Hall in London. Eight hundred "professing Christians," representing fifty-two different denominations, unanimously passed the following resolution:

> The members of this Conference are deeply convinced of the desirableness of forming a confederation on the basis of the great Evangelical principles held in common by them, which may afford opportunity to members of the Church of Christ of cultivating brotherly love, enjoying Christian intercourse, and promoting such other objects as they may hereafter agree to prosecute together. And they hereby proceed to form such a confederation under the name of the *Evangelical Alliance*.[18]

American participation in the international organization was delayed because of the controversy over slavery that occurred in the founding session.

The Alliance sought to promote the interests of a "Scriptural Christianity" against the encroachments of Popery and Puseyism, a perjorative term designating the Anglo-Catholic teachings of the churchman Edward Bouverie Pusey (1800–1882). The Alliance was the only ecumenical organization to arise out of the evangelical awakening of the nineteenth century. It stimulated united prayer observances, worked rigorously on behalf of oppressed religious minorities in European

---

[17]Thomas Campbell, *Declaration and Address*, with an introduction by William Robinson (Birmingham: Berean Press, 1951), p. 17.

[18]*Brief Historical Sketch* [of the Evangelical Alliance] (London, n.d.), p. 4.

countries that had established churches, promoted the study of missions, and encouraged sabbath observance.

THE ECUMENICAL MOVEMENT IN THE TWENTIETH CENTURY

For most chroniclers of the story of ecumenism, the important date in the twentieth-century is the Protestant world missionary conference held in Edinburgh, Scotland, in 1910. The concern of the conference was for the development of a common missionary strategy that would avoid the overlap, duplication, and competition of the past. From this conference, as a result of continuing conversation and follow-up, the International Missionary Council was organized in 1921. For a period of forty years this council functioned to coordinate the activities of the mission groups, to develop corporate strategies, and to think through the meaning of the mission of the church in the modern world.

Another important movement issuing from the Edinburgh Conference was the Life and Work movement. This was an attempt on the part of Protestant and Orthodox churches to discover ways in which they could cooperate in the practical areas of service to the world. Under the leadership of Archbishop Nathan Söderblom (1866–1931) of the Church of Sweden, the famous Life and Work Conference was convened in 1925 in Stockholm. The second important Life and Work Conference was held in Oxford in 1937.

Whereas the Life and Work conferences focused on matters of ethics and socioeconomic concerns, another movement was generated by the Edinburgh Conference, and this was referred to as the Faith and Order movement. This movement concentrated on issues of doctrine and ecclesiastical structure. The historic conference in this movement was the one meeting in Lausanne, Switzerland, in 1927. A second conference was convened in Edinburgh in 1937.

From these two ecumenical movements the World Council of Churches was formed at Amsterdam, Holland, in 1948. The report on the "nature of the Council" included the following remarks:

> The World Council of Churches is composed of churches which acknowledge Jesus Christ as God and Savior. They find their unity in Him. They have not to create their unity; it is the gift of God. But they know that it is their duty to make common cause in the search for the expression of that unity in work and life.
> The Council desires to serve the churches. . . . But the Council is far from desiring to usurp any of the functions which already belong to its constituent churches, or to control them, or to legislate for them. . . .
> The Council disavows any thought of becoming a single unified church structure independent of the churches which have joined in constituting the Council.[19]

[19] As quoted in Robert McAfee Brown, *The Ecumenical Revolution* (Garden City, N.Y.: Doubleday, 1967), p. 36.

Successive World Council meetings have been held at Evanston, Illinois, 1954; New Delhi, India, 1961; and Uppsala, 1968.

The ecumenical movement, beginning with Edinburgh in 1910 and followed by its successive conferences up to the founding of the World Council of Churches, was one in which American Protestant and Eastern Orthodox leadership participated to a significant degree. There is little danger in overestimating its influence on two generations of American Christian leaders who attended these international conferences.

Nationally, there have been two councils that have been organized to further cooperative efforts among American Christians. In 1908 the Federal Council of the Churches of Christ in America was organized in Philadelphia "to promote the spirit of fellowship, service, and cooperation." The Federal Council was started by denominational representatives who were strong proponents of the social gospel movement. Throughout its history it maintained a tradition of outspoken liberal advocacy on social issues.

The Federal Council was succeeded by the National Council of the Churches of Christ in 1950. The National Council actually was an organizational consolidation combining the Council of Church Boards of Education, the Federal Council of Churches, the Foreign Missions Conference of North America, the Home Missions Council, the International Council of Religious Education, the Missionary Education Movement, the United Council of Church Women, and the United Stewardship Council. Although the Federal Council was essentially a Protestant union, largely a successor to the Evangelical Alliance, the National Council had been transformed into an agency that included in its membership a variety of ethnic branches of the "ancient Eastern churches."

Other councils of churches have been established on the basis of opposition to the National and World Councils of Churches. In 1941 Carl McIntire, an independent and fundamentalist Presbyterian minister, organized the American Council of Christian Churches as a group that opposed the "apostasy" of the Federal Council of Churches. The ACCC is "pro-Gospel and anti-modernist." When the World Council of Churches was formed, McIntire countered with the establishment of the International Council of Christian Churches. The National Association of Evangelicals was organized in 1942 as a conservative effort to organize the Protestant churches opposed to the church unity efforts of the World and National Councils of Churches. In addition to these, other Protestant associations have been organized around the purpose of opposition to the social pronouncements of the National Council of Churches.[20] This aspect of ecumenism is to some degree a perpetuation of the old Modernist-Conservative controversy.

---

[20]See Edgar C. Bundy, *Collectivism in the Churches* (Wheaton, Ill.: The Church League of America, 1958); also "Billy James Hargis" in James Morris, *The Preachers* (New York: St. Martin's, 1973), pp. 257–314.

ECUMENISM IN THE 1980s

The difficulties of ecumenism in recent years are well documented. Councils of churches in many major metropolitan areas have folded. Enthusiasm for interdenominational liturgies such as the annual Week of Christian Unity in January has waned. There was a resurgence of denominationalism in the 1970s, and most main-line religious groups focused on their own institutional priorities. The Vatican, as we have seen in Hans Küng's address, has pulled back from programmatic involvements with the World Council of Churches.

COCU's problems have been both visible and symptomatic. The original plan for union had two flaws: (1) it tried to bring about merger from the top down and (2) it underestimated the nontheological reasons for division among the churches. Albert C. Outler's comments concerning COCU were reminders that religious organizations are as subject to the vices and virtues of institutionalism as any other groups. At the very time when flexibility, originality, and creativity are most needed, bureaucrats can and do exhibit what Thorstein Veblen called a "trained incapacity" to recognize the need for innovative response.

There is another problem which is more basic than institutionalism as an obstacle to church unity. The ecumenical movement was by and large a movement led by theological liberals who represented main-line denominations. As we have seen, Hans Küng has more in common with progressive Protestants than he does with conservative Roman Catholics. In every main-line denomination there are those persons who are probably in closer fellowship with members of another denomination than they are with their own denominational counterparts. George W. MacRae, a Jesuit priest and professor at the Harvard Divinity School, has observed:

> In the decade of the eighties and beyond, the crucial alignment of Christians will no longer be Protestant and Orthodox vs. Catholic, or if you prefer Protestant vs. Catholic and Orthodox, but rather liberal—in the sense of accepting critical methods and their consequences—vs. fundamentalist, across any and all denominational lines. Ecumenism as it is currently practiced is confined to the former.[21]

For many years, conservatives have attacked the World Council of Churches and the National Council of Churches. One of the most recent criticisms has come from Ernest W. Lefever, who argues that the WCC has become a sounding board for the Third World since 1966.[22] Lefever feels that the WCC gives too much encouragment to the socialistic tendencies of the Third World.

[21] Geo. W. MacRae, "Convocation 1980: Reflections on Ecumenism," *Harvard Divinity Bulletin,* Vol. XI, No. 1 (September–October 1980), p. 12.

[22] Ernest W. Lefever, *Amsterdam to Nairobi: The World Council of Churches and the Third World,* forward by George F. Will (Washington, D.C.: Ethics and Public Policy Center, Georgetown University, 1979).

Carl F. H. Henry points to the same division as a key issue in the 1980s. With the attempted rehabilitation of COCU, Henry predicts that

> discontented evangelicals in theologically pluralistic mainline denominations will more seriously consider broader evangelical liaison either with consistent evangelicals from other mainline denominations or with evangelicals in the newer and (usually) smaller denominations committed as denominations to evangelical positions. Both evangelical and nonevangelical crosswinds are currently too confusing, however, to give a clear signal about any ecclesiastical realignment."[23]

Despite the realities of institutional intransigency and theological crosswinds, the fruits of the ecumenical movement are also real. In Vatican II, the Catholic Church emerged for the first time as a truly ecumenical church, gathering native church leaders from all over the world—the whole inhabited earth. The same global representation is now a reality in World Council of Churches meetings. The church is no longer a Western—that is, European and North American—church. It is a world church. The Catholic theologian Karl Rahner maintains that Roman Catholic Christianity is about to experience a transformation as great as the change that occurred when Christianity was transformed from a small Palestinian sect to a major Greco-Roman religion.[24] This transformation also confronts ecumenical Protestantism.

There are other recent accomplishments on the part of ecumenical bodies. In the summer of 1979, the World Council of Churches convened a noteworthy conference on "Faith, Science, and the Future" at the Massachusetts Institute of Technology which focused on the vision of a just, participatory, and sustainable society. On the grass-roots level, hundreds of ecumenical experiments are happening throughout the country. Joint liturgies, common social ministries, shared professional staff, and cooperative Christian education programs comprise the ecumenical movement on main street.

Interfatih Cooperation in America

NATIVISM AND ANTI-CATHOLICISM IN THE NINETEENTH CENTURY

During the first half of the nineteenth century an intense and anti-Catholic nativism surfaced in the United States and ushered in a period of violence and religio-ethnic discord that threatened to reshape even the political structure of America. The obvious occasion for nativism was the growth of Roman Catholicism to the point where it became the largest single church in America. Protestant American suspicion of Catholicism was deeply rooted in Puritanism, nourished by Enlighten-

---

[23]Carl F. H. Henry, "The Concerns and Considerations of Carl F. H. Henry," *Christianity Today*, Vol. XXV, No. 5 (March 13, 1981), p. 19.
[24]Karl Rahner, *Theological Studies*, Vol. 40, 1979, pp. 716–27.

ment prejudices regarding medieval superstition, and brought to full force by frontier evangelicalism.

Added to these religious prejudices were the social stresses occasioned by increasing numbers of immigrants who settled in the large cities, the broadening political base that threatened the reigning political tradition, and the competition engendered by the newly arrived "cheap labor."

There was in America what Sydney Ahlstrom has called a Protestant "quasi-establishment" that enjoyed a peak strength between 1815 and 1860. In describing this establishment, Ahlstrom writes, "Its moral attitudes and basic teachings were honored by lawmakers, and dominated newspapers and textbooks. The faculties and curriculum of the public schools and even state universities were molded according to its specifications."[25]

In the third decade of the nineteenth century a type of anti-Catholicism manifested itself in action as well as in ideology. Many leaders of Protestantism, such as Horace Bushnell and Lyman Beecher, were spokesmen for this position. As we have seen, the Evangelical Alliance received much of its initial support from those who were motivated by anti-Catholic convictions. Special nativist journals were founded and many evangelical periodicals gradually printed more and more material of an anti-Catholic nature.

One of the more vulgar literary efforts was the "horror literature" that attempted to describe the atrocities of Roman Catholic monastic establishments. Frequently the material was as salacious as it was inaccurate, but it was accepted by the Protestant establishment.[26]

One of the most unhappy events in the American religious memory is the burning down of the Ursuline convent in Charlestown, Massachusetts, on August 11, 1834. The men who were hired for arson were acquitted and accorded hero status by Boston's Protestant working class.

Nativist sentiment found political expression in the establishment of a secret "patriotic" society in 1849 which named itself the Order of the Star-Spangled Banner. The order was a "lodge" for which only American-born Protestants, who had neither Catholic wives nor parents, were eligible. After elevation to a certain degree, a member was qualified to be an officer in the organization and to be sponsored by the order as a candidate for public office. Because of the order's elaborate secrecy and frequent response, "I know nothing," it was popularly called the Know-Nothing party.

In the period of 1850–1855 the Know-Nothing party realized impressive election victories, particularly in Massachusetts. But the rise of the Republican party and the eclipsing of Protestant-Roman Catholic tensions by the slavery controversy led to a swift demise of the Know-

[25] Ahlstrom, *A Religious History of the American People* (New Haven: Yale University Press, 1972), p. 558.
[26] See Ray A. Billington, *The Protestant Crusade, 1800–1860* (New York: Macmillan, 1938), p. 108.

Nothing party by 1856. Even though nativist anti-Catholic feeling cooled throughout the Civil War, it never completely disappeared and was to erupt again in later periods of American religious history.

TWENTIETH-CENTURY ANTI-CATHOLICISM

In the third and fourth decades of the twentieth century, American Protestants were forced to make a painful adjustment to Roman Catholic growth. During the last half of the nineteenth century the Catholic population in America had increased from 2 million to over 10 million. By World War I it was over 17 million.

After World War I American nativism once again manifested itself, this time in the form of the revival of the Ku Klux Klan. The anti-Catholicism of the Klan in these years was a more central and constant motif of its party line than its anti-Negro outlook. There can be little doubt that among the sources that provided recruiting opportunities for the Klan was Protestant fundamentalism.[27] By the late 1920s the strength of the Klan was in decline.

The next nationally focused expression of anti-Catholicism manifested itself at the time of the 1928 presidential campaign. New York Governor Al Smith was the Catholic candidate nominated by the Democratic party. Anti-Catholic propaganda was widely distributed in 1926. Methodist Bishop Adna Leonard of Buffalo purportedly said that "no Governor can kiss the papal ring and get within gunshot of the White House."[28] The bishop was concerned that America should "remain Protestant." That the secular press also focused so much attention on the issue of Smith's Catholicism indicated how widespread America's concern for the growth of Catholic power had become. Governor Smith was prodded into making the most explicit statement regarding his religious beliefs that a presidential candidate had ever had to make. The statement, offered in the form of an open letter published in the *Atlantic Monthy,* concluded:

> I summarize my creed as an American Catholic. I believe in worship of God according to the faith and practice of the Roman Catholic Church. I recognize no power in the institutions of my Church to interfere with the operations of the Constitution of the United States or the enforcement of the law of the land. I believe in the absolute freedom of conscience for all men and in equality of all churches, all sects, and all beliefs before the law as a matter of right and not as a matter of favor. I believe in the absolute separation of Church and State and in the strict enforcement of the provisions of the Constitution that Congress shall make no law respecting an establishment of religion or prohibiting the free exercise thereof. I believe that no tribunal of any church has any power to make any decree of force in the law of the land, other than to establish the status of its own communicants within its own church. I believe in the right of every parent

[27] John Hingham, *Strangers in the Land: Patterns of American Nativism, 1860–1925* (New Brunswick, N. J.: Rutgers University Press, 1955), p. 293.

[28] Edmund A. Moore, *A Catholic Runs for President: The Campaign of 1928* (New York: Ronald Press, 1956), pp. 47–48.

to choose whether his child shall be educated in the public school or in a religious school supported by those of his own faith. I believe in the principle of noninterference by this country in the internal affairs of other nations and that we should stand steadfastly against such interference by whomsoever it may be urged. And I believe in the common brotherhood of man under the common fatherhood of God.

In this spirit I join with fellow Americans of all creeds in a fervent prayer that never again in this land will any public servant be challenged because of the faith in which he has tried to walk humbly with his God.[29]

Linked to Smith's Catholicism were his alleged connections with Tammany Hall and his stand in behalf of the repeal of the Prohibition laws. Although most Americans did not go so far as to label him a "rum-soaked Romanist," Smith's religion, his accent, and his anti-Prohibition stand were enough to make him unacceptable to American nativist sentiment.

After the 1928 campaign—indeed, in many ways as a result of the campaign—efforts toward interfaith understanding were initiated by the responsible leadership of America's three major religious groups. In 1928 the National Conference of Christians and Jews was established. The conference carried on a number of activities, perhaps the most notable of which was the establishment of Brotherhood Day (later to become National Brotherhood Week). The 1930s, by and large, were characterized by the absence of the open religious conflict that characterized the 1920s.

In the 1940s, however, a new era of conflict erupted. By the fifth decade of this century the Roman Catholic Church in America had a new sense of security and an attitude of aggressive confidence. Many Protestant leaders became concerned about an alleged effort of the Catholic hierarchy to "win America." Issues over federal aid to public and parochial schools continued to be aired throughout the 1940s. In 1948 the organization Protestants and Other Americans United for the Separation of Church and State (POAU) was born.

The organization of POAU brought anti-Catholicism to a new level of respectability in the United States. Lerond Curry writes of the contrast between the anti-Catholicism of the 1920s and that of the 1940s:

> The birth of POAU epitomized the main distinction between the Protestant reaction to Catholic growth in the 1920's and Protestant reaction to the new religious pluralism of the 1940's. In the former case, a nonecclesiastically based reactionary leadership, often lacking extensive formal education, gave rise to physical force in groups such as the Ku Klux Klan. In the latter case an ecclesiastically oriented, highly educated leadership skilled with words and phrases, brought about a manifesto and an apparently sophisticated organization. In essence, POAU was a nationwide admission that Catholicism had gained enormous strength in America and was fast becoming an influence equal to that of Protes-

---

[29] Alfred E. Smith, "Catholic and Patriot: Governor Smith Replies," *Atlantic Monthly*, Vol. 139 (May 1927), p. 728.

tantism. Had POAU's leaders felt otherwise, they would never have founded the organization in the first place.[30]

A person who intensified anti-Catholic sentiment in America was Paul Blanshard, who had been a Congregationalist minister and a State Department official of some reputation. Blanshard's book, *American Freedom and Catholic Power,* published in 1949, created a great deal of public controversy by boldly expressing the fears and anxieties of much of non-Roman Catholic America. The following document is excerpted from the concluding chapter of Blanshard's controversial book.

Document 62

From "Tolerance, Appeasement and Freedom" by Paul Blanshard

The American Catholic problem is this: What is to be done with a hierarchy that operates in twentieth-century America under medieval European controls? We have reviewed the major facts which seem to demonstrate that many of the hierarchy's social and political policies are incompatible with Western democracy and American culture. Many liberal Catholics are in essential agreement with this analysis of the problem and feel that their Church must be rescued from an authoritarian-minded hierarchy.

What policy should non-Catholics adopt in facing this situation? Is it possible to find a basis for unity or a working plan for co-operation with the Catholic hierarchy? Is compromise desirable in order to avoid the bitterness and social waste of religious conflict?

There is no doubt that most non-Catholic Americans want co-operation among all religious groups and dread the effects of sectarian bickering. They feel that any division of the nation into hostile factions is an injury to all citizens. In spite of the Catholic hierarchy's official intolerance and separatism, many liberals would make almost any compromise with the hierarchy which would lead to the give-and-take of mutual adjustment.

Unfortunately, the whole history of the Roman organization in the United States indicates that co-operation is not feasible in the major areas of Catholic authority. The Church co-operates gladly with civic and military power, but it refuses to yield a single inch in compromising its claims to absolute supremacy in religious, educational and moral life. Its rigidity of doctrine and discipline is as unmistakable today as it was when the Reformation split the Christian world in the sixteenth century. The hierarchy has rejected all co-operation based on equality and mutual self-respect.

SOURCE: Paul Blanshard, *American Freedom and Catholic Power* (Boston: The Beacon Press, 1949), Chap. 13, Copyright,©1949, 1958 by Paul Blanshard. Reprinted by permission of McIntosh and Otis, Inc. Although the essay is written in the present tense, it describes conditions at the middle of the twentieth century.

[30] Lerond Curry, *Protestant-Catholic Relations in America: World War I Through Vatican II* (Lexington: University Press of Kentucky, 1972), p. 57.

The story of non-Catholic attempts to co-operate with Rome is long and tragic. Eager Christian idealists, visualizing the glories of a united Christendom, have again and again put their pride in their pockets and made humble advances to Rome in order to find a basis for compromise between the Roman and non-Roman branches of the faith.

Can the Catholic problem in America be met by the formula of limited co-operation and avoidance of the main areas of conflict? One organization in America, the National Conference of Christians and Jews, is operating on that assumption. It is a tripartite body of Protestants, Catholics, and Jews with a membership of some 160,000, offices in sixty-two American cities, joint committees in 280 communities and a proposed budget of $3,500,000 a year. It has grown rapidly in recent years and has received much favorable publicity in the American press. It attempts to operate entirely on the level of the *status quo,* never questioning the fundamental doctrines of its three constituent religions.

The Catholic Church has given relatively little active support to this movement, although the hierarchy in seventy-five dioceses has announced its willingness to permit Catholics as individuals to take part in its activities. In twenty-five dioceses the bishops are openly opposed to the Conference, and in twenty-five other dioceses they are officially "neutral." The *American Ecclesiastical Review,* in September, 1948, warned Catholics against the organization because it held school meetings in which ministers, priests and rabbis appeared on the same platform and spoke of "the common positive elements of all the faiths." Catholics were reminded that they must oppose such indifferentism and "defend the basic truth that there can be only one true religion, and that is Catholicism."

The Conference blandly ignores these attacks and acts as if devout Roman Catholics could be full fledged, bona fide members of the triple alliance. The few Catholic leaders who actively co-operate with the Conference are given unusual publicity, and the public impression created by the publicity is that the Catholic Church believes in the same kind of interdenominational co-operation that is endorsed by liberal Protestants and Jews. The Conference, of course, never criticizes the Roman Catholic Church for intolerant and separatist policies. The official who has charge of the organization's activities in the fields of the press, radio, motion pictures and advertising is a Catholic who was formerly secretary of the National Council of Catholic Men.

The organization's most conspicuous activity for fifteen years has been the promotion of "American Brotherhood Week," a concentrated campaign period during which subscriptions are solicited for interfaith work with the commitment: "I pledge allegiance to this basic ideal of my country—fair play for all. I pledge unto my fellow Americans all of the rights and dignities I desire for myself."

No one can doubt the high motives of the Conference's leaders. The question that honest critics are bound to ask about such a movement is whether it has a moral right to ignore the discriminatory practices of the Catholic hierarchy while conferring upon the hierarchy the protective coloration of "fair-play" slogans. The Conference is extremely vigorous in criticizing anti-Semitism in Europe as well as in the United States, but it never includes in its literature or speeches any criticism of the basic anti-Semitism of priestly doctrine. It is true that Pius XI deplored anti-

Semitism and said that "spiritually we are Semites"; and it is true also that Catholic anti-Semitism is only one feature of a large discriminatory program. But it is anti-Semitism nevertheless. The hierarchy teaches Catholic children (1) that they should not marry Jews (Canon 1070); (2) that they must not go to school with Jews in a neutral atmosphere (Canon 1374); and (3) that they must not read any Jewish literature that states the case for Jewish as against Catholic faith (Canon 1399). The fact that the Catholic hierarchy teaches the same discrimination against Protestant activity, with only a slight modification, does not alter the fundamental fact of the clergy's anti-Semitism. It only proves that the hierarchy is bigoted in regard to both Protestantism and Jewry. The Church did not drop the phrase "perfidious Jews" from the translation of its Good Friday prayers until 1948.

The pledge of the National Conference of Christians and Jews offers "unto my fellow Americans all of the rights and dignities I desire for myself," but the Conference makes no attempt to induce its Catholic members to keep that pledge in intermarriage. A Protestant bride, marrying a Catholic groom, is not given the same "rights and dignities" to bring up her children in her own faith. Likewise, as I have pointed out in the chapter on censorship, the Conference itself is defeated in its attempts to develop mutual understanding between faiths by the exchange of representative literature of each faith. The distinctively Jewish and Protestant books advertised by the Conference in its "Religious Book List" may not be read by Catholics, but the public is not told of this censorship; nor has the Conference ever challenged the narrow dictum of the hierarchy on this point. Instead, the Conference has quietly surrendered the enforcement of its fair-play pledge in this area, and has broken down its lists of religious books into four groups, Protestant, Jewish, Catholic and "Goodwill Books for All." The goodwill books, approved by an interfaith committee, are subject to Catholic veto, and any Catholic may read them without endangering his soul. Protestant and Jewish readers are encouraged to read the books on all four lists; Catholics are forbidden to read any but the books on their own and the goodwill list.

Thus the whole underlying concept of the free exchange of ideas between the three faiths is vitiated, while the Conference officials remain silent. The casual reader of the organization's literature is not told that Catholics are forbidden to read the Jewish and Protestant lists, and he would naturally infer from the publication of the tripartite list of titles in a single cover that Catholic authorities give complete freedom for cultural reciprocity in this matter.

Those who have followed my analysis of the Catholic problem thus far will agree that it is already too late to solve the problem by passive measures. The Catholic hierarchy is not passive. It is well organized and well regimented, and it uses astutely the power that it possesses over a nominal American Catholic population of twenty-six million. It seeks to impose its own social, political and cultural program upon the American community in the name of religion, although a large part of the program has no necessary connection with religion.

It seems clear to me that there is no alternative for champions of traditional American democracy except to build a resistance movement designed to prevent the hierarchy from imposing its social policies upon our schools, hospitals, government and family organization. It is scarcely necessary to say that a resistance movement can have no place for bigots or for the enemies of the Catholic *people*. Nor can it have any place for those who would curtail the rights of the Catholic Church as a *religious* institution. Its sole purpose should be to resist the antidemocratic social policies of the hierarchy and to fight against every intolerant or separatist or un-American feature of those policies.

Where should such a resistance movement begin? I would not presume to answer that question if the answers were not more or less self-evident. I think it should not begin with any one class of people, with clergymen or the "unchurched" or business men. It should begin in the minds of all democratic-minded Americans, Catholic and non-Catholic, who appreciate the danger to our institutions inherent in the hierarchy's policies, and who are resolved to resist without compromising or evasion. The will to defend American freedom from a danger that can no longer be ignored is more important than the method of resistance that may be adopted.

Such a resistance movement should base its activities upon certain broad general principles that will enlist the service of high-minded men of every church and of no church. Its platform of principles and policies might well include certain major objectives in the fields of medicine and general welfare, culture and information, politics and law.

In the field of medicine and welfare, a resistance-movement platform should include the right of every American family to secure information about birth control either from a family physician or from a properly staffed clinic. It should oppose all discrimination against non-Catholic clergymen and doctors in Catholic hospitals. It should resist any solicitation of funds from non-Catholics for Catholic hospitals, unless written assurances are given to contributors that both the surgical and the religious practices of non-Catholic professional persons will be permitted on the same basis as approved Catholic practice. As a matter of public policy such a platform should include a provision opposing the licensing by the state of any medical school in which teachers or priests teach the homicidal doctrine that the life of a mother in childbirth must always be sacrificed in order to avoid therapeutic abortion. The platform should oppose every attempt by the hierarchy to suppress scientific education concerning sexual problems and venereal disease.

In the field of culture and information, the platform should stand for the American public school, from kindergarten through college, as the foundation of American democracy. It should oppose the use of public funds for salaries, textbooks, bus transportation or other routine services for all nonpublic schools. It should favor state laws requiring equivalent training for Catholic parochial-school teachers and public-school teachers. It should favor continuous and scientific inspection of all parochial schools to see that the standard requirements of the state are maintained, that classes are taught in the English language and that textbooks do not distort history, science and sociology in an un-American manner for the benefit of the hierarchy. It should favor the exclusion from public classrooms of all teachers who wear distinctively religious costumes. It should oppose all organized denominational censorship of press, screen and radio; and champion actively those newspapers and magazines that have the good old American courage to treat Catholic policies, personalities and derelictions with impartial candor.

In the field of politics and law, the platform should favor "a wall of separation between church and state," and make it real with no compromise. It should oppose the sending of a formal or informal ambassador to the Vatican, or the holding of any official political conferences with the Papacy. It should favor the registration of all Roman Catholic higher officials operating in the United States under the provisions of the Foreign Agents Registration Law until such time as these higher officials are chosen by the Catholic people of the United States. It should resist the appointment or election of Catholic judges in all states where sterilization laws, applied to the unfit, are on the statute books, unless those Catholic judges publicly repudiate their Roman directives to defy such laws. It should favor the careful review of all tax-exempt real-estate holdings of Catholic bishops in the United States in order to make certain that only property used directly for religious, educational and charitable purposes is exempt from taxation.

Can a resistance movement with such a platform avoid narrow partisanship? Can it challenge the antidemocratic policies of the Catholic people? Can it discriminate between an enemy of American freedom and the victims of the enemy?

Frankly, I do not know. Inherent in every vital social movement are the forces that may pervert and destroy it. Even the most idealistic association of free people is subject to exploitation. Extremists often begin by opposing a man's ideas and end by hating the man himself. There is no doubt that any resistance movement against the policies of the Catholic hierarchy in this country would include some extremists of the type who have made anti-Catholicism a national disgrace in the past.

The danger of such corruption and perversion of any resistance movement must be faced squarely by democratic-minded Americans. In cities where ethnic and national distinctions coincide with religious divisions, it is almost inevitable that any defense against priestly policy will be treated by Catholics as an "attack" upon the Catholic community itself. The identification of honest criticism with religious bigotry is exactly what the Catholic hierarchy wants. It can maintain its hold upon democratic-minded Catholics just so long as it can persuade them that it speaks for *them* against their enemies.

At least once in our history the American people have thrown off an alien system of control without losing their moral perspective or their sense of respect for their opponents. In the days of the American Revolution there were some patriots who lost their emotional balance and began hating Englishmen as Englishmen. Most Americans knew that they were fighting not Englishmen as such but an undemocratic system of alien control. When the crisis had passed, the American and British people soon realized that their common purposes far outweighed their incidental disagreements. As the years passed, two great peoples grew closer together because they shared a common heritage. The analogy is not exact, but it contains a suggestion and a hope for the solution of the Catholic problem in the United States.

The move toward rapprochement between American Roman Catholics and non-Catholics experienced in the 1960s could not have been predicted by the mood of the late 1940s and early 1950s. Much of it must be attributed to the Roman Catholic Church's movement away from Counterreformation defensiveness to a more open and confident willingness to engage in dialogue. The event that communicated this change in attitude was Vatican II. The achievement of a new degree of maturity between American Catholics and non-Catholics was symbolized by the election of John F. Kennedy as the first Roman Catholic President in 1960.

Although the 1960 campaign was not without some incidence of concern over Kennedy's Catholicism, it was remarkably free of the bitterness of the 1928 campaign. Kennedy confronted the issue in a forthright manner by arranging to appear before a meeting of the Greater Houston Ministerial Association. This body had in its membership a significant number of conservative Protestant leaders. In his prepared speech as well as in his answer to questions Kennedy expressed a strict allegiance to the principle of separation of church and state. His remarks included the following statement:

> I believe in an America that is officially neither Catholic, Protestant, nor Jewish—where no public official either requests or accepts instruction on public policy from the Pope, the National Council of Churches or any other ecclesiastical source—where no religious body seeks to impose its will directly or indirectly upon the general populace or the public acts of its officials—and where religious liberty is so indivisible that an act against one church is treated as an act against all.
>
> For a while this year it may be a Catholic against whom the finger of suspicion is pointed; in other years it has been, and may someday be again, a Jew—or a Quaker—or a Unitarian—or a Baptist. It was Virginia's harrassment of Baptist preachers, for example, that led to Jefferson's statute of religious freedom. Today I may be the victim—but tomorrow it may be you—until the whole fabric of our harmonious society is ripped apart at a time of great national peril.[31]

JEWS IN AMERICA AND ANTI-SEMITISM

As we have learned in Chapter 5, the first mass migration of Jews to America began in 1836, and almost all of these immigrants came from German states. The final large-scale Jewish immigration to America occurred from 1881 through the early 1920s. In sharp contrast to the earlier immigration of German Jews, this was a migration of eastern European Jews. Unlike their immigrant precursors, the eastern European Jews were religiously orthodox and were practitioners of a Judaism that comprehended and permeated the whole of their lives. Further, there was a strong ethnic identity because eastern European Jews had not been accustomed to the homogeneous society that had characterized life in Germany. They had little concept of what middle-class social status and possible equality could mean. These Jews tended to form a proletariat that was more vulnerable to radicalism—socialism, anarchism, and various versions of Zionism. The established American Jewish community distrusted both the religious orthodoxy and the secular radicalism of the immigrants.

For the Jewish American, life as a member of a minority group has been, on the whole, free of the persecution that Judaism has experienced in other times and places. This is not to say, however, that life

---

[31] *The New York Times,* September 13, 1960.

for the American Jew has been free from various forms of anti-Semitism. In his book *A Jew in Christian America,* Arthur Gilbert reviews the history of anti-Semitism in the United States.

Document 63 _____

From "Anti-Semitism in the United States" by Arthur Gilbert

Shocked by the evidence everywhere around him of religious intolerance, Thomas Jefferson early in 1776 bitterly wrote:

Why have Christians been distinguished above all people who have ever lived for persecutions? Is it because it is the genius of their religion? No. Its genius is the reverse. It is the refusing of toleration to those of different opinion which has produced all the bustles and wars on account of religion.

Jefferson at that moment was being quite critical. The truth is that Christianity has inspired men to glorious examples of sacrificial love for one another and for that purpose they have journeyed even to the darkest ends of the earth. It is also the truth that Christians have behaved scandalously toward each other and particularly toward the Jew, whose presence in Christian civilization remains a disturbing phenomenon. One can discover among Christians both those who hate their brother and those who have learned that the proper service of God requires the love of their neighbor.

In order to justify their hatred and to clothe themselves in sanctity, anti-Semites in the United States, like anti-Semites everywhere, have invoked particular aspects of the Jewish-Christian relationship—the role of Jews at Calvary, their decisive rejection of Jesus as the Christ, and Jewish insistence on maintaining a distinctive group identity. But a review of American history reveals also that anti-Semitism partakes of many of the same qualities that are present in any form of inter-group prejudice; in fact, it is helpful to realize that some of the same secular purposes and methods involved in the Catholic-Protestant conflict and then the Jewish-Christian antagonism are now also evident in the struggle between racial-segregationists and Negroes. Hatred, no matter against whom it is directed, must ultimately produce within the bigot the same irrationality, paranoiac belief that a conspiracy is at work, close-mindedness and readiness to use violence, that we have witnessed throughout all our history.

In assessing anti-Semitism in the United States, therefore, I wish to underscore two paradoxes: (1) There have been periods of American history when Jews were confronted by Christians both as enemy and as friend. (2) As a victim of prejudice, the Jew has suffered not only because he was a Jew, but also because he was a member of a weak minority group and, therefore, the object of political, economic, and psychological manipulation no different from that suffered by other minorities.

The answer to the problem of anti-Semitism requires, therefore, a more sophisticated religious commitment, sensitivity to the particular historic factors involved in Jewish-Christian relationship, and finally, an active participation in every effort to eradicate discrimination in American society by strengthening our democracy.

It is impossible in this brief review to provide a detailed account of Jew-hatred in the United States. The following illustrations indicate however, that at last we have reached the point in American history where we can dare hope that discrimination will be brought to an end—if only there be the will!

The first settlement of Jews in the United States . . . consisted of refugees from the Spanish Inquisition in Brazil. Fleeing Catholic oppression, they landed in 1654 in Dutch Reformed New Amsterdam, only to find that Governor Peter Stuyvesant considered them to be members of a "deceitful race" who would "infest and trouble" his colony. The same Peter Stuyvesant had also clapped into jail Dutch Lutherans when they in their turn sought the right to hold worship. Eventually, Peter Stuyvesant was ordered by the Amsterdam Chamber of the West India Company to give the Jews their freedom. Unbelievably he wrote to his superiors: "To give liberty to the Jews will be detrimental . . . giving them liberty, we cannot refuse the Lutherans and Papists."

Even after the adoption of the Bill of Rights, the state constitutions of many of the American states provided civil equality only for Protestants. Catholics and Jews were restricted in their privilege to vote or in their right to hold elective office, as in New Hampshire, New Jersey, Maryland, North Carolina, and South Carolina.

It was not until 1826 in Maryland, for example, that the Scotch Presbyterian legislator, Thomas Kennedy, after repeated efforts, was able to convince his colleagues to extend "to those persons professing the Jewish religion the same privileges that are enjoyed by Christians." If the Jews paved the way for Lutherans in New York, it was a Presbyterian in Maryland who opened the door to the Jews.

In 1834 the famous inventor, Samuel F. B. Morse, gave nationwide expression to a Protestant fear that the Jesuits were plotting to deliver America to the Pope. His book *Foreign Conspiracy against the Liberties of the United States* became the model for all bigoted exposes and alleged conspiracies to destroy this land—charges to be leveled later in American history against the Knights of Columbus, Jewish Bankers, Jewish Bolsheviks; in this day one hears similar rumors of an alleged Zionist-Communist conspiracy to mongrelize the races, or poison water with fluoride or weaken the military.

In 1887 the American Protective Association specifically sought to curb the immigration of Catholics and to defend the public schools from subversion—namely, to maintain unchanged Protestant religious exercises within the public school. To further these purposes Protestant nativists had developed seventy weekly magazines and the American Protective Association had chapters in twenty-four states of the Union. This was also the period of Jewish migration from Central Europe. These Jewish migrants were the disillusioned refugees from the failures of the democratic uprising against reactionary government in Prussia, Austria, Hungary, and Italy. More than 200,000 Jews sought the haven of these shores. A vital, educated, and liberal migration, these Jews organized there a network of fraternal and charitable associations, benevolent societies, and the institutions of Reform Judaism. It is not insignificant that one of the earliest social action efforts of the (Reform) Central Conference of American Rabbis was designed to remove sectarian services and teachings from public education, thus, placing them in direct opposition to the program of the nativists.

Unfortunately for the Jews, the Populist Party's candidate for vice-president in 1896, polling one million votes, was a notorious anti-Semite, Thomas E. Watson. He was also a candidate for the presidency in 1904. This Georgia Baptist lawyer edited the most popular of the nativist magazines, assessing therefrom a private fortune of $250,000. By his successful sale of poisoned literature, he set an example for another techinque in the bigots' quest for power. Later in history, a congressional committee was to report that anti-Semites were distinguished, through the sale of hate literature, by an ability to fleece their constituencies of vast sums of money. Unfortunately, hatred "pays off" in the United States and in recent years it has become big business.

It was Watson also who introduced notes of sexuality in his diatribes against the Jews—another conspicuous feature of hate literature. One need only to recall the anti-Catholic exposés of Maria Monk or the response still to be attained by invoking the image of the Negro's alleged lust for white American women. The occasion was the unfortunate rape and murder of a 14-year old Southern girl charged against a Northern urbanized 29-year old Jew, Leo Frank. Watson lasciviously wrote: "Leo Frank was a typical young Jewish man of business, who lives for pleasure and *runs after gentile girls*. Every student of sociology knows that the black man's lust after the white woman is not much *fiercer than the lust of the licentious Jew for the gentile.*" (Italics in original).

Not only Watson's paper, but many others as well, linked the "Israelitic Americans" and "Romanist Americans" as the "enemies" of "Christian America."

Particularly during the Civil War, Jews were made the whipping boy both in the North and in the South; the shortages of supplies and produce felt by both sides were attributed to the manipulations of "Jewish traders." This myth achieved to such an influence, in fact, that on December 17, 1862, General Grant ordered Jewish merchants "as a class" to be expelled from the battle area. The *New York Times* called this incident "one of the deepest sensations of the war." Of course, Grant was soon to realize that Jews were not the only speculators and, in fact, there were many Jews whose commercial dealings were honest and whose assistance—much of it of a sacrificial nature—was required in the war effort. Grant apologized profusely to the Jewish community, but he provided an example of two more factors at work in any kind of prejudice: the improper tendency based on experiences with only a few to make judgment on an entire people, and the use of anti-Semitism or any form of hatred to serve economic or political ends. In this case, the beneficiaries of the restrictive order against Jews—perhaps the instigators of that order—were gentile speculators and traders who rid themselves of Jewish competition by a little anti-Semitism.

It was during the Civil War, also, that Congress enacted its first and only edict of religious discrimination. On July 1861, Congress established a chaplains corps for the Union Army, the chaplains to be appointed from "regularly ordained ministers of some Christian denomination." As a result of this restrictive order, Michael Allen of Philadelphia, who had been serving "the Cameron's Dragoon," was compelled to resign. At the urging of Jewish leaders and with the support of some Christians, President Abraham Lincoln called for the amendment of the law. Congress acted quickly, but it is instructive to note that even as some applauded this action, there were many official Christian bodies who considered the appointment of a Jewish chaplain as a sure sign that America was abandoning its Christian commitment. Those who abhorred this action also recalled the "infamy" of the Jews at Calvary.

If there were some Protestants who defaced the image of Christ by their hatred, there were others in this same period who recognized His image in the plight of their Jewish brother. Protestant clergymen in 1840, for example, rallied to a demonstration in Philadelphia condemning the blood-libel charge that had been brought against the Jews in Damascus. Franciscan monks, supported by the French Consul there, had charged the Jews with the murder of their superior, allegedly for the purpose of using his blood in the Passover rites. For eight months the Jewish community of Damascus suffered murder and pillage. Moved by Christian representations, President Martin Van Buren, in one of the earliest actions of the Federal Government in behalf of an oppressed minority, extended "the active sympathy and generous interposition of the Government of the United States." Van Buren noted that among the Jews "are found some of the most worthy and patriotic of our citizens."

Again in 1858, Protestants joined with the Jews in seeking governmental intervention in behalf of the Moratara family, whose six-year-old son Edgar had been stolen away from his parents in Bologna and placed in a convent. Evidently Edgar had been secretly baptized by his Catholic nurse when severely ill and although the baptism had been administered without his parent's consent, the Holy Office of the Inquisition ruled that he must be raised as a Catholic. He was never again to see his parents.

Early in 1881, a series of pogroms erupted in Eastern Europe. . . . [In Russia], Alexander III had adopted as his policy for dealing with the Jewish problem the proposals of the Procurator of the Holy Synod of the Greek Orthodox Church, Constantin Pobyedonostzev: to force one third of the Jews to migrate, to baptize one third, and to starve the remaining third to death. On February 1, 1882, 100 prominent Christian leaders in New York, led by ex-President Grant, called for American action. Although this country could do little to stop the persecution of Jews—for some years we actually delayed the ratification of a treaty with Russia on this account—America could welcome to its shores Jewish families.

The period between 1881–1914 was a time of mass migration and industrial expansion and 22,000,000 migrants of every religious persuasion, chiefly from Eastern and Southern Europe, rushed through "the Golden Door."

Emma Lazarus, a German Jewish poet, was so moved by America's hospitality, that in 1883 she composed her sonnet "The New Colossus," whose immortal words were later to be inscribed on the Statue of Liberty. She sang:

> . . . Give me your tired, your poor,
> Your huddled masses yearning to breathe free,
> The wretched refuse of your teaming shore,
> Send these, the homeless, tempest-tossed, to me.

2,000,000 Jews accepted this invitation and, indeed, for them America was a golden land. No other ethnic or religious group can boast the same rapid climb-up the ladder of cultural, economic, and social sucess. It was exactly this rapid advancement of the Jew, however, that provided the occasion for a new form of social discrimination in the United States. As the historian, John Higham, points out: "Anti-Semitic discriminations offered another means of stabilizing the social ladder. . . . The evidence suggests that insecure social climbers, rather than relatively more secure Patricians, first resorted to this means of reducing competition."

Thus, once again, the paradox. Even as America gave with one hand, there were some who would take away with the other.

Anti-Semitic agitators, Protestant nativists, the socially insecure, and even fearful liberals in the Labor Movement joined forces to close the door to immigration. In 1924 Congress adopted a shameful racist immigration bill.

From the World War I period on until the adoption of the Johnson Immigration Measure, America had witnessed a continual harangue of anti-foreign, anti-Semitic, anti-Catholic, and anti-Negro hatred. The address of Imperial Wizard Evans, before 75,000 Klansmen in Dallas, Texas, October 24, 1923, is representative: "Negroes, Catholics, and Jews," Evans asserted, "are the undesirable elements in America, defying every fundamental requirement of assimilation. They are incapable of attaining the Anglo-Saxon level." Jews were specifically accused of being an "absolutely unblendable element" for whom "patriotism as the Anglo-Saxon feels it, is impossible."

Henry Ford's *Dearborn Independent,* a weekly newspaper with a circulation of 700,000, added another ingredient to the stench of hatred. Jews, Ford claimed, are engaged in an international conspiracy to rule the world. "Not only does the Jewish question touch these matters that are common knowledge, such as financial and commercial control, usurpation of political power, monopoly of necessities, and autocratic direction of the very news that the American people read; but it reaches into the cultural region and so touches the heart of American life." Ford's publication of *The Protocols of Zion,* an exposé of an alleged international Jewish conspiracy, has now become a classic in the literature of the anti-Semite. Ford himself repudiated the forgery, but Jews never really believed him, particularly when he later accepted Hitler's Grand Order of the Great Eagle of Germany on the occasion of his 75th birthday.

Inevitably the participation of some Jews in the Bolshevik revolution and then the depression of 1929, provided anti-Semites with all the evidence that they needed to step up their claim that "Jewish bankers" or "Jewish Communists" were involved in a worldwide financial manipulation or revolution, the exact charge depending, of course, on the bigot and the gullibility of his audiences. Even the halls of Congress echoed with such charges. So widespread were these canards, that the editors of *Fortune* in February 1936 devoted an entire issue to the role of Jews in American finance. Almost with disbelief, considering the currency of these rumors, *Fortune* exclaimed: "Indeed, there are practically no Jewish employees of any kind in the largest commercial banks and this in spite of the fact that many of the customers are Jews." *Fortune* also revealed that the largest Jewish investment house in America, Kuhn & Loeb, held only 2.8% of the foreign loans outstanding among American investment banks. We see here another model of the hatemongers' technique—the exaggeration of the power and influence of the object of his hatred.

Hitler's rise to power in Germany had its serious repercussions in the United States. As the House Un-American Affairs Committee has revealed, hundreds of anti-Jewish organizations bounded into existence. The Committee listed 135 of them. They were not insignificant. Fritz Kuhn's "German-American Bund" claimed a membership of 25,000. Its Madison Square Garden rally was attended by 19,000 and from the rafters a sign shouted: "Wake Up America. Smash Jewish Communism. Stop Jewish Domination of Christian America."

William Dudley Pelly's "Silver Shirts" reported to the Internal Revenue a $50,000 a year financial turnover. He distributed one million pieces of anti-Semitic literature each year.

Father E. Coughlin spewed forth anti-Semitic diatribes every week to a radio audience of three million. His charge that the Jews were aligned with the Communists, stimulated a latent anti-Semitism to be found among Catholic Americans and planted the seeds of suspicion that remains among some Catholics to this day.

No wonder, then, that the Jewish community expanded the work of defense agencies such as the Anti-Defamation League, the American-Jewish Committee, and the American-Jewish Congress.

With the end of World War II, however, America entered a new era. The Jews had demonstrated their allegiance with their blood. America realized the bitter price civilization must pay for hatred allowed to run rampant. Without question, a resolve was evident nationwide that once and for all discrimination should be buried in this land.

The national effort to end racial segregation is evidence of this resolve in action. Yet again, hatemongers and right wing extremists are at work. Some of these are the same Nazis and anti-Semites who were in operation prior to World War II. Their newspapers cry out the alarm that the Civil Rights Movement is allegedly under the domination of Zionist-Communists. The National Council of Churches, it is claimed, has sold out to the Jews, and America itself is in danger of subversion from within.

I have no doubt that good Americans will repudiate decisively the National States Rights Party, the revived Ku Klux Klan, the John Birch Society, and any other extremist group that will rear its head.

Jewish community relations agencies reveal that anti-Semitism is now at its lowest point, particularly in those areas where they have devoted their major educational energies. In the most recent 20-year period, restrictive quotas on admission of Jews in professional schools has almost been eliminated and resort hotel discrimination is virtually extinct. Unlike a former period, the use of anti-Semitism in a political campaign today is sure to doom the candidate to failure.

Yet recent surveys reveal, also, that 72% of private clubs and 60% of city clubs still discriminate on grounds of religion. Jews are still barred from upper echelon positions in banking, insurance, and in the best law firms. They are still denied housing in the most exclusive communities. 32% of Americans in 1960 confessed that they were uncertain or would not vote for a president nominated by their own political party if he were a Jew, even if he were well qualified. Jews cannot forget so easily that just five years ago, in 1960, during the German swastika epidemic, there were also 700 incidents of anti-Jewish desecration reported in the United States over an eight-week period.

It appears to me that the time is now for Americans to end such nonsense. "What ye do to the least of these, ye do to me."

It is also well here to recall H. A. Overstreet's warning that the main problem stems not from those who impose restrictions against Jews, but from those who acquiesce to them. Said Overstreet:

> He who permits evil, commits evil. This is what makes for the haunting sense of guilt in our culture. Many a member of the dominant group will earnestly aver that *he* never intended that Negroes should be insulted and maltreated . . . that *his heart* is sore and ashamed when he reads of the defiling of Jewish synagogues by hoodlums. He did not intend these things, but *he created the social sanction for these things.* By adopting a twisted principle of human association, he and the people like him open the Pandora's box out of which have flown the intolerance and cruelties that have defiled our culture.

In the past half century, there have been a number of studies that document the incidence of anti-Semitism in American history. There is consensus among scholars who have written about the Jewish experience that anti-Semitism crested in America during the half century preceding World War II.[32] Four factors have made anti-Semitism American style different from European anti-Semitism.[33] (1) In America, Jews have always fought anti-Semites freely; (2) American anti-Semitism has always had to compete with other forms of animus such as racism, anti-Catholicism, anti-Mormonism, and anti-communism; (3) Anti-Semitism is more foreign to American ideals than to European ones; and (4) American politics resists anti-Semitism. Jonathan D. Sarna concludes his discussion of anti-Semitism in America with the comment: "If the remedy has not been utter heaven for Jews, it has been as far from hell as Jews in the Diaspora have ever known."

PLURALISM AND CONSENSUS

America has struggled to realize a pluralistic social order. Achieving social consensus and cohesiveness in such a pluralistic society is the enduring challenge of the American experience. John Courtney Murray wrote a classic statement of the challenge in his essay, "America's Four Conspiracies." In this document, Murray specifies the need for America's four great conspirators—Protestant, Catholic, Jewish, and secularist—to form a consensus that will achieve a civil society. The document is difficult but rewarding reading.

[32] See Jonathan D. Sarna, "Anti-Semitism and American History," *Commentary*, Vol. 71, No. 3 (February 1980), pp. 42–47.
[33] Ibid., pp. 46–47.

From "America's Four Conspiracies" by John Courtney Murray

I

The "free society" seems to be a phrase of American coinage. At least it has no comparable currency in any other language, ancient or modern. The same is true of the phrase "free government." The fact itself suggests the assumption that American society and its form of government are a unique historical realization. The assumption is generally regarded among us as unquestionable.

However, we have tended of late to pronounce the phrase, "the free society," with a rising interrogatory inflection. The phrase itself, it seems, now formulates a problem. This is an interesting new development. It was once assumed that the American proposition, both social and political, was self-evident; that it authenticated itself on simple inspection; that it was, in consequence, intuitively grasped and generally understood by the American people. This assumption now stands under severe question.

What is the free society, in its "idea?" Is this "idea" being successfully realized in the institutions that presently determine the pattern of American life, social and personal? The web of American institutions has altered, rapidly and profoundly, even radically, over the past few generations. Has the "idea" of the free society perhaps been strangled by the tightening intricacies of the newly formed institutional network? Has some new and alien "idea" subtly and unsuspectedly assumed the role of an organizing force in American society? Do we understand not only the superficial facts of change in American life but also the underlying factors of change—those "variable constants" that forever provide the dynamisms of change in in all human life?

The very fact that these questions are being asked makes it sharply urgent that they be answered. What is at stake is America's understanding of itself. Self-understanding is the necessary condition of a sense of self-identity and self-confidence, whether in the case of an individual or in the case of a people. If the American people can no longer base this sense of naive assumptions on self-evidence, it is imperative that they find other more reasoned grounds for their essential affirmation that they are uniquely a people, uniquely a free society. Otherwise the peril is great. The complete loss of one's identity is, with all propriety of theological definition, hell. In diminished forms it is insanity. And it would not be well for the American giant to go lumbering about the world today, lost and mad.

At this juncture I suggest that the immediate question is not whether the free society is really free. This question may be unanswerable; it may even be meaningless as a question, if only for the reason that the norms of freedom seem to have got lost in a welter of confused controversy. Therefore I suggest that the immediate question is whether American society is properly civil. This question is intelligible and answerable, because the basic standard of civility is not in doubt: "Civilization is formed by men locked together in argument. From this dialogue the community becomes a political community." This statement exactly expressed the mind of St. Thomas Aquinas, who was himself giving refined expression to the tradition of classic antiquity, which in its prior turn had given elaboration to the concept of the

SOURCE: John Cogley, *Religion in America* (New York: Meridian Books, 1958), pp. 12-41.

"civil multitude," the multitude that is not a mass or a herd or a huddle, because it is characterized by civility.

The specifying note of political association is its rational deliberative quality, its dependence for its permanent cohesiveness on argument among men. In this it differs from all other forms of association found on earth. The animal kingdom is held together simply by the material homogeneity of the species; all its unities and antagonisms are of the organic and biological order. Wolves do not argue the merits of running in packs. The primal human community, the family, has its own distinctive bonds of union. Husband and wife are not drawn into the marital association simply by the forces of reason but by the forces of life itself, importantly including the mysterious dynamisms of sex. Their association is indeed founded on a contract, which must be a rational and free act. But the substance and finality of the contract is both infra- and supra-rational; it is an engagement to become "two in one flesh." The marital relationship may at times be quarrelsome, but it is not argumentative. Similarly, the union of parents and children is not based on reason, justice, or power; it is based on kinship, love, and *pietas*.

It is otherwise with the political community. I am not, of course, maintaining that civil society is a purely rational form of association. We no longer believe, with Locke or Hobbes, that man escapes from a mythical "state of nature" by an act of will, by a social contract. Civil society is a need of human nature before it becomes the object of human choice. Moreover, every particular society is a creature of the soil; it springs from the physical soil of earth and from the more formative soil of history. Its existence is sustained by loyalties that are not logical; its ideals are expressed in legends that go beyond the facts and are for that reason vehicles of truth; its cohesiveness depends in no small part on the materialisms of property and interest. Though all this is true, nevertheless the distinctive bond of the civil multitude is reason, or more exactly, that exercise of reason which is argument.

Hence the climate of the City is likewise distinctive. It is not feral or familial but forensic. It is not hot and humid, like the climate of the animal kingdom. It lacks the cordial warmth of love and unreasoning loyalty that pervades the family. It is cool and dry, with the coolness and dryness that characterize good argument among informed and responsible men. Civic amity gives to this climate its vital quality. This form of friendship is a special kind of moral virtue, a thing of reason and intelligence, laboriously cultivated by the discipline of passion, prejudice, and narrow self-interest. It is the sentiment proper to the City. It has nothing to do with the cleavage of a David to a Jonathan, or with the kinship of the clan, or with the charity, *fortis ut mors,* that makes the solidarity of the Church. It is in direct contrast with the passionate fanaticism of the Jacobin: "Be my brother or I'll kill you!" Ideally, I suppose, there should be only one passion in the city—the passion for justice. But the will to justice, though it engages the heart, finds its measure as it finds its origin in intelligence, in a clear understanding of what is due to the equal citizen from the City and to the City from the citizenry according to the mode of their equality. This commonly shared will to justice is the ground of civic amity as it is also the ground of that unity which is called peace. This unity, qualified by amity, is the highest good of the civil multitude and the perfection of its civility.

If then society is civil when it is formed by men locked together in argument, the question rises, what is the argument about? There are three major themes.

First, the argument is about public affairs, the *res publica,* those matters which are for the advantage of the public (in the phrase as old as Plato)—and which call for public decision and action by government. These affairs have their origin in matters of fact; but their rational discussion calls for the Socratic dialogue, the close and easy use of the habit of cross-examination, that transforms brute facts into arguable issues.

Second, the public argument concerns the affairs that fall, at least in decisive part, beyond the limited scope of goverment. These affairs are not to be settled by law, though law may be in some degree relevant to their settlement. They go beyond the necessities of the public order as such; they bear upon the quality of the common life. The great "affair" of the commonwealth is, of course, education. It includes three general areas of common interest: the school system, its mode of organization, its curricular content, and the level of learning among its teachers; the later education of the citizen in the liberal art of citizenship; and the more general enterprise of the advancement of knowledge by research.

The third theme of public argument is the most important and the most difficult. It concerns the constitutional consensus whereby the people acquires its identity as a people and the society is endowed with its vital form, its entelechy, its sense of purpose as a collectivity organized for action in history. The idea of consensus has been classic since the Stoics and Cicero; through St. Augustine it found its way into the liberal tradition of the West.

The state of civility supposes a consensus that is constitutional, *sc.,* its focus is the idea of law, as surrounded by the whole constellation of ideas that are related to the *ratio iuris* as its premises, its constituent elements, and its consequences. This consensus is come to by the people; they become a people by coming to it. They do not come to it accidentally, without quite knowing how, but deliberatively, by the methods of reason reflecting on experience. The consensus is not a structure of secondary rationalizations erected on psychological data (as the behaviorist would have it) or on economic data (as the Marxist would have it). It is not the residual minimum left after rigid application of the Cartesian axiom, *"de omnibus dubitandum."* It is not simply a set of working hypotheses whose value is pragmatic. It is an ensemble of substantive truths, a structure of basic knowledge, an order of elementary affirmations that reflect realities inherent in the order of existence. It occupies an established position in society and excludes opinions alien or contrary to itself. This consensus is the intuitional *a priori* of all the rationalities and technicalities of constitutional and statutory law. It furnishes the premises of the people's action in history and defines the larger aims which that action seeks in internal affairs and in external relations.

It is to this idea of consensus, I take it, that the Declaration of Independence adverts: "We hold these truths to be self-evident. . . ." I know, of course, that a good bit of sophisticated fun has been poked at this eighteenth-century sentence. But when the sophisticated gentry has had its fun, the essential meaning of the sentence remains intact and its political significance stands unimpaired. The original American affirmation was simply this: "There are truths, and we hold them as the foundations of our political existence as a constitutional commonwealth."

This consensus is the ultimate theme of the public argument whereby American society hopes to achieve and maintain the mark of civility. The whole premise of the argument, if it is to be civilized and civilizing, is that the consensus is real that among the people everything is not in doubt, but that there is a core of agreement, accord, concurrence, acquiescence. We hold certain truths; therefore we can argue about them. It seems to have been one of the corruptions of intelligence by positivism to assume that argument ends when agreement is reached. In a basic sense the reverse is true. There can be no argument except on the premise, and within a context, of agreement. *Mutatis mutandis,* this is true of scientific, philosophical, and theological argument. It is no less true of political argument.

On its most imperative level the public argument within the City and about the City's affairs begins with the agreement that there is a reality called, in the phrase of Leo XIII, *patrimonium generis humani,* a heritage of an essential truth, a tradition of rational belief, that sustains the structure of the City and furnishes the substance of civil life. It was to this patrimony that the Declaration of Independence referred: "These are the truths we hold." This is the first utterance of a people. By it a people establishes its identity, and under decent respect to the opinions of mankind declares its purposes within the community of nations.

II

The truths we hold were well enough stated. Three are immediate: the limitation of government by law—by a higher law not of government's making, whereby an order of inviolable rights is constituted; the principle of consent; and the right of resistance to unjust rule. These are the heritage of classical and medieval constitutionalism; they center on the idea of law. One truth is remote and metapolitical—that man is not the creature of the City but of God; that the dignity of man is equal in all men, that there are human purposes which transcend the order of politics; that the ultimate function of the political order is to support man in the pursuit of these purposes; that it is within the power of man to alter his own history in pursuit of his own good. You will not find this pregnant truth elsewhere than in the Western and Christian heritage.

Initially, we hold these truths because they are a patrimony. They are a heritage from history, through whose dark and bloody pages there runs like a silver thread the tradition of civility. This is the first reason why the consensus continually calls for public argument. The consensus is an intellectual heritage; it may be lost to mind or deformed in the mind. Its final depository is the public mind. This is indeed a perilous place to deposit what ought to be kept safe; for the public mind is exposed to the corrosive rust of skepticism, to the predatory moths of deceitful *doxai* (in Plato's sense), and to the incessant thieveries of forgetfulness. Therefore the consensus can only be preserved in the public mind by argument. High argument alone will keep it alive, in the vital state of being "held."

Second, we hold these truths because they are true. They have been found in the structure of reality by that dialectic of observation and reflection which is called philosophy. But as the achievement of reason and experience the consensus again presents itself for argument. Its vitality depends on a constant scrutiny of political experience, as this experience widens with the developing—or possibly the decaying—life of man in society. Only at the price of this continued contact with experience will a constitutional tradition continue to be "held" as real knowledge and not simply as a structure of prejudice. However, the tradition, or the consensus, is not a mere record of experience. It is experience illumined by principle, given a construction by a process of philosophical reflection. In the public argument there must consequently be a continued recurrence to first principles. Otherwise the consensus may come to seem simply a projection of ephemeral experience, a passing shadow on the vanishing backdrop of some given historical scene, without the permanence proper to truths that are "held."

On both of these titles, as a heritage and as a public philosophy, the American consensus needs to be constantly argued. If the public argument dies from disinterest, or subsides into the angry mutterings of polemic, or rises to the shrillness of hysteria, or trails off into positivistic triviality, or gets lost in a morass of semantics, you may be sure that the barbarian is at the gates of the City.

The barbarian need not appear in bearskins with a club in hand. He may wear a Brooks Brothers suit and carry a ball-point pen with which to write his advertising copy. In fact, even beneath the academic gown there may lurk a child of the wilderness, untutored in the high tradition of civility, who goes busily and happily about his work, a domesticated and law-abiding man, engaged in the construction of a philosophy to put an end to all philosophy, and thus put an end to the possibility of a vital consensus and to civility itself. This is perennially the work of the barbarian, to undermine rational standards of judgment, to corrupt the inherited intuitive wisdom by which the people have always lived, and to do this not by spreading new beliefs but by creating a climate of doubt and bewilderment in which clarity about the larger aims of life is dimmed and the self-confidence of the people is destroyed, so that finally what you have is the impotent nihilism of the "generation of the third eye," now presently appearing on our university campuses. (One is, I take it, on the brink of impotence and nihilism when one begins to be aware of one's own awareness of what one is doing, saying, thinking. This is the paralysis of all serious thought; it is likewise the destruction of all the spontaneities of love.)

The barbarian may be the eighteenth-century philosopher, who neither anticipated or desired the brutalities of the Revolution with its Committee on the Public Safety, but who prepared the ways for the Revolution by creating a vacuum which he was not able to fill. Today the barbarian is the man who makes open and explicit the rejection of the traditional role of reason and logic in human affairs. He is the man who reduces all spiritual and moral questions to the test of the practical results or to an analysis of language or to decision in terms of individual subjective feeling.

It is a Christian theological intuition, confirmed by all of historical experience, that man lives both his personal and his social life always more or less close to the brink of barbarism, threatened not only by the disintegrations of physical illness and by the disorganization of mental imbalance, but also by the decadence of moral corruption and the political chaos of formlessness or the moral chaos of tyranny. Society is rescued from chaos only by a few men, not by many. *Paucis humanum vivit genus.* It is only the few who understand the disciplines of civility and are to sustain them in being and thus hold in check the forces of barbarism that are always threatening to force the gates of the City. To say this is not, of course, to endorse the concept of the fascist élite—a barbarous concept, if ever there was one. It is only to recall a lesson of history to which our own era of mass civilization may well attend. We have not been behind our forebears in devising both gross and subtle ways of massacring ancient civilities.

Barbarism is not, I repeat, the forest primeval with all its relatively simple savageries. Barbarism has long had its definition, resumed by St. Thomas after Aristotle. It is the lack of reasonable conversation according to reasonable laws. Here the word "conversation" has its twofold Latin sense. It means living together and talking together.

Barbarism threatens when men cease to live together according to reason, embodied in law and custom, and incorporated in a web of institutions that sufficiently reveal rational influences, even though they are not, and cannot be, wholly rational. Society becomes barbarian when men are huddled together under the rule of force and fear; when economic interests assume the primacy over higher values; when material standards of mass and quantity crush out the values of quality and excellence; when technology assumes an autonomous existence and embarks on a course of unlimited self-exploitation without purposeful guidance from the higher disciplines of politics and morals (one thinks of Cape Canaveral); when the state reaches the paradoxical point of being everywhere intrusive and also impotent, possessed of immense power and powerless to achieve rational ends; when the ways of men come under the sway of the instinctual, the impulsive, the compulsive. When things like this happen, barbarism is abroad, whatever the surface impressions of urbanity. Men have ceased to live together according to reasonable laws.

Barbarism likewise threatens when men cease to talk together according to reasonable laws. There are laws of argument, the observance of which is imperative if discourse is to be civilized. Argument ceases to be civil when it is dominated by passion and prejudice; when its vocabulary becomes solipsist, premised on the theory that my insight is mine alone and cannot be shared; when dialogue gives way to a series of monologues; when the parties to the conversation cease to listen to one another, or hear only what they want to hear, or see the other's argument only through the screen of their own categories; when defiance is flung to the basic ontological principle of all ordered discourse, which asserts that Reality is an analogical structure, within which there are variant modes of reality, to each of which there corresponds a distinctive method of thought that imposes on argument its own special rules. When things like this happen men cannot be locked together in argument. Conversation becomes merely quarrelsome or querulous. Civility dies with the death of the dialogue.

All this has been said in order to give some meaning to the immediate question before us, sc., whether American society, which calls itself free, is genuinely civil. In any circumstances it has always been difficult to achieve civility in the sense explained. A group of men locked together in argument is a rare spectacle. But within the great sprawling City that is the United States the achievement of a civil society encounters a special difficulty—what is called religious pluralism.

III

The political order must borrow both from above itself and from below itself. The political looks upward to metaphysics, ethics, theology; it looks downward to history, legal science, sociology, psychology. The order of politics must reckon with all that is true and factual about man. The problem was complicated enough for Aristotle, for whom man in the end was only citizen, whose final destiny was to be achieved within the City, however much he might long to play the immortal. For us today man is still citizen; but at least for most of us his life is not absorbed in the City, in society and the state. In the citizen who is also a Christian there resides the consciousness formulated immortally in the second-century *Letter to Diognetes:* "Every foreign land is a fatherland and every fatherland is a foreign land." This consciousness makes a difference, in ways upon which we need not dwell here. What makes the more important difference is the fact of religious divisions. Civil discourse would be hard enough if among us there prevailed conditions of religious unity; even in such conditions civic unity would be a complicated and laborious achievement. As it is, efforts at civil discourse plunge us into the twofold experience of the religious pluralist society.

The first experience is intellectual. As we discourse on public affairs, on the affairs of the commonwealth, and particularly on the problem of consensus, we inevitably have to move upward, as it were, into the realms of some theoretical generality—into metaphysics, ethics, theology. This movement does not carry us into disagreement: for disagreement is not an easy thing to reach. Rather, we move into confusion. Among us there is a plurality of universes of discourse. These universes are incommensurable. And when they clash, the issue of agreement or disagreement tends to become irrelevant. The immediate situation is simply one of confusion. One does not know what the other is driving at. For this too is part of the problem —the disposition amid the confusion to disregard the immediate argument, as made, and to suspect its tendency, to wonder what the man who makes it is really driving at.

This is the pluralist society as it is encountered on the level of intellectual experience. We have no common universe of discourse. In particular, diverse mental equivalents attach to all the words in which the constitutional consensus must finally be discussed—truth, freedom, justice, prudence, order, law, authority, power, knowledge, certainty, unity, peace, virtue, morality, religion, God and perhaps even man. Our intellectual experience is one of sheer confusion, in which soliloquy succeeds to argument.

The second experience is even more profound. The themes touched upon in any discussion of Religion and the Free Society have all had a long history. And in the course of discussing them we are again made aware that only in a limited sense have we severally had the same history. We more or less share the short segment of history known as America. But all of us have had longer histories, spiritual and intellectual.

These histories may indeed touch at certain points. But I, for instance, am conscious that I do not share the histories that lie behind many of my fellow citizens. The Jew does not share the Christian history, nor even the Christian idea of history. Catholic and Protestant history may be parallel in a limited sense but they are not coincident or coeval. And the secularist is a latecomer. He may locate his ancestry in the eighteenth or nineteenth centuries, or, if his historic sense is strong, he may go back to the fourteenth century, to the rise of what Lagarde has called *l'esprit laique.* In any case, he cannot go back to Athens, Rome, or Alexandria; for his laicism is historically conditioned. It must situate itself with regard to the Christian tradition. It must include denials and disassociations that the secularism of antiquity did not have to make; and it also includes the affirmation of certain Christian values that antiquity could not have affirmed.

The fact of our discrepant histories creates the second experience of the pluralist society. We are aware that we not only hold different views but have become different kinds of men as we have lived our several histories. Our styles of thought and of interior life are as discrepant as our histories. The more deeply they are experienced and the more fully they are measured, the more do the differences among us appear to be almost unbridgeable. Man is not only a creature of thought but also a vibrant subject of sympathies; and in the realm of philosophy and religion today the communal experiences are so divergent that they create not sympathies but alienations as between groups.

Take, for instance, the question of natural law. For the Catholic it is simply a problem in meta-physical, ethical and juridical argument; he moves into the argument naturally and feels easy amid its complexities. For the Protestant, on the contrary, the very concept is a challenge, if not an affront, to his whole religiosity, to which it is largely alien and very largely unassimilable.

Another example might be the argument that has been made by Catholics in this country for more than a century with regard to the distribution of tax funds for the support of the school system. The structure of the argument is not complex. Its principle is that the canons of distributive justice ought to control the actions of government in allocating funds that it coercively collects from all the people in pursuance of its legitimate interest in universal compulsory schooling. The fact is that these canons are presently not being observed. The "solution" to the School Question reached in the nineteenth century reveals injustice, and the legal statutes that establish the injustice are an abuse of power. So, in drastic brevity, runs the argument. For my part, I have never heard a satisfactory answer to it.

This is a fairly serious situation. When a large section of the community asserts that injustice is being done, and makes a reasonable argument to substantiate the assertion, either the argument ought to be convincingly refuted and the claim of injustice thus disposed of, or the validity of the argument ought to be admitted and the injustice remedied. As a matter of fact, however, the argument customarily meets a blank stare, or else it is "answered" by varieties of the fallacy known as *ignoratio elenchi.* At the extreme, from the side of the more careerist type of anti-Catholic, the rejoinder takes this form, roughly spoken (sometimes the rejoinder is roughly spoken): "We might be willing to listen to this argument about the rights of Catholic schools if we believed that Catholic schools had any rights at all. But we do not grant that they have any rights, except to tolerance. Their existence is not for the advantage of the public; they offend against the integrity of the democratic community, whose warrant is fidelity to Protestant principle (or secularist principle, as the case may be)." This "answer" takes various forms, more or less uncomplimentary to the Catholic Church, according to the temper of the speaker. But this is the gist of it. The statement brings me to my next point.

The fact is that among us civility—or civic unity or civic amity, as you will—is a thing of the surface. It is quite easy to break through it. And when you do, you catch a glimpse of the factual reality of the pluralist society. I agree with Prof. Eric Voegelin's thesis that our pluralist society has received its structure through wars and that the wars are still going on beneath a fragile surface of more or less forced urbanity. What Voegelin calls the "genteel picture" will not stand the test of confrontation with fact.

We are not really a group of men singly engaged in the search for truth relying solely on the means of persuasion, entering into dignified communication with each other, content politely to correct opinions with which we do not agree. As a matter of fact, the variant ideas and allegiances among us are entrenched as social powers; they occupy grounds; they have developed interest; and they possess the means to fight for them. The real issues of truth that arise are complicated by secondary issues of power and prestige, which not seldom become primary. Witness, for instance, Catholic defense of the Connecticut birth-rate control statute. It was passed in 1879, in the Comstock era, under Protestant pressure. Its text reveals a characteristic Comstockian ignorance of the rules of traditional jurisprudence; in general, the "free churches" have never understood law but only power, either in the form of majority rule or in the form of minority protest. Since it makes a public crime out of a private sin, and confuses morality with legality, and is unenforceable without police invasion of the bedroom, the statute is indefensible as a law. But the configuration of social power has become such that Catholics now defend it—with a saving sense of irony, I hope.

There are many other examples. What they illustrate is that all the entrenched segments of American pluralism claim influence on the course of events, on the content of the legal order, and on the quality of American society. To each group, of course, its influence seems salvific; to other groups it may seem merely imperialist. In any case, the forces at work are not simply intellectual; they are also passionate. There is not simply an exchange of arguments but of verbal blows. You do not have to probe deeply beneath the surface of civic amity to uncover the structure of passion and war.

There is the ancient resentment of the Jew, who has for centuries been dependent for his existence on the good will, often not forthcoming, of a Christian community. Now in America, where he has acquired social power, his distrust of the Christian community leads him to align himself with the secularizing forces whose dominance, he thinks, will afford him a security he has never known. Again, there is the profound distrust between Catholic and Protestant. Their respective conceptions of Christianity are only analogous; that is, they are partly the same and totally different. The result is *odium theologicum,* a sentiment that not only enhances religious differences in the realm of truth but also creates personal estrangements in the order of charity.

More than that, Catholic and Protestant distrust each other's political intentions. There is the memory of historic clashes in the temporal order; the Irishman does not forget Cromwell any more readily than the Calvinist forgets Louis XIV. Neither Protestant nor Catholic is yet satisfied that the two of them can exist freely and peacefully in the same kind of of City. The Catholic regards Protestantism not only as a heresy in the order of religion but also as a corrosive solvent in the order of civilization, whose intentions lead to chaos. The Protestant regards Catholicism not only as idolatry in the order of religion but as an instrument of tyranny in the order of civilization, whose intentions lead to clericalism. Thus an *odium civile* accrues to the *odium theologicum.*

This problem is particularly acute in the United States, where the Protestant was the native and the Catholic the immigrant, in contrast to Europe where the Catholic first held the ground and was only later challenged. If one is to believe certain socio-religious critics (Eduard Heimann, for instance) Protestantism in America has forged an identification of itself, both historical and ideological, with American culture, particularly with an indigenous secularist unclarified mystique of individual freedom as somehow the source of everything, including justice, order, and unity. The result has been Nativism in all its manifold forms, ugly and refined, popular and academic, fanatic and liberal. The neo-Nativist as well as the paleo-Nativist addresses to the Catholic substantially the same charge: "You are among us but you are not of us." (The neo-Nativist differs only in that he uses footnotes, apparently in the belief that reference to documents is a substitute for an understanding of them.) To this charge the Catholic, if he happens to set store, *pro forma,* on meriting the blessed adjective "sophisticated," will politely reply that this is Jacobinism, *nouveau style,* and that Jacobinism, any style, is out of style in this day and age. In contrast, the sturdy Catholic War Veteran is more likely to say rudely, "Them's fightin' words." And with this exchange of civilities, if they are such, the "argument" is usually there.

There is, finally, the secularist (I here use the term only in a descriptive sense). He too is at war. If he knows his own history, he must be. Historically his first chosen enemy was the Catholic Church, and it must still be the Enemy of his choice, for two reasons. First, it asserts that there is an authority superior to the authority of individual reason and of the political projections of individual anathema. Second, it asserts that by divine ordinance this world is to be ruled by a dyarchy of authorities, within which the temporal is subordinate to the spiritual, not instrumentally but in dignity. This assertion is doubly anathema. It clashes with the socio-juridical monism that is always basic to the secularist position when it is consistently argued. In secularist theory there can be only one society, one law, one power, and one faith, a civic faith that is the "unifying" bond of the community, whereby it withstands the assaults of assorted pluralisms.

The secularist has always fought his battles under a banner on which is emblazoned his special device, "The Integrity of the Political Order." In the name of this thundering principle he would banish from the political order (and from education as an affair of the City) all the "divisive forces" of religion. At least in America he has traditionally had no quarrel with religion as a "purely private matter," as a sort of essence or idea or ambient aura that may help to warm the hidden heart of solitary man. He may even concede a place to religion-in-general, whatever that is. What alarms him is a religion as a Thing, visible, corporate, organized, a community of thought that presumes to sit superior to, and in judgment on, the "community of democratic thought," and that is furnished somehow with an armature of power to make its thought and judgment publicly prevail. Under this threat he marshals his military vocabulary and speaks in terms of aggression, encroachment, maneuvers, strategy, tactics. He rallies to the defense of the City; he sets about the strengthening of the wall that separates the City from its Enemy. He too is at war.

IV

What it comes to then is that the pluralist society, honestly viewed under abdication of all false gentility, is a pattern of interacting conspiracies. There are chiefly four—Protestant, Catholic, Jewish, secularist, though in each camp, to continue the military metaphor, there are forces not fully broken to the authority of the high command.

I would like to relieve the word "conspiracy" of its invidious connotations. It is devoid of these in its original Latin sense, both literal and topical. Literally, it means unison, concord, unanimity in opinion and feeling, a "breathing together." Then it acquires inevitably the connotation of united action for a common end about which there is agreement; those who think alike inevitably join together in some manner of action to make their common thought or purpose prevail. The word was part of the Stoic political vocabulary; it was adopted by Cicero; and it passed into my own philosophical tradition, the Scholastic tradition, that has been formative of the liberal tradition of the West. Civil society is formed, said Cicero, *"conspiratione hominum atque consensu,"* that is by action in concert on the basis of consensus with regard to the purposes of the action. Civil society is by definition a conspiracy, *"conspiratio plurium in unum."* Only by conspiring together do the many become one. *E pluribus unum.*

The trouble is that there are a number of conspiracies within American society. I shall not object to your calling Catholicism a conspiracy, provided you admit that it is only one of several. (Incidentally, I never have seen the validity of Prof. Sidney Hook's distinction: "Heresy, yes; conspiracy, no." The heresy that was not a conspiracy has not yet appeared on land or sea. One would say with greater propriety of word and concept: "Conspiracy, yes; heresy, no." Heresy, not conspiracy, is the bad word for the evil thing. No one would be bothered with the Communist conspiracy if its dynamism were not a civilization heresy, or more exactly, an apostasy from civilization.)

Perhaps then our problem today is somehow to make the four great conspiracies among us conspire into one conspiracy that will be American society—civil, just, free, peaceful, one.

Can this problem be solved? My own expectations are modest and minimal. It seems to be the lesson of history that men are usually governed with little wisdom. The highest political good, the unity which is called peace, is far more a goal than a realization. And the search for religious unity, the highest spiritual good, always encounters the "messianic necessity," so called: "Do you think that I have come to bring peace on earth? No, but rather dissension (*diamerismon*)" (Luke 12:51). In the same text the dissension was predicted with terrible explicitness of the family. It has been the constant lot of the family of nations and of the nations themselves. Religious pluralism is against the will of God. But it is the human condition; it is written into the script of history. It will not somehow marvelously cease to trouble the City.

Advisedly therefore one will cherish only modest expectations with regard to the solution of the problem of religious pluralism and civic unity. Utopianism is a Christian heresy (the ancient pagan looked backward, not forward, to the Golden Age); but it is a heresy nonetheless. We cannot hope to make American society the perfect conspiracy based on a unanimous consensus. But we could at least do two things. We could limit the warfare, and we could enlarge the dialogue. We could lay down our arms (at least the more barbarous kind of arms!), and we could take up argument.

Even to do this would not be easy. It would be necessary that we cease to project into the future of the Republic the nightmares, real or fancied, of the past. In Victorian England John Henry Newman noted that the Protestant bore "a stain upon the imagination," left there by the vivid images of Reformation polemic against the Church of Rome. Perhaps we all bear some stain or other upon our imaginations. It might be possible to cleanse them by a work of reason. The free society, I said at the outset, is a unique realization; it has inaugurated a new history. Therefore it might be possible within this new history to lay the ghosts of the past—to forget the ghettos and the autos-da-fé; the Star Chamber and the Committee on the Public Safety; Topcliffe with his "Bloody Question" and Torquemada with his rack; the dragonnades and the Black and Tans; Samuel F. B. Morse, the convents in Charleston and Philadelphia, the Know-Nothings and the Ku Klux Klan and what happened to Al Smith (whatever it was that did happen to him).

All this might be possible. It certainly would be useful. I venture to say that today it is necessary. This period in American history is critical, not organic (to use Prof. Toynbee's distinction). We face a crisis that is new in history. We would do well to face it with a new cleanliness of imagination, in the realization that internecine strife, beyond some inevitable human measure, is a luxury we can no longer afford. Serious issues confront us on all the three levels of public argument. Perhaps the time has come when we should endeavor to dissolve the structure of war that underlies the pluralistic society, and erect the more civilized structure of the dialogue. It would be no less sharply pluralistic, but rather more so, since the real pluralisms would be clarified out of their present confusion. And amid the pluralism a unity would be discernible—the unity of an orderly conversation. The pattern would not be that of ignorant armies clashing by night but of informed men locked together in argument in the full light of a new dialectical day. Thus we might present to a "candid world" the spectacle of a civil society.

Summary

The movement toward religious unity and cooperation has had a long and precarious history in America. Broadly speaking, it has been a development from acrimonious competition and conflict to a position of general toleration and, at times, earnest interfaith dialogue. The journey, however, has neither been smooth nor without setbacks.

The ecumenical impulse among Christians was arrested in the 1970s after dramatic expression in the 1960s. Structural union or reunion thus far has occurred largely among members of denominational families. The recent romance with localism should cool as church people rediscover that many problems cannot be engaged effectively at a local level by denominational agencies.

The dialogue between Christians and Jews takes different directions, depending on where the participants are on the liberal-conservative scale. Liberal Christians tend not to see Jews as objects of conversion while conservative Christians develop special missions to Jews. Anti-Semitic motifs in both Catholic and Protestant worship and doctrine have largely disappeared. American religious pluralism has become more pronounced, as we shall see in the chapter that follows.

American Religion in Ferment

Into the 1980s

The 1970s was a decade in which American religion—indeed American society as a whole—reached a level of pluralism which John Courtney Murray hardly could have envisaged in 1958. In the 1960s many mainline liberal theologians had believed that increasing secularity was the primary reality in American life.[1] From the vantage point of the early 1980s, it is clear that pluralism rather than secularity characterizes the contemporary scene: People are not necessarily less religious, but there is a great increase in the number of options for religious identity and commitment. Martin E. Marty wrote early in the 1970s:

> For centuries, a believer simply inherited the parental faith and either intensified it or let it wane; the range of other choices was usually quite small. The New England farm boy could not easily have entertained Zen Buddhism, and the southern rural black did not have available to him the literary ties that make black African religion a possibility for his grandson.[2]

Contemporary American religious belief and practice are not only highly pluralistic but also constitute a significant force in national life. The 1970s were the occasion for something of a religious revival. *Homo religiosus*—religious man/woman—is alive and well in America.

PLURALISTIC AND EXPERIENTIAL

American religion has always been pluralistic, but contemporary pluralism is radical. Much of the religious, social, and political conservatism that characterizes the United States in the 1980s must be understood at least in part as a response to rampant pluralism. The decade of the 1960s was the time when radical pluralism became painfully apparent. In his book *A Religious History of the American People*, Yale historian Sydney E. Ahlstrom argues that the "turbulent sixties" marked a new stage in American life:

> The decade of the sixties was a time, in short, when the old foundations of national confidence, patriotic idealism, moral traditionalism, and even of historic Judaeo-Christian theism, were awash. Presuppositions that had held firm for centuries—even millennia—were being widely questioned. Some sensational manifes-

[1] See Harvey Cox, *The Secular City* (New York: Macmillan, 1965).
[2] Martin E. Marty, *The Fire We Can Light* (Garden City, N.Y.: Doubleday, 1973), p. 181.

tations came and went (as fads and fashions will), but the existence of a basic shift in mood rooted in deep social and institutional dislocations was anything but ephemeral.[3]

In previous chapters we have discussed many of the events that produced this turbulence. The election of John F. Kennedy in 1960, the pontificate of Pope John XXIII, Vatican II, the black civil rights movement, and the 1962 ruling of the Supreme Court on the "one man-one vote" principle—which cut deeply into the rural bases of Protestant political power—were all important events. Added to these influences were the exploration of space, the prosecution of the Vietnam war, and the experience of the Six-Day War in Israel in 1967. Ahlstrom remarked, "By 1970 the nation's sense of unity had fallen to its lowest point since 1861."

The decade of the 1970s—with Watergate, the energy crisis, stagflation, and decreasing economic productivity—was the occasion for American worry, a sense of national exhaustion, and growing social and political conservatism.

American religion, which always tended to place a priority on experience over tradition, became even more experiential in emphasis. An increasing number of people in the 1970s seemed to be more interested in religious practice than they were in religious belief or theory. There was more interest in experiencing religion than in talking about it or hearing about it at second-hand.

MAIN-LINE DECLINE, CONSERVATIVE GROWTH

In the 1970s most main-line Protestant churches declined in membership and financial resources. These religious groups experienced dissension among members over their understanding of the church's mission, the issue of religious belief, and the nature of religious authority.[4] Roman Catholicism, which had experienced a decline in vitality in the late 1960s, made a slow but sustained comeback in the 1970s. Synagogue Judaism did not experience a dramatic revival or declension.

The important change in the 1970s was the growth of evangelical and Fundamentalist churches. The resurgence of ultraconservative Christian groups was still going strong in the early 1980s. This trend was documented by Dean M. Kelley in two editions of his book *Why Conservative Churches Are Growing*.[5] Kelley suggests that he might more accurately have titled his book, *Why Strict Churches Are Successful*. Kelley found that those religious communities which are character-

---

[3] Sydney E. Ahlstrom, *A Religious History of the American People* (New Haven, Conn,: Yale University Press, 1972), p. 1082.
[4] See Jeffrey K. Hadden, *The Gathering Storm in the Churches* (Garden City, N.Y.: Doubleday, 1970).
[5] Dean M. Kelley, *Why Conservative Churches Are Growing* (New York: Harper & Row, 1977).

ized by seriousness, strictness, costliness, and bindingness are the ones that achieve the goals of their ministry and realize institutional growth.

The charismatic movement—the designation for Pentecostalism among main-line churches—was noteworthy during the 1970s. What had previously been an emphasis largely limited to the Holiness-Pentecostal churches is now to be found among Roman Catholics, Episcopalians, Methodists, Presbyterians, Baptists, and Congregationalists. The distinguishing mark of the charismatic Christian is speaking in tongues—glossolalia. Charismatics also characteristically believe in spirit-guided decision making and faith healing.

LIBERATION THEOLOGIES

Among many main-line liberal Christians, liberation theologies have had a great deal of influence on Christian ethics. The emphasis on liberation from oppression has taken various forms among black, Third World, and feminist theologians respectively. One of the first spokespersons for a theology of liberation was the Peruvian theologian Gustavo Gutierrez, whose book *A Theology of Liberation* had great impact in American theological circles. Gutierrez notes that the social problem or the social question has been discussed among Christians for a long time, but

> it is only in the last few years that people have become clearly aware of the scope of misery and especially of the oppressive and alienating circumstances in which the great majority of mankind exists. . . . Moreover, today people are more deeply aware both of personal responsibility in this situation and the obstacles these conditions present to the complete fulfillment of all men, exploiters and exploited alike [feminist liberationists would have preferred humankind and men and women].[6]

The following document is an introduction to the various theologies of liberation; its author is a member of the Harvard Divinity School faculty.

Document 65 _____

"Theologies of Liberation" by Jane Redmont

In recent years, the term "theology of liberation" has become familiar to the public through reports on Pope John Paul II's visits to Mexico and Brazil and articles on the church and its relation to the political situation in countries of the Third World. The term liberation itself made its appearance in the political and theological languages of Latin America a dozen years ago. The 1960s had been the

SOURCE: Jane Redmont, "Theologies of Liberation," *Harvard Divinity Bulletin*, Vol. XI, No. 1, pp. 8–9. Copyright, 1981, The President and Fellows of Harvard College.

[6]Gustavo Gutierrez, *A Theology of Liberation*, translated and edited by Sister Caridad Inda and John Eagleson (New York: Maryknoll, 1973), pp. 64–65.

Decade of Development of the United Nations. In his 1967 Encyclical, *Populorum Progressio*, Popo Paul VI called development "a new word for peace." However, by the end of the decade, "development" had taken on a pejorative meaning in those very countries for whom it was intended to signify hope and increased well-being. For many in Latin America, development came to mean a mere reformism which did not begin to touch the international system of trade—a system which, according to the critics of development, left Latin American countries in a secondary role in the system of international exchange, a situation of dependence, of economic colonialism.

Meeting at Medellín, Colombia, in September 1968, the Catholic bishops of Latin America expressed salvation in terms of "liberation," and by according liberation a central place in their statement, gave their blessing to a movement that was already under way.

In the beginning was the experience of a people held in bondage. Through their liberation from slavery, they experienced the power of a living God in their lives. Later, as they reflected together on this experience, they came to see it as both sacred and social history. They wrote it down and remembered it regularly as a community. This experience—the struggle of the people of Israel as written down in the Biblical book of Exodus—provides a primary model for the theologies of liberation in Latin America. Like the community which lived through the Exodus, theologians of liberation assert the unity of history; they deny the existence of two parallel histories, one sacred and the other profane. Their use of the particular, localized historical model of the Exodus is consistent with their belief that all theology must begin in a given sociological situation.

Properly speaking, there is not one theology of liberation. Rather, liberation theologies are many; this is consistent with the practice of starting with a particular historical situation. Latin American countries vary greatly in their racial, economic and political compositions, and the theologies born in each situation are reflective of their place of birth. However, theologies of liberation do agree on several points:

1. They agree on how one ought to go about doing theology: Theologies of liberation begin from within pastoral activity, from within a particular social/political situation, with the intent to transform that situation. In a second step, one reflects on the situation in the light of Christian faith—using the resources of the scriptures, church teachings and the insights of the People of God. Finally, one returns to the political/social and pastoral action with a new understanding of both the situation and the faith.

2. The Exodus story serves as a paradigm for what God does: God acted on behalf of the oppressed Israelites and continues to act within the communities of the oppressed today.

3. The Kingdom of God is not brought to us by our efforts. It is a gift of God: liberation theology remains a Christian theology.

Critics of the theologies of liberation often accuse them of not holding this third point, but of placing undue emphasis upon human efforts. To North American observers, the most controversial aspect of the theologies of liberation is its frequent use of Marxism as a tool of analysis. Liberation theologians in Latin America have disagreed on the content of liberation: Brazilian Rubem Alves, whose book, *A Theology of Human Hope*, was published in 1969, believes liberation must remain undefined and places the emphasis on working toward a "permanently open society." Peruvian Gustavo Gutiérrez, on the other hand, asserts that although we cannot know entirely what liberation will entail, some intermediary steps are highly recommended. Only Marxism, he says, can provide an analysis which explains the situation of dependency in which the Third World finds itself today. Only Marxism can explain why there has not been "development" by now. Gutiérrez advocates the recognition of class struggle and the building of a socialist society. Gutiérrez, whose book, *A Theology of Liberation*, was published in Spanish in 1971 and in English in 1973 was, with Alves, among the first to treat liberation theology systematically in book form.

Liberation theologians—in Latin America and elsewhere—share the view that theology involves not only understanding of faith but also a political commitment to change society. The question for these theologians, then, says English author Peter Hebblethwaite, in *The Christian-Marxist Dialogue*, is no longer "what is to be believed?" but "what is to be done?" Theology of liberation breaks with traditional Western thinking in claiming what it calls the "primacy of action." Spiritual liberation and the liberation of oppressed people go hand in hand—indeed, liberation of people from social systems which oppress them must be the first priority for Christians, and for other people of good will.

While the term "liberation theology" was coined in Latin America, other regions of the world—particularly Asia and Africa—are beginning to produce original works of theology which use a similar type of analysis, but base themselves in their own social and political situations.

Theology of liberation carries with it a commitment to political struggle. When taught or studied only as theology *about* liberation, it is, according to its proponents, no theology of liberation at all. Theology of liberation is, according to Enrique Dussel, "a barbarian's theology, which shocks and scandalizes the 'wise according to this world,' " a theology born, lived, and made true in struggle—not in the comfortable chairs of universities and ecclesiastical institutions.

There is a great deal of talk these days about the response of North American theologians to the theologians of South America. However, two theological movements which are native—though not limited—to North America may also be considered theologies of liberation. They are Black theology and feminist theology.

Black theology, like the Latin American theologies of liberation, uses the Exodus story as a model. In its current form, Black theology developed after the era of Martin Luther King, when Black religious thinkers developed the conviction that the "suffering love and nonviolence" which he preached were not sufficient. This does not mean that Martin Luther King's life, thought, and struggle have been rejected by today's Black theologians. Indeed, they often serve as a paradigm for the political emphasis of Black theology. Unlike Latin American liberation theology, which exists in relation to a church which had very little involvement in radical change before the late 1960s, Black theology views itself as part of the realization of a revolutionary past in the context of the Black church. Black theology in this new phase, begun in the late 1960s, calls Black people to reclaim and proclaim their cultural and religious traditions, and to assert themselves in the face of white oppression.

The milestone in Black theology was James Cone's *Black Theology and Black Power*, which employed the term "Black Theology" for the first time. The basic problem which Black Theology addressed then and still addresses today is, according to Gayraud S. Wilmore, "the ideological role that racism plays in the culture of the North Atlantic Christian community." This particularism is deliberate. A central criticism leveled by Black theologians against classical Christianity is that it has been too abstract. The statements about the nature of God and God's love have not extended to how these come to bear upon the concrete sufferings of human beings. Black theology is a call back to human need, a re-examination of the challenge of Jesus and his Gospel. It also calls for a new valuing of Black traditions—Black history and Black culture—in this examination of the Gospel.

In a recently published anthology of Black Theology, Gayraud S. Wilmore sums up the three specific contributions that Black theologians have made to the theological enterprise in Europe and North America since the mid-1960s:

"First, Black Theology discovered on undisputable biblical grounds that the liberation of the poor and oppressed, of which Blacks are a prominent example in Western Civilization, is at the heart of Christian faith. It is not that this truth had not been known before, but it had been either suppressed or ignored . . . Black theology has helped us to rediscover that this is what our faith is about: the liberation of human beings from every form of oppression.

"Second, Black Theology demonstrated that Jesus Christ can be de-Americanized without losing his essential meaning as the incarnate Son of God who takes away the sin of the world by his cross and resurrection. Black theology authenticated an apprehension of Jesus of Nazareth in cultural symbols and contexts other than those of White American society. In so doing, it provided an example or model for the indigenization of theology in other societies and cultures. . . .

"Third, Black Theology has legitimated a return to the religious genius of the ancestors who came from places other than Europe. It discovered traces of God's visitation in the primal non-Christian traditions of the past.Because of the work Black historians and theologians have done on the African inheritance in Black religion in the New World, the beliefs, insights, and religious imagination of 'primitive' Blacks can be appropriated as correctives to the deficiencies of the western version of the Christian faith."

Both the Latin American theologies of liberation and Black Theology agree that the content of Christian theology is liberation and that it is inseparably connected with the struggle of victims of oppression. But the methods of explication are different, with Marxism the more frequent tool of analysis in Latin America and race the primary category among Black Theologians here.

Feminist theological scholarship initially uses the same method of doing theology from the point of view of an oppressed group—a group which has not had a chance to be a major shaper of culture. But the primary category which it uses is that of gender. All feminist theologians begin with a common critique: they recognize and begin with the fact that the Jewish and Christian traditions have functioned in a way which has oppressed women. In terms of their image in the tradition, their status as human beings, their roles in the community of the faithful, women have been relegated to second place in Western religion. The feminist critique also points out that Judaism and Christianity (both traditions have produced feminist theologians) have influenced powerfully the image and role of women in our culture, and helped to legitimate the secondary role of women in society.

Feminist theologians begin to differ after this point. The major debate centers on the nature of the religious tradition itself. While Black Theology and theologies of liberation in Third World countries ask what the deeper meaning of the religious tradition is, feminist theologians ask whether the tradition can have any meaning at all for women. Is Christianity a religion of liberation for all people—including women? Or is it simply an ideology which sanctions male privilege? Is the relegation of women to a secondary status in Jewish and Christian communities intentional? Is the oppression of women so irreduceably at the heart of the traditions that they are not "salvageable"? Can Judaism and Christianity continue as viable religions?

The two principal trends in feminist theology are determined by the answers given to these questions. For feminist liberation theologians such as Letty Russell, Rosemary Ruether, and Elisabeth Schüssler Fiorenza, there are elements of liberation in the Jewish and Christian traditions. The task at hand is a task of reinterpretation.

Another group believes that the religious traditions are irreduceably agents of oppression, constructed to sustain male supremacy. This group no longer identifies its thinkers as theologians, but rather as radical post-Christian feminist theorists. Mary Daly, the major representative of this group, now characterizes herself as a meta-ethicist, having moved from a reformist stance about the tradition (*The Church and the Second Sex*, 1968) to a "post-Christian feminist" perspective critical of the tradition and directed beyond the critical task toward the creation of new language and new space for women to express themselves spiritually (*Beyond God the Father*, 1973); and finally to a radically separatist position which asserts that our cultural tradition dominated by men and shaped by the Judaeo-Christian tradition, is bringing the world to self-destruction. She is not concerned specifically with constructing a viable religion but with encouraging women to live in such a way as to express themselves without the restraints of patriarchal culture (*Gyn/Ecology*, 1978).

Other feminist theologians who believe that the Western traditions are at their heart incapable of bringing women to wholeness are concerned with constructing or reconstructing a religion which meets the needs of women, giving them not necessarily dominance and supremacy, but the same capacity as men for fullness of being.

Recovering women's experience is one of the central tasks of feminist theology. Feminist theologians remind us that we do not really know the nature of *human* religious experience: what has been presented as "universal human religious experience" is generally the experience of male human beings (usually white, Western men). We need, feminist theologians believe, to know women's perspectives—past and present—on themselves, on men, on social and spiritual reality. The first stage of feminist theology is the critique of theology and religious institutions from a feminist perspective. The second stage is the naming of reality from this perspective —giving a voice to women.

Feminist theology as we know it is a phenomenon of the 1970s—the theological companion to the contemporary women's movement, just as the Black and Latin

American liberation theologies appeared in the wake of a new consciousness within these groups.

All theologies of liberation call into question the presupposition that the experience of white, Western man is the human experience. They assert the distinctiveness of the experience of Black people, women and Third World people and their contribution to our understanding of human reality. They believe that all theology is contextual, particular, bound to a particular social situation.

Theologies of liberation are concerned with understanding the experience of oppression and with throwing off the bonds of oppression. They believe that all theology is political and that all political settings call for theological reflection. They assert that the truth of all theology must be tested in the realm of action.

Finally, theologies of liberation give a voice to people who have not traditionally shaped Western culture or "classical" Western theology. They do not simply relate the experiences of these oppressed peoples, but express their creativity and their distinctive ways of symbolizing and celebrating their faith.

The feminist critique could have the most far-ranging effect of any of the liberation theologies. Sexism is pervasive in Western culture.[7] One consequence of the feminist critique is a project of the National Council of Churches to develop a nonsexist translation or paraphrase of the three-year biblical lectionary used in many main-line churches.[8] The adoption will be from the Revised Standard Version of the Bible, using "language which expresses inclusiveness with regard to human beings and which attempts to expand the range of images beyond the masculine to assist the church in understanding the full nature of God."[9] Such projects generate opposition from many conservative Christians.

NEW RELIGIOUS MOVEMENTS

New religious movements became prominent during the counterculture era of the late 1960s and captured much media attention in the 1970s.[10] New, in this case, refers to one of the three kinds of groups: (1) religious groups that are imported to America from another culture; (2) religious groups that represent an unforeseen development in cultural trends; (3) religious groups offering a different packaging of be-

[7]Sexism is the exploitation of one sex by the other. The term is commonly used to mean the subordination of women by men through ideology, stereotyping, family structures, and unfair legislation.

[8]A lectionary is a schedule of appointed scripture readings to be used in common worship or personal devotion.

[9]As reported in The Christian Century, Vol. XCVII, No. 41, p. 1239.

[10]See Charles Y. Glock and Robert N. Bellah, eds., The New Religious Consciousness (Berkeley, Calif.: University of California Press, 1976). Jacob Needleman and George Baker, eds., Understanding the New Religions (New York: Seabury, 1978). Robert Wuthrow, Experimentation in American Religion (Berkeley, Calif.: University of California Press, 1978). Robert S. Ellwood, Jr., Alternative Altars: Unconventional and Eastern Spirituality in America (Chicago: University of Chicago Press, 1979). Irving I. Zaretsky and Mark P. Leone, Religious Movements in Contemporary America (Princeton, N.J.: Princeton University Press, 1974).

liefs and practices which in themselves are familiar components of conventional faiths. There was a steady progression of groups to center stage, and these then faded out of range of the media spotlight. In the early seventies, it was the Jesus People and the Divine Light Mission. By the mid-1970s, it was the Society for Krishna Consciousness and Sun Myung Moon's Unification Church.

New religious movements, particularly those identified as cults, got a very bad press in November, 1978, when the world learned that 913 members of People's Temple Christian Church died in Jonestown, Guyana—victims of ritual suicide orchestrated by their leader Jim Jones. Jones ordered them to drink a strawberry-flavored potion laced with cyanide and tranquilizers: "Everyone has to die. If you love me as much as I love you, we must all die or be destroyed from the outside." Sociologists, theologians, and social psychologists will be pondering the significance of the Jonestown tragedy for many years.

Included among the new religious movements in America are the old "new" religions that have venerable traditions in their own cultures. Hinduism has had a longer and greater impact on American religious life than any other Eastern religion. Americans were reading Hindu religious classics before there were Hindu bodies in the United States. Emerson and other members of the New England Transcendentalist movement were intrigued with Hindu metaphysics. The beginning of organized Hindu societies in America dates to the 1893 Parliament of Religions held in Chicago. The Vedanta Society, the largest Hindu group in America, was established before 1900, growing out of the vision of Sri Ramakrishna (1836–1886). Over forty other Hindu groups exist in America, one of the most recent and visible of which is the International Society of Krishna Consciousness (ISKCON), founded by A. C. Bhaktivendanta Swami Prabhupada (1896–1977).[11]

The presence of Buddhism in America was occasioned by Japanese immigration to the West coast as early as 1868. The beginning of Buddhism for non-Oriental Americans came with the convening of the World's Parliament of Religions referred to above. There may be as many as 500,000 Buddhists in America, and Buddhism in the 1980s shares the diversity of liberal and conservative trends which characterizes other religious groups.[12]

Muslims in America number less than one million. The economics and politics of oil have made them more visible since 1973. The Islamic revolution in Iran, accompanied by the taking of American hostages in November, 1979, also increased American interest in Islam. The first attempt to establish Islam in America followed the conversion of Mohammed Alexander Russell Webb in 1888. Webb was the American consul in Manila when he was converted. In 1889 Webb edited and

[11] See, J. Gordon Melton, *The Encyclopedia of American Religions* (Wilmington, N.C.: McGrath Publishing Company), Vol. 2, 1978, pp. 355–391.

[12] See Emma McCloy Layman, *Buddhism in America* (Chicago: Nelson-Hall, 1976).

published the periodical, *The Moslem World*. Webb also represented Islam at the Parliament of Religions. Orthodox (Sunni) Muslim centers were organized as early as 1912. Orthodox (Shi'a) Muslims organized in the 1970s as Iraqi and Iranian immigrants arrived in large numbers in the United States. The story of the Black Muslims, now the World Community of Islam in the West, has been told in Chapter 7. There are several other Muslim groups, including Baha'i World Faith, an eclectic religion originating in Persia under the influence of a Sufi Muslim named Mirza Ali Muhammed (1819–1850).[13]

Other religious groups constitute different species altogether and occur by mutation, migration, or a combination of the two. The second type merits the sociological designation of "cult" in that these groups bring a new element to the religious scene. Sociologists Rodney Stark and William Sims Bainbridge clarify the meanings of cult with their distinctions between *audience cults*, *client cults*, and *cult movements*.[14] An *audience cult* is part of a "diffuse occult milieu that toys with vague images of the ultimate." In *client cults* the relationship of the cult member to cult leadership resembles that "between therapist and patient, or between consultant and client. Considerable organization may be found among those *offering* the cult service, but clients remain little organized."[15] There is no sustained effort to organize the clients into a social movement and clients often maintain a primary commitment to other religious organizations. *Cult movements* are full religions in that they have beliefs about the ultimate nature of reality, they have rites and ceremonies, and they have well-developed organizational structures. Cult movements also make greater demands on their followers.

Audience cults offer comparatively vague and weak compensators (a term used by sociologists of religion for the benefits derived from participation in a religious body), while client cults provide very specific compensators. An example of a cult audience would be those who "follow" astrology without making any primary commitment to it. An example of the client cult would be the therapy of "dianetics," which was to develop into the controversial cult movement of Scientology.

Audience and client cults do not tend to generate hostility in the wider culture. Establishment religious leaders do not get too perturbed over the astrology cult, and client cults (if they do not violate fraud or licensing statutes) are seldom harassed. Client cults, because they charge for their services, serve a middle- or upper-class clientele. From the spiritualists of late-nineteenth and twentieth-century America to the human potential cults of the '70s, these groups do not generate opposition from established institutions.

---

[13] J. Gordon Melton, *Encyclopedia of American Religions*, pp. 337–354.

[14] Rodney Stark and William Sims Bainbridge, "Of Churches, Sects, and Cults: Preliminary Concepts for A Theory of Religious Movements," *Journal for the Scientific Study of Religion*, Vol. 18, No. 2 (1979), pp. 117–133.

[15] Ibid., p. 126.

In the case of the cult movements, however, Stark and Bainbridge maintain that "the more a cult mobilizes its membership, the greater the opposition it engenders."

> Cults whose members remain in the society to pursue normal lives and occupations engender much less opposition than do cults whose members drop everything and become full-time converts. In part, this is probably because cults that function as total institutions rupture converts' ties to conventional institutions. This generates personal grievances against the movement. It is one thing to know your son or daughter, for example, attends a weird church and has odd beliefs, but it is quite something else to lose contact with a child who takes up fulltime participation in an alien faith. . . . Thus the rule seems to be, the more total the movement, the more total the opposition to it.[16]

One such cult movement which has generated conflict with the wider American society is the Unification Church of the Korean religious leader, Sun Myung Moon. The "Moonies," as his followers are known, are being singled out here because the Unification Church has been in the public eye since the early 1970s, when Moon first came to America. The Unification movement also exemplifies two themes that are common among the cult movements: 1. surrogate family relations and 2. a comprehensive ideology.

The central theme in Moonist theology is the family: the God-oriented family as the locus of salvation. Salvation for the Moonist does not consist in the receiving of forgiveness but rather in becoming a member of the "True Family."

THE RESTORATION TO TRUE FAMILY

Unification theology is eclectic, syncretistic, and esoteric. The theology is based on the receiving of "new, ultimate, and final truth" by the God-chosen messenger, Sun Myung Moon. The movement's official doctrinal statement, and a part of the revelation, is the *Divine Principle. Divine Principle*, which is both an oral and a written tradition, published in several versions, is the Completed Testament. The Rev. Moon claims he has come not to destroy or abrogate the Old and New Testaments, but to fulfill them—to complete them. The Rev. Moon is seen primarily as "true father," probably the Messiah, and only secondarily as a theologian. In an effort to systematize Moon's teachings, several members of the Unification Church in Korea have put together a developing theological system in the *Divine Principle* which is impressive in its imaginativeness, coherence, and consistency, if not in its Christian orthodoxy. As the most complete expression of Moonist teachings to date, *Divine Principle* is the basic text of the Unification Church.[17] The two major divisions of the system are the doctrines of

---

[16] Ibid., p. 128.

[17] *The Divine Principle* (New York: The Holy Spirit Association for the Unification of World Christianity, 1973). The fifth edition is 536 pages in length and evidences fuller development than an earlier English edition.

Creation and Restoration. There are many subsets to these major divisions, but Creation and Restoration are the foci for the Moonist theological system.

Moon's theological system is based on a relational ontology which understands God's nature to have "dual essentialities"—containing both subject and object—and every creation is a "substantial object" of the invisible deity of God, the Creator. God's creation must reflect God's dual essentialities. The purpose of the creation of the universe was God's joy in the reflection of his own nature: "God wanted to feel happiness whenever he looked at His creation." (*D.P.*, 41) The purpose of the creation of man, after the image of God's own nature, was that man should enjoy his position as an object of God and thus increase God's happiness. God therefore gave to Adam and Eve three great blessings: to be fruitful, to multiply and fill the earth, and to subdue it and have dominion. These three great blessings should have been fulfilled on the basis and with the completion of the four position foundation: "The four position foundation is manifested as God, husband and wife, and their offspring." (*D.P.*, 32) Man was created as both spiritual and physical being, each dimension having its own structure and function and each in reciprocal relationship with the other: ". . . unless a man leads a good life, the living spirit element cannot provide anything for the betterment of physical man. . . . Likewise, our spirit man can be perfected only through our physical life on earth." (*D.P.*, 62)

The primal act which was the occasion for the fall of man was fornication: an improper act of love. Lucifer seduced Eve and she responded by committing illicit sexual intercourse and then, thinking that she might reverse the process which had been set in motion, Eve seduced Adam and he in turn responded by having sexual relations prematurely. The point is that Adam and Eve were in a growth period during which they were to relate as brother and sister. The original sin, then, was unprincipled love. According to *Divine Principle*, the fall is both spiritual and physical in its nature.

> Since God created man in spirit and flesh, the fall also took place in spirit and flesh. The fall through the blood relationship between the angel and Eve was the spiritual fall, while that through the blood relationship between Eve and Adam was the physical fall. (*D.P.*, 77)

The result of the fall was that the world of creation was now based on the four position foundation, centered on Satan (Lucifer) rather than on God. Formally, Moon's understanding of original sin is that of unprincipled love; materially it is "unrighteous intercourse."

According to Moon, God has been working to restore creation ever since the original fall. Human history is the history of attempted restoration. This history is divided into three dispensations: the Old Testament Age; the New Testament Age; and the age of the Second Advent—the Completed Testament. According to the *Divine Principle* the entire period of human history is 6,000 years: 2,000 years from Adam to Abraham, 2,000 years from Abraham to Jesus, and 2,000 years from Jesus to the Second Advent. The end of World War I marks the beginning of the Age of the Completed Testament.

The New Testament Age was not the age of restoration because of the cross. To fulfill God's mandate, Jesus, with the divine blessing, should have been united with a woman who, in the position of Eve, reared children; thus he would have re-established a God-centered four position foundation. All men could have been restored to the original perfection by being grafted both spiritually and physically with Jesus. The death of Jesus on the cross, due to the disloyalty of his followers, meant that he could accomplish only the spiritual restoration of creation. He failed to accomplish the physical restoration. This is why the Moonist reveres Jesus, yet cannot believe in the full sufficiency of his work. Jesus is a tragic figure betrayed and lost; and God's hopes are crushed—a state of affairs which causes God to suffer.

To meet the conditions for full restoration there must be a Second Coming of the Messiah—the Third Adam. In the age of the Second Advent the Kingdom of God on Earth will be established. The *Divine Principle* describes the conditions to be met if the Second Advent is to occur. The first condition is the arrival of the Lord of the New Age. This was preceded by the Satanic counteraction of Wilheim I who initiated World War I. The second condition is the start of the Lord of the Second Advent's mission, which was Satanically counteracted by Hitler with the initiation of World War II. The third condition was met by an event which initiated the Cosmic restoration in 1960, again preceded by the counteraction of the communist regime in the Soviet Union. These formal conditions for the time of the Second Advent were fulfilled as follows: 1) the birth of Sun Myung Moon on January 6, 1920; 2) the vision of Jesus that Moon experienced Easter Sunday, 1936, at which time Jesus revealed that Moon was to accomplish the restoration of the world; 3) the marriage of Moon to Hak-Ja Han, April 11, 1960, which began her twenty-one year course of preparation to become "True Mother" to "True Father," the new Eve to the Third Adam.

The climax of the revelation contained in the *Divine Principle* is the announcement that "the nation of the East where Christ will come again would be none other than Korea." (*D.P.*, 520) as Moon is the Third Adam, Korea is the third Israel. In order to demonstrate that Korea is the birth place of the Second Messiah, the *Divine Principle* cites the following considerations: 1) the "fact" that Korea has suffered forty years of Japanese colonial domination; 2) the "fact" that Korea is a nation which is both God's front line (South Korea) and Satan's (i.e., North Korean communism's) front line for the final confrontation; 3) the "fact" that Korea is a nation which always has valued "loyalty, filial piety, and virtue" qualifies it as a nation which is close to God's heart; 4) the persistent Korean folk belief in the prophecy that the "King of righteousness" would appear in Korea. (*D.P.*, 520–528)

Moonist theology is eclectic in that it is composed of motifs selected from many sources. One can easily discern elements from primitive Korean Shamanism, Confucianism, Mahayana Buddhism, Taoism, Roman Catholic Christianity, and Presbyterian Calvinism. Another way of saying this is to say the Moon's theology is typically Korean. Korean culture reflects the fact that, in its documented history of more than two thousand years, it has experienced a series of invasions and depredations by stronger nations. Korean culture is eclectic.

Moonist theology also is syncretistic in that it attempts to reconcile or unify these apparently different motifs into a coherent system. The Korean people have always experienced a desperate need for religious, cultural, and political unification. Koreans have demonstrated a continuing ability to assimilate what is alien into their own sense of reality and tradition. It is instructive to note that the Reverend Sun Myung Moon's movement is not the first religious movement which has sought the unification of Korean culture. Ch'ŏdogyo, the "Religion of the Heavenly Way," played a significant role in the development of Korean nationalism and in Korea's struggle for independence. It began in 1860 as a religious movement, but Ch'ŏdogyo early acquired a strong political emphasis. The movement was founded by Ch'oe Che-u, who, as is the case with the Reverend Moon, received a supernatural revelation. Ch'ŏdogyo bore a resemblance to Christianity, but it was essentially a syncretistic religion which proclaimed a new age which was to be established through human effort.[18]

Moonist theology also is esoteric, not only in that it is difficult to understand, but also in that there are levels of its teaching expressions which are thought to be understood only by the especially initiated. Certain teachings are to be reserved for those who are established in the faith. Among these, for example, are lectures that instruct members in such matters as proselytizing, witnessing, and fund raising.

To observe that the Moonist theology is eclectic, syncretistic, and at least quasi-esoteric is not to assert that it doesn't have integrity. The unifying concept of Moonist teaching is that of the family, and this concept is rooted deeply in Korean culture. The essential basis of oriental society rests on blood relationship. The ethical basis for Korean society was ancestor worship and friendship among family members, the deep Confucian substratum of Korean social philosophy. Therefore, the meaning of marriage is found only in relationship with the "Family" and marriages are to be performed by families, not by individuals.

[18] See Benjamin B. Weems, *Reform Rebellion, and the Heavenly Way* (Tuscon, Ariz.: The University of Arizona Press, 1964).

Traditionally the three greatest expressions of morality for the Korean people have been loyalty to the king, filial piety to parents, and chastity and obedience toward one's husband. True marriage, then, was only possible in accordance with obedience to the family-nation and to the parent. It is in this context that we understand the Reverend Moon's answer to a fractured and pluralistic world, an answer which is a poignantly Korean answer.

> So far in the universe, no central parents have existed. We have only had false parents, who brought the elements of distrust and betrayal day in and day out. Therefore there have been no true brothers and sisters and no true husband and wife. True parents were not there, and true sinless children were not there. In other words, the heavenly family was lost. . . . Mankind, throughout history, has been blind, not knowing why they lived, where they came from, or where they were going. . . . Why? Because they did not have one central point—true parents as their true ancestors. (Once) you know the central point of this universe, the True parents, from this central point as an axis or starting point, you cannot only understand, but you are given the power to win that past, present, and future. [19]

The one sacrament in the Unification Church is the blessing of marriages arranged by the True Parent, after the member has demonstrated the ability to live a disciplined life of principled love with other brothers and sisters for at least three years.

Unification thought and community must be understood in large measure as a synthesis resulting from almost two hundred years of Christian missionary teaching as it has interacted with indigenous Korean culture.

A number of American youth have been attracted to the Korean Messianic movement described above. There probably are no more than 8,000 committed Moonists in the United States, and the movement seems to have peaked around 1977. There have been, nevertheless, an impressive number of young adults who are attracted to high-intensity religion and who have found the answer to their vocational and ideological needs in the Unification church. Most of them "met the family" when they were between the ages of eighteen and twenty-five. One such Moonie wrote the following letter to one of the authors of this text. His real name is not used, but he has a childhood background in the Episcopal Church; he graduated from a good preparatory school; he has a B.A. degree in a natural science and joined the Unification Church as a graduate student. The letter was written shortly after the Jonestown tragedy in November 1978. It is an earnest, even poignant letter from a member of a cult who, as he writes, would rather follow "Donald Duck" than participate in a system from which he is alienated.

---

[19] A speech by the Reverend Moon, March 24, 1974.

Tom Kellogg's Letter to Leo Sandon

12-10-78

Dear Leo:

It does seem to me that now is probably the most interesting and important time period, *Divine Principle* or no *Divine Principle*, Unification Church or no Unification Church, in American religious history. I would not trade my life for some other more glorious existence in the past or the future because I am "on the dime." All my life I have seen hatred in one form or another. Sometimes it was the gang of kids chasing me and a friend down the road, and at other times things were turned around. But always somebody was hating somebody. Freud called it "thanatos." Now this situation we call life never used to bother me until I joined the Unification church. Truthfully, I was rather autonomous.

Suddenly, I began to see the kind of hate that one only imagines in daydreams over *A Tale of Two Cities*. There they were knitting away and clapping as the heads rolled and the axes fell. Young people like me getting spat on, thrown off 20-story roofs, kidnapped and stripped and never really forgetting . . . there is nothing "good" about indemnity. [Indemnity is a Moonist principle that teaches that indemnity must be paid by contemporary believers for the sins of past generations if restoration is to be effected.] But what bothers me is the fact that people go so crazy to protect their concept of the human norm. What is the norm? And why are Americans so serious about defending an "apple pie" and "family" tradition that has never really been more than an illusory comfort? We are everybody's dream smashers. We are the children who would pass away into suburbia but turned "to new religions instead." And rather than pass into selfishness, we continue to dream on.

If Donald Duck was really the messiah, I would follow him. Why? Because I think most people need to see it. They need to see it because it is their only hope. Otherwise, they can never stop hating. Think of it, your generation hit the road South to Birmingham, and here I would be, following Donald. Why? I am a dream smasher, and I love God radically. Jesus "Christ" was a dream smasher like me. He saw all the people following meaningless paths and sought to challenge their complacency. He was a "redefiner" and a mystery and a heretic in every way. But my God, he made his point.

Now I am 26 years old, and I have worked as a boat builder, a dog groomer, a lawn mower, a surveyor, and a classical guitarist, and I can do whatever I want. When I look at this world, the only thing that really matters to me, finally, is shaking the foundations, smashing dreams of normalcy (because they are inevitably selfish ones)—after all, Jesus could have been a carpenter forever, but he just couldn't.

Now I am aware that we sometimes create the most intense hatred possible. Almost nobody can agree on anything, but everyone can agree that we are easy targets. That's why we are the church that nobody can replace. No Lutheran, no Muslim,

SOURCE: Permission from Tom Kellogg to publish his letter to Leo Sandon, December 10, 1978.

no Jew, no People's Temple . . . because our guy is a real live Don Quixote de la Mancha who cries real tears for humanity.

Best Wishes,
Tom Kellogg

Robert J. Lifton, professor of psychiatry at Yale, has studied what he calls totalistic environments[20] and reminds us that cults should be understood in the context of our times. Lifton argues that cults "are a product of historical dislocation—of the loss and frequent dishonoring of traditional symbols of family, religion, authority, government—the life cycle in general. In the past, these symbols have provided means of continuity beyond the self, or what I call symbolic immortality. That is, they connected ordinary life with eternal structures and spiritual principles."[21] In the 1970s many persons have been led to adopt what Lifton calls the *constricted* style of life. The constricted life-style is an attempt to hold on to a single, absolutely unchanging sense of self. Lifton writes that cults are part of a worldwide impulse toward Fundamentalism or restorationism, an attempt to "fend off currents of change through the construction of an airtight moral and social order, through restoring the perfect harmony of a past that never was or through moving to a future based on the imagery of a past golden age."[22]

New religious movements are a part of the contemporary ferment in American religion. There has been a tendency, however, to assume that they play a larger role than they actually do. The main-line churches lose more members by attrition each year than the total number of persons seriously involved in cult movements. The fact remains that thousands of Americans have found in cult movements the answers to their religious questions.

THE ELECTRONIC CHURCH

The phenomenal success of a new type of religious television broadcasting is an important part of the current religious ferment. An electronic church has emerged from a revolutionary computer technology that permits the rapid storage and retrieval of information. This technological development has revolutionized all communication, and religious programmers have adapted it to evangelism. Sociologist Jeffrey Hadden observes:

The mailrooms of the more successful electronic church practitioners are paragons of modern communication technology. Mail is sorted first by the presence or absence of money. Then letters are sorted by topics, and appropriate paragraphs are retrieved by computer and woven into some appropriate prepared re-

[20] Robert J. Lifton, *Thought Reform and the Psychology of Totalism: A Study of "Brainwashing" in China* (New York: Norton, 1963).
[21] Robert J. Lifton, "The Appeal of the Death Trip," *The New York Times Magazine*, January 7, 1979, p. 27.
[22] Ibid.

sponse that can thus be "personalized." On-line printers dash off these individ- ualized answers. Several organizations reportedly have a capacity for processing 20,000 or more letters a day.[23]

As Hadden points out, this technology is compatible with evangelical Christians' theological stance toward proselytizing. The electronic church, therefore, is dominated by conservative evangelicals.

One superstar of the electronic church world is Pat Robertson of Virginia Beach Virginia, whose television ministry has grown into the Christian Broadcasting Network (CBN). Robertsons's 700 Club appears in 90-minute segments on 130 stations, 3,500 cable television systems, and 4 CBN-owned stations. In 1978 he raised $58 million by constant appeals for money through a telethon format.

Jim Bakker of Charlotte, North Carolina, left Robertson's 700 Club in 1972 and established his PTL Club, now organized as the PTL Television Network. Bakker's *Praise the Lord* or *People That Love* operation grosses more than $25 million a year.

The Reverend Jerry Falwell's *Old-Time Gospel Hour* is carried on 304 television stations in this country and 69 abroad. In Lynchburg, Virginia, Falwell presides over the Thomas Road Baptist Church, a private Christian academy called the Liberty Baptist College, and the headquarters of his vast electronic church empire. Falwell's *Old-Time Gospel Hour* grosses almost $46 million a year.

The electronic church actually raises more money than the combined general mission budget of several main-line denominations. Main-liners feel threatened by the loss of dollars to television ministries that may become "electronic denominations." There are questions concerning the ethics involved in much of the fund raising which, at its worst, has as its sole end the perpetuation of programming. Critics of the electronic church charge that its message is simplistic, providing "instant gratification" rather than resources to meet complex problems. There also is a linkage between some of the electronic evangelists and a rigid type of right-wing politics, as we shall see below.

THE POLITICAL MOBILIZATION OF ULTRACONSERVATIVE EVANGELICALS

In 1980 rallies and seminars sponsored by a group called *Moral Majority* were held throughout the United States. The rally format began as "God Bless America" was sung with Kate Smith gusto. One of the spellbinding pulpiteers associated with the movement exhorted the audience to become politically informed and active. Smiling college students sang and danced to patriotic themes.

The climax of the evening was a 90-minute $110,000 multimedia presentation entitled *America, You Are Too Young to Die*. Images of Charles Manson, Times Square sex emporiums, young men in ap-

[23]Jeffrey K. Hadden, "Soul-Saving via Video," *The Christian Century*, Vol. XCVII, No. 20, pp. 609–613.

parent homosexual embrace, and bloody fetuses lying in hospital pans were juxtaposed with images of an American past that was centered on God, family, Christian piety, and morality in public life. A quotation from Gus Hall, former head of the Communist party in the United States, was flashed on the screen: "I dream of the hour when the last congressman is strangled to death on the guts of the last preacher."

Before the rally, those interested in the organization attended separate (men and women are segregated) four-hour seminars designed to teach them how to organize Moral Majority chapters in their communities. They were briefed by a national Moral Majority officer on policy issues, on the dangers of secular humanism, and on the nuts and bolts of political organization. The seminars focused on practical aspects of organizational development: the preparation of questionnaires, the planning of news conferences, the strategy for registering voters.

Though Moral Majority is the most visible organization, there are other significant organizations in militant evangelical/political coalition. There is also the Religious Roundtable—composed of fifty-six members, corresponding to the fifty-six signers of the Declaration of Independence—which includes prominent television evangelists and many of the politicians who are associated with the far right. The Roundtable, which functions as a coordinating body for the militant evangelicals, sponsored the famous National Affairs Briefing in Dallas on August 21–22, 1980. The Briefing was attended by approximately 12,000 conservative ministers who heard Ronald Reagan call for a return to the "old-time religion" and the "old-time Constitution." Those attending also heard the Reverend Bailey Smith declare "God almighty does not hear the prayer of a Jew, for how in the world can God hear the prayer of a man who says Jesus Christ is not the true Messiah?"

Yet another organization is Christian Voice, a political organization of ultraconservative evangelical ministers that was organized in 1979. The formation of Christian Voice was occasioned by the Internal Revenue Service's investigation of evangelical schools in 1978. In the recent national election, Christian Voice compiled a rating system of the voting records of congressmen with special reference to homosexuality, abortion, and pornography.

Moral Majority has attracted much attention and is credited with having a significant impact on the 1980 presidential and congressional elections.[24] Founded in 1977, the organization's national membership has grown to 400,000, 72,000 of whom are ministers. Moral Majority claims

---

[24] Apparently the impact of Moral Majority on the 1980 elections has been overrated. Seymour Martin Lipset and Earl Rabb argue, on the basis of their analysis of election results, that Americans who "turned right" in 1980 did not agree with the Moral Majority or New Right programs: "These Americans were not supporting specific political solutions any more than they usually do. They wanted a government that would demonstrably reflect their *mood*: a more assertive America on the world scene, and on the domestic front a serious campaign to fight inflation and refurbish American industry. That is the extent of their political conservatism." Seymour Martin Lipset and Earl Rabb, "The Election & the Evangelicals," *Commentary*, Vol. 71, No. 3 (March 1981), p. 47.

to have registered 3 million voters, during the 1980 presidential election. In Alaska, ultraconservative evangelicals following the Reverend Jerry Fallwell's personal direction and inspiration captured the Republican state convention and led it to the early support of Ronald Reagan. In Gainesville, Florida, forty-two members of the Southside Baptist Church won seats on the Alachua County Democratic Central Committee in an election that filled fifty-three vacancies. Their pastor, the Reverend Gene Keith, who ran unsuccessfully for the Florida Senate, had attended a Moral Majority seminar before he became active in politics. The Baptist activists, eight of whom were formerly Republicans, caught regular party officials by surprise.

Evangelical religious leaders were active in the Reagan presidential campaign. A representative group of conservative preachers met three times during the year with Bill Brock, Republican national chairman. They felt they were influential in shaping the party platform. Falwell, founder and head of Moral Majority, was in Detroit for the Republican Convention and attempted to persuade Reagan not to choose George Bush as his running mate. Bush was deemed too liberal by the New Right leaders. The evangelicals lost their case, but their presence in Reagan's Renaissance Plaza Hotel suite as the decision was made attests to their influence.

The politically aroused evangelicals believe that America is morally adrift and that time is running out for the opportunity to restore national righteousness. They are against abortion, pornography, the acceptance of homosexuality, and the Equal Rights Amendment: this is their "pro-family" package. They are for prayer in public schools, unconditional support for Israel as a nation, unrestricted private enterprise and a superior national defense. They will support candidates who are "right" on these issues and pray for those who are wrong.

Their rubric for all that is evil in American life is humanism—secular humanism: "The little tugboat of humanism is pulling America into moral degradation." Humanists, according to the ultraconservative evangelicals, are persons who believe in atheism, evolution, situational ethics, the autonomous person, and socialistic one-worldism. A rather typical evangelical exposition of humanism is provided by Glenn E. Fox, executive director of the Association of Christian Schools International:

_____ *Document 67*

From "Secular Humanism" by Glenn E. Fox

The official religion of the public schools is humanism. To many, the word religion means a belief in God. However, religion really means that which is basic and ultimate. That which is most important to us is our religion. What we have in the

SOURCE: Glenn E. Fox, *Encyclopedia for Christian Schools* (Dallas: Life Inc., 1980), p. 506.

public schools (or government schools) is religious humanism: a militant, anti-Christian faith.

The French scholar, Jacques Ellul, wrote a book called *The New Demons*. He is not a Christian but his insight about humanism is remarkable. He says, "Humanism is the unquestionable faith of our time. It has saturated the minds and perspectives of people. People, without intending to be humanists, spout humanism." In essence, this faith has six principles, he says:

1. Man is the measure of all things. The word of man is law—is authoritative.
2. Man is autonomous—totally independent of God. It is God who needs man.
3. Man is a rational being.
4. Man is free to choose between good and evil. His being is not tainted with sin and therefore corrupt. Barring error, ignorance, passion, and superstition—by these terms the humanist means Biblical faith—man will choose good. Therefore, if you purge Biblical faith from man he is going to choose good. Thus, education must eliminate Biblical faith and the Word of God in order to allow the children of humanism to choose good.
5. If evil exists, it is not the fault of man, but of institutions (church and family), society, education, economic systems, division of society into classes, etc. If you abolish these institutions and bring about total equality, then evil will disappear.
6. Whatever is normal is good. Normal means whatever the majority of our group accepts.

The ultraconservative evangelical believes that too many humanists are teaching in our schools, supervising government bureaucracies, and holding public office. Secular humanism's dominance in our national life must be repudiated, and we must effect a restoration to a "one nation, under God" America.

There is nothing particularly new about religious and political conservatism operating together in the United States. Christian anticommunist crusades flourished in the 1950s and the early 1960s. The late J. Howard Pew, founder of the Sun Oil Company, established and financed the Christian Freedom Foundation, which is engaged in the advocacy of the free enterprise system. There are, however, four new factors present in current conservative evangelical political activism.

First, there is the new breed of an American religious type, the independent evangelist: Today's version of the independent evangelist is the big-time television preacher. These preachers have created an electronic constituency of at least 10 to 14 million regular viewers. The television congregations have proved to be a reservoir of financial resources for incredible fund-raising feats.

A second important factor is the linkage between these electronic ministries and leaders of the New Right. Men who are former school administrators, business executives, and political organizers have organized the conservative evangelical constituency into a cohesive coalition. The three key leaders of New Right political activity are Richard Viguerie, the successful professional fund raiser and publisher of the *Conservative Digest*; Terry Dolan of the National Conservative Political Action Committee (NCPAC); and Paul Weyrich, director of the Committee for the Survival of a Free Congress (CFSFC). Weyrich and Viguerie founded the CFSFC and the Heritage Foundation, the New Right think tank, in 1974. Weyrich, a political conservative and Eastern Rite Catholic, discovered "the sleeping giant" of the ultraconservative constituency. Two other names of some importance are the Religious Roundtable's president, Ed McAteer, and Howard Phillips, the head of the Conservative Caucus. Weyrich organized Christian Voice in 1979, giving the New Right access to the religious Fundamentalist constituency. McAteer introduced Phillips to Jerry Falwell, and soon thereafter Falwell organized Moral Majority with the Reverend Bob Billings as the executive director. Up until that time Billings had been Weyrich's deputy at CFSFC.

Falwell thus founded Moral Majority on the advice of and in consultation with a group of New Right veterans who are professional organizers and managers. These men know how to use computer mailing lists, and they are skilled in organizational development. The constituency is no longer a diffuse Bible Belt population led by charismatic leaders who are short on organizational competence.

A third factor contributing to the movement's success is the willingness of militant evangelicals to enter into coalition with those who do not share the same theological beliefs. In the past the Fundamentalists' obsession for doctrinal purity hampered their ability to form alliances or enter into coalition. A Utah Moral Majority chapter has recently been organized even though Mormon theology is a scandalous heresy to an independent Baptist. Mormons as politically conservative Americans are "right" on all of the key moral issues. Ultraconservative evangelicals are now willing to enter into political coalition with those with whom they cannot enter into full fellowship. Cooperation with Roman Catholics, which in the past would have been problematical if not unthinkable, has become part of the working strategy. Weyrich refers to this development as reverse ecumenism "because the original ecumenical movement was a very liberal movement. And now we have cooperation among . . . all kinds of people who frankly didn't speak to each other."

A fourth factor is the establishment over the past fifteen years of a network of private Christian academies. There are over 16,000 Christian schools in the United States, and they have both defined and consolidated the conservative evangelical subculture. Leaders of the Christian school movement claim that a new Christian school is established in the United States every seven hours. Certainly the movement is a significant force in American society. The interests of the private evangelical academy both provoked the ultraconservative evangelical political movement and provided its leadership network.

The 1978 decision of the Internal Revenue Service to challenge the tax-exempt status of private Christian schools—especially segregated schools in the South—provoked a strong response. Weyrich moved quickly to express the New Right's sympathy and support for the schools. One of Moral Majority's admonitions to its members is that they must resist the government interference that would "stifle and harass" them in their mission of Christian education. The leadership of Moral Majority consists largely of men who were administrators of private Christian schools.

The term *evangelical* is notoriously imprecise. In American life it has come to mean those Christians who describe themselves as "born again" or "twice born." The focus is on the believer's personal conversion to Jesus Christ as Lord and Savior. The evangelical tradition in the United States is deeply rooted in our nation's frontier experience and can be traced to eighteenth-century awakenings and revivals. Between 40 million and 75 million Americans, depending on how rigorously the term *evangelical* is defined, consider themselves to be part of this tradition.

The Fundamentalists constitute a subset of this broad evangelical population. Fundamentalism emerged as a movement in the nineteenth century; it was a more militant and narrowly gauged expression of Protestant Christianity than main-line evangelicalism. The core of Moral Majority can be described as Fundamentalist in heritage, belief, and life-style.

Not all evangelicals are conservative in their politics. The most theologically articulate evangelical in Congress, Senator Mark Hatfield, a Republican from Oregon, has a progressive if not liberal voting record. One of the most interesting developments the past fifteen years has been the emergence of an evangelical left—a group of political activists who would disagree with Moral Majority on many issues. Although many Southern Baptists are members of Moral Majority, others are critical of the organization.

Black evangelicals do not play an important role in the new political coalition. The coalition is not strictly white, but it has not attracted minority groups.

Not all conservative evangelicals have become politically organized. Oral Roberts and Rex Humbard, to name two prominent television evangelists, have chosen not to participate in the political movement. Billy Graham has publicly cautioned the partisan, politically active leaders not to become too closely identified with a particular viewpoint.

Moral Majority's message is appealing to millions of Americans who do not belong to the Fundamentalist subculture. Belief in the importance of personal morality, a devotion to free enterprise capitalism, and a conviction that we must maintain military superiority are positions held by what probably is a majority of Americans.

It is difficult to gauge the influence the conservative Christian coalition has had and will continue to have on American politics. Television evangelists tend to exaggerate the number of their followers, and it is hard to get accurate data on the actual number of grass-roots activists. It is unclear what the actual impact of the ultraconservative evangelicals was in the 1980 elections. What is clear is that a particular electorate is being organized; its views on issues have been developed; it is learning a common language and establishing a common network of communication; it is raising money to support candidates and to affect policy on federal, state, and local levels; and, finally, it is training workers in the ways of political organization. Ultraconservative evangelicals will probably be a visible and significant force in American politics in the 1980s.

SCIENTIFIC CREATIONISM AND EVOLUTION

Christian Fundamentalists have mounted an attack on evolution more than a half century after the Scopes "monkey trial" in Dayton, Tennessee (1925) and more than a century after Charles Darwin published his *Origin of Species*. By March 1981, Fundamentalist groups persuaded legislators in fourteen states to indroduce laws requiring that creationist views be taught in science classes. At the National Affairs Briefing in Dallas of August 1980, candidate Reagan, when asked his view on evolution, replied: "It is a scientific theory only, and it is not believed in the scientific community to be as infallible as it was once believed. But if it is going to be taught in schools, then I think the biblical story of creation should also be taught."

In March 1981 in Sacramento, California, Judge Irving Perluss presided over *Seagraves* v. *California*, a five-day non-jury trial in which Kelly Seagraves charged that the policy of the California Department of Education and Board of Education on scientific textbooks violated the rights of Fundamentalists, who object to the teaching of evolution. Seagraves is the director of the Fundamentalist Creation-Science Research Center in San Diego, California. Judge Perluss found that for the past eight years it had been Board of Education policy that evolution be taught as theory, not dogma.[25]

Creationists are attacking evolution on allegedly scientific grounds. At least six scientific organizations have warned that creationism is not science. In 1981 the intellectual and social revolution begun in the nineteenth century with the publication of Darwin's *Origin* is resisted by those who feel that the evolutionary hypothesis is responsible for most of the societal ills of the modern age.

THE THIRD WORLD, THE HOLOCAUST, AND STORYTELLING

Robert McAfee Brown (1920–   ) is a theologian whose writings over the past twenty years have been helpful to earnest main-line Christians seeking to understand the mandates of Christian faith and ethics. Brown,

[25] *The New York Times*, Saturday, March 7, 1981, p. 6.

a Presbyterian clergyman and professor of theology and ethics at the Pacific School of Religion, is something of a bellwether theologian who reflects the current theological consensus among main-liners. Our last document is Brown's statement of the theological task for the 1980s.

Document 68

From "Starting Over: New Beginning Points for Theology" by Robert McAfee Brown

Redefining the Task

So, out of reflection on what is going on in a world of injustice, my own theological task has been redefined. Three points of special emphasis are emerging, each enriching and informing the others. One is geographical, a second is historical and cultural, a third is methodological. Here is that agenda, set out with telegraphic brevity:

1. The geographical ingredient I have to take with utmost seriousness is the power of *the voices of the Third World*. Latin America has been my special point of listening, but similar voices are being raised in Asia and Africa. Indeed, to be open to "the voices of the Third World" means to be open to the outcry of those near at hand in the United States as well, to *all* who are dispossessed and exploited, wherever they are, whether for racist, sexist or cultural reasons. Theologies that fail to hear the cries of the hurting, or fail in their responses to seek to overcome the need for those cries, are no longer theologies worthy of attention.

2. The historical-cultural ingredient to which I want to respond is *post-Holocaust Judaism*. Christians, of course, need to listen to Judaism as a whole, since our historical record vis-à-vis Judaism is worse than our record vis-à-vis any other faith—a devasting indictment. We have killed, tortured, manipulated, proselytized and discriminated against Jews in ways and to a degree that are the shame of our history. But all of this is brought to pinpoint focus in the event of the Holocaust, and what Christians do about it in a post-Holocaust era. The deliberate murder of 6 million Jews, by those who were shaped by an ostensibly Christian culture, makes forever impossible some of our previous theological assertions about (a) the inherent goodness of human nature, (b) a universe in which all things work together for good, (c) any equations between justice and virtue, or (d) just about anything else. A pall is forever cast over complacent or triumphant orthodoxies. There is little of past Christian theology, let us face it, that is "credible in the presence of burning children."

3. For me, the methodological ingredient of this endeavor is *story*. In claiming this I seek not to embrace a "fad" but to recover a lost emphasis. Our faith, after all, did not initially come to us as "theology," and particularly not as "systematic theology." It came as story. Tell me about God: "Well, once upon a time there was a garden . . ." Tell me about Jesus: "Once upon a time there was a boy in a little

SOURCE: "Starting Over: New Beginning Points for Theology," *The Christian Century*, Vol. XCVII, May 14, 1980. Reprinted with permission from the Christian Century Foundation.

town in Palestine called Nazareth . . ." Tell me about salvation: "Well, when that same boy grew up, he loved people so much that the rulers began to get frightened of him, and do you know what they did? . . ." Tell me about the church: "Well, there were a great many people who were attracted to Jesus and started working together: Mary and Priscilla and Catherine of Siena and Martin Luther and Martin Luther King and John (several Johns: John Calvin, John Knox, John XXIII) and Gustavo and Mother Teresa, and do you know what they did? . . ."

Out of such stories the systems begin to grow, with results we know only too well: stories about a garden become cosmological arguments; stories about Jesus become treatises on the two natures; stories about salvation become substitutionary doctrines of atonement; stories about the church become by-laws of male-dominated hierarchies. Who could care less?

In losing the story we have lost both the power and the glory. We have committed the unpardonable sin of transforming exciting stories into dull systems. We have spawned system after system: Augustinian, Anselmian, Thomistic, Calvinistic, Lutheran, Reformed, orthodox, liberal, neo-orthodox, neo-liberal. Historically they were very different; today they share in common an inability to grab us where we are and say, "Listen! This is important!"

Retelling the Christian Story

We must *recover the story* if we are to recover a faith for our day. Each of us has his or her story. Alongside them is the Christian story, a story of the heroes and heroines of faith. Could the pair of stories impact one another? Sometimes we hear another person's story and we say, "Aha! That's *my* story too. In hearing about Abraham Lincoln or Jane Addams or Billie Jean King or Coretta King, I am learning about myself." Our theological task is to find ways to "tell the old, old story" so that the listener says, "Aha! That's *my* story too. In hearing about Abraham or Sarah or Jeremiah or Judas I am learning about myself."

The three approaches are interrelated. Story is the interrelating factor. Third World Christians reflect on their situation of oppression and the need for liberation; they reread the biblical story of people-under-oppression-who-are-being-liberated, and find their present story being informed and guided by the ancient one. The Exodus story becomes their story. A similar thing has happened among post-Holocaust Jews, attempting to recover a sense of identity after all identity has been stripped away. Elie Wiesel's writings have become for me a galvanizing example. In a series of novels he explores what it means to be a Jew living in a world in which Auschwitz could take place. The stories at first are very contemporary. But soon the 18th and 19th century Hasidic tales begin to be woven in. Then earlier midrashic commentary on Scripture makes its appearance. Recently he has been retelling tales from the Hebrew Scriptures. None of this is an evasion of the present. It is an attempt to *understand the present by making use of the past*. In retelling the ancient tales, Wiesel informs us, he comes to understand who he is today. The old story becomes his story.

Both Third World theologians and post-Holocaust Jews have been recovering stories from the past that help them understand their own stories in the present. The convergence is too marked to be capricious. It suggests the appropriate theological task for Christians in the future: to explore the ways that stories are told, all kinds of stories, to see if that could help us uncover a way of retelling the Christian story so that listeners, confronted by such retelling, could say, "Aha! That's my story too."

Once we have done that, there will be plenty of time to worry about systems.

As Brown mentioned, his interests in the Holocaust and storytelling are shared by the Jewish novelist Elie Wiesel (1928–   ) who has introduced many Americans to the wisdom and power of Hasidic teachings. Wiesel writes,

> It must be pointed out that all the conditions that existed in the eighteenth century, when Hasidism came into being, prevail again today. Physical and emotional insecurity, fallen idols, the scourge of violence. Where can one go, where can one hide? "Hell exists and it is of this world," said Rebbe Nahman, "but none dares speak of it." Wrong. Today everyone dares. Never before has mankind known such anguish. Such ugliness. Man walks the moon but his soul remains riveted to earth. Once upon a time it was the opposite. Despairing of the present, man seeks beauty in legends. Like the Hassid long ago.[26]

Much attention in the late 1970s and early 1980s has focused on the meaning of the Holocaust.

The Roman Catholic priest John S. Dunne (1929–   ) is a third writer who makes story—biography and autobiography—the interrelating factor in his theology. In his book *A Search for God in Time and Memory*, Dunne writes that the search "will carry us on quests and journeys through life stories, through hells, purgatories, and heavens, through ages of life, through stories of God. It is the sort of thing you might undertake if you were writing an autobiography or composing a personal creed."[27]

CONTINUITIES WITH THE PAST

The decade of the 1980s, for all of its pluralism and religious ferment, shares obvious linkage with the past. American civil religion is alive but hardly well. Vietnam and Watergate both have had a negative effect on "the religion of the republic." Even the observance of the nation's bicentennial in 1976 did not revive a waning faith in civil religion.

Church and state relations continue in a dynamic tension, with a focus on the issue of tax exemption for religious property emerging as the key issue. Moral Majority forces are seeking to get prayer back into the public schools.

An older Billy Graham still conducts revivals using the same format

---

[26] Elie Wiesel, *Souls on Fire: Portraits and Legends of Hasidic Masters* (New York: Random House, 1972), pp. 256–257.

[27] John S. Dunne, *A Search for God in Time and Memory* (Notre Dame, Ind.: University of Notre Dame Press, 1977), p. vii. See also *The City of God*, *The Way of all Earth*, and *Time and Myth* by Dunne.

that Charles G. Finney developed and Dwight L. Moody perfected. The newer generation of independent evangelists—the electronic preachers—have moved to a talk-show format.

One indigenous American religion that has been rediscovered is Amerindian religion, as many persons strive for a holistic theology that is sensitive to ecological issues. The other "made-in-America" religions are doing well. Pentecostalism has been our most successful religious export and has, since 1960, crossed the tracks into upper-middle-class respectability as the charismatic movement.

The "positive thinking" tradition is kept alive by a number of practitioners. Oral Roberts, having moved from his earlier career as a Pentecostal Holiness faith healer, now is a spokesman for an Oklahoma version of positive religion—"Something good is going to happen to you." Robert Schuller preaches "possibility thinking," a California twist to Norman Vincent Peale's positive thinking, and the television evangelist Rex Humbard shows signs of giving an Akron, Ohio, working-class version of peace, power, poise, and prosperity perpetually possessed.

Liberals and conservatives continue either to revise or defend the faith when confronted by the forces of modernity. Conservative religious communities were riding the crest of the social and political conservative waves in the early '80s.

A *Time* essay, recognizing the widening racial chasm in America, said that the great secret is that whites and blacks may need each other. Amid all the ferment and change, many of the themes were familiar.[28]

---

28 "The Great White and Black Society," *Time*, March 16, 1981, pp. 93–94.

Postscript

The late Paul Tillich maintained: "Religion is the substance of culture, culture is the form of religion."[29] This aphorism has two implications, the first being that at the heart of culture is religion—the ways we give meaning to ultimate reality and the values by which we live. The second implication is that both personal and ecclesial religion are culturally formed. Religion and culture are, therefore, inextricably related in a dialectical way. To say that they are in a dialectical relation means that they have a mutual impact each on the other. We hope that you have learned something about religion in American culture and that you will continue your investigation of the relationship with an open and inquiring mind.

[29] Paul Tillich, *Theology of Culture* (London: Oxford University Press, 1969), p. 42.

Index